AGAINST THE DELUGE

Polish and Lithuanian armies during the war against Sweden 1655–1660

Michał Paradowski

'This is the Century of the Soldier', Fulvio Testi, Poet, 1641

HELION &
COMPANY

Helion & Company Limited
Unit 8 Amherst Business Centre
Budbrooke Road
Warwick
CV34 5WE
England
Tel. 01926 499 619
Email: info@helion.co.uk
Website: www.helion.co.uk
Twitter: @helionbooks
Visit our blog http://blog.helion.co.uk/

Published by Helion & Company 2022
Designed and typeset by Mary Woolley, Battlefield Design (www.battlefield-design.co.uk)
Cover designed by Paul Hewitt, Battlefield Design (www.battlefield-design.co.uk)

Text © Michał Paradowski 2022
Images as individually credited
Colour artwork by Sergey Shamenkov © Helion & Company 2022
Maps by George Anderson © Helion & Company 2022

Every reasonable effort has been made to trace copyright holders and to obtain their permission for the use of copyright material. The author and publisher apologize for any errors or omissions in this work and would be grateful if notified of any corrections that should be incorporated in future reprints or editions of this book.

ISBN 978-1-804510-03-2

British Library Cataloguing-in-Publication Data.
A catalogue record for this book is available from the British Library.

All rights reserved. No part of this publication may be reproduced, stored in a retrieval system, or transmitted, in any form, or by any means, electronic, mechanical, photocopying, recording or otherwise, without the express written consent of Helion & Company Limited.

For details of other military history titles published by Helion & Company Limited contact the above address or visit our website: http://www.helion.co.uk.

We always welcome receiving book proposals from prospective authors.

Contents

Acknowledgements		iv
Foreword		v
Chronology of the Polish–Lithuanian Commonwealth's Wars from 1655–1660		vii
1	Sources	12
2	Organisation, Recruitment and Overall Strength of the Armies	19
3	Commanders	63
4	Lances, Sabres and Muskets	80
5	Military Life and Death	203
6	Pitched Battles	241
7	Small War	274
8	Siege Operations	290
9	Example of a 'Low-Level' Campaign: Actions in Livonia and Courland 1657–1660	316
Conclusion		324
Colour Plates Commentary		326
Flag Plates Commentary		332
Appendices:		
I	Stefan Czarniecki's Division in Denmark (1658–1659) and in the Campaign against the Muscovites (1660)	334
II	Polish Auxiliary Corps Sent to Support the Lithuanians in Late Autumn 1654	337
III	Polish and Imperial Army Besieging Toruń (Thorn), Summer–Winter 1658	340
IV	Lithuanian Forces Loyal to Grand Hetman Janusz Radziwiłł – Autumn 1655	343
V	Two Lithuanian Army Lists from 1661	346
VI	Letter of Passage for Patrick Gordon (July 1661)	355
VII	Register of the Prisoners Taken at the Battle of Werki on the Day 21 October 1658	357
VIII	Letters of Marshal Lubomirski and General Würtz	359
IX	Administrative Division of the Polish-Lithuanian Commonwealth	361
Bibliography		364

Acknowledgements

As always, my massive thanks to Helion & Company for allowing me to continue this great adventure with the *Century of the Soldier* series, with yet another volume about the Polish–Lithuanian Commonwealth's warfare. Special thanks to series' editor Charles Singleton for his constant support, encouragement and patience while waiting for the delayed manuscript. My heart goes to Sergey Shameknov, who, despite the terrible peril he and his countrymen are in right now, provided such fine contribution with his well-researched colour plates.

I would like to thank Michał Molenda, Zbigniew Hundert, Konrad Bobiatyński and Bartosz Staręgowski for their help in gathering materials for the book. Special thanks to Krzysztof Kucharski, for his translation from German and providing very interesting information about the city of Gdańsk's army, and to Tomasz Łomnicki for great insight and inspiration in the topic of seventeenth-century clothing.

Finally, to my wife Patrycja and son Ezra: yet again thanks for all your love, understanding and patience ('Another book, Dad, really?').

Foreword

The war between the Polish–Lithuanian Commonwealth and Sweden that took place between 1655 and 1660 became known as the Swedish Deluge (*potop szwedzki*) and became one of the most important and devastating conflicts involving the Commonwealth in the seventeenth century. At the same time, it was part of the interlinked series of wars, both with internal and external enemies, that took place between 1648 and 1667. They very much shaped the situation of Poland and Lithuania for the rest of the seventeenth century, echoing well into the eighteenth century as well. Within this volume, I did not plan to describe the whole war, with all its campaign, battles and sieges. Instead, it is an attempt to provide the non-Polish readers with as many as possible details of the very complex picture of the Polish and Lithuanian armies in this period. Despite its title, while the main focus is on the war against the Swedes, readers will also be able to find here much information about the Commonwealth's armies during their conflicts with the Cossacks and the Muscovites between 1648 and 1667. It is my belief that this allows me to paint a more detailed picture of the soldiers and army that served during the reign of King Jan II Kazimierz.

A few additional notes regarding terminology are used in the book. Where possible, current geographical names available in the English version are used, usually accompanied by the Polish or German name from the period as additional reference. Polish, German and Latin terms (except for geographical and people's names) are written in italics. The names of Polish and Lithuanian officers and soldiers are written in their Polish version. Certain Eastern-European and German words that are already established in English-language nomenclature are not marked in italics (e.g., 'hetman', 'haiduks' and 'reiters'). For many Polish military words that do not have an English equivalent, the original form will be used (e.g., '*pancerni*' and '*rotmistrz*').[1] On their first appearance, each of these words will be accompanied by a footnote explaining their meaning. The same approach is taken with terms used to describe measurements or any other Polish words. The currency mentioned in the text is the Polish *złoty* (abbreviated to 'zł'), which is divided into 30 *groszy* (abbreviated to 'gr'). In that period,

---

1   While a *rotmistrz* is the equivalent of a Western-European cavalry captain, we decided to keep the original form, especially as, in the Polish and Lithuanian military, 'captain' was normally used only in regard to foreign troops.

one *grosz* equalled 0.27 grams of silver, so one *złoty* was approximately 8.1 grams of silver. If a different currency is mentioned, its equivalent in Polish currency will be given as well. In the primary sources, Polish and Lithuanian commanders, even on the banner level, tend to be called by their official title (e.g., 'Voivode of Ruthenia' and 'Castellan of Cracow') without their name being mentioned. For the purpose of this book, even when quoting original documents, the name of the official is used instead, and normally the title, except for military ones (e.g., 'Hetman', 'Camp Master' and 'Guard'), is tended to be ignored. I decided on such an approach to simplify a bit the already confusing way of the official documents and diaries. The names of all provinces, voivodeships and lands can be found in Appendix IX. All dates are given according to the Gregorian calendar, which was already used at the time in the Commonwealth.

Chronology of the Polish–Lithuanian Commonwealth's Wars from 1655–1660

The main events of the 1655–1660 wars, including the Swedish–Muscovite and Swedish–Danish conflicts. Additionally, the main events of the war between the Commonwealth and Muscovy are included to provide a more detailed picture of the situation.

1655

11 July – The Lithuanian garrison of Daugavpils (Dyneburg) surrenders to the Swedes.
13 July – Minsk (Mińsk) is captured by the Muscovites.
24–25 July – After a brief fight, the levy of nobility from Wielkopolska surrenders to the Swedes at Ujście.
7–9 August – The Lithuanian army (Janusz Radziwiłł and Wincenty Gosiewski) is defeated and forced to retreat by the Muscovites (Jakow Kudeniekowicz Czerkasski) at Vilnus (Wilno). The town is captured without a fight by the Cossacks and Muscovites then sacked and burned.
17 August – Hetman Janusz Radziwiłł signed the Treaty of Kiejdany (Kėdainiai), accepting Swedish protection for Lithuania.
2–3 September – The Swedish army (Karl X Gustav) is victorious at the Battle of Sobota and Piątek despite initial Polish success on the first day of the fight. The Poles (Jan Kazimierz) retreat south.
8 September – Warsaw is captured without a fight by the Swedes.
16 September – The Polish army (Jan Kazimierz) is defeated by the Swedes (Gustaf Otto Stenbock and Magnus Gabriel de la Gardie) at Żarnów.
25 September – The Swedish siege of Kraków begins.
29 September – The Polish division of Grand Hetman Stanisław Rewera Potocki is defeated by combined Muscovite (Wasyl Szeremietiew) and Cossack (Bohdan Chmielnicki) armies at Gródek Jagielloński.
30 September – The Swedish division of Gustaf Otto Stenbock defeats the levy of nobility from Masovia (Mazowsze) led by Jan Kazimierz Krasiński at Nowy Dwór.

3 October – Swedes led by Karl X Gustav defeat the Polish division of Field Hetman Stanisław Lankoroński at the Battle of Wojnich.

3–4 October – Polish partisans under Krzysztof Żegocki destroy the Swedish outpost at Kościan.

10 October – Kościan is recaptured and burned by the Swedish relief force.

17 October – Kraków surrenders to the Swedes. The garrison led by Czarniecki is allowed to leave the town on terms.

Mid-October – Jan II Kazimierz is leaving Poland and finding asylum at Głógówek in Silesia.

20 October – Janusz Radziwiłł signs the Union of Kiejdany (also known as the Agreement of Kiejdany), which supersedes the Treaty of Kiejdany.

26 October – In the camp near Kraków, the division of Hetman Lanckoroński, under the command of Aleksander Koniecpolski, gives their oath to Karl X Gustav.

13 November – Hetman Potocki and Hetman Lanckoroński, in the camp at Nowe Miasto-Korczyń, give their oath to Karl X Gustav (taken by Robert Douglas).

18 November–27 December – The unsuccessful Swedish siege of Jasna Góra.

2 December – Toruń (Thorn) surrenders to the Swedes.

22 December – Elbląg (Elbing) is taken by the Swedish army without a fight.

29 December – Hetman Potocki, Hetman Lanckoroński and their troops sign on to the Tyszowce Confederation against the Swedes, where they address all nobles in the land to stand against the invaders. The Tyszowce Confederation was partially in reaction to the siege of Jasna Góra and had a strong religious background.

End of December – Jan II Kazimierz returns to Poland.

Night from 30 to 31 December – Janusz Radziwiłł dies in Tykocin while being besieged by Lithuanian forces loyal to King Jan II Kazimierz.

1656

17 January – Elector Friedrich Wilhelm signs the Królewiec (Königsberg) Treaty with Sweden and becomes vassal of Karl X Gustav.

19 February – The Swedish led by Karl X Gustav defeat Czarniecki's division at Gołąb.

End of February – The vast majority of Polish troops leave Swedish service.

March – Paweł Jan Sapieha is nominated as a new Lithuanian Grand Hetman.

15 March – Czarniecki manages to destroy the Swedish vanguard at Jarosław.

28 March – Inconclusive battle at Nisko (Czarniecki versus Karl X Gustav).

30 March – The Swedish field army led by Karl X Gustav is surrounded by the Polish and Lithuanian armies in the camp at Gorzyce between the Wisła and San rivers.

April – The Muscovites start their offensive in Finland and Ingria (Ingermanland).

June – The beginning of the Muscovite offensive in Livonia.

CHRONOLOGY OF THE POLISH–LITHUANIAN COMMONWEALTH'S WARS FROM 1655–1660

4–6 April – Karl X Gustav manages to break out his army from a trap in Gorzyce. He is opposed only by the Lithuanian army of Hetman Sapieha, as the Polish forces are at the time away fighting the Swedish relief attempt.

7 April – Stefan Czarniecki and Jerzy Lubomirski, with their Polish divisions, destroy the Swedish relief force (Frederick VI, Margrave of Baden-Durlach) at Warka.

18–21 April – The start of the short-lived anti-Swedish rebellion at Samogitia (Żmudź).

24 April – The beginning of the Polish siege of Warsaw. The garrison is under the command of Arvid Wittenberg while the Poles are led by Jan Kazimierz himself.

7 May – The Swedish army led by Prince Adolf Johan defeats Czarniecki's and Lubomirski's forces at the Battle of Gniezno, also known as the Battle of Kłecko.

Summer – The unsuccessful siege of Kraków by Lubomirski's forces.

1 June – Czarniecki is defeated by Karl X Gustav at Kcynia.

30 June – The surrender of the Swedish garrison of Warsaw.

13 July – Swedish forces led by Prince Bogusław Radziwiłł force the Lithuanian forces to lift the blockade of Tykocin.

Late July – Allied Crimean Tatars led by *Subhan Ğazı Ağa* join the Polish army at Warsaw.

28–30 July – Joint Swedish and Brandenburg armies (Karl X Gustav, Frederick Wilhelm) in a three-days' battle defeat the Polish–Lithuanian–Tatar army led by Jan Kazimierz.

25 August – Czarniecki's division, supported by allied Tatars, destroys the Swedish force led by Hans Böddeker in the Battle of Łowicz.

15 October – The Muscovites end their unsuccessful siege of Swedish-held Riga.

8 October – The Polish–Lithuanian army (Gosiewski), supported by Tatars, is victorious in the Battle of Prostki against the Swedish–Brandenburg force (Waldeck). Prince Bogusław Radziwiłł is captured by Tatars.

Mid-October – Tatar raids ruthlessly pillage part of Ducal Prussia.

22 October – The Swedish–Brandenburg force led by Otto von Stenbock is defeated by Gosiewski's Lithuanians at Filipów.

November – Nobles from Wielkopolska raid the Brandenburg region of Neumark (Nowa Marchia).

3 November – A truce in Niemież (Nemėžis) between the Commonwealth and Tsardom of Russia, allowing for a temporary cease of military operations between both sides, as they were both focusing on their wars against Sweden.

1 December – The signing of the alliance between the Commonwealth and Holy Roman Empire.

6 December – The Treaty of Radnot is signed between Sweden, Brandenburg, Transylvania and Zaporozhian Cossacks.

1657

2 January – The Swedish vanguard, led by Rutger von Ascheberg, surprise and inflict heavy losses on the Polish troops near Chojnice (Konitz). The main Polish force, under the command of Czarniecki, safely withdraw before the arrival of the main Swedish field army.

27 January – The Lithuanian army under the command of Hetman Sapieha, after a bloody assault, captures Tykocin.

End of January – George II Rákóczi and Transylvanian army enter Poland.

June – Denmark declares war against Sweden.

14-17 June – After a short siege, Warsaw surrenders to the Swedish–Transylvanian–Cossack army.

July–August – The Swedish field army, led by Karl X Gustav himself, force the Danes to leave Bremen and follow after them into Jutland.

11 July – Polish and Tatar victory over Transylvanians at Magierów.

20 July – Polish and Tatar victory over Transylvanians at Czarny Ostrów.

23 July – The remaining Transylvanian army is destroyed by the Tatars at Skałat.

25 August – Polish and Imperial forces recapture Cracow.

July–August – Poznań is recaptured by the Poles.

18 July – The Commonwealth and Denmark sign an anti-Swedish treaty.

19 September (Treaty of Welawa) and 6 November (Treaty of Bydgoszcz) – Thanks to these agreements, Elector Friedrich Wilhelm ceases to be vassal of the Polish Crown. Brandenburg switches sides and joins the anti-Swedish coalition.

3 November – The Danish fortress Frederiksodde is captured in a bloody assault by the Swedes.

1658

9-25 February – In a surprising move, the Swedish army of Karl X Gustav moves through the frozen Great and Little Belts. Facing Swedish army at the gates of Copenhagen, the Danes decide to negotiate for peace.

8 March – The Treaty of Roskilde: The Kingdom of Denmark and Norway loses one-third of its territory to Sweden.

July – Allied Polish and Imperial armies begin the siege of Toruń.

17 August – The Swedes, breaking the Treaty of Roskilde, attack Denmark but are unable to capture Copenhagen.

15 September – The Danish fortress Kronborg is captured by Swedish forces.

Autumn – Imperial-, Brandenburg- and Polish-allied contingents arrive at Denmark to fight against the Swedes.

Early October – The Swedish division of Robert Douglas captures Courland.

21 October – The Lithuanian force from Gosiewski's division is defeated by the Muscovites (Jurij Dolgorukov) at Werki. Field Hetman Gosiewski and many of his officers are taken prisoner.

8 November – The Dutch fleet breaks the sea blockade of Copenhagen.

14 December – Allied forces land on the island of Als.

CHRONOLOGY OF THE POLISH-LITHUANIAN COMMONWEALTH'S WARS FROM 1655-1660

25 December – Fortress Kolding is captured by an assault of Czarniecki's Polish division.
27 December – The surrender of the Swedish garrison of Trondheim.
30 December – The surrender of the Swedish garrison of Toruń.

1659

21 February – The Swedish army takes heavy losses during an unsuccessful assault on Copenhagen.
20 March – The Swedish counteroffensive in Prussia recaptures Dirschau (Tczew).
18 May – The Lithuanian victory at Szkudy stops the Swedish offensive into Samogitia.
29-30 August – The Polish army captures Grudziądz (Graudenz).
September-November – Unsuccessful Swedish siege of Szczecin (Stettin).
19 September – After few months of siege, the Swedish garrison of Kuldīga (Goldingen) in Courland surrenders to Lithuanians.
December – The beginning of the sieges of Malbork (Marienburg) and Elbląg. The Swedish garrisons manage to hold both places until the end of the war.
10 December – The surrender of the Swedish garrison of Brodnica.
20 December – Gdańska Głowa (Danziger Haupt) is captured by the allied army. The main role in the siege is played by the mercenary army of the city of Gdańsk.

1660

9 January – The Lithuanian army is captured at Mitau.
23 February – The death of Swedish King Karl X Gustav.
3 May – The Polish-Lithuanian Commonwealth and Sweden sign a peace treaty in Oliwa. It is ratified in June at Warsaw.
6 June – A peace treaty between Sweden and Danemark is signed in Copenhagen.

1661

21 June – A Swedish-Muscovite peace treaty is signed in Kärde (Kardis).

1

Sources

The Deluge itself had some previous coverage in English. Probably the most popular publications are two books by Robert Frost.[1] Very interesting, as it is presenting the role of Lithuania in conflict, is the work of Andrej Kotlhjarchuk.[2] The *Century of the Soldier 1618-1721* series also helped English-speaking readers with better understanding the conflict, with two volumes of Michael Fredholm von Essen's work about the wars of Charles X.[3] Thanks to these books, topics like the reasons and outcome of the 1655–1660 war, main events and fighting armies already had some proper description and were the subject of more or less detailed analysis. I still believe, though, that there is a fairly wide gap in the more in-depth picture of the Polish and Lithuanian armies of this period, especially when considering that the Commonwealth was in the state of near-constant wars between 1648 and 1667, with many internal and external factors affecting its military machine, army structure and ways of waging war. Therefore, I came up with the idea of presenting a more detailed work, describing the Commonwealth armies that fought against a multitude of enemies. When I started working on this book, I faced a rather interesting dilemma. Considering how well the topic of the Deluge is covered in Poland, with a large number of very well-researched books already published (especially those from the second part of the twentieth century), one could easily fall into the temptation of relying on such secondary sources to make his own work much easier. I do not think it would be the ideal approach, though, as I strongly believe in working with as many primary sources as possible to have better 'feel' of the period and to be able to provide my own conclusions and findings, not to mention the rich base of quotes and comments from eyewitnesses. As such, I tried my best to access and use a large number of primary sources from the period – from

---

1   Robert Frost, *After the Deluge. Poland-Lithuania and the Second Northern War, 1655-1660* (Cambridge: Cambridge University Press, 1993) and *The Northern Wars. War, State, and Society in Northeastern Europe, 1558-1721* (London: Routledge, 2000).
2   Andrej Kotlhjarchuk, *In the Shadows of Poland and Russia. The Grand Duchy of Lithuania and Sweden in the European Crisis of the mid-17th Century* (Huddinge: Södertörns högskola, 2006).
3   Michael Fredholm von Essen, *Charles X's War. Volume I – Armies of the Swedish Deluge, 1655-1660* (Warwick: Helion & Company, 2021) and *Charles X's War. Volume II – The Wars in the East. 1655-1657* (Warwick: Helion & Company, 2022).

published diaries, chronicles and letters to army muster rolls and financial documents. In this short chapter, I would like to discuss the most important sources (both primary and secondary) that readers can find within this volume, as it can provide some background and comments about the authors and their works.

Amongst the most useful primary sources are those written by soldiers who took part in the campaigns, as they provide us with a very interesting perspective from those involved in the fight. I will often be referencing the most famous Polish diarist of this time, Jan Chryzostom Pasek, who served as a companion in the cossack cavalry banner of *Rotmistrz* Stanisław Widlica Domaszewski. This unit was part of Stefan Czarniecki's division, fighting against the Swedes, Muscovites and Cossacks. Pasek gives amazing insight into mind of a seventeenth-century Polish noble-soldier, and his diary is full of well-observed details, often with a dash of exaggeration though.[4] His colleague in arms from the same division, also serving as a cossack and *pancerni* companion, Jakub Łoś, is much more laconic in his diary, but it is worth it to compare his view of the events with those from Pasek's memoir.[5] Jan Władysław Poczobut Odlanicki served in the Lithuanian army, initially in levy of nobility, then shortly in the cossack-style cavalry of the regular forces and from early September 1659 as a winged hussar. While the majority of his military service took place against the Muscovites, between 1658 and 1660, he fought against the Swedes in Livonia and Courland. His memoir is, just like Pasek's one, full of the details of the usually less-covered aspects of the military service, from duels between companions to the daily struggle of an unpaid army and the motivation driving individual soldiers.[6] A great source of the information about both sides of the conflict is also the memoirs of the soldiers that started the war in the Swedish ranks but ended in the Polish ones. Luckily, we have access to two such detailed relations, those of German Hieronim Chrystian Holsten[7] and famous Scotsman Patrick Gordon.[8] Not only does it allow us to see the initial stage of the war from the Swedish perspective, but it also helps with understanding the process behind the switching of sides by those soldiers of fortune. A further Swedish point of view can be found in the diary of another mercenary, cavalry officer Rutger von Ascheberg, who served during the Deluge and on many occasions fought against the Poles.[9] Finally, there are the memoirs of famous Swedish engineer Erik Dahlbergh, who took part in the Polish campaigns from 1656.[10]

---

4 Jan Chryzostom Pasek, *Pamiętniki* (Warszawa: Państwowy Instytut Wydawniczy, 1963).
5 Jakub Łoś, *Pamiętnik towarzysza chorągwi pancernej* (Warszawa: Wydawnictwo DiG, 2000).
6 Jan Władysław Poczobut Odlanicki, *Pamiętnik Jana Władysława Poczobuta Odlanickiego (1640-1684)* (Warszawa: Drukarnia Michała Ziemkiewicza, 1877).
7 Hieronim Chrystian Holsten, *Przygody wojenne 1655-1666* (Warszawa: Instytut Wydawniczy Pax, 1980).
8 *Diary of General Patrick Gordon of Auchleuchries 1635-1699* (Aberdeen: University of Aberdeen, 2009), vol. I, and (Aberdeen: University of Aberdeen, 2009), vol. II, both edited by Dmitry Fedosow.
9 Rutger von Ascheberg, *Dziennik oficera jazdy szwedzkiej 1621-1681* (Kraków: Wydawnictwo Eternum, 2014).
10 *Erik Dahlberghs dagbok (1625-1699)* (Upsala & Stockholm: Almqvist & Wiksells Boktryckeri AB, 1912).

Amongst the other soldiers' memoirs used in the book, there will be those of Lithuanians Michał Obuchowicz,[11] Aleksander Dionizy Skorobohaty[12] and Bogusław Kazimierz Maskiewicz[13] and those of Polish companions Joachim Jerlicz,[14] Mikołaj Jemiołowski[15] and Jan Florian Drobysz Tuszyński.[16] There are also the diaries of non-military individuals, with different points of view and interesting additional information. The two main ones that will be used here were written by Maciej Vorbek-Lettow[17] and Jan Antoni Chrapowicki.[18] The former is particularly important, as its author served in levy of nobility and it provides its readers with many details regarding the organisation of this formation. Pierre des Noyers, secretary of Queen Marie Louise Gonzaga (or rather Ludwika Maria, as she was known in Poland), left a large collection of correspondence, including many important letters written during 1655–1660. They provide interesting insight into the Court's politics and its view of the war.[19] There are few other relations written by foreigners that will be used as well. French engineer Guillaume Le Vasseur de Beauplan (1600–1675) between 1630 and 1648 served in the Polish army – building the fortress of Kodak in 1639, taking part in campaigns against Cossacks and drawing very detailed maps of Ukraine. His *Description des contrés du Royaume de Pologne* (later titled *Description d'Ukranie*) was for the first time published in 1651, and it provides many interesting descriptions of Zaporozhian Cossacks, Tatars and the Polish military. His comments on the latter will be used as a part of the description of certain formations of the Polish army in chapter four.[20] Sebastian (Sebastiano) Cefali was Italian, serving initially in royal chancellery of Jan Kazimierz and then for years as the secretary of Jerzy Sebastian Lubomirski. In 1665, at the outbreak of Lubomirski's Mutiny, Cefali wrote an interesting relation about the 'political and military affairs in Poland', in which he described in much detail the Polish army from the mid-1660s.[21] During the 1663/1664 campaign against the Muscovites, two

---

11 'Dyaryusz Michał Obuchowicza, Strażnika Wielkiego Księstwa Litewskiego, pisany przez czas więzienia w Moskwie', in *Pamiętniki historyczne do wyjaśnienia spraw publicznych w Polsce XVII wieku posługujące, w dziennikach domowych Obuchowiczów i Cedrowskiego pozostałe* (Wilno: Nakładem A. Assa Księgarza, 1859).
12 Aleksander D. Skorobohaty, *Dziennik* (Warszawa: Wydawnictwo DiG, 2000).
13 *Pamiętniki Samuela i Bogusława Kazimierza Maskiewiczów* (Wrocław: Zakład Narodowy im. Ossolińskich-Wydawnictwo, 1961).
14 Joachim Jerlicz, *Latopisiec albo kroniczka* (Warszawa: Kazimierz Władysław Wóycicki, 1853), vol. I, and (Warszawa: Kazimierz Władysław Wóycicki, 1853), vol. II.
15 Mikołaj Jemiołowski, *Pamiętnik dzieje Polski zawierający (1648-1679)* (Warszawa: Wydawnictwo DiG, 2000).
16 *Dwa pamiętniki z XVII wieku Jana Cedrowskiego i Jana Floriana Drobysza Tuszyńskiego* (Wrocław-Kraków: Zakład Imienia Ossolińskich-Wydawnictwo, 1954).
17 Maciej Vorbek-Lettow, *Skarbnica pamięci. Pamiętnik lekarza króla Władysława IV* (Wrocław-Warszawa-Kraków: Zakład Narodowy im. Ossolińskich-Wydawnictwo, 1968).
18 Jan Antoni Chrapowicki, *Diariusz. Część pierwsza: lata 1656-1664* (Warszawa: Instytut Wydawniczy Pax, 1978).
19 *Portfolio królowej Maryi Ludwiki* (Poznań: Drukarnia i księgarnia Nowa, 1844), vol. I, and (Poznań: Drukarnia i księgarnia Nowa, 1844), vol. II.
20 Eryk Lasota and Wilhelm Beauplan, *Opis Ukrainy* (Warszawa: Państwowy Instytut Wydawniczy, 1972), pp.165–70.
21 'Relacya o stanie politycznym i wojskowym Polski przez Sebastyana Cefali, sekretarza Jerzego Lubomirskiego, marszałka i hetmana polnego koronnego, z roku 1665', in *Relacye nuncyuszów*

sons of the famous French commander and diplomat, Antoine III Agénor de Gramont, Duke of Gramont, joined the Polish army as volunteers and observers. They were elder, Guy Armand de Gramont, Count of Guiche, and younger, Antoine Charles IV de Gramont. The latter wrote a memoir full of interesting insight into both the organisation of the Polish army and history of an unsuccessful military venture against the Muscovites.[22] Official chronicles of the war that will be most often used in this volume are three main works, representing both sides of the war. Samuel Pufendorf will present the Swedish point of view,[23] while Wespazjan Kochowski[24] and Wawrzyniec Jan Rudawski[25] will be supporting us with the Polish point of view. While full of interesting details and in overall very comprehensive, at the same time, these sources are full of bias towards the opponents and include a large number of exaggerations (e.g., when describing the scale of battle victories and losses). Therefore, they need to be used with care. It is worth adding, though, that Kochowski did serve in the Polish army as a companion in Władysław Myszkowski's hussar banner between 1653 and 1657 (or even up to 1660), fighting as a part of Czarniecki's division. Many years later, he turned his attention to history, publishing his *Annalium Poloniae ab obitu Vladislai IV Climacteres* during the early 1680s and taking part as an official historian (*historiographus privilegiatus*) in Jan II Sobieski's Vienna campaign in 1683. Particularly valuable were also modern editions of the archival sources from the wars against the Cossacks and Muscovites, especially relations from the Cossack Uprising of 1648–1651[26] and two volumes of the correspondence of Hetman Janusz Radziwiłł from the period 1646–1655, diary of his hancellery[27] and collection of letters.[28] Amongst older editions of primary sources, it is worth mentioning the Lithuanian documents published by the Archaeographic Commision in Vilnius.[29]

---

apostolskich i innych osób w Polsce od roku 1548 do 1690 (Berlin-Poznań: Księgarnia B. Behra, 1864), vol. II, pp.308–39.

22 For the purpose of this book, all quotes from Gramont will be based on the Russian translation of his memoir, published in 1929, Antoine de Gramont, *Iz istorīi moskovskago pokhoda Īana Kazimira, 1663-1664 g.g.* (Yuriev: Tipografīâ K. Mattisena, 1929).

23 Samuel Pufendorf, *Siedem ksiąg o czynach Karola Gustawa króla Szwecji*, translated and edited by Wojciech Krawczuk (Warszawa: Wydawnictwo DiG, 2013).

24 Wespazjan Kochowski, *Historya panowania Jana Kazimierza* (Poznań: N Kamieński, 1859), vol. I, and (Poznań: N. Kamieński, 1859), vol. II; Wespazjan Kochowski, *Lata Potopu 1655-1657* (Warszawa: Wydawnictwo Ministerstwa Obrony Narodowej, 1967).

25 Wawrzyniec Jan Rudawski, *Historja Polska od śmierci Władysława IV aż do pokoju oliwskiego* (Petersburg-Mohylew: Nakładem Bolesława Maurycego Wolffa, 1855), vol. II.

26 Mirosław Nagielski (ed.), *Relacje wojenne z pierwszych lat walk polsko-kozackich powstania Bohdana Chmielnickiego okresu "Ogniem i Mieczem" (1648-1651)* (Warszawa: Wydawnictwo VIKING, 1999).

27 Mirosław Nagielski, Konrad Bobiatyński, Przemysław Gawron, Krzysztof Kossarzecki, Piotr Kroll, Andrzej A. Majewski, and Dariusz Milewski (eds), *Korespondencja wojskowa hetmana Janusza Radziwiłła w latach 1646-1655*, vol. I, *Diariusz kancelaryjny 1649-1653* (Warszawa: Wydawnictwo Neriton, 2019).

28 Konrad Bobiatyński, Przemysław Gawron, Krzysztof Kossarzecki, Piotr Kroll, Andrzej A. Majewski, Dariusz Milewski, and Mirosław Nagielski (eds), *Korespondencja wojskowa hetmana Janusza Radziwiłła w latach 1646-1655*, vol. II, *Listy* (Warszawa: Wydawnictwo Neriton, 2020).

29 *Akty izdavaemye Vilenskoju Arheografičeskou Kommissieu*, published in 38 volumes between 1845 and 1914. In further footnotes, this source will be described as *AVAK*, with the date

Archival sources were of course a crucial part of the research – as, although many of them were lost during series of wars ravaging Poland in the nineteenth and twentieth centuries, there is still a large number of them available in collections in Poland and elsewhere. Sadly, as this book was written mostly during the world-wide COVID-19 pandemic, it limited my capabilities to travel and research them directly. Luckily, many of the documents are available online, thanks to digitalisation projects that make access to them much easier for the general public. As such, many documents from the Central Archives of Historical Records in Warsaw (*Archiwum Główne Akt Dawnych*)[30] are of special significance, including those related to the Polish *Sejm*, army muster rolls and correspondence between officials and army commanders. Amongst other used sources are those from the National Archive in Poznań (*Archiwum Narodowe w Poznaniu*),[31] the National Archive in Cracow (*Archiwum Narodowe w Krakowie*), Kórnik Library (*Biblioteka Kórnicka PAN*), Czartoryski Library (*Biblioteka Książąt Czartoryskich*), Jagiellonian Library (*Biblioteka Jagiellońska*) and Riksarkivet in Stockholm.

Iconography from the period is also an important source, especially regarding clothes, weapons and equipment of the soldiers involved in the conflict. First and foremost, the name that needs to be mentioned here is Erik Dahlbergh, as his drawings were the base for the numerous engravings in Samuel Pufendorf's book. Dahlbergh took part in the campaigns of the Swedish army from 1656 onwards and had a great eye for details, so a large number of his works can be found here – both with battle scenes and with individual soldiers. Abraham von Westervelt accompanied the Lithuanian army in 1651 against the Cossacks, and his drawings are one of the best presentations of the Commonwealth's soldiers in the period. Stefan della Bella and Jean Boisseau had the opportunity to see and draw Polish envoys in 1640s, giving us a glimpse into the details of attire and equipment from diplomatic events of that time. Less known but still interesting are the drawings from Józef Naronowicz-Naroński's *Architektura militaris, to jest budownictwo wojenne* published in 1659. Some of the plans of the army camps and a few other illustrations from his work are included as well.

At the start of this chapter, I mentioned a large number of well-researched works available on the topic of the war in Poland. I would like to name few brilliant historians that, through the years, added to the better understanding of the topics like the Polish and Lithuanian armies, the battles and campaigns of the Swedish Deluge or the 1654–1667 war against Muscovy. This list of course will not be full, as there will be many more historians that I reference to in the pages of this book, but I felt the need to highlight some of the most important ones and the most crucial for me during my work on this volume. Jan Wimmer was always my most favourite researcher, so it is not surprising that I relied on his works a lot: not only his crucial study of the

---

of publishing and volume number (e.g., *AVAK* (Vilna: Tipografia A. G. Syrkina, 1909), vol. XXXIV).

30 In the footnotes, it will be described as AGAD.
31 In the footnotes, it will be described as APPoz.

Polish army in the second part of the seventeenth century[32] but also his research into the structure and organisation of the Polish army during the 1655–1660[33] war and the conflicts with Sweden in seventeenth century.[34] His other works and articles were also, in a smaller extent, used during the writing of this book and, if used as a direct source of information, will be referenced in the footnotes. Mirosław Nagielski wrote extensively about the Royal Guard of Władysław IV[35] and Jan II Kazimierz, providing many interesting details about this formation during the Deluge.[36] His research, to name just few most important from the point of the view of this book, also includes monographs of the Battle of Warsaw in 1656,[37] Royal hussar banners[38] and foreign troops in Polish army.[39] Andrzej Rachuba extensively researched topics related to the Lithuanian army, delivering, amongst many others, detailed articles about the organisation and strength of this army in the period 1654–1667,[40] Lithuanian officers moving to and from the Swedish army[41] and foreign officers in the Lithuanian army.[42] Another great research into the matters of Lithuanian forces comes from Konrad Bobiatyński. Amongst his works used during the writing this book are the history of the early Lithuanian–Muscovite campaign,[43] Polish auxiliary corps supporting the Lithuanian army[44] and winged hussars.[45] Very useful – both as a source of direct information and archival references – were three biographies of the commanders from the Deluge period. Adam Kersten wrote about

---

32 Jan Wimmer, *Wojsko polskie w drugiej połowie XVII wieku* (Warszawa: Wydawnictwo Ministerstwa Obrony Narodowej, 1965).
33 Jan Wimmer, 'Materiały do zagadnienia liczebności i organizacji armii koronnej w latach 1655-1660', *Studia i Materiały do Historii Wojskowości*, IV (1958).
34 Jan Wimmer, *Polska-Szwecja. Konflikty zbrojne w XVI-XVII wieku* (Oświęcim: Wydawnictwo Napoleon V, 2013).
35 Mirosław Nagielski, 'Gwardia przyboczna Władysława IV (1632-1648)', *Studia i Materiały do Historii Wojskowości*, XXVII (1984), pp.113-45.
36 Mirosław Nagielski, *Liczebność i organizacja gwardii przybocznej i komputowej za ostatniego Wazy (1648-1668)* (Warszawa: Wydawnictwo Uniwersytetu Warszawskiego, 1989).
37 Mirosław Nagielski, *Bitwa pod Warszawą 1656* (Warszawa: Dom Wydawniczy Bellona, 2007).
38 Mirosław Nagielski, 'Chorągwie husarskie Aleksandra Hilarego Połubińskiego i króla Jana Kazimierza w latach 1648-1666', *Acta Baltico-Slavica*, 15 (1983), pp.77-137.
39 Mirosław Nagielski, 'Losy jednostek autoramentu cudzoziemskiego w drugiej połowie 1655 roku (lipiec-grudzień)', in Bogusław Dybaś (ed.), *Wojny północne w XVI-XVIII wieku* (Toruń: Towarzystwo Naukowe w Toruniu, 2007).
40 Andrzej Rachuba, 'Wysiłek mobilizacyjny Wielkiego Księstwa Litewskiego w latach 1654-1667', *Studia i Materiały do Historii Wojskowości*, XLIII (2007), pp.43-60.
41 Andrzej Rachuba, 'Oficerowie armii litewskiej z armii szwedzkiej i oficerowie armii szwedzkiej z armii litewskiej w latach 1655-1660', in Bogusław Dybaś (ed.), *Wojny północne w XVI-XVIII wieku* (Toruń: Towarzystwo Naukowe w Toruniu, 2007), pp.151-63.
42 Andrzej Rachuba, 'Oficerowie cudzoziemskiego autoramentu w armii Wielkiego Księstwa Litewskiego w latach 1648-1667', in Zbigniew Karpus and Waldemar Rezmer (eds), *Od armii komputowej do narodowej (XVI-XX w.)* (Toruń: Wydawnictwo UMK, 1998), pp.57-71.
43 Konrad Bobiatyński, *Od Smoleńska do Wilna. Wojna Rzeczypospolitej z Moskwą 1654-1655* (Zabrze: Inforteditions, 2004).
44 Konrad Bobiatyński, 'Działania posiłkowego korpusu koronnego na terenie Wielkiego Księstwa Litewskiego w latach 1654-1656', *Studia i Materiały do Historii Wojskowości*, XLI (2004), pp.61-81.
45 Konrad Bobiatyński, 'Husaria litewska w dobie walk z Kozakami oraz wojskami moskiewskimi w latach 1648-1667', in *W boju i na paradzie. Husaria Rzeczypospolitej w XVI-XVII w.* (Warszawa: Arx Regia, Wydawnictwo Zamku Królewskiego w Warszawie – Muzeum, 2020), pp.109-28.

Stefan Czarniecki,[46] Konrad Bobiatyński about Michał Kazimierz Pac[47] and Adam Andrzej Majewski about Aleksander Hilary Połubiński.[48] Many other books and articles, written (mostly) by Polish researchers, will of course be referenced in the footnotes and the bibliography.

---

46 Adam Kersten, *Stefan Czarniecki 1599-1665* (Lublin: Wydawnictwo Uniwersytetu Marii Curie-Skłodowskiej, 2006).

47 Konrad Bobiatyński, *Michał Kazimierz Pac. Wojewoda wileński, hetman wielki litewski* (Warszawa: Wydawnictwo Neriton, 2008).

48 Andrzej A. Majewski, *Marszałek wielki litewski Aleksander Hilary Połubiński (1626-1679). Działalność polityczno-wojskowa* (Warszawa: Instytut Historyczny Uniwersytetu Warszawskiego, 2014).

2

Organisation, Recruitment and Overall Strength of the Armies

The Commonwealth's Military System during 1654–1660

The Polish–Lithuanian Commonwealth was created as the outcome of the Union of Lublin, signed on 1 July 1569. The Kingdom of Poland and the Grand Duchy of Lithuania were therefore joined by a real union and reigned by an elected monarch. One of the points of the union was resolving military matters of the new state. It was decided that both the Crown (Poland)[1] and Lithuania would have separate military forces, each with its own command and slightly different military establishment.[2] When researching seventeenth-century Polish and Lithuanian warfare, one has to first realise the very complicated structure of its military establishment. There were many elements of the armed forces – commanded, recruited and paid for by the king, central and local authorities, towns and cities and even by wealthier individuals. Some of them had regular or semi-regular character; others could be raised only in specific situations. It is also important to understand how the units were raised, as there were a few different methods, depending on the type or even formation. I also want to write in much detail about the process of enlisting prisoners of war (POWs), as they were an important part of the expanded foreign *autorament* from 1656 onwards and, thanks to the diaries of two former Swedish soldiers (Gordon and Holsten), we have a unique view into the ways such men could switch from one army to another.

Throughout the majority of the first part of the seventeenth century, only Poland had a standing regular army. It was a so-called 'quarter army' (*wojsko kwarciane*), named after the method of its financing, which was drawn from

---

1 Both names will be used to describe Polish troops.
2 Each army would have its two hetmans: Grand Hetman in command and Field Hetman as second in command.

a special tax on the income from Crown estates (lands owned directly by the king). It was established in 1563, with the tax set up as 25 percent of the income (hence the name), although in 1567 the rate was changed into 20 percent without changing the name of the army. It was a small force, composed mostly of cavalry units (hussar and cossack cavalry), and its main role was to protect the border against Tatar raids. In case of more open conflict or prolonged campaign, it was supported by raising new regular units known as supplement troops (*wojsko suplementowe*). The army created in this way, which was to take part in the campaign, was known as the *komput*, from the Latin word *computus*. Gradually, the term '*komput*' started to be used as a description of the regular army, and in 1652, after a massacre of a large part of the Polish standing troops at Batoh, the 'quarter army' ceased to exist and the *komput* was from then on used to describe the regular army. As mentioned before, in the early seventeenth century, Lithuania did not have a standing army. Sometimes, there were some garrison units paid by the National Treasury, while during times of war, the regular army was raised and then disbanded after conflict ended. From 1648 onwards, facing a series of wars against the Cossacks, Muscovites and Swedes, the regular *komput* was in service in Lithuania as well, increased or decreased depending on the situation.

Polish nobles or unarmoured cavalry in 1655. Erik Dahlbergh's drawing for Samuel Pufendorf's *De rebus a Carolo Gustavo Sueciae rege gestis*, published in 1696 (Biblioteka Narodowa, Warszawa)

If the country was in serious danger – like facing the full Ottoman's might in 1621, the Muscovites in 1654 and the Swedes in 1655 – the king, with approval of the *Sejm*, could order raise of the levy of nobility. In theory, it was composed of all able-bodied nobles in the land, who, depending on their wealth and standing, would arrive on their own or with retinues of the different size. Additionally, towns were to supply a levy of infantry, paid for from their own coffers. During the time of peace, nobles in each voivodeship and land were obliged to take part in musters, usually annual ones, where they were to arrive *armatus et hastatus* (armed and mounted), so they could be counted and checked. Depending on their equipment, they arrived as hussars, cossacks or even reiters, although poor ones could even show up on foot or barely armed. They were then grouped into banners, with some prominent nobles chosen as *rotmistrz*, and all units from one region formed into one regiment (*pułk*). More details about organisation and military actions of the levy of nobility will be provided in chapter four.

The Cossack Uprising of 1648 ended, at least for few decades, the so-called 'Cossack register', as regular troops on Polish pay were known. As such, no Cossack regiments (*pułki*) were in service when war with Sweden started in 1655, although of course some individual Cossacks could be found in the ranks of Polish units. Another formation that was under central control was the so-called '*wybraniecka* infantry', established by Stephan Bathory after he became the King of Poland in 1576. It was militia raised from the peasants from Crown-owned lands. By the time of the Deluge, it was relegated to auxiliary duties, often noncombat like engineering troops or helping with artillery, and it did not play any important role during military operations.

As levy of nobility could not be used as a reliable force and because the nobles serving in it were often rather unwilling to leave their homes for long campaigns, they quickly established a type of regular troops that could be raised instead of them. These 'district troops' (*wojska powiatowe*) were set up individually by each region, paid by special taxes agreed upon by the local *sejmik*. They were often raised for a short period of time, usually for one quarter (three months), and normally just for the defence of the region. As we shall see with many examples from the Deluge, their size, organisation and way they took part in campaigns greatly varied from region to region. Another type of troops raised by districts were *łanowe* troops. Most of them were, at least during the Deluge, serving as infantry, so in this volume I will use the term 'lan infantry' for the simplicity of it. It is named after the word '*łan*', which was a Polish unit of field measurement that, depending on the region, could vary between 18 and 28 hectares. As with other already mentioned formations, it will be described in much more detail in chapter four.

In the seventeenth century, the Commonwealth had a rather wide array of troops that could be called 'private', although their specific classifications varied. First, there was the Royal Household Guard, financed from the king's own coffer. During the 1650s, as sources of royal income diminished, a majority of those guard troops were incorporated into the regular army (*komput*) and were paid by the National Treasury from then on. Private armies of wealthy magnates were often very large in the first half of the seventeenth century, with some of those nobles fielding at times even up to a few thousand men, including banners of hussars and Western-style infantry, supported by their own artillery. The Cossack Uprising of 1648 led to a loss of large territories and many sources of income; therefore, such large private armies became a rather rare sight in the second part of the century. Nonetheless, during the wars of 1654–1667, we can still find numerous examples of private troops of many types – both Polish and Lithuanian. Often, it was just one or two banners in the service of a noble or magnate, but wealthy ones, like Zamoyski, Lubomirski or Sapieha, were still able to afford keeping a few hundred men, with some units protecting their owner's lands and others taking part in fighting alongside the regular army. In some cases, of which again some examples will be provided later in this volume, private units could be converted into part of the *komput*.

AGAINST THE DELUGE

The Polish cossack cavalry, described here as les Carabins, part of the embassy, entering Paris in 1645. Jean Boisseau, 1645 (Bibliothèque nationale de France. Photo by Tomasz Ratyński)

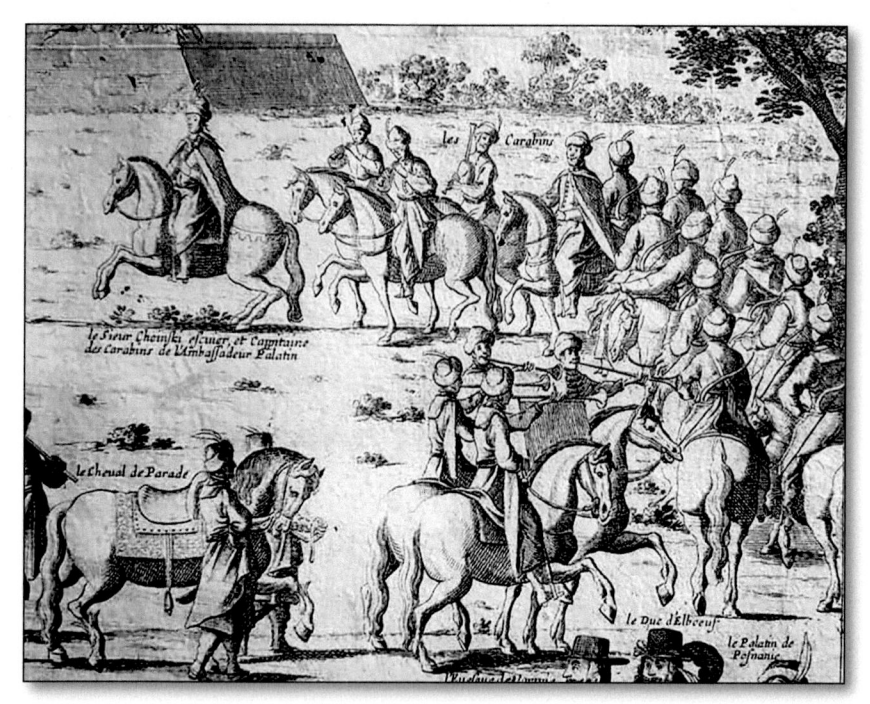

During the Deluge, whether fighting against the Swedes or the Muscovites, a very important role was played by volunteers, often organising themselves into local groups resisting the invaders. We can broadly divide them into two main types. First were the partisans (*partyzanci*), which started to emerge already in 1655 as an *ad hoc* local defence. Some of them would be organised and led by local nobles or even clergy, while others would be peasants defending their homes. Many partisans took part only in local actions, and their activities ceased once fighting armies were gone from the region. Others attached themselves to the regular troops, following the Polish army in many actions. Some groups fighting as mounted partisans, with a larger presence of nobles, could even be reformed into cossack cavalry or light horse banners of the regular army. There were also some attempts to utilise better organised groups of peasant partisans and to form from them new units of infantry. The second type of such irregular troops were those called in Polish as *wolontarze* or *wolentarze*, which actually translates to 'volunteers'. They formed quasi-regular cavalry units that could vary in size from a few hundred to a few thousand armed men. Initially created in Lithuania to face the invading Muscovite army, they were serving without pay, although they were allowed to loot the enemy (and were often a huge nuisance to the local population). They could even be created based on the recruitment letter, although it was issued by a hetman not by the king. We have a few examples of such documents bearing the name of Lithuanian Grand Hetman Janusz Radziwiłł, dated in the second part of 1654. It is worth mentioning, though, that they were very specific – as while they allowed the raising of volunteer units in face of the Muscovite offensive, they were not as detailed as recruitment letters for regular units. For example, one issued on 17 August 1654 for Jan Meżyński allowed him to 'gather as many volunteers as he can, from amongst fleeing [from the Muscovites] nobles, also from amongst commoners, under this condition

ORGANISATION, RECRUITMENT AND OVERALL STRENGTH OF THE ARMIES

that he will not recruit those from the army of Grand Duchy of Lithuania and those that are to defend the fortresses'. The newly appointed commander was to as quickly as possible join the Hetman in the army camp and follow all of his orders.[3] Another newly appointed *rotmistrz*, Michał Kotarski, also received allowance to 'gather as many volunteers as he can' and to march them to the main army, where he was obliged to to follow the Hetman's order, 'under all articles of war and severity of [military] law'.[4] Often, the officer who was in charge of the volunteers also had command of the banner or banners of the regular army, which formed the backbone of his volunteer *ad hoc* regiment. For example, Samuel Oskierko, commander of one of the largest volunteer forces fighting against the Muscovite and Swedes, was at the same time the *rotmistrz* of a cossack cavalry banner and company of dragoons in the Lithuanian *komput*, while famous partisan commander Krzysztof Żegocki built his fighting force around the core of three regular units: one banner each of cossack cavalry, reiters and dragoons. In chapter four, I will present a few of the most (in)famous volunteer commanders and their forces.

Finally, there were troops in the service of towns. Usually, the defence of such places was in the hands of the town militia, with each guild (tailors, butchers, etc.) and some minorities (e.g., Jews and Armenians) defending an allocated part of the city walls. Members of such a militia had to provide their own weapons and ammunition. They also had to take part in musters, where both they and their equipment were counted and where they were due to take part in some military exercise (usually shooting). In the majority of towns, such a militia would number only a few hundred, maybe just over thousand or so, armed men. Of course, wealthier and larger towns could deploy a much stronger militia. Here, the unquestionable leader was Gdańsk (Danzig), which had its militia divided into five regiments of 12 companies each for total of 6,000 men. They were a mostly defensive force, though, with their main role to protect the town walls. At the same time, in case of the direct danger to the city, Gdańsk was able to afford a large number of mercenaries to protect it and its interests. During 1655–1660, there were at least 2,000 to 3,000 of such soldiers on the city's payroll. While most of them were Western-style infantry, recruited in German-speaking countries, there were also some companies of cavalry (reiters) and dragoons. Troops from Gdańsk were, on same occasions, also used as support to the regular Polish troops. During allied offensives against the Swedish positions in Prussia, Jakub Łoś mentioned '500 excellent infantry' sent from the town to the army camp in November 1656.[5] It is more than probable that they were foreign mercenary troops.

A city guard, or haiduk, armed with a sabre and bardiche axe. From Józef Naronowicz-Naroński's *Optica lubo perspectiva to iest opisanie nauk widzenia…*, 1659 (Biblioteka Uniwersytetu Warszawskiego)

---

3   *AVAK* (Vilna: Tipografia A. G. Syrkina, 1909), vol. XXXIV, p.16.
4   *AVAK*, vol. XXXIV, p.33.
5   Łoś, *Pamiętnik towarzysza chorągwi pancernej*, p.74.

The Recruitment and Organisation of Troops

A letter of recruitment (*list przypowiedni*) was approved by the king and issued by the chancellery.[6] It would normally state the name and rank of the chosen officer, type and size of the unit, details of quarterly or monthly pay (per horse in cavalry and per portion in infantry) and conditions of service – when and where the unit was to muster and for how long it was due to serve. We can also sometimes find details of the equipment required for the unit (both weapons and armour), although some descriptions are rather vague, stating just 'proper [winged] hussars equipment' and so on. On many occasions, the recruitment letter did not even include any information on what weapons and equipment were required, as it was treated as 'common knowledge'. The letter issued in February 1656 to Marcin Zamoyski, for raising a 120-horse-strong banner of cossack cavalry, mentioned only that the *Rotmistrz* should recruit men 'experienced in the knightly [military] ways' and that they should be properly equipped, without any specific details.[7]

On rare occasions, a hetman could issue his own recruitment letter to an officer, although such a situation could later lead to an exchange of rather harsh letters with an unhappy monarch. When on 25 August 1654, Hetman Janusz Radziwiłł issued a recruitment letter for a 120-horse-strong banner of hussars for Michał Kazimierz Radziwiłł, he added that it was only because 'due to [war] time it was not possible to issue recruitment letters from the Chancellery of the Royal Highness [Jan II Kazimierz]'.[8] A hetman could, though, and often did, suggest suitable candidates for the rank of *rotmistrz* (in charge of cavalry banners) or foreign *autorament* officers. Some of them would be his political 'clients' or allies, other experienced soldiers that proved themselves in previous campaigns. There was always a certain degree of favouritism when nominating new candidates for the banner and regiment-level officers: many were supported in their bid by a magnate, high-ranking officials or even royal princes, who could write the recommending letter or even speak directly to the king about their suggestions. At the same time, there was a fairly large group of professional soldiers who tended to receive commissions based on their experience and merits, not just thanks to the good word of their political patron. Sometimes, a hetman may receive a recruitment letter with so-called 'windows' (*okienka*) without the name of a *rotmistrz*. Such a letter would have all the information about the type, strength and planned time of service of the unit, but it was up to the hetman

---

6   Avid readers of the *Century of the Soldier* series will probably notice that this part is very similar to those from the author's previous books, *Despite Destruction, Misery and Privations…: The Polish Army in Prussia during the War against Sweden 1626-1629* (Warwick: Helion & Company, 2020) and *We Came, We Saw, God Conquered: The Polish-Lithuanian Commonwealth's Military Effort in the Relief of Vienna, 1683* (Warwick: Helion & Company, 2021). Throughout the whole seventeenth century, the recruitment system of the Commonwealth's armies was organised in such a way, although the author believes it is important to repeat this information to draw a full picture of the army and to point out any Deluge-related differences.

7   AGAD, Archiwum Zamoyskich (AZ) 463, pp.1–2.

8   AGAD, Archiwum Warszawskie Radziwiłłów (AR) 2.1, no. 1287.

to add the name of a suitable candidate and issue him with a full recruitment letter.⁹

Many *rotmistrz*-level officers, especially those leading winged hussar units, were in fact only nominal in position, held by wealthy nobles and important country or court officials. It was traditional, then, that official sources (like army musters) and even mentions in diaries were describing such units by the office held by its leading officer. So, for example, Stefan Czarniecki's units would be named as banners or regiments of Voivode of Ruthenia, while Jan Sobieski's units from 1656 onwards would be Crown Grand Standard-Bearer's units. Thanks to that, we can often find many units with the same *rotmistrz* or colonel, even when he was not taking part in the campaign. Because of this, the main job of recruiting of the banners was in the hands of the lieutenant (*porucznik*), who was second in command of the unit and usually led troops during the campaign. The letter of recruitment was registered in the local court¹⁰ of the district he was planning (or was allocated) to raise the unit in. The letter was then added to the district's record, in a process called '*oblatowanie*', which made it official. It gave the officer the rights to look for volunteers and described the timeframe within which he should be creating the unit. Candidates for companions of the unit could be looked for in many different ways: from amongst people known to the officers (including their families and neighbours) to former soldiers from previously disbanded units to finally amongst local nobles looking for possible military careers. The recruiting officer could look for candidates during any gatherings or meetings of nobles; sometimes, his appeal for volunteers could be even read in church during Mass. Those that agreed to join the unit and were accepted then received some sum of money in lieu of the pay and had to provide their own retinue (*poczet*), composed of retainers called '*pocztowi*'. One of the companions was designated as the standard-bearer (*chorąży*), who would carry the unit's standard. Despite taking on such an important role, he normally was not treated as an officer, though. In certain circumstances, the standard-bearer, even though he was not a ranking officer, could lead the unit in absence of the other commander, although it was a fairly rare occurrence. Konstanty Dederko was, between 1659 and 1661, the standard-bearer in Jan Zamoyski's hussar banner. The *Rotmistrz* was just a nominal commander, and due to the absence of the lieutenant, Dederko 'served at that time in place of lieutenant'.¹¹ While it was a temporary solution, it seems that Zamoyski trusted him well enough to keep him in such an *ad hoc* position for a fairly long period of time.

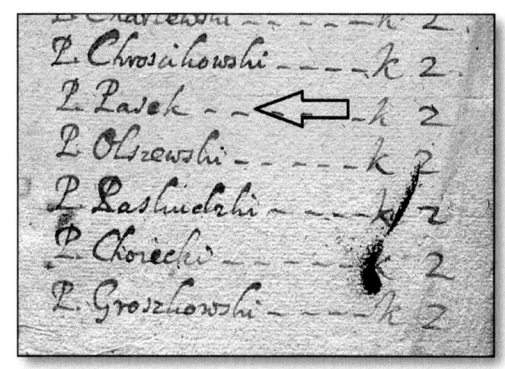

A fragment of the muster roll of *Rotmistrz* Stanisław Widlica Domaszewski's cossack cavalry banner from 1656. The name marked with an arrow is Jan Chryzostom Pasek, author of famous diary. He served with just one retainer and seems to be rather low in unit's hierarchy. Not counting officers' retinues, Pasek is named as twenty-second of 33 companions (AGAD, Warsaw).

---

9   *Korespondencja wojskowa hetmana Janusza Radziwiłła w latach 1646-1655*, vol. I, *Diariusz kancelaryjny 1649-1653*, p.641.
10 So-called '*sąd grodzki*'.
11 Marek Wagner, *Słownik biograficzny oficerów polskich drugiej połowy XVII wieku* (Oświęcim: Wydawnictwo Napoleon V, 2013), vol. I, p.63.

Traditionally, in case of the absence of the *rotmistrz* and lieutenant, one of the companions was designated as deputy (*namiestnik*), who was in charge of the troops. Retinues in each banner were part of a *rolla*. It was the list of all retinues written down by the importance of the companions – so it starts with the *rotmistrz*'s and lieutenant's retinues, but the next place could be taken by a wealthier or somehow more important companion, not necessarily by the standard-bearer. It was all part of the rather delicate and often very confusing social structure of the unit, in which normally officers could only ask their soldiers to follow the orders since, because all officers and companions were nobles, they were (at least in theory) equal.

A position in a banner's *rolla* could help in future promotions (e.g., to replace lieutenant or standard-bearer). The higher one was in the hierarchy, the better chance one had to become deputy or the unit's envoy sent to pick up and deliver pay. We even read about examples of the duels between companions fighting for a better place in the *rolla*. On 15 September 1660, Lithuanian soldier and diarist Jan Poczobut Odlanicki had to defend his position in his hussar banner in a duel against another companion, Kazimierz Jurewicz. It led to an open fight between companions from a few units, but, at the end of it, Poczobut Odlanicki managed to retain his position in the *rolla*.[12]

While many lieutenants had a long connection with their units and their *rotmistrz*, often serving in same banner for decades, others – especially those not linked so close to their patron – could move between the units. Konstanty Górski started his service in the Polish army in 1655 as companion in the cossack cavalry banner of Jan Dembiński. He quickly was promoted to the standard-bearer of the unit. In the second part of 1658, he even became lieutenant, but the unit was disbanded soon after due to death of the *Rotmistrz*. Górski transferred to the cossack banner of Jan Tuczyński, again as a lieutenant. He served there until early 1660, when he moved units again, becoming the lieutenant of Stanisław Czarniecki's cossack cavalry banner, where he stayed until the beginning of 1662.[13] Konstanty Szybiński also started military service in 1655, initially as a companion in the cossack cavalry banner of Feliks Potocki. Between 1657 and 1658, he was the lieutenant of this unit, but in early 1659 we can find him as the lieutenant of the cossack cavalry banner of Jan Sobieski. Later same year, he switched to Mikołaj Daniłowicz's cossacak cavalry banner, where he was lieutenant until at least end of 1661.[14]

While normally issues of recruitment were in their hands, in rare instances, the officer in the charge of the unit could receive an order to take certain companions into the ranks of his banner. It would normally happen in relation between the titular *rotmistrz* (not present in the army) and his lieutenant, the de facto commander of the unit. In June 1655, King Jan Kazimierz wrote such a special 'recommendation' to Aleksander Hilary

---

12   Poczobut Odlanicki, *Pamiętnik Jana Władysława Poczobuta Odlanickiego*, p.37.
13   Wagner, *Słownik biograficzny oficerów polskich drugiej połowy XVII wieku*, vol. I, p.106.
14   Wagner, *Słownik biograficzny oficerów polskich drugiej połowy XVII wieku*, vol. I, p.261.

Połubiński, lieutenant of the newly raised Royal hussar banner.¹⁵ The King mentioned in his letter that Konstanty Odachowski, who just disbanded the district cossack cavalry banner from Samogitia, offered to join the Royal hussars 'in retinue of three horses'. The Monarch 'ordered and will it' for the companion to be added to the banner. Of course, while it was a rather unusual way of recruitment, we can assume that it could happen if the *rotmistrz* liked the new candidate or had some connection with him. It is worth adding, though, that the deputy (*namiestnik*) who was in charge of the banner in the absence of the officers did not have to be in the top of *rolla* (i.e., his retinue did not have to be placed straight after the officers' ones). In 1659, in the cossack cavalry banner of Stanisław Jabłonowski, there was no lieutenant in the *rolla*. In the first quarter of 1659, the deputy leading the unit was Jerzy Srokowski, who was ninth in the order of companions (not counting officers). For the next two quarters, the deputy was Aleksander Jordan, second amongst the companions in the order of the unit. In the final quarter of 1659, it was Jerzy Srokowski again, and what is even more unusual is that his retinue was not even mentioned in the banner's muster roll.¹⁶

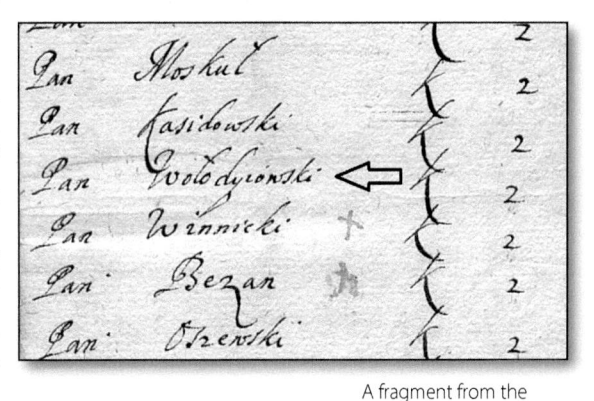

A fragment from the muster roll of the cossack cavalry banner of Franciszek Dziewanowski from the second quarter of 1659. The name marked with an arrow is Jerzy Wołodyjowski, later known as one of the defenders of Kamieniec Podolski in 1672 and who was used by Henryk Sienkiewicz as a base for Michał Wołodyjowski in his 'Trilogy'. We can see that, unlike in the novels, during the Deluge, he was just a companion in the cossack banner. He served with just one retainer (hence the two-horse retinue), and his position in the *rolla* – fifteenth of 38 companions – means that he was not high in the unit's hierarchy (AGAD, Warsaw).

When receiving a recruitment letter, the officer that was to be in charge of new unit was normally obliged to muster his troops in the army camp within a certain date. In fact, they were often given a fairly short notice to do so. On 12 March 1651, chancellery of the Lithuanian Field Hetman Janusz Radziwiłł issued a recruitment letter for the banner of 100 horses of cossack cavalry to Tatar *Rotmistrz* Abrahamowicz. He received a so-called '*przystawstwo*', which were villages that were designated to provide food and forage for the new unit: Propojsk, Pluje, Wosoczort, Białowczyzna, Chirów and Hużyn, also some local land that belonged to clergy. The *Rotmistrz* had only a month to gather his soldiers, as by 12 of April 1651 he was supposed to muster his banner in the army camp. Finally, he also received *asygnacje* (assignation) from the Lithuanian treasury, so he could be paid the recruitment money required to assist his troops in preparation for military service.¹⁷ In same way, Jan Lipski received a recruitment letter for the banner of a 100-horse cossack cavalry. The order was issued on 18 March 1651, and the unit was to muster in the army camp on 18 April. The *Przystawstwo* was assigned for Korzen, Błonie, Staszynki and clergy land 'of both types' in Miński Voivodeship. The *Rotmistrz* was issued assignation for recruitment money 'as normal'.¹⁸

---

15   AGAD, Archiwum Warszawskie Radziwiłłów (AR) III, no. 4, p.14.
16   AGAD, Archiwum Skarbu Koronnego (ASK) 85, no. 80, pp.111–16v.
17   *Korespondencja wojskowa hetmana Janusza Radziwiłła w latach 1646-1655*, vol. I, *Diariusz kancelaryjny 1649-1653*, p.513.
18   *Korespondencja wojskowa hetmana Janusza Radziwiłła w latach 1646-1655*, vol. I, *Diariusz kancelaryjny 1649-1653*, p.533.

A unit could also receive assigned terrain when it was being reinforced or rebuilt. On 27 January 1656, Stefan Czarniecki was assigned the village of Rybotycze 'with its surroundings' and villages in the same area belonging to the Krasicki family as a staging area of his dragoon regiment. The unit was being strengthened to 500 horses, so it needed the larger territory to feed the incoming soldiers and horses. Czarniecki even mentioned in his assignation order that he hoped that 'those areas will provide all [required] help for the posthaste creation of this regiment'.[19]

The recruitment of reiters, foreign infantries and dragoons looked slightly different from that of a *rotmistrz*. The colonel of the units, known under the Germanized term '*oberszter*', received a recruitment letter, but often such a regiment was allocated to magnates and court officials, especially to those that were at the same time the *rotmistrz* of hussar banners. As the equipping and keeping of those cavalry units in service was expensive, having at the same time the rank of the infantry or dragoon colonel – where the officer could claim some part of the unit's nominal strength as his pay (the so-called 'dead pay') – was a way of rewarding him and providing some unofficial, yet well-known to everyone, way of reimbursement. Additionally, one-fifth from each soldier's pay was deducted towards the colonel's pay, such a process was known under the German name of *kopfgeld*.

As with many cavalry banners, the recruitment and organisation of infantry and dragoons was handed over to the second in command, usually the lieutenant colonel (*oberszter lejtnant*) or major. Typically, the colonel signed a special document called 'capitulation' (*kapitulacja*) with such an individual, in which they specified the conditions that the second in command would then recruit the regiment (e.g., special pay or the period of time within which a unit needed to be created). From then on, the lieutenant colonel took over and looked for lower-rank officers to help him create the regiment. It was up to each captain to raise their own company. Despite being called 'foreign', these units were normally recruited locally in Poland and Lithuania, although many officers and NCOs were indeed foreign, mostly German speaking. Volunteers for the service could be officially looked for only on royal and church lands – it was forbidden to recruit from amongst peasants living on the owned land of magnates and nobles, although many fugitives from such areas ended up in the ranks anyway. Troops were recruited by the method of 'free drum', with officers leading recruitment parties into the area designated in their recruitment letter and announcing a call-out for new soldiers.

A recruitment letter could be also issued to reinforce an already existing unit. If the officer had under his command a banner of 100 horses and it was due to be expanded to 120 horses, he would receive a new recruitment letter, replacing his original one. Such a document could sometimes have

A fragment of the muster roll of Władysław Myszkowski's cossack cavalry banner from 1658. The name marked with an arrow is Jakub Łoś, author of another famous diary. He served with just one retainer and seems to have been fairly low in the unit's hierarchy. Not counting officers' retinues, Łoś was named as thirty-first of 44 companions (AGAD, Warsaw).

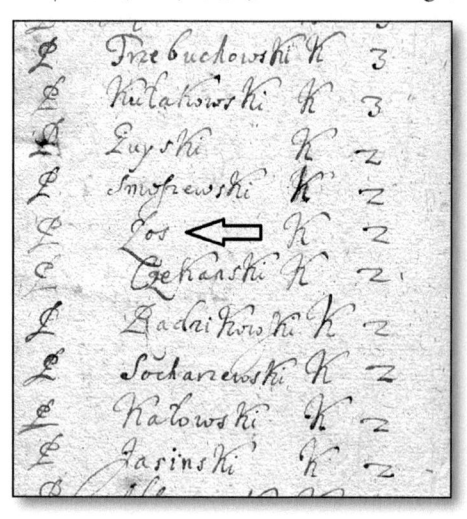

---

19   Andrzej Borcz, *Przemyśl 1656-1657* (Warszawa: Dom Wydawniczy Bellona, 2006), p.195.

different conditions of service, depending on the situation and circumstances. On 3 February 1651, Hetman Janusz Radziwiłł issued order to nine officers of old units (six of *rotmistrz* rank and three captains of foreign troops), informing them that they were to speed up the process of supplementing their units, as per the attached recruitment letter signed by the King.[20] In that way, units reduced during the winter time were to be put again on war footing with full strength and be ready to take part in the new campaign in the spring. In an example from the Polish army, on 20 March 1658, Colonel Józef Łączyński received an amended recruitment letter from King Jan II Kazimierz. As he already had 400 dragoons under his command, he was now ordered to raise 200 more and add them to his unit.[21]

Another unusual one would be a letter ordering a merger of units in service. In July 1661, Michał Kazimierz Radziwiłł was nominal commander of two units in the Polish army: regiment of foreign infantry and regiment of dragoons. On 22 July 1661, he was issued a recruitment letter in which he was ordered to disband the dragoon unit and incorporate its soldiers into the infantry regiment, raising the overall strength of the expanded regiment to 1,000 portions. The official document stated that such a move was dictated 'for better ease of recruitment and lowering of the cost', as infantrymen were paid less than dragoons.[22]

Even the recruitment moves to replace losses or put units back to strength had to be often regulated, as rarely officers were allowed to take new recruits from where and when they pleased. Between 25 and 29 January 1656, officers from Stefan Czarniecki's dragoon regiment – Krzysztof Wąsowicz, Jerzy Godlewski, Jan Skalski and Aleksander Czarnecki – received recruitment letters allowing them to raise supplements for their units. On 7 March the same year, another captain of this regiment, Paweł Dawid Pomyski, was also sent for a recruitment mission as per royal order. It was all a part of the plan to reach an expected strength of 500 (January) and finally 600 horses (March), as the regiment was to take part in a new campaign against the Swedes. Royal letters specified that Czarniecki was allowed to find and recruit a 'certain number of men as he is [currently] some [men] short for [the regiment's] supplement'. The King advised that local nobles were to support these recruitment actions and not 'set any obstacles in recruiting and gathers of those men'.[23] On 30 August 1659, Crown Grand Hetman Stanisław Potocki issued, in written form, special allowance for Captain Jerzy Godlewski to recruit several dozen men from Ukraine, to replace losses in his dragoon regiment.[24]

Officers could also receive a sort of 'renewal' letter, as a confirmation of their prolonged service. Lithuanian *Rotmistrz* Mustafa Baranowski had command of a banner of Tatars that, in 1653, had 130 horses. In December

---

20   *Korespondencja wojskowa hetmana Janusza Radziwiłła w latach 1646-1655*, vol. I, *Diariusz kancelaryjny 1649-1653*, pp.452–53.
21   *Akta grodzkie i ziemskie z czasów Rzeczypospolitej Polskiej* (Lwów: Księgarnia Seyfartha i Czajkowskiego, 1884), vol. X, p.282.
22   AGAD, Archiwum Warszawskie Radziwiłłów (AR) VII, no. 86, pp.5–7.
23   Borcz, *Przemyśl 1656-1657*, pp.195–96.
24   *Akta grodzkie i ziemskie z czasów Rzeczypospolitej Polskiej*, vol. X, p.286.

1654, he received a new letter, this time for a slightly smaller unit of 100 horses. His recruitment letter – 'proof of your faithful service' – was lost, though, so on 23 February 1656 he received yet another recruitment letter, for the same size banner of Tatar light horse, made 'from experienced, well trained men, that he will keep in proper order'.[25]

On rare occasions, command of the unit could be transferred from father to son or from one member of the family to another, when the original *rotmistrz* died or resigned from further military service. In May 1656, Jachia Ułan, Lithuanian 'Tatar *rotmistrz* of His Royal Highness', received a recruitment letter for an 'old recruitment'[26] Tatar banner of 150 horses', after the death of its original commander, his father Czymbaj Ułan.[27] It is more than probable that, in such a situation, the core of the unit was based on the retinues already in service from the deceased's banner.

Finally, there were some cases of a private unit switching to the regular army, which of course was regulated by another type of recruitment letter. For example, in November 1658, Lieutenant of winged hussars Aleksander Ludwik Niezabitowski was ordered by Jan II Kazimierz to strengthen his private squadron of dragoons so that the unit could be incorporated into the regular army.[28] It was, in fact, just a 100-man-strong company. Nonetheless, it shows that, even in the later stage of the war, some privately raised units could find their way into the *komput*.

It is worth noting that, as the war or campaign progressed, many retinues in banners became smaller. The overall strength of units often lost 20 to 30 horses or even more, not only due to 'battle' losses but also due to companions leaving ranks or reducing the size of their retinues. This is especially noticeable with light cavalry, where many three-horse retinues 'downgraded' to two horses, while many two-horse retinues dropped to a sole companion. If a unit was destroyed during a campaign, the effort of rebuilding it was usually very expensive, especially when the National Treasury could not support it. Such a recruitment operation was normally a massive burden for even wealthy magnates. Prince Bogusław Radziwiłł in his memoir wrote that, when his two regiments – infantry and reiters – were destroyed at Batoh in 1652, in order to rebuild them he had to pawn his hereditary land possessions: Zuprany, Hrubieszewice, Dylatycze and Wiazyn. There was no other way for him to obtain a large amount of cash, as 'there was no money [available] in treasury'.[29]

Hardships of a campaign, especially during long marches and pursuits, often with barely any provisions for both men and horses, further diminished the size of units. Jakub Łoś wrote about the summer campaign of 1657, when the Polish army was chasing the Transylvanians, that due to lack of food 'half

An example of the 'wear and tear' of units during a long campaign, the muster roll of Kazimierz Rusinowski's cossack cavalry banner (from the Polish army), January 1655. Many retinues had lowered their number of horses, and we can see in the document how they were changed from three to two. Even the *Rotmistrz*'s retinue was lowered from 12 to nine. At the bottom of the document, the names of five companions are crossed out, indicating that they died or left the service (AGAD, Warszawa).

25 Andrzej Rachuba (ed.), *Metryka Litewska. Księga wpisów nr 131* (Warszawa: Wydawnictwo DiG, Instytut Historii PAN, 2001), pp.42–43.
26 This term means 'existing unit'.
27 Rachuba (ed.), *Metryka Litewska. Księga wpisów nr 131*, p.112.
28 *Akta grodzkie i ziemskie z czasów Rzeczypospolitej Polskiej*, vol. X, p.284.
29 Bogusław Radziwiłł, *Żywot xięcia Bogusława Radziwiłła, przez niego samego napisany* (Poznań: Drukarnia na Garbarach, 1841), p.21.

ORGANISATION, RECRUITMENT AND OVERALL STRENGTH OF THE ARMIES

of the men of the *komput* were left behind on the road' and that banners that had 20 or 30 horses were treated as 'well prepared [to fight]'.[30] Companions were trying to keep their retinues in good shape, but often the lack of funds meant that there were no opportunities to replace lost men, horses and equipment.

Wintertime, when units were stationed on quarters, was often the period when companions were allowed to leave the unit and return home, often in order to deal with their personal business, to see family and their estate and to make necessary purchases. In November 1661, Pasek left his retainers in the unit, while he and his servants (*czeladź*) returned to his family home. Here, he 'fed his horses well, also bought some new ones; as there was, thanks to God, some money from Denmark and my father also gave me some', and then he returned to his banner.[31]

At the same time, the size of a *rotmistrz*'s retinue could be increased, as a way to ensure that the extra pay ended up with the lieutenant in charge of the unit in the field. In the hussar banner of Jan Zamoyski, such a retinue in the first quarter of 1655 was 14 horses, in the next quarter 18 horses, and from the third quarter of this year it was set up on 24 horses.[32]

We rarely have a chance to look into detailed lists of losses amongst units, as diarists tended to usually mention only the most important killed and wounded, like officers and companions, or only provide us with overall army losses. I managed to find one interesting *rolla*, though, where all losses are mentioned in great detail. It describes the cossack cavalry banner of Jan Zamoyski, from the muster in January 1660. Its structure was typical for Polish cavalry of that time, with the *Rotmistrz*'s retinue of 24 horses, the lieutenant's of five and the standard-bearer's of three. The remaining 55 retinues were mostly two or three horses, and the whole unit had almost 200 horses of 'paper strength'. Additional annotations to the *rolla* indicate the number of losses: five killed companions (including the standard-bearer), two wounded companions and five killed and seven wounded retainers. Most of the killed and wounded are described as 'shot'.[33] It worth adding that the vacancy for the killed standard-bearer was not filled for more than a year, and, even on the muster for the second quarter of 1661, the unit did not have his replacement.[34] One of the companions had to 'step in' for the standard-bearer's duty yet for some unknown reason was not officially promoted.

Tracing the exact number of losses in units of infantry and dragoons provides more problems, as often musters of those formations are not as detailed as those of cavalry. An interesting example from 1653 shows the unit after winter quarters with much a diminished strength, as usual illnesses and desertions took its toll. The company of Lithuanian Grand Hetman Janusz Kiszka, mustered on 22 January, was led by a lieutenant, who had just the

---

30 Łoś, *Pamiętnik towarzysza chorągwi pancernej*, pp.78–79.
31 Pasek, *Pamiętniki*, pp.189–90.
32 AGAD, ASK 85, no. 77, *passim*.
33 AGAD, ASK 85, no. 83, pp.296–97.
34 AGAD, ASK 85, no. 83, p.302.

wachmeister[35] and one drummer with him, without any other officers or 'specialists'. There were only 25 rank-and-file dragoons, divided into two files of five, three files of four and one file of three men[36] – all that remained from the unit that should have been around 100 men strong. Another indication of the losses within a unit during a prolonged period of time comes from one of the dragoon companies of Michał Kazimierz Radziwiłł. After the siege of Toruń, during the muster on 3 January 1659, amongst rank-and-file dragoons, 13 are mentioned as killed, six as dead due to illness, eight as deserters – leaving only 42 dragoons in the unit. From amongst company staff, only the lieutenant is mentioned as wounded ('shot'), though.[37]

During the campaign, in order to replace losses, units often incorporated men from disbanded banners or new volunteers found locally. It could lead to a situation in which a unit that was part of the Lithuanian army could, in fact, in large part consist of Polish soldiers. A good example of such a situation is the hussar banner of Aleksander Hilary Połubiński, serving in the Lithuanian army between 1648 and 1655. From the 80 companions of this unit, 29 were from the Lithuanian Nowogródek Voivodeship, nine from Samogitia and eight from Vilnius Voivodeship. The Polish contingent seems to be fairly large, though, including nine companions from Mazowsze and five from Podlasie.[38] When, in February 1655, Połubiński received a recruitment letter for a Royal banner of hussars in the Lithuanian army, in order to find enough willing volunteers to fill the ranks of a 200-horse-strong unit, he had to search far and wide. His own hussar banner was disbanded, and some of the companions joined the new unit, alongside some from Połubiński's cossack cavalry banner. Further recruitment took place again in previously used areas, especially in Nowogródek and Vilnius Voivodeships. The intake of Polish soldiers, especially from Mazowsze, seems to have been mostly connected with replenishing the ranks after the Battle of Warsaw in 1656, where the unit took significant losses during the famous charge against the Swedes.[39] The period when units of the Lithuanian army operated in Poland for a longer time was, especially in 1656, fairly long, so it is more than likely that many Poles found their way to Lithuanian units during that time. It is also possible that some Lithuanians joined the banners of Polish Czarniecki's division in 1660, when it was supporting Sapieha's forces in today's Belarus.

In many units of national cavalry, we can find companions from one family, usually described as 'older' and 'younger', indicating father and son, two brothers or other kinsmen. The cossack cavalry banner of Prince Mikołaj Świątopełk Czetwertyński, at the beginning of 1659, was composed of 144 horses, divided into 56 retinues. Amongst them, there were six 'sets' of

---

35 The NCO responsible for guard duties and sentries around the camp. The term comes from the German *wachtmeister* and was Polonised into *wachmistrz*. I decided to use the version '*wachmeister*' as it was the most commonly present in the primary sources.
36 AGAD, Archiwum Warszawskie Radziwiłłów (AR) X, no. 632, pp.61–62.
37 AGAD, AR VII, no. 63, p.6.
38 Nagielski, 'Chorągwie husarskie Aleksandra Hilarego Połubińskiego i króla Jana Kazimierza w latach 1648-1666', pp.82–83.
39 Nagielski, 'Chorągwie husarskie Aleksandra Hilarego Połubińskiego i króla Jana Kazimierza w latach 1648-1666', pp.84–88.

Polish regular troops surrendering to the Swedes in 1655. Erik Dahlbergh's drawing for Samuel Pufendorf's De rebus a Carolo Gustavo Sueciae rege gestis, published in 1696 (Muzeum Narodowe, Kraków)

those named 'older' and 'younger', additionally one with 'older', 'middle' and 'younger'.[40] Members of a family could also join a banner to replace someone who died or resigned from service. Pasek mentioned that, when veteran companion Jan Rubieszowski died in 1660, he was replaced by his kinsman Wąsowicz (most likely taking over his retinue).[41]

On such a note, one could wonder what happened with a retinue if their companion died. It is unlikely that they would remain in service, although such a situation became more common in the late part of the seventeenth century, when companions left the service but still kept their retainers as a retinue under the banner. Sometimes, a retinue could be taken over by a member of the family of the deceased, like a brother, son or even more distant relative. On other occasions, which were probably the most common, the retinue was disbanded. Pasek mentioned that, after the death of companion Jan Wojnowski, 'his retinue and merits[42] were sent to his wife'.[43]

A retinue could also be sold if the original companion decided to end his military career. In September 1659, Jan Poczobut Odlanicki bought from his brother 'with full order' a three-horse-strong hussar retinue (i.e., one companion and two retainers), giving for it – 'not overpaying, as brother' – 1,600 zł. Three days after this transaction, the new hussar and his retinue enlisted into the banner of Lithuanian Field Hetman Gosiewski.[44]

Members of the same family usually served in the same unit or at least the same division, as it was almost customary that younger siblings were learning military craft from the older already serving in the army. Stefan

---

40 AGAD, ASK 85, no. 89, pp.220–20v.
41 Pasek, *Pamiętniki*, p.137.
42 The term '*zasługi*' used by Pasek, while translated as merits, meant in this context the period of service that the companion was under the banner for. Considering that the army was not paid for a very long time, Mrs. (or rather 'Ms.' at that point) Wojnowska could have attempted to claim the money owed to her dead husband.
43 Pasek, *Pamiętniki*, p.137.
44 Poczobut Odlanicki, *Pamiętnik Jana Władysława Poczobuta Odlanickiego*, pp.28–29.

Czarniecki, later famous as *regimentarz* of the Polish army of the Deluge, as a youth served in the cossack cavalry of his brother Paweł Czarniecki, an experienced officer of this type of cavalry, during the 1626–1629 war against the Swedes in Prussia. One of the diarists of the Deluge and later conflicts, Lithuanian Aleksander Dionizy Skorobohaty, joined the army in 1654 at the age of 15, serving next to his older brother Benedykt Kazimierz, while third brother – Piotr Jerzy – also served during the 1650s in the Lithuanian army.[45] Stanisław Drobysz Tuszyński, who served in a cossack cavalry banner, took his younger brother, Jan Florian, under his wing, and they initially both served in the same unit.[46] Jan Florian became a companion at a very young age, as he was just 17 years old.[47]

Sometimes, every adult member of one family could serve at the same time in the military. By the *Sejm* in 1661, Michał Cerkies, lieutenant in a cossack cavalry banner, was ennobled for his military deeds, 'from Chocim war [of 1621] until the old age', being praised for his bravery and long service. Alongside him, the *Sejm* ennobled his three sons, Konstanty, Kazimierz and Iosef (Józef), who 'also proved their merit in the military service'.[48]

Very rare, at least during the 1650s and 1660s, was the situation wherein an officer of one unit was at the same time a companion in the other. Franciszek Szeligowski was, in the period of 1654–1659, lieutenant of a cossack cavalry banner and, in the period of 1659–1667, *rotmistrz* of Grand Hetman Potocki's haiduk banner. At the same time, between 1651 and 1667, he was a companion in the hussar banner of Grand Hetman Potocki, which clearly indicates that, at least after 1654, his retinue served without companions, just with retainers. Of course, it is easy to understand why he would try to keep his place in the hussar banner. Since it was a unit of the Grand Hetman, service in its rank was prestigious and provided good political connections with powerful and wealthy patrons.

As the campaign progressed, units could be disbanded due to losses, especially if the *rotmistrz* could not afford to replenish the ranks. It is interesting to see the motivations behind officers leaving the service or disbanding their units. In the diary of the chancellery of Hetman Janusz Radziwiłł, there is a document from June 1650, when each *rotmistrz* and colonel of the existing Lithuanian units was declaring if they would stay with their banners in the service, after they would be paid just partial overdue pay. While the majority offered to keep serving under the command of Radziwiłł, some advised that they would not be able to do so. Colonel Jerzy Teodor Tyzenhauz, after a discussion with companions from his reiter regiment, asked for the whole unit to be disbanded. It seems that the reiters were counting on being formed into new units, for which they could receive additional pay. It was met with displeasure from Hetman Radziwiłł, who answered that he was not happy that the whole unit was to leave the service and that there was no chance for a new recruitment (and new money). Another reiter officer, Teofil Szwarcoff,

---

45 Skorobohaty, *Dziennik*, p.26.
46 *Dwa pamiętniki z XVII wieku Jana Cedrowskiego i Jana Floriana Drobysza Tuszyńskiego*, p.25.
47 *Dwa pamiętniki z XVII wieku Jana Cedrowskiego i Jana Floriana Drobysza Tuszyńskiego*, p.31.
48 *Volumina Legum* (Petersburg: Nakładem i drukiem Jozafata Chryzki, 1859), vol. IV, p.411.

ORGANISATION, RECRUITMENT AND OVERALL STRENGTH OF THE ARMIES

advised that, while he was willing to stay in the army, he could not declare the same for the companions of his unit, so he needed to discuss it with them further. The cossack cavalry banner of Adam Łukański Pawłowicz was to be disbanded due to death of its *rotmistrz*, same as the cossack cavalry banner of another dead officer, *Rotmistrz* Aleksander Gosiewski. *Rotmistrz* Andrzej Jarosławski Kurpski said that 'he do not have any means' to keep his cossack cavalry banner in the army. Leon Jan Pogirski, from another cossack cavalry banner, declared that he wanted to stay in the service but also 'do not have means' to retain his cossack cavalry banner, as they only received pay for three-quarters of the service. A regiment of the district troops from Brześć Voivodeship (four banners of cossack cavalry) asked to be dismissed from the service, although one *rotmistrz*, Adam Pociej, and his banner wanted to stay as part of the regular army. All Tatar, dragoon and infantry officers decided to continue with their service.[49]

As we can see, the financial factor was, next to the death of the *rotmistrz*, the most crucial motif, as unpaid soldiers were unable to purchase replacement horses and equipment and afford to keep their retainers and servants. Looking into examples from the Polish army during the Deluge, the cossack cavalry of Stanisław Detyniecki took heavy losses during the Battle of Gołąb in 1656 and disappeared from the army soon after. The *Rotmistrz* was lucky enough to receive a new command, though, as in early 1657 he took over another cossack cavalry banner after Ludwik Lipski.[50] Another unit that disbanded after the Battle of Gołąb was the cossack cavalry banner of Michał Stanisławski, although not due to heavy losses but due to the fact that the *Rotmistrz* was taken prisoner.[51]

As mentioned before, the death of the *rotmistrz* could also lead to the disbandment of a unit, although on some occasions a banner could serve even a few months under the name of the deceased until it was either disbanded or taken over by a new officer. In a rare situation, when, despite a hetman's orders and letters, a unit never joined the army and never started its service, it could be forcefully disbanded. On 10 September 1649, Hetman Janusz Radziwiłł wrote to Zygmunt Adam Słuszka, who was the nominal *rotmistrz* of a cossack cavalry banner in the Lithuanian army. The document stated that, because the unit, despite repeated letters, never showed up and because the campaign was now over, Słuszka – 'or in his absence his lieutenant and all [the companions of the] company' – was no longer required in the army: 'Therefore, by the power of my office, I order you to, wherever this letter will find you, to disband the banner, let go companions [and ensure] that they do not hurt [the local] population during their return and that you to be ready to return to the treasury money that you received to raise the banner'.[52] At least Słuszka, holding the office of Lithuanian Court standard-bearer, was a

---

49 *Korespondencja wojskowa hetmana Janusza Radziwiłła w latach 1646-1655*, vol. I, *Diariusz kancelaryjny 1649-1653*, pp.306–09.
50 Wagner, *Słownik biograficzny oficerów polskich drugiej połowy XVII wieku*, vol. I, p.65.
51 Wagner, *Słownik biograficzny oficerów polskich drugiej połowy XVII wieku*, vol. I, p.131.
52 *Korespondencja wojskowa hetmana Janusza Radziwiłła w latach 1646-1655*, vol. I, *Diariusz kancelaryjny 1649-1653*, p.231.

Different types of defensive camps set up from tabor wagons. From Józef Naronowicz-Naroński's *Architektura militaris, to jest budownictwo wojenne*, 1659 (Biblioteka Uniwersytetu Warszawskiego).

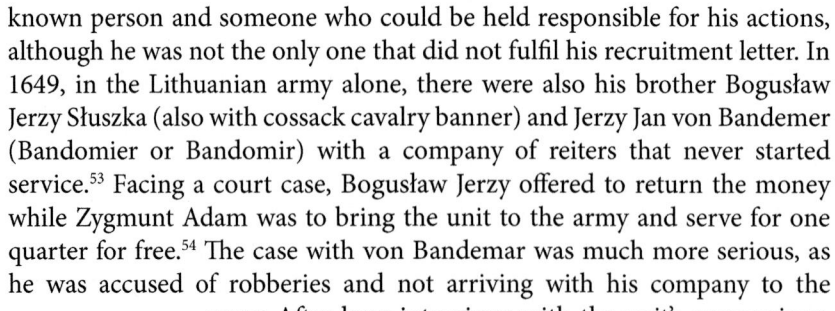

known person and someone who could be held responsible for his actions, although he was not the only one that did not fulfil his recruitment letter. In 1649, in the Lithuanian army alone, there were also his brother Bogusław Jerzy Słuszka (also with cossack cavalry banner) and Jerzy Jan von Bandemer (Bandomier or Bandomir) with a company of reiters that never started service.[53] Facing a court case, Bogusław Jerzy offered to return the money while Zygmunt Adam was to bring the unit to the army and serve for one quarter for free.[54] The case with von Bandemar was much more serious, as he was accused of robberies and not arriving with his company to the army. After long interviews with the unit's companions, who put the blame on the officers, the court came to a sentence. The *Rotmistrz* received the death penalty, and his lieutenant, Czechowicz, infamy (*infamia*)[55] and the loss of his belongings.[56] Such cases, when officers took advance pay to raise their units and disappeared with the funds, were even more common in the first half of the seventeenth century, and it was often very difficult to later find and put such officers in front of the court.

As on many occasions, it was the lieutenants that led banners in the field, and they were the most at risk of death or wound from amongst all cavalry officers. Diarist Jakub Łoś, who was serving in the *pancerni* banner of Władysław Myszkowski, lost two of his commanding officers within two months. On 6 April 1656, during a skirmish with the Swedish reiters and dragoons at Kozienice, Lieutenant Stefan Stapkowski died. His replacement, Lieutenant Jan Borowski, was amongst those killed during the Battle of Kłeck on 7 May 1656.[57] The next officer of this unit, Lieutenant Joachim Łącki, died in the battle against the Transylvanians and Cossacks at Potylicz (Magierów) on 12 July 1657.[58] Standard-bearers also often took heavy losses, as a unit's flag was always considered important loot. Łoś mentioned that, during the Battle of Kłeck, the standard of his cavalry banner first lost two bearers and was only saved by companion Jan Biegański, 'who took it [away] on foot'.[59]

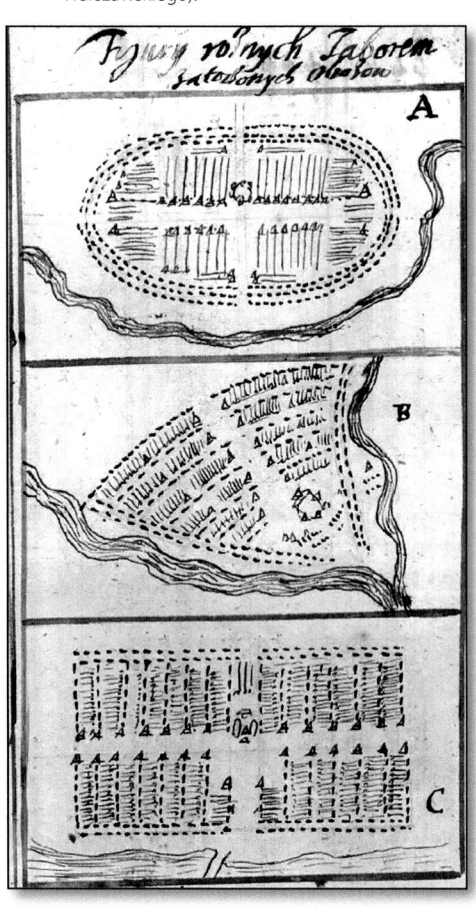

---

53 *Korespondencja wojskowa hetmana Janusza Radziwiłła w latach 1646-1655*, vol. I, *Diariusz kancelaryjny 1649-1653*, p.274.
54 *Korespondencja wojskowa hetmana Janusza Radziwiłła w latach 1646-1655*, vol. I, *Diariusz kancelaryjny 1649-1653*, pp.281–82.
55 In the Commonwealth, nobles could be sentenced to infamy for crimes like murder or robbery. It was a 'loss of good name', and a noble known as *infamis* lost his status, could not held official ranks, etc. Infamy could be revoked, though, and status returned.
56 *Korespondencja wojskowa hetmana Janusza Radziwiłła w latach 1646-1655*, vol. I, *Diariusz kancelaryjny 1649-1653*, pp.287–88.
57 Łoś, *Pamiętnik towarzysza chorągwi pancernej*, pp.65–66.
58 Wagner, *Słownik biograficzny oficerów polskich drugiej połowy XVII wieku*, vol. I, p.180.
59 Łoś, *Pamiętnik towarzysza chorągwi pancernej*, p.66.

ORGANISATION, RECRUITMENT AND OVERALL STRENGTH OF THE ARMIES

In case of the death of the lieutenant, his replacement could be sought from amongst companions, although often it could be someone moving from another unit (an active or disbanded one). The standard-bearer would normally be replaced by promoting one of the companions, although in some cases the banner could serve without a new official standard-bearer for a prolonged period of time, with different companions stepping in to fill the role at a time without official promotion. In the case of foreign troops, promotion was often within the ranks of the same company or regiment, while new recruitment was often the way to fill in the vacancies. Of course, some soldiers were able to, during longer service, go from private to officer rank, granted it was fairly rare. Konstanty Vorbek-Lettow, son of diarist Maciej Vorbek-Lettow, who was serving in the 1640s in foreign infantry, started as a musketeer, then pikeman, followed by the rank of corporal, sergeant, lieutenant, ensign in the colonel's company and captain lieutenant, to die in the French service in 1650 as captain (*rotmistrz*) of a reiter company composed of 'Poles, Livonian, Courlanders'.[60] Michał Brandt, from a German merchant family settled near Wejherowo in Prussia, started his military career as a dragoon in Ludwik Weyher's regiment. In 1658, he was an ensign in one of the companies of the Royal Guard. In the 1660s, we can find him in the unit of the Royal *arkabuzeria*, where he gradually obtained the rank of major. He continued service in Jan III Sobieski and August II's armies, finishing his career as general major.[61]

As with all armies of this period, a very important method of reinforcing the Polish and Lithuanian armies was the recruitment of POWs. It was especially useful for filling the ranks of foreign units, so infantry, dragoons and reiters. On some occasions, soldiers captured during the battle could be straight away included into the ranks of their captors. Jemiołowski mentioned such an episode from February 1656, when Czarniecki's forces captured a small Swedish garrison near Zawichost. All officers were sent to Lwów to be delivered to King Jan II Kazimierz, while around 100 rank-and-files were spread between the companies of Czarniecki's dragoon regiment.[62] The Finnish dragoons and infantrymen that were taken prisoner at the Battle of Warka in April 1656, after some time spent in captivity in Luboml, were later incorporated into Lubomirski's foreign infantry regiment.[63]

The surrender of a besieged fortress was usually a good opportunity to replace losses with those of the defenders that wanted to switch sides. In September 1659, when the Swedes surrendered Goldynga (Goldlingen) to the Lithuanians, 400 reiters and more than 700 infantry 'were taken and spread between [Lithuanian] regiments'.[64] When, in late September 1659, the Swedish garrison of Ventspils (Windau or Windawa) surrendered to the Swedes, all the rank-in-files who were ex-Danish soldiers forced into

---

60 Vorbek-Lettow, *Skarbnica pamięci*, pp.167–69.
61 Marek Wagner, *Słownik biograficzny oficerów polskich drugiej połowy XVII wieku* (Oświęcim: Wydawnictwo Napoleon V, 2014), vol. II, p.35.
62 Jemiołowski, *Pamiętnik dzieje Polski zawierający*, p.173.
63 *Diary of General Patrick Gordon*, vol. I, pp.98–99.
64 Poczobut Odlanicki, *Pamiętnik Jana Władysława Poczobuta Odlanickiego*, p.29.

the Swedish ranks decided to join the Lithuanian army.[65] When recapturing the Swedish-held fortresses in Denmark in 1659, Czarniecki's division was accompanied by Danish officers who were recruiting ex-Swedish soldiers on the spot to use them as new garrisons. Despite that, the Polish general took care of his own troops, 'taking 100 good Swedes and mixing them in [the ranks of his regiment of] dragoons, to replace those that were lost here and there [during the campaign].'[66] During the campaign of 1660, against the Muscovites and Cossacks, Holsten mentioned that all captured Germans from the Muscovite ranks were 'saved [from the Tatars allied to the Poles] and divided between our German regiments'.[67]

Former Swedish and Muscovite soldiers, especially NCOs and privates, who could not count on ransom or exchange, were often given an ultimatum: stay in prison (often in very poor conditions) or join the ranks. On 25 April 1656, Captain Stanisław Kazimierz Zamoyski, recruiting men for Jan Zamoyski's regiment, asked his colonel to send him some Swedish prisoners kept in Zamość so he could 'make them into corporals or sergeants in the unit'.[68] In such a manner, both Holsten and Gordon started their service in the Polish army, and the Scotsman had even done it twice. For the first time, he ended up in Polish captivity in January 1656, when he was captured after being separated from his unit. After 18 weeks spent in 'miserable condition', we finally have a chance to talk to Konstanty Jacek Lubomirski, the youngest brother of the famous Jerzy Sebastian Lubomirski. Gordon's memoirs provide us a very interesting 'interview' that led to him finding a new employer:[69]

> *Starost* [Lubomirski] himself asked me in Latine if I would serve the Crowne of Polland, I answered, 'Most willingly'. He asked me farther if I would rather serve under Kings guards or under him. I replyed, rather under him, Then againe he asked me if I would stay here in garrison or go to the fields with him. I said, I being a yong man, had rather, if it were his will, serve in the fields, where honour and preferment is soonest acquired.

This way, the Scottish adventurer ended up in Lubomirski's private company of dragoons, but he did not stay there long, as in the summer of 1656 after the Battle of Warsaw, he was back in the Swedish service. This time, he remained there for longer, but, in November 1658 after a skirmish with Polish cavalry, he was captured again. It is worth noticing that the Swedes made two attempts to have him ransomed, clearly valuing him as a good soldier. On the first occasion, the Polish officer in charge of the forces in Dzierzgoń (Christburg) advised that he did not have the 'commission to deal in such matters'.[70] On the second attempt, a 'Brandenburgish ensigne' was offered for Gordon, but the Polish officer refused negotiations in that matter.[71] Seeing himself

---

65 Pufendorf, *Siedem ksiąg o czynach Karola Gustawa króla Szwecji*, p.585.
66 Pasek, *Pamiętniki*, p.90.
67 Holsten, *Przygody wojenne 1655-1666*, p.64.
68 AGAD, Archiwum Zamoyskich (AZ) 334, p.7.
69 *Diary of General Patrick Gordon*, vol. I, p.87.
70 *Diary of General Patrick Gordon*, vol. I, p.274.
71 *Diary of General Patrick Gordon*, vol. I, p.274.

ORGANISATION, RECRUITMENT AND OVERALL STRENGTH OF THE ARMIES

without any other options, the Scotsman decided to look yet again for a place in the Polish army. The first offer he received came from Jan Sobieski (later famous King Jan III Sobieski), at the time still a fairly minor commander. In Gordon's response to the Polish proposition, we can see echoes of the previous conversation with Konstanty Jacek Lubomirski:

> Sobieski offered me service and promised me a company of dragownes, which lay on his land of Javorova [Jaworów] and thereabouts; which I excused, telling him that I being a yong man, was come out of my owne countrey to seeke honour, and that by lying upon lands and in quarters, nothing of that nature was to be expected; as also I perceived him to be very niggardly person.[72] He told me he had no other service for me. So I desired he would be pleased to deliver me of to the King or field marshall [Jerzy Sebastian Lubomirski], saying I would willingly serve in the fields and be worth my meat; wherewith he was pleased and said he would with convenience speake with Lubomirsky concerning me.

After 11 weeks in Polish prison, Gordon finally received an audience with Jerzy Sebastian Lubomirski. Initially, he was offered the rank of ensign in the life company of Lubomirski's foreign infantry regiment. He refused, though, saying, 'I had served for ensignie to dragouns under Crowne of Sweden and would not serve for ensignie to no prince in Christedome any more'.[73] It seems that Lubomirski took liking to the stubborn Scot, as he then suggested giving him the rank of quartermaster in his dragoon unit. In his diary, we read about the 'regimental quartermaster', but in fact it was an independent banner, initially of 100 men and later 200.[74] Without hopes for ransom or exchange, not owing anything to the Swedes anymore and seeing Lubomirski as 'the nobleman of greatest power and esteeme amongst all the Polls', Gordon decided to take the offer. It is interesting to read about the other reasons behind this agreement. The Scotsman explained that:

> being a sojor [soldier] of fortune and a stranger to both nations, my interest was nothing in the one or other … only religion made me encline more to the Polls as the other.[75] So that by all meanes, so farr as my honour could permit, I behoved to seek my advancement and strive to make some fortune, w-ch as the case stood now [in early 1659] with the Swedes was very unlikely, yea, impossible to do amongst them.[76]

After half a year of service in Lubomirski's banner, the Scot was sent to take over a newly created company that was to be entirely composed of former Swedish soldiers. Gordon was sent to pick 'a company of the Swedish

---

72 Interestingly enough, he previously called Konstanty Jacek Lubomirski, 'being extreamely covetous and niggard and loveing ease'. *Diary of General Patrick Gordon*, vol. I, p.88.
73 *Diary of General Patrick Gordon*, vol. I, p.278.
74 Lubomirski expected to expand the unit to regimental size, but it never happened due to the lack of available men.
75 Gordon was Roman Catholic.
76 *Diary of General Patrick Gordon*, vol. I, p.279.

prisoners who were in the Meve [Gniew]'.⁷⁷ He managed to recruit 76 men, 20 of them were sick though and had to be transported on wagons. Gordon divided them into files (sections) and, as acting commander, appointed some as officers and NCOs: 'I made Pawl Banser, who had been a quartermaster under the Swedes, *wachmaster* [sergeant major]; Adam Young, who had been freetrowper, being of Scots parents and haveing the Polls language, I made *forier* or quaterm-r; Elias Funk and William Rundt, who had been corporals, in the same charge, and the lyklyest and sharpest like men to be file-leaders'.⁷⁸ What is interesting to note is that around 20 men from Gordon's new unit were Danes – Swedish POWs that were shipped to Poland to serve in one of their regiments. Now, they again changed the army that they were to serve in, in a pattern very common in Europe during the time.⁷⁹ In 1660, the unit was merged with Lubomirski's life company (the one in which Gordon initially served after his release from captivity) into one large banner of 200 portions.

By some odd coincidence, another one of the ex-Swedish soldiers, Hieronim Chrystian Holsten, also ended up under Lubomirski's command. He was captured near Cracow in late autumn 1656 with other prisoners transported to the *ad hoc* prison in the Polish camp. Hearing news that the Transylvanian army was en route to Poland, Polish commanders were eager to use former Swedish soldiers to strengthen existing and to raise new foreign units. Therefore, the prisoners were given a short ultimatum: 'we were obliged to quickly decide to join [Polish] service and give our oath or to wait for something worse, as there was no chance to ransom us'.⁸⁰ It is not surprising that Holsten chose the first option. He and other 'recruits' were transported near Częstochowa, where three companies, 'mostly of the German soldiers from Swedish army', were created as a part of Lubomirski's own reiter regiment under Colonel Stefan Franciszek de Oedt. Holsten joined the life company of the regiment, where 'they force me to became senior corporal' (i.e., the corporal in charge of

Hetman Janusz Radziwiłł and his officers entering Kiev (Kijów) in 1651. From Abraham von Westervelt's painting lost during the Second World War (Zamek Królewski, Warszawa).

---

77   *Diary of General Patrick Gordon*, vol. II, p.20.
78   *Diary of General Patrick Gordon*, vol. II, p.21.
79   *Diary of General Patrick Gordon*, vol. II, p.26.
80   Holsten, *Przygody wojenne 1655-1666*, p.44.

the first corporalship of the company).[81] He was quickly promoted, though, as during Lubomirski's raid into Transylvania he became the company's quartermaster and in later summer 1657 the *wachmeister* in the same company.

Both officers and rank-and-files could switch between opposing armies a few times during a campaign. While Gordon and Holsten are the clearest example of such a practice, there were many other, less known soldiers who were in the same situation. *Rotmistrz* Felicjan Kazimierz Bogusławski was in charge of the haiduk banner that was stationed in Brest (Brest-Litovsk or Brześć Litewski) between 1655–1657. After the fortress surrendered to the Swedish–Transylvanian army, Bogusławski and his men promptly changed sides and joined the Transylvanians. In the ranks of their army, they took part in an assault on Warsaw in June 1657, but later on, after Rakocy's defeat, they rejoined the Polish army. Such an episode did not even affect Bogusławski's career: between 1661 and 1669, he was *rotmistrz* of Jan Kazimierz's household haiduk banner, stationed in Warsaw.[82]

Such opportunities to replace losses or strengthen a unit could happen at any time during a campaign and normally did not require any written order of confirmation. Sometimes, though, especially when stationed for a longer time in friendly territory, commanders of foreign units could receive special allowance to recruit reinforcements whenever and from wherever possible. In May 1659, Krzysztof Jeśman, in charge of a dragoon regiment in the Lithuanian army, was allowed to 'recruit supplement for his regiment in different places, where it will be the easiest to recruit [men] useful for warfare'. This order was explained both by the heavy losses of the unit and the good career record of Jeśman, whose 'service to Commonwealth and to us [the king] was well known'.[83]

Officers and NCOs recruited from amongst the prisoners often joined a new army with the same or similar rank, which often was in fact a condition of them switching armies. Gordon mentioned two former Swedish soldiers from the garrison of Toruń that 'were accommodated in their former charges [ranks]' when joining the Polish army after the surrender of the fortress in 1659. They were Lieutenant Johan Hendrich Griechs and Ensign John Kenedy, who found their way into Lubomirski's dragoon life company.[84]

Soldiers involved in the inner conflicts between Polish or Lithuanian magnates, especially those that allied with the Swedes during the early stages of the war, could be worried that they may be prosecuted once they switched sides again. In fact, on 4 February 1656, King Jan II Kazimierz issued a special proclamation addressing those 'from Crown [Poland] and Grand Duchy of Lithuania, also from both Ducal Prussia and Żmudź, [and] other our subjects' still serving the Swedes. He announced that all of them are to immediately abandon the Swedish side. Anyone who would not do it before 1 of April 1656 would be named as an 'enemy of Homeland' and sentenced to death

---

81 Holsten, *Przygody wojenne 1655-1666*, p.44.
82 Wagner, *Słownik biograficzny oficerów polskich drugiej połowy XVII wieku*, vol. I, p.26.
83 Rachuba (ed.), *Metryka Litewska. Księga wpisów nr 131*, p.189.
84 *Diary of General Patrick Gordon*, vol. II, p.1.

Polish light horse or unarmoured cossack cavalry. Caspar Merian, 1664. (Herzog August Bibliothek Wolfenbüttel: Graph. A2:126).

so that in the future, if one was captured by Polish troops, 'no mercy will be given'.⁸⁵ While it sounds like a serious statement, in reality, in most cases the worst punishment for soldiers switching sides too late was sentencing them to serve one quarter without pay. Moreover, in order to encourage them to rejoin the royal armies, special amnesties could be issued, giving them certain guarantees. In October 1656, Lithuanian Field Hetman Gosiewski, writing in the name of King Jan II Kazimierz, announced than any 'officers, servants and soldiers' formerly serving under Prince Bogusław Radziwiłł (at that time in Brandenburg service) upon 'their return to His Royal Higness [armies] will receive perpetual amnesty and will not be prosecuted for any of their previous deeds'.⁸⁶ In 1658, Jan Kazimierz issued a special decree to the soldiers from the regiment of Prince Bogusław Radziwiłł, praising them for the defence of Słuck and promising them that after the war they would be treated as soldiers of the Polish Crown and receive the same pay as rest of the army.⁸⁷ It seems that this announcement sat well with the soldiers, as Słuck was never captured by the Muscovites, and during the campaign of 1660, it played a vital role as a supply point for the joint Lithuanian and Polish army. The *Sejm* of 1659 confirmed the royal decree, mentioning in its proclamation that, throughout the whole war, Prince Bogusław Radziwiłł kept in Słuck 'foreign troops, [of] infantry, dragoons and reiters, also Hungarian infantry, on his own pay, without pay or bread from the Commonwealth' and that, due to the enemy destroying the local area, Radziwiłł was no longer able to sustain the garrison. As such, his soldiers 'of no more than 1,000 men' were included into the regular Lithuanian army and treated as in its service since 1658.⁸⁸

In the often very harsh conditions of constant conflict, it was particularly difficult to properly equip soldiers in new units and to replace lost weapons and equipment within already existing ones. It was not easy to purchase them locally or to capture enough of them from the enemy, so soldiers often

---

85 *AVAK*, vol. XXXIV, pp.80–81.
86 Biblioteka Kórnicka, no. 350, document 37, p.75.
87 AGAD, Archiwum Warszawskie Radziwiłłów (AR) II, no. 1349, p.1.
88 *Volumina Legum*, vol. IV, pp.317–18.

ORGANISATION, RECRUITMENT AND OVERALL STRENGTH OF THE ARMIES

had to rely on pillaging and theft. Holsten, with brutal honesty, admitted that, at the beginning of his Polish service, ex-Swedish soldiers 'straight away received permission to change our horses if we see better ones, well, we could even travel to the border with Silesia or across it, in order to get some loot and clothes. It was approved by our officers. At this point whoever was the best thief, he was the best soldier.'[89] No surprise that, in short time, three newly created companies of Lubomirski's reiter regiment were ready to fight, with Holsten himself now uniformed and having a 'good servant and [servant] boy', with a supply wagon as well.[90] In Gordon's diary, we can also find many details about the problems with proper weapons and equipment for soldiers. When he was sent to create new a dragoon company from the Swedish POWs in Gniew (Mewe), he received for them only 24 muskets, 'but never one of them fixed'.[91] The Scot despatched his servant and company's drummer to Toruń 'to buy white taffety and necessaryes for the colour and a drumme'.[92] He then gradually purchased more weapons and equipment when the unit was on its march to the main Polish army. In Poznań, he bought five muskets, gunpowder and lead – for his own use a 'pair of Scots pistolls with an English horsegraith [horse equipment]'.[93] In Pyzdry, he managed to acquire 28 pairs of boots, as only that many were readily available.[94] In Tarnów, he purchased some more muskets, gunpowder and lead. A visit in Cracow, at the beginning of 1660, brought a much bigger haul, with 60 new muskets bought from a merchant named Blackhall, with an additional six old muskets, more gunpowder and lead bought from another merchant.[95] When he finally was able to present the company to Lubomirski near Piotrków at the beginning of March 1660, there was an interesting dialogue between the general and Scotsman:[96]

> He asked me if they had armes. I told him, I provided them with all with musquets and powder bagges. 'And swords?', said he. I said, 'Some of them have swords.' But asking if they had horses, I answered, 'Where should I gett horses in such tyme, when I had enough ado to gett shifted for bread?' Yet I told him that the under officers [NCOs] had horses too. He then asked what number I had. I said, 'A hundred men with officers'.

Another very important aspect was the replacement of lost horses. During a campaign, many mounts could be killed, wounded (and no longer suitable for service) or even captured. Rutger von Ascheberg mentioned in his diary that, in late December 1655, he defeated a group of Polish troops near Malbork: two companies of cavalry and three companies of German dragoons. The Swedish reiters managed to capture 'two hundred sixty three beautiful horses

---

89 Holsten, *Przygody wojenne 1655-1666*, pp.44–45.
90 Holsten, *Przygody wojenne 1655-1666*, p.45.
91 *Diary of General Patrick Gordon*, vol. II, p.20.
92 *Diary of General Patrick Gordon*, vol. II, p.26.
93 *Diary of General Patrick Gordon*, vol. II, p.29.
94 *Diary of General Patrick Gordon*, vol. II, p.30.
95 *Diary of General Patrick Gordon*, vol. II, p.47.
96 *Diary of General Patrick Gordon*, vol. II, p.53.

– Polish, Moldavian, Turkish and Tatar [ones]'.[97] When, in February 1656, his regiment defeated the Polish partisans at Zakrzew, the haul of captured mounts was even bigger with 'four hundred thirteen beautiful Polish and Tatar horses'.[98]

Losses amongst horses were often very severe and not only lowered the battle effectiveness of units but were also a massive financial burden for companions and officers, who had to replace the lost mounts. In November 1653, Aleksander Hilary Połubiński estimated that his hussar banner lost 180 horses (both from companions and retainers), his cossack cavalry banner 10 horses that belonged to retainers while his dragoon company lost more than 40 horses.[99] Such massive losses were even worse when one had to consider that units did not see any combat and, for few months, were just stuck in the army camp. As such, soldiers lacked the opportunity to try to capture replacement horses from the enemy or to obtain them from the more-or-

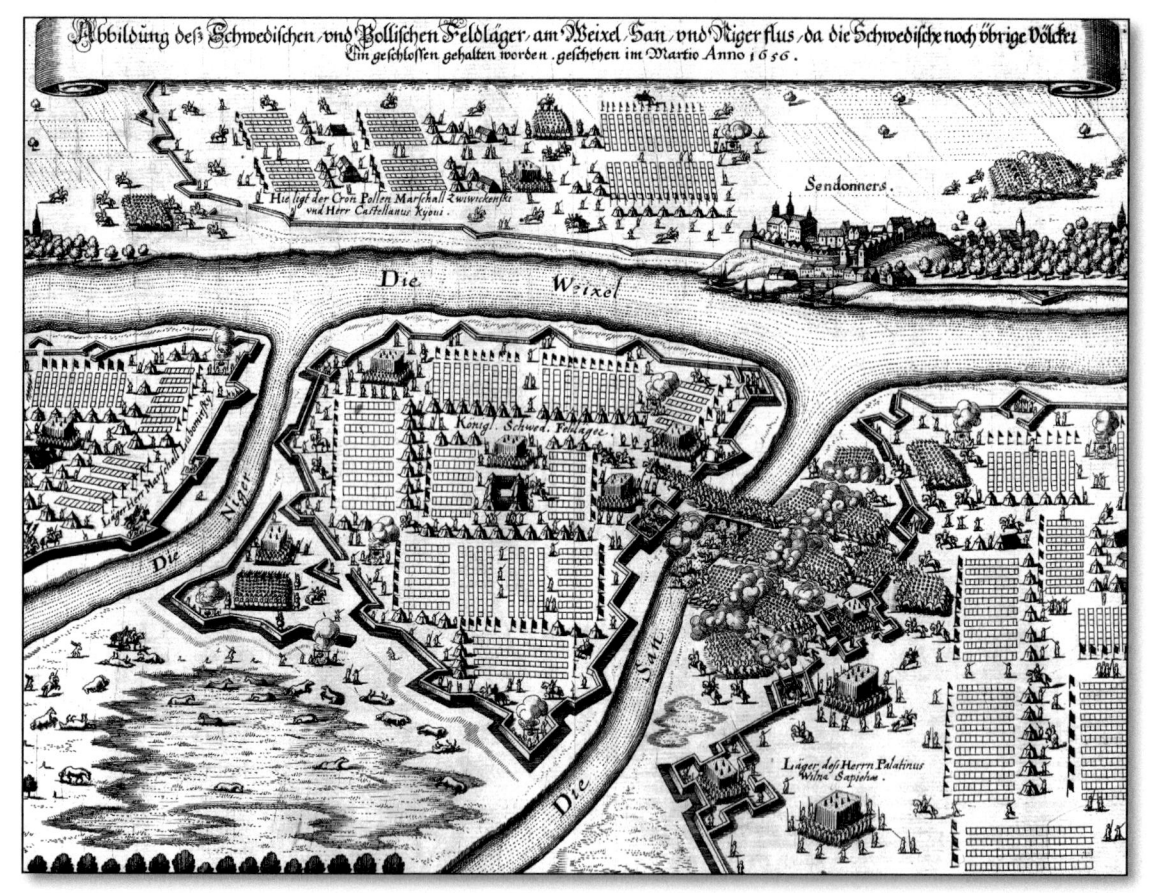

In March 1656, the Swedish field army led by Karl X Gustav was trapped in the camp at Gorzyce between Wisła and San rivers. On the left, the Polish camp of Lubomirski; on the top, Czarniecki; on the right, the Lithuanians under Sapieha. Engraving from volume VII of *Theatrum Europaem*, published in Frankfurt am Main in 1672 (Biblioteka Narodowa, Warszawa).

---

97 Ascheberg, *Dziennik oficera jazdy szwedzkiej 1621-1681*, p.63.
98 Ascheberg, *Dziennik oficera jazdy szwedzkiej 1621-1681*, p.65.
99 Majewski, *Marszałek wielki litewski Aleksander Hilary Połubiński (1626-1679)*, p.70.

less-willing local population. The loss of hussar horses was an even bigger problem, as the 'battle' mounts used by companions were expensive and not easily available. In further chapters, I will often mention cases of purchasing new mounts or their battle losses.

While infantry and dragoons tended to, at least from time to time, receive an allocation of cloth for their uniforms (more of that in chapter four, with the description of each formation), cavalry had to rely on their own resources to obtain clothes. It often led to finding replacements not normally used in times of peace, like Western-type troops in local Eastern clothing or national cavalry companions using clothes and materials captured or looted during the campaign. Pasek described a rather unusual, at least for the Polish army, mix of clothing worn by Czarniecki's division in 1659 and 1660 once they returned from Denmark. While fighting abroad, the diarist mentioned the story of a Danish woman that offered to make shirts for the Polish soldiers. They were grateful for her help, as they had plenty of cloth ('liberated' during reconnaissance missions) but 'no one to make shirts from them, as we had only one woman in [the Polish] troops, [serving as] trumpeter'.[100] Once the troops arrived back to Poland, he mentioned the contrast between Czarniecki's division returning from Denmark and Lubomirski's division that was marching into winter quarters after a long and unsuccessful siege of Malbork:

> When the banners [from both divisions] mixed up during the march, one did not have to ask which one was from which command, as one look was enough to tell: if gaunt, poor, without shoes and without mounts, they were Malbork [Lubomirski's] ones; if mounted, well-armed and in good clothing, they were Danish ones or, as we were called, *czarniecczykowie* [Czarniecki's ones].[101]

The latter were *in veste peregrina* (in foreign clothes) and in Polish clothes made from materials found abroad. Pasek wrote about *żupan* and *kontusz* garments made from drill fabric (*drelich*), the latter knee short; a *jupka* jacket made from buff-coat; and long boots with shanks in a German style 'almost to the waist' known as *sztywle*. He explained that the change in the outfit was made mostly due to the shoes. Those normally worn by the Poles quickly wore out and had to be replaced with long German cavalry boots. As such, it was very difficult to wear the long Polish garments with such footwear, as parts of the *żupan* and *kontusz* 'on those thick shanks [on the boots] were hitting both on front and on the back'.[102] He also commented that such fashion, as presented by Czarniecki's soldiers on the royal court, was picked up by civilians, showing how foreign influence in clothing could spread throughout the country during the war.

During the war, sometimes units changed their army placement, moving from the Polish to the Lithuanian army and vice versa. In Appendix II, I describe the Polish auxiliary corps that supported the Lithuanian army in late 1654 and early 1655. Some of its units stayed as part of the Lithuanian army

---

100 Pasek, *Pamiętniki*, p.80.
101 Pasek, *Pamiętniki*, p.122.
102 Pasek, *Pamiętniki*, pp.124–25.

while others were ordered to return to Poland in the summer of 1655. In July 1655, King Jan Kazimierz requested that his hussar banner under Połubiński, which served in the Lithuanian army, was to move to Poland to join the Monarch preparing his army against the Swedes. In place of this banner, the foreign infantry regiment of Prince Bogusław Radziwiłł that arrived as part of the auxiliary corps was to stay in the Lithuanian army.[103] In October 1656, the Tatar light horse banner of Michał Kuminowicz switched from the Lithuanian division of Hetman Sapieha to the Polish army. In October 1657, two Lithuanian units of Michał Kazimierz Radziwiłł – a regiment of foreign infantry and a regiment of dragoons – were by royal decree also moved to the Polish army.[104] In November 1658, the cossack cavalry banner of Roman Antoni Jelski also switched from the Lithuanian to the Polish army, while in August 1659 the cossack cavalry banner of Karol Łużycki followed the same route. In overall, though, it was not a common situation and was normally linked to a political decision made by the commander of the unit.

While many officers tended to serve throughout their whole time in the army in the same formation, others moved between different cavalry units or even between cavalry and infantry. Usually, they tended to switch within one *autorament*, so either just between national or just between foreign troops. We have some evidence of such activities based on surviving documents and muster letters. For example, Aleksander Dzierzbicki was initially the *rotmistrz* of the free company of dragoons in the Polish army between 1652 and 1653. At the start of the war, in 1655, he was captain in Stefan Czarniecki's dragoon regiment. In 1657, we can find him as the *rotmistrz* of one of the companies in Jerzy Lubomirski's reiter regiment.[105]

While it was fairly rare, lower-rank officers could switch between foreign and national troops as well. Kazimierz Bazalski, from a Scottish family settled in Livonia and Prussia in the early seventeenth century, initially served in the cossack cavalry banner of Kazimierz Piaseczyński in the Polish army. Between 1655 and 1658, he was its standard-bearer, then lieutenant from 1658 and 1660. Then, in mid-1660, he moved to Feliks Potocki's dragoon regiment, where he served as captain in charge one company until the end of 1662.[106]

Switching from cavalry to infantry could be seen as a sort of demotion, but a lot depended on the status of each unit. Between 1654 and 1659, Franciszek Szeligowski was lieutenant (and de facto commander) of Andrzej Potocki's cossack cavalry banner. Then, between 1659 and 1667, he was the *rotmistrz* in charge of Grand Hetman Stanisław Potocki's haiduk banner. With this role, he was also promoted to a so-called 'military captain', who was in theory in charge of all the Polish–Hungarian infantry in the army while also dealing with military discipline, as the Hetman's unit was acting as sort of military police.[107]

---

103 AGAD, AR III, no. 4, p.23.
104 AGAD, AR III, no. 5, p.32.
105 Wagner, *Słownik biograficzny oficerów polskich drugiej połowy XVII wieku*, vol. I, p.80.
106 Wagner, *Słownik biograficzny oficerów polskich drugiej połowy XVII wieku*, vol. I, p.12.
107 Wagner, *Słownik biograficzny oficerów polskich drugiej połowy XVII wieku*, vol. I, p.258.

Army Organisation and Strength between 1654 and 1660

At the beginning of spring 1655, after the winter campaign against the Muscovites, the Polish army was 'on paper' composed of 25,559 horses and portions:[108]

Formation	Number of units[109]	Total number of horses/portions
Hussars	5	857
Pancerni and cossack cavalry	86	8039
Reiters	5	1227
Tatar light horse	11	1285
Wallachian light horse	12	1183
Foreign infantry	8 [regiments]	7275
Dragoons	10	3661
Polish-Hungarian infantry	15	1982

In reality, the army was in very poor shape, tired and bloodied after the Ochmatów campaign in January and February. Kochowski wrote that the 'army was much depleted; with infantry died out and frozen out [to death], with lean and scalded horses, [while] unpaid soldiers did not want to listen to their officers, saying that they already served through [agreed] quarters [periods of service]'.[110] Due to the losses and lack of pay, many infantry units were disbanded (four regiments of foreign infantry, one dragoon regiment and five banners of haiduks), lowering the overall strength of the infantry 'corps' in the Polish army by approximately 4,500 portions and horses.[111] The strong auxiliary corps – composed of a large contingent of foreign infantry, dragoons and reiters, supported by a few banners of Tatar light horse – was sent to support the Lithuanian army (see Appendix II), further lowering the number of soldiers available to face the approaching Swedish offensive. Not surprising, then, that the regular army had to be supplemented by levy of nobility, district troops and lan infantry – which were to serve as the primary defensive force in summer 1655.

At the outbreak of the war against Sweden, the Polish army was divided into two main divisions. One – under the command of Field Hetman Lanckoroński, Aleksander Koniecpolski and King Jan II Kazimierz, who had under his command roughly half of the regular army – was to oppose the

---

108 Wimmer, *Wojsko polskie w drugiej połowie XVII wieku*, p.88.
109 Banners in case of national units (hussars, *pancerni* and cossack cavalry, light horse, haiduks), regiments, squadrons and free companies in case of foreign units (infantry, dragoons and reiters).
110 Kochowski, *Historya panowania Jana Kazimierza*, vol. I, p.204.
111 Wimmer, *Wojsko polskie w drugiej połowie XVII wieku*, p.89.

AGAINST THE DELUGE

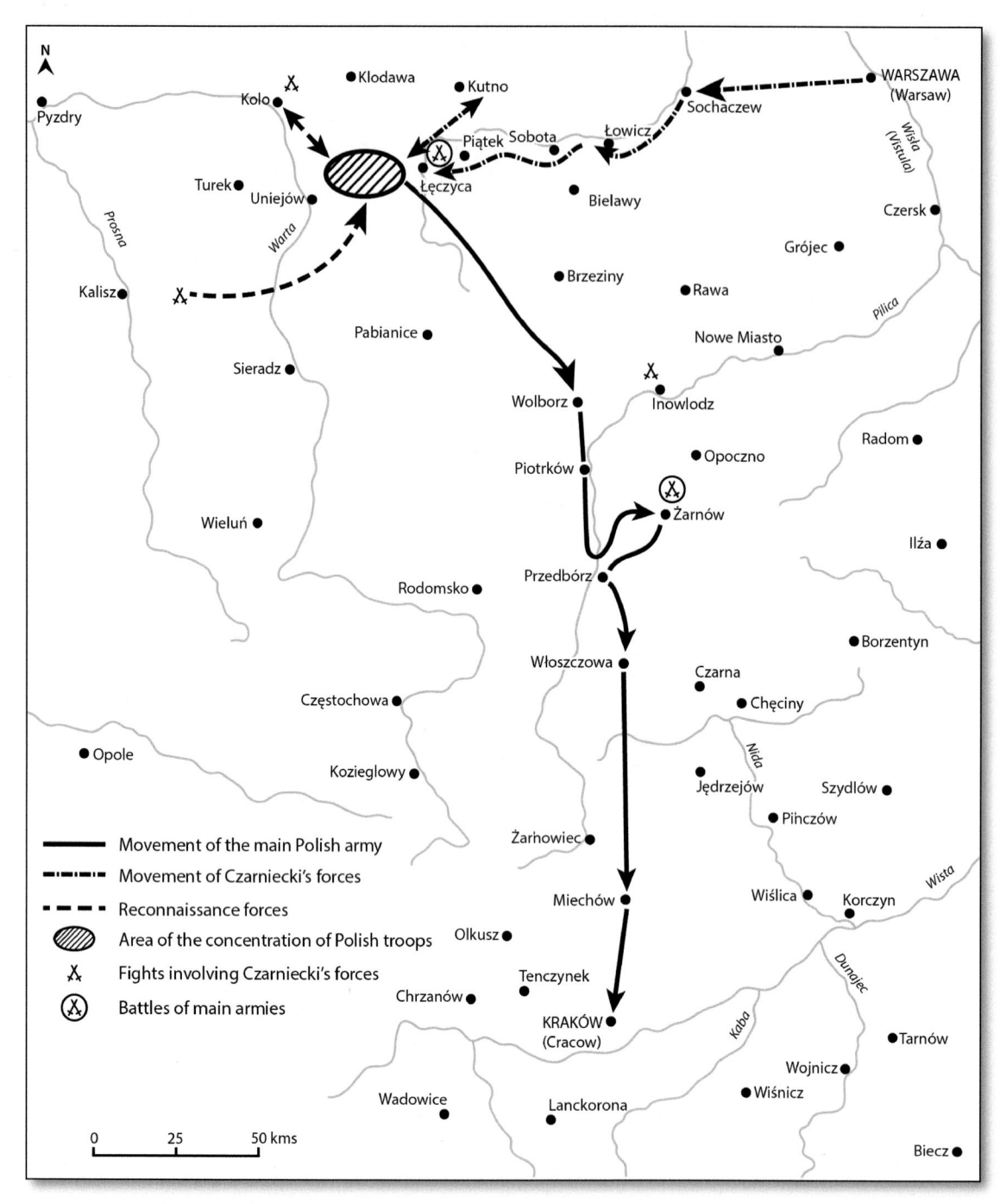

The retreat of the Polish army in summer 1655. Source: Adam Kersten, *Stefan Czarniecki* 1599-1665.

ORGANISATION, RECRUITMENT AND OVERALL STRENGTH OF THE ARMIES

Swedes entering Poland. It was supported by a majority of the Polish levy of nobility, by *wybraniecka* and *łanowa* infantry and by district and private troops. The other part of the regular army, under the command of Grand Hetman Potocki, with a small support of levy of nobility, was facing the Muscovites. To present it with more detailed information, the structure of those forces was as follows:[112]

Army facing the Swedes:
- regular army troops: four banners of hussars; approximately 60 banners of *pancerni*, cossack cavalry and Tatar light horse; five banners of Wallachian light horse; two squadrons of reiters; one regiment and one free company of foreign infantry and four regiments and three free companies of dragoons – in total approximately 9,750 horses and portions
- levy of nobility (mostly mounted), with approximately 33,000 men
- *łanowa* (lan) and *wybraniecka* infantry, with approximately 4,380 men
- district and private troops, including mercenaries on the payroll of the city of Gdańsk, with a total of approximately 5,300 men

Army facing the Muscovites and Cossacks:
- regular army troops: approximately 5,140 horses of national calvary (including two banners of hussars); one banner of 200 horses of *arkabuzeria*; four regiments of foreign infantry (all on garrison duties) with 3,235 portions; one dragoon regiment of 306 portions and approximately 10 banners of Polish–Hungarian infantry with approximately 1365 portions
- approximately 300 men of *łanowa* (lan) infantry
- 3,000–4,000 men of levy of nobility

We need to remember that the forces facing the Swedes were spread out between different locations, with the defence of the border in the hands of levy of nobility and lan infantry, while the regular troops were in the process of gathering in one place to form the field army. After a brief fight, the levy from Wielkopolska surrendered to the Swedes at Ujście on 25 July 1655, opening a route for the Swedish army into the Polish interior. The regular army, supported by levy from different regions, was slowly retreating towards Cracow after the decision to abandon Warsaw without a fight. There were some small-scale fights between Polish and Swedish cavalry, while at Żarnów, on 16 September 1655, the main army led by Jan II Kazimierz himself was defeated by the Swedes. It led to further retreat and opened Cracow for a Swedish siege operation.

After another defeat of the Polish regular army, at the Battle of Wojnicz (3 October 1655), Charles X Gustav sent his envoys to the commanders of the Polish regular army fighting under Jan Kazimierz's command, attempting to convince them to switch sides. His letters were to mention that the Polish soldiers should surrender to the Swedes 'to renew the glory of Polish nation, so weakened during miserable rule of Jan Kazimierz and [for it] to rise

---

112 Wimmer, *Wojsko polskie w drugiej połowie XVII wieku*, pp.91–95.

The Polish embassy entering Paris in 1645. François Campion, 1645 (Bibliothèque nationale de France. Photo by Tomasz Ratyński)

again under [the reign of] Charles Gustav, brave and lucky king'.[113] After some negotiations – in which the Polish soldiers were looking for assurance that they would receive overdue pay, while the non-military nobles wanted a royal promise that they would be protected from the marching armies and, which was a very important paragraph, that they would be allowed to publicly worship as per their religion – the soldiers were to abandon Jan Kazimierz's cause and cease contact with him and his supporters. All garrisons were to open their gates to the Swedes, and officers of the regular army were to confirm this agreement in writing. On 26 October 1655, near Cracow, Koniecpolski's troops mustered in front of Charles X Gustav's 5,174 horses and 211 dragoons.[114] Soon after, on 13 November, a second division of Polish troops, under the command of Grand Hetman Potocki and Field Hetman Lanckoroński, also switched sides with a muster of 11,000 men presenting in front of the Swedish monarch.[115] This last figure seems to be exaggerated, though, as Potocki would have had under his command just over 7,000 soldiers: 7,500 horses of cavalry, 260 portions of dragoons and 200 portions of Polish infantry. It is possible, however, that some levy of nobility were present as well.[116]

After those events, a majority of the Polish regular army was serving next to the Swedes, although there were some groups that were under the very loose control of the Swedish crown or refused to serve it outright. Approximately 3,700 infantrymen were in the garrisons in Lwów (three regiments of foreign infantry) and a few castles in Podolia. While they were included in the agreements between Potocki and other officers with the Swedes, in fact, they never moved under Swedish command. In Royal Prussia, there was

---

113 Pufendorf, *Siedem ksiąg o czynach Karola Gustawa króla Szwecji*, p.73.
114 Pufendorf, *Siedem ksiąg o czynach Karola Gustawa króla Szwecji*, p.75.
115 Pufendorf, *Siedem ksiąg o czynach Karola Gustawa króla Szwecji*, p.75.
116 Wimmer, *Wojsko polskie w drugiej połowie XVII wieku*, pp.97–98.

ORGANISATION, RECRUITMENT AND OVERALL STRENGTH OF THE ARMIES

still a strong group of regular and provincial troops, just over 3,500 men, composed of national cavalry, reiters, dragoons and infantry. They defended Malbork, Gniew, Dirschau and Puck (Putzig) – the latter managed to be held in Polish hands until the end of the war. On top of it all, Gdańsk kept under arms a contingent of mercenaries and a few thousand of burgher militia, with the wealthy town yet again, like in previous conflicts, opposing the Swedes. After Malbork surrendered, Gdańsk provided refuge for the remnants of its garrison. Troops previously defending Cracow, composed of the Royal Foot regiment, lan infantry from Sandomierz and Czarniecki's dragoon regiment, were stationed at the border with Silesia as per the capitulation agreement. A majority of those soldiers were, in December 1655, forced by the Swedes to switch sides, though. Czarniecki managed to only save 100 men (probably mostly dragoons) and flee with them to Silesia to rejoin the King. Finally, there were some private troops and newly created regular units that did not have the time to join the main army yet. For example, Jerzy Lubomirski had his cossack cavalry banner, dragoon banner and Polish infantry banner; they were all stationed in lands owned by him.

As already mentioned, the strongest contingent of the Polish army still not under Swedish control was stationed in Royal Prussia, defending the

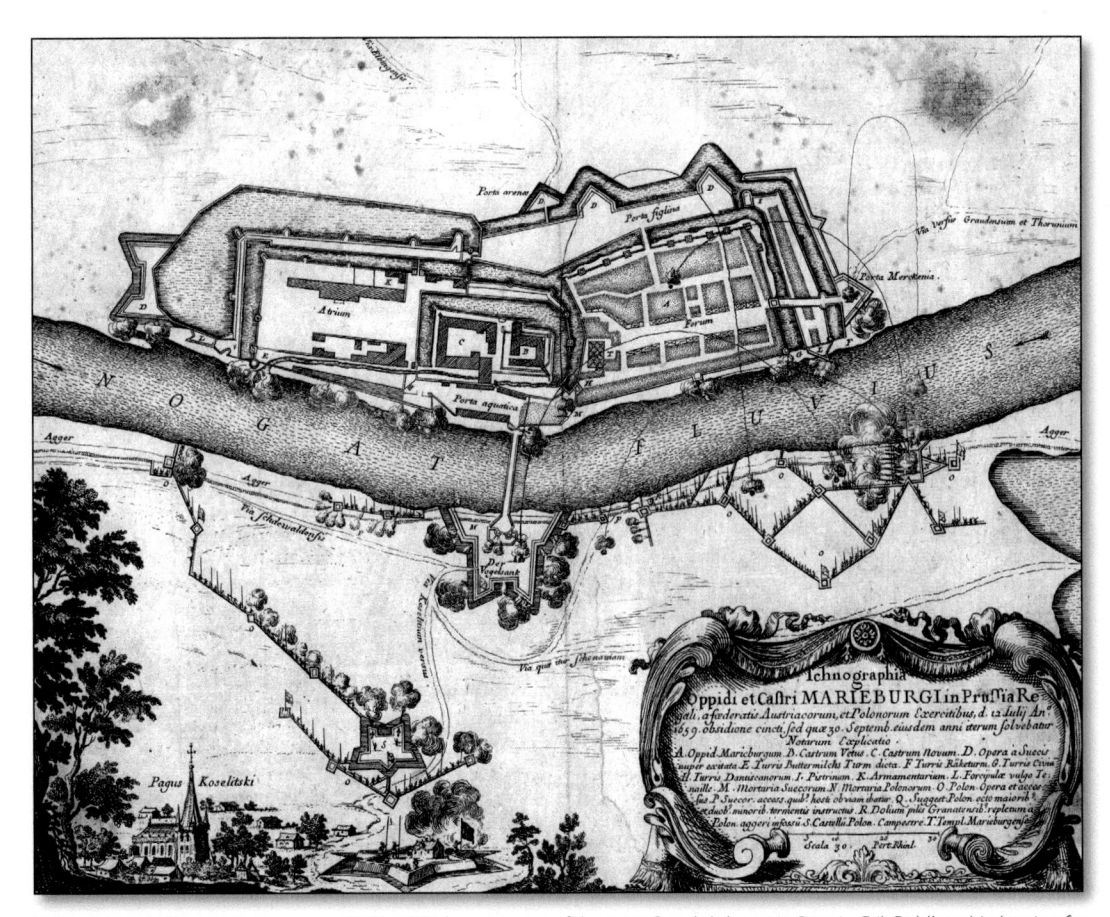

Malbork, in a similar way to the war in 1626–1629, became one of the main Swedish bases in Prussia. Erik Dahlbergh's drawing for Samuel Pufendorf's *De rebus a Carolo Gustavo Sueciae rege gestis*, published in 1696 (Biblioteka Narodowa, Warszawa).

province under the command of Jakub Wejher, Voivode of Malbork.[117] As it was an interesting mix of regular army units and district and private troops, it is worth looking closer into the composition of this corps. Most important is the document titled '*Comput ludzi naszych*' (*Komput* of our men), indicating the units raised in the Voivodeships of Malbork, Pomerania and Chełmno, also in Prince-Bishopric of Warmia:[118]

Formation	Nominal commander	Paper strength	Notes
Infantry (foreign and Polish-Hungarian)	Wacław Leszczyński, Bishop of Warmia	200	Unit raised as private, with many to be paid back from National Treasury 'when available'[119]
	Jan Gembicki, Bishop of Chełmno	200	Possibly private unit
	Jakub Wejher, Voivod of Malbork	500	
	Ludwik Wejher, Voivod of Pomerania	200	
	Jan Dembiński	100	Polish-Hungarian infantry
	Obuchowski	260	
	Żuławski	400	
	-	100	Garrison in Gniew (Mewe)
Dragoons	Jan Gembicki, Bishop of Chełmno	200	Unit raised as private, with many to be paid back from National Treasury 'when available'
	Jakub Wejher, Voivod of Malbork	500	Regular army unit
	Ludwik Wejher, Voivod of Pomerania	200	Regular army unit
Reiters	Jan Kos, Voivod of Chełmno	100	
	Jakub Wejher, Voivod of Malbork	200	Regular army unit
	Gablenc (?)[120]	100	
	Kochański (?)[121]	100	
'Polish banners'	Seven cavalry banners	100 horses each	Possibly cossack cavalry, some of them may be in fact *arkabuzeria*

---

117 Other versions of Jakub's surname, often used in both primary and secondary sources, are 'Weyher' or 'Weiher'.
118 Biblioteka Książąt Czartoryskich (BCzart.), no. 352, p.79.
119 Bishop was supposed to raise 400 men 'trained in foreign fashion', Biblioteka Kórnicka, no 352, p. 79.
120 Name unclear.
121 Name unclear.

ORGANISATION, RECRUITMENT AND OVERALL STRENGTH OF THE ARMIES

Those units were supported by remnants of the Royal Guard dragoon regiment under Jan Henryk von Alten Bockum. The unit was a part of the Polish auxiliary corps supporting the Lithuanian army against the Muscovites, but, in summer 1655, it returned to Poland (see chapter four and Appendix II). There is no indication of the presence of any other regular units that were sent to Royal Prussia; the few foreign units from the auxiliary corps that were supposed to deploy there disbanded en route from Lithuania to Poland. There could of course be some groups of levy of nobility and other locally raised troops, but they are much harder to trace. Gdańsk had its own private army, a mix of mercenaries and city militia from the city and its suburbia, but they focused the defence of the area around Gdańsk itself. The main defensive stronghold for the Poles was Malbork, which faced a Swedish blockade and later siege. It surrendered on 6 March 1656, with part of its garrison (mostly reiters and haiduks) joining the Swedes, while the rest of the troops, under Jakub Wejher (Ludwik died during the siege) were allowed free passage to Gdańsk.

Throughout the war, the Polish army fought divided usually into two or three divisions, with additional troops detached as garrison forces, support for irregular forces and so on. Stefan Czarniecki, nominated by the King as *regimentarz*, tended to lead his own strong division, usually composed of two to three regiments of national cavalry (including a strong Royal regiment) and his own dragoon regiment. The rest of the army was under the command of the King and both the Grand and Field Hetman, either as one larger or two smaller divisions, although the size and organisation of their forces changed, and some *ad hoc* divisions could be detached from it for a specific mission. For example, Jerzy Lubomirski, who at the end of 1656 took command of the Polish troops attempting a blockade of Cracow, had in his division one regiment of national cavalry (16 banners), one regiment of foreign infantry, one banner of dragoons, a few banners of Polish infantry and few thousand men from levy of nobility and district troops.[122] In autumn 1658, the Polish army was divided into three main divisions:[123]

- Grand Hetman Potocki had a large part of regular cavalry, with a paper strength of approximately 9,400 horses (one banner of hussars, 43 banners of cossack cavalry, 17 banners of Tatars and 15 banners of Wallachians) and 10 units of dragoons (approximately 1,900 portions). They were stationed on the border with Ukraine and were supported by up to 1,000 portions of Polish–Hungarian infantry serving as garrisons.
- Stefan Czarniecki took his division to support allies in Denmark. He had three regiments of national cavalry (three banners of hussars, 28 banners of cossack cavalry, two banners of Tatars, two banners of Wallachians and one banner of *semeni* dragoons), one regiment of dragoons and one independent dragoon banner, with a total paper strength of 5,067 horses and portions.[124]

---

122 Wimmer, *Wojsko polskie w drugiej połowie XVII wieku*, p.107.
123 Wimmer, *Wojsko polskie w drugiej połowie XVII wieku*, pp.116–19.
124 More details of this division in this period can be found in Appendix I.

- Field Hetman Lubomirski was in charge of the siege of Toruń. He had with him 12 regiments of foreign infantry; one banner of Polish infantry; three regiments, one squadron and two companies of dragoons; one regiment and one banner of reiters and six regiments of national cavalry (two banners of hussars, 49 banners of cossack cavalry, five banners of Tatars and three banners of Wallachians), with a total paper strength of 20,765 horses and portions.

At the first *Sejm* that took place during the war, in summer 1658, there were plans to change the composition of the cavalry, with one of the resolutions stating that the hetman should increase the number of hussars and *petyhorcy*, as a 'type of lancers that by ancient law was rightly ours but [recently] missing [in the army]'. At the same time, all Wallachian banners in the Crown army, except those under each hetmans' name, should be disbanded.[125] In theory, it was a sound idea. In practice, none of it saw the light of day. Due to the financial strain caused by the constant warfare, there was a very slim chance to increase the number of hussars since the effort of raising even one new banner would be very expensive. At the same time, light cavalry – both cheap to raise and keep in service – was too useful to be rid of. The number of foreign infantry and dragoons was gradually increased as well in order to better face the numerous siege operations. In the second quarter of 1659, with forces spread between Denmark, Ukraine and Prussia, the Polish army reached its maximum size during whole the 1655–1660 war. It had 40,305 horses and portions of paper strength, divided into the following:[126]

Formation	Number of units	Total strength [horses or portions]
Hussars	6 [banners]	999
Pancerni and cossack cavalry	122 [banners]	13,106
Tatar light horse	23 [banners]	2682
Wallachian light horse	18 [banners]	1705
Reiters	7 [regiments, squadrons and free companies]	2246
Foreign infantry	12 [regiments]	10,737
Dragoons	21 [regiments, squadrons and free companies]	7872
Polish-Hungarian infantry	9 [banners]	1048

Of course, such a large army was not concentrated in one place. It was in fact divided into three main components. Czarniecki with his division

---

125 *Volumina Legum*, vol. IV, p.242.
126 Wimmer, *Wojsko polskie w drugiej połowie XVII wieku*, p.122.

ORGANISATION, RECRUITMENT AND OVERALL STRENGTH OF THE ARMIES

was serving as auxiliary corps in Denmark (see Appendix I). Lubomirski and General Grodzicki were operating in Prussia, mostly focused on siege operations against the remaining Swedish fortresses and detaching some troops for garrison duties. Their combined forces had approximately 15,400 horses and portions, in three regiments of national cavalry (two banners of hussars, 26 of *pancerni* and cossack cavalry, four Tatar and one Wallachian light horse banners), eight regiments of foreign infantry, three regiments and two squadrons of dragoons and two regiments of reiters. The rest of the Polish army, under the command of Grand Hetman Stanisław Potocki and Andrzej Potocki, were deployed on Ukraine in preparation to face the Muscovites. It was approximately 11,500 horses of national cavalry, 3,040 portions of foreign infantry, 4,800 portions of dragoons and an almost full contingent of Polish–Hungarian infantry (which were used as garrison forces).[127]

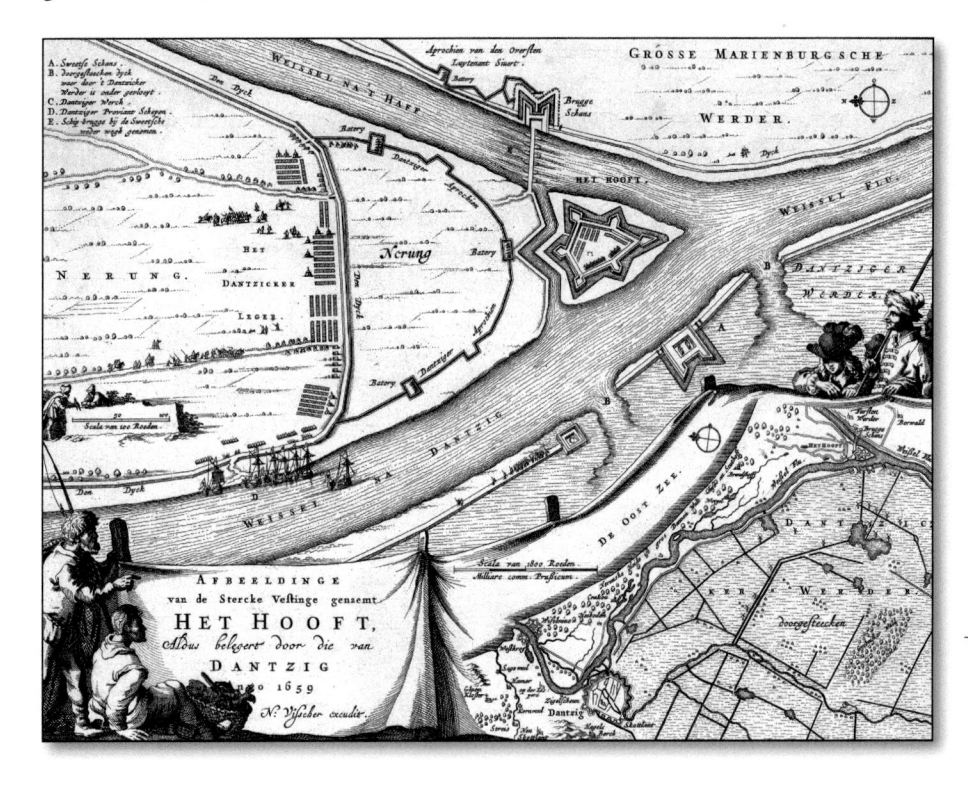

The siege of Gdańska Głowa in 1659. Author unknown (Rijksmuseum)

The Lithuanian army was traditionally divided into two divisions: one under the command of Grand Hetman and the other led by Field Hetman. We can see such a system throughout the majority of the seventeenth century, and it was usually caused by the internal politics of the country, with one commander usually in opposition to the current monarch and the other in support of the king. In 1654, at the start of the Muscovite offensive against Lithuania, Grand Hetman Janusz Radziwiłł was on not-so-friendly

---

127 Wimmer, *Wojsko polskie w drugiej połowie XVII wieku*, pp.122–23.

terms with King Jan II Kazimierz, with Field Hetman Wincenty Korwin Gosiewski being royal nominee. One could think that replacing Radziwiłł with Paweł Jan Sapieha would strengthen the royal party, but it was not the case. Sapieha, a wealthy magnate with political ambitions, quickly continued with pro-Lithuanian and rather anti-royal politics. Gosiewski had a limited way of influencing the army in the period of 1658–1662, as in autumn 1658 he was captured by the Muscovites at Werki and kept prisoner for almost four years. During his absence, his division, despite Sapieha's attempts, managed to keep its independence from the Grand Hetman division being led by a few officers of *regimentarz* rank. After Gosiewski's death in autumn 1662, Michał Kazimierz Pac was nominated as the new Field Hetman, taking over command of the division. This two-way system ended in mid-1660, when, after Sapieha's death in December 1665, Pac was able to gradually disband a majority of the units of the former Grand Hetman's division in a much-reduced Lithuanian army retaining mostly services of units from his own command.

The size and the organisation of the army went through many changes during the war, especially after 1655 when troops were divided into those pro-Radziwiłł and those loyal to the King after the Treaty of Kiejdany. Some stayed with Janusz or Bogusław Radziwiłł; others mutinied against the Grand Hetman and fled to Poland or Samogitia. Gradually, a large contingent gathered in Podlasie around Paweł Jan Sapieha. At the end of 1656 – after restructuring, with many units being disbanded and changing their commanders and a new one being created – both divisions had the following structure:[128]

- Right wing division under Grand Hetman Sapieha with a paper strength of 8,359 horses and portions

Formation	Number of units	Total strength [horses or portions]
Hussars	3 [banners]	469
Pancerni and cossack cavalry	34 [banners]	4230
Tatar light horse	12 [banners]	1540
Foreign infantry	3 [free companies]	380
Dragoons	7 [squadrons and free companies]	1060
Polish-Hungarian infantry	4 [banners]	590

---

128 Rachuba, 'Wysiłek mobilizacyjny Wielkiego Księstwa Litewskiego w latach 1654-1667', p.52.

ORGANISATION, RECRUITMENT AND OVERALL STRENGTH OF THE ARMIES

- Left wing division under Field Hetman Gosiewski with a paper strength of 6,499 horses and portions

Formation	Number of units	Total strength [horses or portions]
Hussars	2 [banners]	400
Pancerni and cossack cavalry	14 [banners]	1840
Tatar light horse	5 [banners]	620
Reiters	6 [free companies]	694
Dragoons	18 [regiments, squadrons and free companies]	2945
Polish-Hungarian infantry	4 [banners]	590

When compared to the Polish army, we can see a complete lack of the Wallachian light cavalry and a large absence of foreign infantry, though with a fairly strong presence of dragoons, widely employed by both Sapieha and Gosiewski. The structure and strength of both divisions did change fairly often, with units disbanding, switching between divisions and even moving from the Lithuanian to the Polish army, also with a large number of new units being created. By the second half of 1657, Sapieha's division had 9,807 horses and portions, while Gosiewski's one had 10,592 horses and portions, including one 5-company-strong regiment of foreign infantry.[129] In the second half of 1659, Sapieha's division had 11,493 horses and portions, while Gosiewski's division (under Komorowski and Pac) had 9,982 horses and portions.[130] Of course, we need to remember that, as with the Polish army, it was in fact just paper strength while the real numbers had to be much lower not only due to 'dead pays' but also due to a high level of attrition, with both combat and noncombat losses. On the other hand, the regular army was supported by a few thousand volunteers, who were not included in the official strength of the armed forces. The Lithuanian army reached its maximum strength by the end of 1661, with Sapieha's division at 12,718 horses and portions and new Field Hetman Pac's division (formerly Gosiewski's division) with 10,082 horses and portions.[131] Two army lists from this year can be found in Appendix V.

The national calvary in both armies were grouped together into regiments (*pułki*), although such larger units did not have regimental staff like the ones that could be found in foreign infantry, dragoons and reiters. The number and size of the cavalry regiments could change from campaign to campaign (e.g., banners could be moved between regiments or disbanded, or new

---

129 Rachuba, 'Wysiłek mobilizacyjny Wielkiego Księstwa Litewskiego w latach 1654-1667', pp.53–54.
130 Rachuba, 'Wysiłek mobilizacyjny Wielkiego Księstwa Litewskiego w latach 1654-1667', pp.55–56.
131 Rachuba, 'Wysiłek mobilizacyjny Wielkiego Księstwa Litewskiego w latach 1654-1667', p.58.

Highly adorned horses of Polish magnates or officials. Such expensive tack, saddles and pelts were also often present in winged hussars banners. Stefano della Bella, 1651 (Rijksmuseum).

units could be added). Some regiments even had up to 20 banners, while the smallest one could contain only two or three of such units. As a rule, the banner or banners that were under the name of a nominal commander of the regiment were always included in his regiment (e.g., the Grand Hetman's hussar and *pancerni*/cossack cavalry banners served in his regiment). Due to the organisation and strength of the cavalry, the majority of regiments contained only cossack cavalry banners, with just three of four regiments in the army having one or two hussar banners.

Light cavalry was likewise spread between different regiments and did not come under its own 'specialised' units. The Polish army fighting against the Cossacks and Muscovites in the autumn of 1654 to the winter of 1655 was divided into 12 regiments, each with different strength.[132] There were known under the name of their nominal commander and were as follows (in parentheses the paper strength of each regiment): Royal regiment under Stefan Czarniecki (3,500); Grand Hetman Stanisław Potocki (3,000); Field Hetman Stanisław Lanckoroński (2,000); Krzysztof Tyszkiewicz (2,000); Piotr Potocki (1,500); Aleksander Cetner (1,800); Aleksander Koniecpolski (1,300); Jan Sobieski (1,100); Dymitr Wiśniowiecki (1,500); Andrzej Potocki (1,000); Jerzy Bałaban (500) and Jacek Szemberk (400).[133] By the time of the Battle of Warsaw in 1656, the Polish army was divided into 17 regiments, which again varied in their size and number of banners (unfortunately, detailed organisations of those units did not survive to our time). There is some more detailed information from the second part of 1658, which allows the following presentation of the structure of at least a few regiments to show how varied they were:[134]

---

132 Unfortunately, we do not know the exact banner structure of those regiments.
133 Rafał Rabka, 'Kampania Ochmatowska 1654-1655. Część I', *Studia i Materiały do Historii Wojskowości*, XLIII (2007), p.194.
134 Wimmer, *Wojsko polskie w drugiej połowie XVII wieku*, pp.117–19.

ORGANISATION, RECRUITMENT AND OVERALL STRENGTH OF THE ARMIES

Commander of the regiment	Hussars' banners	*Pancerni* and cossack cavalry banners	Wallachian banners	Tatar banners	Other	Total
Jerzy Lubomirski	1	16	-	1	-	18
Aleksander Koniecpolski	-	11	1	-	-	12
Jan Zamoyski	1	3	-	-	-	4
Jan Sobieski	-	7	-	1	-	8
Jan Sapieha	-	7	1	3	-	11
Dymitr Wiśniowiecki	-	5	1	-	-	6
Royal regiment under Stefan Czarniecki	3	15	1	1	1 (*semeni* dragoons)	21
Krzysztof Żegocki	-	1	1	1	1 (dragoons)	4

During a campaign, especially prior to a pitched battle, other units – like reiters and dragoons, or even infantry – could be attached to national cavalry regiments. In some cases, especially large regiments could be the size of the division. A good example of such a practice can be found in the list of the regiments prior to the Battle of Beresteczko, dated 14 June 1651:[135]

- Royal regiment: three banners of hussars, nine units of reiters, three banners of cossack cavalry, four banners of Tatar light horse, at least three companies of dragoons,[136] three regiments of foreign infantry and eight banners of Polish–Hungarian infantry
- Regiment of Grand Hetman Mikołaj Potocki: three banners of hussars, 15 banners of cossack cavalry and 300 horses of *arkabuzeria*[137]
- Regiment of Field Hetman Marcin Kalinowski: two banners of hussars and 12 banners of cossack cavalry
- Regiment of Jan Szymon Szczawiński: one banner of hussars and 11 banners of cossack cavalry
- Regiment of Jeremi Wiśniowiecki: three banners of hussars and nine banners of cossack cavalry

---

135 Mirosław Nagielski (ed.), 'Podział wojska na pułki z 14 VI 1651 przed batalią berestecką z włączeniem doń jednostek zaciągu cudzoziemskiego', in *Relacje wojenne z pierwszych lat walk polsko-kozackich powstania Bohdana Chmielnickiego okresu "Ogniem i Mieczem" (1648-1651)*, pp.346–52.
136 The list mentioned three by the names of their commanders and then added 'and others'.
137 Cavalry equipped like armour reiters but recruited in the same way as Polish national cavalry.

AGAINST THE DELUGE

- Regiment of Stanisław Rewera Potocki: two banners of hussars and 10 banners of cossack cavalry
- Regiment of Stanisław Lanckoroński: two banners of hussars and at least 10 banners of cossack cavalry[138]
- Regiment of Jerzy Lubomirski: two banners of hussars, two banners of *arkabuzeria* and 10 banners of cossack cavalry
- Regiment of Kazimierz Leon Sapieha: four banners of hussars, one banner of reiters and four banners of cossack cavalry
- Regiment of Aleksander Koniecpolski: 10 banners of cossack cavalry

Polish cavalry versus Swedish reiters. Detail from Erik Dahlbergh's drawing for Samuel Pufendorf's *De rebus a Carolo Gustavo Sueciae rege gestis*, published in 1696 (Biblioteka Narodowa, Warszawa).

Other examples of regiments, this time from Czarniecki's division in 1659, can be found in Appendix I. The national cavalry in the Lithuanian army was organised in a similar way, with the stronger regiments of each hetman, which included a majority of the hussar banners, alongside some cossack cavalry (and rare pancerni units) and the rest of the regiments composed of cossack cavalry and light horse banners. During military operations, units of reiters and dragoons could be temporarily attached to the national cavalry regiment as support. In a way, it was much easier to organise in the Lithuanian army,

---

138 One banner is mentioned as '300 horses', which could indicate anything between one and three units.

ORGANISATION, RECRUITMENT AND OVERALL STRENGTH OF THE ARMIES

where foreign troops were mostly serving as free companies (independent units) instead of regiments. In February 1655, when Lithuanian Grand Hetman Janusz Radziwiłł was leading his army to besiege Mohylew, his army was marching following this order.[139] The force was divided into two main parts: the Hetman led the main body of cavalry and dragoons, while Colonel Berk was marching behind with the majority of the infantry and baggage train. The Hetman's troops marched in the following order:

- Vanguard of four banners of cossack cavalry (420 horses) and an 'all Hungarian infantry' (so at least two to three banners)
- All units of dragoons
- All units of reiters
- National cavalry (hussars, cossack cavalry and light horse) divided into six regiments

The national cavalry in the Lithuanian division of Grand Hetman Sapieha was, in 1657, divided into seven regiments of:[140]

- Royal, under Antoni Hilary Połubiński: two banners of hussars and seven banners of cossack cavalry (including one *pancerni* banner)
- Grand Hetman Sapieha, under Władysław Jerzy Chalecki: one banner of hussars and seven banners of cossack cavalry
- Jerzy Karol Hlebowicz: five banners of cossack cavalry
- Zygmunta Adam Słuszka: six banners of cossack cavalry
- Michał Kazimierz Radziwiłł: five banners of cossack cavalry
- Samuel Kmicic: three banners of cossack cavalry
- Michał Leon Obuchowicz: four banners of cossack cavalry

Additionally, each regiment had at least one banner of Tatar light cavalry (a whole division had 12), while dragoons and infantry were only attached to those regiments on an *ad hoc* basis.

As with the Polish army, the structure and size of regiments could easily change, with units sometimes switching, due to different reasons, from one division to another. Parts or even full regiments from one division could be, for the period of the campaign, attached to the other. This happened in autumn 1656, when banners from four regiments of Grand Hetman Sapieha's division were attached to Field Hetman Gosiewski's division while fighting in Prussia against the Swedish and Brandenburg forces. While Gosiewski was captured by the Muscovites in 1658, during the Battle of Werki, the units under his name were retained in the service and the left wing division was still – at least in name only – known as Gosiewski's one. It was under the command of officers designated as *regimentarz*, first Samuel Komorowski, then Michał Kazimierz Pac. Even in Sapieha's division, when he was not present for a long period of time in the army, we can see the presence of such

---

139 Vorbek-Lettow, *Skarbnica pamięci*, pp.214–15.
140 Andrzej Rachuba, 'Uwagi do problemu kampanii Wincentego Gosiewskiego w Prusach Książęcych jesienią 1656 roku', *Kwartalnik Historyczny*, CIX:3 (2002), pp.175–76.

ad hoc nominated commanders, like Antoni Hilary Połubiński during the Courland campaign or Mikołaj Władysław Judycki in 1661. A more detailed structure of the command in both the Polish and Lithuanian armies will be described in the next chapter.

3

Commanders

The main officers in the charge of the army were called hetman.[1] There were four of them in total within the Commonwealth, with a separate Grand Hetman in command of both the Polish and Lithuanian armies and their Field Hetman acting as second in command. Throughout the seventeenth century, the office of hetman, in both countries, was a lifelong appointment. Per unwritten tradition, once the Grand Hetman died due to natural causes or (rarely) fell in battle, the Field Hetman was to be promoted to his office and another officer would take over the newly vacated seat of Field Hetman. If neither of the hetmans were present within army (e.g., their presence being required at the *Sejm* or vacancies due death or being taken as prisoners), they were normally replaced by an *ad hoc* nominated *regimentarz* (literally, commander of the regiment) who would command the army until the return of a hetman. Sometimes, the officer could keep the rank of *regimentarz* for a longer period, despite the presence of an officially nominated hetman. We will see examples of this during the Deluge when Stefan Czarniecki, between 1655 and 1665, was in command of his own division in the Polish army, while in the Lithuanian army this rank was in hands of Samuel Komorowski and Michał Pac. If the King was present in the field, he had overall command of the force – whether it was just the Polish army, like in the Battle of Beresteczko in 1651 and the Żwaniec campaign of 1653, or the joint Polish and Lithuanian armies, like in the Battle of Warsaw in 1656.

Crown hetmans were assisted in their day-to-day operations by a small group of officers and officials, who were counted as high-ranking commanders of the army. Crown Grand Guard (*strażnik koronny*, known under the Latin name '*praefectus excubiarum seu vigiliarum*') was an important member of a hetman's staff that appeared for the first time in the regular army in the sixteenth century. His traditional role was to support the Field Hetman in securing the border and protecting army routes during the campaigns, especially in the face of Tatar raids, although it gradually became just an official rank held by magnates. During the Deluge, this rank

---

[1] This part will be very familiar to readers of the author's previous book, *We Came, We Saw, God Conquered*, pp.21–23, but we believe it is important to repeat certain aspects of the organisation in this volume to allow it to function as a standalone book.

was held by Aleksander Zamoyski, who was Grand Guard between 1648 and 1656, while between 1657 and 1661 the title was in hands of Dymitr Wiśniowiecki (1631–1682).[2] There was also the Military Guard (*strażnik wojskowy*), known also as the Field Guard (*strażnik polny*), whose main job was to take care of the important 'leg work' associated with reconnaissance, capturing vital prisoners and protecting the army during marching and camping. Throughout the period of 1648–1664, it was held by Stanisław Mariusz Jaskólski, an experienced soldier and diplomat.[3] Another vital member of a hetman's staff, also nominated by the monarch, was the Field Clerk (*pisarz polny* or *notaries campestris* in Latin), whose role was to deal with the administrative aspects of the army, like checking muster rolls and dealing with pay and reports about state of the army that could be submitted to the King and *Sejm*. Despite his 'desk job', he was in fact obliged to serve as an officer, usually leading his own banner or banners and often being in charge of the regiment of cavalry. Between 1652 and 1663, the Field Clerk office was held by Jan Fryderyk Sapieha (1618–1664), a very experienced soldier who, in the 1640s, served in the French army and, since 1648, was an officer in the Polish army fighting against the Cossacks, Tatars, Muscovites and Swedes. The Military Camp Master (*oboźny wojskowy*) was in charge of the army camp – from choosing the place of it, through setting it up, to building its defences. He also took care of the army tabor train during a march. Between 1653 and 1666, this office was in the hands of another experienced officer, cavalry *Rotmistrz* Szymon Kawecki. The final member of a hetman's staff was the Military Captain (*kapitan wojskowy*), which was a rather peculiar office in the Polish army. Often held by the *rotmistrz* of the Grand Hetman's Polish–Hungarian (haiduk) infantry banner, he had a dual role. Mainly, he was in charge of the personal security of the hetman, but he also seems to have been the commander of some sort of military police that could assist military judges during their proceedings. Interestingly enough, though, during the Deluge this title was held by officers of cavalry. Between 1652 and 1658, the Military Captain was Gabriel Silnicki, lieutenant of a hussar banner, while between 1659 and 1667, it was Piotr Komorowski, a former *rotmistrz* of a cossack cavalry banner.

These officials received regular annual pay (*jurgielt*) from the National Treasury:

- Crown Grand Guard – 1,400 zł
- Military Guard – 9,60 zł
- Field Clerk – 1,140 zł
- Military Camp Master and Military Captain – 800 zł each

---

2   He was gradually promoted within the high command, as, in 1668, he became Crown Field Hetman and, from 1676 until his death, he was Crown Grand Hetman.
3   With two breaks, though. In the period of 1648–1649, it was held by Jan Sokół when Jaskólski was captured at Korsuń and in 1652 when he was recovering from a wound taken at the Battle of Batoh.

Such pay was, in fact, their 'operational budget', from which they had to cover any additional costs associated with their office.[4] The pay of hetmans was, of course, much higher, as they received two forms of pay: *jurgielt* and, since 1654, additional salary:

- Grand Hetman had an annual salary of 12,000 and a *jurgielt* of 1,800 zł.
- Field Hetman had an annual salary of 8,000 and a *jurgielt* of 800 zł.[5]

A very special role was played by the general of artillery, who was in charge of the artillery and engineering corps. This office will be described in more detail in chapter four. Between 1652 and 1659, it was held by Krzysztof Grodzicki. After his death, the office was taken by another experienced infantry officer, Fromhold von Ludinghausen Wolff, who was general of artillery until his death at the end of 1665.

The majority of these offices were present in the Lithuanian army as well, which was under the command of Grand and Field Hetman exactly in the same way as in Poland. Between 1635 and 1656, the office of Grand Guard was held by Hrehory Mirski, a very experienced officer that served for many years under the command of Janusz Radziwiłł. He was banned from the office as a punishment for siding with Jnausz Radziwiłł after the Treaty of Kiejdany. His replacement was Władysław Jerzy Chalecki, who served as Grand Guard until 1668. Since 1656, the office of Military Guard was in the hands of Krzysztof Wiktoryn Zbigniew Vorbek-Lettow, one of the new generation of officers that learned their military trades in the almost continuous campaigns from 1649. Prior to 1656, the Lithuanian army, except in 1624 and 1627, did not

A high-ranking official or army officer with mace. Stefano della Bella, 1651 (Rijksmuseum)

---

4   Wimmer, *Wojsko polskie w drugiej połowie XVII wieku*, pp.339–50.
5   Wimmer, *Wojsko polskie w drugiej połowie XVII wieku*, p.247.

have a regular Military Guard. The candidate that took over as Field Clerk in 1654 was a bit unusual, as it was Aleksander Hilary Połubiński, who at that point was 28 years old and did not have much military service under his belt. He became one of the most important commanders of the Lithuanian army, though, fighting in every campaign and famous from leading a hussars' charge during the Battle of Warsaw in 1656. Military Camp Master, during the Deluge, was held by two officers: Samuel Komorowski from 1654 until his death in 1659 and after him another one of the new generation of officers, Michał Kazimierz Pac. There was also an office of the general of artillery, which was held by Mikołaj Judycki between 1654 and 1670.

Jan II Kazimierz Waza (1609–1672) was the youngest son of King Zygmunt (Sigismund) III. He was elected the King of Poland and Grand Duke of Lithuania in 1648 after death of his brother King Władysław IV. The 20 years of the reign of Jan Kazimierz (1648–1668) was an extremely difficult time for the Commonwealth, full of military conflicts with both internal and external threats. The new monarch took over the throne during the most serious of the Cossack Uprisings, known as the Khmelnytksy Uprising. Already, in 1649, Jan Kazimierz himself had to take part in the military campaign, leading the Polish army in the relief of the besieged Zbaraż. In the bloody Battle of Zborów, he was stopped by the Cossacks and Tatars, and the Poles had to negotiate a treaty with Khan Islam III Girat and Hetman Bohdan Khmelnytsky. The temporary truce did not last long, though, and in 1651 hostility broke out again. While the Polish–Lithuanian army managed to defeat the Cossacks and Tatars at Beresteczko in summer 1651, even another Battle of Biała Cerkiew (Bila Tserkva) in September 1651 did not bring them conclusive victory over the Cossacks. War continued, with a huge Polish defeat in 1652 at Batoh, where a large part of the Polish army was murdered after surrendering. Both sides also fought a 'proxy war' in Moldavia, attempting to secure their own supporter in the throne of the country. Another large Polish military effort in 1653, again led by the King himself, known as the Żwaniec campaign, ended in disappointed failure without any gains. In 1654, Muscovy started an offensive on Lithuania, starting a new conflict that would last until 1667. In 1655, the Commonwealth was almost forced onto its knees when Sweden entered the war. After a string of defeats, King Jan Kazimierz left Poland and spent some time in exile in the Duchy of Opole and Racibórz.[6] He did return to the country after

King Jan II Kazimierz, portrait by Daniel Schultz (Wikimedia Commons).

---

6   The Duchy belonged to the Crown of Bohemia but, from 1645, was under Polish control as a part of a 50-years' land deposit in lieu of the unpaid dowry of Queen Cecilia Renata of Austria

a few months, when the anti-Swedish opposition became stronger. On 1 April 1656, in a cathedral in Lwów, Jan Kazimierz gave the so-called 'Lwów Oath', in which he entrusted the Polish–Lithuanian Commonwealth to the protection of the Blessed Virgin Mary, who was named 'Queen of the Polish Crown'. The King vowed to improve the livelihood of burghers and peasants once the country was saved from the invaders.

At times, Jan Kazimierz led the army himself, taking overall command in the three-days battle at Warsaw (28–30 July 1656), the siege of Cracow in June–August 1657 and the siege of Toruń between September and December 1657. He also led the Polish army in the campaign of 1661 and in the last unsuccessful offensive against the Muscovites in 1663/1664. All other major campaigns were led by professional officers, including hetmans and royal favourite, *Regimentarz* Stefan Czarniecki. De Garmont, who on a few occasions met and spoke with the King during the campaign of 1663/1664, wrote an interesting characteristic of the Polish monarch: 'This was not a man of outstanding education; but he possessed great secularism, was kind, full of humanity, brave as his sword, and counted in his life many valiant deeds in which he always stood out personally'.[7] There is no doubt that Jan Kazimierz was personally brave, often leading from the front, and his presence calmed the waving troops at Zborów. At the Battle of Warsaw in 1656, he commanded 'with fire in his eye and voice (it was heard that he was giving orders with "In God's name" on his lips)'.[8]

Marie Louise Gonzaga, known in Poland as Ludwika Maria (1611–1667), was a French noblewoman and the daughter of Charles I Gonzaga, Duke of Mantua, and Catherine de Guise. She was married to two Polish Kings: to Władysław IV between 1645 and 1648, and to Jan II Kazimierz from 1649 until her death in 1667. Her first marriage was not very successful, as Władysław was mainly interested in the money brought by his new wife as a dowry and the subsequent loans she provided for his grand military plans. The Queen wanted to have more say in the cases of the internal and external politics of the country, which led to conflicts with the Polish and Lithuanian magnates and nobility. Her relationship with Jan II Kazimierz was much closer than that with her previous husband, as the Queen was always supporting him during series of conflicts and played an important role in shaping court policies. Intelligent and well educated, she seems to have had a big influence on her husband, being his close confident and aid in many political matters. During the Deluge, she left with the King in exile but returned and took an active role in the war, always supporting Jan II Kazimierz. She was present during the siege and subsequent Battle of Warsaw in 1656, when she even directed the Polish battery shooting at the enemy. The Queen accompanied Jan II Kazimierz in his later campaigns of the war, being present at the siege of Toruń in 1658. Her activities there were very visible, as the Queen 'in her piety gathered shot, wounded, miserable soldiers, giving care to wounded, support to impoverished, food to hungry, [and bringing]

(1611–1644), the first wife of King Władysław IV.
7 Gramont, *Iz istorīi moskovskago pokhoda Īana Kazimira, 1663-1664 g.g.*, p.16.
8 Kochowski, *Lata Potopu 1655-1657*, p.198.

everyone as much help as she could'.⁹ It is very likely that many of the ideas of the royalist party in regard to internal changes – like election *vivente rege* and attempts to change elections and voting systems – were inspired by her, in a bid of reinforcing the status and role of the King in the Commonwealth. She was, for obvious reasons, in support of closer ties with France, which put her against Hapsburg's influences in Poland. The Queen was also very religious, and she became a benefactor of many monasteries in Poland. With Jan II Kazimierz, they had two children, but both died in infancy. The Queen herself died on 10 May 1667, which seems to have completely broken the King's spirit as he abdicated the next year. Interesting, although sometimes very confusing, may be the case of changing her name when coming to Poland. Originally, she was Marie Louise (Maria Ludwika). In Poland, she had to use Louise Marie (Ludwika Maria), as 'Maria' was 'reserved' for Holy Mary and would not be well seen by the Poles if the Queen insisted on using it as first name.

Crown Grand Hetman Stanisław Rewera Potocki (1589–1667) started his military career in the early 1620s while taking part in an unsuccessful private campaign of his uncle Stefan in Moldavia.[10] He later fought in Royal Prince Władysław Waza's expedition to Moscow (1617–1618) and in Hetman Koniecpolski's victory over the Tatars at Martynów in 1624. Between 1626 and 1629, he was *rotmistrz* of a hussar banner and colonel in charge of one of the national cavalry regiments fighting in Prussia against the Swedes. As temporary commander of the army in Prussia (during Koniecpolski's absence), he was defeated in February 1629 by Herman Wrangel at Górzno. It did not stop his military career, though, as he continued serving in the quarter army and fighting against the Cossacks between the 1630s and 1650s, which included being present on the King's side in the Battle of Zborów in 1649. In 1652, after the death of Crown Field Hetman Kalinowski at the Battle of Batoh, Potocki was nominated to replace him. Two years later, he was promoted to Crown Grand Hetman, as the office was vacant since 1651 after the death of Mikołaj Potocki. By that time, Stanisław Potocki was already elderly, often troubled with sickness and lacking proper energy to lead the army. Despite that, he took part in many campaigns in the 1650s and 1660s, fighting against the Muscovites,

Crown Grand Hetman Stanisław 'Rewera' Potocki, portrait by unknown author (Wikimedia Commons).

---

9   Jan Stefan Wydźga, *Historia Abo Opisanie wielu Poważnieyszych Rzeczy ktore się działy podczas Woyny Szwedzkiey w Krolestwie Polskim od Roku Pańskiego 1655. w Miesiącu Lipcu, aż do Roku 1660, Miesiącu Maiu trwaiącey, w sobie zamykaiące, y do wiadomości potomnym Wiekom Podane* (place of publish unknown, date between 1661 and 1665), p.87.

10 'Rewera' was a nickname, from the Latin phrase '*re vera*' ('in fact' or 'in reality'), which was the Hetman's favourite saying.

Cossacks, Swedes and Brandenburgians. On 29 September 1655, his division was defeated by the Muscovites in the battle at Gródek Jagielloński. The Hetman fought bravely, leading his regiment of national cavalry as a rearguard of the Polish force. His life was in danger, but he was saved by the timely intervention of *Rotmistrz* Aleksander Kryczyński and companion Modrzejewski, who killed the Muscovite directly attacking the Hetman and thus allowed Potocki to flee.[11] Like the majority of Polish commanders and soldiers, in 1655, he switched sides and joined the Swedes – although he later switched back and commanded the Tyszowce Confederation, again serving Jan II Kazimierz. He was present during further fights against the Swedes, but he tended to command only a part of the army while the rest of the troops tended to be led by Lubomirski and Czarniecki. Though personally brave, often leading his soldiers from the front (like at Cudnów in 1660), Potocki was never ranked amongst the best or most able of Polish generals, often relying on talented sub-commanders.

Crown Field Hetman Stanisław Lanckoroński (1590–1657), another officer from Stanisław Koniecpolski's school, took part in this Hetman's campaigns against the Tatars, Cossacks and Swedes in the 1620s and 1630s. He started to play a more significant role during the Cossack Uprising of 1648, when he successfully defended Kamianets-Podilskyi, and in 1649, as *regimentarz* of the Polish army, took part in the defence of Zbaraż. He fought at Beresteczko in 1651 and in the Żwaniec campaign of 1653. In 1654, he took over as Field Hetman after Rewera Potocki's promotion to Grand Hetman. Lanckoroński continued fighting the Muscovites and Swedes, barely survive with his life the Battle of Wojnicz in 1655. Later, he shared the fate of Potocki and went over to the Swedes alongside him. After his return to the Polish service, Lanckoroński fought at Warsaw in 1656. He died of natural causes in early 1657.

Crown Field Hetman Jerzy Sebastian Lanckoroński, portrait by Wolfgang Phillip Kilian (Biblioteka Narodowa, Warszawa).

Field Jerzy Sebastian Lubomirski (1616–1667) received the office of Field Hetman after Lanckoroński's death. At the same time, he held (since 1650) the title of Crown Grand Marshall, which was the most important civilian office in Poland. A wealthy magnate and very well educated, he was one of the most important politicians of his era. His military career started in 1648 against the Cossacks. He also took part in campaigns in 1649, 1651 and 1653. His main focus was on politics, though, both internal and external. In the initial phase of the Deluge, he stayed neutral – not switching to the Swedes, recruiting troops on his own expense and keeping an open line

---

11   *Rotmistrz* Aleksander Kryczyński was in charge of a Tatar light cavalry banner.

of communication with King Jan Kazimierz in his exile. From 1656, much more active, he became one of the most important Polish commanders of the war. Alongside Czarniecki, he defeated the Swedes at Warka but shared the defeat at Gniezno/Kłecko. He also led an unsuccessful blockade and siege of Cracow. In 1657, fighting against George II Rákóczi's troops, he organised a punitive expedition into Transylvania. In the same year, he received a nomination to Crown Field Hetman. In 1658 and 1659, he led Polish troops in Prussia and captured Toruń and Grudziądz. In 1660, alongside Rewera Potocki, he led the Polish army in Ukraine against the Muscovites and Cossacks, winning the Battles of Słobodyszcze and Cudnów.

Lubomirski was often opposed to King Jan II Kazimierz's plans, which led to an increasing conflict between the two in 1663. In 1664, a royal faction, despite the large support for Lubomirski amongst Polish nobility, decided to strike directly at Lubomirski. He was accused of conspiracy against the King and, in a show trial, by a majority of the senators' votes, was sentenced to infamy, to the confiscation of all titles and belongings and finally to death. Lubomirski left the country and went into exile in Silesia. In 1665, with a large support from nobles, he started an open rebellion, known from his name as *Rokosz Lubomirskiego*. He entered Poland while leading his private troops and was quickly joined by masses of nobles and many mutinied units of the regular army. He presented himself as a defender of the old freedoms of the nobility (the so-called 'Golden Liberty') and a strong opponent of the royal plans of *vivente rege*. In September 1665, he defeated the Polish–Lithuanian royalist troops in the Battle of Częstochowa, and, after a temporary truce in November 1665, he yet again left for Silesia. Returning in spring 1666, in the bloody Battle of Mątwy (12–13 July 1666), he severely defeated the royalist forces led by Jan II Kazimierz and new Field Hetman Jan Sobieski. On 31 July 1666, both sides signed an agreement in Łęgonice. Jan II Kazimierz had to promise amnesty for all rebels and abandon his politics of *vivente rege*. Lubomirski's infamy was cancelled, and he 'got back his honour' and his possessions – although he had to leave for exile, where he died on 31 January 1667 in Wrocław (at that time known under the German name 'Breslau'). He was a very able field commander and organiser of the troops, focusing much of his efforts in 1656 and 1657 on raising new foreign troops for the Polish army. If the situation required, he was not shy from leading his troops from the front rank, like at the Battle of Warka where he commanded his regiments 'with the sabre in his hand'.[12]

Regimentarz Stanisław Czarniecki, portrait by Brodero Matthisen (Wikimedia Commons).

---

12 'Relazione dei felici successi dell' armi…', in *Relacye nuncyuszów apostolskich i innych osób w Polsce od roku 1548 do 1690* (Berlin-Poznań: Księgarnia B. Behra, 1864), vol. II, pp.294–95.

Stefan Czarniecki (1599–1665), probably the most famous Polish commander during the war, became such an important symbol of the efforts against the invaders that he is even included in the Polish national anthem, *Mazurek Dąbrowskiego*.[13] As such, I believe it is worth looking at his military career in much more detail to understand his journey from cavalry companion to hetman. It started very early, as Czarniecki took part in the Chocim campaign in 1621. The next few years he spent as a companion in the cossack cavalry banner of his brother, Paweł, serving as a part of the quarter army against the Cossacks and Tatars, while between 1626 and 1629 he fought against the Swedes in Prussia. There he had the chance to learn the craft of 'small war', as his brother's banner was often involved in reconnaissance missions and hit-and-run attacks against the Swedes.

Between 1630 and 1632, Czarniecki was in the Imperial army as a part of Lisowski's mercenary Cossacks (*lisowczycy*). He returned to the Polish army in 1633, being promoted to lieutenant in charge of the cossack cavalry banner of Crown Field Hetman Marcin Kazanowski. Leading this unit, Czarniecki took part in the Smoleńsk War (1632–1634), fighting against the Muscovites. He continued service in the quarter army, in 1636 raising in status and serving as lieutenant of Stanisław Lubomirski's hussar banner. In the ranks of this unit, Czarniecki fought against the Cossacks in 1637 and 1638. He continued in this role until 1648, when he was taken prisoner by the Tatars after the Battle of Żółte Wody. He quickly escaped from captivity but, in October 1648, was taken prisoner again, this time by the Cossacks during the capture of the fortress Kudak. He returned to Poland in 1649 and again rejoined the army, although serving as lieutenant in Grand Hetman Mikołaj Potocki's winged hussar banner. In late 1650, he was also promoted to Military Judge as a part of his hetman's inner circle of officers. In 1651, Czarniecki also organised a dragoon regiment that was to serve under his name until his death in 1665. Czarniecki continued fighting against the Cossacks and Tatars, leading his hetman's regiment of national cavalry. In late 1652, Mikołaj Potocki died, but his units were taken over by King Jan II Kazimierz, so Czarniecki became lieutenant of the prestigious Royal winged hussar banner. He was also promoted to another prestigious military rank, that of Camp Master. In spring 1653, while leading a strong punitive raid into Cossack-held territory, he was heavily wounded in his palate.[14] It was a very dangerous injury – he barely survived, and recovery took him a few weeks. He later took part in the Żwaniec campaign of 1653, then in 1654 and early 1655 against the Cossacks and Muscovites. During the Swedish invasion in summer 1655, Czarniecki was initially fighting as part of the Polish field army facing Charles X Gustav and Wittenberg's forces. He had a few minor successes in ambushing the Swedish reconnaissance units, already showing his trademark understanding of 'small war' tactics.

---

13   The anthem was written in 1797 by Józef Wybicki as the *Song of Polish Legions in Italy* (*Pieśń Legionów Polskich we Włoszech*). After Poland regained independence following the Great War, it was officially chosen as the Polish national anthem in 1927.
14   Either by an arrow or, most likely, a shot from a gun. Kersten, *Stefan Czarniecki*, p.215.

Then, in mid-September, in a rather unusual turn of events, Jan II Kazimierz nominated Czarniecki as a commander of the defence of Cracow. Considering that Czarniecki was a cavalry officer and did not have much experience in siege work, it was more a political than military choice, as the King was leaving the town in the hands of a trusted soldier.[15] Cracow was besieged for three weeks, during which Czarniecki was doing his best to keep up the morale of his troops and prolong the defence as long as he could. The Polish side was even able to surrender on honourable terms, being allowed to leave Cracow with their flags and arms.

In late autumn 1655, Czarniecki twice visited King Jan II Kazimierz in his exile in Silesia to discuss further plans of the fight against the Swedes. He tried to take his troops from the garrison of Cracow, which were stationed in quarters on the Silesian border, to join the King. However, the units were overtaken by the Swedes and mostly forced to switch service to the Swedish army. Czarniecki was only able to take approximately 100 dragoons with him. Jan II Kazimierz awarded his loyal commander, giving him the rank of *regimentarz* and ordering him to start organising new troops in Poland. It gave start to the separate command of Czarniecki, as his division – despite some changes in its organisation – was to fight as a force independent from both the Grand and Field Hetmans. Here, he quickly became known as the undisputed master of the 'small war', leading an expedition to Wielkopolska and fighting against the main Swedish field army. In the pitched battles, though, at least against the Swedes, his record was not very impressive. Fighting side by side with Lubomirski, he decisively crushed the Swedish division at Werki, but he was defeated at both Gołąb and Gniezno/Kłeck. No surprise, then, that he was arguing against an open battle with the Swedish–Brandenburg coalition at Warsaw. Moreover, he did not take part in the battle, sending away with some reconnaissance force just before the beginning of the fight.

In early autumn 1656, Czarniecki was wounded in a fight against the Swedes, probably near Łowicz, and recovery took him two months. He rejoined the fight in December 1656, leading a cavalry raid against the Swedish forces in Prussia. Between March and August 1657, he fought against invading Transylvanians, yet again relying on his favourite tactic of harassing the enemy with sudden cavalry strikes. On 11 July 1657, he defeated the Transylvanian rearguard at Magierowo, capturing and looting their large tabor. He was amongst the Polish commanders negotiating the surrender of the Transylvanian army at Międzyboż. In October 1657, he led a division in a raid to Swedish Pomerania, while between September 1658 and September 1659 his division fought as part of the allied army in Denmark (see Appendix I). In December 1658, his soldiers took part in the fight for island Als and captured the fortress Kolding. In September 1659, a majority of his division left Denmark with only the regiment under Piaseczyński remaining as a part of the allied army to continue fighting against the Swedes. From 1660 onwards, Czarniecki's attention turned against the Muscovites, with

---

15   Kersten, *Stefan Czarniecki*, pp.260–61.

his division supporting the Lithuanian army of Grand Hetman Sapieha. The Poles were instrumental in winning the Battles of Połonka and Basia, with Czarniecki showing good skill in utilising cavalry and dismounted dragoons as combined arms.

After 1661, he became more involved in internal politics, supporting the royalist party and its plans for election *vivente rege*. He was also dragged into a conflict within the army, facing confederations of unpaid troops. He took part in the campaign of 1663/1664 but, like the rest of the Polish and Lithuanian armies, without much success. In autumn 1664, he was wounded during the siege of Lisianka. Finally, on 2 January 1665, he received the highly sought for office of Crown Field Hetman after it was stripped from Lubomirski. While en route from Ukraine to Warsaw, to take command of the royal forces in conflict with Lubomirski, Czarniecki died in Sokołówka near Lwów on 16 February 1665. There were rumours that he was poisoned although it is highly likely that he, in fact, succumbed due to a battle wound.

Czarniecki was, without a doubt, one of the most important of the Commonwealth's commanders during the Deluge – although, for many historians, he is still rather controversial, especially taking into consideration his poor attempts to engage in politics. While he excelled in 'small war' and harassing the enemy (like how his campaigns against the Swedes and Transylvanians showed), he was often reckless on the battlefield and during siege operations, which led to defeats and heavy losses of his troops. Pasek, who served for years under Czarniecki's command, praised him with his usual, a bit exaggerated, style – writing:

Lithuanian Grand Hetman Janusz Radziwiłł, portrait by Daniel Schultz (Wikimedia Commons).

> through the all years of [the Swedish] war I kept with Czarniecki and with him I sometimes went through poor times and sometimes through great times; as he was type of grand commander and [was] lucky, enough to say that during the time in his division I fled [from the battlefield] only once, while I could count thousand time when I gave chase [to the enemy].[16]

Czarniecki was also known, even amongst his soldiers, as a looter, as he often kept the lion's share of the captured prisoners and their belongings. In some way, he explained himself by famously saying, 'I am not from salt or from soil but from my own wounds.'[17] He indicated in this way that he was his own man and that he earned all from his military service, unlike the family of Lubomirski (who earned from a salt mine in Wieliczka) or Potocki (from their large land holds).

16 Pasek, *Pamiętniki*, p.70.
17 Polish: '*Jam nie z soli ani z roli, ale z tego co mnie boli.*'

AGAINST THE DELUGE

Janusz Radziwiłł (1612–1655), son of famous Lithuanian Hetman Krzysztof II Radziwiłł (Field Hetman 1615–1635, Grand Hetman 1635–1640), was one of the most talented and most controversial Lithuanian generals and politicians. Well educated, he spent a few years in Western Europe, studying and travelling. He also took part in the Smoleńsk War, during which he was nominal commander of a few units in the Lithuanian army. A Calvinist like his father, he was a natural leader of the Protestants in Lithuania and was many times elected as a representative on the *Sejm*. In 1646, he was nominated Lithuanian Field Hetman, and for the next few years, he was de facto in charge of Lithuanian military affairs, as the elderly Grand Hetman Janusz Kiszka did not take a much active role in campaigns. Radziwiłł led the Lithuanian army in the victorious campaign of 1649 against the Cossacks, winning the Battle of Łojów. In 1651, he again won at Łojów and captured Kiev. His troops, next to the Polish army, took part in the Battle of Biały Cerkiew on 23 September 1651.

In later years, he often conflicted with Jan II Kazimierz, as the King tried to curb Radziwiłł's influence in the Lithuanian army by promoting royal supporters like Gosiewski to important offices. In 1654, he was promoted to Grand Hetman. Facing a massive invasion of Muscovites in Lithuania, Radziwiłł won the Battle of Szkłów on 12 August 1654 but was defeated, with heavy losses, at Szepielewicze/Ciecierzyn 12 days later. Trying to reorganise and strengthen the Lithuanian army, he led an unsuccessful winter campaign in 1655, with a support of Polish auxiliary corps besieging Stary Bychów and Mohylew. Conflict with Gosiewski led to his defeat at the Battle of Vilnius on 7 August 1655: the city was captured and largely destroyed by the Muscovites and Cossacks. Facing the triumphant Muscovites, while the Swedes were at the same time having much success invading Poland, Radziwiłł decided to negotiate with Charles X Gustav. Under the Treaty of Kiejdany from 20 October 1655, the Grand Duchy of Lithuanian broke out from the Commonwealth and became a Swedish protectorate. While many Lithuanian nobles supported the move, seeing it as the only hope in the war against Muscovy, many – led by the magnate family of Sapieha – were against it, leading to fights between both factions. In the night of 30 to 31 December 1655, Janusz Radziwiłł died in his fortress of Tykocin, which was besieged by troops loyal to the Polish King.

While looking into his decisions in 1655, it is important to remember the wider picture – the situation of the Commonwealth at the time, facing two enemies and losing battle after battle. Of course, it is obvious that, at least partially, he had the interest of his family in mind, hoping for the Radziwiłł family to become the most powerful magnates in Lithuania, maybe even carving their own dukedom there. On the other side, he was facing not only external enemies – Muscovites, Cossacks and Swedes – but also internal ones. Chief amongst them was King Jan II Kazimierz, at odds with Janusz Radziwiłł on many fields, from religion, through the administrative mechanisms of the Commonwealth, to the control of the army. While for many, especially after reading Henryk Sienkiewicz's *The Deluge*, it is easy to just call Radziwiłł a traitor, the truth was much more complicated and needs to be understood within the many aspects of the seventeenth-century Commonwealth.

COMMANDERS

Paweł Jan Sapieha (1609–1655), from the powerful Lithuanian magnate family, was often at odds with Radziwiłł's family. He took part in the Smoleńsk War, during which he was heavily wounded due to a mine explosion during the siege of Biała (today Bely in Tver Oblast) in 1634. From 1635, in Władysław IV's court, he was elected as a representative for the *Sejm* a few times. In 1651, he took part in the Battle of Beresteczko. In 1654, he fought as a commander of the private troops of the Sapieha family that were not under Janusz Radziwiłł's army. After the Treaty of Kiejdany, on which he did not sign, he gathered loyalist Lithuanian troops, private units and levy of nobility in Podlasie, opposing both the Swedes and Muscovites. In September 1655, he was *regimentarz* of the Lithuanian army. On 23 November 1655, he managed to defeat the Muscovite army of Siemion Urusov near Brest, forcing them to retreat from the vicinity of this strategic town. Four days later, though, at Wierzchowicze, Urusov successfully counterattacked, scattering Sapieha's forces and causing heavy losses in the Lithuanian army.

Lithuanian Grand Hetman Paweł Jan Sapieha, portrait by Pierre Landry (Biblioteka Narodowa, Warszawa).

Sapieha later joined the Confederation of Tyszowce, and, in March 1656, he was nominated as Lithuanian Grand Hetman. He took part in a campaign against the Swedes in spring 1656, during which his army was not able to stop Charles X Gustav retreating from entrapment between the rivers Vistula and San. He did not take part in the Battle of Warsaw, as, prior to the fight, his horse had fallen on him and the Hetman suffered a sprained shinbone. He conflicted with Field Hetman Gosiewski, so the Lithuanian army continued to be divided into two separate divisions for the rest of the war. His conflict with Jan II Kazimierz was also often affecting the performance of the Lithuanian army, as the King and the Hetman clashed repeatedly over the financing of the army, control of Grand Hetman over all Lithuanian troops, fighting on two fronts (against the Swedes and the Muscovites) at the same time and external politics as Sapieha was often seen as pro-Hapsburg or even pro-Muscovite. He took part, without much success, in campaigns against the Muscovites in 1659/1660. Only in the second part of 1660, when his division was supported by Czarniecki's Poles, was the joint force victorious at Połonka and Basia.

After 1661, Sapieha focused on politics, only taking part in the 1663/1664 campaign against the Muscovites. By then, the army was mostly under the command of Field Hetman Pac, as the ill Sapieha was not fit enough to lead the army. The Grand Hetman died on 30 December 1665. Overall, he was good at organising the army: in 1655, he spent a large amount of money from his own purse to help reform loyalist Lithuanian troops. In the field, he was a very cautious commander, often relying on talented sub-commanders like Aleksander Hilary Połubiński or Samuel Kmicic.

Wincenty Korwin Gosiewski (1620–1662) started his military career in the Lithuanian army in 1648, fighting against the Cossacks. He was quickly recognised by Janusz Radziwiłł as an able commander: in 1651, he was nominated as Lithuanian general of artillery, replacing the recently deceased Mikołaj Abramowicz. In 1654, after Radziwiłł was promoted to Grand Hetman, Gosiewski became Lithuanian Field Hetman. As a political nominee supported by Jan II Kazimierz, he was in open conflict with Janusz Radziwiłł. This conflict led to a partition of the Lithuanian army into two divisions, each under the command of one Hetman. Both commanders did not want to work with each other, which weakened the Lithuanian defence against the Muscovites and polarised the nobles, with some supporting the King and Gosiewski while the others were on Radziwiłł's side. This lack of proper cooperation led to the defeat at the Battle of Vilnius in August 1655, and as a consequence this important town was captured by the Muscovites.

Later the same month, Gosiewski found himself in Kiejdany, where he initially was one of the signatories of the first treaty with the Swedes. Interestingly enough, he was hoping to receive the office of Lithuanian Grand Hetman in the case of Janusz Radziwiłł's death, so he was asking King Charles X Gustav for reassurance in regard to that. At the same time, he was also in talks with the Muscovites, though, hoping to sign an armistice with them, so the Lithuanians could focus on their fight with the Swedes. He was probably also counting on the start of a conflict between Sweden and Muscovy.

In September, Radziwiłł decided to arrest Gosiewski and, in October, signed a second treaty in Kiejdany, in effect breaking up the Commonwealth. Gosiewski fled from prison in spring 1656 and soon again took command over part of the Lithuanian army. He rejoined Jan II Kazimierz at Warsaw during the siege of the city but did not take part in the three-day battle against the Swedish and Brandenburg army. In autumn 1656, leading a strong force of Lithuanian, Polish and allied Tatars, he invaded Ducal Prussia. On 8 October 1656, he won at the Battle at Prostki, defeating a Swedish–Brandenburg division and capturing Prince Bogusław Radziwiłł. Two weeks later, though, after Polish and Tatars troops left him, he lost the Battle of Filipów. In 1657, Gosiewski was a very active as diplomat, being one of the Royal Commissioners signing the Treaties of Welawa and Bydgoszcz with the Brandenburg Elector. Later, in 1657 and in 1658, he took his division to Livonia, capturing many fortresses from Swedish hands. On 21 October 1658, he was surprised and defeated by the Muscovites at Werki, where he was taken prisoner. He stayed in captivity until 1662.

After Gosiewski's return to the Lithuanian army, as a member of the royal party, he attempted to end the mutiny of unpaid troops (a confederation known as the *Związek Braterski* – Brotherly Union). The group of mutineers – led by vice marshal of the Brotherly Union, Konstanty Kotowski, opposing any plans to end the mutiny – captured Gosiewski and marshal of the Union, Kazimierz Chwalibóg Żeromski. The latter was initially wounded then killed at Dubny. The captured Gosiewski was shot to death at Ostryna on 29 November 1662. The murder of the Field Hetman was a real shock for everyone in the Commonwealth and quickly led to the end of the mutiny. While the majority of the soldiers were pardoned, that did not cover those responsible for the death of Gosiewski. Four main leaders of the assassination were captured and sentenced to death. They were executed in Warsaw on 3

January 1665, with Kotowski publicly tortured with fire then beheaded and his body quartered after the death.

Aleksander Hilary Połubiński (1626–1679) started his military career on a very high note, as in 1648 he received a recruitment letter for a banner of hussars in the Lithuanian army. He was very young (22 years old) but came from family known for its military prowess and had enough wealth to be able to raise such an expensive unit. He led the unit in the campaigns of 1648 and 1649, fighting against the Cossacks. Despite the reduction of the Lithuanian army, his hussars remained in service, and his unit was strengthened before the campaign of 1651. Połubiński and his soldiers took part in the Battle of Łojów on 6 July 1651 and, as a part of the joint Polish–Lithuanian army, at Biała Cerkiew on 23 September 1651. His personal command in the Lithuanian army was also gradually growing, as he raised a company of dragoons in 1652 and a banner of cossack cavalry at the beginning of 1653 as well. The Lithuanian army did not see much action in 1653, though, so Połubiński did not have a lot of chances to show off his military talents. However, he did take a very active part in the campaign against the Muscovites in 1654, fighting at Szkłów and Szepielewicze. At the latter, the battle charges of his reserve regiment of national cavalry managed to stop the Muscovite attacks and cover the retreat of the Lithuanian army. He also managed to gather the remnants of the defeated units and, for two months, had command over them in the camp at Śmiłowicze.

Since Maciej Frąckiewicz Radzimiński, Lithuanian Field Clerk, died at Szepielewicze, Połubiński was appointed to this military office. It promoted him to a more important role in the Lithuanian army, and it seems that, despite some attempts at having him engage into internal politics (as part of the pro-royal, anti-Radziwiłł party), Połubiński stayed focused on military affairs. He was also allowed to increase the size of his cavalry banners, while his dragoons were reinforced into a two-company squadron (later into a regiment). Połubiński later took part in the winter campaign of 1654/1655, fighting at Nowy Bychów and Mohylew. On 22 February 1655, he led a group of Lithuanian cavalry and dragoons, defeating the Muscovite relief force marching to Mohylew.

In late February 1655, Połubiński received another royal favour: he was nominated as lieutenant in charge of the Royal hussar banner in the Lithuanian army. Due to problems with the recruitment for this unit, he disbanded his own banner and took its companion to the Royal banner. This new unit was recalled to Poland to fight against the Swedes, where it took part in the Battle of Wojnicz. The banner took heavy losses there, with its standard-bearer, Chreptowicz, and many of its companions killed. Soon after, alongside the rest of the Polish army, Połubiński and his hussars switched sides and joined the Swedish army. The Lithuanian officer served there until February 1656, when he and his unit rejoined the Lithuanian army stationed on Podlasie. Połubiński served from then on in the division of new Lithuanian Grand Hetman Paweł Jan Sapieha, leading a Royal regiment of national cavalry, which included a hussar banner. To the units under his nominal command, he added a Tatar light cavalry banner.

Połubiński's most famous action was leading the charge of Lithuanian hussars during the second day of the Battle of Warsaw (this fight will be described in more detailed in later chapters). In January 1657, Połubiński with his regiment was present at the capturing of Tykocin, while in February same year he led a punitive raid of Sapieha's division into Ducal Prussia. In summer 1657, leading the vanguard of Grand Hetman's troops, Połubiński supported Czarniecki in his fight against the Transylvanians. In 1658, he fought against the Muscovites, taking command of the siege of Mińsk and capturing the city at the end of November. Gradually, through 1657 and 1658, the tension between Hetman Sapieha and Połubiński was growing, leading to almost open conflict. Połubiński, as part of the royal party, was in opposition to the very independent politics of Sapieha – there was even a plan for pro-royal colonels to take their regiments from Sapieha's command and create a new division under Połubiński. In 1659, Połubiński, showing a lack of political insight, tried to be a 'player' of both parties, attempting to calm the tensions between Sapieha and himself. (In chapter nine, I will describe in more detail his military actions as *regimentarz* in Courland and Livonia up to 1660.)

Later in 1660, again under the command of Sapieha, Połubiński fought against the Muscovites at Połonka and Basia. In 1662 and 1663, he played an important role in calming the situation within the mutinied Lithuanian army. While he hoped to receive the office of Lithuanian Field Hetman, now vacated after the murder of Gosiewski, it went to Michał Kazimierz Pac instead. In early 1664, leading Sapieha's division, he took part in an unsuccessful campaign against the Muscovites. In summer 1665, he led Lithuanian corps to support Jan II Kazimierz in his fight against Lubomirski's mutiny. Here, Połubiński suffered the worst defeat of his military career: on 2 September 1665, his joint Polish–Lithuanian force was severely beaten by pro-Lubomirski soldiers. Połubiński was wounded in the head and taken prisoner. He and his soldiers were soon released from it but had to make an oath that they would not be fighting against the Poles anymore.

In his later years, Połubiński was less active in military affairs, focusing instead on the domestic politic scene and becoming a supporter of the Pac family in their conflict with the Radziwiłł clan. In 1669, he received the office of Lithuanian Grand Marshall, the most important civil office in the Grand Duchy. Połubiński still kept a large contingent of the soldiers under his name in the Lithuanian *komput*: in the early 1670s, he had a hussar banner, foreign infantry regiment (formed from his previous dragoon regiment), *petyhorcy* banner, Tatar light cavalry banner and Hungarian infantry banner. All of those units took part in the Chocim campaign of 1673, although Połubiński, due to unknown reasons, never joined the army to fight against the Ottomans. His units took part in the later campaigns of the 1672–1676 war, but Połubiński focused on diplomatic works (during negotiations with the Muscovites) and especially on internal affairs in the Commonwealth.

Samuel Aleksander Komorowski (unknown–1659) was a very experienced officer in the Lithuanian army, who started his career during the Smoleńsk War. He was present in all the main campaigns of the Lithuanian army from 1648 onwards, fighting against the Cossacks, Muscovites and Swedes. He served as lieutenant of Janusz Radziwiłł's hussar banner and *rotmistrz* of his own cossack cavalry banner. From 1654, he was also Lithuanian Camp Master and colonel in charge of the national cavalry regiment. He was often commanding separate detachments of the Lithuanian army, fighting against the Muscovites and Swedes. He did sign the Treaty of Kiejdany in 1655, hoping that Charles X Gustav would award him with the office of Lithuanian Field Hetman. Since it did not happen, he later rejoined the loyalist forces, serving in the 'left division' of Field Hetman Gosiewski. After Gosiewski's capture, it was Komorowski, as *regimentarz* in Lithuanian army, leading the left wing division until his death in Courland (see chapter nine).

Michał Kazimierz Pac (1624–1682) was one of the military commanders of the new generation that emerged during the Deluge. He started his career in 1648 or 1649, serving as a companion in one of the cossack cavalry banners in the Lithuanian army, fighting against the Cossacks. In 1654, he joined the newly raised hussar banner of Field Hetman Wincenty Gosiewski, taking part in the campaign of 1655 and fighting the Muscovites and Cossacks. He did not sign the Treaty of Kiejdany and joined the part of the Lithuanian army loyal to King Jan Kazimierz. For a short time, he served as lieutenant in one of the cossack cavalry banners, and, in summer 1656, he became *rotmistrz* of a 150-horse-strong banner of such cavalry. Leading it, he probably took part in the Battle of Prostki and Filipów. He then fought in the ranks of the Lithuanian army in Livonia and Courland, often leading vanguard troops and showing good skill in leading cavalry units. By 1658, he was, alongside leading his own banner, also colonel of the national cavalry regiment fighting the Swedes in Courland.

The young officer had good political support from his uncle, Krzysztof Zygmunt Pac, who since 1658 was Lithuanian Grand Chancellor. Furthermore, Michał Kazimierz Pac was well liked by his soldiers, who saw him as 'one of them', always present in campaigns and leading from the front. He also had a string of successes fighting the Swedes led by Douglas in Courland, showing to be a good cavalry commander that knew how to play to the strength of his troops. After the death of *Regimentarz* Komorowski in October 1659, soldiers of the 'left division' of the Lithuanian army chose Michał Kazimierz Pac as their new *regimentarz*. By that time, he was already seen as a part of the 'royal faction' loyal to Jan Kazimierz and opposing Grand Hetman Sapieha. The King not only approved of the soldiers' decision for Pac's command, but he also promoted him to the office of Lithuanian Camp Master. Pac continue to fight the Swedes until the end of the war and then took part in campaigns against the Muscovites. He survived the confederation (mutiny) of soldiers in 1662, when Gosiewski was killed by the mutineers. Pac played a role in negotiating end of the mutiny; he also organised the arrest of the leaders of the confederation. In 1663, he was promoted to the vacant office of Lithuanian Field Hetman, replacing the deceased Gosiewski. During Lubomirski's Mutiny (*Rokosz Lubomirskiego*), he did not take a direct role in the fight but stayed loyal to Jan Kazimierz. In 1667, he was promoted to Lithuanian Grand Hetman and quickly reorganised the army, disbanding troops loyal to Hetman Sapieha. Later, he did take a reluctant part in the war against the Ottomans, often clashing with Crown Grand Hetman Jan Sobieski. He was his political rival and, after Sobieski's election, remained in opposition, often blocking any internal and external political plans of the new king.

4

Lances, Sabres and Muskets

In this chapter, I would like to cover in detail all the formations that were present in the Polish and Lithuanian armies. It will be done with a somewhat different approach from the similar chapters in my previous books. Next to the typical list of the different types of cavalry and infantry, I want to also include some more information about the troops that were often a mix of different formations – like levy of nobility, Royal Guard and district troops. While perhaps confusing, it should help to build a more detailed picture of the Commonwealth's armies, especially as it will draw on numerous primary sources from the period of 1648–1660. Scarce information about the uniforms of soldiers will be, when available, included in the subchapters of each formation. At the end of the chapter, I will write in a bit more detail about the flags used in the Polish and Lithuanian armies.

(Winged) Hussars

Hussars (*husaria*) were the most iconic units of the Commonwealth's armies during the seventeenth century. Well-armoured cavalry, armed with a plethora of weapons including long lance and carrying the pelts of oriental cats and famous wings – it always impressed eyewitnesses, those of allies and enemies alike. It became so associated with the Polish military that the symbol of the winged hussar is even in modern times used on badges of the Tank Corps of the Polish Army, not to mentioned adverts of different businesses and merchandises, from martial art schools to alcohol. It is always interesting to see how foreign guests had described hussars in the seventeenth century, as they often provided us with comments that cannot be found in Polish and Lithuanian diaries, whose authors were so used to the sight of the hussars that they rarely wrote detailed descriptions of it. Guillaume Le Vasseur de Beauplan, who had many occasions to see Polish soldiers from the quarter army, mentioned a good armour of hussars, equipped with 'cuirasses,[1] bracers, greaves, helmets, etc.' Amongst their weapons, the most

---

1 Which most likely covered here both breast and backplates.

LANCES, SABRES AND MUSKETS

important was the 'sabre on the side or pallasch next to left thigh, attached to saddle'. There was also the estoc, long for five feet,[2] 'used to thrust into still alive enemy, laying on ground … it is easier to thrust with it towards the ground and cut through chainmail'. What Beauplan described as a heavy war hammer (*marteux d'armes*) seems to be in fact a horseman's pick (*nadziak*), as it was 'sharp and with long handle, used to crush enemy helmet and armour. This weapon is used to pierce through them'. Of course, crucial was the *kopia* lance:

> 19 feet long and hollowed from sharp end to the handle, rest made from strong wood. On their top they have pennants, which are either white-red or 'blue-green' or 'red-white'. They are always two-coloured though and four to five feet long. They seem to be there to scare enemy horses. As soon as [hussars] lower their lances in charge, those pennants swirl around, causing fear in enemy horses.

Interestingly enough, the Frenchman did not mention wings being used at all. He instead highlighted the importance of proper horses: 'the cheapest of them cost no less than 200 ducats. All of them are Turkish horses, from Anatolian province of Karaman'.[3]

Antoine Charles IV de Gramont, seeing Polish and Lithuanian soldiers during the campaign of 1663/1664, was very impressed with the sight of hussars. He made some interesting observations, especially about how soldiers prepared their estoc sword before a charge:[4]

Cavalry Colonel Szczodrowski in Polish attire. As he was part of Polish embassy entering Rome, he did not wear armour, but we can see a great example of a hussar's wing and horseman's pick (*nadziak*), often used by nobles. Stefano della Bella, 1651 (Biblioteka Narodowa, Warszawa).

> Hussars act at the head of all troops or armed forces in Poland and are the oldest [most important] in this institution. They must meet the following requirements: to be a cavalryman in a hussar detachment – which is colloquially called companion – you must be a nobleman, well-built, strong and able to wear a full cuirass,[5] arm-guards, leg-guards, iron-trimmed mittens,[6] a helmet on the head, on both legs spurs in German [style] (that is, which can be easily removed, while spurs according to the Polish model are nailed to the boots) and a large tiger or leopard skin lined with dark red velvet or silk, with which the hussar covers his left shoulder. His horse must be tall, beautiful, strong and fast; a velvet saddle with chest and tail

---

2   A French *pied* equalled 326mm.
3   Lasota and Beauplan, *Opis Ukrainy*, p.170.
4   Gramont, *Iz istorii moskovskago pokhoda Iana Kazimira, 1663-1664 g.g.*, pp.12–13.
5   So, in this case, breast and backplate.
6   By which he meant *karwasze* protecting the forearm.

straps (as we do in foreign way), so that the rider has a solid support when hitting the enemy with a lance at full gallop. The hussar must have a pistol at the left saddle pommel, a long and pointed sword under the right hip[7] and, as usual, a sabre at the side. During the battle, he pulls his sword from behind his thigh and hangs it on his right hand in order to have his hand free to use the lance, which is the main weapon used by the hussars during the battle, to break through the enemy squadrons. This military equipment is a bit reminiscent of jacquemart [bellstriker]; however, as experience has shown, it really is useful.

The salary of the hussars is fifty livres per quarter, that is, for three months.[8] In addition, they have winter quarters, on which there is nothing definite. These quarters are charged by order of the great general [hetman] per unit of land area. If the country is not ruined, then sometimes fifty, sometimes even a hundred livres are taken from the unit of land; but if the desolation is great everywhere, then twelve livres, so as not to burden the subjects.

It is highly likely that he also wrote mostly about hussars. When before meeting with King Jan Kazimierz leading the army, both De Garmont brothers were 'admiring for some time the beauty and exceptional splendour of the Polish cavalry, about which it can truly be said that it surpasses all cavalry in the whole world'.[9]

In 1665, Italian Sebastian Cefali, for years serving as secretary of Crown Grand Marshal and Field Hetman Jerzy Sebastian Lubomirski, wrote an

Other examples of unarmoured hussars, drawn by Stefano della Bella in 1651 (Biblioteka Narodowa, Warszawa).

---

7   A reference to the estoc.
8   Gramont seems to have treated one French livre as the equivalent of one Polish złoty.
9   Gramont, *Iz istorīi moskovskago pokhoda Īana Kazimira, 1663-1664 g.g.*, pp.15–16.

LANCES, SABRES AND MUSKETS

interesting relation about the political and military situation in Poland. Understandably, he gave an extensive description of winged hussars:[10]

> Hussars are especially worth of the attention, due to their unmatched bravery and their individual dignity. They are similar to old Italian cavalry, although their weapons and discipline are different. Next to sabre, they have lance known as *kopia*, which is hollow inside, on the outside covered with leather strap and covered with tar, rider using it from the galloping horse can pierce through an armour. It is longer than a pike, under point it have silken pennant, cut in the middle, narrower through the bottom and so long that it touches horse's ear. Banners[11] differentiate by colour of pennants and staff of the lance, which is carried by putting through tube made of the folded leather, attached to the pommel of the saddle and to the stirrup. On the left side of the saddle they have pistol [and] under left thigh, attached to the saddle, long estoc, which is used after lance is shattered. On the armour they wear pelt of tiger or leopard, which is connected by the animal's claws [legs] on the right shoulder. They used to carry on their back large vulture wings, that made loud noise during the charge but these days not many [hussars] are using it. Each is serving in at least three men, which means that he should bring with him two good men,[12] well equipped and on good horses, who unlike their master have pelts of bears or wolves, wings and amongst all other weapons they have carbine.
>
> Hussar banners were almost completely abandoned during the wars against the Cossacks and Tatars, as they were of not much use against the enemy not fighting by proper rules of war, but when war against Sweden and Muscovy started, [hussars] was yet again if importance. The best of nobles serve in those banners, and experience officers, who previously commanded cossack [cavalry] or other regiments, do not see serving as simple hussars as something beneath them. Banners of hussars costs way more than even regiment of [other] cavalry or foreign infantry, *rotmistrz*'s spending being especially high, as next to providing his soldiers with lances, he need to provide them with banquets and gifts ....[13] Banner composed of 200 men have no more than 60 nobles, rest is made up by armed men [retainers] brought by them. Noble soldiers, both in hussars and cossack cavalry, are known as companions [*towarzysze*], and they are held in such esteem that even hetman, when giving them orders, calls them brethren. When in march, companions are leading the unit, after them there are musicians, playing on trumpets, shawms and kettle drums, only after them there are non-nobles [retainers].

Throughout the first half of the seventeenth century, hussars tended to be a large part of the whole army, both Polish and Lithuanian alike, often making up half of the overall strength of the cavalry. This situation started to change for the worse with the start of the Cossack Uprising of 1648. All 14 hussar banners of the quarter army were destroyed during the initial phase of the

---

10 'Relacya o stanie politycznym i wojskowym Polski przez Sebastyana Cefali', pp.330–31.
11 In this context, Cefali meant companies.
12 Cefali was writing about retainers called '*pocztowi*'.
13 We will ignore the part where Celafi mentioned which banners were in service in 1661.

conflict, at the Battles of Żółte Wody and Korsuń. While the loss in manpower was not that high, with the majority of men taken prisoners and later returned to Poland, it brought about a large loss in horses and equipment. A vast recruitment of district troops in summer and autumn of 1648 was supposed to provide 2,500 horses of hussars, although not all of the units were raised on time. Those that took part in the campaign in autumn 1648 were scattered after the Battle of Piławce, again taking heavy losses in horses, weapons and armour. Both the regular army and private banners had a strong presence of hussars in the defence of Zbaraż in 1649, but many soldiers died in the fights or succumbed to the illnesses ravaging the defensive force. The presence of hussars was also very important during the Battle of Beresteczko in 1651, although by then hussars were already vastly outnumbered by *pancerni* and cossack cavalry in a 1:6 ratio. The defeat at Batoh in 1652 was the most severe blow to the Polish army. Many officers and soldiers were killed in battle, with thousands more massacred after they were taken prisoner. At least 8,000 men were lost, the majority of them experienced soldiers. Next to the loss of manpower, a huge number of horses and equipment were lost. Many units of the Polish army were wiped out and never rebuilt, amongst them eight banners of hussars. No surprise that the post-Batoh presence of hussars in the Polish army was much reduced, with only five banners, averaging in total between 800 and 900 horses, present until 1654. Some short-lived units served in 1654 and 1655, but, by spring 1659, the Polish army only had six banners, with a total paper strength of 999 horses. During the late 1640s and early 1650s, 'corps' of Lithuanian hussars were varying in size but rarely exceeded 1,000 horses.

It is understandable that, as the elite of the army, hussars were required to include the best men and the best equipment. The recruitment letters for Aleksander Ciekliński and Stanisław Górski from May 1649 specified that their units should be recruited from amongst experienced men and that none of them should come from the ranks 'of those that [previously] made mutinies and brawls in the army'. The latter remarks were clearly addressing the subpar performance of the Polish army in 1648. The letters also noted that officers should also attempt to have companions with the smallest retinues as possible, so 'there is as many companions in the banner as available'. As usual in such documents, there was a request that companions and retainers alike should have a 'good horse and all equipment required for hussar'.[14] The recruitment letter for a 100-horse-strong banner of hussars, issued to Aleksander Hilary Połubiński on 16 August 1648, mentioned that he should take care to have 'good companions and retainers under his banner, on good horses and with proper equipment required by hussars and all in proper order, and when they will march to the [army] camp, each companion should have on his wagon spade, hoe, axe [and] chain'.[15] When this banner was to be supplemented to 120 horses in January 1651, the newly released recruitment letter was more specific in terms of equipment. It still required for each companion and retainer to have a 'good horse', while the detailed armour and weaponry list

---

14 AGAD, Archiwum Publiczne Potockich (APP), no. 7.3, pp.6–7.
15 BCzart., no. 2749, p.41.

stated that each hussar should have a '*kopia* lance, good pallasch or estoc, armour,[16] *szyszak* helmet, vambraces [and a] pair of pistols'.[17] The document did not mention the sabre, as it was the primary weapon used by each soldier, also indicating noble status. The hussars of Jakub Rozdrażewski, raised in summer 1648 as a part of the district troops in Wielkopolska, were very well equipped. The description of the muster roll mentioned armoured men, with gilded arm-guards. Companions were wearing tiger and leopard pelts, while retainers had scarlet *welens* capes. All hussars were armed with *kopia* lances.[18] Lubomirski's hussars, under Lieutenant Andrzej Sokolnicki, took part in the King and Queen's entry to the captured Toruń on 1 January 1659. They were all armed with lances with white and blue pennants, while their armour was covered in the pelts of leopards, lynx and bears.[19] No surprise that the sight of such well-equipped and splendidly looking units was always the main point of any foreigner's description of the Polish or Lithuanian forces.

As already mentioned in the remarks of the foreign guests, hussars were armed with a fairly large arsenal of weapons. Their main armament in the role of 'shock cavalry' was the lance (*kopia*), which could vary in length between 4.5 and six metres. It was a 'one-use' weapon to be discarded after an initial charge when it was stuck in or broken on enemies. While, in theory, hussars should have had replacements in their tabor wagons, as we will see in a moment, it was not very easy to obtain them, and hussars often had to fight without them.

Like every other cavalryman, hussars would have had sabres, which was their main hand-to-hand weapon. Cefali mentioned additional weapons, carried under the left thigh. This could be the long estoc, used for thrusting and especially useful against infantry. But a hussar could also instead carry a heavy pallasch. Another type of melee weapons that could be used were the horseman-pick and the hammer-axe known as a *czekan* or *czekanik*. As a rule, each hussar should have had two pistols in holsters next to the saddle. They would also normally have long firearms – like muskets – or even bows, but these weapons were normally carried on the tabor wagons and were used during sieges and defensive operations. If the situation required it, hussars could even fight dismounted, relying on their firearms and sabres. In January 1657, Lithuanian soldiers from Hetman Sapieha's and the Royal banners, supported by dismounted cossack cavalry, took part in an assault on Tykocin, 'facing heavy fire [and] marching in such good order that it is hard to describe it'.[20]

As seen in examples of recruitment letters, retainers were supposed to have the same weapons as their companion, although theirs would often be of a lower quality. Lances seem to have been the weaponry that were often rather scarce, and some units had to fight through a whole campaign

---

16 In this case, most likely breast and backplate.
17 BCzart., no. 2749, p.163.
18 APPoz., Gr. Pozn., 693, p.626.
19 Tadeusz Nowak, *Oblężenie Torunia w roku 1658* (Toruń: Nakładem Wydawnictwa Naukowego w Toruniu, 1936), p.204.
20 Otton Laskowski (ed.), 'Relacja obrotów wojennych pod Tykocinem roku 1656', *Przegląd Historyczno-Wojskowy*, X:2 (1938), p.256.

without them. It is not surprising, considering that, in most cases, the cost of purchasing lances for the whole unit was in the *rotmistrz*'s hands and he already had to dig deep into his pocket to support his officers and companions. Interestingly, it seems that sometimes units had two types of lances. In the expenditures of Bishop Piotr Gembicki's hussar banner, which served in the Poland army in late 1654 and early 1655, we can find lances for companions that cost 8 zł and those for retainers that costs 5 zł. The bill also mentioned the purchase of the 50 of the former and 70 of the latter.[21] We can assume that difference was due to the quality and possibly some additional ornaments on the lances. Additionally, crimson and white silk (*kitajka*) was purchased for the pennants of lances in the unit. In October 1655 – in the letter to Hilary Antoni Połubiński, the lieutenant in charge of the Royal hussar banner – King Jan Kazimierz mentioned the high cost of the lances bought for unit during two quarters of its service.[22] Łoś also wrote that, during the Battle of Warsaw in 1656, only the Lithuanian banners were equipped with lances while none of the Polish ones had them.[23] In 1660, when the Polish division under Czarniecki was supporting the Lithuanians under Hetman Sapieha, the latter was slowing down the campaign, making excuses that he needed to wait to equip his men in lances and other equipment. Enraged, Czarniecki told him that there was no time to waste and even lances would not be of much help. He even suggested to improvise some *ad hoc* lances, saying that 'there is enough of hop's poles [sticks used as support] in Lithuania'. Pasek mentioned that the Lithuanian army followed this advice, 'preparing poles, painting them in spotted and white [colours], like those old men when making their walking sticks, adding pennants [made] from cloth; brining lance's head from towns … so they looked good, if there was no other way [to have them].[24] According to Łoś, though, the situation looked completely opposite. Four banners of Lithuanian hussars were equipped with lances, while the Polish hussars from Czarniecki's division used improvised ones. They had 'poles painted with elderflowers, instead of [proper] lance's heads they had fired out ends'.[25] During the Battle of Cudnów in 1660, Lubomirski's and Potocki's hussars were mentioned using lances while Zamoyski's banners did not have them at all.[26]

However, even when armed with lances, hussars could sometimes decide not to use them. During the Lithuanian assault against Pinsk (Pińsk) on 9 and 10 November 1648, a group of fleeing Cossacks was charged by the hussar banner of Aleksander Hilary Połubiński. The *Rotmistrz* led his men in a successful charge in which some hussars used their lances while others

---

21 Biblioteka Jagiellońska (BJ), no. 8842/IV, p.57.
22 AGAD, AR III, no. 4, pp.32–33.
23 Łoś, *Pamiętnik towarzysza chorągwi pancernej*, p.68.
24 Pasek, *Pamiętniki*, p.154.
25 Łoś, *Pamiętnik towarzysza chorągwi pancernej*, p.100.
26 Samuel Leszczyński, *Potrzeba z Szeremetem, hetmanem moskiewskim i z Kozakami w Roku Pańskim 1660 od Polaków wygrana*, edited by Piotr Borek (Kraków: Collegium Columbinum, 2008), pp.75–77, 90.

dropped them and cut the Cossacks with their pallasch swords instead.[27] Overall, it is more than probable that some banners were serving without lances for longer periods of time, relying on their other weapons, from the pallasch and estocs to sabres and pistols.

Hussars were also to provide their retinue with all the items necessary to build the camp – from tents to tools – along with the items to be used for engineering work during siege operations. The lance was not an easy weapon to master – although with many hussars being veterans who had served in the army for years, it was probably easier to train any newly raised men. Kochowski once mentioned the show of arms that was presented by one of Czarniecki's hussars in 1658 when the Polish division arrived in Denmark: in front of a 'few German princes', companion Paruszewski rode towards a wreath lying on the ground, picked it up with his lance, turned around and charged towards observing allies, 'riding like he was going to strike them' and then suddenly stopped the horse in front of them while lifting his lance up.[28]

Serving as a hussar was very expensive, as a companion had to spend a large amount of money on equipment, weapons and horses. Stanisław Druszkiewicz, who in 1651 joined Crown Field Hetman Marcin Kalinowski's banner, mentioned that he spent a few thousand złotys 'on horse, on wing' and that all of it was lost at Batoh in 1652 when he was captured by Tatars.[29] Raising and equipping the unit was also a quite costly affair for the *rotmistrz* himself, as they tended to provide large sums of money for their companions to encourage them in joining the unit and to support them, especially when they needed to buy new equipment or replace lost ones. The cost of equipping hussars was so high that, in March 1651, Wincenty Korwin Gosiewski complained that he 'could raise for [the same] cost three banners of light horse than 40 [horses of] hussars'.[30] No surprise, then, that many of those that were offered rank of *rotmistrz* with new hussar units declined such an honour, as they could not afford it. In summer 1649, Prince Bogusław Radziwiłł wrote to Hetman Janusz Radziwiłł, asking if he could be allowed to raise a banner of cossack cavalry instead of a hussar one, as 'I cannot afford

A hussar charging against a Turk. Well visible is the *wytok* that he is holding at end of the lance – one of the rare example of iconography that shows this vital part of hussars' equipment. From the cover of *Ioachimi Pastorii Florus polonicus seu polonicae historiae epitome nova*, first time published in 1641 (Biblioteka Jagiellońska, Kraków).

---

27 'Zabytek historyczny o Pińsku', in *Athenauem* (Wilno: Nakład i druk T. Glucksberga, 1841), vol. VI, p.96.
28 Kochowski, *Historya panowania Jana Kazimierza*, vol. I, p.338.
29 Stanisław Zygmunt Druszkiewicz, *Pamiętniki 1648-1697* (Siedlce: Wydawnictwo Akademii Podlaskiej, 2001), p.89.
30 *Korespondencja wojskowa hetmana Janusza Radziwiłła w latach 1646-1655*, vol. I, *Diariusz kancelaryjny 1649-1653*, p.562.

to keep hussars [in service]'.³¹ In March 1651, Aleksander Ogiński, in a polite letter to Hetman Janusz Radziwiłł, declined a royal recruitment letter to raise a banner of hussars for the planned campaign against the Cossacks. He excused himself due to his advanced age (he was 64 or 65 years old by then) and due to the difficulties with raising the unit in such a short period of time, 'as better soldiers are already [serving] in units, and it is difficult to find good companions now'.³² In February 1656, King Jan II Kazimierz wrote to Jakub Weyher that none of the nine newly planned banners of hussars were created since 'nobody want to take care of [being *rotmistrz*]'.³³

The loss of equipment during a prolonged campaign, without many opportunities to replace any of it, could of course lead to a rather sorry state of even the majestic units of hussars. Jakub Łoś mentioned that, during the campaign of 1660 against the Muscovites, two banners of hussars in Czarniecki's division lacked equipment, with 'only tenth of them in armour'.³⁴ One of the worst things that could happen – to both the magnate creating the unit and to his noble companions – was a skirmish or battle in which a unit would lose a large number of horses and equipment. If this happened in the early stage of a campaign, it could even lead to a situation in which the unit was not able to fight or had to spend additional time (and money) to get battle ready. On 11 November 1648, the newly raised banner of hussars of Wincenty Gorwin Gosiewski was completely surprised by an attack of Cossacks and Tatars on their muster point in Kobryń. The unit was almost completed by then, although still missing *Rotmistrz* Gosiewski himself, who was in Warsaw. As one of the companions was Krzysztof, son of diarist Maciej Vorbek-Lettow, we have fairly detailed information on the disaster that struck the hussars. Some soldiers were killed, others were scattered, but the loss of horses and equipment was much worse: 'All *rotmistrz* wagons, battle horses and almost whole equipment [weapons and armour] of the company, [including] clothes, wagons and horses were taken or pillaged'. Krzysztof Vorbek-Lettow, who served with a four-horse retinue, managed to flee but also lost 'all battle and wagon horses, equipment, clothes and all other items'. One of his retainers and two servants were captured, with another servant killed.³⁵ Some of the surviving hussars, including Krzysztof, arrived in Warsaw asking Gosiewski for help and support. Sadly, none of it was provided, but Gosiewski still managed to convince Krzysztof to stay in service. Vorbek-Lettow then returned home and raised another four-horse retinue for the hussar banner. One can only imagine how huge of a dent was made in his family budget by the requirement of purchasing horses and equipment for two retinues in such a short period of time.

---

31 *Korespondencja wojskowa hetmana Janusza Radziwiłła w latach 1646-1655*, vol. I, *Diariusz kancelaryjny 1649-1653*, p.193.
32 *Korespondencja wojskowa hetmana Janusza Radziwiłła w latach 1646-1655*, vol. I, *Diariusz kancelaryjny 1649-1653*, p.477.
33 Rabka, 'Kampania Ochmatowska 1654-1655. Część I', p.185.
34 Łoś, *Pamiętnik towarzysza chorągwi pancernej*, p.100.
35 Vorbek-Lettow, *Skarbnica pamięci*, p.159.

LANCES, SABRES AND MUSKETS

The horse of a Polish or Lithuanian soldier, captured by the Swedes during the Battle of Warsaw in 1656. Well visible is rich *dywdyk*, feathers attached to the horse, pistol in a holster, bow and arrow case attached to the saddle – all indicating good quality equipment, that had to belong to a companion. Erik Dahlbergh's drawing for Samuel Pufendorf's *De rebus a Carolo Gustavo Sueciae rege gestis*, published in 1696 (Photo by Tomasz Ratyński).

The cost of horses was the biggest part of all hussars' expenses. We need to remember that a companion not only had to provide horses for himself and his retainers but also provide those used just for travelling (as hussars did not ride on their 'battle' horses) and those for servants accompanying the retinue. Depending on the size of retinue, we are looking at between 10 and 30 horses, but of course it is worth noting that the cost of mounts varies. Companion horses were the most expensive and could cost between a few hundred and a few thousand złotys. In September 1659, one day after joining Hetman Gosiewski's hussar banner, Jan Poczobut Odlanicki by mistake shot a horse belonging to another companion, Konstanty Zaleski. The horse was allegedly worth 600 zł, but Poczobut Odlanicki paid a compensation of 300 zł instead.[36] When Poczobut Odlanicki had his own horse shot during a battle at the river Basia in 1660, he mentioned that it was the 'loss of 600 zł', granted he was also counting in that figure the equipment that was robbed from the dead animal by some marauders.[37] Another horse he lost, this time during the Battle of Kuszliki in 1661, was worth 500 zł,[38] while the final horse that he had at the end of his military service in 1671 cost 600 zł.[39] Conversely, retainer horses were cheaper. For example, in 1664, Poczobut Odlanicki bought such a horse for 350 zł and another one of much lower quality (known in Polish as *podjezdek*) for just 32 zł.[40] There was then the cost of horses used for wagons,

---

36 Poczobut Odlanicki, *Pamiętnik Jana Władysława Poczobuta Odlanickiego*, p.29.
37 Poczobut Odlanicki, *Pamiętnik Jana Władysława Poczobuta Odlanickiego*, p.40.
38 Poczobut Odlanicki, *Pamiętnik Jana Władysława Poczobuta Odlanickiego*, p.52.
39 Poczobut Odlanicki, *Pamiętnik Jana Władysława Poczobuta Odlanickiego*, p.128.
40 Poczobut Odlanicki, *Pamiętnik Jana Władysława Poczobuta Odlanickiego*, p.88.

although oxen were also used in this capacity. Yet again, we can use Poczobut Odlanicki's diary to find information about the price of such horses. In July 1661, one of his servants deserted, taking with him a 'Samogitian[41] cart horse' valued at 60 zł.[42] Then, 10 years later, he mentioned a pair of 'Samogitian cart horses', paying 100 zł for the both of them.[43]

The parts of equipment that are always connected to the hussars are the wings and pelts of exotic cats, wolves and bears, worn by both companions and retainers. The previously mentioned Stanisław Druszkiewicz wrote about wings, confirming that they were part of the retinue's equipment. Most commonly used were eagle and vulture feathers, but those of storks and cranes were used as well. We can also find interesting evidence in iconography from the period. Etchings by Stefano Della Bella dated 1648–1651, show large single wings attached to the back of the riders. Erik Dahlbergh drew hussar horses captured during the famous charge on the second day of the Battle of Warsaw in 1656: they have two wings attached to the back of the saddle and are most likely from the Lithuanian units taking part in the charge. Wings can also be seen on the backs of both armoured and unarmoured hussars from the Battle of Beresteczko and on the relief on the tomb of the heart of King Jan II Kazimierz in the Saint-Germain-de-Prés church in Paris, although we need to remember that the relief itself was made in the 1670s. Interestingly, though, none of the Lithuanian hussars from 1649–1651 that were drawn by Westervelt are shown with wings.

The pelts worn over armour were usually from exotic cats: tigers, leopards, panthers and possibly cheetah. More local animals were also suitable: wolves, bears and lynx. A *rotmistrz* would often support his companions with more expensive pieces of equipment, like the pelts of exotic cats that could be borrowed while they served in the unit. King Jan Kazimierz, in early 1655, sent his secretary to the newly created Royal hussar banner to deliver 18 leopard pelts for companions.[44] Many exotic pelts are mentioned in the register

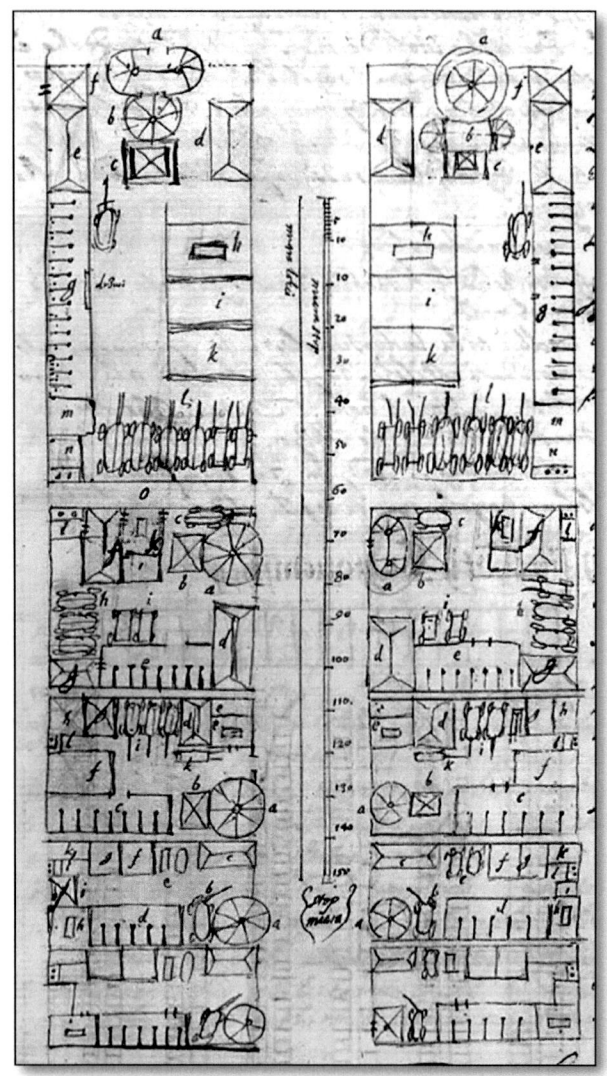

The plan of the camp place for a banner of hussars or cossack-style cavalry. Each companion was to have a separate space for himself and his retainers and servants. The biggest space was for *rotmistrz* and lieutenant; there were even spaces set up for tabor wagons. Like all Naronowicz-Naroński's plan, it is scaled in feet. From Józef Naronowicz-Naroński's *Architektura militaris, to jest budownictwo wojenne*, 1659 (Biblioteka Uniwersytetu Warszawskiego).

---

41 From Samogitia, a region of Lithuania.
42 Poczobut Odlanicki, *Pamiętnik Jana Władysława Poczobuta Odlanickiego*, p.45.
43 Poczobut Odlanicki, *Pamiętnik Jana Władysława Poczobuta Odlanickiego*, p.128.
44 Nagielski, 'Chorągwie husarskie Aleksandra Hilarego Połubińskiego i króla Jana Kazimierza w latach 1648-1666', p.92.

of Hetman Janusz Radziwiłł's possession, left after his death in Tykocin. Amongst them were one lion, three tigers and 37 leopards; there was also one more local lynx pelt.⁴⁵ Six wolves pelts are specifically described as 'retainers' wolves'.⁴⁶ Retainers would probably often have to cover their armour with *delia* or *kilim/welens* (one coloured or striped) capes, usually made from wool. Pasek mentioned the red 'Gypsy-like' *kilim* worn by servants in the hussar banner of Jan Zamoyski, so it is possible that such one-coloured clothing was a part of the retainers' equipment as well.⁴⁷ In late 1654, in Bishop Gembicki's hussar banner, all 70 retainers were to receive *welens* made from cloth bought for the unit, which could indicate that they were all to be in the same colour. There was also additional silk and cloth bought for them, for additional parts of the clothing. Musicians of the units were to receive turquoise cloth for their clothes.⁴⁸ We need to take under consideration that it was a unit created before the country was overtaken by the Swedes, and thus it could rely on easier ways of obtaining weapons and clothing. Moreover, the nominal *rotmistrz*, Bishop Gembicki, was wealthy and an important person who could afford to put a lot of money into the unit serving under his name.

As national cavalry was recruited 'in companion style', with each companion providing his own retinue, it affected the internal structure of the banners. Two or three units that, in theory, had the same paper strength of 150 horses could in fact vary in the number of companions and the size of their retinues; in the same way, retinues of officers could also have different sizes. I would like to present a few structures of hussar banners to help in better understanding the way in which Polish and Lithuanian cavalry was organised within those units. The first example is an old hussar banner of His Royal Highness at the beginning of 1656. While under the name of King Jan II Kazimierz, its nominal *rotmistrz* was Stefan Czarniecki, who of course did not lead banner in battle but could still receive at least part of the pay from the retinue in the unit. The rest of the pay from this retinue was probably used to supplement the lieutenant's pay and to finance the musicians of the banner (as they are not mentioned separately). As we can see below, it was a very large unit, with a total of 201 horses, divided into 55 retinues:⁴⁹

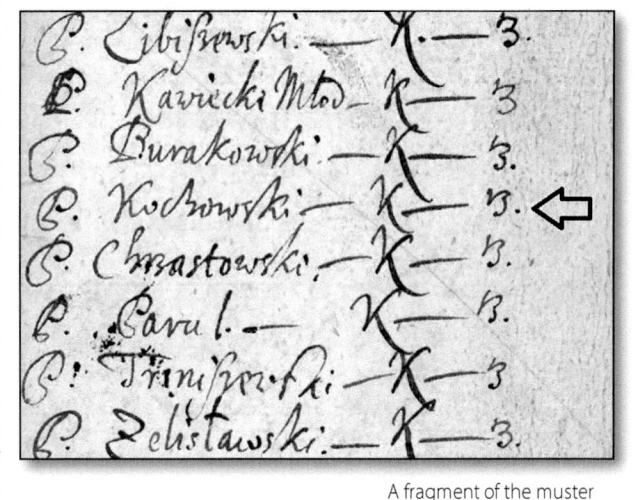

A fragment of the muster roll of *Rotmistrz* Władysław Myszkowski's hussars banner at the beginning of 1655. The name marked with an arrow is Wespazjan Kochowski, who later authored one of the most important historical works about the 1655-1660 war. He had a three-horse retinue and, not counting the officers, was fifteenth of 40 companions in the roll, indicating a fair importance in the unit's hierarchy (AGAD, Warsaw)

---

45 Edward Kotłubaj (ed.), 'Rejestr rzeczy pozostałych po śmierci X. Janusza Radziwiłła w Tykocinie', in *Życie Janusza Radziwiłła* (Oświęcim: Wydawnictwo Napoleon V, 2016), p.329.
46 Kotłubaj (ed.), 'Rejestr rzeczy pozostałych po śmierci X. Janusza Radziwiłła w Tykocinie', p.328.
47 Pasek, *Pamiętniki*, p.74.
48 BJ, no. 8842/IV, p.57.
49 AGAD, ASK 85, no. 74, pp.228–28v.

Number of horses in retinue	Number of retinues of that type in banner	Additional comments
24	1	*Rotmistrz* retinue
4	1 (see comments)	Lieutenant's retinue
4	1 (see comments)	Standard-bearer's retinue
4	1 (see comments)	Retinue of Jan Kaski, Military Judge, who was serving as companion in this banner
4	20	
3	24	
2	6	
1	1	

Next to the Royal banner, those that were under the name of Grand Hetman and Field Hetman were amongst the largest. Looking at the banner of Crown Grand Hetman Stanisław Rewera Potocki in the last quarter of 1657, it was a unit of 188 horses, divided into 55 retinues, with no separate musicians or surgeon mentioned in the roll:[50]

Number of horses in retinue	Number of retinues of that type in banner	Additional comments
24	1	*Rotmistrz* retinue
6	1 (see comments)	Lieutenant's retinue
4	1 (see comments)	Standard-bearer's retinue
3	50	
2	2	

Battle losses and long campaign attrition, combined with the problems of recruiting reinforcements for such an expensive formation like that of hussars, could lead to a gradual decrease in the strength of the unit. The banner of Władysław Myszkowski reached its highest strength at the beginning of 1656 when it had 220 horses. As we can see from the muster below, by the last quarter of 1657, the banner's size had dropped to 124 horses:[51]

---

50 AGAD, ASK 85, no. 76, pp.18–18v.
51 AGAD, ASK 85, no. 76, pp.2–2v.

Number of horses in retinue	Number of retinues of that type in banner	Additional comments
13	1	*Rotmistrz* retinue
6	1 (see comments)	Lieutenant's retinue
4	1 (see comments)	Standard-bearer's retinue
3	31	
2	4	

So far, we have looked into the Polish hussars, so it is time to see the muster roll for a Lithuanian unit as well. We start with Aleksander Hilary Połubiński's banner, from the muster dated 30 October 1648:[52]

Number of horses in retinue	Number of retinues of that type in banner	Additional comments
12	1	*Rotmistrz* retinue
4	1 (see comments)	Lieutenant's retinue
4	1 (see comments)	Standard-bearer's retinue
3	24	
2	2	

This unit had a paper strength of 100 horses, but, on muster, there were 96 horses since two companions (each with a two-horse retinue) took advance pay for raising retinues but never joined the unit.

It is worth comparing this muster roll to another muster of the same unit after a few years of campaigning. *Rolla* March 1653 was as follows:[53]

Number of horses in retinue	Number of retinues of that type in banner	Additional comments
12	1	*Rotmistrz* retinue
5	1 (see comments)	Lieutenant's retinue
5	1 (see comments)	Standard-bearer's retinue
4	4	
3	19	
2	2	
1	1	
Musicians (no details)		

---

52 BCzart., no. 2749, p.73–74.
53 BCzart., no. 2749, pp.285–86.

The banner was again with 100 horses (not counting an unknown number of musicians), with the lieutenant's and standard-bearer's retinues strengthened by one horse each. A few four-horse-strong retinues were now present as well.

Next is the *rolla* of the banner of Lithuanian Field Hetman Wincenty Korwin Gosiewski in February 1655:[54]

Number of horses in retinue	Number of retinues of that type in banner	Additional comments
12	1	*Rotmistrz* retinue
6	1 (see comments)	Lieutenant's retinue
5	1 (see comments)	Standard-bearer's retinue
4	14	
3	31	
2	11	

It was a large unit, with 194 horses, divided into 59 retinues. Unlike with Polish hussars, there was a large number of four-horse-strong retinues, although it may be linked to the fact that it was, as a Field Hetman's banner, the most prestigious unit in the army.

Another interesting muster roll of Lithuanian hussars comes from 21 November 1654, and it describes the banner of Michał Kazimierz Radziwiłł. It served for only one quarter, after which it was disbanded. Unlike other documents of that type, it had a detailed number of 'specialists' serving in unit, but it lacked retinues for the lieutenant and standard-bearer. There is a surviving written order from Hetman Janusz Radziwiłł, who was urging the unit to quickly march and join the Lithuanian army in their camp. It seems it was at least the second of such a request from him, so he was probably already losing patience with the slowly forming banner.[55] Looking into the *rolla*, it is full of annotations indicating that many companions were absent during the muster, which probably explains why the banner served for such a short period of time.[56]

---

54 Vorbek-Lettow, *Skarbnica pamięci*, pp.212–14.
55 AGAD, AR II, no. 1293.
56 AGAD, AR VII, no. 227.

LANCES, SABRES AND MUSKETS

Number of horses in retinue	Number of retinues of that type in banner	Additional comments
12	1	*Rotmistrz* retinue
4	1	
3	22	
2	9	
1	3	
Additional staff (in brackets number of horses)		Chaplain (2), drummer (1), surgeon (1), three trumpeters (1), three shawm players (1)

The banner was supposed to have 120 horses, but the muster lists 103 horses, divided into 36 retinues and nine retinues of additional staff.

The final example of a Lithuanian hussar banner comes from the list of the unit with the named *rotmistrz* of Lithuanian Grand Hetman Janusz Kiszka. Unfortunately, the document is not dated, but it is possible that it was from 1653. The banner was small, having just 61 horses, which may indicate that the surviving document is only a part of the original and we only have one of two pages. Unusual, the lieutenant's retinue was noted as first, with four horses. After it, there was the *rotmistrz*'s retinue, with the typical 12 horses. The standard-bearer had, as per usual, a rather modest retinue of three horses. Following them were 10 retinues of three horses and six retinues of two horses.[57]

Hussars were used as the most important shock cavalry of the Polish and Lithuanian army – although in the post-1652 period, due to the fairly small number of its banners in service, these units were often spread over the battle line, making it difficult to deliver a proper 'punch' against the enemy. Even when present in small numbers, hussars could play an important role on the battlefield. Łoś wrote that, during the Battle of Warka, 'we fought valiantly, especially hussars that broke the [Swedish] cavalry'.[58] There were only four banners of hussars that took part in

Polish and Lithuanian winged hussars breaking through the left wing of Swedish-Brandenburg army during the Battle of Warsaw in 1656. Erik Dahlbergh's drawing for Samuel Pufendorf's *De rebus a Carolo Gustavo Sueciae rege gestis*, published in 1696 (Muzeum Narodowe, Kraków).

---
57 AGAD, AR X, no. 632, p.63.
58 Łoś, *Pamiętnik towarzysza chorągwi pancernej*, p.66.

this battle, and at least one of them – Lubomirski's one – was most likely without lances.⁵⁹ Additionally, these banners were not grouped together but fought supported by cossack cavalry, and only in the later stage of the battle could they be deployed as some sort of quasi-squadrons of two banners each.

For many years, authors assumed that, during the famous charge of hussars during the second day of the Battle of Warsaw in 1656, the Poles and Lithuanians deployed up to eight banners (four Polish and four Lithuanian), numbering between 800 and 1,200 horses.⁶⁰ The most up-to-date research has lowered this number significantly, though, as it seems that only two Lithuanian banners, with a real strength of approximately 300 men, took part in the attack. These banners were the Royal banner under Połubiński (who led the charge) and Hetman Sapieha's banner (the former banner of Hetman Janusz Radziwiłł) under Lieutenant Władysław Jerzy Chalecki. Each should have had a paper strength of 200 horses, but their muster strength (so including the 'dead pays' for the officers) was smaller: the Royal banner had 147 and Sapieha's banner 193 horses. All of the men were armed with lances, and that is probably why, despite the small number of soldiers taking part in the charge, they managed to break through first line of Swedish reiters and hit the second line. Yet under the heavy fire of the Swedish cavalry and infantry and without the support of the rest of the Polish and Lithuanian cavalry, the hussars were forced to retreat, taking heavy losses.⁶¹ Two, Wojciech Lipski and Jakub Kowalewski, even managed to attack King Charles X Gustav but were stopped and killed by his entourage.⁶² It is estimated that the Royal banner could have lost, in terms of killed and wounded companions and retainers, up to one-third of its strength.⁶³ Sapieha's banner had 18 killed companions, whereas the number of killed retainers and wounded men of both 'classes' is unknown.⁶⁴ According to Patrick Gordon, Charles X Gustav, in anticipation of the attack from the famous Polish–Lithuanian cavalry, 'gave orders to all commanders of brigades and regiments than when the hussars or lanciers should charge them, they should open [ranks] and give way to their fury, which he knew was not to be withstood with any force of other policy at that tyme'.⁶⁵ While Swedish sources indicate that the hussars did not manage to inflict any serious losses during this charge,⁶⁶ Holsten claimed that the 'hussars harmed us the most'.⁶⁷

Of course, if possible, hussars were grouped together, forming squadrons that could be used as an 'armoured fist' during a charge. In 1660, during the battle at the river Basia fought against the Muscovites, the combined Lithuanian

---

59 Marcin Gawęda, *Od Beresteczka do Cudnowa. Działalność wojskowa Jerzego Sebastiana Lubomirskiego w latach 1651-1660* (Zabrze-Tarnowskie Góry: Wydawnictwo Inforteditions, 2013), pp.103–08.
60 Nagielski, *Bitwa pod Warszawą 1656*, pp.141–42.
61 Majewski, *Marszałek wielki litewski Aleksander Hilary Połubiński (1626-1679)*, pp.112–14.
62 Majewski, *Marszałek wielki litewski Aleksander Hilary Połubiński (1626-1679)*, pp.114–16.
63 Nagielski, *Bitwa pod Warszawą 1656*, p.149.
64 Majewski, *Marszałek wielki litewski Aleksander Hilary Połubiński (1626-1679)*, p.117.
65 *Diary of General Patrick Gordon*, vol. I, p.113.
66 Fredholm von Essen, *Charles X's War. Volume II*, pp.134–35.
67 Holsten, *Przygody wojenne 1655-1666*, p.36.

LANCES, SABRES AND MUSKETS

and Polish army deployed nine banners of hussars. They were grouped into three squadrons of three banners each, additionally supported 'behind each squadron' by a *pancerni* banner.[68] We know that, in later years, during Sobieski's reign, it was common to combine one banner of hussars with two supporting *pancerni* banners flanking it. It is possible, especially due to the small number of hussars available during the Deluge, that such units were also deployed on the battlefield, although I was unable to find any evidence of such a practice in any primary sources. During the Battle of Cudnów in 1660, the hussar banner of Grand Hetman Stanisław Potocki was leading the attacks of the Hetman's national cavalry regiment, with cossack cavalry banners providing fire support, while the hussars 'charged with their lances three times so hard, that [despite] lances not breaking, the enemy was forced back'.[69]

Polish cavalry in 1655. The lance-armed riders are unarmoured, while the second man from the left is armed with a bow and a horseman's pick. Erik Dahlbergh's drawing for Samuel Pufendorf's *De rebus a Carolo Gustavo Sueciae rege gestis*, published in 1696 (Biblioteka Narodowa, Warszawa).

We need to remember that, especially considering the fairly small number of hussars in the army, the toll that campaigns took on them was usually quite high. Even a victorious battle could lead to heavy losses within the units. Poczobut Odlanicki, fighting in the ranks of Hetman Gosiewski's hussar banners in the battle at the Basia against the Muscovites in October 1660, mentioned that his banner had in killed and wounded 'seven companions, 24 retainers, 46 horses'. While only one of those companions – Jan Łosowski – was killed, it is interesting to see the list of the wounded: Bogusław Wolan was shot, Krzysztof Szumski had his hand ripped out by a cannonball, Uzdowski was wounded in the hand by another cannonball, Chrząstowski was wounded in the leg with a pike, Święcicki was wounded with a pike and Pakosz was wounded (likely with a sabre) in the hand.[70]

As always, the loss of horses is worth highlighting since, due to their quality (and price), the death or wounding of these mounts deeply affected companions and often led to lowering the battle effectiveness of the units. The same previously mentioned unit had even higher losses (at least amongst companions) during the first Battle of Kuszliki in October 1661. Three companions – Małyński, Piołuch and Starczewski – were killed, while

---
68 Pasek, *Pamętniki*, p.159.
69 Ambroży Grabowski (ed.), *Ojczyste spominki w pismach do dziejów dawnej Polski* (Kraków: Nakładem Józefa Cypcera, 1845), vol. I, p.157.
70 Poczobut Odlanicki, *Pamiętnik Jana Władysława Poczobuta Odlanickiego*, pp.40–41.

eight others were wounded: Parczewski (shot), Kirliło (wounded in the hand by a cannonball), Okmiński (shot), two Łukomski brothers, Tomaszewicz, Uzdowski and Poczobut Odlanicki (shot three times). The latter also lost all three horses: two killed and one wounded in such way that it was no longer suitable for service. Lithuanian hussars, as some sort of afterthought, added the information that his retainer named Bortkiewicz was wounded in nose.[71] Such losses were often difficult to replace, both in regard to men and horses, not to mention all the lost and damaged equipment.

Despite their small number, hussars were still playing an important role during the whole 1655–1660 war and the conflict with the Muscovites between 1654 and 1667. As iconic and elite units, they were the linchpin of the cavalry, serving as both shock troopers and as a sort of 'morale booster' for other troops. Serving in their ranks, despite the large expenses, was often a good way for opening one's career in the military and civil service; it also played important role in building a net of connections between magnates and nobles. While the overall number was low, hussar banners on many occasions played the role of the 'tip of the spear', opening gaps in the ranks and allowing cossack cavalry and reiters to break through the enemy. The presence of hussars could even boost the morale of the other troops. However, in the case of a defeat of their charge or breaking their ranks, it could of course have a very negative effect on the self-confidence and battle spirit of the rest of the army. The number and strength of hussar banners were often very important for the opponent and their battle plans as well. In his recent research into the topic of Polish hussars, Piotr Kroll pointed out that, in November 1663 when Muscovite officers were interviewing captured Poles, one of the main topics they focused on was the presence of hussars, their strength and morale and if they were equipped with *kopia* lances.[72]

Pancerni and cossack Cavalry

Before we look into a detailed description of this formation, I would like to clarify some misunderstandings in regard to its name, both in Polish and in English. Hopefully, readers of my previous book will forgive me for dealing with this issue yet again.[73] Originally, this cavalry was called '*jazda kozacka*' (cossack cavalry), with its soldiers being known as the *kozacy* (written in lowercase). It was a term used to describe free men 'serving for money' and was adopted for both military use and to name household servants, often mounted. In the sixteenth century, the word started to be used to describe free men settled in Ukraine near the Dnieper River, but these men were called '*Kozacy*' (written in uppercase). As such, in original Polish texts, one could find both *kozacy* and *Kozacy* serving together in one army. Obviously, it made

---

71 Poczobut Odlanicki, *Pamiętnik Jana Władysława Poczobuta Odlanickiego*, p.52.
72 Piotr Kroll, 'Wykorzystanie husarii koronnej na ukraińskim obszarze działań wojennych w latach 1648-1667', in *W boju i na paradzie. Husaria Rzeczypospolitej w XVI-XVII w.* (Warszawa: Arx Regia, Wydawnictwo Zamku Królewskiego w Warszawie – Muzeum, 2020), p.145.
73 Paradowski, *Despite Destruction, Misery and Privations*.

it very confusing when translating it into English, when normally one form – Cossacks – is always being used, leading to many errors in identifying who is in fact described in the original text and attributing many military features of the Polish cossack cavalry to the Zaporozhian Cossacks. As such, in this book we will be using the term 'cossack cavalry' or 'cossacks'[74] to describe the regular cavalry in the Polish army and 'Cossacks' to describe Zaporozhian Cossacks.

In regard to *pancerni* (which means 'armoured'), many modern historians tend to repeat the theory that it was a name introduced in 1648 to name all cossack cavalry in order to distinguish between *kozacy* (Polish cavalry) and rebel *Kozacy* (Zaporozhian Cossacks). Based on primary sources, especially army and banner muster rolls, such a theory seems to have no factual basis. As we will see soon, when describing the equipment of such cavalry, through the whole Deluge, they did not achieve such a level of equipment to live up to its 'armoured' name. It seems that, at least until the mid-1660s, only certain banners of cossack cavalry were named as *pancerni*. Usually, this name was used in connection to units that we can call elite – those where the nominal *rotmistrz* was the King, Grand Hetman, Field Hetman or some of the wealthiest nobles.

Adding to the confusion, the same banner could be in one source called cossack cavalry while in other *pancerni*. For example, Jakub Łoś, one of the most famous diarists of the war, always referred to the banner that he was serving in as a *pancerni* banner, leading to situations in which his memoir is even known as a 'diary of the companion of the *pancerni* banner'. In fact, surviving muster rolls of the unit that he was a part of until 1661, which was under the nominal command of Voivode of Sandomierz Władysław Myszkowski, always called it a cossack cavalry banner.[75]

Sometimes, the border between formations was very fluid, especially when comparing cossack cavalry and light horse. It led to a rather puzzling nomenclature in official documents, like in the 1659 muster roll documents for the banner of *Rotmistrz* Hussein Morawski, where his banner is called 'cossack [cavalry] Tatars'.[76] It seems that this title was fairly common in the Lithuanian army, though: in 1651, *Rotmistrz* David Tarasowski, in charge of Grand Hetman's Janusz Kiszka's Tatar banner, was in official letter called leading a 'cossack Tatars banner'.[77] However, modern researchers tend to count such units as Tatar light horse, although this still indicates that seventeenth-century terminology was far from settled and that the same unit could be counted as a part of different formations depending on who and in what circumstances described it in the primary sources.

---

74 For the purpose of translating into English the wargaming rules of the 'By Fire and Sword' wargame, the author of this book has used the term 'cossack-style cavalry'. While technically not as accurate, such a translation was used to make it much easier to differentiate from the different Cossacks and mounted Cossacks also present in the game's setting.
75 AGAD, ASK 85, no. 79, pp.182–85.
76 AGAD, ASK 85, no. 84, p.87.
77 *Korespondencja wojskowa hetmana Janusza Radziwiłła w latach 1646-1655*, vol. 2, *Listy*, p.112.

AGAINST THE DELUGE

Lithuanians soldiers in the campaign of 1651. On the right, an officer or companion is equipped as a *pancerni*, with chainmail and a *misiurka* helmet. On the left is a likely unarmoured cossack cavalrymen, armed with a *bandolet* and *karwasze* armguards. From the drawing of Abraham von Westervelt. 1651 (Muzeum Wojska Polskiego, Warszawa, photo from author's archive).

Due to the diminished numbers of hussars, *pancerni* and cossack cavalry gradually became the most important part of the cavalry in the Commonwealth, fulfilling many roles from supporting hussars during battles, through being the main 'line' cavalry fighting the Swedes and Muscovites, to taking part in reconnaissance missions and pre-battle skirmishes. In the second quarter of 1659, when the Crown army reached its biggest size during the whole war, it included 122 banners of *pancerni* and cossack cavalry, with a paper strength of 13,016 horses. As a comparison, there were only six banners of hussars (999 horses), 41 banners of light horse (4,387 horses) and seven units of reiters (2,246 horses).[78]

Being such a universal formation, cossack cavalry allowed in certain situations for an 'upgrade' of existing units (e.g., a better equipped banner of cossack cavalry could be at some point named as *pancerni*). At the beginning of 1660, the cossack banner of Stanisław Lubomirski was even upgraded to hussars, in a process known as *pohusarzenie*. It would require providing it with more equipment, including lances, and normally in such a situation the *rotmistrz* would provide financial assistance to those companions who could afford large spending (e.g., for armour and horses). Some light horse units could even be converted into cossack cavalry: in October 1657, the Wallachian banner of Jan Sułowski was 'upgraded' this way. However, the process could work in reverse as well. Cossack cavalry – often due to a loss of manpower and equipment – could be 'downgraded' into light horse, usually a Wallachian one.

Guillaume le Vasseur de Beauplan provided an interesting description of *Rotmistrz* Deczyński, serving as commander of a cossack-style cavalry banner in the quarter army. First of all, he mentioned that it was a type of cavalry equipped with 'bows and arrows', most likely to highlight the main difference between them and hussars. The Frenchman was particularly surprised by the number of items carried by the Polish officer, so he described them in much detail. I think it will be very useful to quote it in full here, to give some idea of

---

78   Wimmer, *Wojsko polskie w drugiej połowie XVII wieku*, p.122.

LANCES, SABRES AND MUSKETS

the full equipment used by Polish cavalrymen of this period:[79]

> First of all he had sabre, carried next to chainmail, on head [he had] *szyszak* [helmet] with chain net on both sides of the head, [made] from the same material as his chainmail, covering his next and back; also carbine and if he did not take it – bow and arrow case. At his belt he had: awl, flint (used to sharpen his sabre and knife, also to set up fire), knife, six silver spoons, put together one into another [and] carried in box made from red saffian. At belt he also carried: pistol, ornamented scarf, small foldable leather bucket, which could easily be filled with large glass. [Poles] Use it to grab water in field. He also had *sabretache* bag (which is a large pouch made from red cloth, and because it is flat, they put there letter, papers, combs and even money), *nahajka* (short leather whip, used to drive his horse) and two or three fathoms of silken rope, as thick as half of small finger. They use it to bind their prisoners, if they manage to capture them. All of those are carried at the belt, on the opposite side to [the side with] sabre. At the saddle, next to stirrup, they have smaller wooden bucket [with a] measure of the half of the [big] one. It is used to water the horse. Also there are three leather tethers, to bind horses during the rest. If they do not have bow, instead they have carbine and flat leather bad, where they keep bullets for carbine and pistols, also key for the carbine and powder horn. Please, decide yourself if a man carrying so many things could easily take part in the fight.

A few examples of Polish horsemen, serving as a good depiction of cossack cavalry and light horse. Stefano della Bella, 1651 (Rijksmuseum).

Though Beauplan witnessed Polish troops in the 1630s and 1640s, their equipment and weapons would not change by the time of the Deluge. The number of all the additional items – including the buckets and even spoons – could easily be explained by the necessities of living in the harsh conditions of the service on the border, when units could be away from the camp for a week or more at the time. Of course, it was up to each companion to provide weapons for himself and his retinue, so the level of armament could vary within the unit. Pasek, when fighting against marauding Lithuanian volunteers in 1662, mentioned that he had three pistols (two in holsters and

---

79 Lasota and Beauplan, *Opis Ukrainy*, pp.169–70.

AGAINST THE DELUGE

one worn at the belt), a *guldynka*[80] as a long firearm and an *obuch*.[81] This last weapon was a type of war hammer very popular amongst the Commonwealth nobility, often known as an *obuszek*. It was one of the family of weapons that were used by all types of cavalrymen and civilian nobles: the *obuch* had a curled downward beak opposite to the hammer head, the *nadziak* was a typical horseman's pick, with a sharp beak, and the *czekan* or *czekanik* had an axe head. In descriptions of the soldiers' armaments, especially in recruitment letters, we will often see the lack of the sabre, but it was such an inseparable weapon and attribute of the Polish and Lithuanian nobles that of course men would not fight without it.

De Gramont, witnessing many actions of cossack cavalry during fights against the Muscovites in 1663/1664, left some descriptions of them as well:[82]

> Then follows the light cavalry, which in the language of this country is called 'Cossacks'. These latter are also nobles and serve in the same way as the hussars in detachments.[83] Their equipment consists of a ringed jacket or chain mail, which covers their arms halfway. In addition, they also have iron mittens, and their head is covered with a cap of rings (the same as the body), and it is called in Polish 'misyurka' [*misiurka*]. Their horses must be hardy, fast and agile. Their weapons are bows, arrows and pistols. The purpose of the Cossacks is to support the hussars when they go into action, to complete the destruction of the squadrons defeated by the hussars. Their salary is forty livres per quarter, per horse and man.

Another foreigner present in Poland, Sebastian Cefali, also looked into this formation, and he did not make any distinction between *pancerni* and cossack cavalry:[84]

> There is lightly armoured cavalry [made of] nobles, known as cossacks. They wear chainmail, on their heads have *misiurka* [mail helmet], with chainmail falling on their arms and which is fastened under the chin. During the musters they [show up with] bows but during battle they use firearms. Non-nobles are dressed and equipped in a similar way, the difference being, in same way as in hussar banners, that some of them [nobles] are marching in front of musicians, while others [non-nobles] behind it. This cavalry grown in number after [Zaporozhian] Cossacks Mutiny, to make up for their loss [from the army].

Different types of a horseman's pick, which was popular amongst nobles in the Commonwealth as both a walking stick and an additional hand weapon. The drawing of the original weapons was made by Władysław Sztolcam, 1910 (Muzeum Narodowe, Warszawa).

---

80 A high-calibre rifled-barrel gun, used for hunting larger animals.
81 Pasek, *Pamiętniki*, pp.224–25, 228.
82 Gramont, *Iz istorii moskovskago pokhoda Iana Kazimira, 1663-1664 g.g.*, p.14.
83 By which he either meant retinues or whole banners.
84 'Relacya o stanie politycznym i wojskowym Polski przez Sebastyana Cefali', p.331.

LANCES, SABRES AND MUSKETS

Recruitment letters normally required 'typical cossack equipment' or sometimes mentioned 'three firearms' (so two pistols and a carbine or musket or arquebus). One issued for the cossack cavalry banner of the district troops in Wielkopolska in July 1648 described the soldiers' equipment as 'three guns, in quarter army's style, in [chain] mail, with *misiurka* helmet and arm-guards, and with good sabre'.[85] It is an interesting document, as it mentioned the sabre, which was not normally included in the list of required equipment. The letter issued in December 1654 for *Rotmistrz* Łukasz Rossudowski (Rosodowski), in charge of a 120-horse banner in the Lithuanian army, stated that the soldiers should have 'good horse, *bandolet* and pair of pistols, both for companions and for retainers'.[86] Cefali mentioned bows as used by companions on musters, but – as another symbolic weapon – it was in fact often employed on the battlefield. Pasek provides us with an interesting description of Czarniecki's division marching through Brandenburg to Denmark in 1658. The soldiers were kept 'in good order' with strict discipline, clearly the Poles wanted to make an impression on their allies. The diarist mentioned that the division marched 'in German manner, [when] moving through towns presenting themselves, with officers with sabres in hand leading in front of the banners, companions with pistols and retainers with *bandolety* in hand'.[87] Since a majority of Czarniecki's troops were composed of *pancerni* and cossack cavalry, it is yet another confirmation of firearms being, next to sabres, their main weapon in this period.

An example of the equipment and weaponry of *pancerni*: chainmail, *misiurka* helmet, sabre, bow, carbine and short *nadziak* (Author's archive).

The presence of chainmail and a *misiurka* helmet was also a personal choice, more often than not regulated by the wealth of the individual companion. During the 1650s and 1660s, such elements of armour were not regulated by any written requirements or laws; therefore, within one unit, the number and quality of it could vary. Long campaigns, with small chances to replace lost and damaged equipment, meant that many soldiers had to go without any armour. When describing the campaign against the Muscovites in 1660, Łoś mentioned (probably with slight exaggeration) that, except for the *pancerni* banner of King Jan Kazimierz, none of the cossack cavalry units in Czarniecki's division had armour.[88]

---

85 Bartosz Staręgowski, *Formacje zbrojne samorządu szlacheckiego województw poznańskiego i kaliskiego w okresie panowania Jana Kazimierza (1648-1668)* (Warszawa: Wydawnictwo DiG, 2022), p.82.
86 *AVAK*, vol. XXXIV, pp.29–30.
87 Pasek, *Pamiętniki*, p.75.
88 Łoś, *Pamiętnik towarzysza chorągwi pancernej*, p.100.

Round Eastern *kałkan* shields were also not a part of the 'official' requirement for equipment but were often used by both companions and retainers. During an assault on Kolding in Denmark, Pasek mentioned that some of dismounted companions used such shields next to their chainmail.[89] Both companions and retainers could also use additional weapons, again chosen according to personal preferences: horseman's picks, axes, even pallasches or estocs.

Despite the penchant of many modern wargaming companies to present *pancerni* and cossack cavalry as equipped with spears or short lances, there is no direct evidence of these formations using such weapons during the Deluge, as it only became part of the equipment in the early 1670s. None of the diarists fighting in the period of 1655–1660 mentioned it; none of the documents I accessed during the writing of this book indicate the presence of this equipment, either. *Petyhorcy*, a type of cavalry normally associated with using the *rohatyna* spear or the shorted hussars' lance, was sometimes present in both the Polish and Lithuanian armies during the end of the sixteenth century and the first four decades of the seventeenth century. They reappeared in the Lithuanian army in 1663, within two banners (a total of 299 horses), and were gradually increasing during the 1670s and 1680s, but none of them seem to be in service during the 1650s.

In a similar way to the hussars, I would now like to look in more detail into the structure of different cossack cavalry banners, as it gives great insight into the unique structure of the national cavalry in the Polish and Lithuanian armies. As with any other national cavalry, companions were seen as the real fighting core of each unit, so it was always good to have as many of them as possible. In January 1649, Lithuanian Grand Hetman Janusz Kiszka sent to Władysław Wołowicz a recruitment letter for three banners of cavalry (300 horses in total) 'in old style of cossack [cavalry], made from knightly and experienced men'. An important note in the letter was that Wołowicz was to get men 'with their retinues not so large, in order to have more companions [in the ranks]'.[90] Of course, this was not the rule within each unit, as officers had the freedom to compose their units as they saw fit. Some of the banners had really 'uniformed' structure, with just the retinues of officers being different of sizes. Here is an example, the cossack cavalry banner of Władysław Rej (Rey) in the second half of 1656, which had 97 horses:[91]

A seventeenth-century *kałkan* shield, probably Turkish or Persian. Those used by the Poles and Lithuanians would be of similar design, even including ornaments, as many were brought to Poland by Armenian merchants (Livrustkammaren, Stockholm).

---

89 Pasek, *Pamiętniki*, p.83.
90 AGAD, AR V, no. 6760, p.88.
91 AGAD, ASK 85, no. 74, p.134.

Number of horses in retinue	Number of retinues of that type in banner	Additional comments
12	1	*Rotmistrz* retinue
4	1 (see comments)	Lieutenant's retinue
3	1 (see comments)	Standard-bearer's retinue
3	26	
Additional staff (not counted towards retinues)	See comments	drummer, *surmacz*[92], trumpeter

Many cossack cavalry banners had more than 100 horses, with a few (e.g., those of a royal, a hetman or some wealthier magnates) reaching even 200 horses. Here is an example of one with 115 horses, under the command of Jan Dembiński. Its muster roll is from July 1655, when unit was raised:[93]

Number of horses in retinue	Number of retinues of that type in banner	Additional comments
12	1	*Rotmistrz* retinue
6	1 (see comments)	Lieutenant's retinue
4	1 (see comments)	Standard-bearer's retinue
3	29	
2	2	
1	2	
Additional staff (not counted towards retinues)	See comments	Musicians, drummer, surgeon

Sometimes, the structure of a unit could be slightly different, lacking the officers. A good example of such a practice is the cossack cavalry banner of Jan Sapieha, as it was lacking the lieutenant's retinue. It also had some additional, non-retinue staff mentioned on muster. Here is the *rolla* from January 1658, with 115 horses divided into 43 retinues:[94]

---

92 He played woodwind instrument, known as *surma* (zurna).
93 AGAD, ASK 85, no. 75, pp.135–35v.
94 AGAD, ASK 85, no. 78, pp.38–38v.

Number of horses in retinue	Number of retinues of that type in banner	Additional comments
12	1	*Rotmistrz* retinue
3	1 (see comments)	Standard-bearer's retinue
3	18	
2	23	
Additional staff (not counted towards retinues)	See comments	Chaplain, musician(s) [no details of type], drummer, surgeon

There were, of course, smaller banners in service as well. Depending on many factors (e.g., rate of losses, availability of reinforcements or situation of the nominal or actual *rotmistrz*), there could be banners as small as 40 to 70 horses. Here is an example of such a smaller unit of 75 horses, the cossack cavalry banner of Piotr Potocki from April 1655:[95]

Number of horses in retinue	Number of retinues of that type in banner	Additional comments
9	1	*Rotmistrz* retinue
3	1 (see comments)	Lieutenant's retinue
3	1 (see comments)	Standard-bearer's retinue
3	18	
2	3	

A very good example of a unit severely depleted during a long campaign can be found in the *rolla* of the cossack cavalry banner of Krzysztof Grzymułtowski from April 1660. The unit was created in the second half of 1658 and initially had a paper strength of 150 horses. Two years of constant fighting took a heavy toll, as, by spring 1660, there were only 41 horses in total, with 17 retinues:[96]

---

95 AGAD, ASK 85, no. 75, p.95.
96 AGAD, ASK 85, no. 82, p.278.

LANCES, SABRES AND MUSKETS

Number of horses in retinue	Number of retinues of that type in banner	Additional comments
5	1	*Rotmistrz* retinue
1	1 (see comments)	Lieutenant's retinue
3	1 (see comments)	Standard-bearer's retinue
3	7	
2	4	
1	3	
Additional staff (not counted towards retinues)	See comments	musician(s) [no details of type], surgeon

A Polish cavalry assisting the Swedish army during the siege of Jasna Góra Monastery in 1655. Jan Aleksander Gorczyn, 1660's (Muzeum Narodowe, Kraków. Photo by Tomasz Ratyński).

Despite diarists like Pasek and Łoś serving their whole military career in these formations, they did not write that much about the tactics of *pancerni* and cossack cavalry in battles. We can typically find fairly generic terms, like 'we charged the enemy' or 'we strike them down'. As already mentioned, when writing about hussars, *pancerni* (and most likely some cossack cavalry banners as well) were in some circumstances used as support for hussars' squadrons, following them on the battlefield. While it is possible that in some situations mixed squadrons were created as well, in a ratio of one banner of hussars to two banners of *pancerni* or cossack cavalry, it is a tactic much more common during the reign of Jan III Sobieski. In 1660, at Połonka, in a fight against the Muscovites, Pasek mentioned that the Royal regiment (composed mostly of *pancerni* and cossack cavalry) initially charged against the Muscovite infantry, which was supported by some cannons: 'Many of ours were killed, others were wounded. Yet we strike them with full impetus, as we know that otherwise we would all be killed, if we try to retreat'.[97] The Polish cavalry managed to break the Muscovites in a vicious hand-to-hand combat that took around 15 minutes, during which the Poles took some heavy losses from the famous Muscovite berdiche axes. Czarniecki's cavalry was then counterattacked by the Muscovite boyar cavalry and 3,000 reiters. The Poles stood fast against the charge, barely any soldier was able to shoot from his pistols, as 'we all shot at the infantry and there was no time to reload'. The Polish cavalry managed to hold on against the firepower of the Muscovite reiters then engaged the enemy in hand-to-hand combat, 'to prevent them from reloading their guns'. It seems that the experience of Czarniecki's veterans was crucial here, as they managed to break the opponents and chase them out of the battlefield. This gave the Poles time to reload their pistols, which were then used again in another charge against the Muscovites, after which the cavalry reverted to sabres.[98]

It seems that the tactic of *pancerni* and cossack cavalry was not by then much different from Western-style cavalry, like the Swedish reiters or Imperial cuirassiers: giving fire from pistols just before closing in for melee. One of the relations describing the Battle of Cudnów in 1660 added that the banners of cossack cavalry were providing fire support to the hussars: while the latter retreated after the charge, the former attacked the Muscovites, 'giving fire from their handguns' and softening the enemy against the new charge of hussars.[99] Poczobut Odlanicki described, in 1664, two Lithuanian cossack cavalry banners that, while facing the Muscovites reiters, charged at them and engaged in an exchange of fire and then, when forced to retreat, rearmed and, supported by further banners, charged again.[100]

During some battles, banners had to engage enemies a few times, especially when the Polish or Lithuanian army was outnumbered. During Janusz Radziwiłł's victory over the Muscovites at Szkłów in August 1654, each of the cavalry banners in his army had to charge at least five or six times over the course of five-hour battles. The Hetman's own cossack cavalry banner, probably the most elite unit of the Lithuanian army at the time, 'attacked more than 10 times'. No surprise that the victorious Lithuanians did not even have the strength to chase the retreating enemy since, according to a post-battle relation, 'we were so tired that [we were] barely alive, happy with the fact that we force such strong [enemy] army from the battlefield'.[101] Soldiers often had to pay a high price for such bravery when facing outnumbering opponents. Janusz Radziwiłł's cossack banner that fought so hard at Szkłów was practically annihilated in the next battle against the Muscovites at Szepielewicze. When the defeated Lithuanian army was retreating from the battlefield, at the river crossing at Ciecierzyn, it took heavy losses from the

---

97 Pasek, *Pamiętniki*, p.147.
98 Pasek, *Pamiętniki*, pp.147–48.
99 Grabowski (ed.), *Ojczyste spominki w pismach do dziejów dawnej Polski*, vol. I, p.157.
100 Poczobut Odlanicki, *Pamiętnik Jana Władysława Poczobuta Odlanickiego*, p.73.
101 Grabowski (ed.), *Ojczyste spominki w pismach do dziejów dawnej Polski*, vol. I, pp.115–16.

LANCES, SABRES AND MUSKETS

pursing Muscovites. The Hetman's cossacks, defending their commander, had only 30 men left after the fight.[102]

Reiters

Western-style cavalry, usually called in Polish 'rajtaria' (and its soldiers known as *rajtarzy*), had a long history of serving in both the Polish and Lithuanian armies. It was always valued as a formation providing solid fire support for other cavalry. However, for many nobles, it was not that trustworthy, as it was a part of the foreign *autorament* and, during the reign of King Jan II Kazimierz, was often associated with his attempts of strengthening royal power and his control over the army. In the first part of the seventeenth century, reiters were, in a majority of cases, recruited from amongst German-speaking lands: starting with those that were a part of the Commonwealth (e.g., Royal Prussia and Livonia), through vassals (e.g., Courland and Ducal Prussia), to neighbouring regions (e.g., Silesia). There were of course also those raised from different nationalities – like the Scots, French or Walloons – but they were fairly rare. Poles and Lithuanians were present as well, usually as part of German-speaking units.

The second part of the century did not bring many changes, with a majority of reiters being raised locally and including native Poles and Lithuanians, but, thanks to opportunities to enlist former Swedish soldiers, it also had a larger variety of German-speaking soldiers. Sometimes, volunteers for the service arrived on their own, looking for a chance of employment. In autumn 1654, Maciej Vorbek-Lettow met a noble from Mecklenburg, Konrad Rosenberg, who came to Lithuania 'willing to enlist as reiter'. He was an experienced soldier, previously serving in the Imperial army. However, it seems that the prospect of serving in the Lithuanian army was not exactly to his liking, as he decided not to join Jan Denhoff's banner and instead left to look for employment in Prussia in the ranks of the elector's army.[103] Conversely, a native Swede named Zass did serve in a reiter unit and saved Hetman Sapieha's life during the Battle of Połonka in 1660, giving him his own horse and sacrificing his life so the Hetman could run from the approaching Muscovites.[104] A good example of the international composition of the reiter units comes from the spring–summer of 1657, when Holsten described a regiment of Lubomirski:[105]

> In our German regiment there were just four companies, each of 100 horses. Our colonel was free baron from Moravia [Franciszek de Oedt]. My Captain lieutenant[106] was baptised Jew named [Jakub] Mautner, our Major was [Wacław

---

102 Grabowski (ed.), *Ojczyste spominki w pismach do dziejów dawnej Polski*, vol. I, pp.126–27.
103 Vorbek-Lettow, *Skarbnica pamięci*, p.203.
104 Chrapowicki, *Diariusz*, p.250.
105 Holsten, *Przygody wojenne 1655-1666*, p.45.
106 Holsten served in the life company.

Bartłomiej] Gaszyński and of two *rotmistrz* one was called de Bron [Gothard Eremiasz Debron] and the other [Władysław Łaszowski].

Cefali mentioned the presence of reiters in the Commonwealth's armies, writing that 'armoured units similar to our [Italian] cuirassiers are all abandoned, in their place there were employed large number of German reiters, but now [in 1665] there are not many of them [anymore].'[107] He then added that, 'next to Grand Marshal [Lubomirski] regiment of reiters, all other banners [of reiters] in the army could only make up [together] another regiment'.[108] It seems that he was referring to the situation at end of the 1650s or beginning of the 1660s, since, by 1665, Lubomirski's regiment was no longer in service.

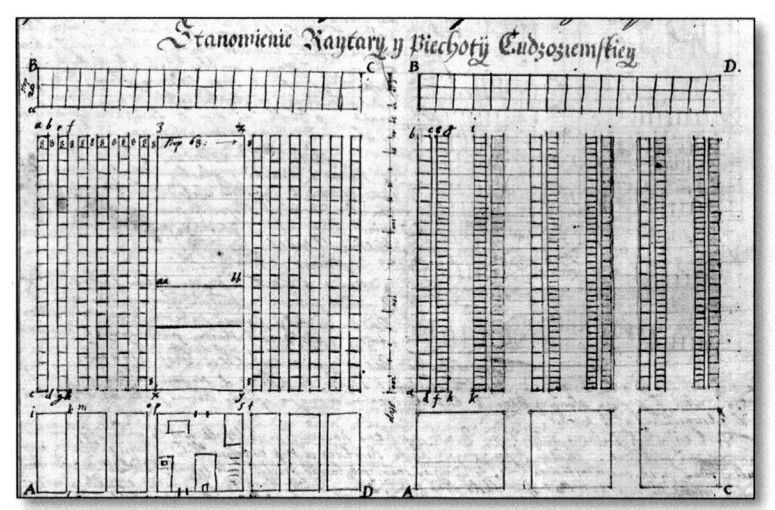

The plan of the camp set up for a regiment of foreign troops: reiters, dragoons or infantry. Compared to national cavalry, it is much more uniformly built. Like all of Naronowicz-Naroński's plans, it is scaled in feet. From Józef Naronowicz-Naroński's *Architektura militaris, to jest budownictwo wojenne*, 1659 (Biblioteka Uniwersytetu Warszawskiego).

As far as the status and importance of the army goes, reiters were in a rather peculiar position. On one hand, as a part of the foreign troops, they were often disliked by the national *autorament*, who saw them as an alien element and, during the 1660s, as part of the pro-royal faction. On the other hand, many of their units had powerful nominal commanders like the king or hetmans, which meant that their regiments and companies could be seen as an important part of the army and counted next to hussars and some *pancerni* or cossack cavalry banners as the elite of the cavalry. All this comes with a price, of course, as reiters often had to fight to keep their status. On 24 March 1651, three companies from Jerzy Teodor Tyzenhauz's regiment mustered in the Lithuanian army camp. One of the units was missing its *rotmistrz* and ensign and 'was very weak on the horses', which indicates the poor quality of the mounts. Hetman Radziwiłł gave the company two weeks to improve the quality of their horses; otherwise, the unit was to be 'shaved down into dragoons'. Considering the difference in pay and status of those two units, it would have been seen as a serious demotion.

As with any other army formation in the Commonwealth, there were no general rules that would force upon commanders a certain organisation of their units. Of course, the recruitment letter would indicate a planned strength of regiment or company, but its internal structure was always in the unit commander's hands. In the campaign of 1653, when the Poles raised a strong army but failed to achieve any success in their operations against the Cossacks and Tatars, there was a large contingent of 3,035 horses of reiters,

---

107 'Relacya o stanie politycznym i wojskowym Polski przez Sebastyana Cefali', p.331.
108 'Relacya o stanie politycznym i wojskowym Polski przez Sebastyana Cefali', p.332.

divided into five regiments and five independent banners. Each unit had a different structure and strength: the regiments had 538, 454, 411, 474 and 507 horses, while the banners had 158, 112, 163, 112 and 106 horses.[109] In autumn 1653, the Lithuanian army had one regiment (660 horses) and three banners (120 horses each). By the end of 1654, it was reinforced by a regiment of 460 horses and a strong banner/squadron of 224 horses and, finally in early 1655, by two banners of 120 horses each and two smaller banners combined into a unit of 158 horses.[110] In July 1660, there were five units of reiters in the Polish army with a paper strength of one regiment of 1,000 horses, one of 800 horses, one of 600 horses, one squadron of 200 horses and one independent company of 200 horses.[111]

Of particular notice is that at least some of the reiter units in the Polish service and many of those in the Lithuanian army were following a 'retinue-type' organisation, in which some reiters were serving with two or three horses. Nobles serving in such units were called 'companions', in the same way as those from the national cavalry types. An example of such a unit is the independent company of Stefan Stanisław Czarniecki (not the famous *regimentarz*) from the Polish army; here is its *rolla* from the second quarter of 1658, with the company listed as 78 horses:[112]

Number of horses in retinue	Number of retinues of that type in banner	Additional comments
12	1	*Rotmistrz* retinue
6	1 (see comments)	Lieutenant's retinue
4	1 (see comments)	Standard-bearer's retinue
4	1 (see comments)	*Wachtmeister*'s retinue
3	1 (see comments)	Quatermaster's retinue[113]
3	3	
2	12	
1	16	
-	-	Drummer, surgeon

Other independent companies were following a Western style of organisation, in which reiters were serving 'with one horse', although the allowance of 'dead pay' in the company staff was usually rather large. As an example, we can look into the banner of Prince Bogusław Radziwiłł, which in 1654 and 1655 was under the command of *Rotmistrz* Otto Butler. As per the muster from

---

109 AGAD, ASK 85, no. 89, p.5.
110 Rachuba, 'Wysiłek mobilizacyjny Wielkiego Księstwa Litewskiego w latach 1654-1667', pp.43–46.
111 AGAD, Archiwum Skarbu Koronnego (ASK) 82, no. 9, p.71.
112 AGAD, ASK 85, no. 79, pp.34–34v.
113 Unit had two NCOs with this rank, each with different size of retinue.

August 1654, the unit had 158 horses.[114] The staff had 34 horses, divided as follows (the number in parentheses is the number of horses assigned to each individual): *rotmistrz* (12), lieutenant (five), clerk (five), ensign (four), *wachmeister* (three), surgeon (one), three trumpeters (one each) and one drummer (one). Reiters were divided into three corporalships, each led by a corporal. Unfortunately, these documents were partially lost, and only the third corporalship's *rolla* survived in full: it was composed of a corporal (two horses) and 39 reiters. The corporal of the first corporalship also received a pay of two horses, which allows us to assume that the structure of the first and second corporalship was practically the same as the third one, with a few more reiters in each and with both corporals serving in two horses. It is worth mentioning that it was a strong unit, as the typical independent company or banner of reiters had 100 to 120 horses of paper strength. It seems that the organisation into three corporalships was the most common one in Western-style companies. This organisation can be found in Samuel Schlichting's unit, in the muster from May 1653,[115] with a first corporalship of 34 reiters while the second and third had 30 reiters each. Interestingly enough, the company staff was much smaller (the number in parentheses is the number of horses assigned to each individual): *rotmistrz* (12), ensign (two), *wachmeister* (one), trumpeter (one) and drummer (one).

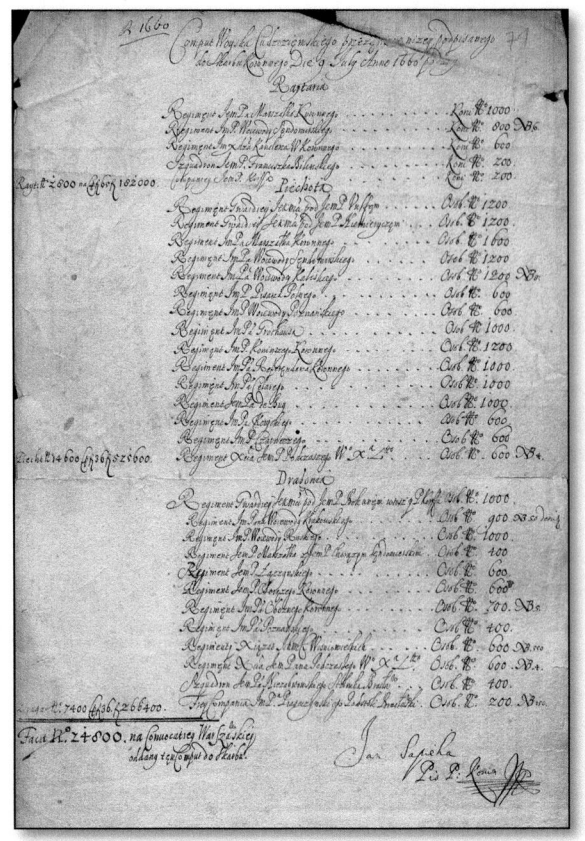

A list of the foreign *autorament* units in the Polish army in July 1660. From top to bottom: reiters, foreign infantry and dragoons. All units are under the name of their nominal commander, all with paper strength. The document is signed by Crown Field Clerk Jan Sapieha (AGAD, Warszawa).

Regimental structure was far from standardised, with each unit having a different number of companies with different strength. Based on some surviving muster rolls, we can compare the structure and size of such units. The first example is a smaller regiment (sometimes called a squadron) of Colonel Teodor Leskwant (Dietrich von Lessgewang), from the first quarter of 1655.[116] Its organisation was as follows, with the number in parentheses as the number of horses (pay):

- Regimental staff: colonel (one), major (one), quartermaster (six), clerk (three), adjutant (three), drummer (two), surgeon (two) and profos (one), with a total of 19 horses.
- Colonel's banner with a staff of colonel (12), captain lieutenant (six), ensign (four), quartermaster (three), *wachmeister* (three), three corporals (two horses each), trumpeter (one), another soldier and possibly another trumpeter

---

114 AGAD, AR VII, no. 228, pp.1–3.
115 AGAD, ASK 85, no. 68, pp.196–97v.
116 AGAD, ASK 85, no. 73, pp.271–75.

(one), with a total of 38 horses. The main fighting part of the units were three corporalships, where each reiters was serving with one horse (the same as in two other banners). The first corporalship had 31 men, second 26 men and third 28 men, so the total paper strength of the company was 143 horses.
- Major's banner with a staff of major (12), lieutenant (five), ensign (four), quartermaster (three), *wachmeister* (three), three corporals (two horses each) and two trumpeters (one horse each), with a total of 35 horses. The first corporalship had 22 men, second 24 men and third 18 men. The total size of the banner was 99 horses.
- The third banner was led by the *rotmistrz*, with a staff of *rotmistrz* (12), lieutenant (five), ensign (four), *wachmeister* (three), quartermaster (three), three corporals (two horses each) and one trumpeter (one), with a total of 34 horses. The first corporalship had 22 men, second 23 men and third 23 men. The total paper strength of this unit was 102 horses.

So, in total, the regiment/squadron had 363 horses but only 217 rank-and-file reiters, with a fairly large part of it being 'dead pay' covering the pay of officers and NCOs, as we can see in each banner's staff. Most likely, a similar structure was also used in other smaller regiments, especially those that served in 1654 and 1655. In 1649/1650, the Lithuanian regiment of Jerzy Teodor Tyzenhauz was composed of four cornets (companies), each with 120 horses.[117] Unfortunately, I was unable to find any surviving documents with a more detailed structure of its companies. In the same way, there is no indication of a separate regimental staff, as the only pay received for the regiment was for the 480 horses of all four companies.

It is worth comparing these smaller regiments with the biggest unit of reiters serving in the Commonwealth during the seventeenth century, the regiment of Crown Field Hetman Jerzy Sebastian Lubomirski. In the first quarter of 1659, it had a paper strength of 1,000 horses, divided into 10 companies. Of course, in typical Polish style, each company had a different size, and the organisation of the regiment was not standardised. The number in parentheses is the horses/units of pay assigned to each officer, NCO and 'specialist'. A star next to the soldier means that he was crossed out from the original document, indicating that, at the time of muster, there was vacancy for this position or that this particular number of horses/pay did not count towards the overall strength of the unit. Since muster rolls were made by different clerks, it is noticeable that they did not even use a standardised way of writing down the structure of units:[118]

- Regimental staff: colonel (18), lieutenant colonel (six), major (five), regimental quartermaster (four), regimental auditor (three), regimental adjutant (three), regimental clerk (three), chaplain (two), surgeon (three), drummer (two), profos (two), tabor master (two) and regimental blacksmith (one)*. In total, 13 men with 54 horses, on muster present 12 men with 53 horses.

---

117 *Korespondencja wojskowa hetmana Janusza Radziwiłła w latach 1646-1655*, vol. I, *Diariusz kancelaryjny 1649-1653*, p.352.
118 AGAD, ASK 85, no. 92, pp.1v–24.

- Life company of Colonel Stefan Franciszek de Oedt: a unit staff of colonel (12)*, captain lieutenant (10), ensign (four), *wachmeister* (three), quartermaster (two), two trumpeters (one each)*, surgeon (one)*, under-ensign (two)*, clerk (two)* and blacksmith (one)*; so while it should have 10 men (not counting the colonel) with 27 horses (plus 12 for the colonel's pay), there were in fact only four men with 19 horses. Fighting men were divided into three corporalships, each led by a corporal with two horses, while all reiters were serving as one horse. The first corporalship should have had a corporal and 21 men, for a total of 23 horses. On muster roll, five men, including the corporal, are crossed, so the actual strength of the corporalship was 17 men. The second corporalship should have had the same structure of a corporal and 21 men, with a total of 23 horses, but the names of 11 men are crossed, leaving a total of 11 men and 12 horses. The third corporalship should also have had a corporal and 21 men, with a total of 23 horses, but the names of 11 men are crossed, leaving 11 men and 12 horses. The total paper strength of this company should have been 108 horses, with 79 fighting men,[119] indicating how large a percentage of the unit was in fact 'dead pays'.
- Company of Lieutenant Colonel Stefan Niemirycz: A company staff of lieutenant colonel (12), lieutenant (six), ensign (four), *wachmeister* (three), quartermaster (two), under-ensign (two), trumpeter (one) and surgeon (one). In total, it should have been seven men (not counting the lieutenant colonel) with 19 horses (plus 12 for the lieutenant colonel's pay). The first corporalship was composed of a corporal (two horses) and 21 reiters, second was composed of a corporal (two horses) and 22 reiters, while third had a corporal (two horses) and 20 reiters. The overall paper strength of the company should have been 100 horses with 73 men.
- Company of Major Wacław Gaszyński: A company staff of major (10), lieutenant (six), ensign (four), *wachmeister* (three), quartermaster (two) and three corporals (two horses each). Reiters were not divided into corporalships in this muster roll; there is a list of 52 of them, all serving on one horse. The total paper strength of the company was 83 horses (including the major's pay) and 59 men (not including the major).
- Company of *Rotmistrz* Eliasz Łącki: A company staff of *rotmistrz* (12), lieutenant (six), ensign (four), *wachmeister* (three), clerk (two), under-ensign (two), three corporals (two horses each), surgeon (one), trumpeter (one) and blacksmith (one). Three corporalships, led by corporals mentioned as part of the staff, had accordingly 25, 23 and 26 reiters. The total paper strength of the company was 112 horses and 86 men.
- Company of *Rotmistrz* Hieronim Olszowski: A company staff of *rotmistrz* (12), lieutenant (six), ensign (four), *wachmeister* (three), quartermaster (three), under-ensign (two), trumpeter (one), surgeon (one), clerk (two) and blacksmith (one), with a total of 10 men and 35 horses. The first corporalship had a corporal (two horses) and 18 reiters, second had a corporal (two) and 17 reiters, while third had a corporal (two) and 16 reiters. The total paper strength was 92 horses, with 64 men.

---

119 Not counting the colonel.

- Company of *Rotmistrz* Władysław Łaszowski: A company staff of *rotmistrz* (12), lieutenant (six), ensign (four), *wachmeister* (three), quartermaster (two), trumpeter (one), clerk (two), surgeon (one), under-ensign (two) and blacksmith (one), with a total of 10 men and 34 horses. The first corporalship had a corporal (two horses) and 19 reiters, second a corporal (two) and 18 reiters and third a corporal (two) and 19 reiters. The total paper strength was 96 horses, with 69 men.
- Company of *Rotmistrz* Gothard Eremiasz Debron: A company staff of *rotmistrz* (12)*, lieutenant (six), ensign (four), *wachmeister* (three), quartermaster (two), trumpeter (one), surgeon (one), under-ensign (two)*, clerk (two)* and blacksmith (one)*. It should have been 10 men with 34 horses, but only six men with 17 horses were present. The first corporalship should have had a corporal (two horses) and 22 reiters, but nine reiters are crossed out. The second corporalship should have had a corporal (two horses) and 21 reiters, but five reiters are crossed out. Finally, the third corporalship should have had a corporal (two horses) and 23 reiters, but the corporal and 11 reiters are crossed out. In theory, the company should have had 106 horses with 79 men, but, due to losses, only 49 men were present.
- Company of *Rotmistrz* Aleksander Dzierzbicki: A company staff of *rotmistrz* (10), lieutenant (six), ensign (four), *wachmeister* (three), quartermaster (two), under-ensign (two), trumpeter (one) and surgeon (one), with a total of eight men and 29 horses. Each of the three corporalships had the same structure, with a corporal (two horses) and 15 reiters. The total paper strength was 80 horses, with 56 men.
- Company of *Rotmistrz* Jakub Mautner: A company staff of *rotmistrz* (12), lieutenant (six), ensign (four), *wachmeister* (three), quartermaster (two), clerk (two), trumpeter (one), surgeon (one), under-ensign (two) and blacksmith (one), with a total of 10 men and 34 horses. The first corporalship had a corporal (two horses) and 21 reiters, second a corporal (two) and 20 reiters and third a corporal (two) and 22 reiters. The total paper strength was 103 horses, with 76 men.
- Company of *Rotmistrz* Teodor Gorajski: A company staff of *rotmistrz* (10), lieutenant (six), ensign (four), *wachmeister* (three), quartermaster (two), clerk (two), trumpeter (one), surgeon (one), under-ensign (two) and blacksmith (one), with a total of 10 men and 32 horses. The first corporalship had a corporal (two horses) and 16 reiters; second and third had a corporal (two) and 15 reiters each. The total paper strength was 84 horses, with 59 men.

Excluding any losses mentioned in the muster rolls of some of the units, the total paper strength of the regiment was 1,018 horses, so slightly more than the expected 1,000. However, it was in fact only 713 men, so almost one-third of the overall strength was used for 'dead pay'. Each company had a different size despite similarities in staff (officers, NCOs and specialists). Even in units of reiters, the rank of *rotmistrz* could be just honorary, though, often used for obtaining extra pay if the same officer was also serving in national cavalry. Holsten mentioned that, in 1660, due to heavy losses taken by Lubomirski's regiment in a campaign against the Muscovites and Cossacks, there were many new officers nominated in the unit. He was promoted to the rank of lieutenant in the company of Teodor Gorajski, who 'was young man, [who] was not staying with company, he only held title and honours [of] *rotmistrz*'.[120] Holsten was de facto commander of the company, but he received some privileges and likely a part of the pay assigned to the *rotmistrz*.

In 1663, four regiment of reiters in the Polish army were disbanded and merged into a new large Royal regiment of *arkabuzeria*.[121] Despite the Polish name, everyone – from the King to the nobles – still used the old name for the formation. De Garmont, who had seen them in action against the Muscovites, wrote about their bravery and order in combat:

> We were in this confusion [fleeing from the Muscovites] when we saw from afar the royal regiment of 1,000 horses, consisting of six impressive squadrons. It was the colour of the old German cavalry of the Swedish king,[122] and in this battle they really showed us that they surpassed all the cavalry of the whole world, since it can be said that the troops never did what they did during this case.
>
> We joined the head units of the first squadrons, which for some time restrained the ardour of those who were so energetically pushing us into the loose. But a little later, when the Muscovite vanguard fell upon us, we had to think about retreating before it and about passing the gorge that we had behind us before we reached the [river] Desna – which was done in perfect order and with all possible valor. We lost a lot of people here, since the enemy had a large number of dragoons, whose very strong fire we endured, and Muscovite squadrons made repeated attempts to disrupt our ranks. But they could not achieve this in any way. As our riders fell in the ranks of the dead, others closed even better – this was our only concern. Finally, we passed the gorge in detachments of thirty fellows, in the face of an entire enemy army, not at a trot, without giving the enemy the opportunity to cut us during the execution of this task, which lasted more than an hour.[123]

Soldiers in Polish and Western-European clothing, from a map of the siege of Gdańska Głowa in 1659. Unknown author (Rijksmuseum).

During his time in Swedish service, Holsten mentioned a typical mix of weaponry used by reiters: a cavalry pallasch, two pistols and a long firearm (carbine). Interestingly, though, he seems to have acquired a Polish horseman's pick, which seems to be especially useful as a 'universal key' used to open any locked chests in Polish houses.[124] Almost the same set of weaponry, but without the *nadziak* and with the

---

120 Holsten, *Przygody wojenne 1655-1666*, p.61.
121 More information about its structure can be found later in this chapter, in the subchapter describing *arkabuzeria*.
122 It could indicate either blue uniforms or blue flags – both highly likely considering that it was the traditional colour of the Vasa kings.
123 Gramont, *Iz istorīi moskovskago pokhoda Iana Kazimira, 1663-1664 g.g.*, pp.22–23.
124 Holsten, *Przygody wojenne 1655-1666*, pp.31–32.

sabre replacing the pallasch, was used by him when he served in Lubomirski's regiment in the Polish army. In summer 1657, Holsten travelled to the town of Cieszyn in Silesia (so across the Imperial border) to purchase saddles, pistols and carbines for the life company that he was serving in.[125] Documents from the Royal Arsenal in Warsaw from December 1649 mention, amongst lists of 'reiters' armour', breast and backplates, *szyszak* helmets and some older arm-guards and tassets. Quantities could also be fairly large, as a regiment of Dietrich Johan Maydel received 500 sets of 'reiters' armour' in 1649, which in this case most likely indicates breastplates, backplates and helmets. It was the armour of rank-and-file reiters, though, as documents also mention 'officers' good armour, black[ened], bought in Gdańsk' that had gorgets as well. Another type was the 'white cuirasses' that had helmets and arm-guards in their sets.[126] In one case, in May 1651, a reiters company recruited in Prussia for the Polish army was described as a *kiryśnicy*, (from the word '*kirys*' – cuirass), which indicates that its soldiers had armour, most likely breast and backplates.[127]

However, we do not know how often armour was used in the period of 1655–1660. There is no information about any helmets or armour, but, when Holsten was captured by the Poles in autumn 1656, he mentioned that the 'thick clothes and wide belt from his carbine' saved his life, so it is possible that he was wearing a buff-coat. Interestingly, his coat had lining from lynx fur, which was very useful during the cold Polish nights.[128] His diary does support the theory about reiters in Polish service using buff-coats, though, as he mentioned those being worn by his soldiers in the second part of 1657.[129] Westervelt, in his drawings, showed Lithuanian reiters in the period of 1649–1651 in Western-style clothes, wearing hats. While Holsten mentioned a few times about obtaining 'uniforms' for the reiters, he did not mention any specific details. In winter 1659/1660, when stationed in winter quarters near Częstochowa, he added that Lubomirski's reiters often travelled through the border to (then Imperial) Wrocław (Breslau) where they obtained 'excellent uniforms', so probably Western-style clothing.[130] In the winter quarters of 1661/1662, when again stationed near the Imperial border, Holsten and other officers were travelling to Wrocław to purchase weapons, equipment and 'the best [available] uniforms' for the existing units and newly recruited reinforcements.[131] Interestingly enough, though, when in 1663, after leaving the Polish service, he and a few former soldiers and their servants arrived in Hamburg, he added some information about their different clothing. Ex-soldiers and their servants were 'dressed in Polish style, in blue coats with yellow satin lining', all armed with firearms and sabres,

---

125 Holsten, *Przygody wojenne 1655-1666*, p.50.
126 Konstanty Górski, *Historya artyleryi polskiej* (Warszawa: Księgarnia E Wende i S-ka, 1902), pp.295–96.
127 *Korespondencja wojskowa hetmana Janusza Radziwiłła w latach 1646-1655*, vol. I, *Diariusz kancelaryjny 1649-1653*, p.692.
128 Holsten, *Przygody wojenne 1655-1666*, p.42.
129 Holsten, *Przygody wojenne 1655-1666*, p.48.
130 Holsten, *Przygody wojenne 1655-1666*, p.53.
131 Holsten, *Przygody wojenne 1655-1666*, p.70.

with Polish saddlecloths on their horses.[132] It seems that, in the same way that Czarniecki's cavalry obtained Western-style clothing during their campaign in Denmark, reiters serving longer periods in the Polish ranks picked up Polish clothing, as it was the easiest available in the region.

As with many other formations of the Commonwealth's armies, there is a frustrating lack of details about the tactics of reiters. Like, cossack cavalry, they seem to be a jack of all trades, fighting as both a main 'strike cavalry' alongside hussars (in the 1660 campaign on Ukraine) and a reconnaissance force, especially in the Lithuanian armies between 1649 and 1655. The important role of reiters providing fire support can be seen during the Battle of Zborów in 1649, when reiters stopped the Crimean Tatars chasing the retreating Polish cavalry by 'standing firm and shooting at the enemy with their firearms'.[133] One would expect that Holsten, who was fighting in the ranks of Lubomirski's reiter regiment, would provide some more details; sadly, he described the battles against the Cossacks and Muscovites in rather generic terms. At least, thanks to his diary, we can confirm that Polish reiters were not shy of striking into hand-to-hand combat, as the German mercenary often mentioned being engaged in bloody melee. During the 1660 campaign, he lost four horses in fights, three of them being shot and one being 'mortally wounded during melee'. The reiters in his diary 'were shooting and striking with sabres' in combat, taking heavy losses during a fight within the Cossack camp. He added that the regiment was pushed back by defenders using 'firearms, spears, bows, scythes, staffs and even [cart] stanchions'. The company standard that he was carrying had a 'few cuts and shots', again showing that the unit was right in the centre of the fight.[134] During the Battle of Cudnów in the same campaign, reiters were a part of the force of Polish cavalry that 'struck with great fury' into the Muscovite and Cossack tabor, breaking into it. Meanwhile, other Polish and allied Tatar forces charged on their own. Holsten wrote about the confusion of the ensuing fight, during which all armies were mixed: 'Muscovites, Cossacks, Tatars, Poles, German and Wallachians.[135] We were deafened by huge scream, noise of cannons and muskets; blinded by fury, dust and shining sabres. We barely could recognise friend from foe. And we fought like this for nearly four hours, none of the [fighting] side wanted to retreat before dusk.'[136] The already quoted De Garmont mentioned that, in 1663, reiters of the Royal regiment fought, next to light cavalry (which seems to in fact include cossack cavalry), so fiercely that 'the enemy had to give way to the Polish sabre'.[137] If needed, reiters could take part in an assault as dismounted 'heavy infantry'. In February 1649, when the initial attacks of the Lithuanian dragoons and

---

132 Holsten, *Przygody wojenne 1655-1666*, p.90.
133 Mirosław Nagielski (ed.), 'Relacyja bitwy pod Zborowem die 15 augusti 1649. Wojciech Miaskowski sekretarz JKM. do niewiadomego z obozu pod Zborowem die 22 augusti 1649', in *Relacje wojenne z pierwszych lat walk polsko-kozackich powstania Bohdana Chmielnickiego okresu "Ogniem i Mieczem" (1648-1651)* (Warszawa: Wydawnictwo VIKING, 1999), p.223.
134 Holsten, *Przygody wojenne 1655-1666*, pp.54–60.
135 From the light horse cavalry of the Polish army.
136 Holsten, *Przygody wojenne 1655-1666*, p.61.
137 Gramont, *Iz istorii moskovskago pokhoda Iana Kazimira, 1663-1664 g.g.*, p.24.

LANCES, SABRES AND MUSKETS

foreign infantry at Mozyrz (Mozyr) were repulsed by the Cossacks, Field Hetman Janusz Radziwiłł ordered all cavalry to dismount and take part in the attack. The following attack, led by Colonel Lieutenant Herman von Ganzkopf (Ganskoff) and his reiters, was successful.[138]

Tatar and Wallachian Light Horse

In the first part of the seventeenth century, light cavalry units were normally not present as a separate formation in the Commonwealth's armies. Instead, they were included as a part of cossack cavalry. Units composed of Tatars were especially common in the Lithuanian armies, usually recruited from amongst families settled in the country, with some of them tracing their Lithuanian military service back to the fifteenth century. Private armies also included a fair number of such light horse units, sometimes raised from amongst the military settlers and subjects of the magnate, on other occasions recruited from foreigners like Hungarians and Wallachians. The Khmelnytsky Uprising, which in its initial phase led to the destruction of the standing quarter army, opened the door for the introduction of light cavalry as a separate formation, though. Fairly easy and cheap to raise, equip and keep in service, banners of Tatars and Wallachians became an integral part of the Commonwealth's military in the second part of the seventeenth century. While the former were present in both the Polish and Lithuanian army, the latter were almost exclusively present in the Polish forces, with just one 100-horse-strong banner of Wallachians being a part of the Lithuanian army in 1661. Whether fighting against the Cossacks, Muscovites or Swedes, light horse was useful for reconnaissance missions, harassing the enemy and after-battle chases. It was also a very flexible formation, as banners could easily be upgraded to cossack cavalry, with a simple addition of better equipment, while still retaining the skills they developed as part of a lighter formation.

Polish light horsemen, armed with bows, sabres and *nadziaks*. Stefano della Bella, 1651 (Rijksmuseum).

Of course, amongst the settled Tatars, there were also those that converted from Islam to Christianity, most likely in order to make their career easier. One such example was Józef Syryn Murza Baranczewicz (Barancewicz), from a Christian Lithuanian

---

138 *Pamiętniki Samuela i Bogusława Kazimierza Maskiewiczów*, p.263.

Tatar family. He was the *rotmistrz* of a Tatar light cavalry banner in the Polish army between 1658 and 1663.[139]

De Gramont made a point to describe both types of light horse, as he saw them during the campaign of 1663/1664:[140]

> Then follow the Tatars, whom, having defeated, the Grand Duke of Lithuania brought with him many whole families, which he then placed in Lithuania to populate the region. They own free estates, but have neither rank nor voice among the nobility. They also constitute the light cavalry, well equipped and armed like the Cossacks [cossack cavalry], and differ from the latter only in that they do not have mail. Their pay is thirty livres a quarter.
>
> Wallachians and Moldavians are also accepted into the Polish cavalry. Their clothes and equipment are the same as those of the Tatars, their pay is the same. Their duties are to burn, rob, supply and serve the army in every possible way, which, of course, does not leave them much time for their entertainment.

Sebastian Cefali wrote extensively about light cavalry in the Polish and Lithuanian armies, probably because they were a fairly 'exotic' topic for him. He also divided his description into Wallachians and Tatars:[141]

> Wallachians are cavalry composed of Wallachian people, that used to be Polish subjects but now are Turkish. It is used for skirmishing, harassing the enemy, capturing prisoners, [so] it is lightly armed. Their weapons are bow, sabre and pistols, [although] some of them used carbine instead of bow, [while] the wealthiest of them [also] have chainmail. They are mighty robbers, but warlike, and there is no more than 20 banners of them in the whole army.[142]
>
> Tatars came from Crimea and, receiving many privileges to entice them into military service, settled in; as the Commonwealth had them for long time in service, [so] those that served in Poland and wanted to stay, received lands, so they can be nearby if needed. They are Muslims, their weapons are bow and arrows. There are no more than 10 banners of them in Polish army, [while] in Lithuanian army there are many more.[143]

Stanisław Druszkiewicz, who, after a few years as a companion in different hussar banners, was serving as the *rotmistrz* of a Tatar banner in the Polish army since 1654, provides us with some interesting insight into the origins of his soldiers. Initially, he raised a banner of 120 horses, enlisting 'very good Tatars' previously serving in the service of Prince Jeremi Wiśniowiecki. However, it seems that there were many more willing volunteers, as 'many good men wanted to serve under my command, Crimean Tatars and Circassians [were] arriving, so I had more men than [required] in recruitment letter'. His

---

139 Wagner, *Słownik biograficzny oficerów polskich drugiej połowy XVII wieku*, vol. I, p.10.
140 Gramont, *Iz istorii moskovskago pokhoda Iana Kazimira, 1663-1664 g.g.*, p.14.
141 'Relacya o stanie politycznym i wojskowym Polski przez Sebastyana Cefali', pp.331–32.
142 He seems to have been referring to the situation during the Deluge or the earlier 1660s, as, by 1665, there was only one banner in the Crown army.
143 In fact, in 1665, there were 25 banners of Tatars in the Polish army and 17 banners in the Lithuanian army.

recruitment letter was thus increased, initially to 150, then 'to almost 200 horses', but he added that sometimes he had even 250 horses, indicating that the unit kept at least some of the additional volunteers.¹⁴⁴ What is even more interesting in his story is the fact that his original recruitment letter, issued on 7 August 1654, was for a banner of 120 Wallachians.¹⁴⁵ It seems that, at the end of the day, a *rotmistrz* could to some extent choose if he preferred to enlist his unit 'in Tatar' or 'in Wallachian' style, as long as the banner was raised as light cavalry. Another example of a unit raised from amongst so-called 'wild Tatars' was the banner led by *Rotmistrz* Michał Antonowicz, in service between 1655 and 1661. The officer in charge was a minor noble from Podlasie, but the rest of the unit was composed of Tatar volunteers from areas near the Black Sea.¹⁴⁶

A light horseman or unarmoured cossack using a bow in fight against Swedish cavalry. Erik Dahlbergh's drawing for Samuel Pufendorf's *De rebus a Carolo Gustavo Sueciae rege gestis*, published in 1696 (Muzeum Narodowe, Kraków)

Light cavalry tended to have a large number of smaller retinues, especially those with two or even one horse. As with all previously described formations, I would like to present a few examples of this internal structure. We will start with the Tatar banner of Murza Bohdanowicz (Bohdan Murza) in January 1658. This banner had 106 horses, divided into 46 retinues.¹⁴⁷ Of particular notice, there is no separate entry for musicians, which seems to have been the usual system in light cavalry. If musicians were present, they would have to be included in the *rotmistrz*'s retinue:

Number of horses in retinue	Number of retinues of that type in banner	Additional comments
12	1	*Rotmistrz* retinue
4	2 (see comments)	Lieutenant's retinue and Standard bearer's retinue
3	14	
2	15	
1	14	

---

144 Druszkiewicz, *Pamiętniki 1648-1697*, p.91.
145 *Akta grodzkie i ziemskie z czasów Rzeczypospolitej Polskiej*, vol. X, p.273.
146 Wagner, *Słownik biograficzny oficerów polskich drugiej połowy XVII wieku*, vol. I, p.7.
147 AGAD, ASK 85, no. 74, pp.150–50v.

Another Tatar banner was under the command of Aleksander Kryczyński. In the last quarter of 1655, it had 105 horses, divided into 49 retinues. It is worth noting the large number of one-horse retinues, especially when compared to the previous banner:[148]

Number of horses in retinue	Number of retinues of that type in banner	Additional comments
12	1	*Rotmistrz* retinue
5	1 (see comments)	Lieutenant's retinue
4	1 (see comments)	Standard-bearer's retinue
3	16	
2	6	
1	24	

Of course, not every banner of light cavalry had such a large number of smaller retinues. There are examples of units that, throughout the whole war, managed to be based mostly on two-horse retinues. Looking into the Tatar banner of Dawid Bykowski, from the last quarter of 1658, it had 91 horses, divided into 35 retinues:[149]

Number of horses in retinue	Number of retinues of that type in banner	Additional comments
12	1	*Rotmistrz* retinue
5	1 (see comments)	Lieutenant's retinue
3	1 (see comments)	Standard bearer's retinue
3	9	
2	21	
1	2	
Additional staff (not counted towards retinues)	See comments	musician(s) [no details of type]

We can compare the structure of Tatar banners with Wallachian banners to see how similar they were. Here is the list of retinues of the banner under the command of Bazyli Hołub from January 1659. It was an average-sized banner, with 74 horses, divided into 42 retinues, again without a separate entry for musicians:[150]

---

148 AGAD, ASK 85, no. 76, pp.123–23v.
149 AGAD, ASK 85, no. 78, pp.67–67v.
150 AGAD, ASK 85, no. 74, pp.201–01v.

Number of horses in retinue	Number of retinues of that type in banner	Additional comments
9	1	*Rotmistrz* retinue
4	1 (see comments)	Lieutenant's retinue
3	1 (see comments)	Standard-bearer's retinue
3	2	
2	15	
1	22	

Another example comes from the *rolla* of the Wallachian banner of *Rotmistrz* Mikołaj Stadnicki from July 1658. Particular to this unit, besides the lieutenant and standard-bearer, none of the companions had a three-horse retinue. The banner had 90 horses, divided into 48 retinues:[151]

Number of horses in retinue	Number of retinues of that type in banner	Additional comments
12	1	*Rotmistrz* retinue
3	2 (see comments)	Lieutenant's retinue and Standard-bearer's retinue
2	27	
1	18	
Additional staff (not counted towards retinues)	See comments	musician(s) [no details of type]

The third banner we will look into was under the command of *Rotmistrz* Franciszek Dziewanowski. The muster roll comes from January 1655, when the unit had 100 horses, divided into 41 retinues. Both the lieutenant and standard-bearer's retinues are larger than usual – with five horses – and one of the companions served with a four-horse retinue:[152]

---

151 AGAD, ASK 85, no. 80, pp.47–47v.
152 AGAD, ASK 85, no. 73, pp.196–96v.

AGAINST THE DELUGE

Number of horses in retinue	Number of retinues of that type in banner	Additional comments
12	1	*Rotmistrz* retinue
5	2 (see comments)	Lieutenant's retinue and Standard-bearer's retinue
4	1	
3	13	
2	11	
1	13	
Additional staff (not counted towards retinues)	See comments	musician(s) [no details of type]

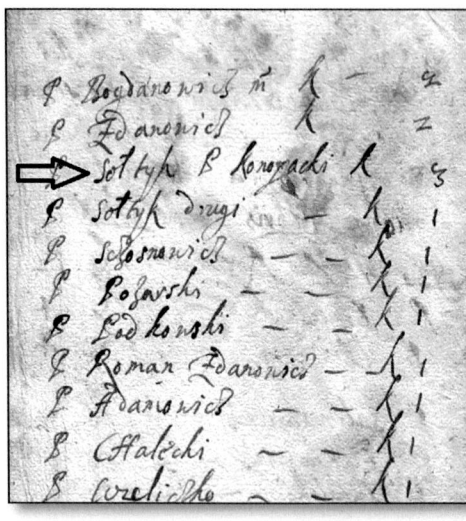

An example of a companion being very low in the hierarchy of a cavalry unit, in a fragment of the muster roll of the Tatar light horse of Aleksander Sulimanowicz in 1658. The companion named 'Sołtyk', despite having a three-horse retinue, is placed just above those that have just a one-horse retinue. This means that, not counting officers, he was thirty-first of 57 companions. Above him, there were 10 companions with three-horse retinues and 20 with two-horse retinues. (AGAD, Warszawa).

A good example of how well-trained units of light cavalry could act on the battlefield comes from July 1649, when, near the Polish camp at Zbaraż, the banner of Prince Jeremi Wiśniowiecki's Tatars faced an overwhelming number of Crimean Tatars: 'There were 2,000 [men] of Khane's Orde, while only 150 [men] on our side'. Wiśniowiecki's veterans 'broke [ranks of the unit] first into three [groups], then into four, then into two and finally attacked as a whole banner'. Despite their well-drilled movements, the Polish Tatars could not resist for long, losing more than 100 men while their lieutenant was wounded in the head six times.[153]

Light cavalry tended to be deployed on the flanks of the Polish and Lithuanian armies, where it could harass the enemy's cavalry using typical hit-and-run attacks and could then, if the battle was won, be thrown after the enemy in pursuit. We can often find Tatar and Wallachian banners sent out as the vanguard of the force, leading reconnaissance missions normally known as *podjazd*. They were also routinely employed during raids against the enemy's logistic lines and territories, where they could employ terror tactics of burning, looting and – if the opportunity arose – destroying smaller outposts. On occasion, they would fight in the same way as cossack cavalry: first shooting at the enemy with bows and firearms, then closing in with sabres in hand to engage in hand-to-hand combat.

---

153 Mirosław Nagielski (ed.), 'Akta Anni 1649 pod Zbarażem Nowym albo raczej diariusz w miesiącu lipcu za regimentu jm. pana Andrzeja z Dąmbrowice Firleja kasztelana natenczas bełskiego, jm. pana Stanisława z Brzezia Lanckorońskiego kasztelana kamienieckiego, jm. pana Mikołaja Ostroroga podczaszego koronnego', in *Relacje wojenne z pierwszych lat walk polsko-kozackich powstania Bohdana Chmielnickiego okresu "Ogniem i Mieczem" (1648-1651)* (Warszawa: Wydawnictwo VIKING, 1999), p.136.

Arkabuzeria

In the first half of the seventeenth century, sometimes there were units of reiter-like cavalry that were recruited in the same way as national cavalry (i.e., with companions and the retinue system). From time to time, they appeared in the Polish army and were usually described as a sort of lance-less hussars (i.e., armoured, with 'three firearms' (two pistols and a carbine or musket) and a sabre). They were known under the Polish name '*arkabuzeria*' or under the Latin name '*Equitibus harkabuseris*', although in modern works they are often incorrectly referred to as '*arkabuzerzy*' or '*arkebuzeria*'.[154] It seems that they were especially valued by the nobles in Wielkopolska, who, as early as 1627, were due to serve in levy of nobility as either hussars or *arkabuzeria*.[155] They reappeared in the Polish army in the summer of 1648, when some units were to be raised as planned district troops gathered against the Cossacks and Tatars. Cracow Voivodeship was to have two banners (100 horses each), Sandomierz Voivodeship one banner (200 horses), Mazowsze Voivodeship one banner (100 horses), Rawa Voivodeship 300 horses (probably three banners), Chełm Land one banner (200 horses), while Poznań and Kalisz Voivodeships decided to raise a large contingent of 12 banners, numbering in total 1,250 horses (one banner of 150 horses and the rest 100 horses each). Interestingly, the Polish voivodeships and lands were planning to raise more *arkabuzeria* (2,900 horses) than hussars (2,500 horses) or reiters (1,450 horses). Depending on the district, there was even a different rate of quarterly pay for the units, from 40 zł in Chełm Land to 50 zł in Mazowsze and 60 zł in Mazowsze – compared to between 40 and 80 zł for hussars, 30 to 60 zł for cossack cavalry and 50 to 60 zł for reiters.[156] Some of the raised units were left to defend their territories while the rest were scattered alongside the main Polish army after the defeat at the Battle of Piławce in September 1649. Between 1649 and 1653, there were still a few units of this formation serving in the regular army. Four banners were destroyed during the disastrous Battle of Batoh in June 1652, while, by autumn of the same year, there were five banners with a total of 700 horses still in the service.[157] They gradually disappeared, though, probably due to the high cost of equipping and retaining these units in the ranks. The *arkabuzeria* raised in Wielkopolska in 1649, as part of the district troops, was well armoured and armed with 'three guns'. When one *rotmistrz* arrived in muster with an undermanned and underequipped banner, he mentioned that he was waiting for the arrival of 'arms, armour and buff-coats from Wrocław'.[158] That last item is interesting, as it indicates that the soldiers were equipped in the style of Imperial cuirassiers, with a buff-coat as 'basic' armour and a breast and backplate worn over it.

---

154 Which, more often than not, seems to be the result of issues with editing the text in print rather than an error made by authors.
155 Paradowski, *Despite Destruction, Misery and Privations*, p.83.
156 Wimmer, *Wojsko polskie w drugiej połowie XVII wieku*, pp.43–54.
157 Tomasz Ciesielski, *Od Batohu do Żwańca. Wojna na Ukrainie, Podolu i o Mołdawię 1652-1653* (Zabrze: Wydawnictwo Inforteditions, 2007), pp.20, 38, 76.
158 APPoz., Gr. Pozn., 693, p.629.

During the Deluge, we can only find a token presence of *arkabuzeria*. At the beginning of the war, one banner of 200 horses, under *Rotmistrz* Władysław Arciszewski, was to be a part of Hetman Potocki's forces fighting against the Muscovites. The unit served only for a short period of time and was destroyed while marching to join Potocki's army.[159] There were plans to raise at least two more units, though. In September 1655, appointed as *rotmistrz*, Krzysztof Grzymułtowski was to raise a banner of 150 horses made of 'men experienced in knightly [military] service, with proper equipment of *arkabuzeria* companions'.[160] It is possible that, due to the changing military situation, Grzymułtowski was unable, or maybe even was unwilling, to create such an expensive unit. Famous partisan Krzysztof Żegocki received, in October 1655, a recruitment letter for 200 horses of *arkabuzeria*, but – due to unknown reasons, maybe caused by problems with the recruitment – he raised a cossack cavalry banner instead.[161] Some of the levy of nobility gathered in Wielkopolska in autumn 1656, in order to attack against Brandenburg's lands, were also equipped as *arkabuzeria*, once again indicating that the style of this formation seems to be very popular in this region of Poland.[162] However, there is no indication that any banners of *arkabuzeria* served in the regular army post-1655.

As mentioned before, in the description of reiters, *arkabuzeria* reappeared in the Polish army in 1663, when four reiter regiments were disbanded and their former soldiers merged into a new unit. The Royal regiment was under the command of Franciszek Bieliński and was divided into nine companies, with a total paper strength of 989 horses. Its structure was as follows:[163]

Company commander	Paper strength (horses)
Regimental HQ	16
Colonel Franciszek Bieliński	137
Colonel-lieutenant Otton Fryderyk Felkersamb	107
Rotmistrz Zygmunt Tetwin (Tedtwin)	98
Rotmistrz Jerzy Leszkwant (Lesquant)	110
Rotmistrz Walter Jan Wrangel	102
Rotmistrz Jerzy Rawa	104
Rotmistrz Jan Falęcki	97
Rotmistrz Eliasz Hagenthorn	114
Rotmistrz Aleksander Duplessis	104

---

159 Wimmer, *Wojsko polskie w drugiej połowie XVII wieku*, p.94.
160 Biblioteka Kórnicka, no. 356, pp.52v–53.
161 Staręgowski, *Formacje zbrojne samorządu szlacheckiego województw poznańskiego i kaliskiego w okresie panowania Jana Kazimierza (1648-1668)*, pp.170–71.
162 Staręgowski, *Formacje zbrojne samorządu szlacheckiego województw poznańskiego i kaliskiego w okresie panowania Jana Kazimierza (1648-1668)*, p.175.
163 Nagielski, 'Gwardia przyboczna Władysława IV (1632-1648)', p.136.

Despite its name, it was just a 'cover up' for keeping reiters in service. No surprise, then, that De Gramont, who saw the regiment during the campaign 1663/1664, was still calling its soldiers 'German reiters'. As such, while *arkabuzeria* was in theory present in the army in following years, it was in fact nothing more than just another, more native name for Western-style cavalry. It is highly likely that *arkabuzeria* fought in the exact same way as reiters, relying during the initial phase of the fight on their firepower, before closing in for hand-to-hand combat with sabres and pallasch swords.

Foreign Infantry

Until 1629, the Commonwealth relied on employing foreign infantry, with both native and foreign officers receiving recruitment letters and looking for volunteers in the British Isles, Prussia, Pomerania, Silesia and other German-speaking neighbouring areas. During the last stage of the 1626–1629 war against Sweden, for the first time, a new way of raising foreign infantry units was used by the Polish *Sejm*. Colonel Reinhold Rosen raised a 1,000-man-strong regiment from Poles 'trained in German manner', with officers and NCOs recruited from the foreigners. While the unit arrived in Prussia too late to take part in actions against the Swedes, its creation was seen as a rather revolutionary move, as it indicated that further regiments could be raised in the same way in the future. In fact, an occasion for this happened soon after during the 1632–1634 Smoleńsk War against Muscovy. During this conflict, the majority of the infantry regiments serving in the Polish army was composed of volunteers gathered in Poland, equipped and trained 'in German manner' by mostly foreign cadre. Of course, even as late as the early 1650s, there were still situations in which whole regiments were recruited abroad; nonetheless, throughout the Deluge and 1660s, the larger part of infantry was composed of local manpower.

Despite its mixed national structure, these units were always called 'foreign infantry' (*piechota cudzoziemska*) or 'German infantry' (*piechota niemiecka*). Amongst the officers, we can find not only native Poles and Lithuanians but also many nobles from German-speaking families settled for centuries in Prussia, Livonia and Courland. Amongst foreign officer 'corps', there were Englishmen, Scots, Italians, Frenchmen, Dutchmen and many Germans (including former Swedish officers). In 1651, the foreign infantry for the Lithuanian army was recruited not only locally but also in Courland and Prussia,[164] as those regions were traditionally seen as good recruitment grounds. Another two were Wielkopolska and the southern regions of Poland on the border with Silesia, which were also very frequent recruitment grounds.

---

164 *Korespondencja wojskowa hetmana Janusza Radziwiłła w latach 1646-1655*, vol. I, *Diariusz kancelaryjny 1649-1653*, p.631.

Foreign infantry was always met with great reluctance and even open hostility by the Commonwealth's nobles. It was seen as unpatriotic to recruit men from abroad, especially as they tended to cost a lot and were often a hindrance to the local population. Many nobles opposed the idea of foreigners serving as officers in the Polish army or were directly opposing the recruitment and training of Poles in the 'German way'. As units often lacked experienced foreigners in their ranks, especially amongst rank-and-files, it led to complaints from both officers and nobles paying for the upkeep of the troops. In March 1651, Łukasz Hulewicz, *rotmistrz* of a cossack cavalry banner in the Polish army fighting against the Cossacks during the siege of Winnica, wrote that 'German trousers and coats are not willing to fight. I write about German trousers, because officers in their [foreign] regiments lack of good and experienced German soldiers, instead they put German clothes on youngsters and journeymen who are struggling not only with the fight but even with small toils [during the campaign]'.[165]

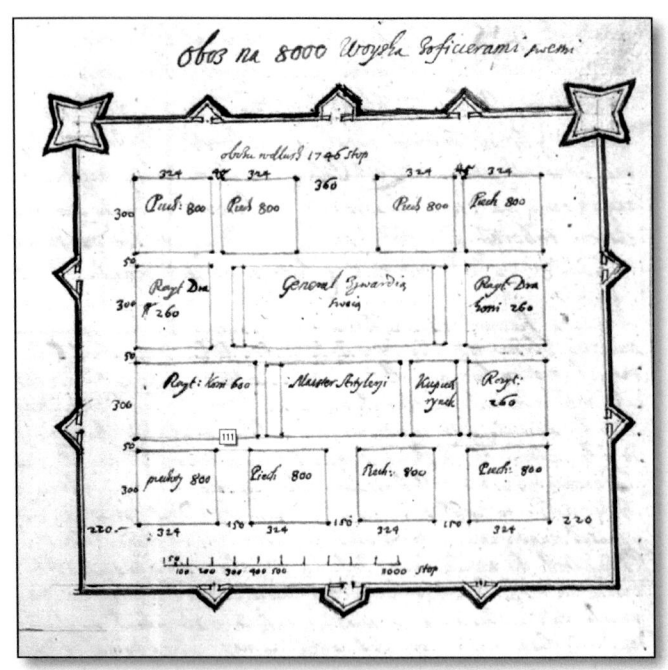

The plan of the camp for 8,000 foreign troops (reiters and infantry). The largest block was designed for the 'general and his guard'; under his place, there was a block for the general of artillery and, on its right, for a 'merchant's market'. From Józef Naronowicz-Naroński's *Architektura militaris, to jest budownictwo wojenne*, 1659 (Biblioteka Uniwersytetu Warszawskiego).

With infrequent musters and a lack of proper control over the units, nobles were also – often rightfully – protesting that foreign infantry had many 'dead pays' and that it allowed officers to defraud large sums of money for nonexistent men. In the 1660s, the Polish core of this formation was also noticed by Cefali, as he mentioned that 'these days it is [a formation] composed mostly from Polish peasants but it kept its foreign name'. He then added that, 'while drilled in German style, it is made from Polish peasants, while the officers came from all [other] nations'. The Italian wrote that foreign infantry was 'very numerous and brave but in last expedition of royal army against Cossacks and Muscovites almost all of it was taken prisoners'.[166] This last statements refers to the unsuccessful offensive from 1663/1664, where the Polish and Lithuanian armies took heavy losses. De Gramont, who took part in this campaign, was very impressed by the bravery of this infantry, and his description is full of praise. He often mentioned their willingness to fight and sacrifice, and he provided an overall picture of this formation:[167]

> It remains for me now to speak only of the German infantry, which was brought into this country by frequent wars with Sweden. At first, these regiments were supposed to consist entirely of German officers and soldiers, but, due to the fact

---

165 Grabowski (ed.), *Ojczyste spominki w pismach do dziejów dawnej Polski*, vol. I, p.70.
166 'Relacya o stanie politycznym i wojskowym Polski przez Sebastyana Cefali', p.332.
167 Gramont, *Iz istorii moskovskago pokhoda Iana Kazimira, 1663-1664 g.g.*, p.15.

that the local residents are very capable of military affairs and are more enduring and tireless, the officers began to accept them in their detachments, and, since they are extremely brave and dexterous in handling muskets, then on occasion they are used better than the Germans. Their pay is thirty-six livres a quarter. But, since not all officers receive their salary and pay from the state, but collect it from their soldiers, the soldiers receive only eighteen livres out of their thirty-six livres per quarter, a corporal – thirty-six, a sergeant – fifty, a soldier – one hundred and fifty, a lieutenant – two hundred and twenty, the captain – six hundred, and also their winter quarters. Colonels have all judicial power in their regiments and dispose of all their subordinates.

While foreigners could be full of praise, locals were often strongly against raising and keeping regiments of infantry in the service. Noble opposition to foreign troops would often reappear during discussions in the *Sejm*. In May 1654, a local *sejmik* of Ruthenian Voivodeship issued a set of instructions for its envoys sent to the *Sejm*. In line with many other local noble gatherings, the Ruthenians were strongly against raising further foreign troops, pointing out their high cost and unreliability. They even suggested that most of the existing units of reiters, infantry and dragoons should be disbanded, 'to leave in service just small number and not those led by German officers but by native Polish nobles'. In place of German infantry, they wanted to raise a Hungarian one, which was seen as more useful. Lastly, they wanted the army to be based, 'as per old custom', on hussars '[armed] with lances' and *petyhorcy* cavalry.[168] There were even suggestions, mentioned by the envoys of other local *sejmiki*, to designate one regiment of foreign infantry 'not only with officers from Polish nation but also serving mostly in Polish clothes'. It was to encourage Polish nobles to serve in infantry, as such a regiment was to act 'as military school, so we can have infantry officers of our nation and in our clothes', which in the long term was to help save money for the expensive foreigners.[169] Even within already existing units, there was a call to assign Polish nobles, not foreigners, as colonels for the regiments.[170] While the idea was sound on paper, it was never put into practice: during the string of armed conflicts between 1648 and 1667, there were no opportunities nor the money to establish such a unit within the Polish army.

The lack of a standardised organisation of the regiments can be clearly seen throughout the 1650s and 1660s, with the size of Polish army units varying between 400 and 1,600 portions. Larger regiments usually had six or eight companies, with only the Royal Guard being even bigger and having 10 companies.[171] However, it seems that, during the 1655–1660 war, sizes varied between four and eight companies. As early as 1653, during the Żwaniec campaign, 10 regiments of foreign infantry in the Polish army had a strength

---

168 *Akta grodzkie i ziemskie z czasów Rzeczypospolitej Polskiej* (Lwów: Księgarnia Seyfartha i Czajkowskiego, 1911), vol. XXI, p.149.
169 *Akta grodzkie i ziemskie z czasów Rzeczypospolitej Polskiej*, vol. XXI, p.244.
170 *Akta grodzkie i ziemskie z czasów Rzeczypospolitej Polskiej* (Lwów: Księgarnia Seyfartha i Czajkowskiego, 1931), vol. XXIV, p.108.
171 *Stanisława Oświęcima Dyaryusz 1643-1651* (Kraków: Akademia Umiejętności, 1907), pp.292–94.

Malbork besieged by Polish and Imperial troops in 1659. Erik Dahlbergh's drawing for Samuel Pufendorf's *De rebus a Carolo Gustavo Sueciae rege gestis*, published in 1696 (Muzeum Narodowe, Kraków).

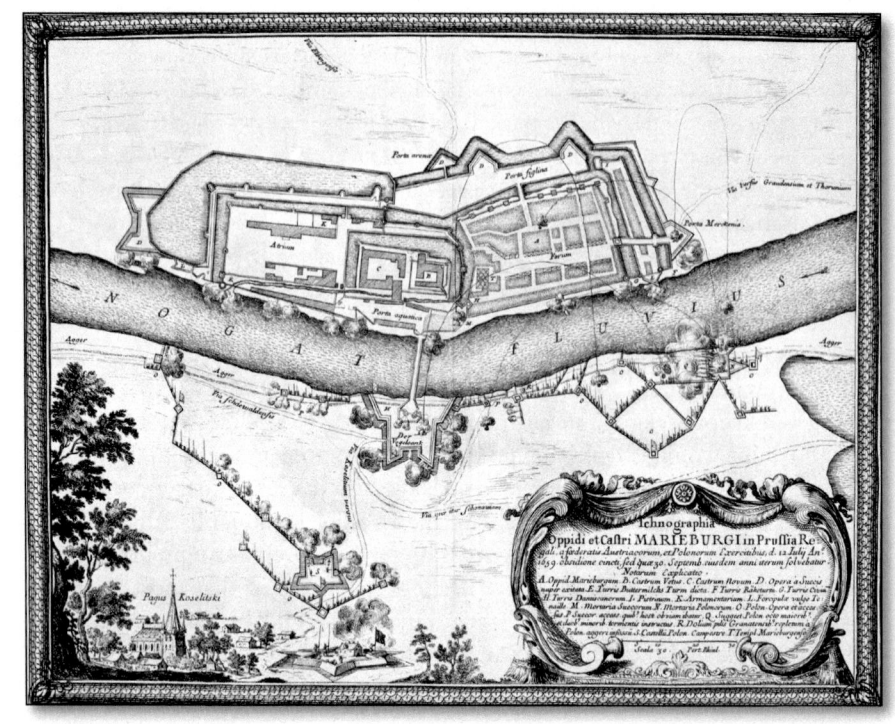

of 1,211; 1,200; 1,120; 884; 839; 785; 634; 605; 539 and 402 portions. There was also one smaller unit, designated as squadron, and it had 294 portions.[172] Next to these larger units, there were also small independent companies of 100 to 200 portions, which we can find mostly in the Lithuanian army. In the campaign of 1649, the Lithuania army had in total 1,510 portions of German infantry, divided into one squadron of 600, two free companies of 200, one of 150 and three of 120 portions each.[173] In September 1653, there were 4,088 portions of German infantry in the Lithuanian army, divided between nine units. Four of them were regiments (1,050; 1,000; 694 and 598 portions) and the remaining were five free companies (200, 176, 150, 120 and 100 portions).[174] But, even in the Polish army, there were some examples of these smaller units, like the 200-portion-strong company of Jan Wielopolski, which was raised 'in German style' and served in 1659.[175] The foreign infantry regiment raised in Wielkopolska in early spring 1649 was composed of only musketeers and was supposed to have one company of 200 men and three companies of 100 men (although one raised only 50).[176] In July 1660, the Polish army had 15 foreign infantry regiments, with a total paper strength of 14,600 portions:[177]

---

172 AGAD, ASK 85, no. 89, p.5v.
173 *Korespondencja wojskowa hetmana Janusza Radziwiłła w latach 1646-1655*, vol. I, *Diariusz kancelaryjny 1649-1653*, pp.355–56.
174 Rachuba, 'Wysiłek mobilizacyjny Wielkiego Księstwa Litewskiego w latach 1654-1667', pp.45–46.
175 AGAD, ASK 85, no. 82, pp.75–76v.
176 Staręgowski, *Formacje zbrojne samorządu szlacheckiego województw poznańskiego i kaliskiego w okresie panowania Jana Kazimierza (1648-1668)*, p.92.
177 AGAD, ASK 82, no. 9, p.71.

Paper strength	Number of regiments	Additional notes
1600	1	Lubomirski's regiment
1200	5	Including Foot Guard
1000	4	
600	5	

The structure of each regiment, its companies and independent companies could vary, as there were no regulations that would standardise the organisation of troops within the army. For example, in the partial muster roll of the infantry regiment of Michał Kazimierz Radziwiłł in 1656, the unit had a very small regimental staff: lieutenant colonel (in charge of the unit), major, regimental quartermaster, regimental clerk, *wachmeister*, surgeon and one fifer.[178] Each of its companies varied in strength, with no attempts to make them more uniformed. As an example, we can look into the first and second company of the regiment. The life company was led by the captain lieutenant, with the rest of the company staff being composed of an ensign, quartermaster, two corporals and three drummers. The rank-and-files were divided into files (*rota*) each led by a file leader known as the *gefraiter*; there were nine files in this company, each with six men, with a total strength of 62 men.[179] The lieutenant colonel's company had a slightly different structure, being led by the lieutenant, with an ensign, under-ensign, two quartermasters, two corporals and one drummer. There were seven files of privates, six of them with six men and one with five men. The total strength of the company was 49 men.[180] In March 1651, the Lithuanian company of foreign infantry of Captain Bogusław Przypkowski had 19 files, so a maximum of 114 men (not counting company staff), while Captain Teofil Bolt's company had 16 files, so a maximum of 96 men, without company staff.[181]

Another interesting structure worth looking into comes from 1658 and 1659: the muster of the Prince Bogusław Radziwiłł regiment that was serving as the garrison of the important fortress of Słuck.[182] In 1658, the regimental staff composed of a quartermaster, auditor, *wachmeister* lieutenant, wagon master, regimental drummer and regimental executioner.[183] There were seven companies (a life company, two led by majors and four led by captains) with a structure of:

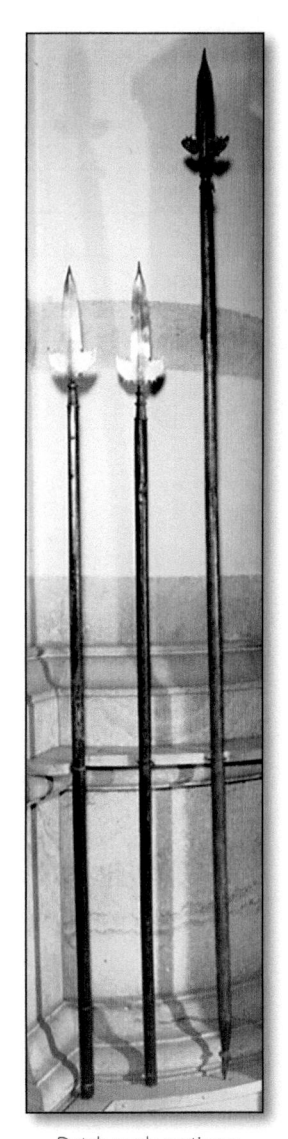

Dutch-made partisans, used by Polish officers and captured by the Swedes in 1655 (Livrustkammaren, Stockholm).

---

178 AGAD, AR VII, no. 225, p.1.
179 AGAD, AR VII, no. 225, pp.2–3.
180 AGAD, AR VII, no. 225, pp.4–5.
181 *Korespondencja wojskowa hetmana Janusza Radziwiłła w latach 1646-1655*, vol. I, *Diariusz kancelaryjny 1649-1653*, p.530.
182 The unit served there since 1655. AGAD, AR VII, no. 473, pp.1–15.
183 Surprisingly, it was missing the lieutenant colonel.

	Life company	Major Gros	Captain Niwicki	Captain Karlik	Major Fridrich Polsen	Captain Detlof	Captain Hempel
Captain	-	1	1	1	1	0	0
Lieutenant	1	1	0	1	0	1	1
Ensign	0	1	1	0	1	1	1
Sergeant	2	1	1	2	3	2	2
Armourer	1	1	1	1	1	1	1
Corporal	4	3	3	2	3	3	2
Quartermaster	1	1	1	1	1	1	1
Sub-ensign	1	1	0	0	0	1	0
Surgeon	0	0	0	1	1	0	0
Drummer	3	1	2	2	1	2	0
Provost	1	0	1	0	1	1	0
Privates[184]	118	78	75	88	71	57	75
Total strength	132	89	86	99	84	70	83

Not counting regimental staff, the total strength of all seven companies was 643. It could indicate that the muster was done either in the third quarter (when the regiment had paper strength of 710 portions) or fourth quarter of 1658 (when the paper strength was 711 portions), as we need to add a certain number of 'dead pays' for the extra portions for officers and some 'specialists'. The life company was clearly much stronger then the remaining six. Oddly enough, there was the presence of two companies led by majors, though this may have something to do with the regiment being stationed as garrison force. It is worth comparing it with a more detailed *rolla* from 21 October 1659 to see how the structure and strength of the units have changed. The regimental staff was composed of a major (in charge of the regiment), quartermaster, auditor, clerk, adjutant, another NCO of a non-specified role, *prowiantmaster*, wagon master, surgeon and drummer. The number of companies was reduced from seven to four, but they increased their overall strength, no doubt taking over the remaining soldiers from disbanded units. They also seem to be more uniformed, being similar in both structure and size:

---

184 Muster do not mentioned how they were divided into files within each company.

	Life company	Major Fridrich Polsen	Captain Karlik	Lieutenant Wojciech Sławkowski
Captain	1[185]	1[186]	-[187]	-
Lieutenant	-	1	1	1
Ensign	1	1	1	1
Sergeant	4	4	4	4
Armourer	1	1	1	1
Corporal	See privates	See privates	See privates	See privates
Quartermaster	2	1	1	2
Clerk	1	-	1	-
Sub-ensign	-	1	1	-
Surgeon	-	-	1	1
Drummer	3	3	3	4
Provost	1	1	1	1
Privates	183[188]	180[189]	180[190]	185[191]
Total strength	197	194	195	200

Another document shows the strength of the combined squadron of 273 men, sent from Słuck in December 1655, to capture Nieśwież.[192] It was part of a small-scale civil war in Podlasie, where Bogusław Radziwiłł was trying to increase his sphere of influence and carve some sort of a semi-independent duchy. Nieśwież belonged to his cousin Michał Kazimierz Radziwiłł, who remained loyal to Jan II Kazimierz. The soldiers sent from Słuck captured the town and its castle without a fight on 5 December 1655, thanks to the betrayal from some of Michał Kazimierz's officers. The 'strike force' was led by a small staff: Captain Jakub Robak, a lieutenant, two ensigns and six NCOs, with soldiers provided by all seven companies of the regiment. The colonel's company composed of a sergeant, quartermaster, drummer and 78 men (including two corporals), divided into 12 files (nine files of six, two of five and one of four men). The lieutenant colonel's company composed of 30 men, divided into five files of six men each. The major's company had an armourer and 36 men (including one corporal), divided into six files of six men each. Captain Niwicki's company also had an armourer and 24 men (including one

---

185 Captain-lieutenant in charge of the unit.
186 Major Polsen is mentioned as captain here.
187 Despite his name in command of company, he is not included in the strength of the unit's muster.
188 30 files of six men each, one file of three men. Number includes five corporals.
189 30 files of six men each. Number includes four corporals.
190 30 files of six men each. Number includes three corporals.
191 30 files of six and one file of five men. Number includes four corporals.
192 AGAD, Archiwum Warszawskie Radziwiłłów (AR) XI, no. 48, pp.76–83, *Anno 1655 die 5 (Decem(bris do Nieswieskiego Zamku weszło żołnierzów według Regestru tego*.

corporal), divided into four files of six men each. Captain's Dotlof's company composed of a sergeant, drummer and 24 men (including one corporal), divided into four files of six men each. Captain Karlik's company had a sergeant, armourer, drummer and 24 men divided into four files of six men each. Captain's Robak's company had a drummer and 36 men (including one corporal), divided into six files of six men each. This clearly shows that, when the situation required it, infantry's structure was very flexible and allowed the division of units even on a company level to fulfil different tasks.

The last regiment that I want to look into is one of the late-war additions, as it was created in early 1658. It was the regiment under Colonel Bogusław Leszczyński, which for short period of time served as his private unit, paid by Lieutenant Colonel Krzysztof Unrug, who was reimbursed for it by his nominal commander.[193] Initially, the regiment was composed of four companies, each of 100 portions. In summer 1658, another company was added, also with 100 portions. By early 1659, the paper strength of the regiment was increased to 890 portions – although, due to the lack of surviving documents, it cannot be confirmed if the existing companies were strengthened or new companies were added as well. There were two particular differences in the organisation of this regiment, though. While the company staff had the same structure and numbers as in the other regiments, it is the arrangement of the rank-and-files that draws attention. The Colonel, Lieutenant Colonel and Capitan Andrzej Drohojowski's companies had their units divided into files of musketeers and pikemen, with the majority of files being of six, and some of five, men. There was also an additional group called the '*furierszycowie*', soldiers designed to take care of the company's supplies, assisting the quartermaster:

A Dutch-made partisan, used by a Polish officer, with the date '1654' on the engraving (Livrustkammaren, Stockholm).

Company	Staff	Number of files of pike	Number of pikemen	Number of files of musketeers	Number of musketeers	F^{194}	Total company strength[195]
Colonel	11	8	46	4	24	6	87
Lt. Colonel	8	9	52	4	24	6	90
Captain Drohojowski	12	4	24	10	59	-	95

---

193 The history and the structure of the regiment from Bartosz Staręgowski, 'Organizacja, struktury i udział w walkach regimentu piechoty Bogusława i Jana Leszczyńskich w latach 1658-1662', *Przegląd Historyczno-Wojskowy*, 2 (2020), pp.10–41.
194 *Furierszycowie.*
195 It means actual fighting strength, rest of 100 portions of 'paper strength' was filled with additional pay for officers.

The fourth original company of the regiment, under Captain Adolf Herman Mięsicki, was composed solely from musketeers: 13 men of staff, 84 musketeers (14 files of six men each) and seven *furierszycowie*, with a total strength of 104 men, thus exceeding the paper strength. Leszczyński's regiment provides us with solid proof of the presence of pikemen in the Polish army. At the same time, it is another example indicating how confusing and fairly chaotic the internal structure of the foreign infantry regiments was.

Patrick Gordon, in the second volume of his diary, presents the unique muster of the foreign infantry from Hetman Lubomirski's division from 20 August 1660, during a campaign against the Muscovites. It is worth quoting it *in extenso*, as it provides some details into the structure of the units at the end of war with Sweden:[196]

The regiments were:

The Field Marshals,[197] commanded by Coll. Giza,[198] well cloathed and armed, in 10 companies 1,000 men.
The Palatine of Sandomirs[199] his reg. commanded by Lt. Coll de Williams,[200] 10 comp., 900 men.
Maior Gen-ll Celary[201] his reg., 8 comp., 800 men, and a company of dragownes, 60 men.
Maior Gen-ll Grothaus[202] his reg., 8 comp. 800 men.
Coll. Nemerits[203] his reg., 8 comp., 900 men.
Coll. Koritsky[204] his reg., 6 comp., 600 men.
Coll. Czarnotsy[205] his reg., 5 comp., 200 men.
The Palatine of Posna[206] his reg., 8 comp. 700 men.
Coll. de Buy[207] his reg., 8 comp., 900 men, and a company of dragownes, 100 men.
Duke Michel Radzivill,[208] 4 companies, commanded by Lt. Coll. Fittinghausen, 200 men.

The discrepancy between the paper strength and actual size of a unit could sometimes be shockingly high, especially after a long campaign and heavy losses. In May 1654, the infantry regiment of Colonel Zygmunt Wall was stationed in Wisznia, and local Ruthenian nobles were alarmed that the unit was taking the pay for 1,200 portions, while there were no more than '15, maybe 20 men under banner [each company]'. The regiment most likely was

---

196 *Diary of General Patrick Gordon*, vol. II, p.68.
197 Jerzy Lubomirski.
198 Mikołaj Konstanty Ghizza/Giza.
199 Jan Zamoyski.
200 De Vilen.
201 Paweł Celary.
202 Ernest Magnus Grotthauz.
203 Stefan Niemirycz.
204 Krzysztof Korycki.
205 Andrzej Cernezzi.
206 Jan Leszczyński. Former regiment of Bogusław Leszczyński.
207 Franciszek de Buy.
208 Michał Kazimierz Radziwiłł.

composed of eight companies; no surprise, then, that the Ruthenians were instructing their envoys in the *Sejm* to point out this issue and request that Colonel Wall return the overpaid money.[209]

At the same time, gradual attrition during years of service can be seen in some of the surviving documents. The company of Captain Hans, from Michał Kazimierz Radziwiłł's infantry regiment, started service in October 1657 with a paper strength of 128 portions. Throughout the whole of 1658 and 1659, it was mustered as 87 portions, for each of eight quarters – which already indicates some interesting bookkeeping, as it highly unlikely that it would have kept the same actual size for such a long time. Finally, in 1660, we can see many changes, connected with the campaign in Ukraine. In the first quarter of this year, it was mustered as 59 portions, in the second and third as 62 portions, with the final quarter of the year as 44 portions.[210] Radziwiłł's regiment saw one of the biggest decreases in size during the Deluge. While it started service as 500 portions in October 1657, by the second quarter of 1660, it had just 182 portions, so it was in the size of the reinforced company. Another badly affected unit was the regiment of Andrzej Karol Grudziński. It entered service in the third quarter of 1658 as 1,200 portions, and, by the second quarter of 1660, it dropped to 385 portions.[211]

Due to only partially surviving records, it is impossible to tell with full certainty that all foreign infantry units in the Commonwealth's armies were the typical 'pike and shot', with a normal ratio of pike to shot of 1:2 or 1:3. However, it is possible that some units, especially free companies so common in the Lithuanian armies, were in fact pure shot units. Abraham von Westervelt's drawings of the Lithuanian army from the campaigns of 1649–1651 shows mostly musketeers, although there is at least one large unit presented as a block of pikemen with shot all around it. As the painter was an eyewitness to the campaign of 1651 and worked directly for Hetman Janusz Radziwiłł, his observations are very

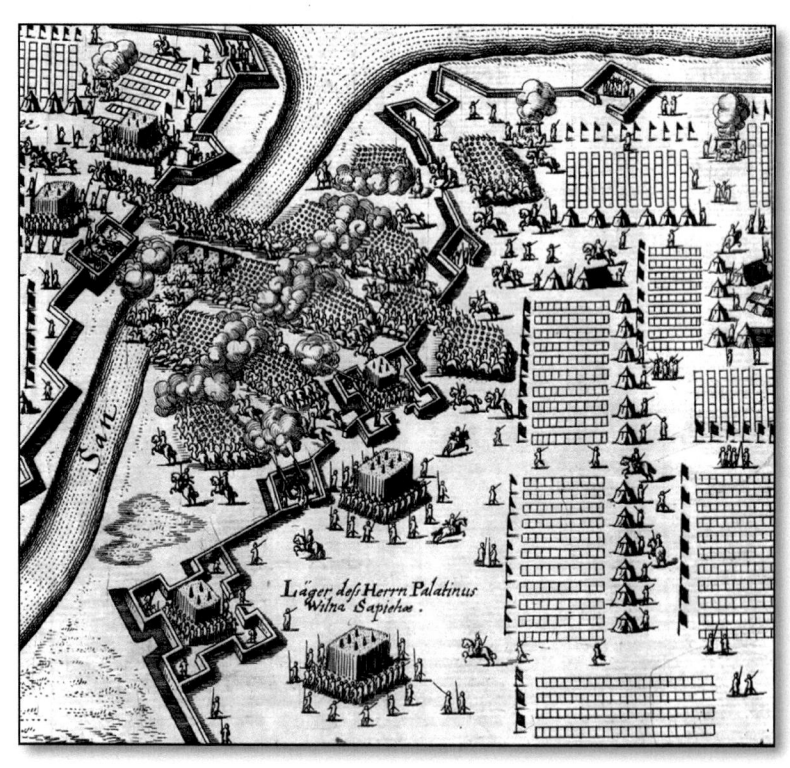

Details of the camp of the Lithuanian army under Hetman Sapieha, March 1656. Despite many visible pike and shot units, they were in fact practically absent from his force at that time. Engraving from volume VII of *Theatrum Europaem*, published in Frankfurt am Main in 1672 (Biblioteka Narodowa, Warszawa).

---

209 *Akta grodzkie i ziemskie z czasów Rzeczypospolitej Polskiej*, vol. XXI, p.154.
210 AGAD, AR VII, no. 57, p.14.
211 Wimmer, 'Materiały do zagadnienia liczebności i organizacji armii koronnej w latach 1655-1660', *passim*.

LANCES, SABRES AND MUSKETS

reliable. The 1,500 foreign infantry raised as district troops in Royal Prussia in 1648 were all equipped with muskets, as surviving bills mentioned 10,500 zł spent on those weapons (7 zł per musket).[212]

The Royal Armoury in Warsaw had, in December 1649, fairly large quantities of the pikemen armour, used by the Foot Guard in 1648 and 1649 while fighting against the Cossacks. There were 4,488 sets of 'white pikemen armour' including helmets; 382 black pikemen armour sets, 1,839 new black *szyszak* helmets and many single pieces of armour (i.e., 51 breastplates, 70 backplates and 120 bad quality (or damaged) helmets). Additionally, the Foot Guard regiment under Colonel Samuel Osiński returned, after the campaign of 1648, 278 breastplates, 271 backplates, 202 helmets, 261 bad quality (or damaged) helmets and 61 gorgets; some of them were then delivered to the rebuilding Foot Guard regiment, now under the command of Fromhold von Ludinghausen Wolff. All of these armour pieces were owned by the King, as they were purchased for his guard units. Further black armour was purchased from the merchant Szymon Bem (Bom) from Toruń. The armoury received 498 full sets (including helmets, gorgets and spaulders), 209 set without spaulders, 262 'armours' (likely just breast and backplates) and 27 spare helmets.[213] Those pieces were owned by the Commonwealth, as they were purchased with money from the National Treasury.

Amongst the weaponry kept in the Royal Armoury in Warsaw, there were of course pikes as well. In December 1649, 349 good pikes and 11 bad ones (possibly meaning they were damaged) were kept in store. The Foot Guard regiment under Osiński, after taking severe losses at Piławce, returned pikes in different conditions: 84 'not so bad', 98 with broken shafts that required repair, 74 'others requiring repair', finally 20 'shafts without any iron [heads]'. A merchant from Toruń, Szymon Bem (Bom), who seems to have had very good deals with the Royal Armoury, delivered 760 new pikes, while a further 299 pikes were brought from Tczew.[214]

The Royal Armoury also had in its stores different types of muskets. In 1648, the majority of its supply was taken by Samuel Osiński's Foot Guard in a campaign against the Cossacks and returned in a very sorrow state. The items handed over were listed as 43 old muskets, five short muskets, 279 musket barrels, 266 locks for those barrels and 10 damaged barrels. No surprise that purchases were required to restock the armoury. Already, in February 1647, 1,700 muskets were purchased from the previously mentioned Szymon Bem (Bom) from Toruń. A further 909 'old Malbork muskets' were delivered from Gdańsk. In June 1649, 295 'good muskets' were delivered from the United Provinces. Documents mentioned that some of those muskets were handed over to the army units while the others were sold to individual buyers (likely for their private units). The armoury also had 1,540 musket rests 'that belonged to His Royal Highness' (i.e., were purchased from his treasury) and 64 old Muscovite rests that, as a war trophy, belonged to the Commonwealth. An additional 1,200 musket rests were purchased from Szymon Bem. A

---

212 Skokloster Samlingen (SkS), 337, p.185.
213 Górski, *Historya artyleryi polskiej*, p.296.
214 Górski, *Historya artyleryi polskiej*, p.296.

store of bandoliers was also divided into 'His Royal Highness' ones and Commonwealth ones. The former included 485 that had their powder bottles and 1,960 spare powder bottles, many of them damaged or of poor quality. The Foot Guard returned, after the campaign, 200 bandoliers and 54 'old ones'. The Commonwealth's stores had initially 1,200 bandoliers with powder bottles, purchased in 1647 in two sets of 600 from Szymon Bem. They were not kept there for long, as they were sold to different buyers, including (the then still) Royal Prince Kazimierz, who bought 500 for his soldiers.[215]

In March 1651, Hetman Janusz Radziwiłł wrote to Mohylew, asking the Town Council to look for '100 German muskets', most likely for his foreign infantry,[216] while not mentioning any pikes at all. The Royal Guard regiment, when leaving Cracow after the city surrendered to the Swedes in October 1655, was described as being armed with muskets and pikes, although again in an unknown ratio.[217] Of particular notice, de Noyers – writing about three 'old' foreign infantry regiments stationed in Lwów – described them specifically as '4,000 musketeers' without mentioning pikemen.[218] However, Leszczyński's regiment, about which I wrote before, indicates the presence of pikemen in the Polish army, although it is very difficult to find some more detailed information about it. Pikemen were present in Niemirycz's regiment at the Battle of Cudnów, where they managed to repulse a counterattack of the Muscovite cavalry.[219] Further evidence of the presence of pikemen can be found in a letter from Captain Stanisław Kazimierz Zamoyski to Jan Zamoyski, from 25 April 1656. The officer mentioned that he already recruited 30 men for a new company and asked for a delivery of muskets and pikes to arm them.[220] Amongst the weapons that were to be delivered to Michał Kazimierz Radziwiłł's regiment in October 1656, there were 120 pikes, 'enough for 20 files [of six men each]', which could supply a few companies.[221] A list of muskets for the same regiment provides us with a very interesting mix.[222] Amongst them, we can find 47 brand-new muskets, purchased for the soldiers; 47 Turkish muskets (possibly those were for the haiduks); 30 newly repaired muskets from one of the national armouries;[223] 41 old muskets from the national armoury and 11 other muskets.[224]

Older types of weapons could probably be more often used by troops stationed for a longer time as garrisons, especially when they were equipped with the guns from the local arsenal. Amongst the weapons kept in the arsenal at Lachowicze in 1658, we can find heavy muskets for the foreign infantry

---

215 Górski, *Historya artyleryi polskiej*, pp.296–97.
216 *Korespondencja wojskowa hetmana Janusza Radziwiłła w latach 1646-1655*, vol. I, *Diariusz kancelaryjny 1649-1653*, p.530.
217 Kochowski, *Historya panowania Jana Kazimierza*, vol. I, p.237.
218 *Portfolio królowej Maryi Ludwiki*, vol. I, p.288.
219 Leszczyński, *Potrzeba z Szeremetem, hetmanem moskiewskim i z Kozakami w Roku Pańskim 1660 od Polaków wygrana*, pp.78, 82.
220 AGAD, AZ 334, p.7.
221 AGAD, AR VII, no. 237, p.1.
222 Although some could have been in fact for Radziwiłł's haiduk banner.
223 They were called '*skarbne*' as in 'belonging to the National Treasury'. It was a term often used for weapons kept in royal armouries.
224 AGAD, AR VII, no. 237, p.1.

stationed as garrison. They are named '*kobyła*' (Polish word for mare), which was the term used to describe heavy Dutch muskets used with rests.[225] During siege operations, when assaulting enemy positions, grenades were frequently used. There is no indication that any special class of grenadiers were created for this task, though, with grenades being allocated between soldiers within the ranks of the companies taking part in assaults. In June 1658, 1,000 hand grenades were despatched from the armoury in Warsaw to be sent to the troops preparing to besiege Toruń.[226]

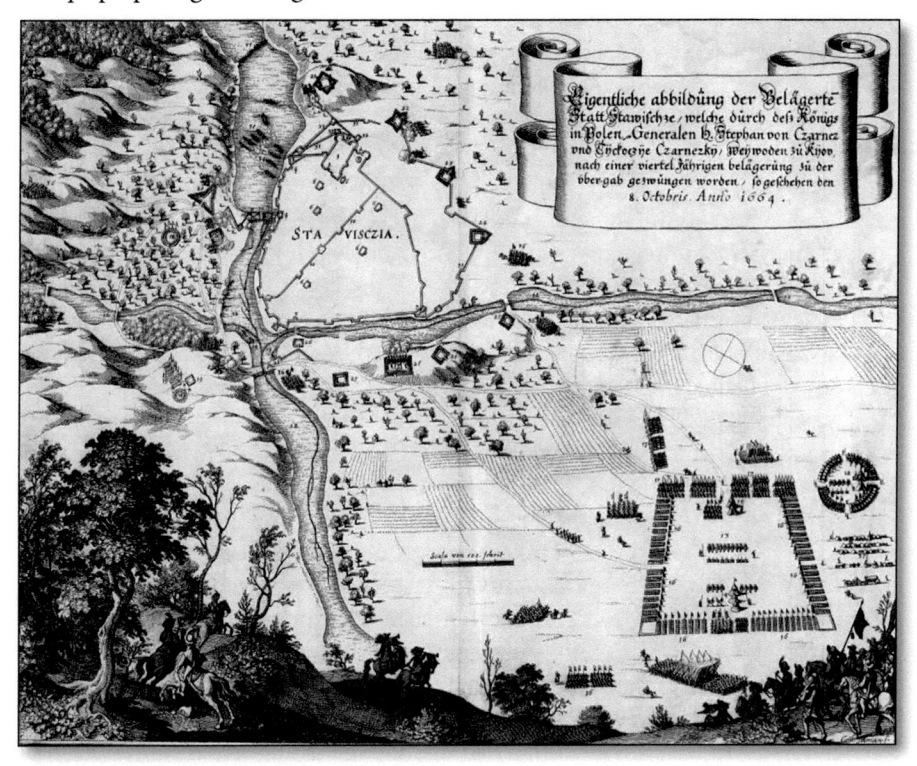

The Polish army under the command of Stefan Czarniecki during the siege of Stawiszcze in Ukraine, October 1664. Caspar Merian, 1664. (Herzog August Bibliothek Wolfenbüttel: Graph. A2:126).

As with all other formations in the Commonwealth's armies, it is difficult to draw a detailed picture of the uniforms in foreign infantry. While the units should have received cloth for such garments, it is highly likely that – due to logistical problems, campaign attrition and a constant lack of money – infantrymen often had a rather strange mix of Eastern and Western clothes, relying on the local clothing that they could 'acquire' during campaigns. Some of the companies, especially at the beginning of a campaign, could of course be in more similar clothing, especially if the nominal colonel or hetman supported them. The foreign infantry raised as district troops in Wielkopolska in spring 1649 received 'good blue uniforms'.[227] Abraham

---

225 *Zbiór dyplomatów rządowych i aktów prywatnych, posługujących do rozjaśnienia dziejów Litwy i złączonych z nią krajów (od 1387 do 1710 r.)* (Vilnius: J. Zawadzki, 1858), vol. I, p.30.
226 AGAD, Archiwum Skarbu Koronnego (ASK) IV, Księga Rekognicji, no. 14, p.90.
227 Staręgowski, *Formacje zbrojne samorządu szlacheckiego województw poznańskiego i kaliskiego w okresie panowania Jana Kazimierza (1648-1668)*, p.92.

von Westervelt's drawings provides interesting sets of foreign infantry from Radziwiłł's troops between 1649 and 1651, with Western-style coats, hats and even the same style haircuts. In April 1651, the foreign company of Captain Hugo Montgomery in the Lithuanian army mustered 'well dressed' – unfortunately, the eyewitness did not mention the colour of the uniforms.[228] In January 1658, Captain Alex Katerla, from Jan Zamoyski's foreign infantry regiment, wrote to the colonel that the whole of his company was now 'well clothed', most likely from supplies purchased in Poznań, but he did not mention the colour of the uniforms.[229] Samuel Leszczyński, describing the Polish army marching against the Muscovites in 1660, wrote that they looked so miserable that, if they did not have uniforms, one would have thought they were beggars. Unfortunately, he did not mention any details regarding the colours of the clothing.[230]

Primary sources are sadly lacking in the details concerning the tactics used by foreign infantry in the Polish and Lithuanian armies, as practically all diarists were serving in cavalry. Their descriptions of battles tend to just mention infantry 'giving fire' and 'facing the enemy'. When describing the attacks on the Cossack tabor at the Battle of Łojów in 1649, Hetman Janusz Radziwiłł wrote that his infantry assaulted the tabor for two hours, without any details on the tactics they employed. We know at least that their attack was supported by a few regimental cannons and that, after more than two hours of constant assaults, with the musketeers running out of musket bullets, they had to call it a day.[231] Westervelt shows in his drawing shot-only units, deployed in six ranks; there is also at least one unit, again with six ranks, where we can see a block of pikemen surrounded by the musketeers. Between infantry units, there are small cannons, most likely indicating regimental pieces. Patrick Gordon had some first-hand experience from 1660, when his dragoons fought next to foreign infantry against the Muscovites and Cossacks. He mentioned infantry deployed in battalions, often supported by small artillery pieces and a vanguard of dismounted dragoons. Yet again, he did not leave any detailed information, like the strength and composition of the battalions or how they interacted with each other on the battlefield.

Using sketchy information from different sources, it seems that foreign infantry in the Commonwealth's armies tended to employ similar tactics to Swedish, Imperial or Muscovite 'new-style' infantry, although they tended to often operate from behind field fortifications (like during the Battle of Warsaw in 1656) or in close cooperation with the cavalry (like during the fights against the Cossacks). Except for siege operations and assaults on fortresses, there seems to be no occasion where Polish foreign infantry faced Swedish counterparts. Instead, during the third day of the Battle of Warsaw, on 30 July 1656, the Brandenburg infantry brigades under Otto Christoph

---

228 *Korespondencja wojskowa hetmana Janusza Radziwiłła w latach 1646-1655*, vol. I, *Diariusz kancelaryjny 1649-1653*, p.638.
229 AGAD, AZ, 1083, p.4.
230 Leszczyński, *Potrzeba z Szeremetem, hetmanem moskiewskim i z Kozakami w Roku Pańskim 1660 od Polaków wygrana*, p.62.
231 *Korespondencja wojskowa hetmana Janusza Radziwiłła w latach 1646-1655*, vol. I, *Diariusz kancelaryjny 1649-1653*, p.114.

LANCES, SABRES AND MUSKETS

von Sparr attacked the positions held by the foreign infantry regiment of Ernest Magnus Grotthauz and Czarniecki's dragoons and forced them to come out from their half-finished position. Apparently, the Poles 'retreated moving slowly [on order]', although due to a lack of available horses they had to abandon the cannons.[232] Infantry units took a much more active role in the campaign of 1660 against the Muscovites and Cossacks, including assaulting the defended tabor of the latter and clashing with regiments of the 'new-style' infantry of the former.

Dragoons

Mounted infantry known as dragoons (*dragonia*) appeared for the first time almost simultaneously in both the Polish and Lithuanian armies in 1617 and quickly became a vital part of the military establishment. It could easily accompany cavalry during a campaign and support it with firepower, so useful when fighting against different enemies facing the Commonwealth. It was widely employed as a part of both the Polish and Lithuanian armies during the wars against Sweden in 1626–1629 and against the Muscovites in 1632–1634; after that, a few units were usually kept as part of the quarter army

Lithuanian army camp in 1649. Abraham von Westervelt, 1651 (Wikimedia Commons).

---

232 Nagielski, *Bitwa pod Warszawą 1656*, pp.168–69.

fighting against the Tatars and Cossack uprisings. No surprise, then, that dragoons were always present post-1648, in both the Polish and Lithuanian armies and in private troops on a magnate's payroll. Foreigners present in Poland do not provide us with much information about this formation, though. Cefali did not give any detailed description of dragoons, but he mentioned that 'almost all of them are Poles'.[233] Similarly, De Gramont only mentioned that they were 'equalized in everything with infantry, without any distinction'.[234]

The composition of dragoons 'corps' varied from campaign to campaign; there were also major differences between the Polish and Lithuanian armies. In a similar way to foreign infantry, the Poles tended to focus more on regimental structure, while the Lithuanian force had mostly free companies. In the campaign of 1649 against the Cossacks, the Lithuanians had 1,646 portions of dragoons, which were divided into 11 free companies: four of 200, one of 150, one of 123, three of 120, one of 113 and one of 100 portions.[235] In September 1653, the Lithuanians had dragoons of 3,074 portions, divided into 12 units: two regiments (750 and 700 portions), one squadron (400) and nine free companies (200, 200, 150, 134, 120, 120, 100, 100 and 100).[236] In July 1660, the Polish army had 7,400 portions of dragoons, divided into 12 units. There were two regiments of 1,000 portions each, one with 900, one with 700, four with 600 portions each and two with 400 portions each. Additionally, there was one squadron with 400 portions and one independent company of 200 portions.[237]

In the same way as was already mentioned with reiters and foreign infantry, there was no standardised structure of units with dragoons, even within one regiment. It seems that most of these units had four while only some larger ones had six companies. The surviving muster roll of Ludwik Weyher's regiment from 21 December 1654 shows four companies, with individual strengths of 119, 117, 140 and 159 men.[238] The unit was, by then, a part of a Polish auxiliary force sent to reinforce the Lithuanian army. There were some minor differences in the staff of each company and much larger differences within the number of files within each corporalship:

---

233 'Relacya o stanie politycznym i wojskowym Polski przez Sebastyana Cefali', p.332.
234 Gramont, *Iz istorii moskovskago pokhoda Īana Kazimira, 1663-1664 g.g.*, p.15.
235 *Korespondencja wojskowa hetmana Janusza Radziwiłła w latach 1646-1655*, vol. I, *Diariusz kancelaryjny 1649-1653*, pp.354–55.
236 Rachuba, 'Wysiłek mobilizacyjny Wielkiego Księstwa Litewskiego w latach 1654-1667', p.44.
237 AGAD, ASK 82, no. 9, p.71.
238 AGAD, ASK 85, no. 72, pp.107–11v.

	1st company	2nd company	3rd company	4th company
Captain	1	1	1	1
Lieutenant	1	1	1	1
Ensign	1	1	1	1
Sergeant	1	1	1	1
Wachmeister	1	-	1	1
Armourer	1	1	1	1
Sub-ensign	1	1	1	1
Quartermaster	1	1	1	1
Surgeon	1	-	1	1
Clerk	1	1	1	1
Drummer	2	3	3	3
1st corporalship	36 men[239]	36 men[240]	33 men[241]	42 men[242]
2nd corporalship	35 men[243]	35 men[244]	36 men[245]	42 men[246]
3rd corporalship	36 men[247]	35 men[248]	38 men[249] + 20 men[250]	62 men[251]
Total strength	119 portions[252]	117 portions[253]	140 portions[254]	157 portions[255]

Unfortunately, there is no information about the number of men and portions in the regimental staff – none of it is included in surviving muster rolls. Such regiments, numbering just over 500 portions, seem to be pretty common in the 1650s and 1660s. For example, in 1653, five regiments of dragoons in the Polish army numbered 563, 568, 502, 563 and 505 portions.[256] This would indicate that a typical company in these regiments was likely to have

---

239 Six files, each of six men. First one led by corporal, rest by file leaders called *gefraiter*.
240 Six file of six men each, first one led by corporal.
241 Four files of six (including corporal's one) and one file of nine men.
242 Seven files of six men, including corporal's one.
243 Six files, with corporal's one of five men and rest of six men each.
244 Five file of six men each, first one led by corporal, and one file of five men.
245 Six files of six men.
246 Seven files of six men, including corporal's one.
247 Six file of six men each, first one led by corporal.
248 Corporal's file of seven men, four files of six men and one file of four men.
249 Five files of six (including corporal's one) and one of eight. One soldier is named as provost.
250 Under this corporalship there's additional sub-unit, composed of another sergeant and three files (five, six and eight men).
251 10 files: seven with six men, one with five, one with seven and one with eight men. One soldier is named as provost.
252 Total strength on muster signed as 122, which incorrect, unless officers were counted as double pay rate.
253 Total strength on muster signed as 116.
254 Total strength on muster signed as 143.
255 Total strength on muster signed as 160.
256 AGAD, ASK 85, no. 89, p.5.

between 115 and 150 portions, with regiments having up to four companies. Another interesting example of regimental sub-units comes from August 1660, when Prince Bogusław Radziwiłł sent from Prussia to Podlasie a unit led by Captain Michał Flok from his dragoon regiment. Flok had with him his own company of 115 men.[257] The staff was composed of a captain, lieutenant, ensign, *wachmeister*, sub-ensign, quartermaster, armourer, clerk, three corporals, three drummers and one surgeon, with 100 rank-and-file dragoons. Furthermore, the unit was strengthened by adding a half company drawn from other units of the regiment, which was composed of a *wachmeister*, sub-ensign, corporal and drummer, with 50 rank-and-file dragoons. Radziwiłł's plan was for the unit to garrison the two villages previously owned by him: Captain Flok with 100 dragoons was to take over Zabłudow, while his lieutenant with 50 dragoons was to be sent to Orle.[258] Another structure from Radziwiłł's family command, this time the squadron (sometimes called 'regiment') of Michał Kazimierz Radziwiłł, was stationed as a garrison of Nieśwież in February 1660. It was missing a separate regimental staff, although some of them can be found on company lists. Surprisingly, two of four companies lacked lieutenants. The first company was composed of a major, lieutenant, ensign, *wachmeister*, armourer, three corporals, two drummers and 85 dragoons. The second and third companies had the same structure: a captain, ensign, three corporals, one drummer and 86 dragoons. The fourth company had a captain, lieutenant, ensign, three corporals, one drummer and 86 dragoons.[259] There is also an earlier document regarding the newly recruited company for this squadron/regiment from April 1657. The company staff was fairly small: an ensign, *wachmeister*, senior NCO[260] and quartermaster, although the anonymous lieutenant writing the document surprisingly did not add himself to the list. The rank-and-files were divided into 12 files, with 11 of them of six men each and one of five men. Probably due to the unit being recently raised, it did not have drummers or armourer yet.[261]

Independent companies had a similar structure to the units within regiments, so it is worth providing at least an example of such. The company of Captain Jerzy Kurcweill, on the muster roll from 21 October 1659, had a strength of 118 men.[262] The staff was composed of a captain, lieutenant, ensign, *wachmeister*, armourer, quartermaster, sub-ensign, three corporals,[263]

---

257 The detailed payroll of the units allows for a correct reconstruction of the unit's structure.
258 Biblioteka Narodowa, Rps III 3092, pp.17–19v, *Kopiariusz korespondencji Bogusława Radziwiłła oraz innych materiałów historycznych i publicystyczno-literackich z lat 1657–1672*.
259 AGAD, AR VII, no. 57, pp.37–40.
260 The document named his rank as '*felweber*', which seems to be a change from the German word '*feldfebel*'.
261 AGAD, AR VII, no. 63, pp.1–4.
262 The summary of the muster roll mentioned '115 horses', but none of the officers or soldiers are mentioned as serving in more than one horse. Additionally, adding staff and all 'files' gives 118 men, not 115.
263 Indicating that, like in the companies mentioned in Weyher's regiment, there were three corporalships here as well.

LANCES, SABRES AND MUSKETS

two drummers and one trumpeter. The dragoons were divided into 18 files, with 17 of six men each and one of three men.²⁶⁴

Janusz Radziwiłł and Zaporozhian Cossack envoys in 1651. On the right, we can see foreign infantry and dragoons from the Lithuanian army. Abraham von Westervelt, 1651 (Wikimedia Commons).

A common problem was the lack of horses, visible especially during long campaigns or prolonged periods of garrison service. The already mentioned newly raised company for Michał Kazimierz Radziwiłł's squadron/regiment in April 1657 had only enough horses for company staff and for five files of dragoons (29 men), while the remaining seven files (42 dragoons) did not have horses.²⁶⁵ In November 1658, the dragoon company serving as part of the garrison in Słuck had 123 rank-and-file dragoons. Only 51 of them are mentioned as mounted, while the rest was serving on foot. From the seven corporals, five are mentioned as mounted and two on foot. The rest of the company staff did not have any annotation,²⁶⁶ which probably means they did have horses.²⁶⁷ The recruitment letter for Aleksander Hilary Połubiński's dragoon company from August 1652 specifically mentioned that the soldiers should have 'good horses, with proper harness and all needed equipment, as required for mounted dragoon'.²⁶⁸

Often, there were vast differences in the quality of horses within one unit, and these differences could lead to a situation when only those with better horses could survive to live another day. During the Battle of Zborów in 1649, when fighting against the Cossacks and Tatars, the Polish army took heavy losses. Amongst the decimated units were dragoons of Jerzy Lubomirski and, according to one of the diarists, 'only those experienced [soldiers], that had

---

264 AGAD, AR VII, no. 473, pp.15–17.
265 AGAD, AR VII, no. 63, p.2.
266 Lieutenant, ensign, two *wachmeister*s, two armourers, sub-ensign, quartermaster, surgeon, four drummers and provost.
267 AGAD, AR VII, no. 473, p.1.
268 BCzart., no. 2749, p.289.

good horses, survived, while the rest, gathered from amongst [Lubomirski's] peasants, were all killed'.²⁶⁹

Gordon provides us with interesting information about attempts to purchase horses for Lubomirski's dragoons. In spring 1660, his unit was quartered in today's Slovakia, near the town of Spišská Nová Ves (Neundorf). He was supposed to buy 160 horses for his unit, but initially, burghers, unwilling to deal with the military, sold him only eight. After receiving new orders, in which he was told 'to take such horses as I had occasion for, or thought fit for service', he set up his dragoons to block all town gates to make sure 'no horses passe out'. The next day, he spoke to the magistrate of the town, ordering him to bring all serviceable horses into the marketplace, and 'gave orders to bring no horses of high prices nor such either as were old or unable for service'. Within two hours, more than 400 horses were gathered, from which he chose 150 or 160. Gordon then proceeded to the 'taxing of them, which I made them do at very reasonable rates, noting downe the markes, colours, ages and owners of the horses with their prices'. Some of the chosen horses were excluded, though, 'as being taken from widdowes and poor men'. Nonetheless, he managed to purchase enough to provide horses for the whole unit.²⁷⁰ Of course, horses bought for dragoons were of much worse quality than those used by cavalry; therefore, their cost was much lower. For the 500 dragoons of district troops in Royal Prussia raised in 1648, horses cost 30 zł per mount.²⁷¹

There is some interesting information about the prices of the equipment for a newly raised company of dragoons in April 1657. Muskets cost 5 zł each, and swords 3 zł each. The officer raising the unit even managed to buy 42 horses for 30 zł each and some saddles costing 3 zł each.²⁷² In 1658, when buying new equipment for another company of dragoons taking part in the siege of Toruń, muskets cost 6 zł (so one zł more), but acquired horses were much cheaper than the year before, as they were only 20 zł each.²⁷³ It is interesting to compare this with the price of the muskets bought for the dragoons raised as district troops in Royal Prussia in 1648, where they cost 7 zł.²⁷⁴ To put it in perspective, dragoon's pay was 36 zł per quarter or 12 zł per month, and, if they received weapons from their commander, it was normally later taken off from their pay.

The main weapons of dragoons, in their role of fire supports, were muskets, mentioned in both Gordon's diaries and surviving documents regarding raising and equipping units. The hand weapon could vary, though, as soldiers would receive what was locally available: sabres or any type of Western-style swords. I refer readers back to chapter two, where I mentioned the big problems that Gordon encountered when trying to equip

---

269 Mirosław Nagielski (ed.), 'Diariusz Ekspedycyjej Zborowskiej', in *Relacje wojenne z pierwszych lat walk polsko-kozackich powstania Bohdana Chmielnickiego okresu "Ogniem i Mieczem" (1648-1651)* (Warszawa: Wydawnictwo VIKING, 1999), p.186.
270 *Diary of General Patrick Gordon*, vol. II, pp.58–59.
271 SkS, 337, p.185.
272 AGAD, AR VII, no. 63, p.4.
273 AGAD, AR VII, no .63, p.5.
274 SkS, 337, p.185.

Lubomirski's dragoons. In April 1657, a newly raised company for Michał Kazimierz Radziwiłł was equipped with muskets and *szpady*, with the latter word used at the time to describe a military sword. The 200-horse-strong unit of Aleksander Hilary Połubiński, which he received the recruitment letter for in October 1654, was to have for each man a 'musket, powder flask, sword [*szpada*], horse good [enough] to ride on him. [For] Each 10 [dragoons] should [also] have spade and hoe'.[275] Unfortunately, other recruitment letters are often of less use, as they provide generic information. One issued in August 1658, for the third banner of dragoons of Aleksander Hilary Połubiński, only mentioned that it should be a unit of 100 men 'experienced, with all equipment required for dragoons'.[276]

Non-standard weapons, often captured or 'acquired' during a campaign, were used as well. Pasek, who commanded a small group of dragoons from Czarniecki's regiment in 1662, during a clash again Muraszko's volunteers, mentioned one dragoon using with great skill a Muscovite berdiche axe. The other men in his unit had blunderbuss, a 'musket with ferocious barrel', that was shooting *hufnal* nails,[277] which came very handy when facing the large group of volunteers.[278] In the same manner, dragoons could have had access to pistols, which were not part of their normal armament but were more than likely often present as an additional weapon. As dragoons were on many occasions used for engineering work, forced to quickly build field fortifications or assault gates or fix bridges, the presence of all kinds of axes had to be widespread as well. At the same time, soldiers could often lack basic equipment, even the ones required as part of their main 'battle role'. When describing an assault on Stary Bychów in 1655, Prince Bogusław Radziwiłł mentioned that the dragoons did not have axes, which were needed to break through the wooden palisade.[279]

Not much information can be found about the uniform of dragoons. Blue and red are mentioned in a description of troops during the ceremonies of the entry of Queen Louise Marie into Poland in 1646. Amongst the troops that welcomed her in Gdańsk on 11 February 1646, we can find three private units 'in blue colours', while dragoons of the Royal Prince Jan Kazimierz 'had red colours [and] iron *szyszak* [zischagge] helmets'.[280] Amongst the troops that greeted the Queen in Warsaw on 10 March 1646, the private unit of Michał Zebrzydowski represented an unusual mix of Western and Eastern clothing. Dragoons had not only Polish *żupan* and *giermak* garments but also elk-hide coats, a version of buff-coats more popular amongst reiters. King Władysław IV's Guard dragoons were in red clothes, 'with polished [shining] *szyszak* helmets'.[281] While the majority of dragoons wore Western-

---

275 BCzart., no. 2749, p.341.
276 BCzart., no. 2749, p.37.
277 Large nails used to attach horseshoes.
278 Pasek, *Pamiętniki*, pp.225–28.
279 Radziwiłł, *Żywot xięcia Bogusława Radziwiłła, przez niego samego napisany*, p.25.
280 *Ingres albo wjazd królowej [Ludwiki Marii] do Gdańsk 11 lutego 1646* (Kraków: Walerian Piątkowski, 1646).
281 *Ingres triumfalny do Warszawy Ludwiki Marii Gonzagi, królowej polskiej w r. 1646* (Warszawa: Piotr Elert, 1646), p.4.

style clothes, Jean le Labourer, who was in the entourage of French envoy Renata du Bec-Crespie de Guebriant, mentioned seeing '60 dragoons in Polish clothing' from the private unit of Stanisław Lubomirski. The dragoon company of Aleksander Kostka, raised as a part of the district troops in Wielkopolska in the summer of 1648, had 'sky blue' (*obłoczyste*) uniforms.[282] While Patrick Gordon did not mention any uniforms for his unit, he did provide one interesting note about a different company of dragoons. In 1656, he saw the private unit of Konstanty Lubomirski, 'which were about 80 men, all Polls with blew cloaks after the Dutch manner and fashion.'[283]

It seems, though, that at least some of the regular army units also received some sort of uniform, or at least the cloth to make ones. In September 1650, Lithuanian Colonel Jerzy Teodork Tyzenhauz wrote to Hetman Janusz Radziwiłł that his unit of 200 dragoons did receive uniforms during the campaign of 1649.[284] Unfortunately, the type or colour of such clothing is not mentioned. Amongst the clothes for the servants and private soldiers of Jan Zamoyski in 1653, we can find 'red dragoon coats'.[285] In June 1657, Captain Andrzej Wergal was in charge of one of Połubiński's dragoon companies, which was being rebuilt after losing a large part of its strength in May the same year when the Swedes and Transylvanians captured Brest. In a document confirming the rebuilding of the company, Wergal wrote that 'Colonel [Połubiński] promised to provide those dragoons with new uniforms'.[286] Two years later, in July, Wergal, already promoted to major and in charge of Połubiński's dragoon regiment/squadron, confirmed receiving a delivery of red cloth for the uniforms of his unit.[287] In 1662, when Pasek arrived at the army camp with a group of dragoons from Czarniecki's regiment that he had under his command, he had a discussion with Czarniecki himself, praising the deeds of his men when facing a large group of marauding volunteers. The Polish *Regimentarz*, seeing that the dragoons managed to capture good horses during the fight, told them that they would receive *barwa* (uniforms) quicker than other men in the regiments.[288] This would indicate that, even if not on a regular basis, even soldiers in this regiment were receiving an allocation of uniforms or the cloth for it. Another example is from November 1661: when Prince Bogusław Radziwiłł presented to King Jan Kazimierz his new units (600 dragoons and 200 reiters), he mentioned that the Monarch was very pleased with the sight of those troops since they were well equipped and 'newly clothed'.[289] Unfortunately, Radziwiłł did not provide any further information about the uniforms of his troops, but at least his brief words provide us with yet another evidence of clothes being issued to the troops.

---

282 APPoz., Gr. Pozn., 693, p.629.
283 *Diary of General Patrick Gordon*, vol. I, p.87.
284 *Korespondencja wojskowa hetmana Janusza Radziwiłła w latach 1646-1655*, vol. I, *Diariusz kancelaryjny 1649-1653*, p.374.
285 AGAD, AZ, 2744, p.43.
286 BCzart., no. 2749, p.367.
287 BCzart., no. 2749, p.383.
288 Pasek, *Pamiętniki*, p.230.
289 Radziwiłł, *Żywot xięcia Bogusława Radziwiłła, przez niego samego napisany*, p.44.

LANCES, SABRES AND MUSKETS

The layout of the army camp for 15,700 soldiers, made up in 'old Polish style', with each square described as one regiment. Due to their structure, the regiments of national cavalry (hussar and cossack cavalry) were allocated a much larger space to allow for servants and tabor wagons. Like all of Naronowicz-Naroński's plan, it is scaled in feet. From Józef Naronowicz-Naroński's Architektura militaris, to jest budownictwo wojenne, *1659 (Biblioteka Uniwersytetu Warszawskiego).*

Units of dragoons were, like all other foreign *autorament* troops, a mix of different nationalities. On one side, there were many German-speaking soldiers, ranging from those who were recruited in Prussia and Silesia to those who were former Swedish soldiers that decided (or were forced) to switch sides. Aleksander Kostka's dragoon banner, part of the district troops in Wielkopolska in the summer of 1648, was composed of 'Finns, Semigallians and [men of] German nations'.[290] Von Ascheberg, in one of his letters, mentioned that the majority of the 150 Polish dragoons captured by his reiters in Prussia late December 1655 were German;[291] he also sometimes specifically wrote about 'German dragoons' in the Polish service.[292] On the other side, in surviving muster rolls, we can find many Polish and Lithuanian names, recruited locally. A large part of the cadre was foreign, though, mostly Germans but also with Scots (like Gordon), Italians, Frenchmen and Dutchmen. The recruitment letter for the 100-horse dragoon banner of Aleksander Hilary Połubiński, issued on 27 August 1652, mentioned that the banner should be composed of 'drilled men and as many of them [as possible] with previous [military] experience'.[293] It did not specify whether the unit should be recruited locally or abroad, so it seems that, like in many other occasions, the officer in charge had free reign when choosing the nationalities that should be included in the ranks of his company. The already mentioned private unit of Konstanty Lubomirski in 1656, despite being composed of Polish dragoons, had a Dutch captain named Zacharias Mitlach.[294] A particularly unusual unit was the banner of *semeni* under *Rotmistrz* Franciszek Kobyłecki, serving under Czarniecki's command since

---

290 APPoz., Gr. Pozn., 693, p.629.
291 Ascheberg, *Dziennik oficera jazdy szwedzkiej 1621-1681*, p.14.
292 Ascheberg, *Dziennik oficera jazdy szwedzkiej 1621-1681*, p.62.
293 Majewski, *Marszałek wielki litewski Aleksander Hilary Połubiński (1626-1679)*, p.62.
294 *Diary of General Patrick Gordon*, vol. I, p.87.

mid-1657. It was composed of mercenary Zaporozhian Cossacks, and it was highly praised by Pasek, who wrote that 'they done miracles, as they are all chosen men, in [the same] age and height like they would be all born from one mother'.²⁹⁵ Lithuanian dragoons played a vital role in the victory over the Muscovites at Szkłów in August 1654. Their regiments and companies were deployed on the flanks of Janusz Radziwiłł's force, hiding in ravines and shooting from ambush at the Muscovite cavalry chasing the Lithuanian horses.²⁹⁶

Of course, dragoons had to be prepared and 'battle ready' to be able to properly support cavalry. At the skirmish near Mozyr, on 17 July 1654, the Lithuanian regiment of Szymon Pawsza (composed of no more than five banners of cossack cavalry and Tatar light horse, supported by one company of dragoons) was surprised by Zaporozhian Cossacks allied with the Muscovites. The dragoons did not have bullets or powder, so they did not even have a chance to open fire. More than 30 of them died, with the rest of the company scattered.²⁹⁷ During the Battle of Szepielewicze in August 1654, yet again Lithuanian dragoons fought valiantly, providing fire support to Radziwiłł's cavalry. Regiments of Hetman Radziwiłł under Herman Ganzkopf/Gantzkow (a paper strength of 600 horses), Bogusław Radziwiłł under Eberhard Puttkamer (600 horses) and Ernest Jan Korff (700 horses) fought until the end but, abandoned by their own cavalry, were finally broken by the Muscovite reiters and thus fled, taking heavy losses during the retreat.²⁹⁸ Stefan Czarniecki's veteran regiment accompanied his division during campaigns of the Deluge, later fighting in Denmark and in 1660 and 1661 against the Muscovites.

Dragoons could also be very useful as part of a garrison force, performing the role of the 'eyes and ears' of the defenders. In February 1659, Kazimierz Kłokocki and Władysław Huryn – commissioners serving on behalf of Prince Bogusław Radziwiłł and at the time in charge of the defence of the important fortress Słuck – wrote to Radziwiłł a long report about the state of the defence and the situation in the areas around Słuck. They mentioned that they lacked mounted units, as the garrison's company of dragoons was away. The commissioners asked Prince Radziwiłł to send them a 'company of horse with able officers', suggesting that it would be good to provide them with dragoons again, as without them 'we are very alert and cautious [now], as we do not know anything about the enemy [Muscovites] nearby'.²⁹⁹ When a unit of dragoons finally arrived to Słuck in May 1659, the commissioners decided to keep it in the fortress, as 'it is badly needed here'.³⁰⁰

Thanks to the fact that Patrick Gordon served in Lubomirski's dragoons in the late 1650s and in 1660, we can find in his diary some first-hand relations about the tactics and battle role of this formation in the fights

---

295 Pasek, *Pamiętniki*, p.111.
296 Grabowski (ed.), *Ojczyste spominki w pismach do dziejów dawnej Polski*, vol. I, p.115.
297 Grabowski (ed.), *Ojczyste spominki w pismach do dziejów dawnej Polski*, vol. I, p.119.
298 Grabowski (ed.), *Ojczyste spominki w pismach do dziejów dawnej Polski*, vol. I, p.123; Bobiatyński, *Od Smoleńska do Wilna. Wojna Rzeczypospolitej z Moskwą 1654-1655*, p.58.
299 AGAD, AR V, no. 6865/I, pp.78–79.
300 AGAD, AR V, no. 6865/I, pp.95.

LANCES, SABRES AND MUSKETS

against the Muscovites and Cossacks in 1660.[301] I do hope that, despite this rather long relation not being connected directly with the conflict against the Swedes, it can be still useful as an insight into the role of dragoons in the Polish army. It is also very interesting and rather refreshing to read a few details from an eyewitness that, for a change, did not serve in the cavalry. Gordon mentioned his men often being used for guard duty, protecting the army camp. They were also used as support for the cavalry group, including hussars, where dragoons dismounted near the enemy and could lend their muskets in firelight or be used in terrain too difficult for mounted troops, like woods and orchards. As such, we often find them in the vanguard of the army, where they could react the fastest to situations on the battlefield. In one case, Gordon was ordered, along with a commanded force of 100 dragoons, to march through orchards to attack and get the attention of a large Muscovite infantry unit. He was not sure if the enemy wanted to waste their ammunition on such a small group of dragoons, but, at the same time, he was conscious of the fact that his unit could be easily overwhelmed by the much stronger enemy. Therefore, he divided his force, leaving his lieutenant with 40 laying in ambush in the orchards, while Gordon himself took the rest of the unit outside of the cover to get the attention of the enemy foot. Here, he ordered his dragoons to 'fyre rank-wise, keeping ground'. After three salvoes, the whole Muscovite battalion turned towards the dragoons and returned fire. Meanwhile, despite Gordon's orders to 'desist and reserve his shot', his lieutenant, a 'giddy headed inexperienced fellow', broke with his troops from the ambush and, standing in out in the open, 'continued still fyreing'. Seeing that the small company of dragoons was in danger of being overwhelmed, Jan Sobieski (who was in charge of one of the national cavalry regiments) arrived next to Gordon and ordered him to retreat. Considering that the unit was 'exposed to with[out] necessity or hopes of doing any good', the dragoons retreated. This small-level affair was a rather costly one, as Gordon's detachment had two killed and 12 wounded while his lieutenant's detachment had six killed and 17 wounded.[302]

Dragoons, alongside infantry, were also often employed as sappers, building field fortifications and trenches and raising batteries for the artillery. Another action of Lubomirski's life company, with Gordon again leading 100 men, took place on 7 October 1660 during the Battle of Słobodyszcze, and it started with the capture and repair of a small bridge held by the Cossacks. He mentioned that the unit arrived mounted as close as possible and that he then ordered his men to dismount and left the 'horses with the usuall guard'. Unfortunately, he never mentioned how strong this guard was, so we do not know what the ratio of horse-holders to horses in such cases was. The dragoons captured the bridge after a short fire fight, as the Cossacks decided to abandon their position after seeing the approaching group of Crimean Tatars, allied with the Poles. Gordon left 20 men to repair the bridge and took the rest to try to support the Tatars attacking the Cossacks – who, by then, after taking heavy losses in the flight, barricaded themselves in a wooden

---

301 *Diary of General Patrick Gordon*, vol. II, pp.71–100.
302 *Diary of General Patrick Gordon*, vol. II, pp.77–78.

church. Help from the dragoons was not needed, though, as the Tatars, enraged at taking losses from the Cossacks' shots, set the church on fire. All the defenders perished in the conflagration or were cut down mercilessly by the Tatars during retreat. Gordon's men, losing only one killed and six wounded during the whole mission, took position 'within musquet shott of the enemyes leaguer [camp]', waiting for the arrival of the main force.[303]

Later the same day, dragoons were then used as the vanguard of the Lubomirski's infantry attacking the Cossack camp. As the gate through which Gordon's dragoons had to march was faced by at least 20 cannons, he decided to move through it quickly and then to move aside, so the approaching infantry had enough space to push through with its battalions. The dragoons were ordered to 'double the files' and then, after crossing the gate and the ditch next to it, to move right. Unfortunately, the officer leading the first four files (so a maximum of 24 men) forgot the orders and, in confusion, started to break ranks, moving with his troops to a nearby orchard. The other dragoons, under the increasing fire of Cossack cannons, bows and firearms, milled in confusion and started to break ranks trying to get to the orchard. Luckily for Gordon, his troops encountered some sort of small ditch, which stopped their movement and allowed him to redress the ranks. Here, he was reinforced by the next squadron of dragoons, led by Major Schults (possibly Schultz), whose troops also broke ranks and were moving in a disordered group. Both officers managed to bring back order despite heavy shooting from the defending Cossacks. Finally, Gordon gave the order to 'fyre orderly, ayming well at so fair markes, which they did, and go good purpose', as musket salvoes managed to force the Cossacks to hide behind a wall and allowed for a renewal of the Polish attack. The dragoons approached 30 to 40 paces from the Cossack field fortification and started to continuously 'fyre rankewyse'. The Cossacks were pinned with musket fire and were only able to fire from bows 'shoot in the hight'. All Polish infantry and dragoons were then ordered to renew their attack on the Cossack fortified camp, a large part of it 'not entrenched but barricadoed with waggons'. Led by the forlorn hope of four files (likely the leading sub-unit, under the command of a forgetful officer), the dragoons managed to break into the camp, forcing the Cossacks to retreat. Here, discipline broke, though, and a majority of dragoons left their units, focusing on robbing tents and wagons. Gordon, Schults and other officers managed to keep under their command only 100 men. Other units had the same problem, so, despite breaking into the camp, Polish troops spread out in search of loot. Meanwhile, the Polish cavalry – hussars, cossacks and reiters – were engaged in a heavy fight with the Cossack tabor, taking heavy losses in bloody hand-to-hand combat. The Cossacks managed to rally and return to camp, surprising the scattered Polish infantry and dragoons. With the tables turned, it was now time for the Poles to flee from the camp, chased by the vengeful Cossacks. Gordon, still barely recovered from the fever he suffered before the battle, managed to run thanks to the help of two file leaders from his unit, Kraus and Steffansky (possibly Stefański). The

---

303 *Diary of General Patrick Gordon*, vol. II, pp.82–83.

units were pushed outside of the camp, where officers managed to rally them. Infantry and dragoons were then twice again thrown at the Cossack camp, but their assaults failed.[304]

Gordon and his dragoons returned after this battle with Lubomirski to the main Polish army, which, under the command of Grand Hetman Potocki, was blocking the Muscovite forces at Cudnów. Here, on 13 and 14 October, dragoons were yet again used as the vanguard of the Polish troops, engaging the retreating Muscovite infantry and dragoons. Again, we can find a mention about 'here wee dismounted and leaving our horses with the usuall number of guards to be brought after us'. Sadly, in this passage, Gordon did not mention the exact number of those horse-holders, although he added that the officers remained mounted. The fight was a rather messy affair, with Polish dragoons sometimes shooting at the Muscovites from 30 to 40 paces and other times running after them until '[they] were out of breath sometymes' and soon after giving fire again. As the dragoons were fighting in that way on their own for a while, they took heavy losses until the main force of infantry, cavalry and artillery approached and engaged the Muscovites and their allied Cossacks, with 'many falling, both officers and sojours [soldiers] on both sydes'. The Poles managed to capture a large part of the Muscovite tabor, including provisions, money, clothes and other 'good booty'. While the bravery of dragoons was most likely richly rewarded with some captured goods, the price they paid for it was high. The unit had a paper strength of 200 portions and, as already mentioned, took some losses before. During the fight with the Muscovites at Cudnów, *Wachmeister* Paul Banzer and 16 dragoons were killed, while 24 more, including Gordon ('twice wounded with musket ball, in the left shoulder and right legg'), were amongst the wounded. From the latter, 'some dyed afterward of their wounds'.[305]

Polish–Hungarian Infantry

In the first part of the seventeenth century, 'native' infantry, usually called 'Polish' or 'Hungarian', tended to play a fairly important role, often containing a large percentage of the whole infantry 'corps'. However, the 1626–1629 war against Sweden in Prussia shows that, due to the lack of experienced cadre, it was difficult to quickly raise and then keep in service large numbers of banners. Gradually, this type of infantry started to play smaller role in the Polish army, often delegated to garrison duties or, in the case of hetman banners, to serving as some sort of bodyguard and military police units. The situation was slightly different in the Lithuanian army, when – due to the overall smaller strength of the whole armed force – even a few banners with a few hundred men could make up a large part of the overall infantry. Interestingly enough, in both armies, this formation was known under a few names, as in sources we can find the terms 'Polish infantry', 'Hungarian

---

304 *Diary of General Patrick Gordon*, vol. II, pp.83–87.
305 *Diary of General Patrick Gordon*, vol. II, pp.88–90.

AGAINST THE DELUGE

infantry', 'Polish–Hungarian infantry' and haiduks. The Hungarian influence, brought into the Commonwealth during King Stephen Bathory's reign, by the second half of the seventeenth century, was mostly visible just in the clothing, like the *magierka* cap. De Gramont wrote:

> In Poland, there has always been a Hungarian infantry, called in this country haiduks. Those troops are very well dressed and armed with large rifled arquebuses, sabres and rather long axes, in the form of halberds. Polish kings from ancient times used these people for their protection, both in the palace and on campaigns, due to their tested loyalty. Their salary is the same as that of the [foreign] infantry.[306]

Sebastian Cefali noticed the diminished role of this type of infantry, writing that 'formerly infantry in Poland was composed of Hungarians, known as haiduks, [but] now used only for parades in public events and as servants'.[307] While in the 1650s and 1660s haiduks were usually recruited locally, sometimes officers were sent abroad to find suitable recruits. In March 1651, Captain Grodzicki was sent to Hungary to raise a banner of 200 haiduks for the Lithuanian army. While he did succeed in finding enough men, his unit was scattered during some rather unspecified event while still in Hungary and never joined Hetman Radziwiłł's army.[308] At the same time, both Holsten and Gordon, while fighting against the Poles, often mentioned haiduks as a part of local forces – alongside nobles and peasants – defending against the Swedish invaders. Later, already in Polish service, Gordon mentioned a haiduk unit that opposed his dragoons near Pińczów and

Polish haiduks, part of the embassy entering Paris in 1645. Jean Boisseau, 1645 (*Bibliothèque nationale de France*. Photo by Tomasz Ratyński).

---

306   Gramont, *Iz istorii moskovskago pokhoda Iana Kazimira, 1663-1664 g.g.*, p.15.
307   'Relacya o stanie politycznym i wojskowym Polski przez Sebastyana Cefali', p.332.
308   *Korespondencja wojskowa hetmana Janusza Radziwiłła w latach 1646-1655*, vol. I, Diariusz kancelaryjny 1649-1653, pp.532–33, 832.

LANCES, SABRES AND MUSKETS

described them as 'souldiers with fyrelocks, shables [sabres] and pollaxes'.[309] This indicates that, on the local level, haiduks, employed perhaps in smaller units as a part of private troops, were serving as some sort of armed militia, helping to keep order and fight off all kinds of marauders. As such, they were not part of the regular army but played vital role in the local defence.

The structure of the haiduk banners were very interesting, as some of them still followed a pattern initially introduced in the late sixteenth century. Large banners had an organisation that allowed them to be divided into two sub-units, known as left and right 'wings'. The banner of Crown Grand Hetman Stanisław Rewera Potocki had a strength of 200 portions throughout the whole war, and its structure was as follows:[310]

- Staff of the unit, officers and musicians, including the captain in charge of the unit (with a pay of three portions), two lieutenants (each with two portions), one clerk, two ensigns, four drummers and 12 other musicians (fifers and shawm players).
- Sub-units known as 'tens' (*dziesiątki*), each led by an NCO known as 'tenth man' (*dziesiętnik*). Despite their name, sub-units had in fact nine men each. There were 20 of them in total.

Counting all additional portions, the paper strength of the units was in fact slightly higher, with 206 portions. On the battlefield, each 'wing' would be led by a lieutenant, with an ensign and a few musicians attached, while its fighting strength would be composed of 10 'tens'.

Even a unit that was smaller than 200 portions could be divided in the same way. A good example of this type of banner was the Hungarian infantry of Jan Kaski. The muster from the third quarter of 1658, when the infantry was listed with a paper strength of 140 portions, presented it as follows:[311]

- Staff of the unit, with a *rotmistrz* (not captain, like in the previous banner; also with a higher pay of four portions), two lieutenants (two portions each), two ensigns, surgeon, four drummers and five other musicians, with a total of 20 portions.
- Right wing, divided into nine 'tens', which in fact were smaller: two of eight men, five of seven, one of six and one of five, with a total of 62 men.
- Left wing, also divided into nine smaller 'tens': four with seven and five with six men each, for a total of 58 men.

Rather unusual amongst units of Polish–Hungarian infantry was the banner of Jerzy Sebastian Lubomirski serving during the Deluge, as it had certain differences in structure. Looking into its muster roll from the second quarter of 1657,[312] the staff of the unit was composed of a *rotmistrz* (with three portions of pay), lieutenant, ensign, two drummers and seven other

---

309 *Diary of General Patrick Gordon*, vol. II, p.39.
310 AGAD, ASK 85, no. 78, pp.56–58v.
311 AGAD, ASK 85, no. 79, pp.2–3v.
312 AGAD, ASK 85, no. 91, pp.38–39.

Another noble from the Polish embassy in Paris in 1645. He is escorted by two axe-armed haiduks,1645 (*Bibliothèque nationale de France*. Photo by Tomasz Ratyński).

musicians.[313] What made it so odd was the presence of two sergeants (each with one portion of pay), normally not present in this type of infantry. The 'tenth man' in this banner was called '*dardzista*', from the word '*darda*', which was the Polish name for a type of halberd or half-pike, used as both a weapon and symbol of rank. Each *dardzista* was in charge of one section or file, composed of himself and five haiduks. There were 15 such files, for a total of 90 men. The banner was officially listed with a paper strength of 100 portions despite having 106 of them.

Another interesting structure can be found in the banner of Jan Skrodzki, from the muster in October 1654.[314] It was a larger unit divided into two sub-banners, each with its own staff. The 'right banner' was composed of a *rotmistrz* (with four portions of pay), lieutenant (two portions), ensign, one drummer and four other musicians. It also had three more 'specialists': a clerk, quartermaster (under the name of '*oboźny*', so literally camp master) and chaplain. There were 90 haiduks, divided into 10 'tens' of nine men each (yes, talk about confusing structure), so the total paper strength of this sub-unit was 105 portions. The 'left banner' had a staff of a *rotmistrz* (with four portions of pay), lieutenant (two portions), ensign, one drummer, clerk and surgeon. Eighty-six haiduks were divided into 10 'tens' but of different sizes: six of nine men each and four of eight men each. This sub-unit had a paper strength of 96 portions, giving the banner a total of 201 portions.

The main weapons of haiduks were muskets and the sabre, but they also often used axes as both a weapon and engineering tool. As mentioned before, the unit's NCOs known as tenth men were equipped with a *darda*, hence the name '*dardzista*' sometimes used to describe them. In July 1649, Lithuanian

---

313 All, including the lieutenant and ensign, with one portion of pay.
314 AGAD, ASK 85, no. 70, pp.32–35.

LANCES, SABRES AND MUSKETS

Field Hetman Janusz Radziwiłł requested from the town of Mohylew the delivery of 200 sabres and 'haiduk axes' for his infantry. As was often the case, he did not send any money but just a written confirmation that the items would be paid for in the future.[315]

Sometimes, information about the specific type of muskets could be found in sources as well. In March 1651, Hetman Janusz Radziwiłł was planning to order in Byhów 60 muskets with wheellocks for the Polish infantry and to 'pay for them as soon as they are ready'.[316] Another 60 wheellock muskets for haiduks were to be ordered at the same time in Mohylew, 'to be bought if available'.[317] The haiduk banner of Michał Kazimierz Radziwiłł, which in October 1656 was sent to join the Polish army, received muskets and six *darda*: the unit had 60 men, so it was enough weapons for each of the six tenth men.[318]

Private haiduks could have access to better quality weapons. At Zborów in 1649, two Hungarian haiduks from the entourage of Zbigniew Oleśnicki acted as sharpshooters. Armed with rifled muskets, they kneeled in front of the unit and shot at the individual skirmishing Tatars.[319] Of course, such weapons were not something normally available in the regular units; therefore, examples of similar actions were fairly rare. In December 1655, Gordon mentioned Polish sharpshooters armed with hunter guns known as *cieszynka* (from the town of Cieszyn in Silesia), utilising their weapons to kill Swedish sentries during an ambush attack: 'Their ryfled gunnes, being heavy and taking a very little bulletnot much bigger as a good pease, and not much powder, shoot very just without making a loud report'.[320]

Haiduks, especially those from Royal and hetman units, tended to be uniformed, as they received allowance for 'colour' (*barwa*), which was the term used to describe the cloth for uniforms. Throughout the whole seventeenth century, the most common colour used for infantry would be blue or 'sky blue', although red or 'scarlet' was also often used. The latter colour was used by the banner of Grand Hetman Potocki during their triumphal entry into Warsaw on 12 June 1661. Some further

A Polish noble armed with a hand-axe. Stefano della Bella, 1651 (Biblioteka Narodowa, Warszawa).

---

315 *Korespondencja wojskowa hetmana Janusza Radziwiłła w latach 1646-1655*, vol. I, *Diariusz kancelaryjny 1649-1653*, p.92.
316 *Korespondencja wojskowa hetmana Janusza Radziwiłła w latach 1646-1655*, vol. I, *Diariusz kancelaryjny 1649-1653*, p.529.
317 *Korespondencja wojskowa hetmana Janusza Radziwiłła w latach 1646-1655*, vol. I, *Diariusz kancelaryjny 1649-1653*, p.530.
318 AGAD, AR VII, no. 237, p.1.
319 Nagielski (ed.), 'Diariusz Ekspedycyjej Zborowskiej', p.192.
320 *Diary of General Patrick Gordon*, vol. I, p.67.

examples of colour combination with district haiduks will be mentioned later in this chapter, along with the description of the troops raised by different voivodeships and lands. In March 1651, Captain Grodzicki, who was to go to Hungary to raise a banner of 200 haiduks for the Lithuanian army, mentioned in his letter to Hetman Janusz Radziwiłł that there was a problem with receiving money for colour. He wrote that the soldiers were due to receive kersey (*karazyja*) and that the old allowance was two *postaw*[321] per three haiduks, which was to cover the cloth required for the full clothing.[322]

A unit serving for a long time in the crucial garrisons could also sometimes receive cloth for uniforms. For example, the Polish infantry stationed in Vilnius castle got their cloth every two years, as we can find evidence of it for the period of 1648–1652. While documents do not mention how many ells[323] were allocated to each of the soldiers, the *rotmistrz* of the banner received 16 ells every two years, and his lieutenant 14 ells.[324] The town guards in Warsaw, hired in August 1655 and later serving under the Swedish occupation, received blue, red and white cloth, made in Wschowa (so-called '*sukno wschowskie*') and yellow wool cloth known as *kir*.[325]

Private units also received an allowance of cloth, although it is highly likely that they had two separate sets: one, of a more expensive type, used in ceremonial services and a second, made from cheaper cloth known as *pakłak* or from kersey, for day-to-day duties or military service. The Polish infantry in the service of Jan Zamoyski in July 1649 received an allocation of cloth for their uniforms. The NCOs (tenth men) received between six-and-a-half and seven ells of red English cloth (*falendysz*) and seven to eight ells of white *pakłak*.[326] Haiduks got 'sky blue' *pakłak*, which was to be used for the full uniform, so the allowance was between fourteen-and-a-quarter and fifteen-and-a-half ells of it. Additionally, each 'squad' of 10 men received seventeen-and-three-quarters ells of red *pakłak*.[327] Considering the fairly small quantity of this last cloth, it was probably used for some small yet visible element of the clothing (e.g., partial lining).[328] Amongst the clothes for the servants and private soldiers of Jan Zamoyski in 1653, we can find red haiduk *delia*, which may indicate that the red English cloth mentioned in 1649 was used for such an outer garment while white *pakłak* was used for *żupan*.[329] The private haiduk banner of Lithuanian Grand Hetman Sapieha, stationed in 1661 and

---

321 Old Polish measurement of cloth, depending on the region, between 27 and 62 ells.
322 *Korespondencja wojskowa hetmana Janusza Radziwiłła w latach 1646-1655*, vol. I, *Diariusz kancelaryjny 1649-1653*, pp.532–33.
323 Old Polish measurement *łokieć* of 59cm.
324 *Rachunki podskarbstwa litewskiego 1648-1652, wydane z współczesnego rękopisy znajdującego się w bibliotece Eustachego Hr. Tyszkiewicza* (Wilno: Nakładem i Drukiem Józefa Zawadzkiego, 1855), pp.42–43.
325 'Najdawniejsza taryfa okupu szwedzkiego z Warszawy w roku 1655', *Starożytności Warszawy* (Warszawa: Aleksander Wejnert, 1856), series 2, vol. IV, p.192.
326 The Polish name '*falendysz*' was the distorted German or Dutch phrase '*vijn londisch*', which was used by merchants to describe good quality woollen cloth from England. By the mid-1650s, it was also used to describe cloth brought from the Netherlands.
327 AGAD, Archiwum Zamoyskich (AZ), 3112, pp.353–55.
328 The author would like to thank Tomasz Łomnicki for his comments on this topic.
329 AGAD, AZ, 2744, p.43.

1662 as the garrison in Lachowicze, received an allocation of clothing for the uniforms for all of the men. Again, it was cheaper English cloth, mentioned under the name '*lundysz*',[330] and wool cloth *kir*.[331] Unfortunately, the colour of it was not mentioned, although it is possible that those haiduks wore red. During autumn and winter, units could also receive additional clothing more suitable for the weather. The already mentioned banner of Michał Kazimierz Radziwiłł, in October 1656, received sheepskis (*kożuchy*) and shoes for all haiduks.[332]

In one of my previous books, I had discussed the problem with the description of the tactics of haiduks.[333] They were 'shot' units, and only the first rank was composed of tenth men, armed with *darda* half-pikes, with all musket-armed haiduks standing in up to 10 ranks. Modern Polish researchers tend to support the claim that a unit would start the fight with just the last rank standing and all the others kneeling in front of it. The shooting sequence would start with the standing rank, then the next one would stand up and give fire, while the initial one would be preparing to shoot again. The main problem with such a tactic would be that, after the final rank discharged their guns, it would force the whole unit besides the last rank to kneel again to restart the whole procedure. As early as 1558, Crown Grand Hetman JanTarnowski suggested that a unit of Polish infantry should in fact open fire with first ranks, which then should kneel and reload, etc.[334] This tactic seems more plausible, although it was written with *rusznica* caliver-armed infantry in mind, so the weapon more likely easier to reload when kneeling. Sadly, none of the Polish diarists served as haiduks, and their relations always seem to mention haiduks 'giving fire' without any attention paid to how these units fought on the battlefield. As such, we are still at a loss on how haiduks were really employed on the battlefield.

Artillery and Engineers

The reign of King Władysław IV (1632–1648) brought extensive reform to the artillery in both the Polish and Lithuanian armies. Until then, 'Master of Ordnance' (*Starszy and armatą*) tended to be just a temporary title, assigned to the commander of artillery in the field. Beginning in 1637 in Poland, the master of ordnance, often called the 'general of artillery' (*generał artylerii*), became a regular army official, in charge of all artillery and engineers. He was also in control of all the armouries (*cekhauzy*) in Poland: Warsaw, Cracow, Puck, Malbork, Lwów and Kamieniec Podolski. The Polish artillery corps was now financed from a separate 'quarter' tax, drawn from royal lands.

---

330 Which was the same cloth as the previously mentioned *falendysz*, with the name also coming from the distorted word '*landisch*'.
331 Andrzej A. Majewski, 'Military accounts of the Grand Lithuanian Hetman Paweł Jan Sapieha of the years 1655-1662', *Res Historia*, 49 (2020), p.580.
332 AGAD, AR VII, no. 237, p.1.
333 Paradowski, *Despite Destruction, Misery and Privations*, pp.101–02.
334 Jan Tarnowski, *Consillium rationis bellicae* (Tarnów: Publisher unknown, 1558), p.19v.

AGAINST THE DELUGE

During times of peace, the general of artillery had under his command a small cadre of cannoneers, engineers and specialists, rarely exceeding 100 men. The Lithuanian artillery had its own general of artillery, who was in charge of the armouries and staff in Lithuania. Each armoury was under the command of the officer known as *cejgwart*.[335] An important role in the corps was played by the *cejgmaster* or *cejgmistrz*[336] (inspector of artillery), later the lieutenant colonel of artillery, who was in fact second in command, often leading artillery detachments in the field. The highest-ranking commanders in the artillery corps often served in the dual role of engineer/artilleryman and officer of infantry.

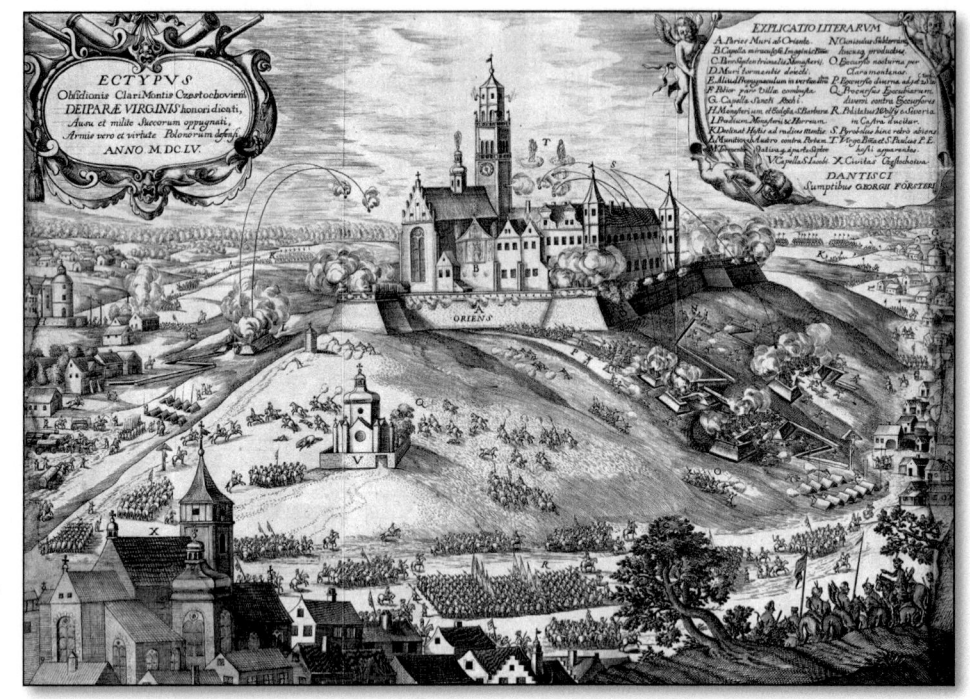

The Swedish siege of Jasna Góra in 1655. Johann Bensheimer, 1659 (Muzeum Narodowe, Kraków)

During the Deluge, the Polish general of artillery was Krzysztof Grodzicki, who held this rank from 1652 until his death in 1660. An experienced officer, he served in the Polish army under Hetman Koniecpolski in the 1620s and then had an episode in the Imperial army as well. After his return to Poland, he was again in the ranks of the quarter army, from 1640 as military governor of the important fortress of Kudak. During the Cossack Uprising of 1648, he defended the fortress for few months against the besieging Cossacks force and surrendered it only once his men had run out of food and ammunition. He returned from captivity in late 1649 and, in 1650, was nominated to colonel of artillery. Two years later, he was promoted to the rank of general of artillery; in this capacity, he was in charge of the artillery and siege works against Swedish-held Toruń in 1658. After his death in 1660, he was replaced by Fromhold von Ludingshausen Wolff, who held this office until 1666. From

---

335 From the German word '*Zeugwart*'.
336 From the German word '*Zeugmeister*'.

LANCES, SABRES AND MUSKETS

the 1640s, he served in the Royal Foot Guard, and he was colonel of this regiment between 1649 and 1655, when the unit was taken over by the Swedes. He rebuilt the regiment in 1658, taking part in campaigns against the Swedes and Muscovites. In 1660, he had the dual role of infantry colonel and general of artillery, taking part in the Battle of Cudnów. In Lithuania, the general of artillery was Mikołaj Judycki, who held the office between 1654 and 1667. Most likely, he received the office thanks to his military experience against the Ottomans. As a Knight of Malta in the 1640s, he had the opportunity to fight against the 'enemy of the Cross' in Algiers and Tunisia and on Crete. He commanded a meagre Lithuanian artillery during the 1650s and 1660s; from 1658, he was also often a regimentarz in the army. Between March and June 1660, he successfully defended the fortress Lachowicz (Lyakhavichy) against the Muscovites.

Many of the engineers and artillerymen were foreigners, usually also serving in foreign infantry or dragoons. The most famous of them was, without a doubt, Fryderyk Getkant (Gettkant), from the Rhineland. He came to Poland around 1625; since 1634, he was working as a cartographer in Prussia and as an engineer on the fortifications of Wejherowo, Kazimierzowo and the important fortress of Kudak in Ukraine. Since 1646, he was *cejgmaster*, and since 1654 lieutenant colonel of artillery. In 1660, he was promoted to colonel of artillery. He fought against the Cossacks and Tatars at Beresteczko, while, in 1655, he defended Cracow against the Swedes. Later

The plan of the full army camp for Polish/Lithuanian troops, including sections for each type of units. From Józef Naronowicz-Naroński's *Architektura militaris, to jest budownictwo wojenne*, 1659 (Biblioteka Uniwersytetu Warszawskiego).

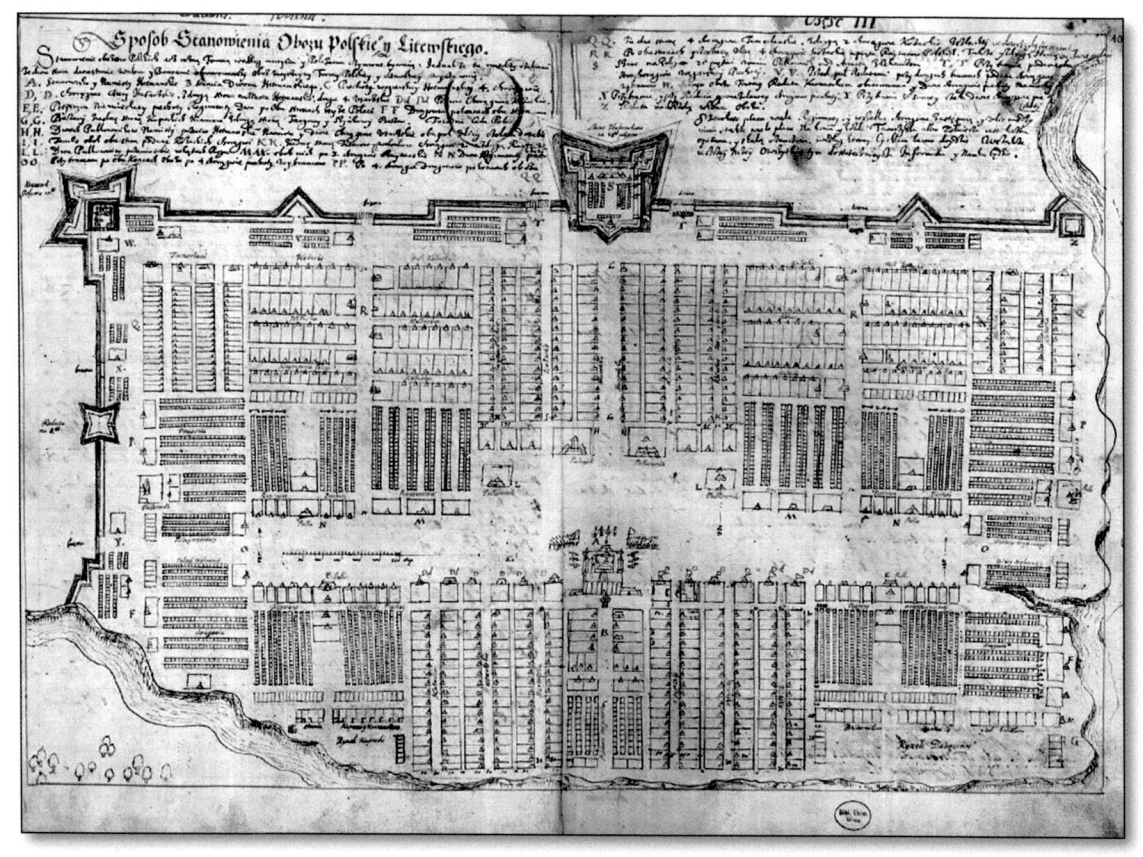

the same year, he switched to the Swedish service and was in charge of ex-Polish cannons during the siege of the Monastery of Jasna Góra. Like the rest of the Polish army, he returned to Jan II Kazimierz's service, taking part in siege operations in Prussia in 1658 and 1659. He played a crucial role in the siege of Toruń in 1658, where besiegers built and used so-called 'earth mortars' during the fight with the Swedes. He also experimented with new types of cannons and mortars; sadly, the manuscript with his written ideas was lost during a fire in Lwów in 1662.[337]

Looking at some of the other foreigners, Henryk de Beaulieu was a French one. He served in the Polish army between 1648 and 1678, and, in 1662, he was ennobled in Poland for 14 years of military service 'against Cossack, Tatars, Muscovites and Swedes' and fortification work in both Prussia and Podolia.[338] Venetian Giovanni Giacomo Bonelli was employed as a military engineer and artillery officer since the reign of Władysław IV, probably since the late 1630s. He built a field fortification for the Polish army in 1653 and, in 1654, took care of the fortification of Smoleńsk. During the Deluge, he worked on strengthening the defences of Brest and took part in the siege of Warsaw by the Polish–Lithuanian armies. His efforts were noticed, as the *Sejm* of 1659 ennobled him for his engineering works from the period of 1654–1656.[339]

Francesco Corossini (Corazzini) was French or Italian and arrived in Poland in 1646. Since 1658, he was captain in the infantry regiment of Andrzej Potocki, at the same time working as an engineer in the employ of Potocki's family. He planned and supervised the fortifications of Halicz and Stanisławów. Starting in June 1661, he was *architectus generalis militarni regni*, so the general military architect in Polish army. He held this office until the end of 1676.[340]

Giovanni Delari (de Lary, Delary) came from a French family living in the Southern Netherlands. He was one of the officers that arrived in Poland with the Queen's entourage in 1646. Initially serving as a royal engineer in the Polish army (campaigns of 1651–1653), from 1654, he moved to the Lithuanian army, where he served as captain of artillery and a miner. In 1661, during the siege of Vilnius, he lost his right hand, ripped by a Muscovite cannonball. Despite that, he continued military service until at least 1671 and was ennobled, with the support of Lithuanian Grand Hetman Jan Paweł Sapieha, in 1662.[341]

Giovanni Battista Frediani came from Lukka in Tuscany, and he was another military engineer that came into the Polish service during the reign of Władysław IV. He took part in campaigns between 1648 and 1658, was taken prisoner by the Muscovites at Werki in 1658, returned from it in 1659 and continued service in the Lithuanian army until 1690.[342]

---

337 Karol Łopatecki and Wojciech Walczak, *Mapy i plany Rzeczypospolitej XVII w. znajdujące się w archiwach w Sztokholmie* (Warszawa: Ministerstwo Kultury i Dziedzictwa Narodowego, 2011), vol. I, p.62.
338 Wagner, *Słownik biograficzny oficerów polskich drugiej połowy XVII wieku*, vol. I, pp.13–14.
339 Wagner, *Słownik biograficzny oficerów polskich drugiej połowy XVII wieku*, vol. I, pp.28–29.
340 Wagner, *Słownik biograficzny oficerów polskich drugiej połowy XVII wieku*, vol. I, pp.52–53.
341 Wagner, *Słownik biograficzny oficerów polskich drugiej połowy XVII wieku*, vol. I, pp.63–64.
342 Wagner, *Słownik biograficzny oficerów polskich drugiej połowy XVII wieku*, vol. I, pp.90–91.

Francesco Trewani a Cassaragi was another Italian that served in campaigns between 1648 and 1664. Like many of his colleagues, he also received *indygenat* (a grant of nobility to a foreign noble) for his military service, especially for the campaign of 1651.[343]

Another French engineer was Jerzy de Cadorette, from a Huguenot family originating in Bretagne. He arrived in Poland in the 1640s, as part of a group of engineers connected with Wilhelm Beauplan. He fought during the Żwaniec campaign in 1653, working on the field fortifications of the Polish army camps. From 1654 onwards, using his engineering skills to reinforce the fortifications of Smoleńsk and Brest, he also took part in the sieges of Nowy Bychów and Mohylew. In 1661, he was present during the recapture of Brest from the Muscovites.[344]

There were, of course, also engineers of Polish origin. Stanisław Baryczka (Barycki) served with the artillery 'corps' since 1649, taking part in campaigns at Zborów, Beresteczko and Żwaniec. During the Deluge, he was present, dealing with both artillery and engineering, at the sieges of Warsaw, Cracow and Toruń.[345] While usually engineers also held the ranks of captain or even colonel in infantry, sometimes there were exceptions. In August 1655, Jan Kazimierz issued a decree to Cracow's city council, advising them that his officer Stefan Franciszek de Oedt will be in charge of the fortification works around the city.[346] This same officer was later put in charge of Lubomirski's reiter regiment and died in 1660 fighting against the Muscovites.

In the late 1630s and during the 1640s, all Polish armouries were increased in size and upgraded with larger warehouses, more staff and – most importantly – with new cannons. It is more than likely that the whole reform was closely linked with King Władysław's plans to wage a large-scale war against the Tatars and Ottomans, during which artillery would be useful in siege operations. During the early years of Jan II Kazimierz's reign, only a fairly small part of the artillery park was deployed against the Cossacks and their allied Tatars. Due to the constant problem with proper financing, negatively affected by lowered taxes, caused by the Cossack Uprising of 1648, the Polish and Lithuanian armies tended to usually deploy a small number of cannons, often of lower calibre (e.g., regimental pieces). As such, it was often problematic to have proper artillery support during siege operations, and the Commonwealth's commanders had to rely on costly and bloody assaults instead. Other issues were connected to providing enough ammunition and powder for the cannons or even purchasing or hiring enough horses to transport cannons and supplies during a campaign.

In 1654, just before the start of the war with Sweden, six Polish arsenals contained 245 brass and 127 iron canons and mortars:[347]

---

343 Wagner, *Słownik biograficzny oficerów polskich drugiej połowy XVII wieku*, vol. I, p.270.
344 Wagner, *Słownik biograficzny oficerów polskich drugiej połowy XVII wieku*, vol. II, p.44.
345 Wagner, *Słownik biograficzny oficerów polskich drugiej połowy XVII wieku*, vol. II, pp.14–15.
346 Archiwum Narodowe w Krakowie, Zbiór dokumentów papierowych, no. 658, document 548, p.1.
347 Tadeusz Nowak, 'Polska artyleria koronna przed wojną 1655-1660 i podczas jej trwania', in Jan Wimmer (ed.), *Wojna polsko-szwedzka 1655-1660* (Warszawa: Wydawnictwo Ministerstwa Obrony Narodowej, 1973), p.125.

Brass cannons:

Type of cannon	Arsenal						Total
	Warsaw	Puck	Malbork	Cracow	Lwów	Kamieniec Podolski	
Whole kartouwen	2						2
Half kartouwen	24		2	1			27
Quarter kartouwen	24			15	7	3	49
Octave kartouwen	8				9	1	18
Regimental 6-pdr					26	11	37
Regimental 3-pdr					16	10	26
Small cannons				8	6		14
Culverin			2	2		2	6
Bastard culverin		2		2		2	6
Falconet		22		14		8	44
Mortars	2				9	2	13
Captured cannons	3						3

Iron cannons:

Type of cannon	Arsenal						Total
	Warsaw	Puck	Malbork	Cracow	Lwów	Kamieniec Podolski	
Cannons		44	62	10	1	1	118
Mortars	8			1			9

We need to remember that these were only the official arsenals, which consisted of artillery that was part of the regular military establishment. Besides that, there were also cannons counted as a part of important fortresses. For example, Smoleńsk, in early 1654, had 61 cannons (mostly older and low calibre ones), three leather cannons in very poor conditions and six mortars.[348] As such, they would not be used as a part of the field operations, except in specific conditions. Towns had their own arsenal, and

---

348 *Zbiór dyplomatów rządowych i aktów prywatnych, posługujących do rozjaśnienia dziejów Litwy i złączonych z nią krajów (od 1387 do 1710 r.)*, vol. I, pp.60–61.

large quantities of cannons were in private hands, as part of the magnate's arsenals. The quality and quantity of the armament in private hands could vary, as often a large part of such arsenals could contain older pieces, including those from the late sixteenth century. The fortress of Lachowicze, which during the Deluge belonged to Sapieha's family, had in February 1658 a total of 31 cannons, from one large 25-pdr to a small 'old one that belonged to the Teutonic Knights'. Detailed inventory mentioned pieces cast between 1560 and 1595, with the larger part of the arsenal made during the two first decades of the seventeenth century, when Lachowicze belonged to Jan Karol Chodkiewicz.[349]

Despite looking good 'on paper', artillery did not have enough staff, and, as mentioned before, its operational use was often affected by a lack of funding. During the Deluge, the logistics of the army were in very poor shape; no surprise, then, that help was sought from privately owned arsenals to provide weapons and ammunition. For example, in July 1657, in order to supply the troops besieging Cracow, Colonel Bokum had to borrow store from Pauline monks in the Jasna Góra Monastery. The supplies that they kindly offered *in fidam publicam*[350] were 20cwt of gunpowder, 8cwt of lead and 60 cannonballs for the half-kartouwe cannons used during the siege.[351] For all this support, the monks were reimbursed 2,440 zł by the *Sejm* in 1661.[352]

However, another problem was with supplying enough horses for artillery park and associated wagons, as it could lead to situations in which available animals were bought 'in the field', which could then lead to increased prices. Amongst the bills presented by General of Artillery Wolff in the *Sejm* in 1661, we can find information that a merchant from Cracow, Tomasz Stodownik, sold 10 horses (for 30 zł) that were 'unharnessed from the wagons full of the merchant's goods'.[353] A further 47 horses were bought from three other sellers, although in these cases the individual cost was higher at 50 zł per horse.[354]

There were also not enough cannons to take to the field, as arsenals in Warsaw, Malbork and Cracow were looted by the Swedes after those towns were captured (in the latter, the Swedes took 96 cannons).[355] Not surprise,

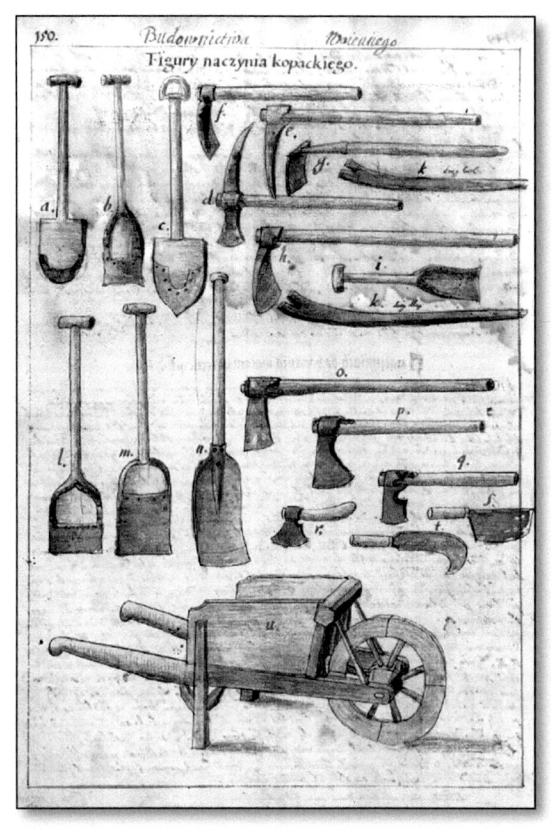

Engineering tools – most of them were usually part of the equipment requirements of any infantry units raised in Polish districts as part of lan infantry and of *wybraniecka* infantry. From Józef Naronowicz-Naroński's *Architektura militaris, to jest budownictwo wojenne*, 1659 (Biblioteka Uniwersytetu Warszawskiego).

---

349 *Zbiór dyplomatów rządowych i aktów prywatnych, posługujących do rozjaśnienia dziejów Litwy i złączonych z nią krajów (od 1387 do 1710 r.)*, vol. I, pp.116–17.
350 Which meant they could be returned or paid off in the rather far away future.
351 AGAD, ASK IV, Księga Rekognicji, no. 14, p.2.
352 AGAD, Archiwum Skarbu Koronnego (ASK) II, Rachunki Sejmowe, no. 55, p.67.
353 Archiwum Narodowe w Krakowie, Zbiór Zygmunta Glogera, no. 619, p.8.
354 Archiwum Narodowe w Krakowie, Zbiór Zygmunta Glogera, no. 619, p.8.
355 *Diary of General Patrick Gordon*, vol. I, p.63.

then, that Jan II Kazimierz had to often ask magnates (like Zamoyski) or other private owners (like the city of Gdańsk) to support his army with their own cannons and trained crews. When the Polish army besieged Warsaw in June 1656, it had to initially rely on smaller field pieces, including those used to support foreign infantry regiments. Only by the end of the month did the besiegers receive heavy cannons from the arsenal in Lwów and further pieces borrowed from Jan Zamoyski from his fortress in Zamość, which allowed them to set up proper batteries to support their assaults on the town.

The plan of Elbląg (Elbing), captured by the Swedes 22 December 1655. Erik Dahlbergh's drawing for Samuel Pufendorf's *De rebus a Carolo Gustavo Sueciae rege gestis*, published in 1696 (Muzeum Narodowe, Kraków).

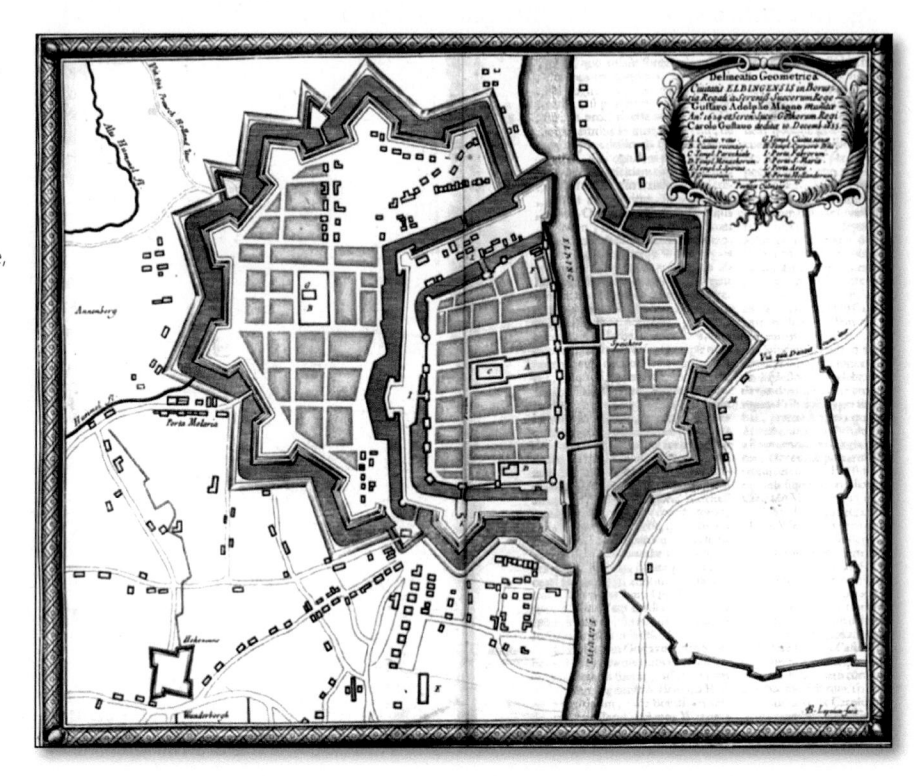

The Lithuanian artillery was also in no better shape than the Polish one, lacking properly trained crews, cannons and ammunition. Poor funding meant that there was not enough money to hire wagons and drivers to transport artillery trains. In 1648, in a campaign against the Cossacks, the artillery staff was composed of a captain (who was also in charge of a foreign infantry company), one petardier, five trained cannoneers, seven hired assistants (for cannoneers), one blacksmith and his assistant, one wainwright and his assistant; they were accompanied by 141 horses hired for transporting cannons and supplies.[356] In the first campaign of 1649, there was a captain, petardier and five cannoneers, including three that were formerly in the service of Hetman Janusz Radziwiłł. They were accompanied by 16 assistants

---

356 *Korespondencja wojskowa hetmana Janusza Radziwiłła w latach 1646-1655*, vol. I, *Diariusz kancelaryjny 1649-1653*, pp.359–60.

arrived at the battlefield, the soldiers could only congratulate the nobles from the levy for their amazing success.[368]

The size and organisation of levy of nobility in each region varied. By the time of the Deluge, the majority of nobles were serving 'in cossack cavalry style', although most likely with a rather large variety of equipment and weapons. Some could still afford to arrive as hussars; others could serve as *arkabuzeria*, reiters or even *petyhorcy*. There were also many examples of nobles or their replacements arriving on foot. In late summer 1654, when Lithuanian nobles from Vilnius District gathered to serve as levy of nobility, they were grouped into one banner of hussars and five banners of cossack cavalry. Maciej Vorbek-Lettow, who took part in their muster, served in the cossack cavalry banner under *Rotmistrz* Jan Tyzenhaus and Lieutenant Stefan Borejko. The unit had 76 horses and four men serving on foot; in addition, 15 nobles that should have served in it never arrived at the muster. Most men were present on their own, serving in a one-horse retinue (so without retainers). Interestingly, one of the replacements in the unit was mentioned 'with musket, as dragoon'.[369] Those units served for one quarter (three months), practically not moving from their own camp, after which they disbanded and the nobles returned home. In August 1655, when facing a Muscovite offensive, nobles from Vilnius District gathered in one banner of hussars and four banners of cossack cavalry. This time, Vorbek-Lettow ended up in the cossack banner of *Rotmistrz* Krzysztof Partykowski and Lieutenant Jan Pietkiewicz. It was 'the strongest and best equipped' unit of the muster, numbering at least 200 horses. To compare, one other cossack cavalry banner, that of *Rotmistrz* Marcin Wołowicz, had 'no more than 70 horses', and most of them were boyars living on Wołowicz's possessions and serving as his subjects.[370]

It was up to each noble or even family to decide who would be sent as a representative for the levy of nobility. Some, especially poorer ones, were present in person; others would send a family member or a replacement – either another noble (their 'client' or subject) or even a servant. In August 1658, when 18-year-old Jan Władysław Poczobut Odlanicki was sent to serve in levy of nobility as a representative of his family, it was a fact decided upon by his older brothers. His mother seems to have been opposed to sending the youngest one to war, but – in the absence of the father of the family, Marek Kazimierz Poczobut Odlanicki, who died in 1648 – the older sons had the right to decide and choose who from amongst the family would represent them in the levy.[371]

In the early stage of the war in 1655, with a large part of the regular Polish army deployed against the Muscovites, the defence against the Swedes had to be supplemented by other formations. According to a resolution from

---

368 Biblioteka Kórnicka, *Extraktschreiben von unrterschiedlichen Orten aus Großpolen*, PAN Kórn, 1119; Tadeusz Nowak, 'Kampania wielkopolska Czarnieckiego i Lubomirskiego w roku 1656', *Rocznik Gdański*, XI (1938), pp.148–50; Kochowski, *Lata Potopu 1655-1657*, pp.165–66.
369 Vorbek-Lettow, *Skarbnica pamięci*, pp.198–201.
370 Vorbek-Lettow, *Skarbnica pamięci*, pp.230–31.
371 Poczobut Odlanicki, *Pamiętnik Jana Władysława Poczobuta Odlanickiego*, p.20.

in such numbers.[364] The biggest effort of the Polish levy took place in the summer of 1655, when approximately 33,000 of them were serving against the Swedes and 3,000 to 4,000 against the Muscovites.[365] On all these fronts, though, their presence was more often a hindrance than real military help, as clearly proved during the surrender at Ujście. No surprise that regular army officers were not keen on having levy under their command, knowing all the problems that they generated.

Amongst the many problems with the presence of levy of nobility during a campaign was their need for non-military gear. Unused to soldier life, they were often trying to make sure that they had all the comfortable 'essentials', from food to clothing. Bogusław Kazimierz Maskiewicz was full of criticism towards the Polish levy taking part in the Piławce campaign in 1648, and it was in their need for luxury that he saw the main reason in their humiliating defeat against the Cossacks:

> Polish nobles arrived *cum taxi luxu*[366] [wearing] scarlet, with golden ornaments on their [tabor] wagons, full of clothes, silver, gold, jewels, ornaments, etc., so almost every companion was trying to equal grand magnates, so even sold the last possessions just to buy spending clothes; and there were such luxuries that God punished them for it mightily, as they all fled, despite no one was chasing them. In such way they brought unforgettable affront and shame on the Homeland.[367]

In the unusual circumstances of the Deluge, levy of nobility could sometimes achieve some success on the battlefield or least during actions of 'small war'. It was levy, supported by district troops and the local population, that played the main role in fighting against the Swedes and Brandenburg forces in Wielkopolska – from the guerrilla fight in late 1655 to the more open uprising in 1656 and 1657. On 9 May 1656 at Kościan, levy led by Jan Piotr Opaliński, Voivode of Podlasie, destroyed a strong detachment of Swedish cavalry sent to pacify the uprising. Polish sources vary in their estimates of the Swedish force, counting it as between 1,500 to 2,000 reiters in four regiments gathered from different garrisons. Their initial night attack on the Poles besieging Kościan was successful, and they caused losses, with some levy fleeing from the battlefield towards Czarniecki's forces. The Swedes woefully underestimated the strength of Polish force, though, as the levy was much more numerous than the attacking Swedes. After a short fight, the outnumbered reiters were completely overwhelmed, taking massive losses during the ensuing retreat. Polish sources claim that only 35 or 40 reiters managed to flee to safety in Poznań. Opaliński's men captured up to 14 flags and many Swedish officers. When the regiment of regular national cavalry of Aleksander Koniecpolski, despatched with a relief mission by Czarniecki,

---

364 Bobiatyński, *Od Smoleńska do Wilna. Wojna Rzeczypospolitej z Moskwą 1654-1655*, p.91.
365 Wimmer, *Wojsko polskie w drugiej połowie XVII wieku*, pp.93–95.
366 'With all splendour'.
367 *Pamiętniki Samuela i Bogusława Kazimierza Maskiewiczów*, p.259.

Scattered in different sources, we can find some information about the artillery support provided to the Polish and Lithuanian army during their campaigns. Foreign infantry tended to use regimental cannons, although it is difficult to estimate the correct number of these per unit. Even such a large encounter as the three-day Battle of Warsaw in 1656 saw a fairly small use of artillery, with 18 heavier field pieces deployed on the batteries alongside the foreign infantry, probably with further regimental guns attached directly to the regiments. When the majority of the Polish field army marched against the Muscovites and Cossacks in the summer of 1660, it was initially accompanied by only 10 cannons (four 6-pdrs and six 3-pdrs), with eight wagons with ammunition.[361] In mid-September, General of Artillery Fromhold von Ludingshausen Wolff brought with him a further, unspecified number of cannons, five mortars and 60 large wagons with ammunition.[362] Finally, on 1 October, Jan Zamoyski, with a mix of the his *komput* and private troops, joined the army; they were accompanied by 'some field pieces and ammunition'.[363] At the same time, Czarniecki's division, supporting the Lithuanian army, did not have any artillery at all, although this could be explained by the solely mounted character of his command, composed of just cavalry and dragoons. While one source mentioned Czarniecki's dragoons being supported by two small pieces (possibly regimental cannons) during the battle at Połonka, it is not described by other sources, so it is difficult to judge how accurate it could be. Meanwhile, Gordon wrote about Polish dragoons being assisted by regimental guns in the Ukrainian theatre of the war during the same year, so it is possible that some infantry-owned guns were temporarily attached to dragoons if needed. In all though, artillery had a very low impact on the military actions of the Commonwealth's armies during the war, being used rarely and in small quantities.

Levy of Nobility and District Units: Enlisted Cavalry, Lan Cavalry and Lan Infantry

On paper, the available number of levy was high, but, in practice, many nobles did not want to serve in military capacity and those that did decide to arrive often were in poor shape, lacking equipment and the proper will to fight. In theory, levy should have been raised as *viritim*, which means that all nobles from the region were to be present. As we will see in historical examples, more often than that, nobles decided to replace it with a choice of armed men, based on the ownership of the land, or instead raised district troops, paid from specially agreed taxes. In July 1654, in the face of the Muscovite invasion, Jan Kazimierz sent out a call to arms known as *wici*, asking the Lithuanian levy of nobility to gather. It should have provided Hetman Radziwiłł with up to 23,000 armed men, but, of course, they never gathered

---

361 *Diary of General Patrick Gordon*, vol. II, p.68.
362 *Diary of General Patrick Gordon*, vol. II, p.73.
363 *Diary of General Patrick Gordon*, vol. II, p.80.

LANCES, SABRES AND MUSKETS

and had 62 horses.[357] In the second campaign of 1649, the artillery staff was composed of a captain and a petardier with only two cannoneers, supported by just two assistants and 60 horses.[358] No surprise that the Lithuanian artillery had very a minimal impact on any military actions. During the siege of Mohylew in 1655, Janusz Radziwiłł complained about the poor skills of his artillerymen, writing in his letter that 'crews and all officials [officers] of this artillery are so poor and practically useless, as during the whole assault only one grenade [cannonball] hit the city, while other overshot or fall too short, hitting our own men'.[359] When taking part in a blockade of the Swedish field army between the Vistula and San rivers in spring 1656, the Lithuanian division under Sapieha had only two small cannons, so it is not surprising that it was severely outclassed by the Swedish artillery when Charles X Gustav's troops managed to break through the blockade.[360]

Cracow in August 1657, defended by Swedish and Transylvanian troops, under siege from the Polish and Imperial armies. Isidor Affeita, between 1657 and 1675 (Herzog August Bibliothek Wolfenbüttel: Graph. A2:1).

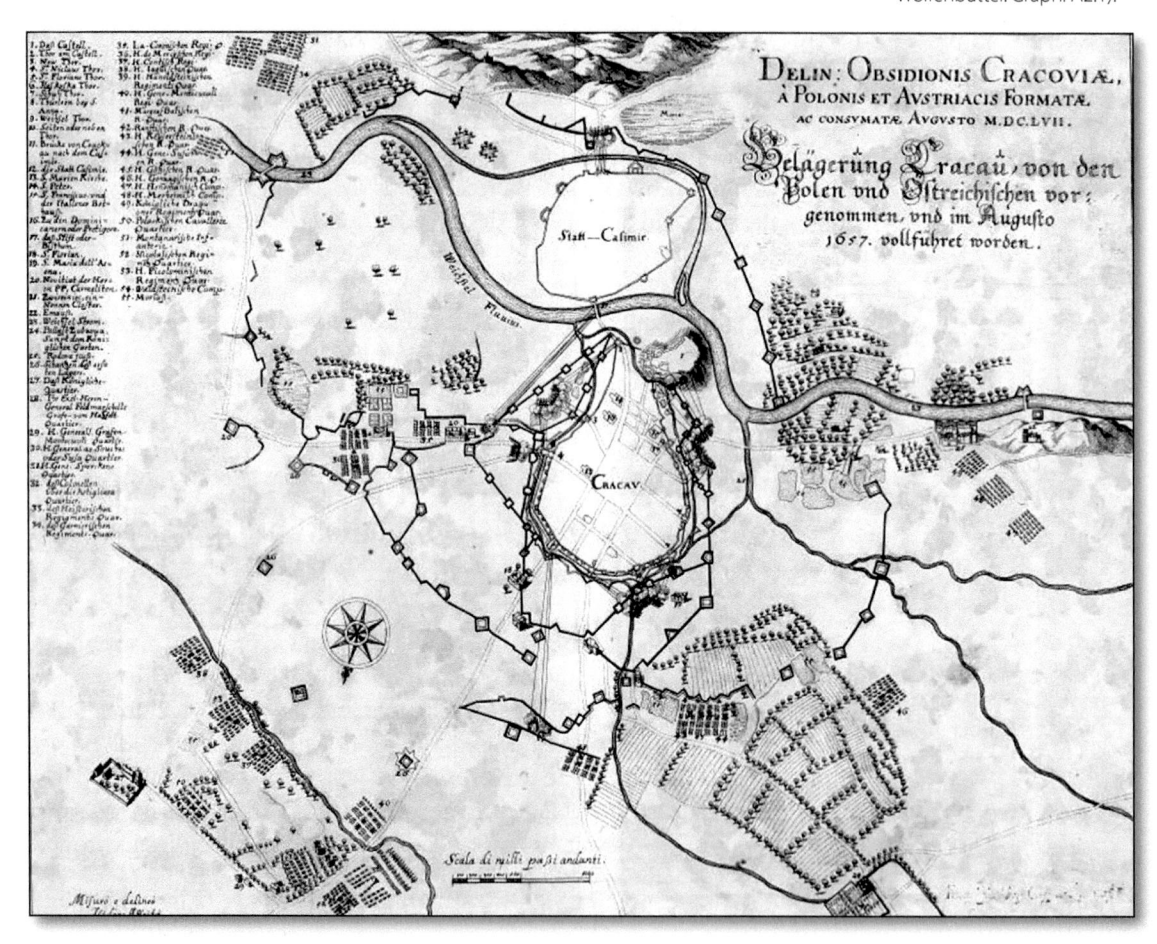

---

357 *Korespondencja wojskowa hetmana Janusza Radziwiłła w latach 1646-1655*, vol. I, *Diariusz kancelaryjny 1649-1653*, pp.359–60.
358 *Korespondencja wojskowa hetmana Janusza Radziwiłła w latach 1646-1655*, vol. I, *Diariusz kancelaryjny 1649-1653*, pp.359–60.
359 Bobiatyński, *Od Smoleńska do Wilna. Wojna Rzeczypospolitej z Moskwą 1654-1655*, p.139.
360 Jemiołowski, *Pamiętnik dzieje Polski zawierający*, p.192.

the *Sejm*, agreed on 19 May 1655, so-called 'lan' (*łanowe*) troops were to be raised from Polish voivodeships and lands. From each 15 *łan*[372] or *włók*[373] of land, there would be one infantryman, equipped with a 'matchlock musket, sabre, axe, gunpowder, bullets, match, with [enough] food for half a year', with the 'colour [of the uniforms] as per decision agreed on *sejmiki*'. As part of their military obligation, large towns were to raise one man for each 25 houses, smaller towns one from each 35, while the smallest one from each 50 houses. Only miners working in places like Bochnia, Wieliczka and Olkusz, were excluded from being used as military force. Local *sejmiki* were to nominate officers, who would be leading units raised in such a matter. The clergy, 'in time of danger for Homeland', was to raise one infantryman from each 15 *łan* of their lands.[374] Levy of nobility was to be raised, as per royal prerogative, with the typical annotation that it would not serve outside of the country. Certain officials, especially bishops, were exempt from taking part in the levy in person, although they were still obliged to send retinues as per their land obligations.[375]

Due to the dangerous situation, with both Muscovite and Swedish aggression, it was also decided that each of the royal (crown) lands in Lithuania would raise one infantryman from each 20 *włók*, armed and equipped in the same manner as those from the lan infantry in Poland. The units were to be led by officers chosen from amongst the nobles living in their lands and to be attached to the Lithuanian levy of nobility.[376] *Wybraniecka* infantry was to be used as well, especially to supplement the defence against the Swedes. The Lithuanian levy of nobility was to look different than usual, as, by May 1655, a large part of the country was already under Muscovite control. As such, the Voivodeships of Połock, Witebsk and Mścisław, alongside five separate districts, were excluded from their levy obligation. Because many towns were also lost, it lowered the overall number of infantry that could be raised as part of their obligation.

Krzysztof Opaliński (1609-1655), Voivode of Poznań. He was one of the commanders of the Polish army at Ujście and a signatory of the surrender of Wielkopolska to Swedes. Portrait by Lucas Vorsterman (Muzeum Narodowe, Kraków).

---

372 Old Polish field measurement. Depending on the region, it could be between 17.9 to 28 hectares.
373 Another old Polish field measurement. Depending on the region, it could be between 7.6 and 17.9 hectares.
374 *Volumina Legum*, vol. IV, p.222.
375 *Volumina Legum*, vol. IV, pp.222–23.
376 *Volumina Legum*, vol. IV, p.224.

It was decided that, in total, only 400 infantry 'with good equipment' would be required, although 100 of them, alongside local levy of nobility, was to be deployed as the defence of Vilnus. Lithuanian Tatars, as per their military obligation, were to join the military effort as well. In the same manner as in Poland, certain officials were allowed to be absent from the levy but were still obliged to despatch their retinues, as per land obligation.[377]

There were also additional decrees and orders issued specifically to regions or towns. According to a royal decree from May 1655, in order to face the Swedes, Cracow was to raise its own force under the command of army officers. One man was to be sent out for each two tenement houses or houses in the city proper and four tenement houses or houses in the suburbia. The soldiers were to be 'in foreign style', armed with matchlock muskets. The King added that, if someone was able to raise more men 'for the defence of the Homeland', he was welcome to do so. Cracow's infantry would be then added to the other local units, most likely to łan infantry.[378]

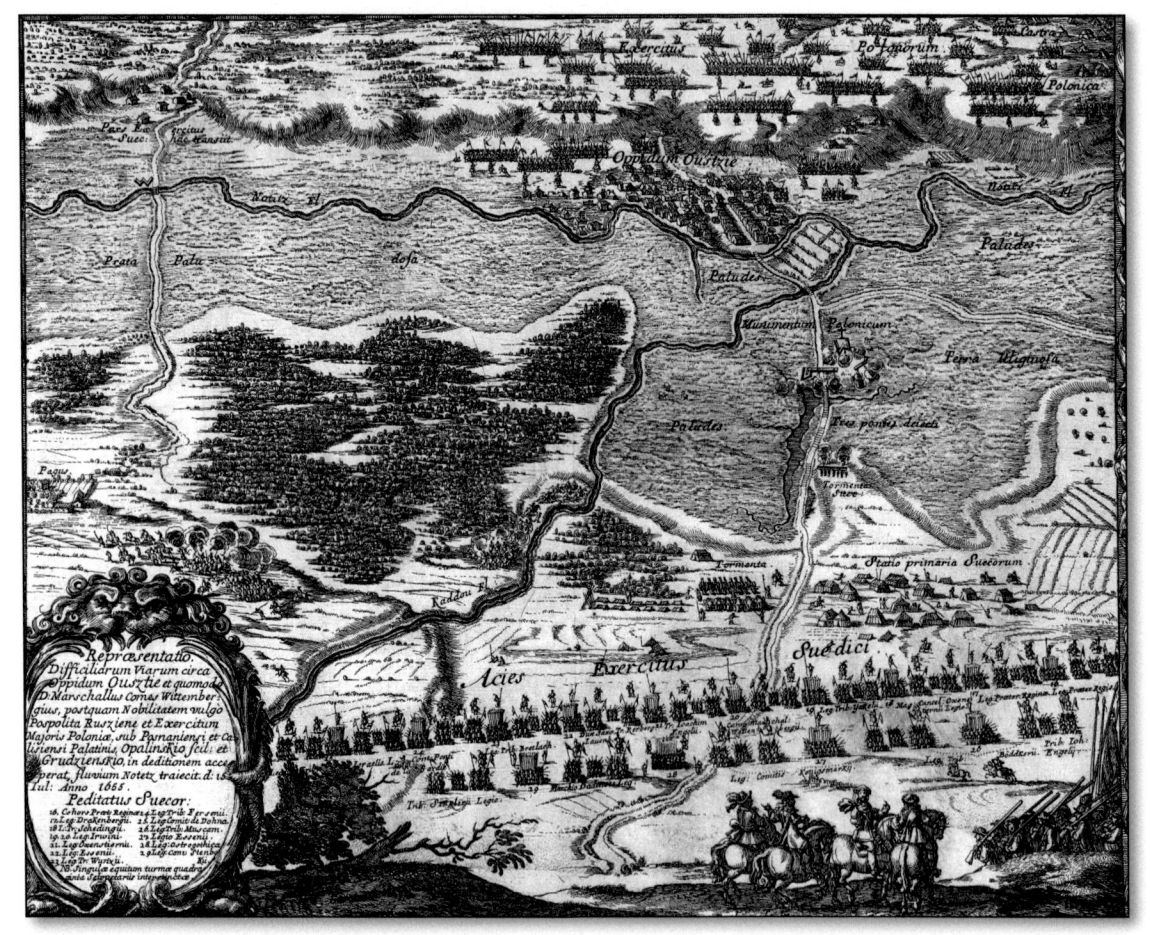

Swedish and Polish forces at Ujście in 1655. Engraving by Willem Swidde, based on Erik Dahlbergh's drawing for Samuel Pufendorf's *De rebus a Carolo Gustavo Sueciae rege gestis*, published in 1696 (Biblioteka Narodowa, Warszawa).

---

377 *Volumina Legum*, vol. IV, p.229.
378 Archiwum Narodowe w Krakowie, Zbiór dokumentów papierowych, no. 658, document 545, pp.1–2.

The Tyszowce Confederation, signed by the Polish army and nobles on 29 December 1655, was an all-out call for war against the Swedes. Two days later, the gathering of nobles there issued a document about levy of nobility, providing very detailed information on what conditions it should be gathered. It was to take the form of lan cavalry, with soldiers provided based on the number of *łan* of the land owned. Each noble, 'whether he was settled or not, should have as many sons as possible ready for war, the best they can and with what [equipment] they can'.[379] From each five *łan* of the land he owned, a noble was to send one horseman 'with good weapons'. The number of such soldiers was to depend on the amount of land owned: if a noble had only two or three *łan*, he was to combine it with a neighbour in order to equip one man. If a magnate or noble had lands in a few voivodeships, he was to combine them all and send the total equivalent of soldiers for the unit of one chosen voivodeship. Towns and newly located villages were to get one man from every 15 houses. Soldiers raised in this way, whether cavalry or infantry, were known as 'chimney-smoke' ones.[380] Particularly interesting, any noble that was banished from the country, had penalty of infamy on him or was in prison, was also to serve as part of this all-noble military obligation. Catholic and Orthodox clergy, with some exceptions, were to send their armed substitutes from every five *łan* or 15 houses. In the same way, noble widows and minors (left without adult kin) were to send their armed replacements. Any non-nobles that were using grounds 'in land of King, clergy or nobility', either as part of their privileges, rent or special allowance, also had to equip one man per the same area of land as the nobles. Settlers that lived on land on the rights of fief or as free boyars were to arrive in person. Anyone having a lease (*arenda*) on a wide variety of businesses (from distilleries to mines) was to send a 'horseman with good weapons' for every 10,000 zł worth of business, with smaller merchants combining in twos or threes to equip one man. The stewards of magnate and noble estates were to 'arrive themselves or send good retinue'. The elderly and sick were to send 'appropriate retinue' by the judgment of the local commissioner of their voivodeship or land. As the army was always in need of artillery, as part of this levy obligation, each voivodeship was to 'provide as many cannons and cannon balls at is had lands or districts'. In each voivodeship, Jews were to take care of the powder and lead, delivering a pound of each for every male Jew in the region. Infantry, 'as it was badly needed', was raised as a 'chimney-smoke' measure, with one man 'with musket, all equipment [required] for war and food'. Soldiers were to be raised in a ratio of one man to 10 'chimneys' (houses), whether they were from royal, noble or clergy lands, also from larger and smaller towns. Additionally, all lan infantry that was created in voivodeships in the spring or summer of 1655 were to continue their half-year service period.[381]

---

379 *Jakuba Michałowskiego, wojskiego lubelskiego a później kasztelana bieckiego Księga Pamiętnicza* (Kraków: Drukarnia C.K. Uniwersytetu, 1864), pp.792–93.
380 From the Polish word '*dym*', which means 'smoke'. One house had one chimney, so it was normal that, for the purposes of raising troops, one house equalled one *dym*.
381 *Jakuba Michałowskiego, wojskiego lubelskiego a później kasztelana bieckiego Księga Pamiętnicza*, pp.792–95.

AGAINST THE DELUGE

Nadziak-armed horsemen. Stefano della Bella, 1651 (Rijksmuseum).

In October 1656, a gathering of nobles from Poznań and Kalisz Voivodeships, so from the Wielkopolska region, decided to raise levy of nobility from their area, as per royal decree. They agreed that everyone who owned lands in those two voivodeships, without any exceptions (so including clergy, widows and orphaned minors) were to send one horseman, armed with a 'pair of pistols, bandolet and all required military equipment'. Three or four such soldiers were to be grouped into a retinue, with one – either volunteer or chosen – to be a companion. Poorer nobles were to group together in threes and send 'one well-armed horseman', while some were allowed to serve as companions themselves. Lands were to choose the officers in charge of the levy units. A *rotmistrz* was to have a banner of no more than 100 horses, while a colonel was allowed 150 horses. If some nobles from the area were already in the regular army, they were to stay with their units and to reinforce their retinue by one horseman, as per the agreement. Lan infantry was to be raised as per a decree issued after the Tyszowce Confederation, with soldiers 'well equipped, with musket, bullets and three pounds of powder'. Interestingly, though, clergy was obliged to send one extra soldier for every 10 chimneys. Areas that still had a strong presence were to send either one horseman or one infantryman, as per the overall rules issued for both voivodeships. Magnates and nobles that had private troops were asked to join the levy to reinforce its strength. The lands had one month to raise the soldiers and send them to muster. Local priests were to read this proclamation in their parishes so that as many people as possible could hear about it.[382] Overall, it is a very interesting document, as it shows how levy and lan infantry were to be organised in the provinces with a still-strong Swedish presence.

Levy from various regions took part in the siege that led to the capture of Warsaw and in the later three-day battle in 1656. Between 25,000 and 30,000 of them were present during the siege of the capitol, where of course they did not play an important role, although their presence was a clear indication of the support for Jan II Kazimierz. Amongst those present were levies from the Voivodeships of Wielkopolska, Sieradz, Łęczyca, Mazowsze, Cracow, Sandomierz, Lublin, Podlasie, Ruthenia, Volhynia and Bełz.[383] A large part of them returned home after capturing Warsaw, so it is estimated that approximately 10,000 to 13,000 were present during the battle on 28–30

---

382 AGAD, Zbiór Anny z Potockich Ksawerowej Branickiej, no. 5, 338, pp.475–81.
383 Nagielski, *Bitwa pod Warszawą 1656*, pp.242–43.

July 1656.³⁸⁴ Some units of levy of nobility paid a heavy price during the retreat after the third day of the Battle of Warsaw, when they were scattered by Swedish and Brandenburg reiters near Skaryszow. While a part of the levy managed to flee without problem, others were pushed into Nadwiśle, an area near the Vistula river, where 'in the bogs and creeks they lost many men'. Badly affected was Bełz Voivodeship, which lost almost 80 important nobles, some of whom were taken prisoners while others were '[stuck] in the mud and the bog were shot [at] like ducks with pistols and carbines'.³⁸⁵ The levy from Sandomierz Voivodeship fought bravely during the retreat, and their standard-bearer, Marcin Dembicki, saved Hetman Potocki's life, but they lost 19 killed companions.³⁸⁶

Polish envoys led by Krzysztof Przyjemski in front of King Karl X Gustav, August 1655. Detail from Erik Dahlbergh's drawing for Samuel Pufendorf's *De rebus a Carolo Gustavo Sueciae rege gestis*, published in 1696 (Biblioteka Narodowa, Warszawa).

When looking into lan troops and the way they were raised and organised, they could of course vary from region to region. For example, in April 1655, a part of Ruthenian Voivodeship³⁸⁷ decided that there should be one haiduk raised from each 10 *łan* and from every 20 houses in larger and 30 houses in smaller towns of the voivodeship. Each land was to create one banner, under the command of the chosen *rotmistrz*: Jakub Orzechowski for Lwów, Piestrzewski for Przemyśl and Dzięciołowski for Sanok. There was a plan for uniforms as well, 'with blue *żupan*, red coat and with sheepskin coat (*kożuch*) in case they had to [still] fight in winter'. Each haiduk was to be armed with a matchlock musket, with 10 pounds of gunpowder and 'enough lead [for bullets]'. For every five haiduks, there would be a supply wagon with enough food to last them for half a year and engineering equipment like spades and hoes.³⁸⁸ In July 1655, the same Ruthenian *sejmik* issued another

---

384 Nagielski, *Bitwa pod Warszawą 1656*, p.243.
385 Jemiołowski, *Pamiętnik dzieje Polski zawierający*, p.211.
386 Kochowski, *Lata Potopu 1655-1657*, pp.206–07.
387 The territorial units (known as lands) of Lwów, Przemyśl and Sanok.
388 *Akta grodzkie i ziemskie z czasów Rzeczypospolitej Polskiej*, vol. XXI, p.163.

call for lan infantry, this time with one haiduk from each 15 łan, with the same specifications for equipment and uniform.[389] While the sabre is not mentioned amongst the equipment, it is more than likely that all the soldiers were equipped with it, as it was customary for this type of infantry. In February 1656, when the Ruthenian *sejmik* issued the call for levy of nobility, it requested the haiduks accompanying tabor wagons to have a 'musket, sabre and axe'.[390] Interestingly enough, another part of Ruthenian Voivodeship, Halicz Land, which had its own local *sejmik*, issued a different recruitment order for its lan infantry, which was supposed to raise one man per each 10 łan. In two documents, one from April and the other from July 1655, the soldiers are mentioned as musketeers, with a foreign type of clothing. They were supposed to have German-style balandran (known as a *palendrak* in Poland) coloured blue and with lining made from white, thick cloth known as *kir*, also with six white buttons. Weaponry included a matchlock musket with 10 pounds of gunpowder and 20 pounds of lead, a sabre and an axe. As with other units of that kind, there was also the request for hoes and spades so soldiers could be used as engineering units if needed. For every five musketeers, there was to be a one-horse wagon with enough food to last for two quarters of service.[391] Notably, one part of Halicz Land, District of Trembowla, due to heavy war damage, received special dispensation and was allowed to raise a smaller, very specific number of men. The nobles were to put together the pay for two musketeers, while 12 towns in the district had to raise six men in total.[392] The nobles from Przemyśl and Sanok lands decided to focus on raising cavalry, agreeing in June 1655 for district troops 'in cossack style, in [chain]mail, *misiurka*, arm-guards, armed with bandolet and pistols'. Only town and local Jews were to finance raising infantry, armed with muskets, match, powder, bullets, spades (tool) and enough provisions. Haiduks were to be clothed in blue *żupan* and red *delia* coats.[393]

Very detailed was the regulation of raising lan infantry from the Voivodeships of Poznań and Kalisz.[394] It was signed in late April 1655 and specified that the soldiers from the region should be 'clothed well' and equipped with sabres, muskets, a minimum of two pounds of powder, 40 bullets and food for the time of service. Especially interesting, each district (*powiat*) specified what colour of clothing should be prepared for its troops:

---

389 *Akta grodzkie i ziemskie z czasów Rzeczypospolitej Polskiej*, vol. XXI, p.171.
390 *Akta grodzkie i ziemskie z czasów Rzeczypospolitej Polskiej*, vol. XXI, p.186.
391 *Akta grodzkie i ziemskie z czasów Rzeczypospolitej Polskiej*, vol. XXIV, pp.116, 119.
392 *Akta grodzkie i ziemskie z czasów Rzeczypospolitej Polskiej*, vol. XXIV, p.122.
393 Stanisław Szczotka, *Chłopi obrońcami niepodległej Polski w okresie potopu* (Kraków: Spółdzielnia Wydanicza "Wieś", 1946), p.24.
394 Staręgowski, *Formacje zbrojne samorządu szlacheckiego województw poznańskiego i kaliskiego w okresie panowania Jana Kazimierza (1648-1668)*, pp.145–47.

LANCES, SABRES AND MUSKETS

District or land	Colour of *żupan*	Colour of outer garment: *delia* or *katanka*
Poznań	White	Red
Kościan	Blue	Red
Wschów Land and district of Wałcz	Blue	Blue
Kalisz	Red	Red
Konin	Red	Blue
Pyzdry	White	Blue
Gniezno	Red	Green
Kcynia	White	Green
Nakło	Blue	Blue

Rather unusual was the unit raised as lan infantry by Sandomierz Voivodeship in spring–summer 1655.[395] The unit was a unique blend of Western and Eastern influences, as it was named a regiment but was divided into four banners of 100 men each. Each banner was under the command of a *rotmistrz*: Andrzej Gnoiński (who was also the overall colonel of the regiment), Jerzy Janiszewski, Adam Pozowski and Walenty Skotnicki. The regiment had small headquarters, with a colonel, captain, surgeon and chaplain. Each banner had a *rotmistrz*, lieutenant, standard-bearer, two sergeants and two corporals. The soldiers, called 'haiduks' (like those from Polish infantry) were to be equipped with matchlock muskets, sabres and axes. Each haiduk was to have 50 fathoms of musket fuse, 10 pounds of powder and 10 pounds of lead. The local *sejmik* even provided very detailed instructions about the uniforms of the planned unit. Each haiduk was to have a blue *żupan* and a red coat (*katanka*) with lining from *kir* and blue ornaments, along with 'red hooded German caps' (probably a Montero cap or *kapuza*). If any of the nobles owning the land from where the recruits were sent to the unit were willing, they could provide haiduks with a *delia* outer garment, 'as long as it was blue'. Each soldier was to receive food for half of a year, which was carried on the tabor wagons. There was one such cart (with two carriage horses) per five haiduks, where next to the food there would be two scythes, two hoes and three spades for all the engineering work that the soldiers could be used for. The regiment even had, again in a rather Western-style, four small cannons, provided by owner of a large ironworks Giovanni Gibboni.[396] The regiment took part in the defence of Cracow, where one of

---

395 Wimmer, *Wojsko polskie w drugiej połowie XVII wieku*, pp.90–91.
396 In the 1630s and 1640s, he built a large ironworks complex known as the manufacture of Bobrza and Samsonów, where, next to ironworks and hammer mills, he had three ore mines. A large part of his production was focused on weapons, from cannons to muskets and other hand weapons. For his achievements in the field, he was ennobled by the *Sejm* in 1654.

the eyewitnesses interestingly noted that the haiduks used covers of badgers' fur for their muskets.[397]

If, due to the direct danger to the land or the changing military situation, troops had to be raised much quicker, this could lead to particular changes in requirements. On 15 January 1657, Przemyśl and Sanok Lands required the formation of haiduk infantry units to work on fortifications and to garrison Przemyśl and Krosno. This time, all the estates in the region, including those owned by the king and clergy, had to send one haiduk per village, as it was seen as an emergency situation. The soldiers were to be equipped with a 'good musket, sabre, hoe, spade, enough food for quarter of the year, five pounds of gunpowder, three pounds of lead and as much match as needed'. The instructions specified that there was no need for uniforms, so each haiduk would be in his own clothing.[398] As mentioned, though, this was an unusual case, especially considering that the hastily raised troops had to 'be mustered by next Thursday, for four days', highlighting the danger that both cities were in. Additionally, each haiduk was to be provided by the noble that sent him with 5 zł for further purchases of gunpowder, lead and match. There is an interesting list of haiduks raised to defend Przemyśl, dated 26 January 1657, so 11 days after the initial request to raise this unit. There were 215 men, sent by 96 magnates, nobles and clergymen. Most of them, owning just one village, sent just one haiduk, although the wealthiest ones dug deeper into their own coffers, sending six, eight, nine (two of them) or even 16 haiduks.[399] Of course, one had to think about the quality of such a hastily raised force and how effectively such an *ad hoc* banner could fulfil its role as a garrison. It could at least serve as a support or, in some conditions, replacement for the regular troops, freeing them from garrison service.

Sometimes, regions could combine together to raise joint provincial troops. In October 1655, the nobles from Brześć Kujawski Voivodeship and Inowrocław Voivodeship decided to pay for provincial troops to protect them from the constant raids of Swedish patrols and garrisons. Their plan was to raise two banners of cossack cavalry (200 horses each) under *Rotmistrz* Stanisław Działyński and *Rotmistrz* Stefan Jaranowski and 220 haiduk infantry (based on the soldiers raised in summer 1655 as łan infantry) in one banner under *Rotmistrz* Wnorowski. Działyński was additionally nominated as colonel, in overall command of

An example of a Polish horseman armed with a bow and *bandolet* gun. Such a combination would not be used during a campaign, though, but it is interesting to see how the gun was worn by raiders. Stefano della Bella, 1651 (Rijksmuseum).

---

397 Kochowski, *Historya panowania Jana Kazimierza*, vol. I, p.237.
398 *Akta grodzkie i ziemskie z czasów Rzeczypospolitej Polskiej*, vol. XXI, p.211.
399 *Akta grodzkie i ziemskie z czasów Rzeczypospolitej Polskiej*, vol. XXI, pp.215–17.

all three units. The order to create these troops and the plan on how much money would need to be raised for them were very detailed. They specified that the officers of provincial banners 'are obliged to defend us from the enemies and with constant patrols oppose them, guarding watchfully from all sides, so our belongings and villages are free from enemy incursions and pillaging'. Documents mentioned where each unit was to be stationed, detailing all the villages that were supposed to provide provisions for troops and, if soldiers were to be kept in service for longer, winter quarters as well.[400]

In autumn 1654, in order to supplement the Lithuanian regular army, local *sejmiki* decided that each district that did not gather their levy of nobility would be required to raise four banners of district troops: one each of hussars, cossack cavalry, reiters and infantry (probably haiduks). Most likely, each of those banners would have 100 horses or portions.[401] While such a plan looked good on paper, there were low chances to make it work. The lack of funds, men and equipment, alongside the large territorial losses due to the fast approach of the Muscovite armies, meant that many districts were unable or unwilling to raise a sufficient number of soldiers. To make things even worse, on some occasions, the gathered nobles had problems on agreeing what formation should be raised for their district troops. Vorbek-Lettow mentioned that the nobles from Vilnius District, gathered on a general muster of levy of nobility at the end of August 1654, could not decide '[as] some for [agreed tax money] wanted to raise 120 horses of cossack cavalry, other [wanted] dragoons while other [wanted] reiters'. Finally, Jan Denhoff suggested that, if given 17,000 zł from tax money, he could – in addition to using his own funds – 'in three Sundays [weeks] raise 120 good and well-armed reiters and take them to Mińsk to [serve under] Hetmans'.[402] Of course, as always, there was a problem with the delivery of the agreed upon money. On 19 October, Denhoff was still refusing to march to join the army, as he was lacking 6,000 zł from the promised 17,000.[403] In total, in 1655, 12 districts and lands of Lithuania that were not occupied by the Muscovites or stood only as levy of nobility were to raise 2,705 horses of district troops,[404] mostly hussars and cossack cavalry. As part of this obligation, Novogródek District raised 300 horses, including one 100-horse-strong banner of hussars, while Oszmiana District and Samogitia raised 500 horses each.[405]

Typically, district troops were recruited for a short period of time, usually one or two quarters. For example, in September 1656, the nobles from Przemyśl Land (a part of Ruthenian Voivodeship) decided to pay for 'enlisted soldiers with good equipment [which should be] 150 horses [serving as] cossack cavalry', but the unit was to serve only for one quarter starting from

---

400 *Rządy sejmikowe w epoce królów elekcyjnych 1572-1795. T.2. Lauda i instrukcye 1572-1674* (Warszawa: Druk Józefa Bergera, 1888), pp.64–67.
401 Bobiatyński, *Od Smoleńska do Wilna. Wojna Rzeczypospolitej z Moskwą 1654-1655*, p.92.
402 Vorbek-Lettow, *Skarbnica pamięci*, p.195.
403 Vorbek-Lettow, *Skarbnica pamięci*, p.202.
404 Plus four banners raised by Vilnius District – their strength is unknown.
405 Rachuba, 'Wysiłek mobilizacyjny Wielkiego Księstwa Litewskiego w latach 1654-1667', pp.47–48.

its muster day.⁴⁰⁶ The situation dictated the prolonging of this service, though, so the banner was financed by Przemyśl Land as late as the end of April 1657. Another part of the same voivodeship, Sanok Land, had in service a banner of 100 dragoons, sent to serve for one quarter as a part of the regular army (under the command of Lubomirski, besieging Cracow) and, additionally, a small banner of 50 haiduks to protect their territory from bandits and marauders.⁴⁰⁷ Halicz Land, in May 1657, raised a banner of 100 horses, most likely cossack cavalry, to defend 'more easily against sudden enemy raids'. However, the *sejmik* in its instructions demanded that the *rotmistrz* of this unit needed to ensure that none of the companions would serve in a retinue stronger than three horses.⁴⁰⁸ Such a request was not unusual, though, as it was a way to have a higher number of companions (i.e., the best part of the unit) present in the ranks. At the same time, the nobles decided to give a special pay of 500 zł to the *rotmistrz* so that he could serve with a fully manned retinue and would not use it as 'dead pay' in the same way as it was custom in regular army units. In June 1657, the unit was split into two smaller banners, 50 horses each, to better 'protect from bandits' attacks'.⁴⁰⁹ As these units were to be used purely as a defensive force, in June 1657, Halicz Land's *sejmik* decided to pay for 200 'dragoons trained in foreign style' that would be serving in the regular army as a unit of Starosta of Halicz, Andrzej Potocki. As with many provincial units, it was to initially serve for one quarter, but the *sejmik* added an additional paragraph to their document, in which they stated that the dragoons could stay in service for longer, if required, and the nobles of Halicz Land would continue paying for it.⁴¹⁰

Another and a rather unusual way of raising a new unit came from Ruthenian Voivodeship. In April 1658, instead of lan infantry, the local *sejmik* decided to raise and finance 'with good officers [a regiment] serving in foreign style for half of the year, [armed] with matchlock muskets, without any specific uniforms, just to clothe soldiers and supply them well with food … gunpowder and lead', allowing for the recruitment in the whole voivodeship.⁴¹¹ While Jews normally were obliged to only defend the city they lived in as a part of a militia, we know about one unusual case when they raised a unit of cavalry. Maciej Vorbek-Lettow mentioned that, in summer 1654, when Vilnius was in danger from the approaching Muscovite army, 'it happened (what no one heard before) that even Jews under their own banner … raised 130 willing and well-armed and equipped Jews'.⁴¹² It is possible that it was a banner in the cossack cavalry style, as the diarist mentioned it being sent out as part of a reconnaissance mission. Even clergy could sometimes help with the military effort, financing their own unit. In summer 1654, Jesuits from Vilnius raised a banner of dragoons that was 'in uniforms and

---

406 *Akta grodzkie i ziemskie z czasów Rzeczypospolitej Polskiej*, vol. XXI, p.198.
407 *Akta grodzkie i ziemskie z czasów Rzeczypospolitej Polskiej*, vol. XXI, p.205.
408 *Akta grodzkie i ziemskie z czasów Rzeczypospolitej Polskiej*, vol. XXIV, p.131.
409 *Akta grodzkie i ziemskie z czasów Rzeczypospolitej Polskiej*, vol. XXIV, pp.133–34.
410 *Akta grodzkie i ziemskie z czasów Rzeczypospolitej Polskiej*, vol. XXIV, pp.132–33.
411 *Akta grodzkie i ziemskie z czasów Rzeczypospolitej Polskiej*, vol. XXI, pp.230–32.
412 Vorbek-Lettow, *Skarbnica pamięci*, p.184.

with good weapons' and that served alongside the regular army.⁴¹³ Another company of dragoons, this time under the name 'Discalced Carmelites of Vilnius', was serving in the Lithuanian army in 1661, probably as a volunteer unit paid by monks.⁴¹⁴

District troops were often frowned upon by regular soldiers, who saw them as lower quality troops. It is possible that there was an element of jealousy here as well, as district soldiers tended to receive a larger pay than regulars and it tended to be paid on time. Joachim Jerlicz noted, in September 1653, that Wołyń Voivodeship was paying 100 zł per quarter to its district cavalry while other regions paid even more, with some giving 150 zł and some even 200 zł per quarter.⁴¹⁵ Furthermore, units raised by districts, especially when just freshly formed, could often suffer from 'weak spirits' and high desertion rates. Pasek mentioned that, when Czarniecki's division was to cross the Polish border to Brandenburg, on its way to Denmark in 1658, a large number of soldiers from the recently created provincial banners from Wielkopolska left the ranks. *Rotmistrz* Kozubski was to be left with just the standard-bearer and one companion of his banner; in other units, there were only two to three companions left. Even when taking into account Pasek's clear disregard to those new soldiers, which could affect the real scale of the desertion that he described in his diaries, we can still understand why such units, created to defend their own regions, could be unwilling to take part in a campaign abroad, especially against battle-hardened Swedish troops led by the King himself.⁴¹⁶ Unfortunately, desertion was a common problem within district troops, especially once soldiers received their initial payment. The cossack banner under Jan Tryzna, raised by the Lithuanian district of Wołkowysk, had on its initial muster on 24 December 1654 only 58 from its paper strength of 100 horses. What is worse, even the *Rotmistrz* himself never joined the unit, and 14 companions left the ranks as soon as they were paid.⁴¹⁷ Albrycht Stanisław Radziwiłł noted, in September 1654, that Lithuanian district troops took a very long time to raise and be battle ready: the hussars and cossack cavalry raised in Kowno were gathered after four months. Moreover, they were pillaging the local population so much that, 'instead of being called soldiers, they should be called robbers and brutes.'⁴¹⁸

A Polish noble with yet another example of a weapon often used as a cane: the *czekan* (hammer-axe). Stefano della Bella, 1651 (Biblioteka Narodowa, Warszawa).

---

413 Vorbek-Lettow, *Skarbnica pamięci*, p.197.
414 See Appendix V.
415 Jerlicz, *Latopisiec albo kroniczka*, vol. I, p.149.
416 Pasek, *Pamiętniki*, p.74.
417 AGAD, AR X, 220, pp.3–3v.
418 Albrycht Stanisław Radziwiłł, *Pamiętnik o dziejach w Polsce. Tom 3. 1647-1656* (Warszawa: Państwowy Instytut Wydawniczy, 1980), p.434.

As district troops were better paid and usually had better conditions of service, they could potentially lure soldiers from already existing regular army units. To prevent this, the king could sometimes issue 'reminders' to individual districts or voivodeships. One such document was sent, in the form of instruction, to the envoys of nobles from Wielkopolska in autumn 1656. Jan Kazimierz stated there that 'it is law, to not recruit any men that are already in [army] service'. He also reminded nobles that they should keep district troops as long as it was required and to serve in levy of nobility for as long as district troops were not ready to replace them.[419]

It is worth mentioning, of course, that there were situations when district troops showed themselves from a good side, fighting with great bravery and valour. The hussar banner from Nowogródek Voivodeship under *Rotmistrz* Stefan Frąckiewicz participated in the assault on Mohylew on 16 February 1655, when it was a part of the small cavalry force that broke into the town and managed to retreat from it after heavy fighting. Another district banner that was serving with the Lithuanian army besieging Mohylew, hussars

Polish nobles from the embassy in France in 1645. François Campion, 1645 (*Bibliothèque nationale de France*. Photo by Tomasz Ratyński).

---

419   AGAD, Zbiór Anny z Potockich Ksawerowej Branickiej, no. 5, 338, p.474.

from Lida District (a part of Vilnius Voivodeship) under the command of *Rotmistrz* Jakub Teodor Kuncewicz, took part in the victorious Battle of Domany on 22 February 1655. When, in May 1655, Lithuanian Camp Master Samuel Komorowski led a successful relief mission to Dyneburg besieged by the Muscovites, more than half of his force of 3,000 horses was composed of district troops: 520 hussars and 1,320 cossack cavalry.[420] Some units raised in Poland, especially in Wielkopolska, gathered a lot of experience during campaigns against the Swedes and Brandenburg – some were even converted into regular army units. In overall, though, district troops were a rather expensive substitute for the normal soldiers, adding another layer to the confusing structure of command in the Commonwealth's armies. It is also another example of the difficult financial and tax system of the country, where real power and control was not centralised but lay in the hands of local gatherings of nobles in each district and land.

Wybraniecka Infantry

In theory, this type of infantry should have served equipped in a similar way as haiduks, with muskets, sabres and axes. Already, during the Smoleńsk War in 1632–1634, King Władysław IV relegated *wybraniecka* to engineering duties, directly ordering them to be equipped with engineering tools and without weapons. In later years, they were still being raised as support troops, often used as garrisons and battle engineers. During the Deluge, they saw some units being raised by a few Polish regions, often serving next to łan infantry (at the start of the war) and supporting artillery. In 1650, based on the report of the number of łan available to raise such infantry, there were only 1,103.5 that could be raised and, by 1660, that number dropped to 853.[421] *Wybraniecka* served in regional banners, probably fairly small, rarely exceeding 150 men, as not all regions managed to prepare such units and some had to be combined from two voivodeships. Jan Wimmer, based on documents regarding pay to the officers of the *wybraniecka*, identified the following banners serving in the period of 1655–1660:[422]

---

420 Bobiatyński, *Od Smoleńska do Wilna. Wojna Rzeczypospolitej z Moskwą 1654-1655*, p.197.
421 Wimmer, *Wojsko polskie w drugiej połowie XVII wieku*, p.303.
422 Wimmer, *Wojsko polskie w drugiej połowie XVII wieku*, p.309.

Year	Voivodship(s)	*Rotmistrz*	Notes
1655	Sandomierz	Wawrzyniec Baranowski	
	Mazowsze	Wojciech Korzuchowski	100-150 men
	Royal Prussia	Unknown	Probably serving alongside Ian infantry
1656	Lublin and Bełż (combined)[423]	Andrzej Świdnicki	Świdnicki was also in command of this infantry in 1654[424]
1657	-	-	No information
1658	Cracow and Sandomierz (combined)	Jan Branicki	
	Lublin and Bełż (combined)[425]	Andrzej Świdnicki	
1659	Cracow and Sandomierz (combined)	Jan Branicki	
1660	Cracow and Sandomierz (combined)	Jan Branicki	

Royal Guard: Household Guard and *Komput* Guard

In the early part of the seventeenth century, Polish kings had their own Household Guard (*gwardia przyboczna*), which was the king's private army – paid from his own treasury and, as such, not a part of the regular army establishment. These soldiers accompanied the monarch during campaigns; they also served during ceremonial duties (e.g., protecting the royal castle). In certain circumstances, some part of the guard units could be sent to support the regular army, even if the king himself was not present. For example, when Royal Prince Władysław Waza took part in the Chocim campaign in 1621, he was accompanied by a few dozen of his Scottish guards. During the 1620s, King Sigismund III kept in the service no more than 1,000 guardsmen: between 400 and 600 Hungarian infantry (haiduks), approximately 100 reiters-drabants, one banner of 'Royal Tatar-cossacks' (used to deliver royal mail) of no more than 100 horses and some halberdiers and musicians stationed in Warsaw.[426] Possibly, there was also a company or two of guard dragoons, as we can find them in 1632 as a part of the guard of newly elected King Władysław IV. The beginning of this monarch's reign, who took over the throne during the early stage of the Smoleńsk War, led to

---

423 AGAD, ASK IV, Księga Rekognicji, no 15, p. 68.
424 He received pay for that campaign in February 1654, see: AGAD, ASK IV, Księga Rekognicji, no 15, p. 70.
425 AGAD, ASK IV, Księga Rekognicji, no 15, p. 67.
426 Nagielski, 'Gwardia przyboczna Władysława IV (1632-1648)', pp.115–17.

LANCES, SABRES AND MUSKETS

a large increase of the units of the guard. For the first time, however, some of them were financed by the National Treasury and, despite their 'guard' name, were treated as part of the regular army. Amongst them, we can find a strong regiment of infantry (1,200 portions) under Reinhold Rosen and a strengthened contingent of dragoons (two banners, with a paper strength of 400 portions).[427] These units were disbanded after the war, though. In the mid-1640s, as part of his preparations for war against the Ottomans, Władysław raised a large number of foreign infantry and dragoons, but – due to strong opposition to his military plans – he was forced to disband most of them after the decision of the *Sejm* in December 1646. He was allowed to retain his Household Guard of no more than 1,200 men, all paid for from his own treasury.[428] He did, in fact, keep a slightly larger force. By the end of Władysław's reign in 1648, it was estimated by Polish researcher Mirosław Nagielski as between 1,600 and 1,800 'horses and portions':[429]

- Foot Guard regiment under Colonel Samuel Osiński: 1,200 portions
- Dragoon squadron under Major Teodor Leszkwant: 200 or 300 horses
- Reiters-drabants company: 50–100 horses
- Banner of Tatars–cossacks (known also as 'Cossacks of His Royal Highness') under Jan Turobojski: 50–100 horses
- So-called 'old Hungarian infantry' (haiduks): 50 men
- Halberdiers and musicians based in Royal Castle in Warsaw: a small number

A unit that sometimes is counted amongst the Guard, but one that technically was not a part of the Household Guard, was the so-called 'Court banner' (*chorągiew dworzańska*). It was a hussar banner composed of the royal courtiers, who did not receive pay for their service but financed their own equipment, horses and retinues. While usually just ceremonial troops, it could sometimes accompany the king during a campaign. A 'Court banner' was present in Prussia with Sigismund III in 1626 and 1629, while its last military action took place in 1649, when it fought as part of King Jan II Kazimierz's army at Zborów against the Tatars and Cossacks.

Jan II Kazimierz took over his brother's Guard units when he was crowned King in 1648, and his troops were almost straight away used in campaigns against the Cossacks and Tatars. The Foot Guard regiment under Osiński took heavy losses at the Battle of Piławce, where it lost approximately half of its strength while the remaining soldiers were

King Jan II Kazimierz in Polish clothing and armed with a horseman's pick. Johann Hoffman, 1650's (Author's archive).

---

427 Nagielski, 'Gwardia przyboczna Władysława IV (1632-1648)', p.119.
428 Nagielski, 'Gwardia przyboczna Władysława IV (1632-1648)', p.138.
429 Nagielski, 'Gwardia przyboczna Władysława IV (1632-1648)', p.142.

lacking equipment and weapons.[430] Moreover, due to a lack of royal funds, the regiment was paid for by the National Treasury, which since then became – despite the unhappiness of the local *sejmiki* – the new norm in the rest of the seventeenth century. As we will see later on, even more units bearing the name of 'Royal Guard' became part of the regular army: all of them were known as the *Komput* Guard (*gwardia komputowa*) to differentiate between those paid as part of the regular army and those few still financed by the king as a part of his Household Guard. In 1649, former Lieutenant Colonel of the Foot Guard regiment, Fromhold von Ludinghausen Wolf, took command from Osiński and became the new colonel of the regiment. He led the unit in the Zborów campaign of 1649, although, due to problems with finding enough reinforcements, the regiment was *ad hoc* strengthened by the 300 infantry of Crown Chancellor Jan Ossoliński. In January 1651, the King ordered the enlargement of the regiment from 1,000 to 1,600. In June 1651, this unit mustered as eight companies, with a total strength of 1,259 portions, although it is possible that two further companies were left in Warsaw and did not take part in the campaign.[431] The strength of the companies taking part in the campaign was as follows:[432]

Company's commander	Strength
Colonel Fromhold von Ludinghausen Wolff	144
Lieutenant Colonel Mikołaj Konstanty Giza	163
Major Jan Butler	153
Captain Jan Ratki	152
Captain Jerzy Zimmerman (Cymerman)	162
Captain Mikołaj Kierzbuch (Kielbruch)	162
Captain Wall (Wahl)	161
Captain Wall (Wahl)	162

Another regiment known as a Guard unit was the dragoon unit under Mikołaj Korf. Created in late 1648, it was in service until the end of 1651. In 1649, when taking part in the defence of Zbaraż, it had eight companies of dragoons (100 portions each) and one company of reiters (100 horses). The regiment was reduced to five companies (500 portions) in 1650, but, by the end of the winter–spring campaign in Ukraine, it was even smaller. In June 1651, it mustered just four companies of dragoons, with a total of 235 portions. It fought at Beresteczko (probably also at Biała Cerkiew) in same

---

[430] Nagielski, *Liczebność i organizacja gwardii przybocznej i komputowej za ostatniego Wazy (1648-1668)*, pp.15–16.

[431] Nagielski, *Liczebność i organizacja gwardii przybocznej i komputowej za ostatniego Wazy (1648-1668)*, pp.18–19.

[432] Stanisław Oświęcim, *Dyaryusz 1643-1651* (Kraków: Nakładem Akademii Umiejętności, 1907), p.290; Nagielski, *Liczebność i organizacja gwardii przybocznej i komputowej za ostatniego Wazy (1648-1668)*, p.18.

year, but, in 1652 after the Battle of Batoh, it lost its Guard status. Instead of it, a new regiment, under the command of Lieutenant Colonel Fryderyk Moh, was created. In October 1652, it had 560 portions, and it was divided into six or eight companies.[433] The third unit of the *Komput* Guard was a reiter regiment, under Colonel Henryk von Walenrodt and his brother, Lieutenant Colonel Marcin von Wallenrodt. The regiment created in 1652, after Batoh, was to have a strength of 600 horses (probably six companies). All three Guard regiments took part in the Żwaniec campaign of 1653, where they took – like other foreign troops – high losses due to illnesses and desertion. In autumn 1654, the regiments were sent to support the Lithuanian army in their campaign against the Muscovites.[434] Mohl's dragoons after his death were, from July 1655, under the command of Jan Henryk von Alten Bockum. During the siege of Mohylew, infantry and dragoons took heavy losses, greatly reducing their strength, with Wolff's regiment losing half of its number. In July 1655, the units were recalled to Poland to strengthen the defences against the Swedes. Officers received orders to enlist new men while en route to Poland, to replace the losses. The dragoons under von Alten Bockum were sent to Malbork, which they helped to defend until March 1656. The infantry regiment was marching very slowly towards Warsaw, but they never managed to get there on time prior to the arrival of the Swedes, and instead Wolff's men rejoined the Polish army during its march to Cracow. Wallenrodt's reiters, while also recalled to Poland, were disbanded by him during the march to Poland, and the unit ceased to exist. Many officers and soldiers, including the Colonel himself, switched to service in the Brandenburg army instead.

One company from Wolff's regiment was a part of the Warsaw garrison and did not take part in the campaign at the side of the Lithuanian army.

The Swedish siege of Cracow in October 1655. Erik Dahlbergh's drawing for Samuel Pufendorf's *De rebus a Carolo Gustavo Sueciae rege gestis*, published in 1696 (Muzeum Narodowe, Kraków).

---

433 Nagielski, *Liczebność i organizacja gwardii przybocznej i komputowej za ostatniego Wazy (1648-1668)*, pp.37–40.
434 See Appendix II.

AGAINST THE DELUGE

When, in summer 1655, the Swedes captured Warsaw, they took prisoner this whole company, which was under the command of Captain Jan Guldyn. The 60 men composing this unit were incorporated into the Swedish army, but Guldyn was released and allowed to return to Jan Kazimierz.[435] The rest of Wolff's infantry regiment took part in the defence of Cracow and, after the surrender of the city, was allowed – alongside the rest of the garrison – safe passage to quarters near the Silesian border. The soldiers were allowed to take their weapons and standards, and they marched out from Cracow 'with a sound of fifes and drums'. Based on the agreement with the Swedes, the regiment was allowed to stay in the border quarters until 18 November 1655, after which the soldiers were allowed to go wherever they wanted. In late November, though, to prevent the regiment from returning to the Polish service, the Swedes managed to bribe and convince the soldiers of two companies stationed in Będzin to switch sides. The rest of the regiment – six companies – when marching to Będzin, was surrounded by Swedish reiters and forced to join the Swedish army as well. The unit was taken over by Arvid Wittenber and became his life regiment, under the command of Major Jan Butler. It took part, probably rather unwillingly, in the siege of the monastery at Jasna Góra. Afterwards, the regiment seems to be disbanded, and its soldiers spread between different Swedish mercenary regiments.[436]

The former Polish Foot Guard regiment of King Jan II Kazimierz after changing colours – here in the Swedish army as the Life Regiment of Arvid Wittenberg during the famous siege of Jasna Góra in 1655. Johann Bensheimer, 1659 (Muzeum Narodowe, Kraków).

When King Jan Kazimierz left Poland, he took only a small unit of his Household troops with him. It was either one company of reiters or one company of dragoons from Alten Bockum's regiment, probably no more than 100 horses. All other Guard units were either disbanded or taken over by the Swedes. After his return to Poland, when preparing to retake

---

435 Wagner, *Słownik biograficzny oficerów polskich drugiej połowy XVII wieku*, vol. I, p.113.
436 Nagielski, 'Losy jednostek autoramentu cudzoziemskiego w drugiej połowie 1655 roku (lipiec-grudzień)', pp.139–41.

the country from the Swedes, Jan Kazimierz decided to create many Guard units that were to be a part of the regular army, the so-called '*Komput* Guard'. On one hand, it was part of the overall process of increasing the number of foreign units, seen as important in fighting against the Swedes (especially infantry, needed in siege operations). On the other hand, it helped to create a 'royal party' in the army, with officers and soldiers more directly connected to the Monarch, which could be useful in case of any internal conflicts. The following Guard units were active during the post-1656 period:

- Reiter company, under Captain Franciszek Bieliński, had a maximum strength of 200 horses. In theory, it was part of a Guard dragoon regiment, but in practice it served as an independent unit, providing direct protection to the King and Queen.
- Dragoon regiment under Jan Henryk Bockum, as already mentioned, was active since 1648. It was composed of eight companies, with the regiment size ranging between 730 and 940 horses (depending on the period and scale of losses) but with a paper strength reaching 1,000 horses in 1660. It was a very active unit, fighting in the siege of Warsaw and the Battle of Warsaw in 1656, siege of Cracow in 1657, siege of Toruń in 1658 and operations in Prussia in 1659. In 1660, it took part in the campaign against the Muscovites.
- Foot Guard regiment, under General Major Wilhelm Butler: It was one of three regular army regiments that, in 1655, were part of the garrison of Lwów and were never taken over by the Swedes. As such, Butler's unit became the core of the infantry corps of the rebuilding Polish army in 1656. In summer 1656, it was renamed as Foot Guard regiment, most likely to ensure that such a prestigious title was again 'active' in the army. The regiment took part in the Battle of Warsaw in 1656, siege of Poznań in 1657 and siege of Toruń in 1658. In 1659, it was on garrison duty in Prussia, in Gniew, Nowe and Dirschau. When the last town was captured by the Swedes in March 1659, 300 men from Butler's regiments were taken prisoner. Later, in 1659, the unit was present at the siege of Grudziądz and Gdańska Głowa. Butler died in early 1660, and the regiment was taken over by Stefan Niemirycz, taking part in further operations of the Polish army against the Muscovites. The regiment was probably composed of eight companies, and, in the period of 1656 and 1660, its strength varied between 740 and 1,200 portions. The regiment ceased to use name of 'Foot Guard' at the end of 1661, but it remained in the regular army, under the command of Jan Stachurski.
- Foot Guard regiment under Fromhold von Ludinghausen Wolff: Former commander of Guard infantry, Wolff in 1658 received a royal order to rebuild a Foot Guard, and the unit was initially based on 400 lan infantry from Ruthenian and Volhynia Voivodeships. As such, it seems to have been on their payroll for the whole of 1658, as district troops. It joined the regular army payroll in 1659, so, alongside Butler's regiment, there were in service two regiments of Foot Guard. The regiment took part in the siege of Toruń in 1658, after it was sent to Wielkopolska to increase its size through new recruitments. In 1659, in siege operations in Prussia, including the unsuccessful siege of Malbork. In 1660, it was with the main Polish army in Ukraine against the Muscovites. Despite additional recruitment, it seems to

- be below strength, as its size varied between 637 and 835 portions while its paper strength was at 1,200 portions.
- Horse Guard regiment under Ernest Jan Korff: In April 1658, Colonel Korff, formerly serving in the Lithuanian army and later in the service of Prince Bogusław Radziwiłł, received a recruitment letter to raise a Guard Life Regiment. It was a mixed unit, initially composed of three reiter and two dragoon companies, with a total strength varying between 400 and 500 horses/portions. In spring 1659, the regiment received another reiter company. The unit took part in Prussia in 1658 and then in Courland in 1659, where it took heavy losses during clashes with the Swedes. The defeat was so serious that a letter of King Jan Kazimierz addressed to the soldiers mentioned the 'King [writing] to the remnants of the life regiment'. Korff was to be court-martialled for losing the regiment and for pillaging in Courland, while the unit was due to be taken over by General Berk. However, the King changed his mind and allowed Korff to reinforce the regiment with new recruitments and former POWs. The rebuilt unit took part in the campaign of 1660 as part of Czarniecki's division.
- Household banner of Hungarian infantry was created in 1656 in Lwów. Initially under the command of Captain Jan Guldyn, it had 200 men divided into two smaller banners, under Guldyn and *Rotmistrz* Wojciech Jezierski. The sub-unit under Guldyn bravely defended the border town of Sambor against the Transylvanians in 1657.[437] The whole banner was then taken over by Samuel Powirski, and, under his command, the unit took part in the siege of Warsaw in 1656 and siege of Toruń in 1658.
- Small unit of Household cossack cavalry was of unspecified size, probably a few dozen men. They were used as couriers, delivering letters between the King, army commanders and high-ranking dignitaries.
- 'Tatars of His Royal Highness' was a banner of Tatar light cavalry within the regular army, under the command of *Rotmistrz* Bohdan Kiński. The unit had a paper strength of 120 horses since its creation in spring 1656. Despite its 'Royal' name, it was just treated as a normal light horse banner.

In July 1656, there was also a plan to create a Queen's dragoon regiment as well. On 2 July 1656, the Swedish garrison of Piotrków, besieged by levy of nobility since May, decided to surrender. All defenders, under the command of Jean Baptiste de Piron, were to switch to the Polish service. According to the Queen herself, the 'whole garrison is made of Italians, although they have Swedes and Finns as officers'.[438] According to the conditions of the surrender, signed by de Piron and Jan Koniecpolski (who was in charge of the besieging forces), ex-Swedish soldiers were to be organised into a dragoon regiment of eight companies, each 100-men strong. Piron was to be colonel of this new

---

437 When the *Sejm*, in 1662, granted Guldyn – at that point a major in Aleksander Lubomirski's regiment – Polish *indygenat*, it was mentioned that he served for many years in the guard unit, fighting against all kinds of enemies, and it especially highlighted the defence of Sambor. See *Volumina Legum*, vol. IV, p.412.

438 Aleksander Przeździecki (ed.), 'Zdobycie Warszawy przez Szwedów w 1656 r. opisane w listach królowej polskiej Marii Ludwiki,' in *Biblioteka Warszawska* (Warszawa: Drukarnia Stanisława Strąbskiego, 1851), vol. III, p.202.

unit, which was to be known as the 'Queen's life guard'. The regiment was to be mustered in German style, and all soldiers were allowed to keep their current religion. To recover from the hardships of the siege, soldiers were to be allocated two months rest, during which the regiment would be formed.[439] Unfortunately, the agreement was broken by the besieging forces, with the Swedish garrison being taken prisoner instead. Therefore, the plan to raise a unit for the Queen was abolished, as soldiers felt betrayed and were now unwilling to serve in the Polish army.

Soldiers from Guard units – both Household and regular army – received uniforms, although we lack detailed information about their colours and types. In summer 1660, the Royal Treasury paid 100 zł advance pay for the clothes for the '200 Hungarian infantry' (Household haiduk banner) marching to Lwów and another 100 zł advance for pay for the clothes for 'His Majesty Guard' (no unit was specified).[440] It worth adding, though, that the cloth they would have received did not have to be very expensive, as there was confirmation of a cheap one, known as *pakłak*, to be issued as well.[441] A painting presenting guardsmen during official celebrations in the 1640s has them in blue uniforms of the Western style, with blue being associated with Vasa kings and being seen as a typical colour worn by infantry in Poland.

Guard units were treated as normal fighting regiments and companies. As such, their tactics employed in battle would be the same as of those from relevant formations in the Polish army.

Irregular Units: Volunteers and Partisans

Volunteers for the first time appeared in large numbers on the Lithuanian side in the summer and autumn of 1654, supporting the regular army in the fight against the Muscovites. Usually, they fought in the secondary theatre of war or behind enemy lines, sometimes supported by a few regular banners or levy of nobility. For example, in the first half of 1655, Hetman Radziwiłł used his volunteer force to cover his approach to Witebsk, Połock and Mścisław.[442] According to Kochowski, a very important role in preparing volunteers in the conflict against the Swedes and Muscovites was played by Paweł Sapieha. When, in 1656, he reorganised the Lithuanian regular army under his command, he despatched a few nominated officers to different regions, where they were to recruit volunteers under their regiments: 'Stankiewicz to Żmudź, Idzkiel to Courland, Libekier to Livonia, [Stefan Wojciech] Czarniawski to Połock Voivodeship, Salamonowicz to Bracław Voivodeship, [Samuel] Oskierko to [the area of] Mozyrz and Rzeczyca'. All of these colonels allegedly received 10,000 zł from Sapieha's private funds; they also gave him their oath 'to not pillage in own country, but allowed abroad; what they will take from the enemy, first need to be checked by him [Sapieha]

---

439 Rudawski, *Historja Polska od śmierci Władysława IV aż do pokoju oliwskiego*, vol. II, pp.109–12.
440 AGAD, ASK 1, no. 344, p.68.
441 *Rachunki podskarbstwa litewskiego 1648-1652*, p.42.
442 Bobiatyński, *Od Smoleńska do Wilna. Wojna Rzeczypospolitej z Moskwą 1654-1655*, p.99.

and he will decide their share'.[443] Of course, we need to remember that this was the opinion of an often very biased historian and former soldier who highly praised Sapieha in all his endeavours.

In reality, regiments of volunteers were as much help as they were hindrance, especially with the low-to-nil control of hetmans over their commanders. This was a recurring theme in all the written sources, where diarists and authors of letters alike tended to complain a lot about unruly volunteers causing misery in their own territories. They did not receive pay, so they had to live 'from the land', looting both the enemy and local population alike. They were not regulated by the disciplinary regulation of the regular army, although in theory they were under the command of regular officers in charge of the relevant theatre of war.

Some volunteer forces were of the size of large regiments, with multiple banners of cavalry, infantry and even light artillery. The composition of such forces often changed in short spans of time, as often they were scattered by the enemy and quickly rebuilt by putting together new groups of nobles and peasants. When Samuel Oskierko led his troops in a raid against the Cossacks of Ivan Zolotarenko and Muscovites forces near the Berezina river in autumn 1654, he allegedly had under his command 4,000 men. His 'regiment' was composed of two banners of noble cavalry, seven banners of Tatars, a dragoon banner, a banner of mounted volunteers, a banner of infantry volunteers and four banners of haiduks.[444] In autumn 1664, Major Karol Karlik, in charge of the garrison of Birże, described men fighting under the commander of famous volunteer Stefan Wojciech Czarniawski: 'there are nine banners in his regiment, composed of many [different] kind, foul tangle of men of Polish, Ruthenian, German and Lithuanian nations; especially [there are] many outlaws from Poland, who, not finding place amongst decent people, come and join here. There is more than 2,000 [men] of this rabble'.[445]

The battle at Zakrzew, 2 February 1656, where the Swedish troops under Lieutenant Colonel Rutger von Ascheberg defeated the Polish partisans of Stanisław Witowski. While the painter is unknown, it seems that at least two versions of this painting were commissioned, most likely by von Ascheberg himself (Author's archive).

---

443 Kochowski, *Historya panowania Jana Kazimierza*, vol. I, p.260.
444 Kochowski, *Historya panowania Jana Kazimierza*, vol. I, pp.121–23.
445 Krzysztof Kossarzecki, 'Działania wojenne nad Dźwiną w latach 1662-1667', in Karol Łopatecki (ed.), *Organizacja armii w nowożytnej Europie. Struktura-urzędy-prawo-finanse* (Zabrze: Wydawnictwo Inforteditions, 2011), pp.329–30.

Plate A
King Jan II Kazimierz and Queen Ludwika Maria.
Illustration by Sergey Shamenkov © Helion & Company 2022
See Colour Plates Commentary for further information.

Plate B
B.1 Aleksander Hilary Połubiński B.2 Hussar Companion
Illustration by Sergey Shamenkov © Helion & Company 2022
See Colour Plates Commentary for further information.

Plate C
C.1 *Pancerni* Companion C.2 Cossack Cavalryman
Illustration by Sergey Shamenkov © Helion & Company 2022
See Colour Plates Commentary for further information.

III

Plate D
D.1 Light Horseman D.2 Reiter
Illustration by Sergey Shamenkov © Helion & Company 2022
See Colour Plates Commentary for further information.

Plate E
E.1 Dragoon E.2 Foreign Infantry
Illustration by Sergey Shamenkov © Helion & Company 2022
See Colour Plates Commentary for further information.

Plate F
F.1 Polish Haiduk F.2 Peasant Partisan
Illustration by Sergey Shamenkov © Helion & Company 2022
See Colour Plates Commentary for further information.

Plate G
See Flag Plates Commentary for further information.

1

TANDEM BONA CAVS TRIVMFAT

2

VINCERE AVT MOREI.

Plate H
See Flag Plates Commentary for further information.

Plate I
See Flag Plates Commentary for further information.

Plate J
See Flag Plates Commentary for further information.

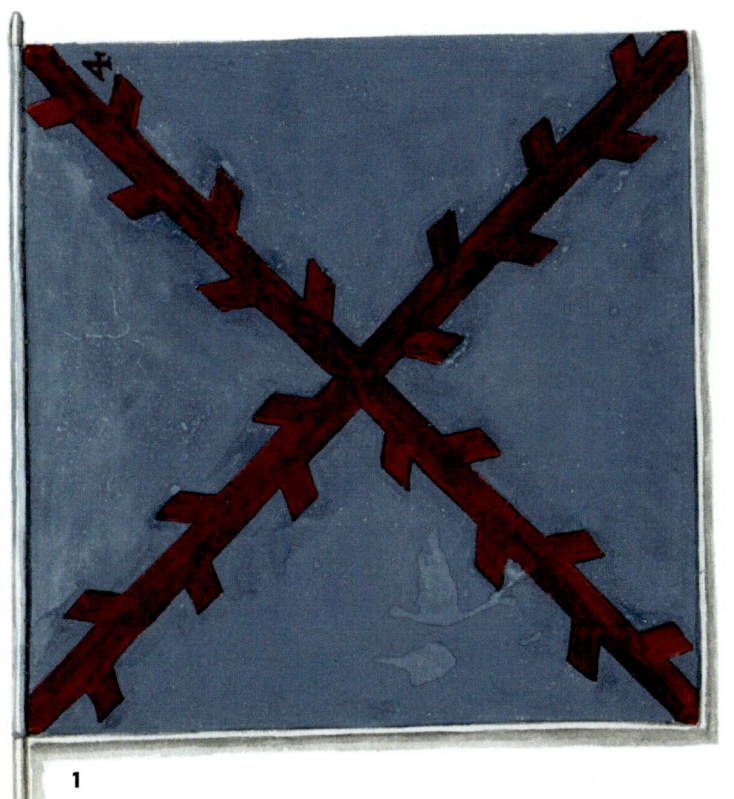

Plate K
See Flag Plates Commentary for further information.

Plate L
See Flag Plates Commentary for further information.

1

CÆLITUSERIGOR

2

PROREGEETPATRIA

Plate M
See Flag Plates Commentary for further information.

XIII

Plate N
See Flag Plates Commentary for further information.

Plate O
See Flag Plates Commentary for further information.

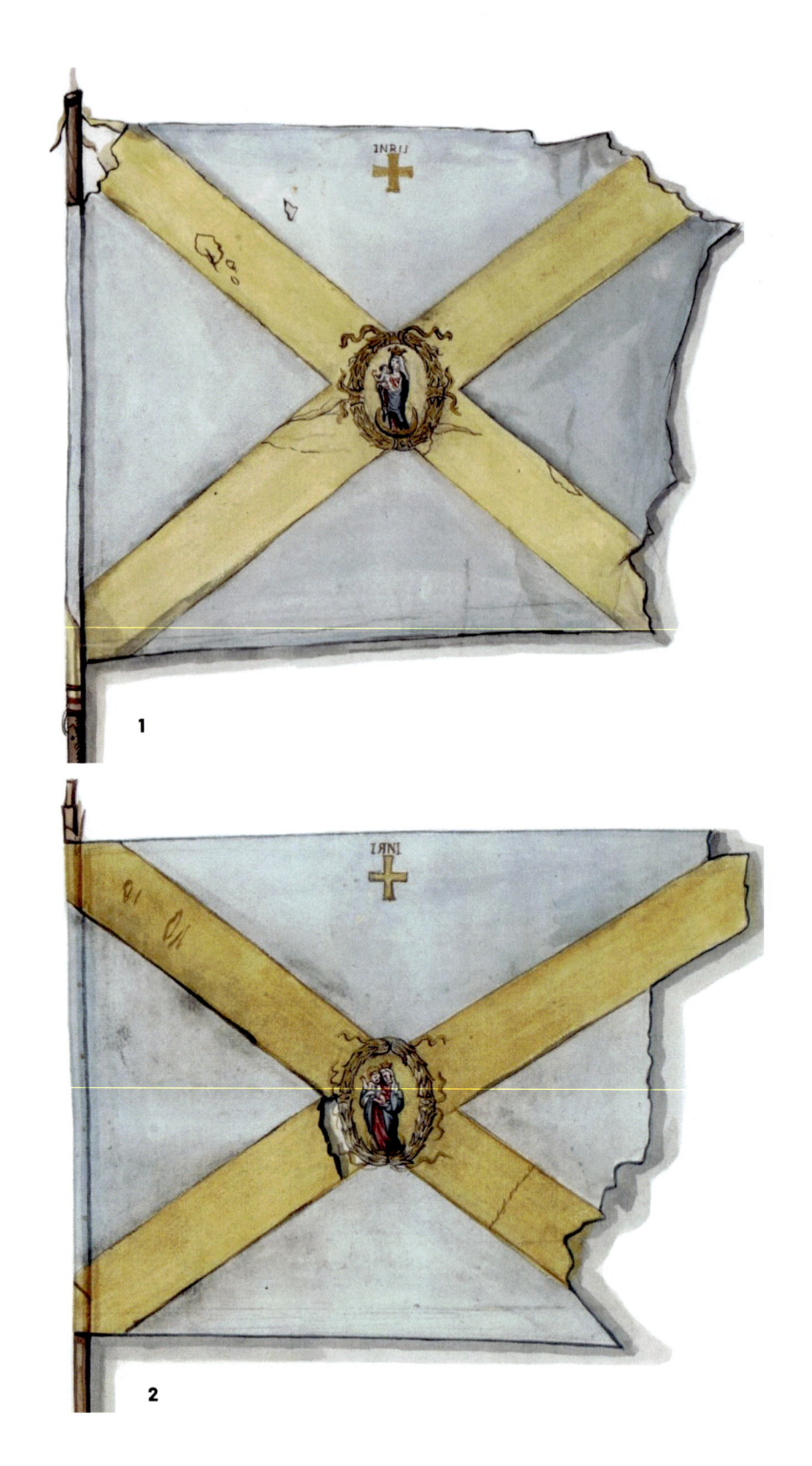

Plate P
See Flag Plates Commentary for further information.

Plate R
See Flag Plates Commentary for further information.

XVII

Plate S
See Flag Plates Commentary for further information.

LANCES, SABRES AND MUSKETS

Volunteers, as those 'living from war', were often an even worse burden on the population of their own country than the Swedish or Muscovite invaders. On some occasions, the border between 'volunteers' and 'bandits' (known as 'loose bands' (*kupy swawolne*)) was often very thin, as the former often pillaged their own population or turned directly to banditry, looting anyone no matter what language they spoke and what side they would support. When caught, they were usually sentenced to death and rarely could count on mercy. As early as August 1654, King Jan Kazimierz sent out a proclamation against volunteers pillaging 'villages of ours, of clergy and nobles'. He mentioned that there were many of those calling themselves *rotmistrz* or captain gathering banners of troops without recruitment letters and hetman's proclamations. Any men like that, attempting 'under any pretext to travel through our lands and trying to loot', were to be treated as 'loose men' and the enemy so that they could be attacked and destroyed.[446] In September 1654, a volunteer called Paszkowski, who was to gather a few thousand men to fight against the Muscovites, became such a menace to the local Lithuanian population that Albrycht Stanisław Radziwiłł had to gather his private troops to fight him off. Radziwiłł commented that 'it is a shame, when one do not know if peasant suffers more from the enemy or from [our own] soldier'.[447]

Sometimes, documents could specify the name of the noble in charge of volunteers turned robbers. In May 1655, a Royal proclamation sent to Pińsk County mentioned that Felicjan Rodakowski gathered 'loose men' as volunteers without a recruitment letter and that he not only never arrived in the army camp but also caused much trouble ignoring local laws – a very polite way of saying that his men were pillaging the area. The King wrote that, if Rodakowski did not decide to move towards the Lithuanian army and did not pay out damages, the locals were allowed to defend themselves against him and his men.[448] In a similar specification, Vorbek Lettow mentioned in his diary that, on 20 July 1655, the leader of one such 'loose band', a 'good noble and old soldier' named Stanisław Odachowski, was beheaded on Hetman Janusz Radziwiłł's court. Odachowski was accused of 'causing much damage, raiding noble's estates, towns and villages'. His son, also named Stanisław, was saved from the executioner's sword, as 'he was forced to help his father in this volunteer wantonness'.[449]

One of the most famous commanders of such troops, Denis Muraszko, was probably equally famous for his military exploits as for pillaging certain areas of Lithuania. Diarist Jan Cedrowski wrote that, in March 1657:[450]

> We suffered vast robberies and raids from our own peasants, whose colonel was rogue Dzienis Muraszka. He set up his camp in Kamień.[451] This Godless man and his rogues not only mutinied our peasants and subjects but also our servants,

---

446 'Akt uniwersału jego kr. Msci, aby swawolne kupy gromili', *AVAK*, vol. XXXIV, p.14.
447 Radziwiłł, *Pamiętnik o dziejach w Polsce. Tom 3. 1647-1656*, p.434.
448 'Akt uniwersału jego kr. Msci, aby p. Rodakowskiego gromili', *AVAK*, vol. XXXIV, p.38.
449 Vorbek-Lettow, *Skarbnica pamięci*, p.225.
450 *Dwa pamiętniki z XVII wieku Jana Cedrowskiego i Jana Floriana Drobysza Tuszyńskiego*, p.12.
451 A village near Borysów in the seventeenth-century Mińsk Voivodeship.

signing them in his [military] register [of the volunteer unit], and were the worst cause of huge hunger and loss of our all peasants. They calmed though, after were defeated at Prusowicze,[452] where few of my subjects, that went rogue, were killed.

Muraszko's troops did take part in fights against the Swedes and Muscovites, being present next to the regular army units in the campaign of 1660. Pasek mentioned that, at the battle at the river Basia, Muraszko had under his command a few banners of volunteers that were prior to the fight reinforced by cavalry servants from both Polish and Lithuanian troops. This large group of armed mounted men visually increased the size of both Czarniecki and Sapieha's armies 'by few thousand'. They even impressed the regular soldiers, as 'Muraszko was riding under tug (*buńczuk*) with mace in his hand, [looking] like new hetman and new troops [arriving]; standing in rank so well looking, that even we took a heart from looking at this rabble'.[453] Despite this rather encouraging appearance during the campaign, not much changed in the behaviour of Muraszko's volunteers. One year later, they were yet again pillaging and looting the local population, as one of their banners clashed with Pasek and his dragoons. The volunteers took heavy losses amongst their men and horses while facing the famous diarist, and it is more than likely that it was not just a single case of such a clash with the regular troops.

A rather unusual force of (more or less willing) volunteers was the 'noble banner' (*chorągiew szlachecka*) created in January 1660 in Słuck. To bolster the defence of the fortress, military commander of the garrison Friedrich Klosing ordered that the noble refugees from terrains captured by the Muscovites gather into a cavalry unit. They chose their own officers: *Rotmistrz* Hieronim Władysław Brzuchański, Lieutenant Jan Śląski and Standard-Bearer Jan Wołek. During the first muster of the unit, its strength was 300 horses, 'including retainers'. It is more than probable that the banner served as cossack cavalry, with the typical structure of retinues composed of noble companions and their associated retainers. Nobles had to commit to the service by signing a list of regulations. They were to send their servants for reconnaissance missions or take part themselves, as long as a *rotmistrz* led the unit. The same applied to serving on fortress walls, by either sending armed servants or being present themselves. They also had to provide their own food for a year, two barrels of rye per person. To ensure proper discipline, they had to abide by the 'Articles of War' as regular soldiers. Anyone that was not happy to agree with these conditions was free to do so, but, in such a case, he had to leave Słuck. New refugees arriving post-January 1660 also had to sign into the unit or were forced to leave.[454]

On 20 November 1655, while still in Opole, King Jan Kazimierz issued his decree raising levy of nobility in Poland to fight against the Swedes. He appealed to the nobles not to wait for the appointed commanders or voivodes, as per previously agreed laws, but 'to gather together, first with second, [then those] two with third, third with fourth, and so on, [all] with their subject to

---

452 A village near Borysów in the seventeenth-century Mińsk Voivodeship.
453 Pasek, *Pamiętniki*, p.159–64.
454 Vorbek-Lettow, *Skarbnica pamięci*, p.287.

LANCES, SABRES AND MUSKETS

An interesting depiction of Polish partisans: nobles (mounted) and peasants (on foot) from a painting of the battle at Zakrzew, 2 February 1656 (Author's archive).

group together and once they in the strong enough band, attack [the Swedes], choosing their own leaders'.[455] As we can see, it was in fact an order to fight as an irregular force as part of the country-wide uprising. The King added that, once more and more nobles and their subjects picked up arms and fought, he would immediately return to Poland, while, in the meantime, he was looking for alliances with other monarchs and preparing more regular troops. There were further, more direct calls of action once the King returned to Poland. On 5 March 1656, he issued a proclamation to the nobility from Przemyśl Land. While appealing to them to take part in the levy, he also asked them to 'gather your subjects, to defend tracks against the enemy, to destroyed crossing through rivers and bogs and to destroy the enemy [where they could]'. He also advised them to hide all available food and possessions 'in safe places or in the woods' so that the approaching Swedes would encounter problems when looking for provisions.[456]

Partisan groups could have had many different backgrounds: from a noble gathering his neighbours and subjects to fight against invaders, through some local populations raised by a charismatic leader or parish priest to protect their homes and possessions, to the unusual cases of former soldiers deserting from the Swedish army and fighting against their former employers. An example of the latter comes from Jan Gotthard Heering (Jan Ering). Until 1655, he was captain lieutenant in Hetman Radziwiłł's infantry regiment. After the Treaty of Kiejdany, he joined the Swedish army, for which he was branded a traitor and, in January 1656, sentenced to lose his possessions.[457] It seems that this new service was not to his liking, though, as after one quarter he decided to desert during an uprising in Samogitia, taking with him a mixed unit of reiters and dragoons. It was the regiment of Colonel Harald Igelström, and the fact that a large part of the unit deserted was not very surprising. Apparently, even the Swedes did not trust the unit,

---

455 AGAD, Zbiór Anny z Potockich Ksawerowej Branickiej, no. 5, 338, p.436.
456 Borcz, *Przemyśl 1656-1657*, pp.198–99.
457 Rachuba (ed.), *Metryka Litewska. Księga wpisów nr 131*, pp.221–22.

as Christer Horn, Governor of Riga, mentioned that it was a mix of 'bad officers and defective Lithuanians'.[458] Cooperating with local Lithuanian partisans composed of nobles from Wiłkomierz District and Upita District, he was a real thorn in the Swedish side. Heering destroyed the garrisons in Wiłkomierz and Dziewiałtów, and he ambushed four companies of Swedish reiters at Uszpol, 'killing their commander by himself, in front of all men', and sending the captured cornet to King Jan Kazimierz at Warsaw. For a few months, he blocked Swedish-held Birże and, in another ambush, scattered 600 infantry of the relief force, taking many as prisoners. In an interesting turn of events, he was then imprisoned by the order of Hetman Gosiewski and, for one year, was prisoner in Birże. In March 1658, after receiving petitions from local nobles describing his military deeds, he was pardoned by the King and, in the rank of colonel, served in Hetman Sapieha's army.[459]

Commanders leading partisan groups could come from all backgrounds: nobles (including former soldiers), clergy or even peasants. One of the most famous ones, who became a serious thorn in the Swedish side in Prussia in late 1657, was peasant born, a man known under the name Michałko. A miller from Tuchola, he was forced into the Swedish ranks, serving as a reiter in Stenbock's regiment. Taken prisoner by the Poles in 1657, he decided to organise a partisan party to fight against the Swedes. He gathered a fairly strong group, including some fighting as light cavalry, and he harassed Swedish outposts and supply lines in Prussia. At some point, he even captured two small castles, Starogard and Lipinko (between Toruń and Grudziądz), from them striking against the Swedes. Gordon wrote that Michałko was 'doing every where great harme and surprising the Sweds even at the gates of their garrisons like thunder, and getting away againe no man knew whither, when the first newes that was to be heard of him was that he had done harme in another place and was gone'.[460] In late November 1657, he was finally captured by the Swedes, who besieged him and his 80 men for two days in Starogard. He was initially transported to Elbląg, from there to Malbork, where he was to be court-martialled as a deserter from the Swedish service. By then, the fame of the self-proclaimed *rotmistrz* reached even the Polish court, so King Jan II Kazimierz intervened on behalf of the famous partisan. The Polish King threatened that, if Michałko was to be executed, he would avenge him on the Swedish officers kept in Polish captivity. Michałko was released by the Swedes and soon returned to leading a partisan group, this time already confirmed with the rank of *rotmistrz*.

Another example of a Polish noble armed with a horseman's pick, used both as a weapon and as a cane. Stefano della Bella, 1651 (Biblioteka Narodowa, Warszawa).

---

458 Kotlhjarchuk, *In the Shadows of Poland and Russia*, pp.146–47.
459 Kotlhjarchuk, *In the Shadows of Poland and Russia*, pp.96–97.
460 *Diary of General Patrick Gordon*, vol. I, pp.159–60.

LANCES, SABRES AND MUSKETS

He was very active in 1658, supporting Polish regular troops in Prussia. According to some sources, he was even ennobled for his military service.[461]

Some units of partisans or levy of nobility were, at some point, converted into regular banners and became part of the standing army. One of the most famous partisans in Southern Poland, Kasper Kasprzycki, gathered and financed from his own money a group of irregulars. He had 30 horsemen and a banner of 120 *harnicy* 'with good guns and good weapons'.[462] In the second quarter of 1656, his infantry was incorporated into the regular army and served for three quarters as a unit of Polish infantry. It was disbanded, though, after Kasprzycki succumbed to mortal wounds taken during the siege of Cracow, where the banner was fighting as part of Lubomirski's force. In 1655 and 1656, Stanisław Pogorzelski led a unit of partisans, which included his son Jarosz, that was fighting in Wielkopolska against the Swedes. It seems to be mostly based on levy of nobility, as, since 1658, Jarosz Pogorzelski led, as *rotmistrz*, a banner of cossack cavalry in the regular army composed of former partisans and levy.[463] In November 1661, a 100-horse-strong banner of volunteers under Andrzej Muraszko was incorporated into the Lithuanian regular army, serving in Hetman Sapieha's division as a banner of cossack cavalry. Groups of irregular infantry were very likely to be used as reinforcements for already existing foreign infantry and dragoon regiments, as they had easily available a number of experienced and armed men.

Irregulars fighting in volunteer and partisan groups used all kinds of weapons – from military-grade muskets, sabres and swords to *ad hoc* adapted tools. Holsten, who had few encounters with Polish peasants during his pillaging adventures as a Swedish reiter, mentioned that they were armed with 'sabres, scythes, spears and rods', which seems to be the typical mix of weapons and tools available for villagers.[464] On another occasion, he wrote about barely escaping with his life from an encounter with a peasant armed with a 'large axe'.[465] Von Ascheberg wrote about Polish irregulars using bows, scythes and sickles attached to long sticks.[466] Jemiołowski, describing peasant partisans that were raised to fight against the Swedes in 1656, wrote that some of them had scythes, sickles and rods, so the same way as in Holsten's diary. Others were 'trained with good guns', indicating semi-regular infantry units, of which some were later included into the *komput*.[467]

---

461 Nowak, *Oblężenie Torunia w roku 1658*, pp.161–67.
462 *Harnicy* were semi-regular units raised from Polish Highlanders, kept as private troops. Their main role was to fight against bandits and marauders in the mountains. AGAD, ASK 85, no. 74, pp.140, 143.
463 Wagner, *Słownik biograficzny oficerów polskich drugiej połowy XVII wieku*, vol. I, p.218.
464 Holsten, *Przygody wojenne 1655-1666*, p.31.
465 Holsten, *Przygody wojenne 1655-1666*, p.32.
466 Ascheberg, *Dziennik oficera jazdy szwedzkiej 1621-1681*, pp.64–65.
467 Jemiołowski, *Pamiętnik dzieje Polski zawierający*, p.181.

AGAINST THE DELUGE

Peasant Levy

An unusual type of troops that did not really fit into any previous category was peasant levy. Its best described examples come from October 1656, when Jerzy Sebastian Lubomirski forced local nobles from Cracow Voivodeship to agree to the massive levy of not only their subjects but also peasants from royal and clergy lands and townsmen in this voivodeship. Polish commanders needed infantry and sappers for a planned assault of Cracow, so such a levy was the answer to all his needs:

- All town and cities (including those that belonged to the King and clergy) were to send one in three men, armed with a musket or *rusznica* caliver, sabre, axe, 30 bullets, one-and-half pound of powder and enough food for one week.
- All villages (again, including royal and clergy ones) were to send every third wealthier peasant[468] and every fifth poorer one,[469] who also should have a firearm or, if they did not have one, a scythe or iron pitchfork. They also were to bring axes, spades, enough food for one week and assault ladders made in each village.
- All blacksmiths with their hammers.
- All millers with pickaxes and spades.
- All huntsmen and forest guards with their guns.
- All miners from Olkusz, Wieliczka and Bochnia with their pickaxes and spades.

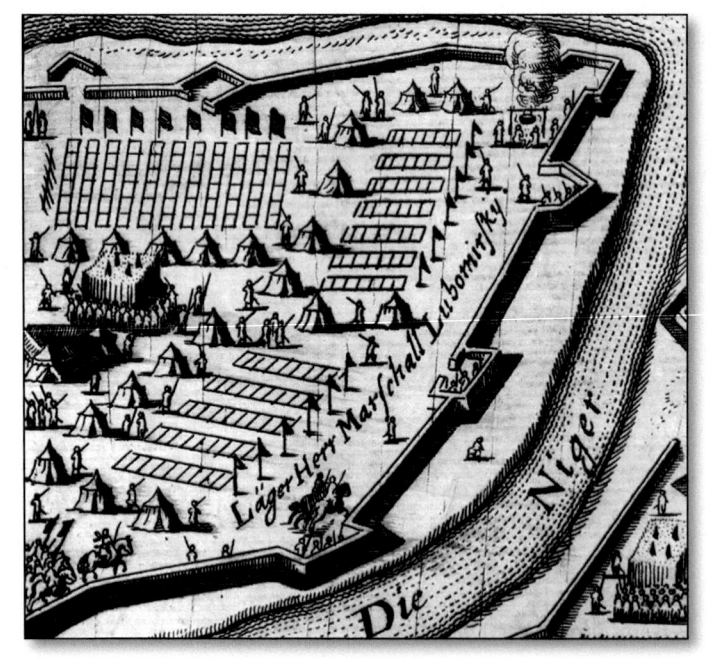

Details of the camp of Lubomirski's division, March 1656. Engraving from volume VII of *Theatrum Europaem*, published in Frankfurt am Main in 1672 (Biblioteka Narodowa, Warszawa).

The nobles and administrators of the lands that would stop their subjects from taking part in the levy could be fined; town mayors and village leaders could be executed, same as the peasants or townsfolk that refused to take part in the levy. No surprise that, facing such harsh penalties, there was very small opposition to Lubomirski's plan, and in short time he had under his command a few thousand 'volunteers'.[470]

---

468 Known in Polish as '*kmieć*'. This person was a peasant that had at least one *łan* of land.
469 There were two types of these. One was called '*zagrodnik*', and he had no more than one-fourth of *łan*. The other was called '*chałupnik*', and he only owned his cottage, without any other land.
470 Tadeusz Nowak, 'Kasper Kasprzycki, nieznany bohater z czasów "Potopu"', *Przegląd Historyczny*, 50:2 (1959), p.244.

Standards, Flags and Cornets

The standard, flag, cornet or banner – whatever its name – carried by the unit was always the most important symbol of the unit's identity and, as such, was always a primary enemy target. Captured flags were amongst the most crucial spoils of war, often mentioned in sources and army despatches. Each cavalry and infantry banner and company had its own flag, received when the unit was created. They were often very expensive pieces, especially in the case of units like winged hussars or life companies, made from silk, with golden embroidery.

Polish flags and horses of winged hussars captured by the Swedes during the Battle of Warsaw. Detail from Erik Dahlbergh's drawing for Samuel Pufendorf's *De rebus a Carolo Gustavo Sueciae rege gestis*, published in 1696 (Biblioteka Narodowa, Warszawa).

In both the Polish and Lithuanian armies, the shapes and sizes of and the motifs on flags were very similar, although there were of course some local variations. The most common pattern was square, usually unfringed. Hussars, also possibly some *pancerni* and cossack banners, were usually with tails or tongue-shaped fly. Cossack cavalry could sometimes have a flag with a half-round end, but their standards were normally smaller square ones, sometimes ending with tails. Some surviving examples are also shaped as triangles. Light horses would follow a similar pattern, but they often had flags with a smaller number of ornaments. Dragoons had smaller square cornets, often very similar to those of light horse. Infantry ones were the biggest: the majority of them were in the shape of a large rectangle.

Both 'national' and religious motifs were the most common. A 'court' hussar banner was, in both 1649 and 1651, serving under a flag blessed by papal nuncio Jan de Torres. It was turquoise, made from damask, although one source also mentioned that it was made from silk. On one side, it had a large white Knight's Cross, on the other side a yellow one. The former had an embroidered satin Royal coat of arms, while the latter had the Madonna with the Infant Jesus and motto '*subscriptio sub praesidio*' and '*tecum a pro te*'.[471]

---

471 Latin for 'under your protection' and 'with you and for you', respectively.

In 1651, there was also one more flag used for a short period of time, when the 'court' banner was temporarily divided into two smaller banners. It was also turquoise and made from silk.[472] An eagle was present on banners of all formations. The Madonna with the Infant Jesus could be used for cavalry banners, especially hussars. The Burgundian Cross or Saint Andrew's Cross, usually red or white, was present on many infantry flags. References to mythology (e.g., Fortuna), saints (e.g., St. George defeating the dragon) or angels were also sometimes present. A cavalry banner raised by the Jewish community in Vilnius in summer 1654 had a 'red [flag] with white edges on both sides, with writing in Hebraw'.[473] A Tatar banner could have the *Shahada* (Islamic creed): 'There is no God but Allah. Mohammed is the prophet of Allah'. The coats of arms of the nobles leading the units were most likely the most common in privately raised troops but could also be present in flags in the standing army, where a magnate or noble was often the commander of a few different units. Such symbols were often accompanied by a wreath, usually green, red or black. Throughout the whole seventeenth century, very common in infantry was the usage of horizontal lines in alternate colours, usually three, sometimes mixed with additional emblems (e.g., the Madonna or Burgundian Cross). Sometimes, when one officer had two or more banners of the same formation in the army, they tended to be named after the colour of their flag for easier identification. For example, in the early 1660s in the Lithuanian army, officers with two cossack cavalry banners were Jerzy Karol Hlebowicz ('black' and 'white') and Zygmunt Adam Słuszka ('red' and 'blue'). Of course, it was just the 'main' colour of the flag, its background. At the same time, the standard was more than likely also embroidered with some other motifs.

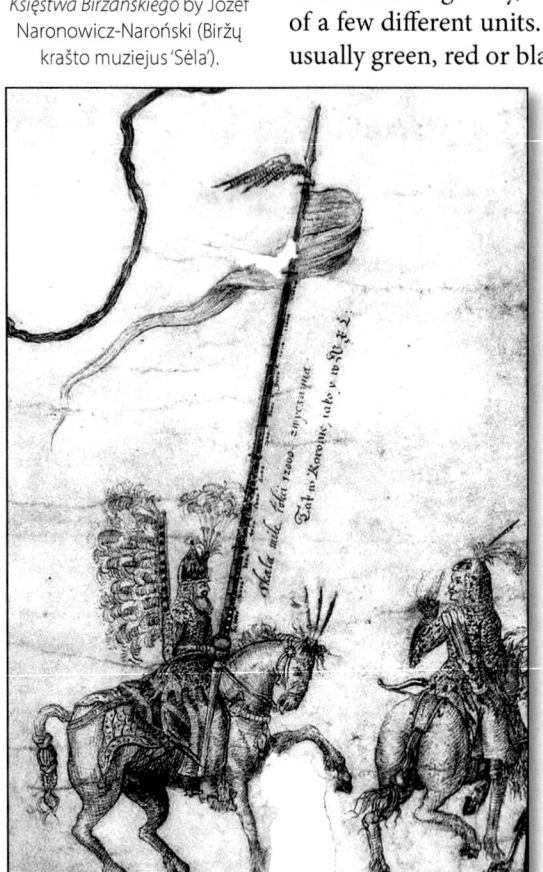

Lithuanian hussars' standard bearer with the hetman's sign and armoured cossack (or *petyhorzec*) from *Mapa Księstwa Birżanskiego* by Józef Naronowicz-Naroński (Biržų krašto muziejus 'Sėla').

There are also some interesting notes about the Commonwealth's flags scattered between written sources. For example, captured Polish flags were used by the Cossacks in the early stage of the 1648 uprising, and they were possibly from cavalry units. One was a 'red flag with coat of arms of [the city of] Lwów and white cross'.[474] The other was '[of the] quarter [army], damask, [with an] eagle that hold sword in one leg'.[475] The detailed muster roll of the regiment of Jakub Rozdrażewski, raised as a part of the district troops in Wielkopolska in July 1648,

---

472 Nagielski (ed.), *Relacje wojenne z pierwszych lat walk polsko-kozackich powstania Bohdana Chmielnickiego okresu "Ogniem i Mieczem" (1648-1651)*, pp.321, 343–44.
473 Vorbek-Lettow, *Skarbnica pamięci*, p.184.
474 *Korespondencja wojskowa hetmana Janusza Radziwiłła w latach 1646-1655*, vol. I, *Diariusz kancelaryjny 1649-1653*, p.55.
475 *Korespondencja wojskowa hetmana Janusza Radziwiłła w latach 1646-1655*, vol. I, *Diariusz kancelaryjny 1649-1653*, p.122.

provides some description of flags in units. Winged hussars had a white standard with a red Knight's Cross, with the Holy Mary drawn in the cloud and with an armed hand with sword in another cloud. Andrzej Przyjemski's *arkabuzeria* banner had a white flag with a black Knight's Cross. Piotr Tomicki and his *arkabuzeria* had a red damask flag with a white Knight's Cross. The *arkabuzeria* of Hieronim Piglowski had a red flag with a white cross, with yellow silk edges. The dragoon company of Aleksander Kostka had a red banner with a white cross.[476] In 1651, as a part of increasing the Lithuanian army, the Royal Treasury paid for three flags for newly created cossack cavalry banners: 'One scarlet with black cross, second red with white cross, third red and blue'.[477] Bishop Piotr Gembicki's hussar banners, in late 1654, was to receive two flags. One was to be made from white and crimson damask, the other from silk (*kitajka*) in the same colours. There was also to be a golden and silver ornament on the top of the flags, known as a *skofia*.[478] To replace the old flag of the Royal hussar banner in the Lithuanian army, which was 'lost in the fight against the Enemy', Jan Kazimierz ordered in April 1656 for a new one to be made in Lwów. As he wrote in his letter to the lieutenant of the hussar banner, Aleksander Hilary Połubiński, it 'wo not be from the same material as first one, as we cannot get it here [in Lwów] but [one we got] is even better to make new one'.[479] Without going into too much detail, Gordon mentioned that, during a fight with Polish troops near Ujście on 24 July 1655, the Swedes captured 'two collours, the one red the other white'.[480] In October 1656, the newly raised foreign infantry company of Michał Kazimierz Radziwiłł, under Captain Lieutenant Neiman (possibly Neuman) received a yellow flag with a red cross.[481] In the register of Hetman Janusz Radziwiłł's possessions, left after his death in Tykocin and captured by the Lithuanian army, we can find a few examples of flags.[482] There was a 'white hussars' flag with black eagle', indicating that it was from one of Radziwiłł's units since his coat of arms included a black eagle. 'Seven yellow regimental flags' most likely belonged to a foreign infantry regiment. There was also one for cossack cavalry, 'black with white cross and red edges'. The register also included the flag of the Polish infantry of Field Hetman Gosiewski, probably taken over by Radziwiłł's troops in 1655. It was 'yellow with white and blue cross, with black edges'. Another one is not mentioned in connection with any unit, 'new blue silk flag, with three yellow crowns'. There was also an 'old embroidered reiter cornet', unfortunately without any further details.

Amongst 28 flags of the Lithuanian army, captured by the Muscovites during the Battle of Vilnius on 8 August 1655, we can find many common motifs present during the seventeenth century. There are a few examples of a white Knight's Cross, on a black, red and yellow background. A few others

---

476 APPoz., Gr. Pozn., 693, pp.625v–30.
477 *Rachunki podskarbstwa litewskiego 1648-1652*, p.24.
478 BJ, no 8842/IV, p.57.
479 AGAD, AR III, no. 4, document 98, p.41.
480 *Diary of General Patrick Gordon*, vol. I, p.31.
481 AGAD, AR VII, no. 237, p.1.
482 Kotłubaj (ed.), 'Rejestr rzeczy pozostałych po śmierci X. Janusza Radziwiłła w Tykocinie', pp.322–35.

had the Madonna with the Infant Jesus, the most common religious motif. Another interesting religious one is a flag with Saint Anne the Prophetess on it. Infantry colours seem to be present as well, with some horizontal lines in green, blue, white, red and yellow.[483] Another haul of Lithuanian flags in Muscovite hands comes from the battle of Chausy that took place on 16 May 1662. It is very likely that most of the units present were volunteers and district troops, so the motifs on the standards are fairly simple. Most of them have a Knight's Cross – either white, blue, red or black – with different backgrounds in white, red, blue and black.[484] Settled cossacks serving as part of the Lithuanian garrison of Smoleńsk in 1654 were divided into three banners, each with a different flag: white, red and yellow. The fourth territorial unit based there was composed of settled boyars, and their flag was black.[485]

Hetman Janusz Radziwiłł with his entourage at Kijów (Kiev) in 1651. Worth noticing is the hetman's sign carried next to the commander. From the drawing of Abraham von Westervelt. 1651 (Muzeum Wojska Polskiego, Warszawa, photo from author's archive).

---

483 'Lithuanian Colours & Standards Lost in the Battle of Wilno, 8 August 1655', *Oderint dum probent*, <http://rusmilhist.blogspot.com/2013/07/lithuanian-colours-standards-lost-in.html>, accessed 6 June 2022.

484 'Lithuanian Colours and Standards Lost in the Battle of Chausy, 16 May 1662', *Oderint dum probent*, <http://rusmilhist.blogspot.com/2015/01/lithuanian-colours-and-standards-lost.html>, accessed 6 June 2022.

485 *Zbiór dyplomatów rządowych i aktów prywatnych, posługujących do rozjaśnienia dziejów Litwy i złączonych z nią krajów (od 1387 do 1710 r.)*, vol. I, p.63.

5

Military Life and Death

Pay

Pay during the whole Deluge was set up on the same level. In fact, there seems to be no changes between 1654 and 1677. Soldiers in cavalry and dragoons would receive their pay every quarter, while infantry would be paid each month. The level of pay depended on the formation:

Formation	Pay (per quarter or month)	Notes
Hussars	51 zl/quarter	
Pancerni and cossack cavalry	41 zl/quarter	
Tatar and Wallachian light horse	31 zl/quarter	
Reiters	65 zl/quarter	50 zl of standard pay + 15 zl of *anritgeld*[1]
German infantry	12 zl/month	
Polish/Hungarian infantry	12 zl/month	
Dragoons	36 zl/quarter	

One złoty from the pay of each horse in national cavalry (hussars, *pancerni*, cossack cavalry or light horse) was taken by the *rotmistrz* as a so-called 'kitchen addition' (*kuchenne*). In foreign units, the colonel (or the other officer in charge) received a so-called '*kopfgeld*', which was one-fifth (sometimes one-sixth) from each pay portion in the unit. There is also evidence that one pay for the full twelfth month (in the case of units serving for the whole year) also landed in the colonel's pocket. It was money used to buy flags and drums for the units, some being paid directly into the lieutenant colonel in charge of the regiment, to supplement his pay and to run the regimental

---

1 Special pay for purchase of equipment.

chancellery.² Such a system provided the nominal colonels of regiments with a nice income, as, even after deducting all the already mentioned spendings, they could end up with extra money earned 'on the side' of their pay. It also explains why, in later years, many officials that raised and kept in the army, with the great cost, banners of hussars received commission as colonel of the infantry regiments so that they could recoup the money spent on the expensive cavalry.

The main problem when dealing with the financial aspect of the Commonwealth's armies was their very poor fiscal system.³ Each *Sejm* was to agree upon the types and levels of taxation; additionally, the local *sejmiki* allowed their deputies to propose what and how much could be raised in each land. As in the second part of the seventeenth century, it was lands and districts that often took over the direct financing of some army units, and this could lead to further delays and disagreements over pay. Since soldiers had to serve for many years without pay, it often led to the mutinies of disgruntled troops. What is worse, they became used to living off of their own land, with local peasants being robbed by the same soldiers that were supposed to defend them from invaders. While officers tried to keep the discipline, often they had to turn a blind eye to illegal 'taking bread' (*wybieranie chleba*) from areas that were not assigned to the unit, in order for their soldiers to not desert or even die from starvation. As we will see later in this chapter, financial problems were long going and really badly affected both the Polish and Lithuanian armies during their struggle against the Swedes, Muscovites, Brandenburgians, Cossacks and Transylvanians.

By November 1654, the Lithuanian army was already due a pay of up to 1,000,000 zł, with the debt covering a period of service since early 1653. During the Commission at Mińsk, which took place between November and December 1654, it was agreed that the soldiers already in service would be paid four of six overdue quarters of pay plus the current quarter (up to 9 February 1655), while the newly raised unit would receive pay for just one quarter, covering the period until 9 February 1655.⁴ It was an outcome that did not satisfy the soldiers, and it led to further voices of discontent from the army. At the same time, there was just no way for the country already ravaged by war, with a large part of its territory captured or destroyed by the Muscovites, to raise enough money from taxes to pay off the troops. As it was, for the next few

An example of a delayed payment for the units of Polish army. The fragment of bills from the *Sejm* in 1661 confirms that five banners of cossack cavalry finally received special pay for one quarter of service for Żwaniec campaign of 1653, previously agreed upon by the *Sejm* of 1654 (AGAD, Warszawa).

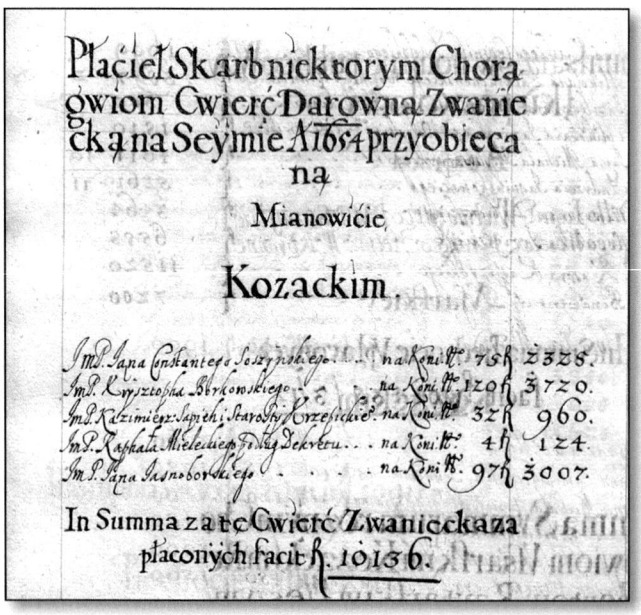

---

2   Wimmer, *Wojsko polskie w drugiej połowie XVII wieku*, p.295.
3   As discussed in Paradowski, *Despite Destruction, Misery and Privations*, pp.115–20.
4   Bobiatyński, *Od Smoleńska do Wilna. Wojna Rzeczypospolitej z Moskwą 1654-1655*, pp.118–19.

MILITARY LIFE AND DEATH

years, soldiers had to 'live from the land', receiving very small amounts of pay and supplementing it with war loot, support received from wealthy commanders and, unfortunately very often, money and provisions robbed from their own population. In August 1656, when the Lithuanian army was sending its envoys to discuss the financial aspect of the service with King Jan Kazimierz, in their petition it was mentioned that the 'army is starving and so impoverished [now], especially as it is serving for such long time without pay [and] for two years it did not had any support in *hiberna* [support in kind or money during winter time]'.[5] The final recognition of the army's debt was resolved after the war with Sweden, at the end of 1662 and beginning of 1663, during the Commission in Vilnius.

Delay in pay was often of such length that there could be disbanded units that still were owed money for years. For example, there is a surviving list of money paid and owned to the units that were serving under the name of Hetman Janusz Radziwiłł. The document, dated 26 February 1663, mentions the following units of the deceased commander:

- Reiters: 660 horses
- Dragoons: 200 portions
- Regiment of German infantry: 1,400 portions
- Life company of German infantry: 200 portions
- Free company of German infantry: 150 portions
- Hungarian infantry banner: 200 portions
- Hungarian infantry banner: 100 portions
- Hungarian infantry banner: 100 portions

Many of these units were serving even prior to 1654, although most of the bills cover the period of 1654–1655. By February 1663, even counting a certain reduction of the strength of each unit, the whole 'contingent' was owed 420,417 zł. Some of it was paid 'in kind', usually with clothing materials. The final bill was reduced by a number of payments made prior to 1663 or by the voluntary decision of the soldiers to stop their claim for the pay of a certain period. In total, according to the Vilnius Commission, after all reductions and partial payments, the final amount due was 211,630 zł.[6] We need to realise that this was the money owed to units already not in service for

A so-called *'asygnata'* from July 1659. It was a document issued by Crown Vice Treasurer Jan Krasiński confirming that the cossack cavalry banner of Szymon Kawecki, Crown Camp Master, was to receive from the Royal Treasury the amount of 10,136 zł and 20 gr. Unfortunately, due to the lack of cash in the Treasury, such documents often were unpaid for rather long periods of time (AGAD, Warsaw).

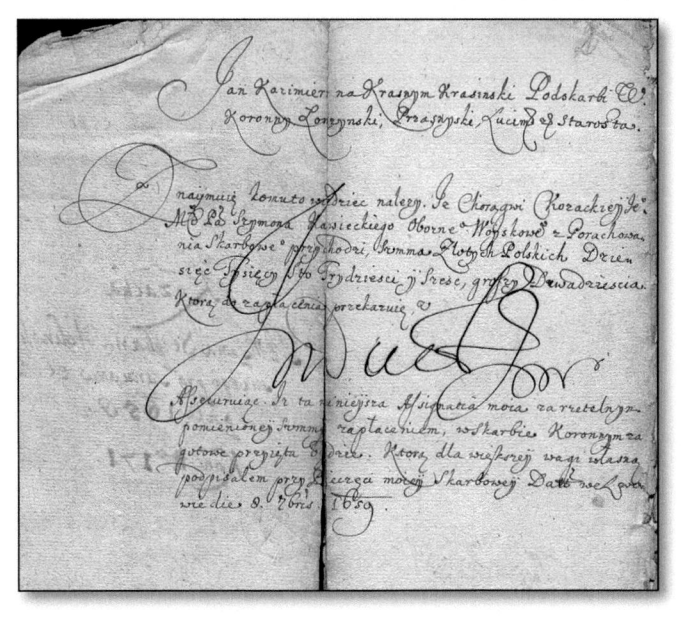

---

5   AGAD, AR II, no. 1317, p.1.
6   AGAD, AR XI, no. 39, pp.121–39.

close to eight years – yet another example of how inefficient the army pay system was during the period.

As the Polish army was much larger, here, the financial situation was even worse. The debt of the National Treasury, due to delayed pay, ran in millions of złoty, as units served for years without pay. In January 1659, the military commission to deal with outstanding pay started its proceedings in Lublin. All Polish army units sent there their envoys, including those present as part of Czarniecki's division in Denmark. Both Grand Hetman Potocki and Field Hetman Lubomirski were there as well. It took a few weeks to calculate how much was owed to the troops. The debt ran from as far as 1653, with some smaller instalments paid in previous years. According to Jan Wimmer, taking under consideration payments already made, the National Treasury owed between 20,000,000 and 21,000,000 zł to the troops. It was a huge amount that taxes, especially in a country ravaged by conflict, were unable to cover even in a small percentage. The army envoys mutinied, declaring a 'confederation' (*konfederacja*) led by Mariusz Jaskólski. Their demand was simple: the soldiers wanted to receive at least part of their owed money before they would return to fight against the Swedes and Muscovites.[7]

Matters of taxes and payments to the army were discussed in great detail during the *Sejm* that started on 22 March 1659 in Warsaw. One of the topics that led to the most heated discussion was the presence of the allied Imperial army in Poland. They were burdensome allies, and their cost – in coin and provisions – was very heavy. No surprise that many nobles arriving at the *Sejm* were especially vocal in suggesting that Leopold I's troops should leave Poland as quickly as possible. In fact, the Commonwealth never paid back the whole amount owed to the Imperial army for its stay in Poland in 1657 and 1658, with the final settling of the remaining debt done in 1683 when the Imperial side cancelled it to encourage the signing of an anti-Ottoman treaty.

In July–September 1659, another special commission of 37 deputies chosen by the *Sejm* held conference in Lwów, where, alongside both the Crown hetman and vice treasures, it was negotiating with representatives of the army. After long talks and (very typical in such a situation) bribes paid to the deputies from the army units, it was agreed that, for now, the soldiers would mostly receive a payment for three quarters of delayed pay, with many units paid only for one and some for four. The problem was that only a part of it was received in coin, the rest in assignat (*asygnata*) or in goods, usually cloth. There are many surviving documents from the 1655–1660 period, signed by the deputies sent from the army units, confirming receiving a partial payment or, in most scenarios, just assignat, which was supposed to allow for the money to be released by local officials.[8] Amongst the most interesting are those from the Lwów Commission showing how large units were behind with their pay, which helps to realise the whole scale of the financial problem. In August 1659, deputies sent by Stefan Czarniecki received one-year's worth of pay for his dragoon regiment. It was an overdue payment for the four quarters of 1658. During that time, there was a total

---

7   Wimmer, *Wojsko polskie w drugiej połowie XVII wieku*, pp.120–21.
8   AGAD, ASK IV, Księgi Rekognicji, no. 12–15.

of 3,695 horses serving in the unit: 790 in the first quarter, 917 in the second, 1,000 in the third and 988 in the fourth. With a quarterly pay of 36 zł per horse, the deputies received 133,020 zł.[9] In a very similar scenario, in September 1659, Jan Fryderyk Sapieha received one-year's worth (four quarters) of pay for his dragoon regiment serving in the Polish army. As with Czarniecki's regiment, it was pay for the previous year, so from January to December 1658. During that time, there was a total of 1,845 horses serving in the unit: 234 in the first quarter, 461 in the second, 553 in the third and 597 in the fourth. The Treasury paid Sapieha 36 zł for each horse in service in 1658, so a total of 66,420 zł.[10] Also in September 1659, Krzysztof Sędziwoj Potocki received 5,400 zł, which was overdue pay for his dragoon company (150 horses) for the last quarter of 1658.[11] On one hand, this shows to what extent troops had to rely on the support of the colonel or commander of their unit in order to survive such long periods of time without pay. On the other hand, this shows how the system was open to attempts of misuse, as officers rarely set up a muster of their units in front of the royal or local land commissioners so that the number of portions or horses they claimed their pay was for was based on muster rolls provided by themselves, where the numbers could be to some extent exaggerated so that the officer could claim pay for 'dead souls'.

Sometimes, officers, even on the company level, went through great lengths to support their troops. An undated document regarding Michał Kazimierz Radziwiłł's foreign regiment, which seems to have been written in late 1659 when the unit took part in the siege of Malbork, shows the rather dramatic situation of the troops. The unknown author of the financial report complained that the regiment barely received any money, so he appealed to Prince Radziwiłł to support the unit. He then added that the 'officers sold or pawned their horses, clothes, [and all that] they had, they are in debt up to their ears to [get money] to keep men in service'.[12]

There are many documents confirming the amount and value of the 'silks, cloth and firearms' provided to soldiers as 'payment in kind' in lieu of overdue pay in 1659 after the Lwów

Another *asygnata* signed by Crown Vice-Treasurer Jan Krasiński confirming that the cossack cavalry banner of Andrzej Potocki was due to receive 4,870 zł and 14 gr. The unit was to receive its delayed pay from taxes gathered in the Voivodship of Lublin (AGAD, Warsaw).

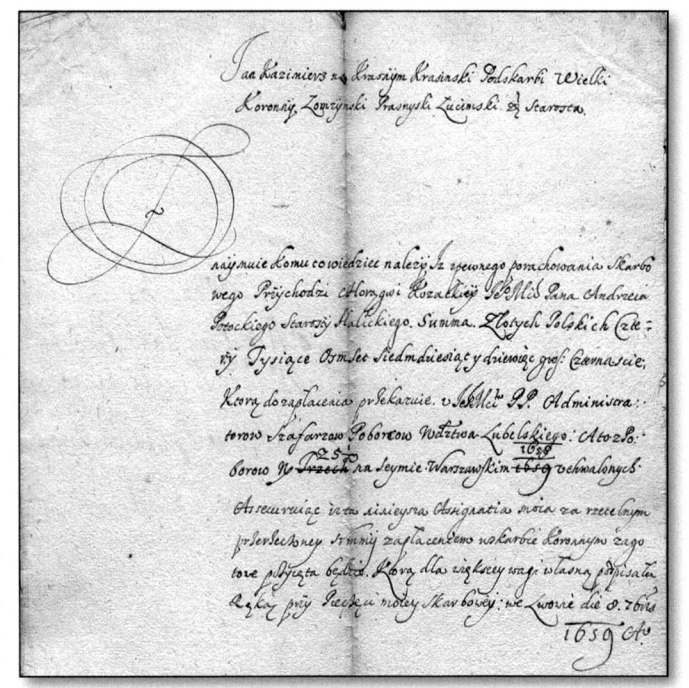

9   AGAD, ASK IV, Księga Rekognicji, no. 14, p.286.
10   AGAD, ASK IV, Księga Rekognicji, no. 14, p.269.
11   AGAD, ASK IV, Księga Rekognicji, no. 14, p.276.
12   AGAD, AR VII, no. 57, p.49.

Commission.[13] We can find there a large quantity of Venetian and Florentine velvet, French and Venetian *tabin* (silk), taffeta silk, different types and colours of satin, English cloth (*falendysz*) in its cheaper Dutch version and the more expensive English and French ones, cheap cloth called '*pakłak*', the thick woollen cloth *kir*, heavy woven silk cloth known as *samis*, soft cloth *barchan* of mixed fibre (wool, cotton or cotton and hemp) and lower quality woollen cloth known as *kromras* or *rasa*. Amongst firearms, there were the *bandolet* used by cavalry, many pairs of Dutch pistols, 'excellent quality' Dutch pistols and 'smaller Dutch pistols of excellent quality'. All the goods were provided by merchants from towns like Lwów and Cracow, with the National Treasury to pay them the value of all the items at a later date once cash was available.

On some occasions, companions in national cavalry, especially in hussar banners, could be supported by their *rotmistrz*, who would provide them with money to purchase equipment, to replenish losses during a campaign. In April 1662, four companions from the Lithuanian Royal hussar banner (under the command of Połubiński) received such financial help. Michał Karol Harabud got 100 zł to rebuild his retinue. Piotr Kaczanowski got 200 zł for the horse he lost during the battle at the river Basia in 1660. Teodor Wołk received 200 zł 'to keep his retinue intact', while Samuel Zabuski got 100 zł 'to improve his retinue'.[14] In other situations, it was the companions that could help one of their own. In January 1662, Poczobut Odlanicki was chosen by his banner to be their deputy sent for 'bread money' for the unit. The companions decided to give all that money to him 'for my losses, as I was in their eyes fallen and lost companion'. The few hundred of złoty that

Polish cavalry assisting the Swedish army during the siege of Jasna Góra Monastery in 1655. Jan Aleksander Gorczyn, 1660s (Muzeum Narodowe, Kraków. Photo by Tomasz Ratyński).

---

13 AGAD, ASK 82, no. 9, pp.61–67.
14 Nagielski, 'Chorągwie husarskie Aleksandra Hilarego Połubińskiego i króla Jana Kazimierza w latach 1648-1666', p.132.

he obtained in this way could help with rebuilding his retinue.[15] Of course, infantry or dragoons, especially if their colonel was a wealthy magnate, could also from time to time count on additional support. In early August 1658, officers from the foreign regiment of Jan Zamoyski, taking part in the siege of Toruń, wrote to their nominal commander (who was not present with the army) asking for financial help. They thanked him for the money already delivered but mentioned that it was not enough and that it did not even cover the expenses of all the officers. They added that, for the last four weeks, the officers were paying from their own pockets for the food for their companies to keep 'poor soldiers' in the ranks. The situation was growing desperate, though, so the officers were looking forward for any more money that Zamoyski could send them.[16]

Very important were the official rewards given by the king to veterans in recognition of their military service. Sometimes, they were given out immediately after (or even during) a campaign, but more often soldiers had to wait years for such an example of the royal favours. The scale of the received rewards varied greatly. Most sought for were military and office titles, as they came with prestige, more money and sometimes a seat in the Senate as well. Examples are Lubomirski, who was nominated as Crown Field Hetman after Lanckoroński's death; Sapieha taking over the office of Lithuanian Grand Hetman; Pac, who became Lithuanian Camp Master and later Field Hetman; and Stefan Czarniecki, who originally came from a lesser noble family and later received the much-coveted office of Voivode of Ruthenia.

Lower ranking officers (e.g., *rotmistrz* or lieutenant) or companions could normally receive a lease of royal land (i.e., a village), which was usually awarded for the life of the recipient. Thirty-six companions from the Lithuanian Royal hussar banner (under the command of Połubiński) received, between 1656 and the 1670s, rewards ranging from office titles to village leases or direct financial payments.[17] A lot depended on the person of their direct commander – the higher the rank, the bigger the chance that the support of an influential colonel or *rotmistrz* could lead to some additional rewards for the service. Common were some financial awards or goods received by the Crown through escheat law (*prawo kaduka*) or through the confiscation of belongings of traitors of the state, in this case the nobles that allied with the Swedes. A large part of the latter were the former estates of the Polish Brethren, members of the Protestant movement who were known in Poland as *arianie*. They were expelled from Poland based on a decree of the *Sejm* from 20 July 1658, when they were branded as pro-Swedish traitors.

Foreigners in the Commonwealth's service could receive, as an award for their service, the Polish ennoblement known as *indygenat*. Documents describing these individuals tended to mention their 'valour in the wars against Cossacks, Muscovites and Swedes', sometimes even specific events (e.g., deeds from a particular battle or their engineering skill). At the same

---

15 Poczobut Odlanicki, *Pamiętnik Jana Władysława Poczobuta Odlanickiego*, p.57.
16 AGAD, AZ, 1083, pp.1–2.
17 Nagielski, 'Chorągwie husarskie Aleksandra Hilarego Połubińskiego i króla Jana Kazimierza w latach 1648-1666', pp.119–25.

time, non-noble Poles and Lithuanians could also be ennobled or added to a specific coat of arms as a reward for their military service. In the *Sejm* in 1658, 31 foreigners received *indygenat*. Some of them were diplomats or courtiers, but the majority were soldiers, especially from the ranks of foreign infantry and engineers. There was a fairly wide scope of nationalities as well, as amongst the ennobled were men from Gdańsk (German-speaking), Brandenburg, Prussia, France, Italy, the Netherlands and England. Additionally, 12 Poles were ennobled or 'added to the coat of arms', again most of them for their military service.[18]

The *Sejm* in 1659 had a large number of ennoblements, most of them linked to the Treaty of Hadiach (Hadziacz), signed in autumn 1658 with the Cossacks. Therefore, many 'new nobles' were Cossack officers that were rewarded this way, with 32 of them being ennobled and only three foreigners receiving *indygenat* at the same time.[19] In 1661, to further award soldiers for their involvement in the wars against the Swedes and Muscovites, the *Sejm* agreed for 13 *indygenat* and 62 ennoblements. From amongst the latter, more than a half was for non-noble Poles and Lithuanians who were serving as lieutenants, standard-bearers and companions in national cavalry units, while at least 18 were for officers of foreign troops (infantry, dragoons and reiters).[20] Such rewards could come with some conditions, though. In February 1662, Jerzy Kleyn/Klein, captain in the Royal Guard dragoon regiment, received *indygenat* for his service in the Polish army since 1648. He was a Calvinist from a Dutch family settled in Ducal Prussia, so he had to promise that he would convert to Roman Catholicism, which he did in 1663.[21]

Sometimes, despite support from regional *sejmiki* or representatives of the army, an ennoblement proposal could be rejected. It happened to Henry de Serocourt, lieutenant colonel of the Royal Guard dragoon regiment. Despite fighting in the Polish army since 1648 and having a good military record, his candidature for ennoblement was rejected by the *Sejm* in 1660. His name was proposed by envoys sent by the army, but, without the support from high-ranking officials (e.g., a hetman), it could not go through.[22]

Provisions

The types, quality and quantity of the food received by soldiers during the war varied. While there were some basic regulations about how much and what food was assigned to units, during campaigns, it was very hard to keep up with regular supplies, and for long periods of time soldiers had to look for their food themselves, and usually it was the local population that suffered because of it. Throughout the majority of this period, there was no centralised

---

18 *Volumina Legum*, vol. IV, pp.263–66.
19 *Volumina Legum*, vol. IV, pp.295–97, 303–05, 319.
20 *Volumina Legum*, vol. IV, pp.407–12.
21 Wagner, *Słownik biograficzny oficerów polskich drugiej połowy XVII wieku*, vol. I, p.146.
22 Wagner, *Słownik biograficzny oficerów polskich drugiej połowy XVII wieku*, vol. I, p.246.

MILITARY LIFE AND DEATH

way of gathering and delivering food to the army. Marching units were normally 'taking bread' from villages during their march, usually leaving just a signed confirmation of its cost and no real money. The hetman or other high-ranking commanders would normally issue orders reminding their soldiers to keep strict discipline while 'taking bread', to ensure that the units used only assigned areas and were not crossing into other units' paths. Unfortunately, reality was much different from even the best laid plans. More often than not, soldiers were just taking what they could and wanted, leading to numerous complaints and court cases from the victims of such activities. Only during the longer stay of the Polish army in Prussia in 1658–1659, connected with many siege operations there, was there an attempt to establish better control of the supply chain, which was agreed upon by the *Sejm* in June 1658.[23] Local *sejmiki* chose their own local quartermasters known as *prowiantmagister*, who were to in charge of gathering and transporting provisions or money on the territorial level. The main quartermaster (*prowiantmaster generalny*), Marcin Dębicki, was coordinating the gathering of those supplies in set-up warehouses and from there delivering it by the Vistula river to the army in Prussia. Voivodeships and lands that had river ports were supposed to focus on providing food, while those without river ports could provide money instead, which was then to be used to purchase provisions. There was even a specific list of food items that were supposed to be provided as part of this obligation, which will be described below. The main quartermaster was ordered to liaison with the hetman, to agree where all those provisions should be delivered by 'ferries, ships and any other [boats]'. Deputies sent

An Eastern-style tabor wagon pulled by four horses. While the one represented here is from Transylvanian army, the Poles and Lithuanians would use exactly the same type, often drawn by oxen. Erik Dahlbergh's drawing for Samuel Pufendorf's *De rebus a Carolo Gustavo Sueciae rege gestis*, published in 1696 (Biblioteka Narodowa, Warszawa).

---

23   *Volumina Legum*, vol. IV, pp.246–47.

from regiments and banners were to provide the quartermasters with special assignations, indicating how much food and for how many men they were supposed to take. At the next *Sejm*, the main quartermaster was then to provide all the paperwork, including signed assignations from the troops and documents indicating the amount of food and money gathered for the campaign. Importantly, the nobles at the *Sejm* pointed out that this whole operation was a 'one time only' attempt to support the army.

It is very interesting to find out what was part of the soldiers' diet at the time. Here, we can use not only some surviving documents but also information scattered in diaries. In August 1648, the newly raised hussar banner of Aleksander Hilary Połubiński received an allowance of 'bread' that it was allowed to gather for its men in so-called '*przystawstwo*' (the area where the new unit was gathering). A document issued by Hetman Janusz Radziwiłł specified the number of voloks (*włók*) that were needed to provide the specific items:[24]

Number of voloks	Type of food	Measurement	Number
2	Rye	Barrel[25]	1
4	Barley	Barrel	1
15	Peas	Barrel	1
8	Buckwheat	Barrel	1
1	Oats	Barrel	1
1	Hay	Cart[26]	1
10	Heifer	-	1
3	Mutton	-	1
1	Goose		1
2	Hen	-	2
12	Butter	*Miednica*[27]	1
1	Cheese	-	2
10	Slab of pork lard	Slab (*połeć*)	1

---

24 Volok was an old Polish land measurement. In Poland, it was 17.955 hectares, in Lithuania 21.368 hectares. Majewski, *Marszałek wielki litewski Aleksander Hilary Połubiński (1626-1679)*, p.32.
25 Probably barrel used here was between 130 and 160 litres for beer. One used as measurement for dry capacity could have up to 300 litres, which again could vary depend on the region.
26 With enough hay for four horses.
27 Old Polish measurement, depends on the region it could between 33 and 46.8 litres

MILITARY LIFE AND DEATH

Another document regarding food for the same unit comes from September 1649, when it was sent to the winter quarters. Like before, there is a very detailed list of items based on the number of voloks:[28]

Number of voloks	Type of food	Measurement	Number
3	Rye	Barrel	1
3	Barley	Barrel	1
4	Buckwheat	Barrel	1
8	Slab of pork lard	Slab (*połeć*)	1
10	Butter	*Faska*[29]	1
10	Cheese	*Kopa*[30]	1
1	Oats	Barrel	1
1	Hay	Cart	1
2	Goose	-	1
2	Hen	-	2
2	Smoked beef ham (*kump*)	-	1
6	Peas	Barrel	1
12	Heifer	-	1
4	Mutton	-	1

In 1650 and 1651, as part of the *hiberna* (the food allowance for national cavalry in the winter quarters), soldiers were to receive the following items from each łan in the lands owned by the King and clergy:[31]

---

28 Majewski, *Marszałek wielki litewski Aleksander Hilary Połubiński (1626-1679)*, p.46.
29 Small wooden vessel, used for keeping butter.
30 One *kopa* equals 60.
31 Wimmer, *Wojsko polskie w drugiej połowie XVII wieku*, p.242.

Item	Measurement	From royal lands	From clergy lands
Oats	*Korzec*[32]	5	4
Rye	*Korzec*	1 ½	1
Wheat	*Korzec*	1 ½	½
Barley	*Korzec*	2	1 ½
Peas	*Korzec*	½	½
Tatar buckwheat (green buckwheat)	*Korzec*	1	1
Groats	*Korzec*	½	½
Butter	Quart (*Kwarta*)	10	10
Cheese	-	20	20
Slab of pork lard	Slab (*połeć*)	½	½
Animal meat	Quarters (of whole animal)	2	2
Mutton	-	1	1
Oil	Quart (*Kwarta*)[33]	2	2
Hen	-	6	6
Goose	-	3	3
Hay	Cart	3	3
Additionally 'vegetables, firewood and straw as per availability [in given area]'			

Połubiński's dragoon company, in their assigned winter quarters in December 1653, was to have delivered the following items, based on voloks:[34]

Number of voloks	Type of food	Measurement	Number
3	Rye	Barrel	1
4	Barley	Barrel	1
6	Peas	Barrel	1
6	Lard	Slab	1
12	Cheese	*Kopa*	1
2	Oats	Barrel	1
2	Hay	Cart	1
3	Hens	-	2
3	Goose	-	1
3	Rump	-	1
12	Heifer	-	1
4	Mutton	-	1

---

32 Old Polish measurement, depends on the region it could be anything between 50 and 100 litres of dry capacity.
33 One *kwarta* was approximately 0.9 litre of dry capacity.
34 BCzart., no. 2749, p.311.

Another detailed list comes from autumn 1654, describing the provisions supplied for the hussar banner of Bishop Piotr Gembicki. The unit was composed of 50 companions and 70 retainers. The supplies delivered to them were as follows:[35]

Item	Measurement	Quantity
Rye	*Korzec*	98
Barley	*Korzec*	34
Butter	*Faska*	33
Cheese	*Kopa*	33
Mutton	-	34
Beer	Barrel	35
Heifer	-	10
Oats	*Korzec*	1095
Hay	*Brog*[36]	6

There was also a special food allowance for a unit's chaplain and surgeon. The former received one *faska* of butter, one *kopa* of cheese, two slabs of meat, one *korzec* of groats, half a *korzec* of millet and 12 *kwarta* of vodka. The latter's allowance was one slab of meat, one *faska* of butter, one *kopa* of cheese, half a *korzec* of groats and a quarter *korzec* of millet.[37]

More interestingly, when a nominal *rotmistrz* stayed with his banner between 9 October and 8 November 1654, there were special deliveries for the pantry set up for him and his entourage. Due to his status, as both Crown Grand Chancellor and Bishop of Cracow, the menu on his table was much more generous than the one used to feed the soldiers. It is more than likely, though, that the officers and some chosen companions could on occasion dine with him. Therefore, it is worth mentioning some of food that was available. This gives us an idea on what could be found on the tables of wealthy magnates and high-ranking officers when they had the time and money to purchase proper supplies during a campaign. Amongst the list, we can find wheat and rye flour for baking bread, 49 hens, 15 capons, 30 geese, 20 ducks, two *korzec* of cooking apples, 2 *korzec* of shallots, 30 wreaths of onions, 12 muttons, two oxen, seven calves (five delivered alive, two already slaughtered) and a barrel of salt. There were three different types of beer, in total 22 *achtel*: two barrels of wine and 67 *kwarta* of vodka. As additional ingredients to preparing dishes, we can find six *kwarta* of cherry juice and six *kwarta* of honey. Finally, there were the more expensive items: two pounds of black pepper corns, three *łut* of saffron, one pound of ginger, four pounds

---

35 BJ, no. 8842/IV, p.56v.
36 Closest equivalent would be hay barrack
37 BJ, no. 8842/IV, p.57v.

of 'large and small raisins', four pounds of olive oil, four pounds of sugar, a quarter pound of cloves, half a pound of cinnamon and two *łut* of mace.[38] As the Bishop was staying with the unit for a long time, there were also large deliveries of fish, used for meals during fasting (as Friday was traditionally a non-meat day). On the menu, we can find carp, pike, trout, bream and perch.[39]

Returning to the not-so-impressive diet of the ordinary soldiers, it is time to look into some documents from the Deluge. First, we have the provisions planned for the district troops from Prussia in 1655, raised in the face of the Swedish invasion. While we need to consider it regional specific (e.g., the presence of the fish in the infantry's diet), this list still provides us with interesting insight into the food eaten by Polish troops. The list was divided into provisions for cavalry and infantry:

Monthly allowance for a 200-horse-strong banner of *arkabuzeria*:[40]

Item	Measurement	Quantity
Oats	*Korzec*	700
Hay	Cart	24
Rye	*Korzec*	75
Wheat	*Korzec*	75
Beer	Barrel	100
Oxen	-	25
Skopy[41]	-	200
Goose	-	400
Chicken	-	400
Slab of meat[42]	Slab (*połeć*)	50
Peas	*Korzec*	25
Barley	*Korzec*	25
Butter	*Achtel*[43]	20
Salt	Barrel	1
Cheese	*Kopa*	20
Garden vegetables		As much as needed

Monthly allowance for a 100-man-strong company of infantry (probably the same set would be for both foreign and Polish–Hungarian infantry):[44]

---

38 *Łut* was an old Polish measurement. One *łut* equalled 0.0127kg.
39 BJ, no. 8842/IV, pp.57–57v.
40 BCzart., no. 352, p.64.
41 Castrated ram.
42 No information about type of the meat, most probably breast or belly of lamb or pork belly.
43 Old Polish measurement, depends on the region it could between 80 and 160 litres.
44 BCzart., no. 352, pp.64–65.

MILITARY LIFE AND DEATH

Item	Measurement	Quantity
Rye	*Korzec*	100
Wheat	*Korzec*	25
Beer	Barrel	25
Oxen	-	2
Skopy	-	50
Geese (for officers only)	-	100
Chicken (for officers only)	-	100
Slab of meat	-	560
Peas	*Korzec*	30
Barley	Not mentioned, probably *korzec*	24
Butter	*Achtel*	15
Herring	Barrel	1 ½
Cabbage and kale		As much as needed
Cheese	*Kopa*	25
Oats for officers' horses	*Łaszt*[45]	2
Hay	Cart	5

An interesting source for the soldiers' diets are the Swedish requisition orders from autumn 1655 and spring 1656, indicating the types and quantity of food and other provisions that were to be provided to the Swedish troops, as after all it was the same type of food that would be provided to the Polish soldiers. The document from 1 November 1655 requested a large contribution towards the Swedish Guard regiment, which was to be provided by six villages belonging to Jakub Michałowski. Amongst the items that were to be provided were rye, malt, hops, oats, fresh meat or lard (not rendered), hay, straw and some cash.[46] Even more interesting is the order issued on 29 November 1655 for the food that was to be delivered to the Swedish troops at Częstochowa besieging Jasna Góra. We can find there '60,000 loaves of bread, 80 barrels of beer, 400 *korzec* of oats, eight oxen, 60 muttons, four barrels of salt, one barrel of vodka, 400 tallow candles, 200 eggs, 40 *faska* of butter, geese and hens as many as needed'.[47] In March 1656, the village of Bochnia was to deliver, on a weekly basis, the following provisions to the Swedish garrison of Łowicz: one ox or 'two good heifers', two calves, four lambs, 10 hens, seven geese, 60 eggs, two *faska* of butter, two barrels of beer (or the financial equivalent of them), 20 carts of fire wood, seven carts of hay, four carts of straw, 30 *korzec* of oats and a mix of pepper, ginger, cloves

---

45   Each ach *łaszt* equals 30 *korzec*.
46   *Jakuba Michałowskiego, wojskiego lubelskiego a później kasztelana bieckiego Księga Pamiętnicza*, pp.773–75.
47   *Jakuba Michałowskiego, wojskiego lubelskiego a później kasztelana bieckiego Księga Pamiętnicza*, p.781.

AGAINST THE DELUGE

Details of the camp of Czarniecki's division, March 1656. Engraving from volume VII of *Theatrum Europaem*, published in Frankfurt am Main in 1672 (Biblioteka Narodowa, Warszawa).

and sugar.[48] Of course, these are just three examples of Swedish requisition orders. During the war, many more of them were issued, usually with a specific timescale and place of delivery. In some cases, they had, like an order from Częstochowa, an additional treating note, indicating that if provisions were not delivered on time, the people from the designated area would be 'severely punished with fire and sword, by the [Swedish] soldiers send to execute [the order]'.

Switching again our attention to the Polish side, the *Sejm* regulation from June 1658, dealing with preparing provisions for the army in Prussia, mentioned the following allocation of food per each volok of the land belonging to the King, clergy and nobles alike:[49]

Number of voloks	Type of food	Measurement	Number
1	Rye	*Korzec*	1 ½
1	Malt (for beer)	*Korzec*	1 ½
1	Oats	*Korzec*	3
1	Peas	*Korzec*	¼
1	Groats	*Korzec*	¼
10	Heifer	-	1
10	Slab of meat	Slab (*połeć*)	1

Another document comes from the end of the war, from the region of today's Belarus. Soldiers from the dragoon squadron (known also as regiment) of Michał Kazimierz Radziwiłł, stationed as a garrison of the fortress in Nieśwież in 1660, were receiving their food once per week, and each file composed of five or six men was to receive the following weekly food allowance:[50]

---

48 *Z Bochynia taki raty chcieli na tydzień do Łowicza*, Riskarkivet Stockholm, Extranea IX Polen, p.143.
49 *Volumina Legum*, vol. IV, p.246.
50 AGAD, AR VII, no. 57, p.47.

MILITARY LIFE AND DEATH

Item	Measurement	Quantity
Rye	*Korzec*	1 ½
Groats	*Miarka*[51]	6
Peas	*Korzec*	¼
Barley	*Korzec*	1
Slab of lard	Slab (*połeć*)	1/2
Salt	Quart (*Kwarta*)	

In chapter four, there were a few mentions of supplies required for lan infantry during the raising of their units in 1655. Sometimes, we can find such information about regular troops as well. When the Polish army was marching to the Ukrainian theatre of the war in the spring of 1660, Holsten mentioned the food required for his reiters. Each soldier was supposed to have flour and bread for four weeks. Additionally, within a company of the regiment, there were two sutlers with large wagons 'full of mead, beer and vodka'. The army was also accompanied by 'many oxen and other cattle'.[52] Men could also supplement their diet by hunting 'animals, of which there were plenty here – hares, capercaillies, grouses, partridges, quails and other of their kind. They are so fat, that they can barely run or fly, so you can hunt them with whip from the horseback.'[53]

As it seems, sometimes soldiers were lucky enough to take part in a campaign that took place in an area not touched by previous conflicts or at least by recent fighting. Bogusław Kazimierz Maskiewicz wrote about a two-week stay in a village near Rzeczyca, where Prince Bogusław Radziwiłł's hussar banner was quartered in late February 1649. Maskiewicz's retinue was stationed in houses of a weaver and a fisherman. The former 'was helping my servants to get some food', but the fisherman was so poor that actually it was the Lithuanian hussar that had to share his bread with him. In return, 'he sometimes fed me proper fish, while more often just pikes [and] so many of them, that me and my retinue got some, other we gave to other [soldiers], while many other I smoked [for later].[54] Jan Florian Drobysz Tuszyński, who as a young companion took part in Lubomirski's expedition to Transylvania in 1657, wrote that there was 'plenty of wine, meat, all kind of cattle and other things, as it is [normally] in enemy's land, but it was very difficult to get some bread'.[55] Pasek mentioned how well supplied Czarniecki's division was when it entered Denmark in winter 1658: 'enough cattle, sheep … plenty of honey … all kind of fish, plenty of bread, poor wine but good mead and *petercymenty* [sweet Spanish wine]'.

---

51 Old Polish measurement of dry capacity, approximately 15 litres.
52 Holsten, *Przygody wojenne 1655-1666*, p.55.
53 Holsten, *Przygody wojenne 1655-1666*, p.55.
54 *Pamiętniki Samuela i Bogusława Kazimierza Maskiewiczów*, p.266.
55 *Dwa pamiętniki z XVII wieku Jana Cedrowskiego i Jana Floriana Drobysza Tuszyńskiego*, pp.30–31.

There were also plenty of opportunities to hunt for hares, roes and deer.⁵⁶ In the winter quarters in 1659, a Polish division continued to have access to the proper supplies. Pasek, who clearly enjoyed a nice meal, mentioned:

> good alcohol, especially mead, as they do not drink it here just make it and send via ships to other provinces; plenty of fish, [as for] two Leipzig shilling, which is four Polish groszy, given to fishermen [he] brought you whole bag [of fish]. They bake bread from peas [flour], as there is plenty of it here. But we also had [bread] baked from wheat or rye, especially [eaten] by nobles.⁵⁷

After the campaign of 1660, when spending the winter of 1660/1661 in the quarters in Ukraine, Holsten mentioned that 'good meat and bread, mead, vodka and tobacco were our normal rations'.⁵⁸

On the other hand, much more often, supplies were very poor, and soldiers – especially from infantry and dragoons – were half starving. Lithuanian soldier Aleksander Skorobohaty mentioned that, in summer 1657 during a pursuit of the Transylvanian army, the joint Polish and Lithuanian troops had to stop at Żółkiew to resupply, as 'for three Sundays [weeks] we did not have bread, eating only cherries'.⁵⁹ Jakub Łoś, describing the same campaign against the Transylvanians, wrote that the Polish soldiers were hungry, as they ate 'only berries'.⁶⁰ Gordon described the very basic diet of his soldiers in late September 1660, when the Polish army allied with the Tatars was fighting the Muscovites and Cossacks in Ukraine: 'Wee had no other victuals but what was purchased from the Moskovites, which was most[ly] dryed bread cutted small lyk [like] dice which tasted excellently at such a tyme'.⁶¹ By the end of October, after two battles against the Muscovites and Cossacks, the situation was even worse, 'for provisions were very scarce, especially among the foot, most whereof had be[e]n long ago eating horse flesh'.⁶² In November, before units were sent into winter quarters, the Scot gave another example of the non-working logistics in the Polish army, writing that 'haveing all this march nothing to eat but what wee had in our waggons. For neither bread not any other victualls was any where to be had, so that to the poor foot-souldiers even horse flesh was very acceptable'.⁶³ Holsten depicts a tragic episode from the winter of 1659/1660 in Prussia, where many Polish, Imperial and Brandenburg troops were stationed after the siege operations of 1659: 'Our infantry spread out on few miles around the camp, looking for roots and turnips in empty gardens, to save themselves from starvation. All they were able to find was just dog and horse carcasses, which they ate with great appetite'.⁶⁴ He even mentioned a case of cannibalism, when three musketeers

---

56 Pasek, *Pamiętniki*, pp.75–76.
57 Pasek, *Pamiętniki*, p.96.
58 Holsten, *Przygody wojenne 1655-1666*, p.65.
59 Skorobohaty, *Dziennik*, p.67.
60 Łoś, *Pamiętnik towarzysza chorągwi pancernej*, p.78.
61 *Diary of General Patrick Gordon*, vol. II, p.76.
62 *Diary of General Patrick Gordon*, vol. II, p.94.
63 *Diary of General Patrick Gordon*, vol. II, p.100.
64 Holsten, *Przygody wojenne 1655-1666*, pp.52–53.

ate the fourth one 'with appetite and pleasure'. It appears that this sudden lack of supplies was just short lived, caused by sudden storms and ice on rivers destroying two pontoon bridges used to deliver provisions from the other side of the Vistula river. After eight days, the weather improved, bridges were set up again and soon supplies were provided to the starving troops.[65] Even Pasek, after his 'good times' during the campaign in Denmark, had to survive on rather poor rations during a few months of the 1660 campaign against the Muscovites. In October 1660, after the battle at the river Basia, Polish soldiers finally had a chance to get some meat from the cattle captured from the Muscovite tabor, as previously 'it was hard to get them, as near Muscovite border [cattle] was either already taken [by other soldiers] or well hidden'. Before that, both the Poles and Lithuanians 'for few months eat only gardening things [vegetables], especially roasted beetroots, from which they make all special things'. Most favourite were baked dumplings (*pierogi*) made from roasted beetroots wrapped in bread-like dough and brushed with ground flaxseed.[66] No surprise that, after a diet of this kind, as soon as 'any of us had ox or heifer, he did not had to invite any guest [for dinner], as those from other regiments arrived, as soon as they know that someone is cooking piece of fresh meat'.[67]

Sometimes, free access to alcohol, combined with a lack of proper food, could lead to dire consequences. Holsten mentioned that, after the Battle of Słobodyszcze, the soldiers were hungry and thirsty, which was especially problematic for the wounded. Reiters brought them some water found nearby, which was 'yellow, very muddy and we had to filter it through cloth. It quench our thirst though'. The next day, a few carts full of large barrels of vodka arrived from the Polish camp: 'Well, it was such amazing meal for us, as we drunk our fill, each according to our own likes and health. Many wounded drunk themselves to death'.[68] At the end of the campaign of 1663/1664, after a sudden thaw that caused all the snow to melt and rivers to overflow, the marching Polish–Lithuanian army had to abandon all their tabor wagons. According to de Gramont, 'since not a single one of them [wagons] was preserved in the whole army, starting with the royal wagons, there was such a severe famine that for two days I saw how there was no bread on the king's table and how everyone was on the eve of starvation.'. He also added, 'as for me personally, out of the six wagons and six horses that I had, I only had one Tatar horse left, which I loaded with a barrel of vodka'.[69]

As we have already seen in Holsten's diary, even in such dire times, certain provisions were clearly prioritised over the others. It is worth finishing this part with a quote from de Noyers, who, after seeing how stubborn the Polish army was while besieging Toruń in autumn 1658, commented in one of his letters:

---

65 Holsten, *Przygody wojenne 1655-1666*, p.53.
66 They were more like Cornish pasties, considering Pasek's description.
67 Pasek, *Pamiętniki*, p.175.
68 Holsten, *Przygody wojenne 1655-1666*, p.60.
69 Gramont, *Iz istorii moskovskago pokhoda Iana Kazimira, 1663-1664 g.g.*, pp.29–30.

AGAINST THE DELUGE

> There is no other nation in the world that can so easily [as the Poles] survive during the hard time, with small dose of vodka and pipe of tobacco then can live without bread; when they have it, they will it more of it than other but when they lack it, they wo not starve to death, they can sleep on the snow like in the best bed.[70]

Polish cavalry in the Battle of Warsaw in 1656. Erik Dahlbergh's drawing for Samuel Pufendorf's *De rebus a Carolo Gustavo Sueciae rege gestis*, published in 1696 (Muzeum Narodowe, Kraków).

Spiritual Guidance

The religious aspect was very important in the war against the Swedish 'heretics', so the motif of fighting in God's name can be often found in letters and diaries. Pasek mentioned a situation when Czarniecki's troops were taking part in a Holy Mass celebrating the capture of Kolding, just three hours after taking the city:[71]

> *Te Deum laudamus* was sung and was heard in whole forest. I kneeled next to Father Piekarski, to attend him; covered in blood [after the fight] I started to help him when Voivode [Czarniecki] said 'Brother,[72] at least wash your hand'. Priest then answered: 'No matter, God does not abhor blood that is spilled for the glory of His name'.

Czarniecki's division was accompanied in Denmark by at least two chaplains, both of them Jesuits: Adrian Piekarski, who was Pasek's uncle and later became a royal priest, and Dąbrowski (first name unknown). In his diary, Pasek often mentioned them blessing troops before assaults, taking their pre-battle confession (from horseback) and celebrating Holy Mass after battles. Łoś also mentioned the presence of chaplains, supporting Pasek's claims as

---

70 *Portfolio królowej Maryi Ludwiki*, vol. II, pp.207–08.
71 Pasek, *Pamiętniki*, p.87.
72 The phrase used by Czarniecki was '*panie bracie*', used when two nobles were talking to each other to show that they were (at least in theory) equal. It is sometimes translated as 'brother sir', although we believe such a version sounds rather awkward and decided to use just 'brother' or 'brethren' throughout the book.

they both served in the same division. The presence of Jesuits was even a subject of bitter comments from the other Polish soldiers, when, in 1661, there were arguments if the unpaid army should mutiny and start a so-called 'confederation'. After Pasek talked the soldiers against mutiny, companions from other units were shouting, 'no surprise that Czarniecki's men [from his division] have such [moral] scruples, in their division all chaplain are Jesuits. They fil all men with such scruples'.[73]

Of course, 'spiritual guidance' was not just limited to the regiment or division level. In some of the surviving muster rolls, we can find chaplains included into unit staff, which indicates the presence of many more priests within the rank. While most of them were present in hussar banners and *pancerni* banners, there was also *Pater Capelanus* in Lubomirski's reiter regiment with an allowance of a two-horse retinue (pay).[74] Of course, there was no general rule for the presence of a chaplain. It all depended on the will of the colonel or *rotmistrz*, as normally priests were outside of the unit's structure and were not included in the overall pay list. They would be normally paid by the magnate or noble from his own expenses, with many of them being in fact part of the retinue of the wealthier commanders, amongst his surgeon, aides and servants. Some of the high-ranking hierarchs of the clergy held even the rank of *rotmistrz* in the army, although it was purely a nominal office and their units were led in the field by professional lieutenants.

The blessing of the troops before a battle was very common, and, of course, we have more examples of such activities during campaigns. During the Battle of Beresteczko in 1651, amongst the priests riding in front of the banners to provide the blessings were Bishop of Chełmno and Crown Chancellor Andrzej Leszczyński and Jesuit Cieczyszowski. Another chaplain, an unnamed Bernardine monk from the regiment of Jerzy Lubomirski, impressed all soldiers when, 'with crucifix on his neck, mounted but without any armour nor weapon' he rode from banner to banner, and his sermons were so passionate that 'almost all of them [soldiers] cried listening to him'.[75] Poczobut Odlanicki mentioned that, before the battle at the Basia against the Muscovites in 1660, 'all [soldiers] took part in the Holy Mass and place their faith in the Lord'.[76]

It is also important to remember the role played by clergy on the local level in the occupied country. Priests were often an important part of the resistance movement, helping to organise or even leading peasant partisans in their struggle against the Swedes. They were sometimes directly engaging the Swedes although not always with successful outcomes. Holsten wrote about his skirmish fight against a 'priest, who was good Polish noble'. The Pole shot at the reiter and missed from both his pistols and then, in a hand-

---

73 Pasek, *Pamiętniki*, p.182.
74 AGAD, ASK, no. 92, p.1v.
75 Mirosław Nagielski (ed.), 'Diariusz wojny pod Beresteczkiem z chanem krymskim i Kozakami zaporoskiemi za szczęśliwego panowania Króla JM. Jana Kazimierza, na którą sam osobą swą ruszeł się z Warszawy in Anno 1651', in *Relacje wojenne z pierwszych lat walk polsko-kozackich powstania Bohdana Chmielnickiego okresu "Ogniem i Mieczem" (1648-1651)* (Warszawa: Wydawnictwo VIKING, 1999), pp.251–52.
76 Poczobut Odlanicki, *Pamiętnik Jana Władysława Poczobuta Odlanickiego*, p.39.

to-hand fight, hit the German soldier in the head with his spent pistol, 'so I started bleeding from nose and mouth'. Holsten managed to take him prisoner only because more reiters came to his rescue. The anonymous priest did not stay in Swedish captivity for long, though, as he paid the ransom of 400 Thalers to General Wirtz.[77] Pauline Fathers, led by Jan Kordecki, were of course instrumental in the defence of the Jasna Góra Monastery, acting as the 'heart and soul' of the siege. The Polish success and forcing the Swedish besiegers to lift their operations had a huge psychological impact on the morale in Poland and on the way that both soldiers and the local population started to see the Swedes as heretical invaders. It seems that other Pauline Fathers were also involved in direct actions against the Swedes. We can find two of them – Marceli Tomicki and Hieronim Wojsza – as 'spirit leaders' of the partisans under Żegocki and Kulesza during their operation in Wieluń in January 1656. Unfortunately, both monks died on 12 January during a battle with the Swedish pacification force.[78] Priest Jan Zapolski, abbot of the monastery in Lądz, gathered a partisan group from amongst local nobles in Wielkopolska and, in May 1656, managed to push out the Swedes from the town of Koło.[79] In autumn the same year, he had a banner of cossack cavalry, led by Lieutenant Kacper Jan Żychliński, serving as part of the levy of nobility of Wielkopolska.[80]

Taking Care of the Dead, Wounded and Prisoners of War

The situation of the wounded left on a battlefield was, in most of cases, very dire, as they often fell victim to pillaging marauders or local peasants. Opponents rarely took care of those seriously wounded unless they were officers. Pufendorf wrote about a rather gruesome attempt of delivering the coup de grâce to the Polish wounded. It was based on Erik Dahlbergh's story from early April 1657, when his troops encountered a badly harmed Polish soldier:[81]

> [The Pole] was lying on his back, shot through heart by two bullets, with his eyes closed and bloody froth on his mouth. [The Swedish] Soldiers decided that it would be merciful to end his suffering, as he did not stand a chance to survive. One of them dismounted, placed the muzzle of his pistol on [the Pole's] forehead and shot him, so man's brain came out [from the wound]. At that moment wounded placed his right hand on this wound [and] stick his fingers into blood and brain. Then second [Swedish] soldier shot him twice, hitting him between the

---

77   Holsten, *Przygody wojenne 1655-1666*, p.38.
78   Damian Orłowski, 'Potop szwedzkie na ziemi wieluńskiej', *Rocznik Wieluński*, 7 (2007), p.40.
79   Staręgowski, *Formacje zbrojne samorządu szlacheckiego województw poznańskiego i kaliskiego w okresie panowania Jana Kazimierza (1648-1668)*, p.166.
80   Staręgowski, *Formacje zbrojne samorządu szlacheckiego województw poznańskiego i kaliskiego w okresie panowania Jana Kazimierza (1648-1668)*, p.174.
81   Pufendorf, *Siedem ksiąg o czynach Karola Gustawa króla Szwecji*, p.254.

eyes, smashing while upper part of the skull. Despite that Pole was still moving both hands. Then Swede thrust his sword three or four times into his heart [but] with each thrust Pole moved his legs and put hand on his chest. He then received many more thrusts, from his stomach up to his neck. Many shots hit his head and heart, so blood was pouring from smashed skull, yet he still was moving his hands and legs and started to moan in a way like he was trying to say something. All [of the Swedish soldiers] were very surprised, that he was still so conscious with his heart and forehead hit so many times. They were observing this event for half an hour and then finally abandoned him [there] while he was still drawing breath.

Care for the wounded was often in the hands of monks and nuns, for which they were usually financially reimbursed. In Poland, it was common that the Brothers Hospitallers of Saint John of God, known as *bonifratrzy*, specialised in providing such medical care in their hospitals. After the assault on Warsaw, their friary in this town 'took care of the shot and wounded' during the fight, for which in December 1657 the monks received 100 zł.[82] There was also an institution of military hospitals set up for 'soldiers, those that are wounded and shot'. The *Sejm* of 1659 requested that the *Instygator Koronny* (Latin: *Instigator Regni*)[83] was to prepare a list of all such hospitals for the next *Sejm*.[84] As most of them were in private hands, they seem to have not fulfilled their assigned role. Therefore, a stricter control of them was needed. The *Sejm* of 1661 did not look into the problem, but the one from 1662 did, asking the *Instygator Koronny* to look into the cases where those hospitals were decreased or ceased to operate. The order mentioned the locations as 'Warsaw, Tykocin, Lwów and others'.[85]

As there was a slim chance to look for support from some official source or service, the survival of the wounded was often just a case of pure luck or help received from their servants or even other companions from the same banner. Pasek mentioned two veterans from his unit, Jan Rubieszowski and Jan Wojnowski, who were severely wounded during the Battle of Chojnice on 1 January 1657. Both were 'cut and struck with rapiers, left for dead on the battlefield'; their wounds were so grave that King Jan II Kazimierz himself sent them money for the funeral. However, they did survive and returned to the ranks, fighting in further campaigns, taking part in the Danish expedition and finally dying – both on the same day – from some unspecified illness or maybe even post-campaign exhaustion in early 1660.[86]

The timely intervention of surgeons could save even severely wounded men, especially when they were taken care of quickly. Jan Odrowąż Pieniążek, serving as lieutenant in a cossack-style cavalry banner of Jan Wielopolski, was hit by a cannonball during the Battle of Warsaw in 1656. It 'crushed his heel, [causing a] massive wound, and his life was in danger', but he was

---

82   AGAD, ASK IV, Księga Rekognicji, no. 14, p.47.
83   Lord Prosecutor of the Crown, who dealt with any crimes against the King or the State.
84   *Volumina Legum*, vol. IV, p.284.
85   *Volumina Legum*, vol. IV, p.395.
86   Pasek, *Pamiętniki*, p.132.

saved by a battle surgeon (possibly from his own unit).[87] On 19 July 1657, Aleksander Skorobohaty was 'shot with two bullets' during a fight against the Transylvanians. Luckily, he was taken care of by his older brother, Benedykt, who took the 'barely alive' Aleksander to Lwów, where one bullet was cut out while the other had to be left within the body.[88] The wounded Lithuanian companion had to stay there for a few months, clearly in very bad shape, although in October he was transported on stretches to rejoin his unit and he was able to recover during their stay in the winter quarters.[89]

Sometimes, recovery could take a very long time. In October 1664, Joachim Jerlicz's son, Bazyli, was seriously shot in the stomach during the siege of Cossack-held Psiarówka in Ukraine. He barely survived, and recovery took him half a year.[90] Samuel Leszczyński, in his poem about the Battle of Cudnów, mentioned the wounds of two officers from Jan Zamoyski's foreign infantry regiment. Captain von Pincier was wounded in his side by a cannonball, 'so much that his intestines were out', but was saved by surgeons who 'put them back in and stitched the wound'. Captain Drezner, while leading the attack on the Muscovite battery, 'shot next to his testicles so the [cannon]ball went out through his backside'.[91] It seems that, despite the severity of their wounds, both officers were saved by army surgeons. Often though, despite proper help, nothing could be done for the seriously injured. Jerlicz mentioned companion Paweł Butowicz, who was wounded at the Battle of Ochmatów in 1655. Eleven days after receiving the wound, he succumbed, as 'two of his ribs were broken by the cannonball'.[92]

Sometimes, wounded companions could be awarded special gratification 'for wound'. There is a detailed list of wounded Lithuanian officers and soldiers that were due to receive money in July 1650 for the previous campaigns against the Cossacks:[93]

- Officers: one was to receive 800 zł and nine others 400 zł each.
- Hussar companions: two were due 250 zł while four 200 zł each.
- Reiter companions: two were due 150 zł each.
- Companions from cossack cavalry: one 200 zł, three 100 zł each and 22 were due 90 zł each.
- From Tatar light horse: 20 (including one lieutenant) were to receive 50 zł each.
- Dragoons and infantry: two were due 60 zł each, three 50 zł each, one 40 zł and five 50 zł each.

---

87 Kochowski, *Lata Potopu 1655-1657*, p.207.
88 Skorobohaty, *Dziennik*, p.68.
89 Skorobohaty, *Dziennik*, p.69.
90 Jerlicz, *Latopisiec albo kroniczka*, vol. II, p.95.
91 Leszczyński, *Potrzeba z Szeremetem, hetmanem moskiewskim i z Kozakami w Roku Pańskim 1660 od Polaków wygrana*, p.121.
92 Jerlicz, *Latopisiec albo kroniczka*, vol. I, p.169.
93 *Korespondencja wojskowa hetmana Janusza Radziwiłła w latach 1646-1655*, vol. I, *Diariusz kancelaryjny 1649-1653*, pp.342–44.

MILITARY LIFE AND DEATH

Details of the Polish cavalry fleeing from the victorious Swedes near Sandomierz, 26 March 1656. (Krigsarkivet, Stockholm).

Also in the Polish army, soldiers could receive such a 'payment for wounded'. For example, the *Sejm* in 1654 confirmed special payments for companions from six banners (one hussar and five cossack cavalry) for the wounds they received during the Battle of Batoh in 1652. The total value of those payments was assigned as 1,000 zł.[94] The *Sejm* in 1661 confirmed the payments to eight previously wounded companions for a total amount of 1,066 zł, of which the biggest amount was 600 zł and the smallest 30 zł.[95] Of course, the main problem with such rewards was that, facing constant financial trouble with cash flow, the National Treasury could delay pay for a fairly long time. Polish companion Marcin Świrski, who was awarded 50 zł for the wound he took during the Battle of Batoh in 1652, received his money after seven years during the Commission in Lwów in August 1659.[96]

While rank-and-files from foreign troops and retainers from national cavalry could rarely receive a ceremonial military burial, officers from both *autorament* and companions from national cavalry were sometimes honoured this way, especially when the army or its part was stationed in winter quarters or in the camp during siege operations. On 13 August 1649, Field Hetman Janusz Radziwiłł honoured a companion from his own hussar banner who died during the battle at Łojów against the Cossacks. The funeral was accompanied by army units and commanders, probably due to the status of the deceased.[97]

Military funerals could even take place in rather unusual situations. When the Polish army was gathering after their retreat from the Battle of Żarnów in September 1655, the troops were gathering near Przedborz. Here, the soldiers seem to have felt so secure from the approaching Swedes that they even found the time 'for the burial with all military grandeur' for companion Andrzej Gromadzki, who died from illness. Again, it seems that the status of

---

94 AGAD, ASK II, Rachunki Sejmowe, no. 51, p.67.
95 AGAD, ASK II, Rachunki Sejmowe, no. 55, p.71v.
96 AGAD, ASK IV, Księga Rekognicji, no. 14, p.500.
97 *Korespondencja wojskowa hetmana Janusza Radziwiłła w latach 1646-1655*, vol. I, *Diariusz kancelaryjny 1649-1653*, p.174.

the deceased could play its role here, as Gromadzki was the standard-bearer of the Royal hussar banner.[98] Jan Florian Drobysz Tuszyński mentioned that, when his brother Stanisław died 'in face of the almost whole army' during the siege of Toruń, his burial was attended by many companions. Patrick Gordon wrote that, in 1659 during operations in Prussia, two of his killed friends, Lieutenant Adam Gordon and Ensign John Kenedy, were 'both honourably buryed according to the souldier fashion'.[99] A rather unusual situation took place during the Lithuanian siege of Swedish-held Goldynga in August 1659. A Swedish foray from the fortress captured a wounded companion named Zawisza. He died from his wounds, so the defenders decided to return his body, 'nicely wrapped in white sheet, they lowered it from the walls, full of regrets that he died when in their hands'.[100] Jerlicz mentioned that, in June 1658, in exchange for '*rotmistrz* Woronicz and Świrski and many other companions', the Poles sent to the Swedes '[Arvid] Wittenberg's bones'[101] and a few colonels kept as prisoners in Zamość.[102] He seems to have some incorrect information, as Wittenberg's body was only exhumed in 1664 when it was transported to Gdańsk and from there to Stocholm, where he was buried in 1671 in Storkyran church.

Very rare was for a companion's servant to receive a proper military burial, yet, thanks to surviving diaries, we know about one such example. At the end of August 1661, Kuczyński, the 'very needed and useful' servant of Poczobut Odlanicki, died from a fever. His master decided to honour the deceased and organised for him a 'funeral in military style, with military music and with 100 servants armed [with guns] escorted his body to the graveyard of the Benedictine Order church'. When the coffin was lowered to the grave, the servants gave a three-volley salute while a few priests led the funeral.[103]

The situation of POWs was already mentioned when describing their recruitment into the ranks of the Polish army. If the Swedes were fighting with regular troops or levy of nobility, in the case of defeat, there was a chance of being taken prisoner, although if the opponents were partisans or volunteers, the chances of survival were rather slim. Captured men were usually kept in the fortresses still in Polish hands, estates of loyal magnates or improvised POW camps near Polish army camps. De Noyers mentioned that, in March 1656, 'our men are capturing Swedes everywhere, amongst many others there is group of them kept in Łańcut, amongst them two Frenchmen, who were freed and entered our [Polish] service'.[104] It is not surprising that many captured soldiers, without any chance for ransom and exchange, decided to join the service of their new employer. Holsten wrote that, after few months in captivity, the decision to switch to Polish service was an easy one.[105] At

---

98 Kochowski, *Lata Potopu 1655-1657*, p.36.
99 *Diary of General Patrick Gordon*, vol. II, p.14.
100 Poczobut Odlanicki, *Pamiętnik Jana Władysława Poczobuta Odlanickiego*, p.27.
101 Taken prisoner after the surrender of Warsaw in June 1656, he was kept in Zamość until his death in autumn 1657.
102 Jerlicz, *Latopisiec albo kroniczka*, vol. II, p.9.
103 Poczobut Odlanicki, *Pamiętnik Jana Władysława Poczobuta Odlanickiego*, pp.45–46.
104 *Portfolio królowej Maryi Ludwiki*, vol. I, p.280.
105 Holsten, *Przygody wojenne 1655-1666*, p.44.

the end of March 1656, de Noyers in one of his letters mentioned that more than 400 prisoners were kept in Łańcut, Przemyśl and Zamość. Additionally, a whole company of 120 men of former Swedish soldiers joined the troops under the command of Prince Dymitr Wiśniowiecki.[106] Of course, not all soldiers – for many different reasons – were keen to change armies, so they could stay in captivity for even longer periods of time.

As in previous conflicts, during the Deluge, we can find evidence of the process of exchanging prisoners. As always, there were issues with the ratio in which men should be exchanged, as the Swedes tended to mention that a Polish or Lithuanian companion was worth more than an ordinary Swedish reiter or infantryman. Pufendorf mentioned that, in winter 1658, Lithuanian Hetman Gosiewski exchanged prisoners with the Swedes near Kircholm, although there is no information about the number and ratio of the exchange.[107] In December 1659, Robert Douglas was negotiating with Połubiński for a swap of the prisoners from their campaigns in Courland and Livonia. The Swedish general wrote to the Lithuanians that he had in captivity, admitting that he understood that 'every prisoner always want to return to their own' but that it took time to arrange everything. However, he was hopeful that the good negotiations with Połubiński, although proceeding slowly, with trumpeters constantly travelling with letters from one general to another, would be successful.[108] When the garrison of Toruń surrendered on 23 December 1658, one of the paragraphs of the agreement between the fighting sides covered the issue of prisoners. All Poles and Imperials captured by the Swedes and all Swedes captured by the besiegers were to be returned to their armies, except for those that, during captivity, decided to change sides and enter new military employment. The remaining Swedish garrison was allowed to leave the fortress and – under the escort of Polish soldiers, to protect them during the march – to move to Malbork.[109]

As with many other conflicts, armies stationed for a longer period in the same place, either as garrison or in the camp, were plagued by all kind of illnesses, affecting both the men and horses. One of the worst cases took place in the Lithuanian army camp near Rzeczyca, where Janusz Radziwiłł's forces gathered between July and November 1653. Already lacking food and stuck idle in one place, the soldiers were decimated by an outbreak of the plague (*dżuma*), which was at the time spreading throughout a large part of Lithuania and Samogitia. As was often the case, infantry was the worst affected. In the regiment of Wilhelm Korff, from 778 men (or more likely portions), 97 men died and a further 131 were sick.[110] *Rotmistrz* Chryzostom Świacki, who at the time was with the Lithuanian army, in his letter to Lithuanian Grand Hetman Janusz Kiszka,[111] wrote about appealing the conditions of service, mentioning

---

106 *Portfolio królowej Maryi Ludwiki*, vol. I, p.296.
107 Pufendorf, *Siedem ksiąg o czynach Karola Gustawa króla Szwecji*, p.475.
108 AGAD, AR V, no. 3341, p.1.
109 Rudawski, *Historja Polska od śmierci Władysława IV aż do pokoju oliwskiego*, vol. II, pp.365–73.
110 Majewski, *Marszałek wielki litewski Aleksander Hilary Połubiński (1626-1679)*, p.70.
111 Born in 1586, Kiszka, despite being Grand Hetman since 1646, did not take part in the campaigns against the Cossacks, so the actual command was in the hands of Field Hetman Janusz Radziwiłł. Kiszka died on 13 January 1654.

that the troops were unpaid and that 'there was big hunger, near one third men [present in the camp] died'.¹¹² Dahlbergh mentioned many 'poisonous pestilence-affected places' during his tour of Swedish-held fortresses in Prussia: Elbląg, Malbork, Grudziądz and Toruń.¹¹³ As such, those plagues tended to always spread over into besieging armies. No surprise that the Poles and their allies suffered due to the outbreaks during the operations in 1658 and 1659. To make matters worse, such illnesses were also decimating the local population, adding to the many other miseries brought into their territories by the warring armies.

Military Discipline

Official disciplinary regulations in the Polish and Lithuanian armies were normally issued by the king (if he was present) or more commonly by a hetman at the beginning of a campaign. They were called the 'Articles of War', and they regulated many aspects of the army: from the way soldiers should behave during marches, what was forbidden as part of military life (e.g., gambling or selling weapons and equipment), to the positioning of the troops during marches and in the camp. They also established a range of punishments that could be applied for different crimes, including *wytrąbienie* (trumpeting out), which means a dishonoured discharge from the army or even the death sentence. The latter was usually reserved for the killing of other soldiers (especially companions) or cowardice in the face of the enemy. Sometimes, there were specific 'articles' just for national troops, while others were reserved specially for foreign troops. Servants in retinues of the national cavalry were, in theory, at the mercy of their own companions, but, as we will see later, sometimes they were also subjects of direct military discipline. Discipline was in the hands of the hetman's court, with culprits normally delivered by the hetman's haiduk banner, serving as a sort of military police in the army. The court's decision was then pronounced in front of the army, and, as we will see in a moment, sometimes deputies from the troops could try to help the sentenced, especially when he was facing death penalty.

It is also worth mentioning a unique and semi-official institution of army discipline, called 'gatherings'.¹¹⁴ There were two main types of them. First were 'military gatherings' (*koła wojskowe*), and these were normally on the level of just one banner or a whole regiment of the national cavalry. It dealt with minor issues and conflicts within the unit, including any conflicts between companions and the choosing of the envoys from the units that would be sent to deliver pay or represent the rest of the soldiers at some important events. Second, and more important, were 'general gatherings' (*koła generalne*).

---

112 AGAD, AR V, no. 15429, p.1.
113 *Erik Dahlberghs dagbok*, p.80.
114 As mentioned previously in Paradowski, *Despite Destruction, Misery and Privations*, p.140, the Polish word for it was *koła* (singular: *koło*), which meant 'circles', as in 'gathering with a circle of equals'. I prefer to use the term 'gathering' in English, as it represents the essence of the original without confusion coming from the direct translation.

They were main events where deputies despatched from all units of the army, so including foreign troops, were to discuss important issues with hetman or ranking commanders. Usually, the main topic discussed here was overdue pay, the chronic issue of the Polish and Lithuanian armies in this period. It also allowed soldiers to point out their issues with the lack of provisions, proper quarters and equipment. During general gatherings, deputies from the army could also have their say in disciplinary matters, as they could for example try to prevent carrying on with the executions of those sentenced to death by the hetman's court.

Often, high-ranking commanders had to remind their troops about proper discipline by sending out special orders with warnings and cautions. On 26 March 1657, Lithuanian Grand Hetman sent a proclamation to all officers and soldiers, 'both cavalry and infantry, both Polish [national] and foreign *autorament*'. He reminded his men, 'with whole severity of my office', that any soldiers caught attacking and pillaging lands that belong to the nobility would be sentenced to death.[115] On 11 May 1658, Crown Grand Hetman Stanisław Potocki issued a written reprimand to his troops, in which he emphasized the need of protecting the lands owned by nobles and ordered them to cease 'loose behaviour'.[116] Some actions, like prosecuting 'heretics' and Jews, seem to be fairly widespread, though, as on 22 April 1656 King Jan II Kazimierz had to issue an order to the high commanders of the army, in which he forbade the harming of Jews.[117]

A servant with a noble's horse adorned with leopard pelt. Stefano della Bella, 1651 (Rijksmuseum).

In a similar way, during the *Sejm*, gathered magnates and nobles also discussed the issues of military discipline and agreed to issue some warnings to the army. In June 1658, amongst the acts of the *Sejm*, we can find a paragraph titled '*Disciplina militaris* in Crown and Grand Duchy of Lithuania'. It mentioned that some 'Polish banners and also foreign [units] in the service of the Commonwealth' did not follow military laws and articles, pillaging lands that belonged to the nobility and clergy, taking money and food without any assignation from the hetman and, in overall, being a heavy burden to 'poor people'. As such, the *Sejm* reminded them about the 'military

---

115 *AVAK*, vol. XXXIV, p.103.
116 *Akta grodzkie i ziemskie z czasów Rzeczypospolitej Polskiej*, vol. X, p.283.
117 *Akta grodzkie i ziemskie z czasów Rzeczypospolitej Polskiej*, vol. X, p.277.

articles' from 1609, 1653 and 1655, encouraging hetmans to make sure they executed those laws in the army.[118]

Of course – despite all those orders, proclamations and laws – discipline amongst troops was often very low, especially when trying to obtain supplies from the territories where they waged war. There were numerous complaints and court cases, where the local population accused soldiers and their servants of taking far more food and supplies than required or even of direct theft. Prince Bogusław Radziwiłł's commissioners in Słuck, Kazimierz Kłokocki and Władysław Huryn, in July 1659 complained a lot about the behaviour of the Lithuanian troops marching through the area of the fortress. The worst seems to be the newly recruited units, who 'changed into [Zaporozhian] Cossacks style' and were a real menace to the local population. The commissioners were dreading the approach of the main force of the Lithuanian army, as they already received news about their many misbehaviours and excessive looting from different areas of the march. The dragoon regiment of Colonel Bockum was mentioned as one of the worst, as from only one village 'they [took] 18 heifers and 40 muttons, with [a further] five muttons butchered'. Radziwiłł's officials added that 'these are foreign troops, that should be under strict discipline; what [will happen] with Polish [national cavalry] regiments, that are all around us, as they listen neither to Royal or Hetman's decree'.[119] On top of this, there were also cases of the theft within the ranks, both during the pillaging of battlefields and during camp life. In December 1659, when serving in the levy of nobility, in the Lithuanian camp at Katna Muiza, Poczobut Odlanicki was robbed by the dragoons from the regular army unit. When on guard duty, due to the recklessness of his servant, who left his horse unattended, the thieves got away with the 'saddle with pistols and hunting bridle', costing the Lithuanian noble 150 zł.[120]

Looking at some of the examples of disciplinary issues between commanders and their troops, the first name that comes to mind is Stefan Czarniecki. He was always known for imposing strict discipline amongst his troops and would not shy from punishing any criminal actions. In spring 1656, when many calvary servants under his command started pillaging 'not only peasants, burghers, nobles and their homes but even churches', he widely used death sentences to try to reimpose the discipline. Jemiołowski mentioned that he ordered the captured men to be hanged while those committing sacrilege were to be 'thrown into the fire' or dragged behind the backs of horses. Despite these executions, the robberies did not stop, so the *Regimentarz* decided to take a rather unusual step. While his division was resting at the camp near Uniejów, after another hanging of a few captured servants, he ordered that companions who were 'hiding, protecting or [even] knowing about [the crimes] of their servants' would be severely prosecuted, paying the ultimate price for the guilt of their servants.[121] When a division under his command was marching through Brandenburg to Denmark, he

---

118 *Volumina Legum*, vol. IV, p.247.
119 AGAD, AR V, no. 6865/I, p.106.
120 Poczobut Odlanicki, *Pamiętnik Jana Władysława Poczobuta Odlanickiego*, p.26.
121 Jemiołowski, *Pamiętnik dzieje Polski zawierający*, pp.198–99.

MILITARY LIFE AND DEATH

ordered that any soldier caught on any misbehaviour 'wo not be beheaded or shot but dragged few times in circle attached by his legs to the horse. We initially thought it would be nothing; but it is in fact great pain, as not only your clothing but even your body is falling off so only bones remains'. One has to wonder if Pasek based this opinion on a very personal experience.[122] It seems to have worked, though, as Czarniecki's troops marched in good order without causing any problems to their Brandenburg hosts.

Even after soldiers returned from Denmark and many were allowed to return to their homes for winter break, they quickly returned to the ranks in early spring. Pasek admitted that he was not too eager to rejoin the ranks, but 'there was such discipline in our division, that God forbid for the companion to be absent for too long from the banner'.[123] Not all of his comrades in arms were so disciplined, though, especially when ordered to take part in another campaign, this time against the Muscovites. In March 1660, Czarniecki sent requests to other colonels to hand over to him any deserters from his division, which indicates that it became a serious problem.[124] In winter 1662, a group of dragoons from Czarniecki's regiment was looting the village of Mścibów, but they were severely defeated, with many of them killed. The 19 remaining dragoons were then attached to Pasek's command, who was travelling to the army camp with a letter from the King to Czarniecki. On their way, they had a bloody clash with marauding volunteers from Muraszko's 'regiment', killing many and capturing horses and weapons. After their arrival into the army camp, hearing about their deeds, Czarniecki told them that 'I should order to hang you all, for that ruckus you made in Mścisłów; but now I will forgive you'.[125] When, in August 1663, unpaid foreign troops started their mutiny

Polish cavalry serving next to the Swedish army during the siege of Jasna Góra. Johann Bensheimer,1659 (Muzeum Narodowe, Kraków).

---

122 Pasek, *Pamiętniki*, p.75.
123 Pasek, *Pamiętniki*, p.127.
124 Kersten, *Stefan Czarniecki 1599-1665*, p.478.
125 Pasek, *Pamiętniki*, p.230.

in the camp at Mikulińce, it quickly spread throughout many other units in Czarniecki's division. The *Regimentarz* ordered to open fire on the mutineers, and the national cavalry was more than happy to settle their old scores with the foreign *autorament*. The mutiny was pacified, and its 80 leaders – officers, NCOs and privates alike – were arrested, tortured (as part of an investigation checking if the mutiny was inspired by Lubomirski) and then hanged.[126]

Another commander well known for his harsh discipline was Hetman Janusz Radziwiłł, although he often used it to highlight his dominant position in the Lithuanian army. Thanks to the fact that a large part of his Chancellery survived in the archives, we can draw on many examples, starting from the campaigns against the Cossacks in 1649. In February that year, he ordered the hanging of a cavalry retainer who stole a scarf from the inn in Bobrujsk. After the execution, the scarf was left next to the dead man.[127] A rather unusual case happened in his army in early July 1649. One of the reiter companies mutinied, and its soldiers decided to switch to a different unit. Such a decision was not welcomed by (at the time) Field Hetman Janusz Radziwiłł, who showed his displeasure to the reiters. The leader of the mutiny was sentenced to death, and the company was ordered to serve for one quarter without pay.[128] On 14 July of that year, hearing that some hussar companions and a large number of army servants left the camp, Janusz Radziwiłł sent three banners of Tatar light horse to chase after them. The next day, the Tatars brought back four captured companions: Czmijewski, Porębski and Piętkowski from Jerzy Karol Hlebowicz's hussar banner and Rypiński from Wincenty Korwin Gosiewski's banner. On 16 July, those companions were brought before the court composed of the Hetman and high-ranking officers. The hussars tried to explain that they were led to desertion due to 'private penury and misery that led them to leave the camp'. Radziwiłł did not even want to listen to them and pushed for their immediate execution, although, 'to not sound impulsive', he agreed for a proper court case. After hearing all arguments and pointing to different paragraphs of the Articles of War, he still decided to sentence four companions to death. Army officers asked for his mercy, but the Hetman did not want to hear it. On the morning of 17 July, a place was set up for an execution by a firing squad composed of haiduks. Army officers and companions tried once more to look for Radziwiłł's mercy, and Jan Bychowiec, a companion from Jerzy Karol Hlebowicz's hussar banner, was allowed to say a few words as the representative of all the companions. While the Hetman was not too keen on changing his mind, seeing it as a proof of weakness, he finally agreed after constant requests from the senior officers. He was able to gain something in exchange, though, as the whole army 'promised steady service'. The four

---

126 Wimmer, *Wojsko polskie w drugiej połowie XVII wieku*, p.143.
127 *Pamiętniki Samuela i Bogusława Kazimierza Maskiewiczów*, p.265.
128 *Korespondencja wojskowa hetmana Janusza Radziwiłła w latach 1646-1655*, vol. I, *Diariusz kancelaryjny 1649-1653*, p.90.

companions were pardoned, but they had to serve one quarter without pay and show 'bravery in the next occasion'.[129]

In late August 1649, the companions from the cossack cavalry banner of Aleksander Mieleszko refused to leave the camp to accompany their reiter company on a reconnaissance mission. Such insubordination did not sit well with Hetman Janusz Radziwiłł, who ordered the arrest of Lieutenant Konstanty Władysław Kotowski, who was in charge of the unit. The officer was then interviewed to provide reasons for the mutiny. The picture that was drawn by both him and his companions was not very good. The unit was unruly, as is it was due to end its service and the soldiers no longer wished to serve under the command of *Rotmistrz* Mieleszko (who was at the time absent from the camp). The companions claimed that the banner was undermanned, as, during musters, Mieleszko filled the missing retinues with his own servants, pretending that the unit was much stronger and drawing more money for its pay. He seems to have been conflicted with many of the companions, often insulting them and 'even drawing the sabre' during quarrels. It led to the underperformance of the unit during the Battle of Łojów, as the soldiers did not trust their *Rotmistrz*. The Hetman, not willing to allow such a disturbance in the army to affect the other units, ordered the companions to serve the remaining three weeks of their quarter, with their complaints towards Mieleszko to be looked into once he returned to the army. The leader of the mutiny, companion Nowosielski, was arrested and kept under guard.[130] He was later sentenced to death, and, while initially was to be hanged, his sentence was changed to the more honourable beheading, which took place on 1 September 1649.[131]

In late March 1651, retainer Sawicki, from Chasien Karat Karacewicz's Tatar light horse banner, was arrested in the army camp after witnesses recognised him from the killing of the civilian in whose service he was before joining the unit. He admitted his guilt and was sentenced to death by quartering.[132]

In December 1654, Radziwiłł was involved in resolving an incident between the officers of both Lithuanian divisions. The lieutenant from Field Hetman Gosiewski's troops had an argument with Captain Marcin Choromański from Radziwiłł's regiment. They argued about the arrest of a soldier from the lieutenant's command. The argument quickly heated up, and, in the ensuing brawl, one of the lieutenant's servants was killed and the other wounded. After an investigation, it was proved that Captain Choromański was at fault and that he started the whole affair with the unlawful arrest of the soldier. He was sentenced to pay the penalty for the killed man, but then the case was presented to Radziwiłł. He took the side of his officer, and he not

---

129 *Korespondencja wojskowa hetmana Janusza Radziwiłła w latach 1646-1655*, vol. I, *Diariusz kancelaryjny 1649-1653*, pp.174–77.
130 *Korespondencja wojskowa hetmana Janusza Radziwiłła w latach 1646-1655*, vol. I, *Diariusz kancelaryjny 1649-1653*, p.191.
131 *Korespondencja wojskowa hetmana Janusza Radziwiłła w latach 1646-1655*, vol. I, *Diariusz kancelaryjny 1649-1653*, p.218.
132 *Korespondencja wojskowa hetmana Janusza Radziwiłła w latach 1646-1655*, vol. I, *Diariusz kancelaryjny 1649-1653*, p.550.

only led to his acquittal but also sentenced Gosiewski's lieutenant to death! Luckily, after some negotiations between the Hetman and army commissars, the sentence was not carried out.[133]

After the bloody defeat of the Lithuanian and Polish assault on Mohylew on 23 April 1655, Radziwiłł planned to severely punish the Royal Foot regiment, as it was this unit that first retreated from the field, leading to heavy losses amongst the attackers. Clearly enraged with such cowardice, he wrote to King Jan Kazimierz that 'tomorrow there will be execution of six or eight officers, [while the] private from those companies will play dice for death'.[134] While there is no confirmation that he carried on such a severe punishment, it is still a clear indication that even being a part of the elite guard unit would not protect men from the death sentence and the wrath of the Hetman.

Mentions about the death sentence can be regularly found in diaries from the period. Of course, justice worked differently depending on the status of the criminal. Poczobut Odlanicki provides a few interesting examples from the Lithuanian army. In April 1660, two servants from one hussar banner of Hetman Gosiewski were sentenced to death for killing Stefan Przystanowski, a companion from the second hussar banner of Hetman Gosiewski. The sentence was carried out, and they were both beheaded.[135] In February 1661, an unnamed reiter was beheaded for killing cossack cavalry companion Narkuski.[136] In early October 1661, Ogiński (probably Jan Jacek Ogiński, lieutenant of Hetman Sapieha's *pancerni* banner) was sentenced to death for losing a few banners of volunteers during a reconnaissance mission. As he was well liked in the ranks, the 'whole army barely [managed] to beg for his life', and he was saved.[137] Later the same month, after the cossack cavalry banner of Michał Leon Obuchowicz fled from the Muscovites during a skirmish fight, its lieutenant, Mikołaj Komorowski, and standard-bearer, Jan Albrecht Baka, were arrested and sentenced to death for cowardice. The execution never took place, though, as the Muscovite main army approached the Lithuanian camp and both officers were returned to their unit.[138]

While death by beheading or hanging was the most common, sometimes other methods were employed as well. Gordon noted a situation from November 1660, when one of the Polish infantrymen was 'harquebused [shot] for breaking of his landlord, a Cosake, his head to blood'.[139] Vorbek-Lettow mentioned the case of two nobles, brothers Stanisław and Hieronim Biliuński, who were sentenced to death in July 1658 by Hetman Gosiewski. They disbanded their unit (most likely a cossack cavalry banner) without orders and raided noble estates. They were to be beheaded, but, in a rather odd turn of events, the executioner present in Kiejdany did not have a sword, so he could not carry on with his task. Instead, they were forced on their

---

133 Bobiatyński, *Od Smoleńska do Wilna. Wojna Rzeczypospolitej z Moskwą 1654-1655*, p.136.
134 Bobiatyński, 'Działania posiłkowego korpusu koronnego na terenie Wielkiego Księstwa Litewskiego w latach 1654-1656', pp.75–76.
135 Poczobut Odlanicki, *Pamiętnik Jana Władysława Poczobuta Odlanickiego*, p.35.
136 Poczobut Odlanicki, *Pamiętnik Jana Władysława Poczobuta Odlanickiego*, p.44.
137 Poczobut Odlanicki, *Pamiętnik Jana Władysława Poczobuta Odlanickiego*, p.50.
138 Poczobut Odlanicki, *Pamiętnik Jana Władysława Poczobuta Odlanickiego*, p.50.
139 *Diary of General Patrick Gordon*, vol. II, p.101.

knees and, 'first Stanisław, then Hieronim … shot from muskets'.¹⁴⁰ Even serving in a hussar unit was not enough to protect soldiers from the death sentence. In April 1652, two retainers from Aleksander Hilary Połubiński's banner were sentenced to death for stealing grain and oxen belonging to a noble named Janikowski.¹⁴¹

Polish soldiers in 1655. Erik Dahlbergh's drawing for Samuel Pufendorf's *De rebus a Carolo Gustavo Sueciae rege gestis*, published in 1696 (Biblioteka Narodowa, Warszawa).

Sometimes, a sentenced soldier could be saved by a mix of circumstances and the good will of his commanding officer. At the beginning of January 1661, some of Hetman Lubomirski's personal cooks got drunk during post-Christmas festivities and got into a squabble with the Hetman's dragoons, mortally wounding one of the drummers, who died after four hours. Gordon, in charge of Lubomirski's dragoon life company, aimed to prosecute the murderers in civil court. The arrested cooks 'without much ado confessed, and 3 of them being found guilty of giving him deadly wounds, were sentenced to be beheaded.' At the same time, a Scottish corporal named Balfowre (possibly Balfour) was sentenced to death for killing an apothecary and haiduk during a campaign. It was suggested to Gordon that his fellow Scot could be pardoned if the officer helped with saving the cooks. Gordon spoke to the widows of the killed apothecary and haiduk, paying 200 florins to the former and 50 florins to the latter. After obtaining their written confirmation that they did not hold any further complaints against Balfowr, the dragoon officer presented it to Lubomirski, asking for both the fellow Scot and the cooks to be pardoned. After some consideration, the Hetman agreed with that, and he even asked Gordon how much it cost him to convince both women to support his claim. It seems that, in this case, honesty was rewarded, as the Scot was paid back 250 florins from the Hetman's personal

---

140 Vorbek-Lettow, *Skarbnica pamięci*, p.280.
141 Majewski, *Marszałek wielki litewski Aleksander Hilary Połubiński (1626-1679)*, p.60.

treasury as a sign of the magnate's favour.¹⁴² Another unusual case, also noted by Gordon, happened in early September 1660, when the main Polish army was marching on Ukraine against the Muscovites and Cossacks. The Scottish officer mentioned the execution of six deserters: five of them were hanged, but the sixth, 'who ether had his hands not bound or gott them loose one way or other, when he was throwne of, catched hold of the next to him and hung so long untill pardon came for him and another from the generall [Hetman Lubomirski] who being advertized of the accident, was perswaded and pleased to send pardon'.¹⁴³ The fact that the deserters were hanged indicates that they were non-nobles, most likely from infantry or dragoons.

News about death sentences carried in the army often reached civilians, at least those with good connections to the military or those that happened to live near the places where executions were taking place. Jan Antoni Chrapowicki in his diary mentioned, for the period of 1656–1661, two such executions. On 21 January 1658, an unnamed 'Hungarian *rotmistrz* of infantry' was beheaded for killing the noble Orda, who was in the service of Lithuanian commander Jerzy Karol Hlebowicz.¹⁴⁴ On 24 April, a servant of companion Skorupski, from Samuel Kmicic's cossack banner, was shot for taking part in the robbery of the house of another noble, Krassowski.¹⁴⁵

Officers sentenced for crimes other than those punishable by death (e.g., pillaging or drunkenness) could be kept in the service but demoted. In 1659, Lieutenant Johan Hendrich Griechs and Ensign John Kenedy from Lubomirski's dragoon life company, after some drunken quarrel with a *rotmistrz* of a haiduk banner, were punished by an enraged Lubomirski. Patrick Gordon was ordered to take over the command of the unit, while both culprits were ordered to serve the rest of the campaign 'carrying muskets'.¹⁴⁶ Soon after, though, they were given their old posts back, as Jan Kazimierz's personal physician, Scottish doctor William Davidson, spoke on their behalf with Lubomirski.¹⁴⁷

Officers could also sometimes, in the right circumstances, have the opportunity to redeem their guilt on the battlefield. In March 1659, Major Henryk de Beaulieu, from Jan Zamoyski's infantry regiment, had to surrender Dirschau to the Swedish force. After a short captivity, he returned to the Polish army and played a vital role in recapturing Tczew from the Swedes in August the same year. As gratitude for his efforts in retaking the town, the military court decided not to prosecute him for his earlier surrender.¹⁴⁸ Conversely, in January 1659, Lieutenant Colonel Jordan was, by the decision of the military court, removed from the command of Michał Kazimierz Radziwiłł's dragoon regiment. Jan Kazimierz, in his letter to the nominal colonel, explained that

---

142 *Diary of General Patrick Gordon*, vol. II, pp.104–05.
143 *Diary of General Patrick Gordon*, vol. II, p.70.
144 Chrapowicki, *Diariusz*, p.149.
145 Chrapowicki, *Diariusz*, p.237.
146 *Diary of General Patrick Gordon*, vol. II, p.5.
147 *Diary of General Patrick Gordon*, vol. II, p.7.
148 Wagner, *Słownik biograficzny oficerów polskich drugiej połowy XVII wieku*, vol. I, p.13.

MILITARY LIFE AND DEATH

it happened due to several complaints about Jordan's excesses. The officer was not only removed from the command but also expelled from the army.[149]

The disciplinary problems often mentioned in primary sources were duels between companions. They could be caused by many reasons, from some family feuds or an honour duel for a better place in the unit's hierarchy to some more or less imagined slight (often when drunk). While they were officially forbidden, officers often turned a blind eye to them. Jan Poczobut Odlanicki, who seems to have been always eager to stand and fight, between 1658 and 1666, took part in eight duels: seven with sabres and one with pistols. He also fought in at least four brawls between groups of companions and retainers from different banners, including one where his hussars fought against a company of dragoons. Even in his civilian life, he was always ready to fight – as, between 1672 and 1680, he mentioned five occasions when he was to take part in duels, although in two of them the opponents managed to calm down before even crossing their sabres.[150]

Duels were, of course, not reserved for the nobles from national cavalry only. At the beginning of the campaign of 1660, Holsten got into trouble for his duel with *Rotmistrz* Aleksander Korff from Jan Zamoyski's reiter regiment. While the German diarist did not divulge what the reason for the fight was, it seems that both duellists took it seriously: 'He shot me in the leg and mortally wounded my horse, while I shot off his finger from hand [carrying] pistol'. Holsten was arrested but, most likely due to both Lubomirski's patronage and the campaign progress, quickly returned to his unit.[151] When Colonel Korff and *Rotmistrz* Eppinger were to take place in a duel in November 1660, Lubomirski sent Gordon to stop them. He managed to just in time, 'as they were going to it', and brought both officers back to the Hetman: 'The colonell was commanded to arrest in his quarters, and the *ruitm-r* put under the guard'.[152]

Personal conflicts could lead not only to duels between soldiers but also to direct murder. Poczobut Odlanicki mentioned two cases from the end of March 1662. In one of them, Ostrowski, a companion of Hetman Gosiewski's hussar banner, killed another companion named Obrępalski: 'Hit him in the back of the head with *obuch*, [so hard] that brain splattered out'. The murderer fled the army after his deed. In the other case, yet another hussar companion, Jarmołowicz, was killed by a noble named Cywiński (probably not serving in the army). In this case, the murderer settled the case with the father of the deceased, paying him 2,000 zł.[153]

There was an even more serious situation when parts of or whole units, from companions to their retainers and servants alike, took part in brawls. Some of them were fights with the local population that was trying to protect itself from soldiers 'taking bread', especially when units were doing it without orders in villages not picked up by commissioners or quartermasters. Others

---

149 AGAD, AR III, no. 6, p.38.
150 Poczobut Odlanicki, *Pamiętnik Jana Władysława Poczobuta Odlanickiego*, passim.
151 Holsten, *Przygody wojenne 1655-1666*, p.55.
152 *Diary of General Patrick Gordon*, vol. II, p.101.
153 Poczobut Odlanicki, *Pamiętnik Jana Władysława Poczobuta Odlanickiego*, p.58.

were conflicts between different units, ending with killed and wounded on both sides. One such fight took place on 22 December 1652 between two units of the Lithuanian army. The reiter company of Bogusław Radziwiłł, under the command of Major Ernest von Osten Sacken, attacked the town of Husk, where the hussar banner of Aleksander Hilary Połubiński (Husk belonged to him) was stationed in winter quarters. Caught by surprise, the hussars seem to have lost many of their servants in killed and wounded. Furthermore, some of the townsmen were robbed by the attacking reiters. In January 1662, a brawl between different banners of the Lithuanian army, which involved some companions from Gosiewski's hussar banner and Hlebowicz's 'black' cossack cavalry banner, ended up with one hussar retainer killed and 17 men (from all involved units) wounded.[154] In 4 March 1665, just after Holy Mass, a hussar banner, the ranks in which we can find Jan Władysław Poczobut Odlanicki, went into an open fight with the dragoon regiment of Field Hetman Pac in the village of Bujwiany, assigned as quarters for the hussars. The conflict started when the officer in charge of the dragoons, Lieutenant Kacper Berg, due to some slight, hit Poczobut Odlanicki's brother-in-law, Stanisław Szykier. It seems that the hussars were only waiting for the occasion, as their charge 'broke 80 [dragoons] of them, capturing Liuetenant [Berg] himself, who was wounded few times; [also] capturing flag and drums'. Two hussar companions, Błażewicz and Rzątkowski, were killed, while a few others were wounded. Amongst them was Szykier, struck 'with thrust to his nose next to eye', while Poczobut Odlanicki himself 'got thrust through his clothes just under armpit but was not [even] scratched'. After the fight, both units agreed to an accord, and the hussars gave back to the dragoons their flag and drums. Peace did not last long, though, as the vengeful dragoons stole 20 cattle from the village assigned to the hussars. In early May, however, Poczobut Odlanicki finally made peace with Lieutenant Colonel Flock, in charge of the dragoon regiment, and probably just in time, as the dragoons were planning to burn Bujwiany and kill all the peasants living in it. The diarist commented on the whole bloody conflict with the rather light phrase 'all went frothy, like a new beer'.[155]

A Polish soldier armed with a bow and spear, from 1750s Coven and Mortier's re-edition of Beauplan's map (Biblioteka Narodowa, Warszawa).

---

154 Poczobut Odlanicki, *Pamiętnik Jana Władysława Poczobuta Odlanickiego*, pp.57–58.
155 Poczobut Odlanicki, *Pamiętnik Jana Władysława Poczobuta Odlanickiego*, pp.91–92.

6

Pitched Battles

Recently, the battles of a large part of the 1655–1660 war received some good overall overview in Michael Fredholm von Essen's book in the *Century of the Soldier* series.[1] He covered not only the main pitched battles of the Polish–Swedish war (Żarnów, Wojnicz, Gołąb, Gniezno, Warka, Warsaw and Prostki) but also some of those fought against the Muscovites (Szkłów and Szepielewicze). The Battle of Warsaw – being the biggest fight of the war, fought over three days and involving the Poles, Lithuanians, Tatars, Swedes and Brandenburgians – will be the subject of another volume in the *Century of the Soldier* in future.[2] It led me to rethink how the topic of pitched battles could be covered in this book, to avoid too much repetition and yet to provide the readers with some interesting information. As such, I decided to look most of all into some detailed, primary-source-based information or some well-researched Polish secondary sources[3] about a few of those battles, to see how they were described by eyewitnesses and how the picture of the battle could look differently depending on the point of view of the opposing sides.

Interestingly, sometimes very important events had very short passages in diaries, even when their authors were present during the fight. To give a few examples, we can look into the notes on three battles from 1656 according to Pasek. About the Battle of Warka, the first main battle won by the Poles, he wrote only that 'chosen Swedish troops were defeated, few thousands of them killed so [the river] Pilica was full of Swedish dead and blood'.[4] Despite being present at Gniezno/Kłeck, his description is very short, more likely due to the Polish defeat. He mentioned that the Swedes took heavy losses and that there were still many Polish units serving in the Swedish army, 'Arians, Lutherans, still have their banners, with many Catholics there as well, some of them *per nexum sanguinis* [due to kinship], others for a chance of loot and pillage'.[5] As Pasek did not take direct part in the Battle of Warsaw, his

---

1   Fredholm von Essen, *Charles X's War. Volume II*.
2   Is it worth keeping an eye on Helion & Company's website for some news in the near future.
3   As they are usually rather difficult to obtain and understand by non-Polish readers, due to the lack of proper translations.
4   Pasek, *Pamiętniki*, p.69.
5   Pasek, *Pamiętniki*, p.69.

AGAINST THE DELUGE

The first day of the Battle of Warsaw, 28 July 1656. Theatrum Europaeum, volume VII, 1663 (Biblioteka Narodowa, Warszawa).

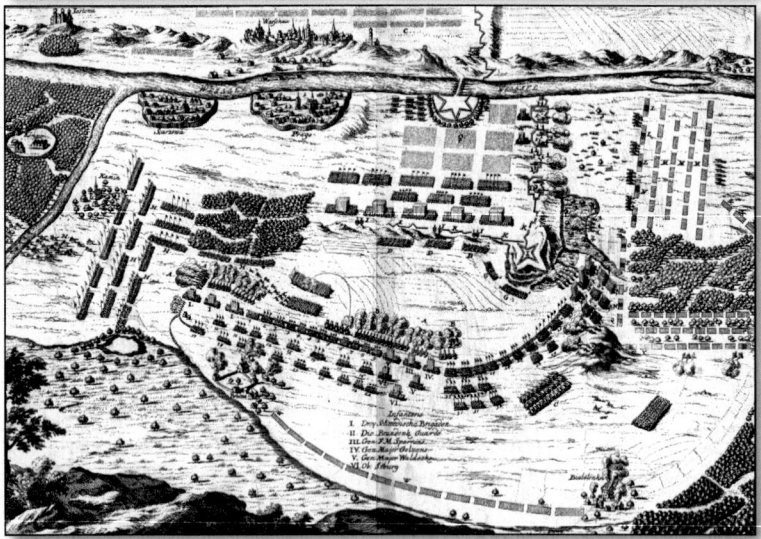

The second day of the Battle of Warsaw, 29 July 1656. Theatrum Europaeum, volume VII, 1663 (Biblioteka Narodowa, Warszawa).

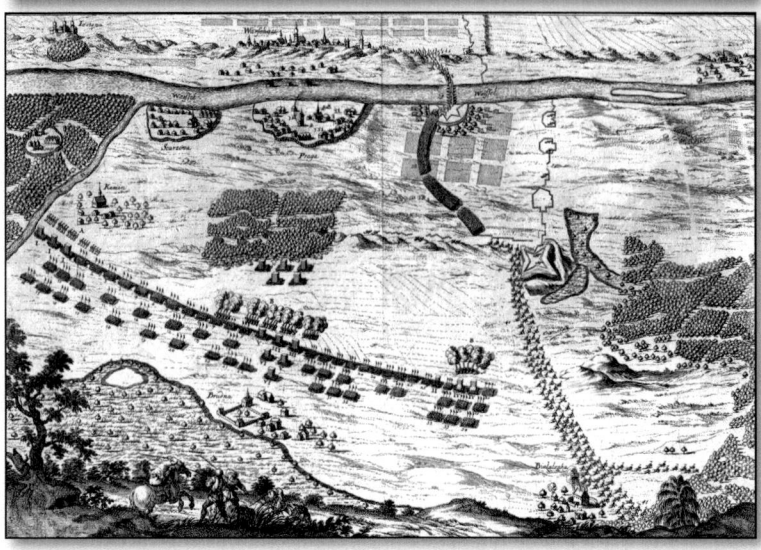

The third day of the Battle of Warsaw, 30 July 1656. Theatrum Europaeum, volume VII, 1663 (Biblioteka Narodowa, Warszawa).

description of the fight is very short. He highly exaggerated the Brandenburg forces, mentioning that the Elector had with him 16,000 men, that arrived to support the Swedes. He blamed the allied Tatars for the loss, writing that the 'first auxiliary Tatars fled from us'. The Poles 'lost many good men' but 'many Swedes too'.[6] He wrote in much more detail about Czarniecki's campaign in Denmark and subsequent battles against the Muscovites from 1660 onwards, and many of his observations regarding those fights were already quoted in this volume.

Describing some of the Polish–Swedish battles, first we will look into two battles from 1655 that took place during the Swedish offensive phase of the war. One of them, at Żarnów on 16 September, opened the way for Charles X Gustav's army towards Cracow. The second one, which took part not long after at Wojnicz on 3 October, led to the defeat of the main Polish field army and indirectly led to the surrender of Cracow, as its defenders had to abandon any hopes for the relief action. During the prelude to Żarnów, the Polish army – a mix of regular soldiers, district troops and levy of nobility – under the command of King Jan Kazimierz and Crown Field Hetman Lanckoroński, was retreating from the main Swedish field army (led by King Karl X Gustav himself) towards Cracow. The Poles had approximately 11,000 men, including 6,000 of regular cavalry and 900 dragoons, but no infantry and only six small cannons. The Swedes had approximately 6,000 reiters, 4,000–5,000 infantry and 400 dragoons, supported with up to 40 cannons – although the highest estimate had them as 31 squadrons of cavalry (approximately 7,750 horses), 12 brigades of infantry (7,200 men) and two squadrons of dragoons (500 horses).[7] Most likely, Jan Kazimierz did not even want to engage in the battle but was somehow forced to by nobles from the local levy, who did not want to march towards Cracow as it would take them too far away from their homes. As we will see from different relations describing the battle, it was infantry and artillery that was to make a real difference in the incoming fight – a pattern often seen in the early stage of the war.[8]

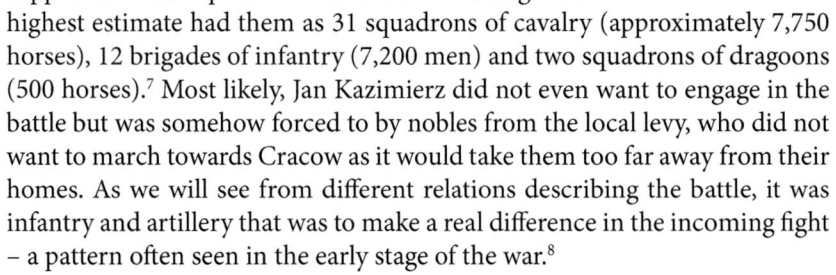

Mikołaj Jemiołowski, who at the time served in the Polish army but was not present at Żarnów,[9] provides some description of the fight, most likely based on the relation of eyewitnesses that he had a chance to talk to about it later. According to him, King Jan Kazimierz had 12,000 men, 'from quarter army and district troops', while the Swedes had 20,000 men. The Polish army was protecting a large tabor retreating towards Cracow, and the Swedes

King Karl X Gustav, portrait by Sebastien Bourdon (Nationalmuseum, Stockholm).

---

6   Pasek, *Pamiętniki*, p.69.
7   Julius Mankell, *Uppgifter rörande svenska krigsmagtens styrka, sammansättning och fördelning sedan slutet af femtonhundratalet* (Stockholm: Tryckt hos C.M. Thimgren, 1865), p.318.
8   Wimmer, *Polska-Szwecja. Konflikty zbrojne w XVI-XVIII wieku*, pp.104–05.
9   The cossack cavalry banner that he served in was fighting against the Muscovites and Cossacks.

AGAINST THE DELUGE

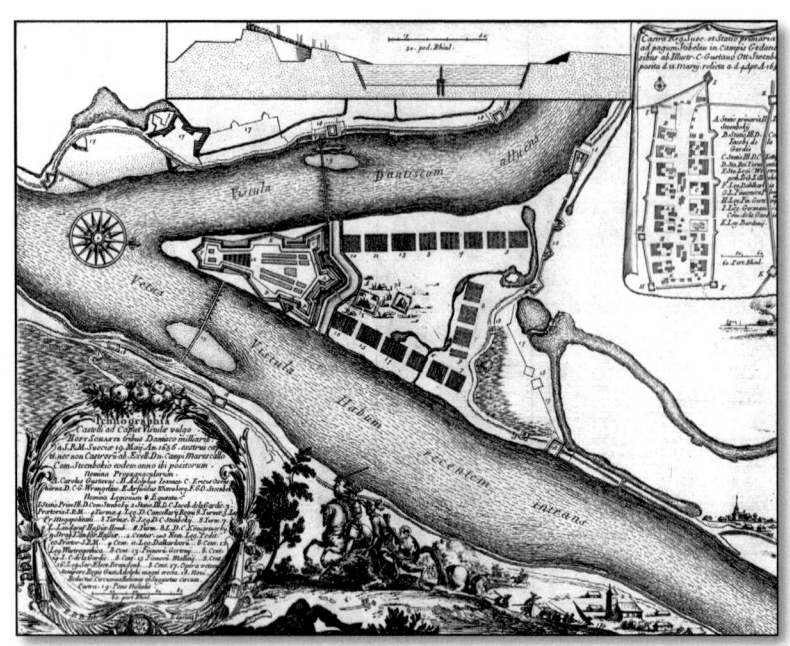

The Battle of Żarnów, 16 September 1655. Engraving by Willem Swidde, based on Erik Dahlbergh's drawing for Samuel Pufendorf's De rebus a Carolo Gustavo Sueciae rege gestis, *published in 1696 (Biblioteka Narodowa, Warszawa).*

used their artillery to fire upon the Polish rearguard. The Swedish attacked 'with whole impetus' against the Poles stuck in bogs. Field Hetman Lanckoroński, along with some troops, tried to stop the Swedes but 'pushed towards bogs and lakes, took heavy losses and many wagons'. While the Polish army did not lose many dead, a large number of men were captured. Many (likely from the regular troops) were enlisted into the Swedish army, while Polish nobles 'were forced to take oath and return home, where they were supposed to sit quietly'.[10]

Wespazjan Kochowski described the battle in very short, almost laconic passages. He wrote that it was taking place near the village of Straszowa Wola. Initially, 12 banners of Polish cavalry surprised the right wing of the Swedish army near ford on the river Drzewica (Drzewiczka), 'hurting them mightily', but no Polish reinforcements arrived to help. The Poles caused heavy losses amongst Wittenberg's cavalry, but, when Karl X Gustav supported his reiters with infantry and artillery, the Polish cavalry was forced to retreat, 'as she did not have the same protection [from other formations]'. Seeing that the Polish army started to waver, King Jan Kazimierz left the battlefield, ordering Field Hetman Lanckoroński to command over the retreat. The Poles had to flee through a thick forest, and their force rested for three days in Przedbórz, where more and more of the scattered troops arrived. After that, the army followed Jan Kazimierz, marching towards Cracow.[11]

Patrick Gordon also provides an interesting eyewitness account of the Battle of Żarnów, although he did not take part in the fight as he was recovering from a wound and observed the fight from the tabor. He wrote that the Polish army did not have infantry, just four or five companies of dragoons. Other formations that are mentioned were three or four banners of hussars and a Royal 'lyfeguard of strangers', protecting Jan II Kazimierz. Gordon mentioned the initial ambush, where the Polish cavalry attacked the Swedish vanguard, which 'forced ours to disorderly retreat, without any great losse', thus supporting what Kochowski wrote about 12 banners fighting successfully against the Swedes. Karl X Gustav then ordered his army 'in two battailes or lynes, besides commanded men in the foretroopers and a strong rearguard'. The centre of the first line was composed of cavalry, with pike and

---

10 Jemiołowski, *Pamiętnik dzieje Polski zawierający*, p.138.
11 Kochowski, *Historya panowania Jana Kazimierza*, vol. I, pp.216–17.

PITCHED BATTLES

shot infantry on the flanks, while the second line was set up opposite, with infantry in the centre and cavalry on the flanks. The Swedes moved their artillery forwards, with regimental cannons 'before the regiments as usuall' and heavy pieces set up in a battery on the skirt of the hill that the Swedish army was marching from, where they could shoot towards the Polish army occupying another hill. While heavy artillery fire could shake Polish morale, it did not cause heavy losses, 'by reason of the distance and inequality of the ground'. The Poles were unwilling to charge against the slowly marching close-ranked Swedes, so, after a quick fight, they retreated. The Swedish army was initially reluctant to pursue, as commanders were worried that the retreat may be a ruse and that other Polish forces were waiting in ambush. Only later, when some of the Polish cavalry were stuck in the woods and marsh, forced to abandon their horses and flee on foot, did the Swedes start a more energetic action. They were faced in a short fight by the Royal Guard, covering the retreat of Jan Kazimierz's army. The 3,000-strong Swedish cavalry was then sent in pursuit of the Polish army, capturing part of the baggage train and 'good booty'.[12]

Holsten, who took part in the battle, provides a rather short description of the fight. He mentioned that the Swedish army managed to wrestle the hill from the Poles and forced them to retreat into the woods. During the pursuit, the Swedes took many prisoners, tabor wagons, flags and kettle drums. Of interesting note is that Holsten wrote 'it was [my] second battle [against the Poles] and by then we were already used to their great yelling'.[13]

Pufendorf depicted the Polish army as more than 10,000 cavalry but without any infantry. He mentioned the initial cavalry fight and subsequent Swedish cannonade. Before both sides could engage in proper battle, though, massive rain stopped both armies in their tracks: 'There were those amongst Poles that wanted to attack Swedes during the rain, with sabres in their hands, as guns would be useless due to all damp. Others pointed out though, that weapons and match can be kept [dry] under coats, so it is better to think about retreat'.[14] Once the rain stopped, the Polish army started a hasty retreat, with the Swedes reluctant to chase them, in order to not break the ranks of their army. According to Pufendorf, approximately 1,000 Poles were killed, and they also lost a whole baggage train of 4,000 wagons.[15]

According to Stanisław Wierzbowski, who would know it from his father, Łukasz Wierzbowski (present at the battle), the Poles lost at least 3,000

Swedish Field Marshal Arvid Wittenberg, portrait by Sebastien Bourdon (Nationalmuseum, Stockholm).

---

12 *Diary of General Patrick Gordon*, vol. I, pp.53–54.
13 Holsten, *Przygody wojenne 1655-1666*, p.32.
14 Pufendorf, *Siedem ksiąg o czynach Karola Gustawa króla Szwecji*, p.70.
15 Pufendorf, *Siedem ksiąg o czynach Karola Gustawa króla Szwecji*, p.70.

carts and many horses, with many men killed during the retreat.¹⁶ After the battle, the levy of nobility left the army and returned home. Jan Kazimierz and Stefan Czarniecki quickly travelled to Cracow to work on the further preparation of the defences of the city. Hetman Lanckoroński was gathering scattered troops and following them towards the town. Soon after, King Jan II Kazimierz decided to leave Poland, leaving Czarniecki as the commander in charge of the defence of Cracow while Lanckoroński was to lead a field army from the camp near Tarnów.

While the Swedes started the siege of Cracow, it was obvious that Lanckoroński's troops could potentially arrive as a relief force, so the Swedish King decided to lead an expedition against them. Both forces were to meet near Wojnicz on 3 October 1655. Field Hetman Lanckoroński had under his command practically all the regular troops that previously fought at Żarnów, although without Czarniecki's dragoon regiment (by now a part of the garrison of Cracow) and the Royal Guard reiters and dragoons that were escorting Jan II Kazimierz to Silesia. The Hetman's force consisted of three hussar banners, approximately 70 banners of cossack cavalry and light horse, and one weak regiment and two independent banners of dragoons. While 'on paper' these units had just over 7,000 horses, their real strength had to be much smaller. Excluding 'dead pays' and the losses taken during the campaign so far, including Żarnów and other losses, Lanckoroński could probably count on no more than 6,000 men, including 300–400 dragoons. The Swedish force under Charles X Gustav had eight reiter regiments (approximately 4,700 horses), one regiment of dragoons and some mounted musketeers (approximately 500 dragoons) – although even lower estimates describe them as 3,000 reiters (12 squadrons), 400 dragoons and 150 musketeers.¹⁷ Both sides were without any artillery support.

Pufendorf provides us with a good description of the battle. The King marching from Cracow was reinforced by Robert Douglas, who, with a strong detachment, was

The Battle of Wojnicz, 3 October 1655. Engraving by Francois de La Pointe, based on Erik Dahlbergh's drawing for Samuel Pufendorf's *De rebus a Carolo Gustavo Sueciae rege gestis*, published in 1696 (Biblioteka Narodowa, Warszawa).

---

16   Stanisław Wierzbowski, *Konnotata wypadków w domu i w kraju zaszłych od 1634 do 1689 r.* (Lipsk: Księgarnia Zagraniczna, 1858), p.93.
17   Mankell, *Uppgifter rörande svenska krigsmagtens styrka, sammansättning och fördelning sedan slutet af femtonhundratalet*, p.319.

despatched earlier to capture Lanckorona. The Swedish vanguard, led by Colonel Christian von Bretlach, had some initial success, defeating the Polish guards. Bretlach then decided to attack the Polish camp, not waiting for the main Swedish army. Seriously outnumbered, without reinforcements (which were marching slowly through the narrow road), he was soundly beaten. His troops lost many men, and King Charles X Gustav had some harsh words with him for his ill-sounded attack.[18] When the main Swedish force approached the camp, they found the Polish army ready for battle. Pufendorf described them as 8,000 men, including four banners of hussars, 'five squadrons of noble cavalry' (perhaps he meant levy of nobility), one regiment of dragoons and a few companies of Wallachians.[19] The right Swedish wing, under Philip von Sulzbach and Israel Ridderhielm, defended against the attack of the Polish light cavalry, with the King leading two regiments of reiters charging against hussars, while Colonel Johan Beddeker attacked the Polish right wing. After some tough fighting, the Polish ranks were broken, and their army forced to retreat through the river. According to Pufendorf, Charles X Gustav was very pleased with his men, as 'he noticed that they are getting used to Polish style of warfare and that they bested hussars, despite scary sight of the charging Poles'.[20] The Swedes took many prisoners, including Colonel Henryk Denhoff. Their battle loot included 20 cavalry drums, many flags – amongst them one that belonged to King Jan Kazimierz[21] – and the whole baggage train.

Further details can be found on Willem Swidde's engraving of the battle from Pufendorf's book, based on Erik Dahlbergh's drawing. It gives some additional information not available in other primary sources, even in Pufendorf's description itself. We can find there a note about the '2,000 quarter army' attacking the Swedish flank from the forest on the hill and about how they were completely broken and forced to retreat by the Swedes. In another part of the drawing, the Swedish dragoons set up in a ravine defeated the Polish hussars who 'were charging with great speed'. Finally, there is a note that the Swedes captured the Polish camp, the whole tabor, the 'banner of the Kingdom' and '[Henryk] Denhoff [colonel of a dragoon regiment]'.

Patrick Gordon was not present at the battle, staying with the main force besieging Cracow. As such, his description is very brief, noting that the King had with him '4,000 horse and dragouns' and that he marched to Wojnicz, where the quarter army gathered, and he routed them.[22] Mikołaj Jemiołowski praised the role of the regiment of Prince Dymitr Wiśniowiecki, who fought against the Swedish vanguard, 'strongly resisting their attack and leaving many Swedes [dead] on the battlefield'. The rest of the army was not eager to fight, though. Their ranks quickly became disorganised, and morale was low, especially as the King was not present on the battlefield. No surprising that

---

18   Pufendorf, *Siedem ksiąg o czynach Karola Gustawa króla Szwecji*, p.71.
19   Pufendorf, *Siedem ksiąg o czynach Karola Gustawa króla Szwecji*, pp.71–72.
20   Pufendorf, *Siedem ksiąg o czynach Karola Gustawa króla Szwecji*, p.72.
21   Probably the cornet from his guard dragoons or reiters.
22   *Diary of General Patrick Gordon*, vol. I, p.59.

the Polish resistance soon broke, and the army retreated, losing many men captured by the Swedes.[23]

Kochowski, who was present at the battle, wrote more extensively about it, although his description is a bit confusing and at some points exaggerated. The fight started when the Polish reconnaissance force under Lieutenant Krzysztof Modrzewski clashed with the Swedish vanguard. While he engaged the enemy, the officer sent a messenger to the main army camp, allowing the Polish troops to prepare and join the fight. According to the diarist, the Swedes were under the command of Colonels Bretlach and Rosen. The Swedish reiters were met in the fight by the national cavalry regiment of Aleksander Koniecpolski. Kochowski wrote that Koniecpolski himself wounded Bretlach, throwing him from the saddle, while companion Burzyński killed Rosen. The losses on both sides seem to be high, though, as the diarist mentioned 'Szandarowski, good lad, shot' amongst the many others killed. The approaching Charles X Gustav saved his vanguard, and the main bodies of both armies joined the fight. It seems that the fight quickly turned against the Poles, however, as they took heavy losses from the Swedish artillery and were endangered by the flanking force. It was decided to move the tabor away, so it would not block the Polish retreat through the Dunajec river. Under Swedish pressure, discipline started to break, and more and more Polish banners started to flee. Field Hetman Lanckoroński was abandoned by his troops and was almost captured by the Swedes. Only the timely intervention of Stefan Bidziński and Kochowski himself saved him; the Hetman was given a spare horse from a retainer and fled the battlefield. It seems that the scattered Polish troops managed to quickly gather back at the camp near Tarnów, although their tabor was captured by the Swedes after the battle.[24]

The defeat was a severe blow to the Polish cause. Cracow was left at the mercy of the besieging Swedes, while the Polish regular army was in a state of turmoil. Field Hetman Lankoroński left his troops and, with a small escort, journeyed to meet Grand Hetman Potocki and his division. The troops remining in the camp near Tarnów, under the command of Colonels Aleksander Koniecpolski and Dymitr Wiśniowiecki, soon started prolonged negotiations with Charles X Gustav and, on 26 October 1655 near Cracow, took an oath to the Swedish Crown, switching their allegiance to Charles X Gustav. The remaining troops, under both Hetmans, soon followed suit, as on 28 October they also agreed on the Swedish conditions and on 13 November, near Sandomierz, mustered in front of General Robert Douglas. After these actions, the vast majority of the regular Polish army was now in the Swedish service.

While Stefan Czarniecki quickly became one of the leading Polish commanders of the war, it is worth adding that his experience in pitched battles against the Swedes was not very impressive. He was, without a doubt, the master of 'small war', in which he could easily control the hit-and-run attacks of Polish cavalry and coordinate harassing tactics. It seems that leading

---

23 Jemiołowski, *Pamiętnik dzieje Polski zawierający*, p.140.
24 Kochowski, *Historya panowania Jana Kazimierza*, vol. I, pp.226–27.

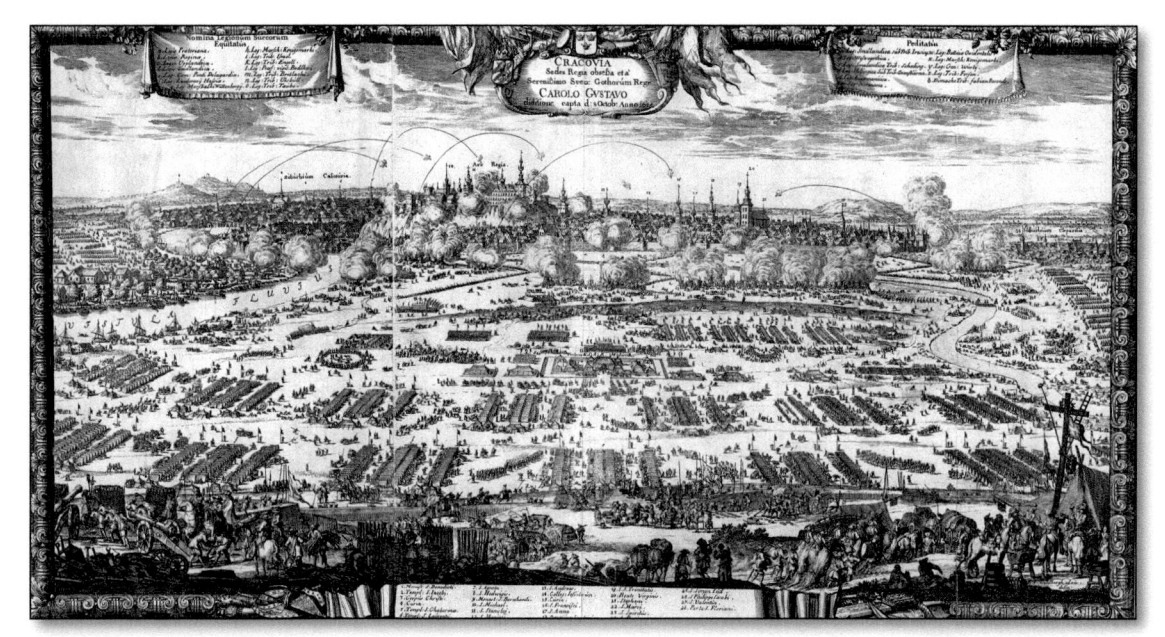

The Swedish siege of Cracow, October 1655. Engraving by Willem Swidde, based on Erik Dahlbergh's drawing for Samuel Pufendorf's *De rebus a Carolo Gustavo Sueciae rege gestis*, published in 1696 (Biblioteka Narodowa, Warszawa).

larger groups of troops in the open fights against the Swedes was something that he had to learn in a rather painful way.[25] At the Battle of Gołąb, which took place in the evening and night of 17 February (into 18 February), he completely ignored the threat from the approaching Swedes, and his soldiers, while resting in quarters, were surprised by the Swedish cavalry led by Count Waldemar Christian of Schleswig-Holstein.[26] Czarniecki's force at hand was fairly small, with two regiments: a Royal one, of which he was nominal commander, and Grand Hetman's Potocki under Sebastian Machowski, plus some newly raised dragoons,[27] in total no more than 2,500 men. Other units, like the regiment of Stefan Witkowski, were nearby, but only some managed to take part in the battle. During an earlier stage of the campaign, he managed to gather approximately 3,000 mounted recruits that were to become a base of new units, but they were despatched to Podlasie and so did not take part in the Battle of Gołąb. Facing him were at least 6,000 Swedish cavalry supported by up to 3,000 Polish troops in Swedish service.

According to Dahlbergh's diagram in Pufendorf's work, the Swedes had 29 squadrons of reiters, one squadron of dragoons and six squadrons of Polish cavalry – although it provides a very high estimate of the Polish side, described as 86 banners with 12,000 men. Facing the sudden attack, Czarniecki managed to quickly mobilise his men, and his counterattack heavily pressed the Swedish vanguard, with 'both sides engaged in the fight, while Poles – as they normally do – shouting their battle cries, keeping on the field and resisting [the Swedes]'.[28] The Polish commander again was surprised

---

25 For a very good overview of his activities during that time, with references to many period sources, see: Kersten, *Stefan Czarniecki*, pp.299–381.
26 Son of Danish King Christian IV and his second wife, Kirsten Munk.
27 On 20 January 1656, Czarniecki received a recruitment letter for a regiment of 1,000 dragoons, although the unit never reached such a strength during 1656.
28 Pufendorf, *Siedem ksiąg o czynach Karola Gustawa króla Szwecji*, p.136.

AGAINST THE DELUGE

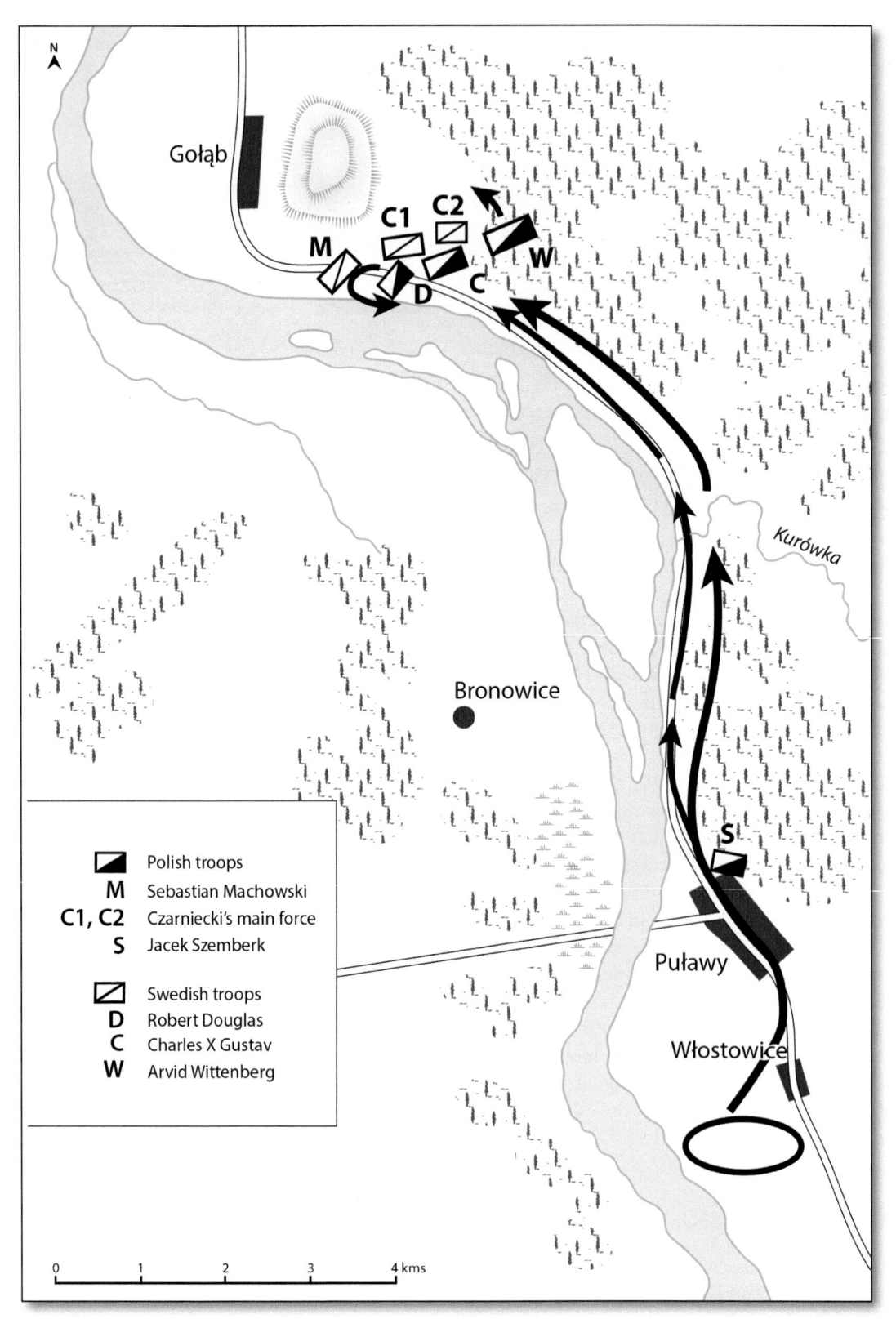

The Battle of Gołąb, 17-18 February 1656. Source: Paweł Skworoda, *Warka-Gniezno 1656*.

by the main force led by Charles X Gustav, who arrived at the battlefield, while the regiment of reiters under Henrik Horn managed to outflank the Poles. Risking being totally cut off, Czarniecki was forced to order a retreat, while losing 'many killed, many officers and 11 flags captured'.[29] The Swedish losses were low, although Adolf Johann suffered a broken leg when he crushed into a Finnish reiter and Count Waldemark was wounded and later died in Lublin.

Unfortunately, the diarists serving in Czarniecki's division did not provide much information about fight. In the case of Pasek, his description of the fight was most likely part of the 50 pages of the original manuscript that did not survive to our time, as his narrative starts from the Battles of Warka and Gniezno. Łoś wrote only that the Polish troops were scattered.[30] Jemiołowski highlighted the presence of Polish troops in the Swedish army, as regiments of Jan Sapieha, Seweryn Mikołaj Kaliński and Michał Zbrożek, 'in which served many Wallachians and Lithuanian Tatars', were leading the march of Charles X Gustav's army, while Jerzy Niemirycz's regiment took an active part in pursuing fleeing Poles. Czarniecki's troops were 'worth of the immortal glory', as, despite heavy losses, they managed to resist the Swedes for a long time but finally were forced to retreat towards the frozen river Wieprz. They were chased by Wallachians and Tatars in the Swedish service, 'who only whipped harmlessly their backs and their horses with the flats of their sabres, shouting "flee your royal traitors"'. According to this relation, many Poles and their horses died when the ice on the Wieprz broke during their retreat, and the Swedes standing on the bank of the river were shooting at those drowning. Jemiołowski wrote that many companions, especially from Royal and hetman's regiments, were killed, including some wounded that were to be killed on the battlefield on the orders of Charles X Gustav.[31] Kochowski's description of the battle seems to be highly inaccurate, with mentions of Swedish reiters from the vanguard being pushed down from the upper bank of the Vistula river, 'many men and horses breaking their necks'. He mentioned that it was the arrival of the Swedish field artillery that turned the tide of the battle, leading Czarniecki to sound the retreat. Kochowski even went so far as to claim that Swedish losses were higher than Polish ones. Amongst the latter, he mentioned a few killed companions (brothers Jan and Samuel Kawecki, Malawski, Rudawski 'and others'), 'but Swedes did not killed many Poles', adding that none of the Poles were captured during the retreat. As such, except for the names of the killed soldiers, his relation is very unreliable.[32] Von Ascheberg highly overestimated the Polish forces, mentioning that Czarniecki had 15,000 men. He wrote that the Swedes chased the retreating Poles for two miles and that the latter lost 1,000 men that drowned when the ice on the river Wieprz broke while they were fleeing on it.[33] Patrick Gordon estimated the Polish army at Gołąb at 80 banners, and he

---

29 Pufendorf, *Siedem ksiąg o czynach Karola Gustawa króla Szwecji*, p.136.
30 Łoś, *Pamiętnik towarzysza chorągwi pancernej*, p.64.
31 Jemiołowski, *Pamiętnik dzieje Polski zawierający*, pp.174–76.
32 Kochowski, *Historya panowania Jana Kazimierza*, vol. I, pp.279–80.
33 Ascheberg, *Dziennik oficera jazdy szwedzkiej 1621-1681*, p.66.

Polish cavalry versus Swedish reiters. Detail from Erik Dahlbergh's drawing for Samuel Pufendorf's *De rebus a Carolo Gustavo Sueciae rege gestis*, published in 1696 (Biblioteka Narodowa, Warszawa).

mentioned that it had to retreat from the fight 'with some losse, many being drowned in the r[iver]'.[34] Czarniecki tried to minimise his defeat, writing letters to the King in which he claimed that he lost only due to the lack of infantry and that his losses were minimal.[35] His offensive plans abandoned, Czarniecki's division was forced to retreat towards Lublin and later Zamość, surrendering the initiative to the Swedes.

The Polish commander had much more success on 7 April 1656, when, alongside Jerzy Lubomirski, he managed to win the first large Polish victory at the Battle of Warka. The strong Polish corps had between 6,000 and 8,000 men, mostly cavalry, supported by some dragoons (between one and three banners) and levy of nobility (up to 1,000 men). A detailed list of the units taking part in the battle mentioned 75 banners of regular cavalry, divided into 10 regiments: Royal (eight banners), Grand Hetman's (eight), Field Hetman's (nine), Lubomirski's (eight), Stanisław Witowski's (eight), Andrzej Potocki's (seven), Jakub Potocki's (six), Krzyszto Tyszkiewicz's (six), Dominik Zasławski's (eight) and Jacek Szemberk's (seven).[36] At least four out of the six banners of hussars that were, at that point, serving in the Polish army were present at Warka as well. We can see that the combined force under Czarniecki and Lubomirski already included regiments that, at Gołąb, fought as a part of the Swedish army and since then switched sides again and returned to the Polish ranks. Facing them was the Swedish division of Frederick Magrave of Baden-Durlach, approximately 2,500 men, mostly reiters from newly raised units, some dragoons and infantry, gathered from different regiments and garrisons.[37] According to Pufendorf, there were 24

---

34 *Diary of General Patrick Gordon*, vol. I, p.94.
35 Kersten, *Stefan Czarniecki*, p.309.
36 Kersten, *Stefan Czarniecki*, pp.327–28.
37 Rudawski, *Historja Polska od śmierci Władysława IV aż do pokoju oliwskiego*, vol. II, p.89 gives the even lower number of 2,000 men, although it does not seem to be supported by other sources.

PITCHED BATTLES

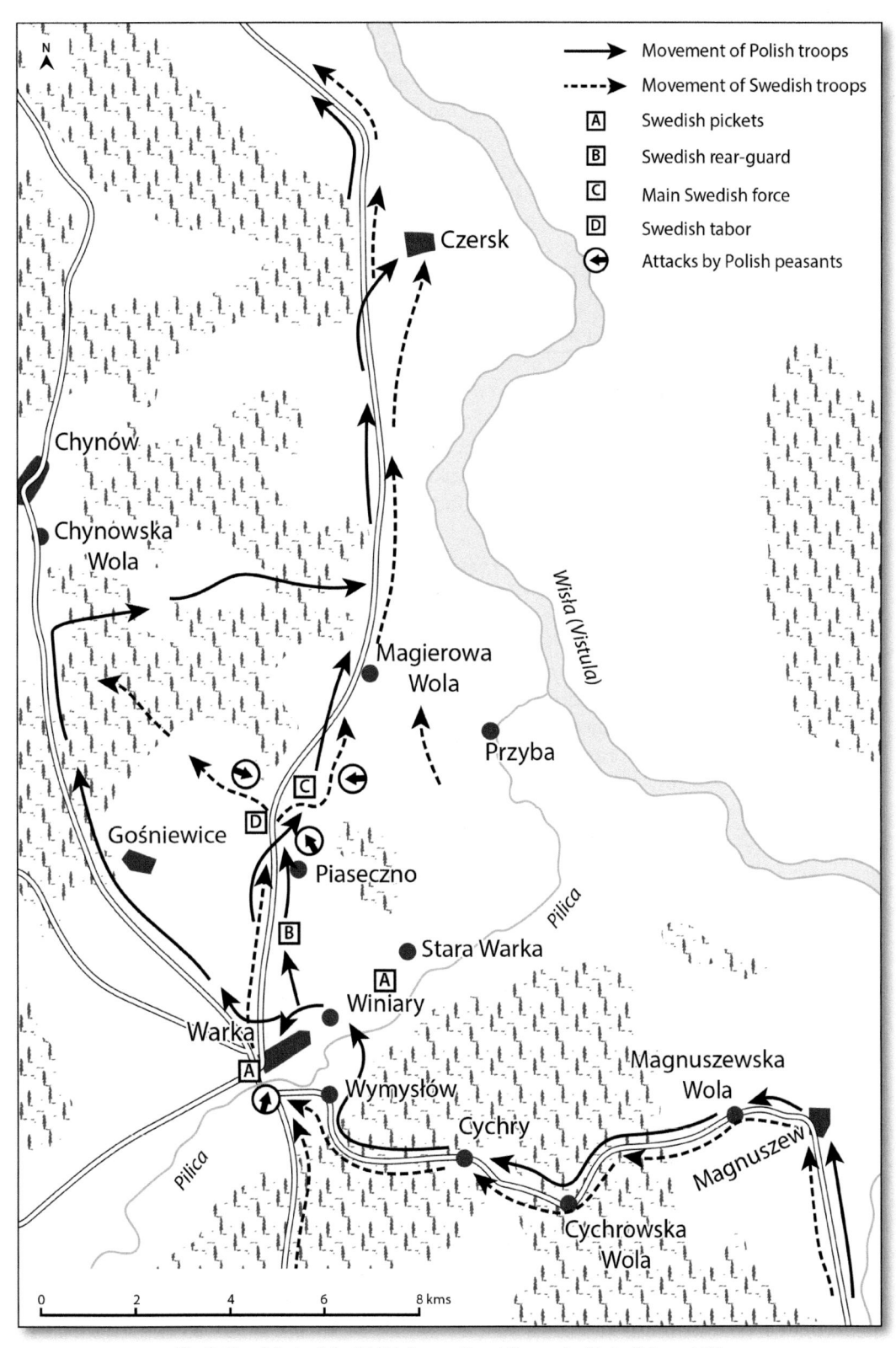

The Battle of Warka, 7 April 1656. Source: Paweł Skworoda, *Warka-Gniezno 1656*.

companies of reiters and 10 companies of dragoons, which seems to be too low an estimate, while at the same time he overestimated the Polish force, giving their strength as 12,000 men.[38] The Swedes had a large tabor full of supplies and loot, something which they were not very keen to abandon even when faced by the Polish force.

On 6 April, the Polish vanguard met and destroyed the Swedish rearguard near Kozienice, although the description of the fight seems to be rather confusing. Kochowski wrote that there were eight companies of Swedish dragoons present and that they were wiped out.[39] Łoś, who was present during the fight, estimated the Swedes as 300 reiters and 50 dragoons, adding that only a single Swedish soldier fled the battlefield.[40] Andrzej Sokolnicki, lieutenant of Lubomirski's hussar banner, stated that there were 240 Swedes and only a few of them survived.[41] Czarniecki, in his letter to the Queen, gave the figure of 600 and wrote that they were all wiped out.[42] Gordon mentioned only 150 reiters.[43] At least the composition of the Polish force is much clearer, as Łoś mentioned three banners being present: the *pancerni* banner of Władysław Myszkowski (in which rank he served), *pancerni* banner of Stefan Czarniecki and Tatar light horse banner of Aleksander Kryczyński.[44] The fight had to be very intense, and it is very possible that even more Polish banners joined the fray since, according to Kochowski, the Poles lost 30 killed companions. It is a surprisingly high number, as it would be the equivalent to a full-banner's worth of companions. Possibly, he meant in fact 30 killed in total; otherwise, Polish losses would have to have been even higher, as there should be some killed retainers alongside the companions as well. We can confirm that one killed officer, as mentioned by both Łoś and Kochowski, was Lieutenant Stefan Stapkowski from Myszkowski's banner.

Chasing the retreating Swedes, the Poles were divided into two sub-divisions. Lubomirski, with a few regiments (including two banners of hussars), engaged the main force of Baden-Durlach, while in the meantime Czarniecki was moving his main force through the Pilica river. The inexperienced Baden-Durlach, lacking knowledge of 'Eastern' warfare, decided to face the Poles with his reiters, while the remaining dragoons and infantry were placed in the rear of his battleline, attempting an ambush from the forest. It is possible that some units of dragoons were also placed on the flank of the Swedish line. Initially, the Swedes managed to resist Lubomirski's attacks, but, once Czarniecki's troops joined the fray, it was just a matter of time before the Swedish line broke under the overwhelming pressure: without a solid defensive position, lacking artillery and pikes, the Swedes could not stop the charging Poles. Reiters started to flee, and, chasing them, the Polish cavalry attacked the dragoons, who were unable to play any important role in the fight. The Swedish tabor was captured and looted, while many officers

---

38 Pufendorf, *Siedem ksiąg o czynach Karola Gustawa króla Szwecji*, p.144.
39 Kochowski, *Historya panowania Jana Kazimierza*, vol. I, p.286.
40 Łoś, *Pamiętnik towarzysza chorągwi pancernej*, p.65.
41 Nowak, 'Kampania wielkopolska Czarnieckiego i Lubomirskiego w roku 1656', p.141.
42 *Portfolio królowej Maryi Ludwiki*, vol. I, p.301.
43 *Diary of General Patrick Gordon*, vol. I, p.97.
44 Łoś, *Pamiętnik towarzysza chorągwi pancernej*, p.65.

and flags were captured during the ensuing chase. Baden-Durlach, with some officers and 108 Finnish reiters, managed to flee to safety, taking refuge in the old fortress of Czersk, but his division was destroyed. According to Pufendorf, 500 fleeing Swedish soldiers arrived the next day in Warsaw; in the following days, some more joined them as well. The Poles captured 160, and the rest 'was killed by the sword'.[45] Łoś wrote that the Poles fought bravely, especially praising the hussars who broke the Swedish reiters and forced them to flee. He also mentioned an episode of the Poles setting fire to the forest where the Swedish infantry was defending against their attacks (see Gordon's relation below). Łoś did not provide any specifics about Swedish losses, adding only that 'not many of them managed to flee'.[46] Jemiołowski's description of the fight is also rather scarce, as he mentioned that the Swedes tried to set up a defending position, 'like a fortress with their infantry', near the forest to give their tabor time to flee to Czerska. Charges of Polish cavalry, especially from the Royal, Grand Hetman's and Stanisław Witowski's regiments, quicky forced the Swedes to retreat. The diarist highly overestimated Swedish losses, giving them as 4,000 killed, 'not counting prisoners'. His description of battle loot is much more interesting, though, as he stated that almost all of the Swedish officers were captured, alongside '16 new cornets [flags], whole tabor with money, silver, cloth and other belonging and plenty of food'.[47] Lieutenant Andrzej Sokolnicki from Lubomirski's hussar banner highlighted the role of the lance-armed hussars and newly raised dragoons, mentioning that the former broke through the Swedish ranks and scattered the enemy's forces. Amongst the captured were almost all of the officers and ensigns; the Poles also took as a battle loot 17 cornets and three infantry flags.[48] A relation of the battle published in Rome and based on a despatch dated 17 April 1656 from Lwów (possibly from Papal Nuncio Pietro Vidoni) praised Lubomirski for leading the first charges of the Polish cavalry, which 'in the blink of the eye killed the large number of Swedes'. It also gave credit to Baden-Durlach, who played a vital role in the fight, 'raising hears and keeping order' of his troops.

There was also an interesting episode with Czarniecki's forces, during which, after the majority of his troops crossed the Pilica river, some soldiers abandoned the ranks and started to pillage the Swedish tabor. This could have jeopardised the chances of Polish success, but Czarniecki threw himself between the looters, whipping a few through their necks with the flat of his sabre and quickly forcing these marauders to return to their units.

The arrival of fresh Polish troops finally broke the Swedish resistance. A relation provides much too high Swedish losses – 4,000 killed – no doubt as a part of propaganda praising Polish victory. There were 250 prisoners, including 40 officers, and captured were 200 tabor wagons, 'many women and camp servants', 17 cornets and three infantry flags.[49] Notably, the number

---

45 Pufendorf, *Siedem ksiąg o czynach Karola Gustawa króla Szwecji*, p.144.
46 Łoś, *Pamiętnik towarzysza chorągwi pancernej*, p.66.
47 Jemiołowski, *Pamiętnik dzieje Polski zawierający*, p.191.
48 Nowak, 'Kampania wielkopolska Czarnieckiego i Lubomirskiego w roku 1656', pp.141–42.
49 'Relazione dei felici successi dell' armi…', p.295.

of captured colours was the same as in Sokolnicki's relation, indicating that it is correct. After all, captured flags were then sent to Lwów to King Jan II Kazimierz, so Nuncio would have been able to see them in person. Czarniecki, in his letter to the Queen, mentioned that he led his men to swim through the Pilica and that he sent some troops to outflank the enemy. He praised the Swedes who 'with great bravery resisted our attack' but added that they finally broke and were chased for seven miles to the suburbia of Warsaw. The *Regimentarz* was certain that those who survived the sabres of Polish soldiers were surely killed by the local population, which did not show any mercy to invaders. Czarniecki finished his letter by adding that the Poles captured many officers, a whole tabor and 30 flags, which he was now sending to the King and Queen.[50]

Polish cavalry in the Battle of Warsaw in 1656. Erik Dahlbergh's drawing for Samuel Pufendorf's *De rebus a Carolo Gustavo Sueciae rege gestis*, published in 1696 (Muzeum Narodowe, Kraków).

Since many Scottish soldiers took part in the battle, Patrick Gordon provides us with some interesting details of the fight, passed to him by his fellow countrymen. The Scot mentioned that, initially, the Swedes sent a reconnaissance group of 150 reiters to check the progress of the marching Poles. They were ambushed and destroyed by the approaching Czarniecki's troops, and 'very few whereof returned'. Delayed by the long wait for the evacuated garrison of Radom (which was burdened with much loot from the town and neighbouring areas), Baden-Durlach's division was slowly moving towards Warsaw. The Swedes moved through the bridge on the Pilica river and destroyed it behind them, but the Polish cavalry, 'not brooking delays, they swimme the reiver on their horses'. Baden-Durlach, understanding that further retreat was no longer an option, set up defensive positions, with the forest protecting one of his flanks. The Swedish reiters and Polish cavalry clashed a few times, and it seems that the inexperience of the many newly raised Swedish units took its toll. The squadron of Major John Watson, from the regiment of Samuel Bosse, was broken by the Polish charge, and only the timely intervention of the Scottish company of Major John Meldrum allowed them to safely retreat. Meldrum's men paid a heavy price for saving their brothers in arms, though. Abandoned by other units, surrounded by

---

50   *Portfolio królowej Maryi Ludwiki*, vol. I, pp.302–03.

the Poles, they managed to break through, but he 'lossed his standard, his lieutenant taken and the most halfe of his troope killed'. The Finnish dragoons defending from the forest seem to have, for the time being, prevented the Poles from dislodging them from their positions. However, the arrival of Lubomirski's dragoons changed the situation, as they set fire to the grass, which was 'very combustible at this season of the year'. The terrified Finns, despite the objections of their officers, decided to lay down their weapons. Gordon added that their commander, Lieutenant Colonel Albrecht Ritter, was executed by the Poles 'for haveing caused hang some gentlemen whilst he was commandant in Radomy [Radom]'. The broken Swedish division was chased within a mile of Warsaw, with its large tabor 'all became a prey to the Polls'. According to Gordon, 500 or 600 Swedish soldiers, along with Baden-Durlach himself, managed to flee to safety at Czersk, while around the same a number arrived in Warsaw. The rest of the division was killed or taken prisoner.[51] Kochowski praised the leadership of Czarniecki, at the same time completely ignoring the important role played by Lubomirski in the battle. According to the historian, the *Regimentarz* bravely led his men through the Pilica river, wearing a coat from tiger or leopard fur and forcing his horse into the river, so within an hour 3,000 of his cavalry were already on the other bank. Despite heavy fire from the Swedes, the Poles managed to outflank the enemy and, after a two-hour-long fight, force him to flee. Many Swedes were killed by the chasing Polish soldiers, others from the vengeful hands of the local peasants. Baden-Durlach fled to Czersk, from which 'after three days of cold and hunger' he retreated under the cover of darkness to Warsaw. Many officers and 400 privates, many of them French, were captured.[52] We do not have much information about Polish losses, except a high number that were killed in the prelude to the battle during a skirmish at Kozienice on 6 April. Jemiołowski wrote that, during the battle, 'not many were killed', naming just Hebdo, the standard-bearer of Zamoyski's hussar banner, as the most prominent casualty. There were many more wounded, though, most of them shot.[53] A relation published in Rome mentioned that there were only a few killed and not many wounded. The worst seems to be the loss amongst the horses, 'as there were almost as many dead as [those of the] enemies, not counting those that perished from exhaustion at Ujazdów'.[54] This last place, half a mile from Warsaw, was the final point until which the Polish cavalry was chasing the fleeing Swedes. Unsurprisingly, many horses, already tired after the battle, died there after the prolonged pursuit. Initially, even the Swedes did not know how much of Baden-Durlach's division was lost. Prince Adolf Johan's letter to King Charles X Gustav, written one day after the battle and later captured by the Poles, stated that 'yesterday near Czersk Magrave's regiments were badly beaten by the enemy, although we do not know where

---

51 *Diary of General Patrick Gordon*, vol. I, pp.97–99.
52 Kochowski, *Historya panowania Jana Kazimierza*, vol. I, pp.286–87.
53 Jemiołowski, *Pamiętnik dzieje Polski zawierający*, p.192.
54 'Relazione dei felici successi dell' armi…', p.295.

our [survivors] are hiding, while some of them that we thought were dead, are arriving [to Warsaw] every hour'.⁵⁵

Despite the differences in sources regarding the size of the fighting forces and their losses, one was clear: for the first time during this war, the Polish army managed to defeat a larger Swedish force in open battle. It was definitely a great boost for the morale of Jan II Kazimierz's troops, although, from a strategic point of view, the success at Warka led to a failure in containing Charles X Gustav's field army between the Vistula and San rivers. Sapieha's Lithuanians were unable on their own to stop the Swedish King from breaking through their blockade and retreating towards Warsaw. In hindsight, it would have been much more logical to send only a part of the Polish army to attack Baden-Durlach, possibly just to harass his division all the way to Warsaw with a few regiments of Polish cavalry. It is very likely, though, that both commanders – Czarniecki and Lubomirski – wanted to make sure that they had their chance for glory against the marching Swedes and did not want their rival to emerge as a possible 'father' of the victory.

The Battle of Nowy Dwór, 30 September 1655. Erik Dahlbergh's drawing for Samuel Pufendorf's *De rebus a Carolo Gustavo Sueciae rege gestis*, published in 1696 (Krigsarkivet, Stockholm).

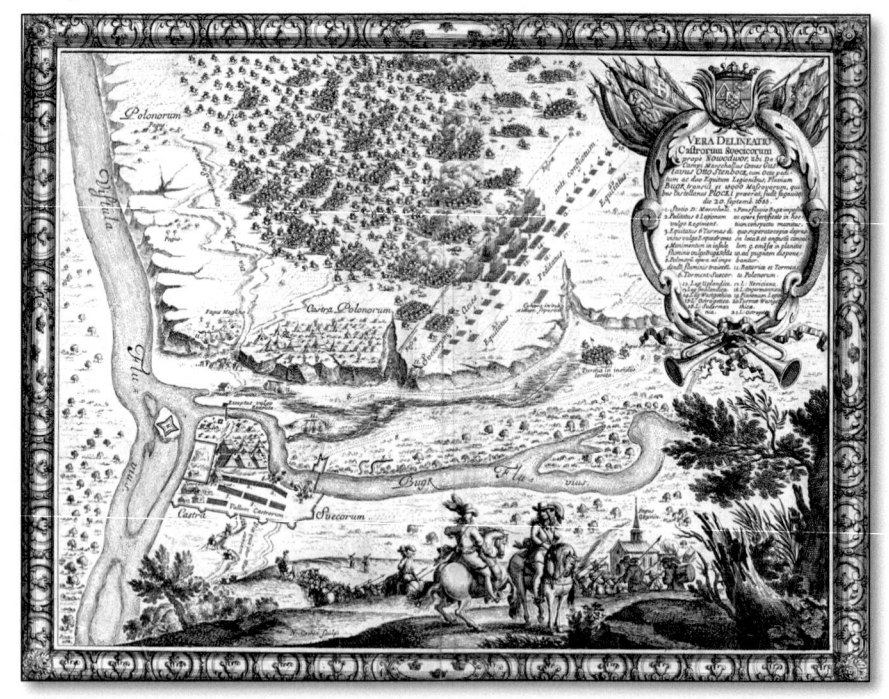

Another occasion to face the Swedes in open fight happened one month later, on 7 May 1656 at the Battle of Gniezno, known also as the Battle of Kłeck. Czarniecki and Lubomirski had here under their command up to 15,000 men,⁵⁶ with two-thirds of this number in regular troops (cavalry and some dragoons), while the remaining one-third were of levy of nobility

---

55 Rudawski, *Historja Polska od śmierci Władysława IV aż do pokoju oliwskiego*, vol. II, p.89.
56 We can completely disregard the statement in Łoś' diary, that the Poles fielded 40,000 men. Such a number would have to include both fighting men and their servants, with the latter not taking part in the fight.

and district troops. The regular troops were divided into 14 regiments of national cavalry. There is no indication of how many regiments of levy and district cavalry were present, but, considering the number of soldiers, it was probably at least five to six regiments.[57] The Swedish army was commanded by Generalissimo Prince Adolf Johan. His force is estimated at approximately 6,000 to 7,000 men[58] (including 1,000 infantry), with strong artillery support (both regimental and heavier field pieces). There were 27 reiter regiments (a total of 39 squadrons), four dragoon regiments and three infantry regiments. Unlike in the few previous encounters from 1656, the Swedes had a 'combined arms' force, and, as we will see in the descriptions of the fight, the presence of artillery and infantry was to play an important role in the events of the battle.

In early May 1656, both Polish and Swedish commanders were trying to establish where and of what strength the opponent's field army was operating in Wielkopolska. Adolf Johan was marching his troops towards Gniezno, destroying groups of Polish partisans. Czarniecki and Lubomirski were, at the same time, moving in the area of Gniezno, where they were hoping to rest and recover after the campaign. The reconnaissance groups from both armies took some prisoners, and, based on the information gathered from them, both sides decided to prepare for pitched battles. The Poles, knowing that they outnumbered the enemy and that the Swedes were not led by King Charles X Gustav himself, were hoping to be able to defeat the Swedish field army. At the same time, Adolf Johan was eager to meet the Poles in open field, believing that the troops he had under his command would be up to the task. The battle was to take place near Kłecko, 16km from Gniezno. The Polish command prepared for the fight by setting an elaborate ambush, hoping to lure the Swedes into a trap and destroy them with charges of cavalry. Two regiments of cavalry (Michał Zbrożek and Jan Szemberk) were sent towards the marching Swedish army to engage their vanguard. A further four regiments (Jan Sapieha, Dymitr Wiśniowiecki, Jan Sobieski and Jakub Potocki) moved through the river Wełnianka near the village of Brzozogaj (on the left bank) and were deployed as an ambush force in the forest there. The rest of the Polish army stayed on the right bank of the Wełnianka to encourage the Swedes to cross the river to get to the battle. The plan was that, when Adolf Johan's troops would be crossing the river to engage the main Polish army, four regiments from the ambush force would strike at them and wreak havoc amongst the crossing troops.[59] The main Polish army was divided into two wings. Czarniecki had command over the left flank, with seven regiments of national cavalry and his dragoon regiment. Lubomirski took over the right flank, with one regiment of national cavalry (his own), all district and levy (so at least five to six regiments).

---

57 Nowak, 'Kampania wielkopolska Czarnieckiego i Lubomirskiego w roku 1656', pp.118–19.
58 Some estimates give them as high as 20,000 men, which is way too high.
59 Stefan Czarniecki described his plan and the battle itself in his after-fight report to King Jan II Kazimierz, written from Środa and dated 10 May 1656: *Stefan Czarniecki do króla Jana Kazimierza, ze Środy 19 maja 1656*, Nowak, 'Kampania wielkopolska Czarnieckiego i Lubomirskiego w roku 1656', pp.146–48.

The Swedish vanguard (Engel's reiter regiment and Berends' dragoon regiment) captured the crossing near Kłecko, as the Poles withdrew without much fight, hoping to lure the Swedish army into a trap. While the Swedish army was setting up their battle line, Engel and his reiters were sent for reconnaissance. They encountered Zbrożek's and Szemberk's regiments, so they quickly were forced to return to the main force of the Swedish army. Expecting that the whole Polish army was already waiting for the fight, Adolf Johan set up his troops. The right wing, composed of two lines of reiters and some dragoons deployed between them, was under the direct command of Prince Adolf Johan and Robert Douglas. The left wing, also made of reiters and some dragoons, was led by Karl Gustav Wrangel and Burchard Müller von der Lühnen. Infantry and artillery were deployed at the centre of the Swedish army, commanded by Barthold Hartwig von Bülow and Gustav Oxenstierna. Wrangel seems to have rushed into the fight, not noticing (or not caring) that the right wing was delayed by the heavy boggy terrain. The Swedish left wing started to outflank the woods, thinking that they were now facing the whole Polish army. Instead, there were just four cavalry regiments awaiting in ambush who now, despite previous orders, charged into a fight against the Swedish reiters and dragoons. They were also soon joined by the two remaining regiments present on this bank of the Wełnianka, so all six regiments were now engaged against Wrangel's wing. Swedish discipline and firepower seem to have won the day, though, so gradually the Polish force was pushed back. Furthermore, the boggy terrain was not an ally of the Poles, as the charging horses were 'getting stuck in the mud up to their necks'.[60] Of course, we can easily disregard Pufendorf's statement, that the two regiments that charged between the Swedish lines were almost completely destroyed in the fight.[61] Nonetheless, one was certain: the initial Polish battle plan failed, and there was no longer a chance to ambush the Swedes since their battle line, supported by strong artillery fire, was slowly moving towards the Wełnianka.

Czarniecki did not give up yet, as he was hoping that the masses of Polish cavalry could still be victorious. He ordered his regiments to move alongside the river and to cross into left bank of the Wełnianka, far away from the eyes of the Swedes, so that he could attack the flank of the Swedish army. At the same time, he hoped that Lubomirski would engage the centre of Adolf Johan's force, keeping the Swedes occupied. The six regiments that initially faced the Swedes now retreated on the right bank, with the Swedish army following after them. Lubomirski's division was able to engage, though, stopped by the heavy fire of the Swedish cannons and muskets. Douglas, in direct command of the Swedish right wing, set up his troops behind a ditch,

Swedish Field Marshal Carl Gustaf Wrangel, portrait by Matthäus Merian the Younger (Skoklosters Slott).

---

60   Kochowski, *Lata Potopu 1655-1657*, p.170.
61   Pufendorf, *Siedem ksiąg o czynach Karola Gustawa króla Szwecji*, p.146.

where they were protected from the lances of the charging Poles and had an open line of fire for their muskets.⁶² In the meantime, Czarniecki charged against the Swedish flank, with the attack being led by Witowski's and Royal regiments. Pufendorf mentioned that the Poles attacked many times 'with loud war cries' and that, despite heavy losses due to Swedish firepower, they showed great resilience. It seems that, based on their previous experience of fighting against Polish cavalry, the Swedes focused on keeping close ranks and an intact battle line, not falling for any hit-and-run Polish tactics.⁶³ Also, Witowski's regiment, despite some initial success, was apparently the hardest pressed and even broke under the heavy fire of the Swedish infantry. It was then supported by the Royal regiment, with two banners of hussars (Royal and Myszkowski's) and Myszkowski's *pancerni* banner (the unit in which Jakub Łoś was serving) leading the countercharge. The timely intervention of these units managed to stop the charge of the Swedish reiters, but again, under the heavy fire of artillery and infantry, they were forced to retreat.⁶⁴ Łoś complained that the Poles 'with their naked bellies [unarmoured] could not do anything against the artillery'.⁶⁵ In his letter to Queen Ludwika Maria, despite the defeat, Czarniecki was to mention that 'this battle only ensure [in the Polish army] conviction that cannons should be despised and that [victory] should be achieved with sabre'.⁶⁶ The Polish army retreated from the

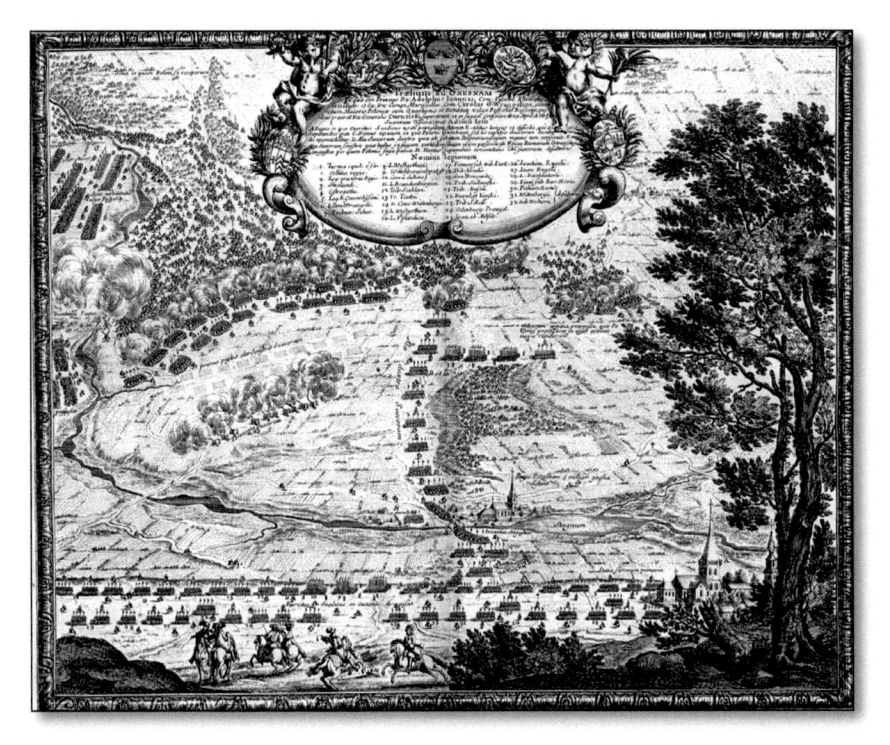

The Battle of Kłeck/Gniezno, 7 May 1656. Erik Dahlbergh's drawing for Samuel Pufendorf's *De rebus a Carolo Gustavo Sueciae rege gestis*, published in 1696 (Muzeum Narodowe, Kraków).

---

62 Kochowski, *Lata Potopu 1655-1657*, pp.170–71.
63 Pufendorf, *Siedem ksiąg o czynach Karola Gustawa króla Szwecji*, p.147.
64 Jemiołowski, *Pamiętnik dzieje Polski zawierający*, p.197.
65 Łoś, *Pamiętnik towarzysza chorągwi pancernej*, p.66.
66 Przeździecki (ed.), 'Zdobycie Warszawy przez Szwedów w 1656 r. opisane w listach królowej polskiej Marii Ludwiki', p.199.

battlefield, moving towards Środa. As the battle took place between 1500 and 2000 hours, the Swedes quickly stopped their pursuit due to the approaching darkness.[67] Their lack of familiarity with the terrain and the danger of ambushes from the local population could be a factor as well.

As so often when dealing with multiple sources, we have very different estimates of losses. Pufendorf gives very high Polish casualties at 600 killed during the battle and 'up to 2,500 killed' during the after-fight pursuit. He explained that not many of the Poles were captured, 'as the spirit of [the fighting sides] was angry – neither Poles asked for mercy nor they gave one'.[68] He did not give any indication of the level of losses amongst the Swedes, though. Those are mentioned by Jemiołowski, who estimated them as a few hundred killed and wounded. As for the Polish ones, he only mentioned high losses in the Royal regiment, with many shot (indicating both killed and wounded).[69] Łoś wrote that the Poles had considerable losses 'in men and horses' while being more specific about the losses in his nominal *rotmistrz* command, which is not surprising considering his banner (Myszkowski's *pancerni*) was in the thick of the fight, losing six killed (including Lieutenant Jan Borowski) and 14 wounded companions, to which we would have to add an unknown number from amongst retainers. Myszkowski's hussars lost two killed, while Wespazjan Kochowski was wounded.[70] Another post-battle relation mentioned 'at Gniezno 130 men were killed, especially [due] to fire from cannons'.[71] Czarniecki, in his letter to the King, tried – for rather obvious reasons – to downplay the defeat and losses amongst his troops, mentioning only up to 70 killed and wounded while estimating Swedish losses (based on relations that prisoners captured sometime after the battle) as more than 500 killed. Moreover, only nine killed Poles were left on the battlefield, with the rest taken away by their comrades in arms.[72] He seems to have been even more imaginative in his despatch to the Queen, informing her that the Polish side lost only 50 or 60 men while Swedish losses could be estimated as up to 1,000 men.[73] According to Kochowski, almost 40 companions were killed, and many more, including Władysław Wilczkowski (lieutenant of Myszkowski's hussar banner), were wounded. Kochowski himself was shot twice in the arm.[74] As we can see, it is very hard to establish the exact level of losses in both armies, but it seems that a few hundred in killed and wounded on each side seems to be as close as it gets. The Swedes would have lost more men in the initial stage of the battle, while Polish losses would have to be the highest during the numerous charges against the Swedish lines. No matter the level of casualties, the Swedes avoided the Polish trap and forced Czarniecki and

---

67 Pufendorf, *Siedem ksiąg o czynach Karola Gustawa króla Szwecji*, p.147.
68 Pufendorf, *Siedem ksiąg o czynach Karola Gustawa króla Szwecji*, p.147.
69 Jemiołowski, *Pamiętnik dzieje Polski zawierający*, p.198.
70 Łoś, *Pamiętnik towarzysza chorągwi pancernej*, pp.66–67.
71 Gawęda, *Od Beresteczka do Cudnowa*, p.143.
72 *Stefan Czarniecki do króla Jana Kazimierza, ze Środy 19 maja 1656*, Nowak, 'Kampania wielkopolska Czarnieckiego i Lubomirskiego w roku 1656', p.147.
73 Przeździecki (ed.), 'Zdobycie Warszawy przez Szwedów w 1656 r. opisane w listach królowej polskiej Marii Ludwiki', p.199.
74 Kochowski, *Lata Potopu 1655-1657*, p.171.

Lubomirski to retreat. They owned the battlefield and could see their victory as at least partial revenge for the battle at Warka.

These three battles with the involvement of Stefan Czarniecki show different Polish approaches and reactions to changing conditions of the battlefield. At Gołąb, when surprised by the approaching Swedes, they quickly decided that discretion was the better part of the valour and quickly retreated from the battlefield. At Warka, outnumbering and outmanoeuvring the enemy, Polish commanders pushed to destroy the enemy, pursuing the fleeing enemy almost to Warsaw. During these two fights, the Swedes could not use the support of their artillery, and the presence of infantry and dragoons at Warka, especially in light of their incorrect deployment by the inexperienced Baden-Durlach, was a non-factor in the outcome of the fight. How important was the effect of solid firepower in the hands of Swedish veteran commanders we could observe at Gniezno/Kłecko, where it played an important role in both inflicting losses amongst the Polish troops and negatively affecting their morale.

An example of chainmail and a *misiurka* helmet, used by Polish and Lithuanian cavalry (Author's archive).

After describing a few battles that involved the Polish army, it is time to look into some examples of those in which Lithuanian soldiers played the most important role. I would like to look more closely into two encounters from October 1656, from Lithuanian Field Hetman Wincenty Gosiewski's campaign in Ducal Prussia. On 8 October, at Prostki, he managed to defeat the Swedish–Brandenburg division, although two weeks later, at Filipów, it was his force that was routed by Swedish and Brandenburg soldiers.[75] The operation was part of the Commonwealth's command's new strategy after the lost battle at Warsaw. While the main Polish army was to march towards Gdańsk, a strong detachment composed mostly from Lithuanians was to raid Ducal Prussia, engaging the Swedish and Brandenburg forces and supporting the uprising in Samogitia. As Lithuanian Grand Hetman Sapieha was still recovering from injury, Field Hetman Gosiewski was to be in charge. The core of the raiding force was to be composed of his division, supported by a few regiments of national cavalry from Grand Hetman's division. The other Lithuanian units from Sapieha's division remained with him in the area of Brest. Gosiewski was supported by Crimean Tatars under Subhan Ğazı Ağa, probably no more than 1,000 warriors. Finally, there was a group of 15 banners of Polish cavalry (cossack cavalry and probably some light horse) under Gabriel Wojniłłowicz, also around 1,000 men. Their main task was to 'keep an eye' on the Tatar allies to make sure that, until they arrived in Prussia, they would not harm the local Polish population. In total, Gosiewski's force was composed of up to 8,000 men (including 6,000 Lithuanians), supported by a few more thousand of armed camp followers.

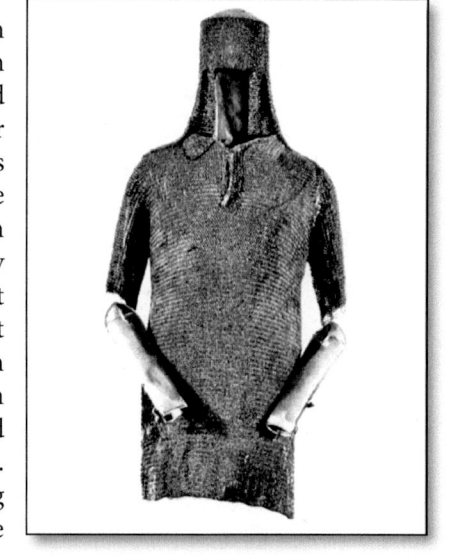

---

75 The whole campaign in Prussia, including both battles, was in-depth described in: Sławomir Augusiewicz, *Prostki 1656* (Warszawa: Dom Wydawniczy Bellona, 2001). This work utilises a large number of German-speaking sources, presenting the Brandenburg point of view, so it will be extensively used as a part of this subchapter.

AGAINST THE DELUGE

It was practically all-mounted corps, which included five banners of Lithuanian hussars; a few units of dragoons and one banner of haiduks were the only units that could be used as infantry.[76] The Brandenburg forces in Ducal Prussia were divided into a few detachments, and the one that was to face Gosiewski was under the command of Georg Friedrich von Waldeck, who was cooperating with the Swedish force led by Prince Bogusław Radziwiłł. Based on the most detailed research by Sławomir Augusiewicz,[77] it can be estimated that Waldeck had with him five regiments and one squadron of reiters, six dragoon companies and (probably) two banners of the local Prussian levy of nobility, all supported by nine light cannons. Two further units (one reiter regiment and one dragoon regiment) were detached from the Brandenburg force and did not take direct part in the battle. As for the Swedes, they probably had five reiter regiments and one dragoon regiment, without artillery support. It seems that the allied force was approximately 4,000-men strong, with a 1:1 ratio of Brandenburg to Swedish soldiers. Overall command was in Waldeck's hands, although, at least based on Radziwiłł's memoir, he did not go well with the Swedish officers and did not coordinate his actions with them. The allied force was deployed on the two sides of the river Ełk: Waldeck's Brandenburg had camp on left side, next to some field fortifications near Prostki, while the Swedes around noon on 8 October arrived on the right side of the river. There were two bridges through river, one (old) north from the Brandenburg camp and the other (newly built, probably by Waldeck's troops) south, near the Swedish position. There was also another Brandenburg detachment, stationed up north near the Ełk, approximately 17–18km from Prostki. It was commanded by Colonel Heinrich von Wallenrodt, who led approximately 2,000 men in two reiter regiments, two dragoon regiments and two infantry regiments.[78] It did not take part in the battle, though, but did provide a safe assembly point for the soldiers fleeing from Prostki. Another Brandenburg force, under Colonel Wolrad von Waldeck (with at least one regiment of infantry), was also marching towards Wallenrodt.[79]

Georg Friedrich von Waldeck, portrait by Jacques Blondeau (Wikimedia Commons).

Initially, both Waldeck and Radziwiłł had news that only the Tatars and Poles were approaching Prostki. They knew that the Lithuanian force was

---

76 Augusiewicz, *Prostki 1656*, pp.73–74.
77 Augusiewicz, *Prostki 1656*, pp.91–94.
78 Colonel Heinrich von Wallenrodt was a former Polish officer, until 1655 serving in a reiter regiment.
79 *Colonel Wolrad von Waldeck* was Georg Friedrich's brother.

nearby but did not have much information about its whereabouts. Waldeck was also counting on the arrival of von Wallenrodt's detachments to increase the overall strength and firepower available for the Brandenburg–Swedish army. Gosiewski, based on his own intel, decided to engage the enemy with the Polish–Tatar force, which was to be followed by the Lithuanians. The idea was to attack the force at Prostki before Wallenrodt's group could join it. Waldeck, after receiving more news about the approaching enemy, decided to abandon the camp at Prostki and move north to regroup with the other Brandenburg force. On the left side of the river, he kept a strong holding force of dragoons and reiters, supported by two cannons. The rest of Waldeck's division started its evacuation by moving its tabor and the rest of its artillery through the northern bridge onto the right bank of the river. The initial attacks by the Tatars and Poles caused some confusion amongst the Brandenburg force and quickly forced the Waldeck's troops that already crossed the river to return to the left bank. Gosiewski's main force arrived on the battlefield on the left bank and started their own attack on the Brandenburg camp. It seems that any plans that Waldeck had for an organised retreat of his troops collapsed at that time, and the allies were forced to disorganise their defence on the left bank of the river next to both bridges. While some of the initial Lithuanian attacks were repulsed, the Brandenburg soldiers – quickly running out of ammunition and powder – started to waver. Regimental officers were asking for orders, putting pressure on Waldeck to order a general retreat. After approximately two hours from the opening of the fight, the first Brandenburg units defending around the northern bridge started to flee. The retreat seems to have started with Colonel Christoph de Brünell being shot dead by one of his officers, which caused the whole unit to flee. The other units – a squadron from the reiter regiment of Christoph von Kannenberg and Waldeck's own reiter regiment – abandoned their positions and followed their fleeing comrades. After an unsuccessful attempt to stop the panicked soldiers, Waldeck moved to the southern bridge to try to rally the soldiers remaining there. He never arrived there, as on his way he encountered a group of Brandenburg officers who advised him that the defence around the southern bridge also collapsed. Waldeck and his entourage then joined the fleeing troops.

In fact, it was just the Brandenburg regiments that were fleeing the battle: Radziwiłł's Swedes were still fiercely opposing the attacks by the Lithuanians, Poles and Tatars. His detachment was completely surrounded and destroyed, with a few hundred men managing to flee but up to 1,500 killed and captured. Amongst the captured were Radziwiłł, General Ridderhielm and a few colonels and lieutenant colonels. The Brandenburg force was scattered, losing a whole tabor and all cannons, but the manpower losses were probably not higher than a few hundred. The already mentioned *Colonel* Christoph de Brünell was killed, while Colonel Josias von Waldeck was captured. Gosiewski's force seems to have had rather low losses, although amongst the killed were two lieutenants: Kosik and Ogiński.[80]

---

80   Augusiewicz, *Prostki 1656*, pp.116–17.

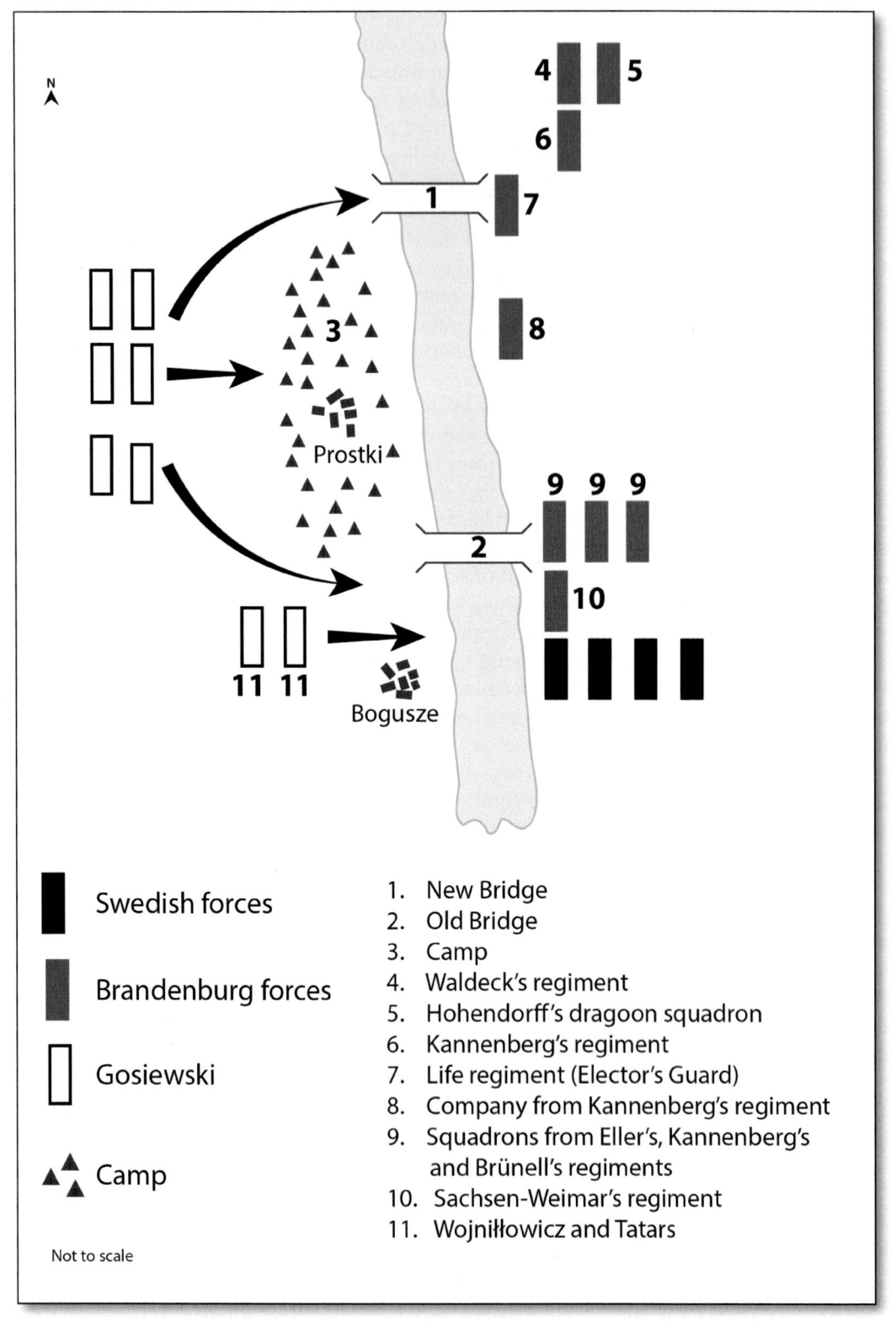

AGAINST THE DELUGE

Legend:

- Swedish forces
- Brandenburg forces
- Gosiewski
- Camp

1. New Bridge
2. Old Bridge
3. Camp
4. Waldeck's regiment
5. Hohendorff's dragoon squadron
6. Kannenberg's regiment
7. Life regiment (Elector's Guard)
8. Company from Kannenberg's regiment
9. Squadrons from Eller's, Kannenberg's and Brünell's regiments
10. Sachsen-Weimar's regiment
11. Wojniłłowicz and Tatars

Not to scale

The second phase of the Battle of Prostki, 8 October 1656. Source: Sławomir Augusiewicz, *Prostki 1656*.

PITCHED BATTLES

Prince Bogusław Radziwiłł, in his autobiography, wrote that he had command of four Swedish reiter regiments, with the senior officer being General Major Israel Ridderhielm.[81] He operated with them near Tykocin to supply its garrison with food. On receiving the news that Gosiewski was approaching Prussia, Radziwiłł marched towards Prostki to join the forces with Waldeck's men.[82] The Brandenburg commander also informed him that the Poles and Tatars were en route, so Radziwiłł hastened the movement of his troops. He seems to have not gotten well with Waldeck, as they could not agree on one plan of battle. Apparently, the allies got confused when the Crimean Tatars attacked the Brandenburg tabor, and Waldeck's troops 'without any reason' started to retreat. Their withdrawal led to Radziwiłł's Swedes being cut off and attacked from all sides by the Lithuanians, Poles and Tatars. The Prince wrote that 600 of his men were killed and that he, seriously wounded in the head, was close to death. While lying on the ground, he was almost stabbed by a blade on top of the pole of the standard wielded by a Tatar warrior, but he managed to grab the blade and break it out from the pole.

Prince Bogusław Radziwiłł, portrait by Jeremiasz Falck (Biblioteka Narodowa, Warszawa).

The captured Radziwiłł was taken as an important prisoner by the Tatars, although, en route to their camp, he was recognised by a retainer from the Polish army, who quickly let his commanders know about the captive. Forty Poles arrived and, by force, took Radziwiłł away from the Tatars, bringing him to Hetman Gosiewski. Here, his wounds were taken care of by the Hetman's surgeon. According to Prince Bogusław, there were those amongst the Lithuanian and Polish soldiers that were eager to kill him, although he was saved by Prince Michał Kazimierz Radziwiłł, his cousin. Under his protection, Prince Bogusław was kept in the Lithuanian camp, but, as we will soon see, his captivity was not very long. Pufendorf put all the blame for the defeat at Prostki on the Brandenburg army – which, 'despite brave resistance of its general [Waldeck]', after a short fight, fled from the enemy, leaving a small number of its men on the battlefield. Far worse was the fight of the Swedish detachment, which was now abandoned and, fighting with the large number of attackers, 'was forced to face serious defeat'. Despite their bravery, the majority of soldiers were killed or captured. Six Brandenburg cannons and a whole tabor were captured. Colonel Dietrich von Rosen and many other officers were killed; amongst the captured were General Major Israel Ridderhielm, Colonel Johan Engel and many more officers. Prince Bogusław Radziwiłł 'was taken captive after hard fight and was badly mistreated by Tatars'. It was Pufendorf that wrote about the rather unusual episode of the

---

81　Ridderhielm, in fact, brought with him two more regiments, and that is why all other sources mention the Swedish force as being six regiments.
82　Radziwiłł, *Żywot xięcia Bogusława Radziwiłła, przez niego samego napisany*, pp.31–34.

battle. When the Brandenburg regiment of Colonel Christoph de Brünell was to attack the enemy, its colonel 'was treacherously shot by one of his own officers, who later paid for it with his head'.[83] As mentioned before, it seems that this act led to the collapse of Brünell's regiment and its subsequent panicked retreat from the battlefield.

Colonel Gabriel Wojniłłowicz, in his after-battle report to King Jan II Kazimierz, written two days after the battle, mentioned that the Swedes had six reiter regiments and a few hundred dragoons while the Brandenburg force was composed of 10 regiments. A whole tabor and nine cannons were captured, alongside many captives, especially officers. Up to 3,000 Brandenburgians and Swedes were supposedly killed, with a further 1,000 captured by the Poles and Lithuanians alone. The Colonel wrote that his brother, serving in the Royal *pancerni* banner, was killed while some men and some horses were wounded. He also reported the conflict with *Subhan Ğazı Ağa*, as the Tatars were unhappy about the situation with Bogusław Radziwiłł and demanded for the important captive to be handed over to them.[84]

Another letter, probably also written by Wojniłłowicz or by another Polish companion present at Prostki, mentioned the important role of the Crimean Tatars that outflanked the enemy, which led to the collapse of the front, already hard pressed by the Poles and Lithuanians. The soldier did notice that the 'Prussians' [meaning the Brandenburg troops] broke first, but he did not think that many of them managed to flee since 'Horde [Tatars] took many captive'. Worth adding, though, the author of this relation estimated the entire Swedish–Brandenburg force at no more than 3,000 men. He was not sure if Waldeck managed to flee (as the relation was written just after the battle) but noticed that the wounded Prince Bogusław Radziwiłł was captured and that the majority of the enemy officers were lost. Amongst the loot were also three cannons. In the *pancerni* banner he served with, one companion and two retainers were killed; in other units, losses were also small.[85] Rudawski did not provide a description of the battle itself. However, he gave some information about the scale of victory, as, according to him, Gosiewski captured '80 flags and two Generals, Izrael [Israel Ridderhielm] and Kannaberg [General Major Christoph von Kannenberg]'. He also added that Prince Bogusław was taken by the Tatars and then 'by force snatched from them by Lithuanians'. The historian also mentioned the number and names of all the Swedish and Brandenburg regiments, with six of the former and five of the latter. There were also supposed to be two banners that served Prince Bogusław Radziwiłł and two banners of Prussian nobles (levy).[86] According to Kochowski, Waldeck's force was supported in the battle by six Swedish regiments under 'colonel Israel' and Bogusław Radziwiłł. In his relation, Gosiewski attacked the Brandenburg force with the majority of his

---

83 Pufendorf, *Siedem ksiąg o czynach Karola Gustawa króla Szwecji*, p.164.
84 Tadeusz Nowak, 'Nieznane materiały do wojny szwedzkiej 1656 z b. Archiwum Radziwiłłów w Warszawie', *Przegląd Historyczny*, 47:4 (1956), p.719.
85 *Pod datą z Woyjska 8 Octobra w Prostkach*, Saint Petersburg Institute of History, collection 32, box 660/2, p.39.
86 Rudawski, *Historja Polska od śmierci Władysława IV aż do pokoju oliwskiego*, vol. II, p.145.

PITCHED BATTLES

troops, while the Poles under Wojniłłowicz and the Tatars were sent down river to find ford and attack the enemy from the rear. The initial Lithuanian charges were stopped by Brandenburg artillery, but the sudden attack of Tatars stopped Waldeck's counterattacks and quickly routed his men. The fleeing soldiers took heavy losses since German horses were far slower than Tatar ones and they were unable to retreat through the boggy terrain. Kochowski wrote about 3,000 killed Swedes and Brandenburg soldiers, with many officers, all cannons and 39 flags captured.[87] The Queen's Court received, as was often the case, rather exaggerated information about the scale of the victory. De Noyers noted that the Tatars captured more than 2,000 soldiers, 5,000 to 6,000 servants and more than 400 women. Hetman Gosiewski's trophy was two carts full of the enemy's flags, amongst them 18 captured by Wojniłłowicz's Poles. Of course, the important information was that Prince Bogusław Radziwiłł was amongst those captured.[88]

Lithuanian Field Hetman Wincenty Korwin Gosiewski, portrait from the workshop of Daniel Schultz (Wikimedia Commons).

Waldeck described the defeat at Prostki in a long letter, dated 20 October 1656, written to Daniel Weimann, a Brandenburg envoy in England and the United Provinces. The General complained that six regiments of his original command suffered much during the initial operations 'due to fatigue and illness' and that they required long rest. Here, they were far away from other Brandenburg troops, facing a large Lithuanian and Tatar force. Waldeck then mentioned that Prince Radziwiłł arrived at his camp with six regiments, totalling 600 horsemen. Colonel Wallenrodt, who was nearby, was ordered by Waldeck to join his force as well, although initially he despatched just two regiments and six canons. Brandenburg and Swedish pickets skirmished against the vanguard of the Lithuanian and Tatar forces, but Waldeck, hoping that Wallenrodt was nearby, decided to wait at the camp. He sent out one regiment of reiters and some dragoons to defend ford on the river, but the 'Tatars having found a suitable place to swim, put themselves between above-mentioned troops and mine'. The enemy attacks quickly overcame the Brandenburg guards and attacked the poorly defended camp fortification. Waldeck lost the cannons deployed with his camp guard in the woods, as their crews abandoned them. Lithuanian dragoons seem to have been leading the attacks on the Brandenburg positions and, supported by cavalry, gradually started to overcome the defenders. Then, Waldeck mentioned that three of his regiments panicked and fled from their position near the bridge and that he barely saved his life. He added that Radziwiłł and Israel (Ridderhielm) were cut off and taken by the Tartars and that his whole tabor was lost. Waldeck estimated his own losses at 'no

---

87   Kochowski, *Lata Potopu 1655-1657*, pp.232–34.
88   *Portfolio królowej Maryi Ludwiki*, vol. II, p.102.

more than 200 horsemen'. The Tatars ravaged the areas in Prussia, taking more than 1,000 captives and burning several villages. Their further raids were only stopped by the arrival of Brandenburg reinforcements (four reiter and two infantry regiments) and Marshal Steinbock's Swedes.[89]

Within the days after the battle, Waldeck and Friedrich Wilhelm exchanged many letters, in which the commander was trying to explain the reasons for the defeats and the Elector was looking to assess the scale of the losses and the ways in which his army could now oppose Gosiewski. Writing one day after the battle, Waldeck mentioned that he was gathering scattered troops and would combine his troops with Wallenrodt's detachment.[90] On 10 October, Friedrich Wilhelm gave assurances to his general, advising him to rally the surviving troops and confirming that he trusted him to do his duties. Other Brandenburg troops were on their way, while Lieutenant Colonel Polentz was despatched to Charles X Gustav to ask for reinforcements.[91] In his letter from 12 October, the Elector insisted that Waldeck needed to investigate who was responsible for the defeat at Prostki and that the guilty should be punished: the reiter that shot Colonel Christoph de Brünell should be, as an example, court-martialled. Waldeck also received information that Stenbock, with Swedish troops and further Brandenburg units, were marching to rejoin Waldeck, so yet again he would be able to take the fight to the enemy.[92] The attempt to regroup the troops after the battle seems to have been fairly successful, as, on 14 October, Waldeck advised that he managed to put together six squadrons from the survivors, with a further five made from the soldiers under Wallenrodt's command. The Brandenburg commander insisted, though, that he could not proceed to attack the Lithuanians without the support of infantry, the formation that he severely lacked at Prostki.[93] In November 1656, during a thorough investigation of the reasons of the defeat, in which many surviving officers were interviewed and provided their own view on the battle, Waldeck wrote that only one regiment – the reiters of Duke Johann Georg zu Sachsen-

A seventeenth-century Turkish *kałkan* shield, of the type commonly used by Polish and Lithuanian cavalry (Muzeum Narodowe, Kraków).

---

89 'Waldeck an Daniel Weimann im Haag. Dat. Stradaunen 20. Oct. 1656', in *Urkunden und Actenstücke zur Geschichte des Kurfürsten Friedrich Wilhelm von Brandenburg* (Berlin: Preußische Kommission bei der Preußischen Akademie der Wissenschaften, 1884), vol. VIII, pp.106–08.
90 'Waldeck an den Kurfürsten. Dat. Angerburg 9. Oct. 1656', in *Urkunden und Actenstücke zur Geschichte des Kurfürsten Friedrich Wilhelm von Brandenburg*, vol. VIII, p.99.
91 'Der Kurfürst an Waldeck. Dat. Königsberg 10. Oct. 1656 (11 Uhr Nachts.)', in *Urkunden und Actenstücke zur Geschichte des Kurfürsten Friedrich Wilhelm von Brandenburg*, vol. VIII, p.100.
92 'Der Kurfürst an Waldeck. Dat. Königsberg 12. Oct. 1656', in *Urkunden und Actenstücke zur Geschichte des Kurfürsten Friedrich Wilhelm von Brandenburg*, vol. VIII, p.102.
93 'Waldeck an den Kurfürsten. Dat. bei Lötzen 14. Oct. 1656', in *Urkunden und Actenstücke zur Geschichte des Kurfürsten Friedrich Wilhelm von Brandenburg*, vol. VIII, p.104.

PITCHED BATTLES

Weimar – remained next to him while the other units, despite him ordering and even begging them not to, fled from the battlefield.[94]

After the battle, the Tatars were unleashed against Prussian territory, destroying villages and taking rich bounty in captives and loot. It is estimated that they managed to capture up to 7,000 people.[95] The local population was completely surprised by their raids, while the Brandenburg army was not ready to defend its territory against these attacks. After less than two weeks of pillaging and looting, the Tatars took their captives and left Prussia, on their way through Poland capturing even more people. At the same time, Wojniłłowicz and the Polish banners under his command left Gosiewski's force as well. The Lithuanian Hetman did not follow up on his success from Prostki, instead spending time on negotiations with the Elector. Some of his troops left as well, marching to Podlasie to rejoin Hetman Sapieha, so Gosiewski was left with no more than 5,000 soldiers. Such a lack of Lithuanian actions allowed the Swedes and Brandenburgians to take the initiative, gather their forces and march against the Lithuanians. By 17 October, Gosiewski started to retreat towards the border between Prussia and Samogitia, setting up camp between Mieruniszki (Miron in Prussia) and Filipów (in Samogitia). Here, on 22 October, he was attacked by the joint Swedish–Brandenburg force, in the fight known as the Battle of Filipów.

As the Swedes played a very important role in the allied victory, Pufendorf provides us with a detailed description of the fight.[96] The Swedish force was under the command of Gustav Otto Stenbock, who had with him eight regiments of reiters and one infantry regiment; he was also supported by further infantry units under Jacob de la Gardie.[97] Near Giżycko (*Lötzen*), the Swedes met von Waldeck's force (the already mentioned 11 squadrons of reiters, probably some infantry as well), and the allied division had in total approximately 6,000 men supported by some Swedish field artillery. Thanks to information from captured Lithuanians, Stenbock knew that the Tatars already left Prussia, although estimates of Gosiewski's strength was way too high, given at 10,000 Poles and Lithuanians. The Swedish general thought that Gosiewski would decide to quickly flee from the approaching allies, but testimonies from more captured Lithuanians convinced him that the Hetman and his troops were camped in nearby Filipów and did not expect any attack. Stenbock decided to take the majority of the cavalry, supported by some dragoons, infantry and artillery, and with this chosen force to chance a surprise attack. His vanguard met the Lithuanians gathering provisions in Mieruniszki and killed most of them, but survivors managed to alarm Gosiewski that the enemy was approaching. The Hetman decided to meet Stenbock in battle, believing that, having the advantage in numbers, he would have the advantage in the coming fight. The Lithuanian division deployed between Mieruniszki and Filipów, in the initial attacks, were hard-

---

94 'Waldeck an den Kurfürsten, (o. D.)', in *Urkunden und Actenstücke zur Geschichte des Kurfürsten Friedrich Wilhelm von Brandenburg*, vol. VIII, p.111.
95 Augusiewicz, *Prostki 1656*, p.146.
96 Pufendorf, *Siedem ksiąg o czynach Karola Gustawa króla Szwecji*, pp.164–65.
97 Augusiewicz, *Prostki 1656*, pp.183–84.

pressing the reiter regiments of Friedrich von Hessen-Homburg (Swedish) and Joachim Ernst von Görzke (Brandenburg). The fight took place in difficult conditions, with 'narrow roads, bogs and broken bridge [through the Rozpuda river]', between Mieruńskie Lake and the boggy terrain near the river. Stenbock followed the reiters with his infantry and six field cannons. Two of the latter he deployed on the small hill on one side of the battlefield. He also despatched a few dragoon companies to support the reiters from the vanguard. Gradually, more and more Swedish and Brandenburg forces managed to be deployed on the battlefield, under the cover of artillery fire that seems to have discouraged the Lithuanians. The left wing of the allied cavalry crossed the Rozpuda and charged against Gosiewski's troops, who started to waver and flee the battlefield. They were chased by the Swedish cavalry under Philip von Sulzbach, although due to the approaching darkness (the battle started in the late afternoon) and tiredness of the horses, the pursuit stopped after just two miles. According to Pufendorf, more than 500 Lithuanians were killed, and many others were captured – including Colonel Dukliński (this name was not recorded amongst the Lithuanian officers' corps, though). A small Lithuanian tabor and a few flags were captured; amongst the released prisoners from Prostki, the Swedes saved Prince Bogusław Radziwiłł.

Waldeck was very quick in reporting the victory at Filipów, writing to the Elector one day after the battle. He mentioned that the allies were 'graciously blessed by God this time' and managed to attack and defeat Gosiewski's force on the afternoon of 22 October. The victorious troops recaptured Prince Radziwiłł and the many flags lost at Prostki, while at the same time took 'prisoners, many flags and drums from the enemy'. He estimated Lithuanian losses at 600 killed and left on the battlefield, also 'quite a lot of prisoners'. Gosiewski's division fled towards Samogitia, so Waldeck asked for a reinforcement of infantry and artillery as soon as possible in case he had to face the Lithuanians again.[98] Prince Bogusław Radziwiłł did not provide us with a description of the Battle of Filipów. He only celebrated that, 'thanks to Providence and Mercy of God', he was recaptured from Lithuanian

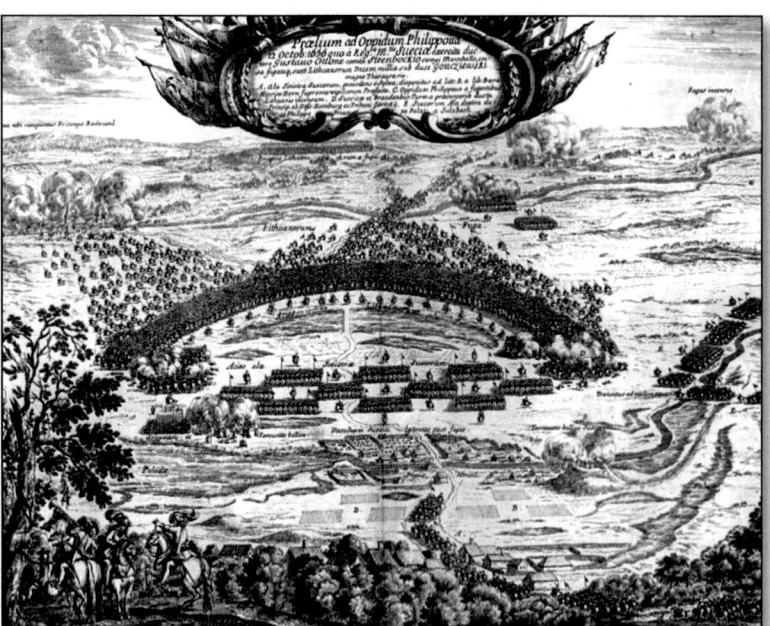

The Battle of Filipów, 22 October 1656. Erik Dahlbergh's drawing for Samuel Pufendorf's *De rebus a Carolo Gustavo Sueciae rege gestis*, published in 1696 (Muzeum Narodowe, Kraków).

---

98 'Waldeck an den Kurfürsten. Dat. 23. Oct. 1656', in *Urkunden und Actenstücke zur Geschichte des Kurfürsten Friedrich Wilhelm von Brandenburg*, vol. VIII, p.109.

hands and that, by the evening of 22 October, he was already safely resting in the Swedish army camp.[99]

Kochowski was very brief with his description of the Battle of Filipów, as he wrote that Gustav Stenbock surprised Gosiewski, scattered his forces and won the battle. He added an interesting piece, though, '[Lithuanian] losses were in this way bigger that when they broke the ranks and scattered, those Swedes kept in captivity since battle of Prostki, gained their freedom'.[100] Gosiewski himself tried to downplay the scale of the defeat, explaining that losses were not very high and that his troops were scattered 'in different directions' but not really destroyed. He also added that the Lithuanians were lacking the support of the Tatars and that many companions left the units and 'with Prussian loot returned to their homes'.[101] This last comment is interesting, as it indicates that there was not much a hetman could do in a situation when unpaid soldiers decided to leave his army, a pattern which seems to have been far too common in the Polish and Lithuanian armies in this period. Amongst confirmed Lithuanian losses were two officers. One *rotmistrz* of a cossack cavalry banner, Samuel Korotkiewicz, was killed; the other, Konstanty Wacław Pokłoński, was captured.[102]

While the Battle of Filipów was not important from a strategic point of view, it definitely helped to rebuild the morale of Brandenburg and Swedish soldiers. Gosiewski apparently overestimated the capabilities of his men, who seem to have been less eager to fight after the already long campaign and were most likely looking forward to resting in winter quarters. Yet again, well-used infantry and artillery played an important role against the cavalry-heavy Commonwealth force. In such fights, a lot depended on the quality of command, though: in 1660, the Polish and Lithuanian armies performed much better against the Muscovite armies despite the fact that the latter employed strong combined-arms forces.

---

99 Radziwiłł, *Żywot xięcia Bogusława Radziwiłła, przez niego samego napisany*, p.34.
100 Kochowski, *Lata Potopu 1655-1657*, p.235.
101 Rachuba, 'Uwagi do problemu kampanii Wincentego Gosiewskiego w Prusach Książęcych jesienią 1656 roku', p.179.
102 Rachuba, 'Uwagi do problemu kampanii Wincentego Gosiewskiego w Prusach Książęcych jesienią 1656 roku', p.179.

7

Small War

Small-scale warfare, especially the actions of Polish partisans and other irregulars (e.g., volunteers), played an important role during the Deluge. It included harassing Swedish lines of communications, attacking small garrisons, convoys and patrols, chasing after marching Swedish troops. Sometimes, it was just an *ad hoc* group of local peasants or nobles, trying to defend their belongings from marauding soldiers. Others were semi-regular 'regiments' or 'warbands', built around the core of some regular banners or private troops. Diarists like Holsten, Gordon and Ascheberg mentioned fighting both reluctant peasants defending their possessions and strong groups of armed horsemen, behaving more in military fashion. Large groups of armed peasants, known as *rabarze*, were sometimes supporting the Polish regular troops – like during Czarniecki's raid to Wielkopolska or during the siege of Warsaw in 1656 – although they were an element very difficult to control, so often they were causing more troubles than providing support. At the same time, especially in 1655 and early 1656, it was all these partisans, often lead by former regular soldiers, that took the brunt of the fighting against the invaders. Small Swedish garrisons and patrols were the most vulnerable to the attacks of Polish partisans, especially as the Poles knew the terrain very well and could use it to their advantage. Scattered groups of Swedish soldiers sent for provisions or marching between different towns could easily fall victim to a sudden attack. Holsten mentioned a situation from late autumn 1655 when he and 15 other Swedish reiters were stationed in Lanckorona. One night, a group of Polish nobles, supported 'by some haiduks and some bandits', attacked the town. All the reiters except Holsten were killed: he – staying in bed due to smallpox – was saved by the lady in whose house he was staying. Truth be told, Holsten admitted that the local nobility hated the Swedes, 'as [the Poles] never felt safe here and we made lots of damage', in a way justifying the attack.[1] At the end of September 1655, Polish partisans led by Krzysztof Żegocki captured the town of Kościan thanks to employing a ruse. Żegocki convinced a peasant entering the town gate to block it with his carriage, due to a broken wheel. It allowed the partisans access to Kościan,

---

1   Holsten, *Przygody wojenne 1655-1666*, pp.34–35.

where they wiped out the Swedish garrison of Kościan – 200 infantry under Major Forbes. On 24 September, Kościan was approached by a small group of Swedish cavalry that was, depending on the source, en route to the main army or returning from the hunting expedition. It was led by Karl Gustav's brother-in-law, Friedrich von Hessen, and Colonel Ludwig von Nassau-Dillenburg. When the Swedish party started knocking on the city gate, looking forward to getting some rest, it was met by musket fire from 'guard of Poles, dressed in Swedish clothes'. Surprised, the Swedes fled, leaving a few casualties behind, including von Hessen, who was 'shot through the thighs and killed'.[2] Of course, soon after, the Polish action was met with Swedish reaction. General Johan Weichard Wrzesowicz put together a pacification force from Swedish garrisons stationed nearby and, on 30 September, under the cover of darkness, attacked Kościan. Their revenge was merciless: 'they killed everyone they found carrying the weapons, hanging the others and torturing some wounded … in total 300 were killed to avenge death of one prince'.[3] Kościan was burned to the ground, which was met with displeasure from Karl X Gustav as he wanted the city intact since it was a vital staging point and a good place for a garrison. Sadly, this was a common situation connected to the actions of partisans, in which vengeful Swedes destroyed villages or even towns near the scene of recent fights.

The religious aspect of anti-Swedish conflict was always a very important factor for local populations, fighting with the Swedes who were looting churches and monasteries. Polish propaganda – both official and ones being part of the local 'point of view' – often presented the Swedes as heretics fighting against the Polish religion. The term *'lutry'* (Lutherans) was used by the Poles as a pejorative description of any foreign soldiers serving under the standards of Karl X Gustav. When, in autumn 1655, Swedish soldiers started to pillage Bernardines Monastery in Kalwaria Zebrzydowska, it led to the almost instant reaction of the local population.[4] Under the command of Wojciech Karwacki, warlike Polish Highlanders from the region (*górale żywieccy*), already under arms as a part of the local defence force, surprised the Swedish soldiers, killing some and capturing the rest. In what was a common scenario when dealing with marauding soldiers (of any army), the prisoners were hanged. It led to a pacification action from the Swedish troops, who burned the monastery and killed the remaining monks. 'Small war' in the area of Lanckorona continued, though, with Highlanders ambushing Swedish patrols and supply convoys. To prevent further damage to the local land and population, local Polish commander Jan Zarzecki was forced to disband his 'land militia', hoping it would prevent further escalation of the conflict.[5] Of course, the level of control that regular officers could have over such volunteers and partisan groups was often limited, although

---

2   Pufendorf, *Siedem ksiąg o czynach Karola Gustawa króla Szwecji*, p.78; *Diary of General Patrick Gordon*, vol. I, p.64; Kochowski, *Historya panowania Jana Kazimierza*, vol. I, pp.273–374.
3   Pufendorf, *Siedem ksiąg o czynach Karola Gustawa króla Szwecji*, p.78.
4   *Bernardyni* is a Polish common name for monks of the Order of Friars Minor, named after its reformer, Bernardino of Siena (1380–1444).
5   Szczotka, *Chłopi obrońcami niepodległej Polski w okresie potopu*, pp.35.

after the return of Jan II Kazimierz to Poland and with Polish attempts of a counteroffensive against the Swedes, there were many attempts to put such groups under control or even to fold them into the army as part of the regular units.

There could even be cases where Swedish soldiers were killed by means other than armed combat. Von Ascheberg, in his letter to King Charles X Gustav dated 25 November 1656, wrote about an event that involved a group of reiters from his regiment. Rittmeister Wilhelm, the lieutenant, the quartermaster and 10 reiters were stationed in the village of Kamlarki, where Polish noble Odrowski tried to poison them. He added rat poison or mercury to their mulled beer. The whole group became instantly sick, but they were saved by the timed arrival of another group of Ascheberg's reiters.[6] It is more than likely that such events happened in different regions of Poland, with poisoned troopers listed as missing in action when their groups disappeared during foraging or reconnaissance missions.

French ambassador to the Swedish King, Hugues de Terlon, provides a very interesting observation about the behaviour of the Swedish troops facing possible Polish ambushers and hostility in occupied territories. In January 1657, he left Toruń, travelling to the Swedish field army, where Charles X Gustav was at that point. De Terlon was given an escort of 50 reiters and 20 dragoons in Toruń; then, en route to the field army, he received another 200 reiters despatched by Charles X Gustav to reinforce the convoy. The Frenchman wrote that 'every night we had to set up camp, which was fortified and with good guar. Commanders of my escort approached it with big caution and we making sure that they used all force in their disposal to protect me.'[7] It seems that, even with a fairly strong cavalry unit, the Swedes still felt wary of possible Polish attacks.

Swedish lines of communication, especially those between smaller outposts, were always in danger of attacks by partisans or even armed peasants. De Noyers noted that, despite Swedish messengers being sent with the usual escort of 50 reiters, on many occasions the Poles managed to capture them.[8] Even as early as early autumn 1655, Holsten was complaining that the Polish regular troops, fighting in small units (possibly banners), caused a lot of trouble to the Swedish supply lines around Cracow.[9] Sometimes, such irregular groups were even able to stand against larger detachments of the Swedish army, utilising the terrain to their advantage. Patrick Gordon mentioned problems in dislodging the partisans attacking Swedish foragers around Cracow during the siege of the city in 1655. General Robert Douglas, despatched by Charles X Gustav with 2,000 reiters and dragoons, was ambushed in the woods by Polish partisans, who not only hid well behind the trees but also fought from a very steep hill near the Swedish temporary camp, rolling large stones on the Swedes. Fighting in such a difficult terrain,

---

6   Ascheberg, *Dziennik oficera jazdy szwedzkiej 1621-1681*, p.25.
7   Hugues de Terlon, *Pamiętniki ambasadora Ludwika XIV przy królu Szwecji Karolu X Gustawie, 1656-1660* (Wrocław: Towarzystwo Przyjaciół Ossolineum, 1999), pp.33–34.
8   *Portfolio królowej Maryi Ludwiki*, vol. I, p.307.
9   Holsten, *Przygody wojenne 1655-1666*, p.33.

SMALL WAR

the Swedish reiters were not of much use, while Gordon added that the Poles, fighting on foot, 'were a great deale nimbler as our dragouns'. This forced the Swedes to regroup and leave their position, after taking some losses. Here, Douglas did manage to avenge his fallen, as he set up an ambush himself – the Swedish rearguard was ordered to 'retreat speedily with some show of confusion' in order to draw the Poles away from the woods. The plan succeeded, as many partisans – both mounted and on foot – left the safety of the forest in pursuit. The Swedish reiters and dragoons quickly regrouped and returned to the fight. Mounted partisans managed to flee to safety without many losses, but those on foot were not so lucky: 'a great multitude whereof were killed in their flight back to the wood'.[10]

An interesting event of 'small war' that is worth mentioning is the local uprising in Samogitia that took place in April and May of 1656.[11] It appears to be a very independent movement that initially was not led by some high-ranking officials or by military commanders. Both the local nobles and peasants united together, striking at the same time at the totally unexpecting Swedish troops. It seems to be mostly caused by the way that the Swedes, spread in small groups in their quarters, were pillaging the local population, behaving like they were in occupied country. Pufendorf wrote that '[the officers] left five to six soldiers in the villages of 30, 40 or 50 farmsteads. They rarely checked on them, so they were of no help [to listen] to peasants' complaints. Besides units were scattered too far away for each other, choosing to stay where it was comfortable and food a plenty'.[12] He also added, with a typical-for-that-time Swedish point of view, that 'intrigues of priests and Jesuits' and the lack of trust between Catholics and Protestants was to blame.[13] At the start of the uprising, there were 2,650 Swedish soldiers, mostly cavalry, stationed in the area. In the initial attack, around 1,000 reiters were killed. Three companies from the regiment of Hans Christoffer Buttler and two from Erik Kruse's regiments were wiped out in their quarters. A part of the newly raised regiment of Colonel Harald Igelström, under Captain

A fight near Człuchów, early January 1656, where the Swedish cavalry under Rutger von Ascheberg surprised the Polish regiments in their quarters. Author unknown, map probably drawn on von Ascheberg's request (Krigsarkivet, Stockholm).

---

10 *Diary of General Patrick Gordon*, vol. I, pp.60–61.
11 For a detailed description of the events, see: Kotlhjarchuk, *In the Shadows of Poland and Russia*, pp.161–68.
12 Pufendorf, *Siedem ksiąg o czynach Karola Gustawa króla Szwecji*, p.177.
13 Pufendorf, *Siedem ksiąg o czynach Karola Gustawa króla Szwecji*, p.177.

Jan Gotthard Heering (Jan Ering), deserted and joined the Lithuanians. Amongst the other destroyed units were three companies of Major Johan von Rosen and four of Colonel Gotthard Vilhelm von Budberg.[14] On 1 May, the German dragoon squadron of Lieutenant Colonel Ludvig Taube was engaged by the Samogitian partisans and almost wiped out, losing three standards. Taube managed to save his life and, with just 80 dragoons, reached Birże. Information about the uprising in Samogitia can even be found in the letters written by Lithuanian nobles living in the area who did not participate in the fight. Tomasz Cedrowski wrote, on 27 April 1656 from Rietavas (Retów), that the 'peasants mutinied so badly, that they have already destroyed few banners [companies] … day before today, five miles from us, they ambushed four banners of reiters and scattered them so much, that barely any [Swedes] fled with life'.[15] He was clearly afraid for his own and his family's life, most likely more from the local partisans than the Swedes as he had links to Janusz Radziwiłł. A few loyalist nobles with some military background, like volunteer Colonel Jan Lisowski, Colonel Aleksander Judycki and Hieronim Kryspin Kirsztensztein, were also involved in the uprising, organising armed groups into something resembling a regular force. The Swedes were pushed out from Samogitia, although they were very quick in organising a counterattack. Magnus de la Gardie managed to gather 3,000 soldiers, including many recruits, and was also reinforced by survivors of the initial attacks during the uprising. He led this force in a punitive expedition into Samogitia. The Swedes burned many villages, killing hundreds of locals, although they also took some losses during both pitched battles and due to hit-and-run attacks. Five hundred captured peasants were sent to Riga, as a workforce for the city's fortifications.[16] While they managed to temporary calm down the situation, they did not destroy all the local armed forces and were still suffering ambushes against their logistics lines. As such, by the end of June 1656, the Swedes decided to abandon their positions in Lithuania except for three garrisons in Birże, Braslaw (Braslaŭ) and Druya (Druja). As a result of the uprising in Samogitia, the Lithuanian territory became mostly free from the Swedish forces.

Another of Rutger von Ascheberg's victories, based on his memoir: 26 March 1656, near Sandomierz, his cavalry defeated a Polish force, taking many prisoners and horses. (Krigsarkivet, Stockholm).

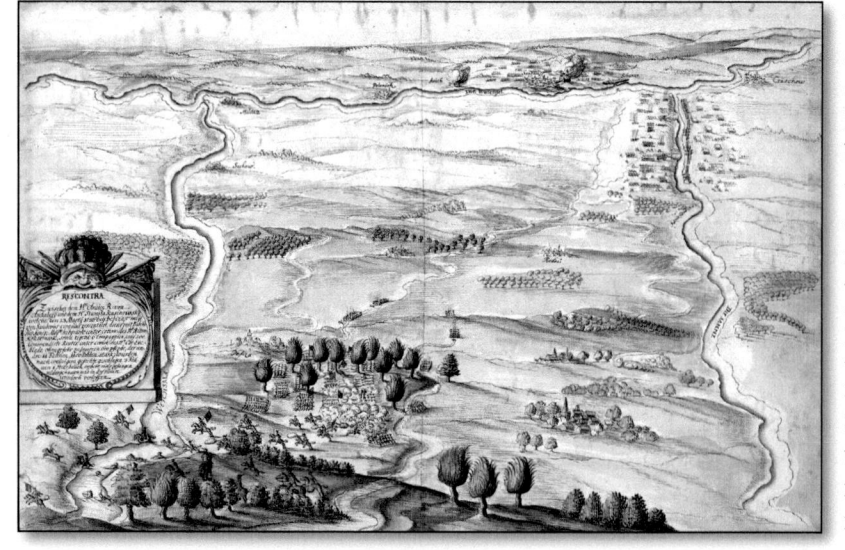

---

14 Pufendorf, *Siedem ksiąg o czynach Karola Gustawa króla Szwecji*, p.177.
15 AGAD, AR V, no. 1871, p.1.
16 Pufendorf, *Siedem ksiąg o czynach Karola Gustawa króla Szwecji*, p.178.

SMALL WAR

The regular units of Polish and Lithuanian cavalry were of course also often engaged in protracted campaigns of 'small war', from being sent out in reconnaissance missions (known in Polish as *podjazd*), through attacking the enemy's lines of communication, to pillaging raids on the enemy's territories. This last type of operations was seen as a very vital task, often fulfilled by light cavalry banners. In autumn 1657, the *rotmistrz* of a Tatar banner, Michał Antonowicz, led a group of Polish cavalry to ravage the Swedish operational base around Szczecin. The light cavalry destroyed more than 160 villages between Szczecin and Nakło, leaving behind just ashes.[17] There were many raids against Ducal Prussia and the Neumark (the New March or East Brandenburg) made by regular troops, levy of nobility and volunteers, leading to serious damages on those lands. Allied Crimean Tatars also took part in raids against Prussia, although normally they were accompanied by Polish or Lithuanian units that were to act as a sort of 'damage control' to prevent the Tatars from looting native the Polish population. This was because the Tatars were rather fickle allies, often refusing to fight or focusing on pillaging and taking prisoners. With the latter, they were not too picky: when 'enemies' were not available, the Tatars would take their quota from the local population. In October 1656, Jan Antoni Chrapowski noted in his diary that the Tatars returning from Prussia had 'too many of ours in captivity, especially Masurians and [caused] unheard losses in Podlasie'.[18] They did have their uses, though, especially as a 'terror weapon' affecting the morale of Swedish troops. In February 1656, Daniel Żytkiewicz, in his relation of the war and the state of current affairs, presented in front of the King and nobility in Lwów, wrote some interesting information about the role of 'small war' tactics against the Swedes. While he referred to Crimean Tatars here, it still gives us some idea on how such tactics were used by the Poles and how the Swedes were at a disadvantage when fighting against them:[19]

> [The Swedes] are very afraid of Tatars and their tactic which is [attacking] from the flanks, from the back, and [the Swedes] already seen from our men what weapon bow is and how quickly and how easy and from further range one can kill with it both man and horse, [so the Swedes] are very much afraid of such way of fighting, especially to be cut off in the field, and first them and their horses to be defeated by hunger than by [strength of] arms. Therefore they want to have them on their side, so there are already Swedish and our [envoys] despatched there [to Crimea], maybe even with money [for bribes].

Patrick Gordon, as a freshly enlisted soldier in the Swedish army entering Poland in summer 1655, noted an interesting observation about the Polish army and its tactics. Field Marshal Arvid Wittenberg, leading one of the Swedish field armies, was to advise his soldiers on 'how to behave themselves

---

17 Wagner, *Słownik biograficzny oficerów polskich drugiej połowy XVII wieku*, vol. I, p.8.
18 Chrapowicki, *Diariusz*, p.102.
19 *Pisma polityczne z czasów panowania Jana Kazimierza Wazy, 1648-1668. Publicystyka, eksorbitancje, projekty, memoriały. Volume I. 1648-1660* (Wrocław-Warszawa-Kraków-Gdańsk-Łódź: Wydawnictwo Polskiej Akademii Nauk, 1989), p.148.

upon all occasions, but especially when they should come to joyne battell or fight with the Polls; that they should not regard their shouting and noise, but keep closse together, because the Polls, being excellent horsemen, ar[e] very nimble upon all occasions, but ar[e] afrayed to deale with closse troups and partyes'.[20] It was directly connected with one of the most favourite tactics of the Polish and Lithuanian mounted-only formation, perfected through the many years of fighting against the Tatars. Groups of cavalry and dragoons were moving quickly, without baggage train, in a tactic known as *komunik*. Such fast marching groups were able to attack stronger Swedish forces, sapping their strength by constant hit-and-run attacks and avoiding pitched battles or, if they had the advantage in numbers, attempting the complete destruction of the Swedish group.

The tactics of Polish cavalry could be, at least initially, rather difficult to use by ex-Swedish soldiers in their new service. Holsten mentioned that, when Lubomirski's division besieging Cracow faced the Transylvanian and Swedish army, they had to leave their camp and 'scatter like Dutch'. He meant by that the partisan tactics of the sixteenth-century Dutch *Geuzen* (Beggars) fighting against Spain. The German reiter added that 'it was not something that me and my Swedish fellows were used to'.[21]

Even in the early stage of the war, during the retreat towards Cracow, Polish cavalry was attempting to harass the Swedes using hit-and-run tactics. According to Pufendorf, at the beginning of September 1655, 120 reiters from the rearguard of Wittenberg's division were ambushed near Opoczno by 10 banners of Polish cavalry. The majority of the Swedish soldiers were killed or captured, with the commanding officer – Colonel Georg Forgell – barely escaping with his life.[22] Patrick Gordon, who did fight in this engagement, provides a much more detailed description, though. According to him, a Swedish regiment of 250 reiters was sent out against a Polish cavalry of 300 men. The Poles pretended to charge, but, once they got up close with the Swedes, 'they let fly some shoot at us, as wee at them, and wheeling of to the right hand of us, they gott in betwixt us and the [Swedish] army'. The cut-off reiters were then charged by a strong force of 18 to 20 banners of Polish cavalry, who, after fierce but quick fight, broke the Swedish ranks. To makes matters worse, the initial Polish group of 300 men now attacked from the rear, helping to destroy the Swedish detachment. There were 132 reiters (including 12 officers) captured; the rest were killed. Only one corporal and eight troopers (Gordon amongst them) 'escaped by chance through the bushes undiscovered', although the Scottish diarist was severely wounded, 'shoot in my left syde under my ribbs'.[23] While in no way a major victory, even such small success helped to raise the morale of Polish troops and to show them that, in the correct circumstances, they could overcome Swedish cavalry. During 1656 and 1657, Stefan Czarniecki became the master of such tactics, although, knowing his history, it should not be such a big surprise.

---

20 *Diary of General Patrick Gordon*, vol. I, p.30.
21 Holsten, *Przygody wojenne 1655-1666*, p.45.
22 Pufendorf, *Siedem ksiąg o czynach Karola Gustawa króla Szwecji*, p.70.
23 *Diary of General Patrick Gordon*, vol. I, pp.51-52.

SMALL WAR

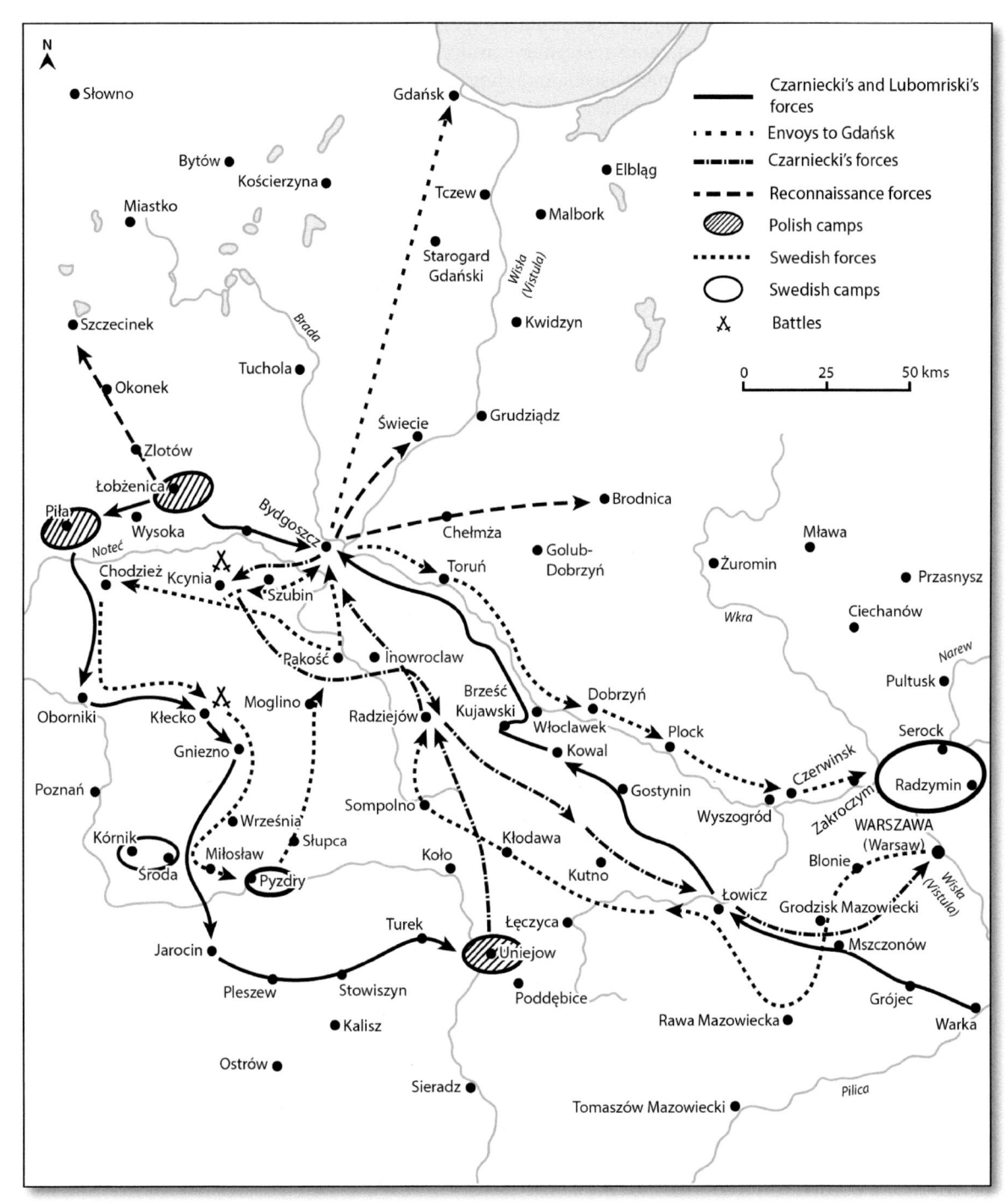

The campaign in Wielkopolska, April–June 1656. Source: Adam Kersten, *Stefan Czarniecki 1599-1665*.

After all, his first military experience from the 1620s comes from serving in a (in)famous mercenary cavalry called '*lisowczycy*', who were well known for being specialists in harassing and ambushing the enemy during the Times of Trouble in Muscovy, the early stages of the Thirty Years' War and the 1626–1629 war in Prussia. The majority of troops under Czarniecki's command were cossack cavalry and light horse, ideally suited to such tactics. They were often accompanied by dragoons, very useful in the role of fire support, especially when an action required capturing and holding certain strategic positions, like small towns, fords or hills. De Noyers also described the Poles fighting 'in Tatar style' during the first phase of the war. According to him, every time when the Swedes were trying to attack, the Polish cavalry feigned flight, 'although as it was all agreed, they knew where they need to flee, to suddenly turn around, attack the enemy with the sabres in their hands and to beat them badly'. By spring 1656, the spirit in the Polish army was much higher, though, so they 'did not thought about flight, instead [they] charged against the enemy straight away'.[24]

Polish 'small war' tactics were especially useful during the campaign in winter–spring 1656, when Charles X Gustav, with his field army, was chasing Czarniecki's forces. After the Swedes defeated Polish forces in the Battle of Gołąb (evening and night from 17 to 18 February 1656), the Polish commander was able to quickly gather his scattered army and revert to harassing tactics, with his cavalry attacking the Swedes day and night. Due to the lack of artillery and infantry, Charles X Gustav was not able to capture the well-defended fortress of Zamość, so he decided to march to Jarosław. In the meantime, further Polish forces led by Lubomirski and Lithuanians under Paweł Sapieha were also moving in the direction of this town. The Polish cavalry was using hit-and-run tactics, trying to attack the Swedish army marching towards Jarosław. Czarniecki managed to capture part of the Swedish tabor, surprising it during fording the river San. Amongst the loot, mostly captured by cavalry servants, was the Swedish King's silverware. This small victory, so important for Polish morale, was then widely advertised in Europe via broadsheets, based on Czarniecki's letters.[25]

At this point, Charles X Gustav realised that a further march into territory held by the Poles could potentially lead to disaster, so he ordered a retreat towards the Vistula river. More and more Polish regular units that were accompanying the Swedish army deserted, strengthening Czarniecki's forces. The Swedes had to march in battle-ready formation, non-stop harassed by the Poles. Kochowski mentioned that Czarniecki used a very unusual trick, ordering his troops to shout in different languages to convince the Swedes that the Poles were supported by many allies: 'Some [were shouting] like Tatars, *hała! hała!*[26] other like Cossacks, other like Wallachians, finally some in Polish'.[27] At one point, even the King's life was in danger, as a group of

---

24 *Portfolio królowej Maryi Ludwiki*, vol. I, pp.318–19.
25 Kersten, *Stefan Czarniecki*, pp.316–17.
26 In Polish, such a Tatar battle cry was known as *hałłakowanie* or *ałłakowanie*, with the word possibly coming from the word 'Allah' used as an encouragement in the fight.
27 Kochowski, *Historya panowania Jana Kazimierza*, vol. I, p.283.

Polish cavalry surprised him during his short stay in the village of Rudnica. He was only saved thanks to the quick reaction and sacrifice of his horse guard.

The slow tempo of the march, with the constant attacks of the Polish cavalry, costs the Swedes dearly. Any marauders left behind or lost during the journey were killed by Polish soldiers or by vengeful peasants. The Swedes had to move their artillery and tabor through difficult terrain, through swamps and forests, with barely any roads. Every time the Swedish army stopped and tried to engage their opponents in open fight, the attacking groups disappeared between trees, not eager to taste the Swedish firepower: 'Different groups, attacking from here and from there, tried to lure [the Swedish cavalry] away from cannons and infantry, tiring Swedish horses and men much more than when fighting them in the battle, with hunger spreading between Swedish soldiers and their mounts'.[28] At one point, Czarniecki even made an attempt to attack the Swedish temporary camp near Nisko, as many Swedish soldiers were away looking for food outside of the camp. On the evening of 28 March 1656, a few thousand Polish cavalry, both regular and levy of nobility, easily broke through the Swedish pickets and attacked the camp. Charles X Gustav managed to set up his infantry in time, though, resisting the Poles long enough to allow his cavalry regiments to return to the camp. The Finnish regiments of Gustav Kurck and Fabian Bernds arrived first; after them, Robert Douglas brought a few more reiter regiments. The Poles feigned a retreat, trying to lure the Swedes into a trap. As Czarniecki lacked infantry, he set up in the forest 2,000 peasants armed with muskets and *rusznica* calivers. They initially managed to stop the Swedish cavalry, although once the Swedes realised that they were facing armed irregulars, Douglas led a counterattack that massacred the peasants from the ambush force. Another ambush force, the Lithuanian cavalry under Połubiński, was late while trying to march through the difficult terrain and arrived after the fight was over. Still, it was a costly win for the Swedes. Even Pufendorf, usually lowering Swedish losses, mentioned, '200 reiters killed in first attack, many captured, also many of those sent for food and forage were missing'.[29] Finally, near Sandomierz, between the rivers San and Vistula, the Swedish army set up camp, trying to gather reinforcements that could be transported to them via river barges. Sandomierz was destroyed during a Polish assault of Lubomirski's forces, which will be described in a bit more detail in the next chapter. The Swedish field army was blocked by two Polish (Czarniecki and Lubomirski) and one Lithuanian (Sapieha) divisions, and the Commonwealth's commanders were hoping to completely cut off Charles X Gustav from the other Swedish forces. The relief force marching from Warsaw was completely destroyed by Czarniecki and Lubomirski in the battle at Warka on 7 April 1656, although, in a way, it was a 'lost chance' victory. The Polish commanders used overwhelming force to attack the small Swedish division, while, at the same time, Charles X Gustav managed to break through the Lithuanian forces and safely march towards Warsaw.

---

28 Kochowski, *Historya panowania Jana Kazimierza*, vol. I, pp.283–84.
29 Pufendorf, *Siedem ksiąg o czynach Karola Gustawa króla Szwecji*, p.140.

'Small war' operations could also have a huge impact on the morale of the Polish army, especially after previously lost battles. One of the most famous actions of a larger detachment of Polish cavalry happened soon after the Battle of Warsaw when, on night from 24 to 25 August 1656, Stefan Czarniecki's troops cornered a large Swedish convoy near Strzemeszno, a village near Rawa in Mazovia.[30] The Polish *Regimentarz* had with him up to 4,000 Polish soldiers, supported by 2,000 Tatars. Against them, under the command of Colonel Peter von Kiessel, were (depending on the source) between 3,000 and 6,000 Swedes.[31] The former number seems to be much closer to the truth, although probably only approximately 1,000–1,200 of those were soldiers while the rest were women and camp followers. The Swedes were marching from Cracow, as their units previously staying at the garrison were replaced by new regiments. The large convoy was full of loot and soldiers' belongings. No surprise, then, that it was a rather juicy target for the Poles and Tatars. The allies completely surrounded the village but did not want to attack under the cover of darkness. At dawn, the Swedes attempted to break through, possibly hoping that they were facing some levy of nobility, not the regular troops. Two Polish relations (Łoś and Kochowski) mentioned that many of the attacking Swedes were drunk. In the fierce fight, von Kiessel's men initially hard pressing the Poles, Łoś mentioned that three Polish regiments were pushed back and started to retreat, so Czarniecki had to use all available forces to break the Swedish resistance. Practically every battle relation, including one written by the *Regimentarz* himself, highlighted the bravery and defiance of the Swedish troops. The Polish cavalry managed to finally drag them down, while outflanking charges made by the Tatars finished the fight. The Swedish defenders were massacred, with some managing to break through and flee only to be chased by the vengeful Poles and local population. As Pasek commented on this final episode of the fight, those 'who managed to flee from the battlefield into woods or bogs, died there cruel death from the peasants' hands'. The whole tabor was captured and looted by the Tatars and Polish cavalry servants; amongst captives were many women, the wives of Swedish officers and soldiers. Czarniecki reported that the Poles and Tatars captured three lieutenant colonels, four majors, 13 *rittmeisters*,[32] 13 lieutenants, 13 quartermasters, 40 corporals and 300 reiters. There were 500 in killed Swedes counted on the battlefield. Polish losses seem to be fairly high, though, yet another evidence that the Swedish veterans dearly sold their skins. Jemiołowski mentioned that 'some [Poles] were killed, many were wounded'. Czarniecki admitted that '[we won] not without loss, as many ours were shot [killed and wounded] as [the Swedes] defended bravely, fighting here well'. Łoś wrote that Polish losses were severe: in his own banner, two companions were killed, and few others, including himself (he was shot in the side) were wounded. Clearly, news of this fight

---

30   The battle is known under few names: Rawa, Strzemeszno or Trzemeszno.
31   Łoś mentioned '1,200 chosen men'; Wierzbowski also wrote about 1,200 soldiers. Kochowski gave the higher figure of 1,200 reiters and 1,200 dragoons on foot, Jemiołowski gave 3,000 to 4,000 men, while Pasek gave the figure of 6,000.
32   Cavalry captains.

echoed to even distant Swedish garrisons, as Holsten – at the time serving in Cracow – wrote down that, despite their brave defence, the Swedish group was completely destroyed with 'no more than 20 men surviving'.[33] While this victory did not have any impact on the strategic situation, it clearly showed how Czarniecki's favourite tactics were dangerous for the Swedes, especially when he was operating with his cavalry in a well-known area and when he was able to dictate the conditions of the fight.[34]

It was these 'small war' tactics that were successfully employed by the Polish commanders, especially Czarniecki, when fighting against George II Rákóczi's Transylvanians in 1657 as well. When, in June and July of that year, his army was retreating through Poland towards Transylvania, the invaders were harassed by the Poles, who 'troubled them from behind, from the front and from the sides, causing large loss in men and tabor [wagons]'.[35] Łoś, who took part in this campaign in the ranks of Czarniecki's division, mentioned only that the Polish forces were keeping close contact with the retreating Transylvanians, blocking all fords en route. The harassing tactics seem to have worked since, by the end of the retreat, when arriving near Czarny Ostrów, the Transylvanians 'had very tired horses and they lost many of their man on the way'.[36] Skorobohaty, fighting as a part of the Lithuanian forces that joined the Poles in the chase after Rákóczi's army, wrote about following the retreating army while constantly fighting the rearguard, often with mixed success, as the diarist himself was seriously wounded during one of the encounters.[37] Kochowski, who also took part in the campaign in Czarniecki's division, pointed out that, despite being outnumbered, the Poles 'were full of eagerness' when attacking the rear or the flanks of the retreating Transylvanians. The Polish commander 'knew from his experience, that when one is overcome with fear, he will focus his sight only on the road of his retreat, not looking after those that chased him'. The diarist also added that any 'choke points' like river crossings, fords or roads running through forests and narrow ravines were used as ambush

Prince George II Rákóczi, portrait by unknown author (Biblioteka Narodowa, Warszawa).

---

33 Holsten, *Przygody wojenne 1655-1666*, p.37.
34 Łoś, *Pamiętnik towarzysza chorągwi pancernej*, pp.71–72; Pasek, *Pamiętniki*, p.69; Jemiołowski, *Pamiętnik dzieje Polski zawierający*, pp.215–16; Kochowski, *Lata Potopu 1655-1657*, pp.220–21; Wierzbowski, *Konnotata wypadków w domu i w kraju zaszłych od 1634 do 1689 r.*, p.103; Nowak, 'Nieznane materiały do wojny szwedzkiej 1656 z b. Archiwum Radziwiłłów w Warszawie', pp.717–18.
35 Jemiołowski, *Pamiętnik dzieje Polski zawierający*, p.246.
36 Łoś, *Pamiętnik towarzysza chorągwi pancernej*, p.77.
37 Skorobohaty, *Dziennik*, pp.66–69.

points, causing heavy losses amongst the retreating invaders. No surprised, then, that the 'Hungarians were moving with great haste; they burnt camp equipment that would slow them down, while cannons and food were sunk in lakes. They abandoned their sick, killed their captives and even left the tabor wagons with loot, taking with them only the most valuable items, that were carried under saddle or under their clothing'.[38]

When it came to fights between small groups of cavalry, there were many factors that could make a difference between victory and defeat. Better command, higher or lower morale, the element of surprise, better local knowledge or sometimes even weather conditions – any of these could affect the final outcome. A good example of such combat factors can be found in the Battle of Malecz, also known as the Battle of Małczyce or Prużany, which took place on 25 January 1660. On one side, there was the Muscovite force of Peter Khovansky, with 2,000 boyar cavalry and reiters, on the other side, the Lithuanian regiment of Colonel Michał Obuchowicz, a part of Hetman Sapieha's division. His force had a paper strength of up to 1,400 horses, but, considering how depleted the Lithuanian army was at the time, Obuchowicz probably had no more than 1,000 men of real strength. His regiment was composed of:

- eight banners of cossack cavalry: Michał Obuchowicz (former unit of his late father, Filip Kazimierz Obuchowicz, a paper strength 123 horses), Andrzej Franciszek Kotowicz under Lieutenant Wołodkowicz (strength unknown), Mikołaj Judycki or Jerzy Władysław Judycki (131 horses), Jan Sosnowski (130 horses), Stanisław Kazimierz Bobrownicki under Lieutenant Górski (strength unknown) and three unidentified
- three dragoon companies of Grand Hetman Sapieha, under Piotr Kasztell/Castelli, Adam Kraszport and Wehling, each 120 horses of paper strength[39]
- two dragoon companies of Jerzy Karol Hlebowicz, possibly under Captain Lieutenant Antoni Arens and Captain Jan Neysztad.

The cossack banner of Judycki and Kotowicz led the attack, defeating the Muscovite vanguard and capturing some prisoners and two standards. They were then supported by Obuchowicz's and Sosnowski's banners, while the remaining units were deployed in a second line, as reserve, soon to follow up the attack. Outnumbered and strongly pressed by the Muscovite reiters, four Lithuanians banners started to retreat towards the dragoons. On their way, they lost their commander: Obuchowicz's horse was killed, and the officer himself 'had few bad wounds, one in the face, three others in the head'. Surrounded by the Muscovite boyars, he surrendered to Siemion Kovdiey, dvorian from Khovansky's *sotnia*.[40] Obuchowicz was, at least according to Maskiewicz's relation, fighting bravely, killing seven and wounding a few

---

38   Kochowski, *Lata Potopu 1655-1657*, pp.296–97.
39   It is possible that there was a different, unidentified unit that was present instead of Wehling's company.
40   'Dyaryusz Michał Obuchowicza, Strażnika Wielkiego Księstwa Litewskiego, pisany przez czas więzienia w Moskwie', p.66.

more Muscovites by himself.[41] The rest of the Lithuanian force panicked and started to flee. In another relation, we can find information that Hlebowicz's dragoons were destroyed, only the captains managed to flee, while the three remaining dragoon units surrendered to the Muscovites.[42] The cossack banners were scatted, which led to the bitter comment from Maciej Vorbek-Lettow 'that is what we have from the regular troops, that when they are on [our own] land, they behave very badly but when they are to face the enemy, they do not even take out their sabres [to fight]'.[43] Sapieha's dragoon units can still be found in the Lithuanian army lists after the battle, so it is possible that only some part of the units surrendered. Obuchowicz mentioned that the Muscovites told him that 'all dragoons started to flee, even without one shot'. When mentioning the captured Lithuanians, he wrote only about 13 companions from cossack cavalry, including three from his own banner. However, like many nobles, he might not have been too worried about the losses amongst the dragoons, seeing them as 'lesser' troops. Despite the small scale of the fight, it had a huge negative impact on the Lithuanian nobility in Brześć Voivodeship, affecting their will to oppose further Muscovite attacks and operations.

Surprising the enemy in such fights was the crucial part in leading to success, especially when striking during the night or at the enemy in their quarters. Of course, the Poles and Lithuanians were not always victorious in such small-scale actions, and often the false state of security was their downfall. On 2 January 1657, Swedish Colonel Rutger von Ascheberg led the vanguard of Charles X Gustav's force against the Polish troops quartered in the villages around Chojnice in Gdańsk Pomerania. He had with him 18 companies of reiters, drawn from four regiments, with a total of 950 men.[44] Led by a local guide, he approached the villages of Pawłowa and Lichnowa, where the national cavalry regiment of Dymitr Jerzy Wiśniowiecki (nine banners, mostly cossack-style cavalry) was stationed in winter quarters. The Swedes laid down straw on the bridge over the river Brda so that their horses could cross it without much noise; they then charged against the completely surprised Poles. The number of defenders varies depending on the source: von Ascheberg claimed that there were 1,600 Poles; the better informed Łoś, whose banner took part in the fight, mentioned only 200 men.[45] Considering that the regiment had nine banners, the first figure most likely indicates its paper strength while the second could mean that the banners were badly weakened after the campaign of 1656, with many companions leaving the units to return to their homes for the winter. The Swedes set the villages on fire and, in the ensuing chaos, decimated the Polish units. Von Ascheberg mentioned that no more than 150 of the 1,600 men managed to flee, with the 'young prince from Zamość' (*Rotmistrz* Marcin Zamoyski) and other

---

41 *Pamiętniki Samuela i Bogusława Kazimierza Maskiewiczów*, p.283.
42 Vorbek-Lettow, *Skarbnica pamięci*, p.288.
43 Vorbek-Lettow, *Skarbnica pamięci*, p.288.
44 Ascheberg, *Dziennik oficera jazdy szwedzkiej 1621-1681*, p.71.
45 Ascheberg, *Dziennik oficera jazdy szwedzkiej 1621-1681*, p.72; Łoś, *Pamiętnik towarzysza chorągwi pancernej*, p.75.

important companions amongst the captured, alongside many horses, so valued as battle loot. Jemiołowski noted that, next to Marcin Zamoyski, another *rotmistrz*, Aleksander Woronicz, also leading a cossack cavalry banner, was captured alongside many companions and retainers.[46] Łoś wrote that the whole regiment was broken, 'companions killed, horses captured, all carts taken, so that only 50 men, running on foot and wearing just shirts, managed to flee'.[47] The Swedes then attacked the regiments of Jan Sobieski and Aleksander Koniecpolski, burning their quarters and killing many men. In the ensuing confusion, fighting during the night, the Poles were supposedly only able to recognise their enemies because of their distinct German haircut.[48] The Swedes finally retreated when faced with further Polish cavalry regiments brought by Czarniecki. Von Ascheberg, praising himself for what he claimed to be a grand victory, estimated Polish losses at 'more than 3,000 men struck dead, perished in fire and losing their lives', 2,600 lost horses and 31 flags captured by the Swedes.[49] While highly exaggerated, it still indicates that the surprised Poles were badly mauled and that their morale suffered greatly as well. It seems that Patrick Gordon's view on the fight is the most balanced, as he wrote that the Swedes 'falleth into the Polls quarters, fyreth some villages, ruineth D[uke] Dimitre Visniovitsky his and other regiments, and retires with some losse and in great confusion to Sluchow, the trowpes haveing lost [each] other and their guides in the woodes, and persued hotly by Polls'.[50] His comments highlighted important aspects of the 'small war', like knowledge of the terrain of the fight, including the presence of local guides, and troubles with keeping units in order when fighting during night time.

Speaking of Patrick Gordon, his diary provides us with a very interesting description of the small-scale fight near Gdańsk, where Swedish reiters from Douglas' command were facing the city's private army. The latter often clashed with Swedish troops, 'small war' taking part in the difficult terrain conditions of the so-called 'Danzig Werder', a lowland area next to the Vistula river that was cut with many ditches and often overflowed. The Scot mentioned a 'very notable incursion' that took place on 4 January 1657. The Swedes deployed a strong force of 2,000 reiters, although the majority of it was not able to take part in the action. Since the terrain was overflowed and frozen, only properly shoed horses could be used, with the majority of the Swedish mounts 'badd and unshooed'. Therefore, when facing Gdańsk's force, only the best mounted Swedish troops were sent out to fight. They were the King's lifeguard company, Douglas' life company (composed of Scots, including Gordon) and two more companies accompanied by some volunteers, in total around 250 men. Facing them were 500 to 600 city reiters (most likely mercenary) 'well mounted and well-armed men', with 'their horses being sharp shooed' and better prepared to the conditions of the fight. Gdańsk's

---

46 Jemiołowski, *Pamiętnik dzieje Polski zawierający*, p.228.
47 Łoś, *Pamiętnik towarzysza chorągwi pancernej*, p.75.
48 Jemiołowski, *Pamiętnik dzieje Polski zawierający*, p.228.
49 Ascheberg, *Dziennik oficera jazdy szwedzkiej 1621-1681*, p.74.
50 *Diary of General Patrick Gordon*, vol. I, p.133.

troops were divided into 10 to 12 companies, when charging, fighting in squadrons of two to three companies. Gordon wrote that the continuous charges of the city reiters were 'repulsed many tymes' although, during the one counterattack, the Scottish unit 'following too farr unadvisedely engaged our selves betwixt two reserves of the enemy'. The company was cut off from the rest of the Swedish troops and was hard pressed by Gdańsk's troopers. The Scots managed to break through, 'chargeing them desperately with our sword', although Gordon himself was wounded in the head during the fight. Another Swedish company, chasing the retreating enemy cavalry, was ambushed by a group of well-hidden musketeers. The 40 or 50 *snaphanes*[51] who gave fire towards the reiters killed six men and some horses. The fight ended without any side claiming victory, with both forces leaving for their own camp when evening approached. The Swedes lost 20 killed and more than 50 wounded; the soldiers from Gdańsk had 26 killed and more than 60 wounded.[52] This is a good example of a low-level skirmish, fought mostly by cavalry – typical for the Deluge. It is interesting due to the fighting in specific conditions and the presence of an infantry ambush, which was not often present during Polish–Swedish fights.

As we can see, 'small war' played a very important role in the fight against the Swedes and, to a smaller extent, against the Muscovites. From partisans to the regular force, many skirmishes and low-scale fights sapped the strength of the invading army, affecting logistic lines, cutting off reinforcements and destroying small reconnaissance forces and garrisons. It contributed in no small way to many Polish victories, though, with the role it played in raising Polish morale and decreasing the Swedish one. At the same time, especially in the first phase of the war, relying on 'small war' tactics was the only way to achieve any success against the invading Swedes, who, in 1655 and part of 1656, held the clear advantage over the Polish army.

---

51 From the word '*snaphance*' or '*snajphaunce*' used to describe a type of firearm lock often used in small-calibre hunter pieces. The term '*snapphane*' was used by the Swedes as a derogatory term to describe Danish partisans during both the 1657–1660 and Scanian War. As such, Gordon may have been using it as a description of the infantry attacking from ambush, like partisans.
52 *Diary of General Patrick Gordon*, vol. I, pp.134–35, 184–85.

8

Siege Operations

In 1655 and early 1656, during the defensive phase of the war against Sweden, the number of the siege operations in which the invaders had to block, besiege or assault fortresses held by the Poles was fairly small. Many towns surrendered without a fight, like Poznań, Warsaw, Bydgoszcz and Elbląg. Others offered just token resistance, like Toruń surrendering on 2 December 1655 after a few days full of exchanging artillery fire and peace negotiations. Rare were places where the Swedes had to invest time and manpower to capture them. Cracow was defended by Czarniecki's forces from 29 September to 17 October 1655. Malbork was under siege from late December 1655 and surrendered on 6 March 1656. In both cases, the garrison was allowed free passage from the city. Finally, there were some places that were either too far for the Swedes to reach (e.g., Lwów and Kamieniec Podolski) or where, despite some attempts, due to different reasons, the invaders did not succeed (e.g., Gdańsk, Puck, Zamość and the monastery at Jasna Góra). Smaller fortresses, often owned by wealthy magnates, were usually abandoned or quickly surrendered without a

The Swedish and Transylvanian armies at the siege of Brest in May 1657. Erik Dahlbergh's drawing for Samuel Pufendorf's *De rebus a Carolo Gustavo Sueciae rege gestis*, published in 1696 (Muzeum Narodowe, Kraków).

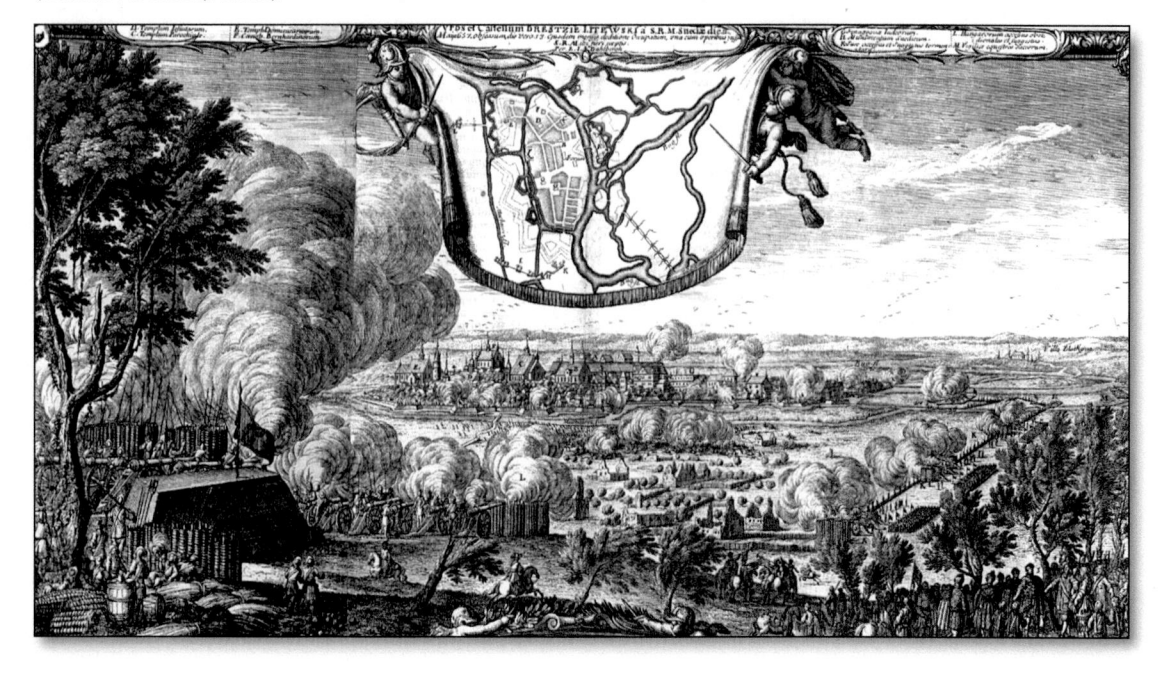

SIEGE OPERATIONS

fight, like Lanckorona and Wiśnicz in late September 1655. Conversely, some attempted the rather hopeless act of defiance in the face of the Swedes, which often ended up badly. The fate of small garrisons – Swedish and Polish alike – was often very tragic, as both sides were not particularly keen on honouring previously agreed upon surrenders. In autumn 1655, Frenchman Franchini Dziuli was defending Tęczyn/Tenczyn with 200 or 300 infantry and some armed townsfolk. While the Poles were initially successful in repelling the first attacks, when facing the outnumbering force, they decided to surrender. Despite agreeing on terms, enraged by taking heavy losses during the siege, the Swedes beheaded all the defenders.[1] Kochowski added that all civilians, 'both male and female, were robbed till last shirt'.[2] Holsten, who served in the reiter regiment of Kurt Christoph von *Königsmarck that captured the castle, explained that the garrison was cut down after the surrender, as von Königsmarck* was angry at the losses his men took during the assault.[3]

Another interesting case relates to Brest. In 1655, the Muscovites approached it, but the Lithuanian garrison refused to surrender, so they did not even attempt a long siege operation. On 12 May 1657, the fortress was besieged by the Swedish and Transylvanian armies. Dahlbergh, who received an order to view the fortification and check how viable a siege operation would be, noted that Brest was built at a suitable place, well fortified and well defended.[4] Facing the overwhelming siege force, the defenders quickly lost heart and surrendered four days later. In 1658, it was recaptured by the Lithuanians. In 1660, Brest was again approached by the Muscovites led by Ivan Khovansky, but, seeing the well-defended fortress (the garrison had 2,000 armed men), they did not attempt a siege and feigned a retreat. The garrison celebrated the success by having a huge drinking party, during which the Muscovites returned and completely surprised the defenders. Khovansky's soldiers easily broke through the gate, capturing Brest and killing both soldiers and civilians

The Swedish and Transylvanian siege of Brest. The defenders surrendered on 16 May 1657. The map includes siege lines and outlines of the planned new fortifications during the Swedish occupation, as drawn by Erik Dahlberg (Krigsarkivet, Stockholm).

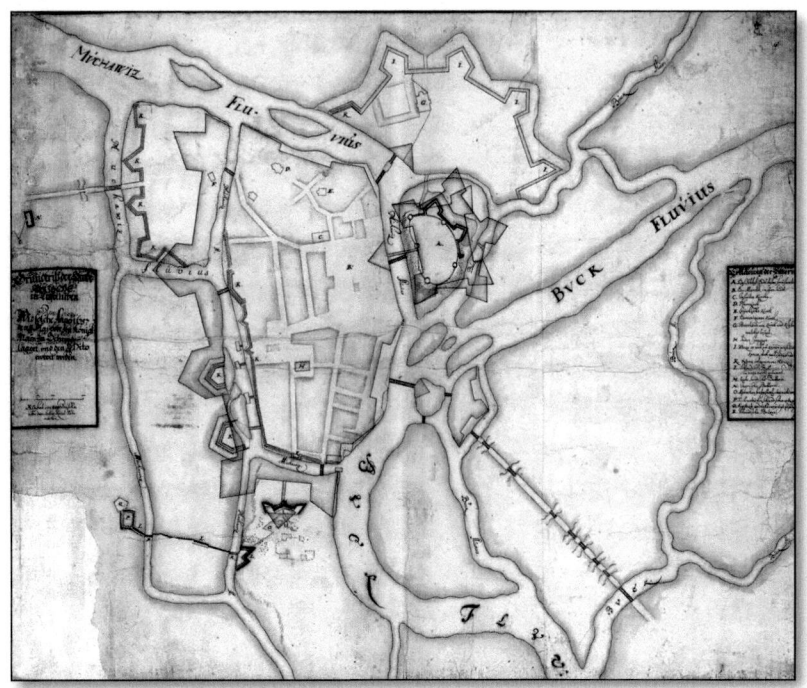

---

1   Wagner, *Słownik biograficzny oficerów polskich drugiej połowy XVII wieku*, vol. I, p.81; Wimmer, *Polska-Szwecja. Konflikty zbrojne w XVI-XVII wieku*, p.113.
2   Kochowski, *Historya panowania Jana Kazimierza*, vol. I, p.241.
3   Holsten, *Przygody wojenne 1655-1666*, p.33.
4   *Erik Dahlberghs dagbok*, pp.95–96.

alike. The drunkenness of the garrison is mentioned in the diaries of Vorbek-Lettow and Chrapowicki,[5] with the latter adding that the Muscovites' success caused much terror and panic amongst local nobles.[6] According to Vorbek-Lettow, 'one thousand and nine hundreds of ours were killed, no mercy was shown even to women and small children'.[7] Bogusław Kazimierz Maskiewicz added that, after the initial retreat of the Muscovite army, the Lithuanian commanders allowed their soldiers wine from Hetman Sapieha's cellar and that no guards were posted on the wall. Seeing the state of the defenders, one of the Muscovite prisoners kept in Brest managed to sneak out and inform Khovansky about the whole situation. When the Lithuanians noticed the Muscovite soldiers climbing on ladders on the wall, it was too late, and, after a short fight, Brest was captured. Also in this diary, we can find information that the 'Muscovites did not gave pardon to anyone, [even] the younglings, so whole castle was running with blood'. Even the attackers were surprised 'that this fortressed so unexpectedly was captured in such odd way'.[8]

Sometimes, fortresses or outposts could be captured by unusual ruses. Very imaginative in capturing the castle of Lanckorona was Jan Zarzecki, leading a group of the local partisans. Pretending to be a noble loyal to the Swedish crown, he offered a fast horse for the commandant of the garrison, Arnold Strumbil. The Swedish officer left the castle to test his new mount, was guided by the Poles away from the watchful eyes of the garrison and was captured. Without their commander, the Swedes were easily convinced to surrender and left the castle.[9] Without a doubt, this story gave Henryk Sienkiewicz the idea for the scene of Andrzej Kmicic attempting to capture Prince Bogusław Radziwiłł in *The Deluge* novel.

When it comes to capturing or recapturing fortresses and defended cities, which started already in mid-1656, we can find the usual list of problems so common for the seventeenth-century

Map of Elbląg from 1657. Published in Amsterdam by Johannes Janssonius (Biblioteka Narodowa).

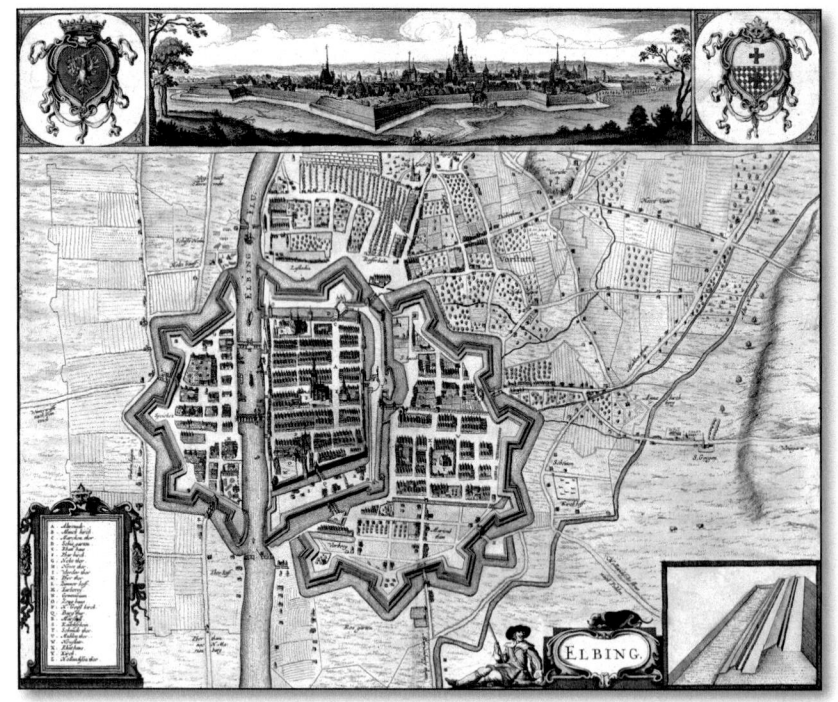

---

5   Vorbek-Lettow, *Skarbnica pamięci*, p.288.
6   Chrapowicki, *Diariusz*, p.219.
7   Vorbek-Lettow, *Skarbnica pamięci*, p.288.
8   *Pamiętniki Samuela i Bogusława Kazimierza Maskiewiczów*, pp.273–74.
9   Kochowski, *Historya panowania Jana Kazimierza*, vol. I, p.276.

Commonwealth's warfare. The constant lack of proper siege artillery and engineers was one of the biggest weaknesses of the Polish and Lithuanian armies. It led to siege operations dragging on for far too long, often tying a large force that thus could not be used elsewhere to take part in the siege. During the uprising in Wielkopolska, local forces made from levy, partisans and district troops had to usually rely on a blockade to force the stronger Swedish garrison to surrender. On many occasions, a lack of the proper tools of war was the major factor leading the Commonwealth's commanders to keep throwing their troops at fortresses' walls in bloody, often unsuccessful assaults. We can almost see a certain pattern in which officers that were more than competent during field operations, pitched battles and 'small war' showed a complete lack of understanding of the proper tactics and patience during siege operations.

On some occasions, despite continuous attacks, they did nothing to break the spirit of the defenders, although they did lead to heavy losses amongst the assault forces. A good example here would be the bloody attacks of Lithuanian and Polish troops on Mohylew in April 1655, where the attackers paid a heavy price in killed and wounded without being able to capture the town. Other assaults, even if they did not succeed, could help in breaking the morale of the defenders and lead to the surrender of the besieged city or fortress. On 29 June 1656, while a heavy assault of Polish troops, armed peasants and camp followers did not succeed in capturing Warsaw, it forced Field Marshall Wittenberg to start negotiations with the Poles regarding the surrender of the capitol.

Even successful assaults could sometimes lead to heavy losses amongst the attackers. In late March 1656, when the Swedish field army was trapped by Polish and Lithuanian forces between the rivers Vistula and San, Charles X Gustav initially ordered for a bridge over the Vistula to be built while the nearby Swedish-held castle in the city of Sandomierz was to stop the Polish army. Facing the overwhelming Czarniecki's and Lubomirski's forces, though, he quickly realised that Sandomierz would not hold for long and ordered the evacuation of the supplies and garrisons. The city was captured by Polish forces on 1 April 1656, and the bridge was destroyed, while the Swedes still held the castle, under the command of Colonel David Sinclair.[10] The first attack of the Polish regular army against it was repulsed, with the loss of Captain Collet, the former commandant of Nowy Sącz, who 'was now shott on the bridge' when leading the Polish soldiers.[11] Charles X Gustav decided to switch to building a bridge over the river San, ordering Sinclair to abandon the castle. As Sandomierz was a Swedish logistic hub in the region, the castle was full of 'many things robbed from the area, especially from churches, nobles' palaces and many towns; also there was lots of food and provisions gathered from nobles' houses and villages'.[12] A large number of irregulars, especially peasant partisans, gathered near Sandomierz, eager to support the regular army in the assault on the castle. The Polish commanders

---

10 Kochowski, *Historya panowania Jana Kazimierza*, vol. I, p.284.
11 *Diary of General Patrick Gordon*, vol. I, p.96.
12 *Diary of General Patrick Gordon*, vol. I, pp.284–85.

allowed them to take part in the attack, in which thousands of soldiers and armed locals stormed the castle. However, they did not know that the Swedes prepared a hellfire trap for them. As Sinclair was not able to evacuate all the ammunition, an artillery lieutenant named Gabriel Anastasius gathered '300 cwt of powder, 50 large and 4,000 small grenades' and set up a fire. He was not able to flee, though, as the last group leaving the castle (30 soldiers) was killed by the Poles, with only Anastasius taken alive.[13] When the masses of attacking Poles entered the castle, hoping for great loot, they only found death and destruction when the gathered explosives were blown up. Between 500[14] and 2,000[15] Poles were killed, with Gordon describing them as 'of the meaner sort, as being vouluntiers'. Holsten, present there as part of the Swedish troops, commented that 'it was great pleasure for us to see it [the explosion] while it caused Czarniecki to be very angry'.[16] The castle was completely destroyed, with many supplies and documents from the archive of Sandomierz Voivodeship perishing in the explosion and subsequent fire.

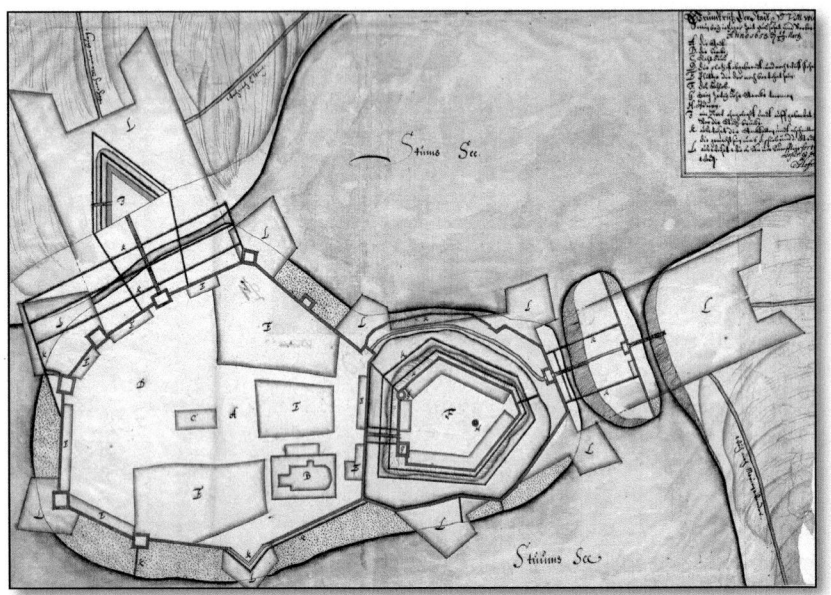

An assault could end up with heavy losses for the defenders and town population if they decided to fight to the last man and did not surrender. Many such bloodbaths took place during the fights with the Zaporozhian Cossacks, when often no quarter was given. When, on 9 November 1648, the Lithuanian force under Hrehory Mirski attacked Pinsk, defended by Cossacks and the local population, the attack started with a cannonade from eight, probably small calibre, cannons, and, after failed negotiations, they decided to assault the city. One gate was attacked by 120 dragoons from Maciej Gosiewski's company and 200 haiduks from Piotr Podlecki's banner, probably supported by some dismounted cavalry. The other was attacked by two mounted units, likely a district of the levy of nobility cossack cavalry banners under Łukasz Jelski. Despite the fact that both gates were well defended and blocked with anti-cavalry obstacles made from fallen trees,

The fortifications of Swedish-held Sztum (Stuhm) in May 1658, with plans of further works suggested to strengthen the defence (Krigsarkivet, Stockholm).

13　Pufendorf, *Siedem ksiąg o czynach Karola Gustawa króla Szwecji*, p.142.
14　Kochowski, *Historya panowania Jana Kazimierza*, vol. I, p.285; *Diary of General Patrick Gordon*, vol. I, p.96. Another diarist mentioned a 'few hundred killed', Jemiołowski, *Pamiętnik dzieje Polski zawierający*, p.187, the same with Holsten, *Przygody wojenne 1655-1666*, p.40.
15　Pufendorf, *Siedem ksiąg o czynach Karola Gustawa króla Szwecji*, p.142.
16　Holsten, *Przygody wojenne 1655-1666*, p.40.

SIEGE OPERATIONS

known as *kobylice*, the attacking Lithuanians managed to break through both of them. The city was set on fire, and three further banners of cavalry – the cossack cavalry of Aleksander Gosiewski, the cossack cavalry of Adam Łukiański Pawłowicz and the reiters of Teofil Szwarcoff – entered the streets, where the 'stubborness of Cossacks and treachery of folks of Pińsk was cut down, [both] rebels and Cossacks punished with fire and sword'. The assault turned into bitter house-to-house combat, in which the defenders were refusing to surrender and the Lithuanians had to capture building after building. Unsurprisingly, the fight was drawn out, as it continued throughout the whole night and most of the whole next day. Many defenders drowned when they were forced into the river Pina; others were cut down when their retreat was blocked by the hussar banner of Aleksander Hilary Połubiński. Only some mounted Cossacks, led by their commander, Maksym Hładki, managed to flee. The town was burned and pillaged by the Lithuanian army servants; it is estimated that between 3,000 and 5,000 of the townsfolk were killed during the fight.[17]

Very interesting and fairly well detailed in description is the successful assault of the Lithuanian troops on Tykocin, which took place on 27 January 1657.[18] It was an important fortress, owned by Radziwiłł's family. It was here that, during a previous, unsuccessful siege, Janusz Radziwiłł died on 31 December 1655. Despite a few previous Lithuanian attempts at a siege and blockade, the fortress held on, on one occasion saved by the relief force under the command of Prince Bogusław Radziwiłł. In autumn 1656, a new blockade was started, this time by a mixed force of Lithuanian regular troops from Sapieha's division and levy of nobility. By that time, Tykocin was held by a mixed Swedish–Polish force. In charge of the garrison was Swedish Colonel Dietrich von Rosen, who had under his command a few companies of Finnish reiters, a large part of the foreign infantry regiment of Prince Bogusław Radziwiłł (under Jan Berk) and two or three banners of Polish–Hungarian infantry, in total between 500[19] and 900 men, well supplied and prepared for a long siege. Tykocin itself was placed in a well-secured location, surrounded by the Narew river, making it difficult to besiege. Next to the castle, on a small river island, there

Castle Tenczyn, captured by the Swedes in 1655, later destroyed by them during an evacuation in summer 1656 (Riksarkivet).

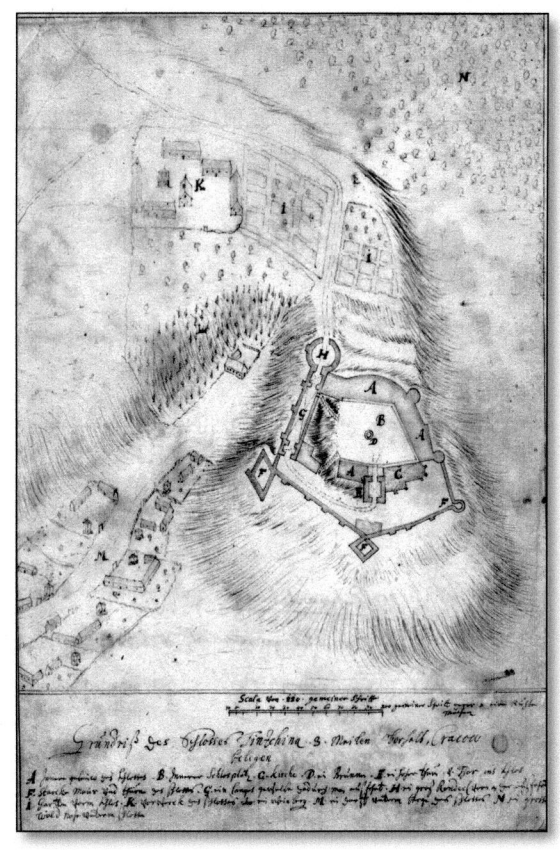

17 'Zabytek historyczny o Pińsku', pp.94–97; Witold Biernacki, *Łojów 1649* (Zabrze-Tarnowskie Góry: Wydawnictwo Inforteditions, 2014), pp.80–84; Majewski, *Marszałek wielki litewski Aleksander Hilary Połubiński (1626-1679)*, pp.39–40.
18 Main source of the event: Laskowski (ed.), 'Relacja obrotów wojennych pod Tykocinem roku 1656', pp.255–57.
19 A rather low estimate, provided by Pufendorf.

AGAINST THE DELUGE

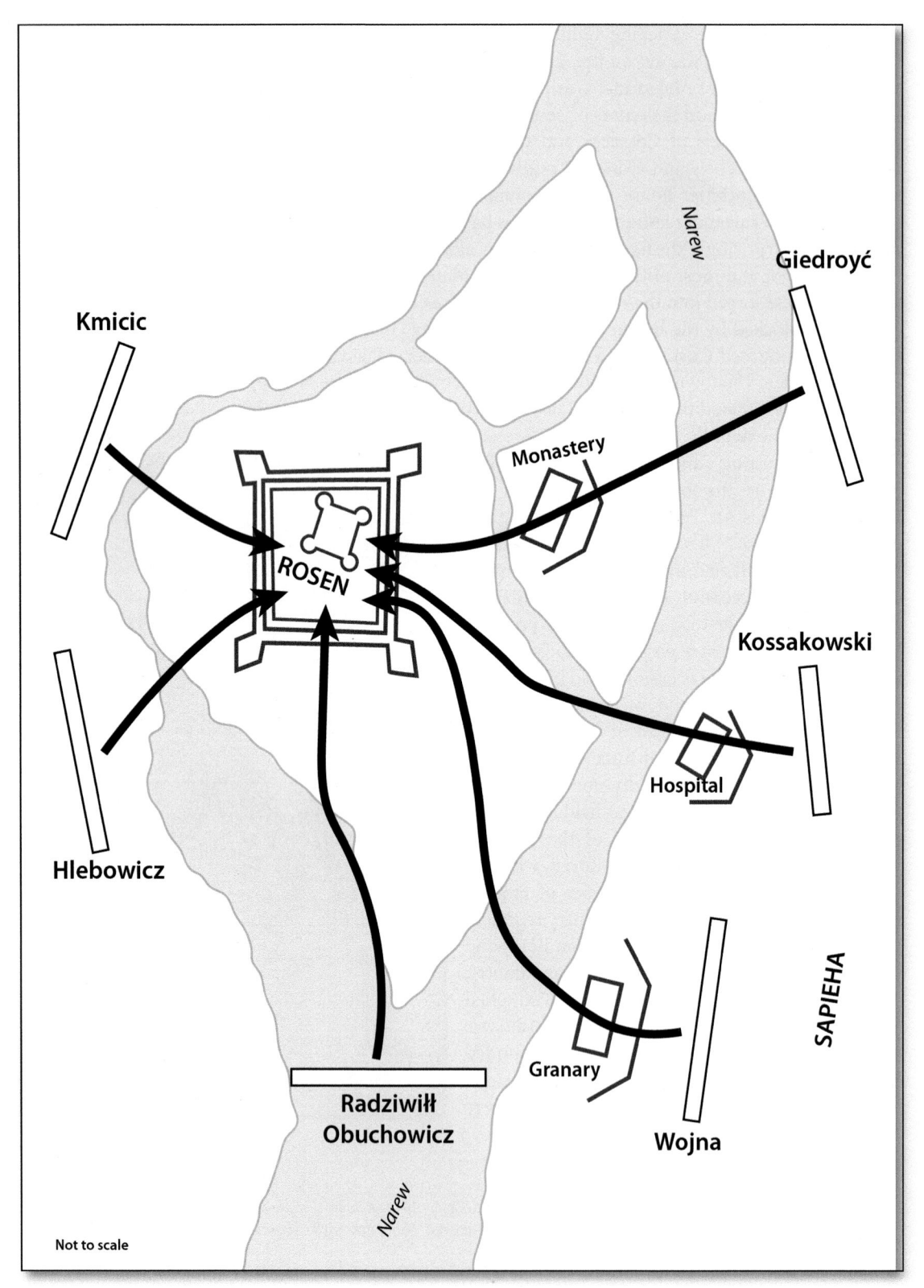

The assault on Tykocin, 27 January 1657. Source: Jacek Płosiński, *Potop szwedzki na Podlasiu*.

was a fortified monastery. On the other side of the river, as the first line of the defence, there was a fortified *alumnat* (military hospital) and the city's granary, both surrounded by palisades and earthworks.

Throughout January, the whole division of Grand Hetman Sapieha gradually arrived to Tykocin, reinforcing the blockade force. The Lithuanians did not have enough infantry, artillery and engineers for the prolonged siege, and the defenders refused to negotiate a surrender. On 26 January, Hetman Sapieha decided that, the next day, his force would simultaneously assault all defended points. Due to heavy frost, the river Narew was frozen, allowing an easy crossing during the attack. The Hetman asked for volunteers for the attack, and it seems that a large part of his cavalry, hoping for loot in Tykocin, joined in. Aleksander Michał Woyna Jasieniecki was leading the first line of attack on the granary, leading a force from three regiments of national cavalry: the Hetman's, Połubiński's and Zygmunt Adam Słuszko's. The soldiers from hussar and cossack cavalry were fighting dismounted, with Hetman Sapieha himself riding his horse next to the attacking soldiers and encouraging them to attack. On the left flank (west force), attacking directly against Tykocin, were dismounted volunteers from two other national cavalry regiments: Michał Kazmierz Radziwiłł's and Michał Leon Obuchowicz's. The attack on the *alumnat* was led by Colonel Albert Kossakowski, who had under his command infantry (probably Polish–Hungarian) and armed servants.[20] The force assaulting the monastery was led by Lieutenant Colonel Mikołaj Dominik Giedroyć, in charge of the dragoons and some levy of nobility and volunteers. Two further national cavalry regiments – probably under Samuel Kmicic and Jerzy Karol Hlebowicz – were set up as a blockade force on the north of Tykocin.

The attack started early in the morning (probably around 0600 hours), with all Lithuanian assault forces striking simultaneously. The hospital and monastery were captured first, and, after bloody hand-to-hand combat, all the defenders were killed. The Lithuanians then focused on breaching the gate into Tykocin, with further attacks from the west and north. Anyone attempting to defend against them was put to sword, with masses of attackers capturing field works and finally breaking through the gate. The

The fortifications of Swedish-held Grudziądz (Graudenz) in December 1657. The town was recaptured by Polish forces under Lubomirski in August 1659 (Krigsarkivet, Stockholm).

---

20   Jacek Płosiński, *Potop szwedzki na Podlasiu* (Zabrze: Wydawnictwo Inforteditions, 2006), p.131.

Lithuanian soldiers and their servants continued with the slaughter, killing both the defenders and any civilians inside the castle. Many ceased fighting and focused on looting instead; some even entered the room with Janusz Radziwiłł's coffin and stole any valuables found there. The scattered defenders were making desperate last stands in a few places. The Lithuanians paid dearly for the assault, especially when Dietrich von Rosen decided to take as many attackers as possible with him. According to Puffendorf, 'he set fire to powder store, blowing up himself, his remaining soldiers, many enemies and part of the castle'.[21] The explosion buried Janusz Radziwiłł's coffin in the rubble. Two further explosions, possibly from mines set up previously by the Swedes, totally wrecked the castle, although they did not cause any further losses to the Lithuanians, who withdrew after the first one.

The garrison was massacred during the fight, and amongst those killed were von Rosen and his brother serving as a captain in the Finnish reiters. The servants of Janusz Radziwiłł – Egierd, Dmuchowski, Mikołaj and Aleksander Łubieniecky – were killed as well, the latter two cut by the Lithuanians after they had already surrendered. *Rotmistrz* Poradowski, of Radziwiłł's Hungarian infantry, was, on the order of Hetman Sapieha, beheaded as a traitor, and his head was stuck on a pike. There were 130 infantrymen from Berk's taken alive, most likely forced to join the Lithuanian army. From civilians, only 30 survived the fight. It was a very costly victory, though. The anonymous author of the relation describing the assault mentioned that especially high were the losses amongst the officers, dragoons and infantry.[22] Allegedly, none of the captains were left unscathed. Lieutenant Colonel Giedroyć was twice shot in leg, Woyna was shot and wounded in the face, Captain Ostel was killed and Hetman Sapieha's Captain Lieutenant (from the dragoon unit) was wounded – with a few other officers wounded by shot, pikes and *rohatyna* spears. The losses of the Lithuanian force had to be severe, as even Chrapowicki in his diary mentioned, likely basing it on despatches directly from Sapieha's forces, that 'Tykocin was taken by storm ad dawn [27 January 1657] and quite a lot of ours were killed'.[23]

Valentin (Walenty) von Winter (1608-1671), a veteran Dutch soldier that was hired by Gdańsk to command city's mercenary army during The Deluge. Portrait by Johann Bensheimer, 1672 (Biblioteka Narodowa, Warszawa).

When fighting against the Swedes, assaults could also end up as massacres when the resistance was strong and the attackers had to pay a high price for capturing the fortress. De Noyers mentioned that, while Grudziądz was captured in 1659 by an assault, the attacking Poles took heavy losses, so in retaliation 'they started to kill

---

21 Pufendorf, *Siedem ksiąg o czynach Karola Gustawa króla Szwecji*, p.247.
22 Laskowski (ed.), 'Relacja obrotów wojennych pod Tykocinem roku 1656', p.257.
23 Chrapowicki, *Diariusz*, p.112.

[both] Swedes and the townsfolk alike'. No surprise that the surviving part of the garrison, holding the castle, decided to surrender to the Imperial force rather than to the vengeful Poles.[24]

It is interesting to notice that one of the most successful and cost-effective siege operations during the war was, in major part, possible thanks to the effort of the private army. The mercenary army employed by the city of Gdańsk during the Deluge had between 2,000 and 3,000 men, supported by a few thousand of the city's militia.[25] The defence of the city was under the command of Colonel Valentin (Walenty) von Winter (1608–1671). He was an experienced officer, previously serving in the Brandenburg and Swedish armies. From 1655 until his death in 1671, he was the commander of Gdańsk's forces. For his successes against the Swedes, he received *indygenat* during the Polish *Sejm* in 1658. The troops from Gdańsk fought against the Swedish forces in Prussia, often clashing during skirmish fights between a few companies of cavalry and supporting musketeers. There was one important siege operation, though, that is worth mentioning here. In autumn 1659, during the Polish and Imperial offensive in Prussia, there were different opinions on which place to attack next. The Poles were eager to besiege the crucial fortress of Malbork, while the Brandenburg commanders preferred Elbląg.[26] Winter offered the support of the city's troops in the retaking of the strategic fortress of Gdańska Głowa. It did not come as a surprise, as it was obvious that the city's council was eager to retake the possession of Głowa, captured by the Swedes in the early stage of the war. Considering that Winter had at his command a strong contingent of infantry, well supported by artillery, his help was more than welcome, and it was decided that the allied force would attack Głowa. On 25 September 1659, his first troops arrived and started a blockade of the fortress. The Swedish garrison was under the command of Claes Danckwardt-Lillieströmm with between 1,000 to 1,500 soldiers (including 200 to 300 reiters) and up to 50 cannons and mortars. During the last days of September, more troops from Gdańsk joined the blockading force, supported by Polish army regulars: the Foot Guard infantry regiment under Butler and the national cavalry regiment under Niemirycz. On 2 October, Winter himself arrived and took command of all Gdańsk's forces, becoming de facto overall commander of the siege operation. There

A musketeer from the mercenary units in the employ of the city of Gdańsk in 1659. From the Petera Voget's *Wahrhafftiger und gründlicher Bericht von Belager- und Eroberung der Haupt-Schantze in der Dantziger Nährung...*, published in 1661 (PAN Biblioteka Gdańska).

---

24 *Portfolio królowej Maryi Ludwiki*, vol. II, p.15.
25 Peter Voget, *Wahrhafftiger und gründlicher Bericht von Belager- und Eroberung der Haupt-Schantze in der Dantziger Nährung zwischen der Theilung des Weissel-Strohmes von den Schweden Anno M DC LVI. auffgeführet und befestiget von den Dantzigern aber Anno M DC LIX* (Danzig: Dawid Fryderyk Rhete, 1661), p.11.
26 Pufendorf, *Siedem ksiąg o czynach Karola Gustawa króla Szwecji*, pp.588.

were also two further allied units present: the Imperial cuirassier regiment Ratschin and the Brandenburg reiter regiment of Colonel Johan von Hill.

Thanks to Peter Voget's work, published in Gdańsk in 1661, we have detailed information about the organisation and strength of the city units engaged in the siege:[27]

- Horse life regiment of Colonel Winter: three companies of reiters and three companies of dragoons.
- Infantry life regiment of Colonel Winter – 656 men: two companies under Winter, one company under Captain Dirsch (Hirsch) and one company under Captain van der Linde. Both life regiments appear to have been composed of mercenary troops.
- Infantry regiment of Major Bobart – 608 men: one company under Bobart, one company under Captain Brendten, two companies under Captain Becheld and one company under Captain Straykowski. It was a militia regiment from Wisłoujście, outside of the Gdańsk proper.
- Infantry regiment of Major Alexander Thompson – 500 men: two companies under Thompson and two companies under Captain Branden. It was a militia regiment from New Gardens (Nowe Ogrody), the suburbia of Gdańsk.
- Infantry regiment of Major Siebers – 501 men: two companies under Siebiers and two companies under Captain Stelzner. It was a militia regiment from the district of Bishop's Hill (Biskupia Górka).
- Infantry squadron of Major Schur (just his company) – 105 men. The unit was from Puck, possibly a mercenary one from the garrison.
- Infantry regiment of Major Fryderyk Gerschau – 499 men: two companies under Gerschau and two companies under Captain John Montgomery. The militia regiment was from Ostrów Island.

Very strong, at least when compared to what was usually fielded by the Polish army, was the artillery contingent. Winter had more than 30 cannons and a few mortars. They were spread between a few batteries, protected by different regiments, attacking Głowa from opposite directions:[28]

- With the main army under Winter in the camp at the Vistula Spit (Mierzeja Wiślana) were large batteries containing six half kartouwen, six quarter kartouwen, three 4-pdrs and three 6-pdrs.
- With Major Siebiers' regiment were six cannons.
- With Major Thompson were five cannons.
- With Major Schur were two cannons.

The army also had in mortars one 220-pdr, a few 70-pdrs, one 60-pdr and a few 30-pdrs.

Captain Jerzy Straykowski was the chief engineer who supervised all siege works. Under his command were a few more engineers employed by the city and peasants from the local area, supporting the troops in preparing

---

27 Voget, *Wahrhafftiger und gründlicher Bericht*, p.234.
28 Voget, *Wahrhafftiger und gründlicher Bericht*, pp.68–69, 86.

trenches and other siege works. Winter's plan was based on meticulous siege work, by isolating the individual Swedish siege works and reducing them by artillery fire. He did not make plans for general assaults, instead a strict blockade and constant barrage was to force the Swedes to surrender. There were, of course, clashes with the Swedish forays, especially in the early stage of the siege when the defenders still had the strength and a high enough morale for such counterattacks. There were also some attacks on the isolated outer bastions. Gradually, despite the harsh conditions (heavy rain, snow and storms), Gdańsk's forces managed to force the Swedes out from the outer fortifications, patiently closing in on the main line of the defence. Pufendorf mentioned the difficult situation of the defenders during the later stages of the fight, as the Swedes took especially heavy losses amongst their officers and 'there was barely enough men left to defend three bastions'. In the difficult weather, which in fact helped the besiegers, the frozen river allowed the attackers to close in upon the defensive positions. It seems that some on the Royal Court were not happy with the length of the siege. In mid-November 1659, de Noyers noted that the siege of Głowa was proceeding slowly 'due to strength of the fortress, numerous garrison and finally due to our own incompetence'.[29] Gdańsk's soldiers were able to frequently use hand grenades against the Swedish positions, adding to the daily barrage of artillery and musket fire. After taking heavy losses, without any chance for relief, Danckwardt-Lillieströmm decided to negotiate his surrender. The truce was signed on 22 December 1659, and the Swedes were allowed to leave the city with their 'arms, standards and drums'. According to Pufendorf, after the surrender, the remaining force of the garrison contained '300 infantry, 50 sick, 100 cavalry – most of them officers', and they were allowed free passage to Pomerania. The Swedes took with them all the standards, 16 cannons and two mortars,[30] so they were granted very good conditions in the surrender. De Noyers added that Danckwardt-Lillieströmm insisted that he be allowed to take with him all the cannons with the Swedish coat of arms, which explains why he could take with him so many pieces.[31]

During the 60 days of the siege, Gdańsk's artillery shot on average 85 shots per day. In fact, Voget provides a very detailed list of all the cannonballs fired upon Gdańska Głowa:[32]

A pikeman from the mercenary units in the employ of the city of Gdańsk in 1659. From the Petera Voget's *Wahrhafftiger und gründlicher Bericht von Belager- und Eroberung der Haupt-Schantze in der Dantziger Nährung...*, published in 1661 (PAN Biblioteka Gdańska).

---

29 *Portfolio królowej Maryi Ludwiki*, vol. II, p.237.
30 Pufendorf, *Siedem ksiąg o czynach Karola Gustawa króla Szwecji*, pp.588–89.
31 *Portfolio królowej Maryi Ludwiki*, vol. II, p.244.
32 Pufendorf, *Siedem ksiąg o czynach Karola Gustawa króla Szwecji*, p.235.

Type of cannon/mortal	Number of cannonballs/grenades
Half kartouwen	1199
Quarter kartouwen	1919
9-pdr	300
6-pdr	225
3-pdr	116
220-pdr mortar	104 stones
220-pdr mortar	16 grenades
70-pdr mortar	211
30-pdr mortar	306
70-pdr mortar	30 fire balls
Fire grenades	60
Hand-mortars	400
Hand grenades	212

As there were no costly assaults on the Swedish positions, all losses were composed of men killed and wounded during the fire exchanges and skirmishes against the garrison's forays. In total, Winter's forces lost 97 killed, including six NCOs (no officers), and 150 wounded; the losses of the other allies are unknown but had to be fairly small. As such, it was a very successful siege operation, which allowed the troops from Gdańsk to recapture a vital strategic point. In the fortress, the besiegers captured 32 cannons and large quantities of match, powder and cannonballs, 'enough to defend for another six months'. There were also good supplies of provisions, with plenty of grain, oats and vegetables and 260 large carts of hay. The Swedish commander explained his decision by being unsure of his own men, as 'they were mix of all nations, amongst them Danes who just shot sand from their muskets'; he was also afraid of a possible general assault.[33] Prince Bogusław Radziwiłł, at the time the Brandenburg Governor of Ducal Prussia, wrote that Głowa was so important that, without it, the remaining Swedish fortresses in Prussia – Malbork and Elbląg – were without any chance for a successful defence and soon would be subdued as well.[34] Although he was far from through, his view was shared by many other commanders in this theatre of the war. Głowa was manned by a strong garrison of 1,500 soldiers from Gdańsk, allowing the allies to control the logistic line from Gdańsk to the inner parts of Poland, supporting them in further siege actions of the Swedish-held towns.

---

33 *Portfolio królowej Maryi Ludwiki*, vol. II, pp.244–45.
34 Biblioteka Narodowa, Rps III 3092, pp.7v–8, *Kopiariusz korespondencji Bogusława Radziwiłła oraz innych materiałów historycznych i publicystyczno-literackich z lat 1657–1672*.

SIEGE OPERATIONS

Probably the most important and extensive siege operation during the whole war was the joint Polish–Imperial siege of Toruń.[35] As it is very well researched in Poland, with many available primary sources and some particularly interesting additional Imperial and Swedish ones, I would like to write a more detailed description of it since, so far, this episode of the war does not have proper coverage in English. Toruń was a crucial Swedish fortress in Prussia, manned by a strong and well-supplied garrison under Governor Bengt Oxenstierna and commander of the garrison General Major Barthold Hartwig von Bülow. The Swedes had approximately 2,500 soldiers in four infantry regiments (including one Scottish),[36] one dragoon regiment and two reiter regiments. Additionally, the defence was supported by the town militia, which should have had 'on paper' five companies of 80 men but rarely deployed more than half of it. The garrison had at least 150 cannons, with enough ammunition to, at least in theory, last for one year. The city was protected by two lines of fortifications. The outer one was composed of new ones, with eight bastions, protected by trenches and palisades, all protected by a moat. The inner line was mostly an older city wall, supported with towers, but kept in good shape. It was also protected by a moat. The Swedish garrison, in theory under a Polish blockade since autumn 1657, was very active, often sending groups of cavalry and dragoons to harass the Poles. In April 1658, their raid surprised the Polish garrison of Bydgoszcz, killing many and capturing 80 prisoners.[37] Gradually, though, the blockade started to limit the Swedish freedom of movement.

The siege was initially started by the Imperial corps under Jean-Louis Raduit de Souches, which was gradually reinforced by large contingents of

The fortress of Gdańska Głowa. Engraving by Noel Cochin, based on Erik Dahlbergh's drawing for Samuel Pufendorf's *De rebus a Carolo Gustavo Sueciae rege gestis*, published in 1696 (Biblioteka Narodowa, Warszawa).

---

35 The most detailed monograph of the siege: Nowak, *Oblężenie Torunia w roku 1658*. Unless where noted, the vast majority of the information regarding the siege in this part of the book is based on Nowak's work.
36 The so-called '*Hans Kungliga Höghet Arvprinsens Skotska livgarde*' (Scottish life regiment of His Royal Highness the Crown Prince). Under the command of Lieutenant Colonel Hamilton, it was very active during the whole siege, often taking part in forays from the city.
37 Pufendorf, *Siedem ksiąg o czynach Karola Gustawa króla Szwecji*, p.470.

Polish troops – a division under Krzysztof Grodzicki and later a division of Lubomirski and further troops sent from Wielkopolska. At the final stage of the siege, there were more than 18,000 Polish and at least 3,000 Imperial soldiers gathered around Toruń. A detailed list of all the regiments taking part in the siege can be found in Appendix III. The Swedes did not have enough forces left in Prussia to attempt any relief action, concentrating instead on the defences of other places, like Malbork and Elbląg, and on 'small war' against Brandenburg forces. The Imperials under de Souches arrived first, on 2 July 1658, although their contingent was severely lacking infantry (having just one regiment) and brought with them just six cannons and two mortars. For a short period of time, they were supported by one Polish regiment of national cavalry, under Jan Sapieha, although it quickly moved away towards Malbork, hearing news that the Swedes landed some reinforcements near the Vistula Spit (Sapieha later rejoined the besieging force). The Imperials approached Toruń from the south (on the left side of the Vistula river), quickly building field fortifications near Dybów castle and near a bridge over the river, to set up batteries against Bazarowa Island and the bridgehead protecting the bridge between the left bank of the Vistula and the island.[38] A part of de Souches' troops set up a pontoon bridge to the north (right) bank of the Vistula and set up another battery south-east from Toruń. All the artillery positions were protected by redoubts and field fortifications. In the first two weeks, the Swedes attempted a few forays against the Imperial forces, but all those attacks were repulsed. On 26 July, de Souches managed to capture the Swedish bridgehead and even temporarily take over Bazarowa Island, although his soldiers were quickly forced to retreat from the island by Swedish reiters. Using fireships, he destroyed the bridge linking the left bank with Bazarowa Island to prevent a possible counterattack from the Swedes. On 1 August 1657, a strong Polish division arrived near Toruń and crossed over the right bank of the Vistula to start building fortifications against the main Swedish positions. The Poles were under the command of General of Artillery Krzysztof Grodzicki, an experienced officer of infantry and engineer. He brought close to 3,300 men, in two foreign infantry regiments, one dragoon regiment and Jan Sapieha's national cavalry regiment. His artillery train was not very impressive, though, as it contained seven small cannons and

Different types of field fortifications designed and used for cannons during siege operations. In Polish, they were called *'baterie'*. From Józef Naronowicz-Naroński's *Architektura militaris, to jest budownictwo wojenne*, 1659 (Biblioteka Uniwersytetu Warszawskiego).

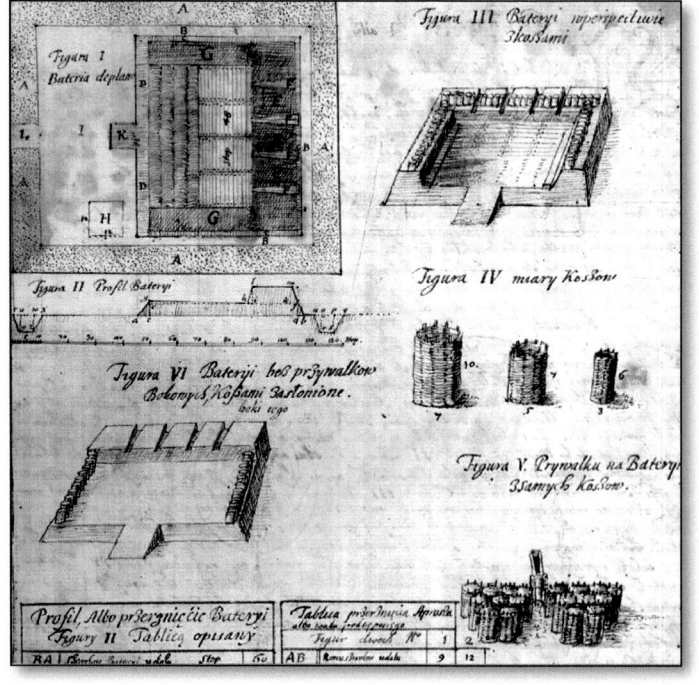

---

38   Dybów castle was a medieval Polish castle built on the left bank of the Vistula river as a guard place against Toruń. In 1656, it was burnt by the Swedes.

SIEGE OPERATIONS

four mortars. Two further foreign regiments and some cannons were, for the time being, left near the Vistula Spit to protect against a possible Swedish relief force.

The arrival of the strong Grodzicki's force led to a start of the proper siege. De Souches left a smaller detachment on the left side of the Vistula and moved the majority of his troops to the right bank, where his soldiers joined Grodzicki's one in building field works. Between 500 and 1,000 paces from the outer line of the Swedish fortifications, the Poles and Imperials bought a complex line of trenches, field bastions, blockhouses and cannon batteries. These earthworks were in some places additionally supported by wooden palisades. The Swedes frequently harassed the besiegers with forays, so strong guards had to be posted to protect the works. While waiting for further reinforcements, both Grodzicki and de Souches focused on cutting off Toruń from other Swedish outposts. In August and September, two further Imperial infantry regiments joined the army, while, between September and October, Lubomirski brought with him seven infantry regiments; two regiments, one squadron and one company of dragoons; a reiter regiment and five cavalry regiments. The Poles brought also between 18 and 27 cannons, mostly of small calibres. Further heavy cannons and a large number of ammunition and supplies were delivered in September and October from Warsaw.

Despite the presence of King Jan II Kazimierz and Queen Ludwika Maria, overall command of the siege was in the hands of Crown Field Hetman Jerzy Sebastian Lubomirski. Luckily for the Poles, he had a good grasp of the Western style of warfare and was patient enough to commence with the siege, instead of the bloody assault so liked by his colleagues as the only proper way to capture a city. The arrival of all the reinforcements allowed for the deployment of all infantry regiments alongside the siege lines, with cavalry kept as a blocking and reserve force. Isidoro Affaitati, serving in Lubomirski's infantry regiment, left a detailed map of the siege, with the placement of all involved units and siege lines (see illustrations in the text). The besieging force was suffering due to a lack of provisions and due to illnesses: the Imperials alone, by the end of September, had 700 ill and were not able to fight. The Swedish defenders, despite being outnumbered and completely cut off and despite letters sent to them by both Jan II Kazimierz and Hetman Lubomirski, were not willing to negotiate a surrender. The Polish cavalry completely cut off the town's supply routes, preventing any contact with other Swedish outposts. A few Swedes captured during a reconnaissance mission were sent to Toruń as a part of psychological warfare, to let the garrison know that Charles X Gustav was too busy in Denmark and would not be able to come to the rescue of the blocked town.[39] By mid-September, de Noyers wrote that the Polish soldiers were eager to assault the city and that, if given the order, they would be able to capture the outer line of defence. The commanders were unwilling to order such an attack, though, 'preferring to proceed slowly, step by step'.[40] In his later letter, dated 22 September, he complained that the 'French would by now capture this fortress, but we

---

39 Kochowski, *Historya panowania Jana Kazimierza*, vol. I, p.349.
40 *Portfolio królowej Maryi Ludwiki*, vol. II, p.169.

AGAINST THE DELUGE

A camp and field fortification of the Polish army during the siege of Toruń in 1658. Isidoro Affaitati, 1659 (Biblioteka Uniwersytecka, Toruń).

[Poles], due to lack of proper engineers, may drag this siege until next year.' He repeated his claim about the soldiers' willingness for a general assault although added the commanders did not want to risk high losses (in the case of defeat) or Toruń being pillaged (in the case of success).[41]

On 26 September, the siege started in earnest, with Polish and Imperial cannons shooting towards Toruń throughout the whole day and night. The Swedes replied in kind, with one 8-pdr cannonball falling just in front of the Queen and her ladies-in-waiting, who were touring the siege works. It led to an exchange of letters with von Bülow, in which the Queen rebuked him for shooting at the ladies. He gallantly apologised and advised it would not happen again, asking her to let him know when the next time the Queen and her companions would be on the siege lines so that the Swedes would not fire in that direction.[42] Within a few days, under the cover of heavy artillery fire, in a few places the besiegers' trenches reached the outer moat. Their approaches were reinforced by small earthworks and connected with another line of trenches for an easier route for the infantry. Having such a new line of field fortifications allowed them to close in with artillery batteries, focusing cannon fire on bastions and the city walls. Artillery was under the command of the experienced Grodzicki, but another Polish engineer came to the fore during the siege. Fryderyk Getkant was in charge of the mortars, and he came up with the idea of the so-called 'earth mortars'. As ammunition, they used large stone water wheels from the water mills, which was to carry a basket of grenades towards the walls. The mortar was in fact a large hole in the ground, of the size of the stone or wheel that would be used as the main bullet. Under the main hole there was a smaller chamber, where the cannoneers would put a bag with powder or petard. Once lit, it would send

---

41 *Portfolio królowej Maryi Ludwiki*, vol. II, p.176.
42 *Portfolio królowej Maryi Ludwiki*, vol. II, pp.183–84.

the stone into the target, where it could crash into walls or implode on impact and shatter into many smaller stones. Another version of the stone was only used as the 'base' of the mortar, while the real projectile was a basket with grenades. The setup was normally used for 25 grenades: one large of 500 pounds, eight that had in total 1,920 pounds and 18 smaller ones that were in total 1,280 pounds. It was a terror weapon, not very effective and using large quantities of powder – it seems that it was employed due to a lack of a sufficient number of proper siege cannons. Amongst the grenades lobbed towards the city were firebombs and even more surprising pieces. Jan Florian Drobysz Tuszyński, who took part in the siege of Toruń, wrote that Getkant 'was sending grenades, firebombs and other smelly and contagious kind; it did not work though, until [the defenders] surrendered themselves'.[43] Another unusual projectile sent towards Toruń was the carcass of a horse, probably a mix of a 'bioweapon' and a psychological one (as the garrison was already low on food). The Swedes answered in kind: they shot with Dutch cheese from their own mortar.[44] Kochowski mentioned that Grodzicki's engineers, especially Getkant, were sending fire balls and a large stone from mortars 'that breaking up [on impact] destroy the buildings, killed people and caused scurvy amongst Swedes due to odour and swelter'.[45]

Despite transports of cannonballs and powder from Warsaw, the besiegers quickly started to suffer from a lack of ammunition; also, they just did not have enough of heavy siege artillery. The Poles asked Prince Bogusław Radziwiłł, who was the Elector's governor of Ducal Prussia, to support the siege – he sent three heavy cannons and ammunition. Royal envoys also travelled to Gdańsk and managed to obtain 100cwt of powder, 50cwt of lead and 1,000 bundles of fuse. The besiegers were also suffering from a lack of food, which led to desertions and even fights between Polish and Imperial soldiers.

The allies were sending small-scale attacks against the Swedish positions, looking for weaker places in their defence. The Swedes were hitting back, focusing on the Imperial positions. It is possible that they were looking to weaken the resolve of de Souches' soldiers and lead to the escalation of the conflicts within the besieging camp. Throughout the whole month of October and in early November, almost every day, the Swedish sallies were attacking different spots in the Imperial lines, every time killing and wounding some besiegers. The allies responded with long cannonades and musket fires, while, in October, they tried a few times to dry out the outer line moat. Their initial attempts of damming the water from the Vistula river directed into the moat were stopped by Swedish counterattacks, though. The constant artillery fire and frequent forays started to take their toll on the defenders, with their losses growing in November. On 6 November, the besieging army received further reinforcements of three foreign infantry regiments of the Polish army, including the strong Andrzej Karol Grudziński's unit (9 companies, a total 1,150 portions). They were stationed next to the Imperial troops to strengthen their line.

43　*Dwa pamiętniki z XVII wieku Jana Cedrowskiego i Jana Floriana Drobysza Tuszyńskiego*, p.31.
44　*Portfolio królowej Maryi Ludwiki*, vol. II, p.165.
45　Kochowski, *Historya panowania Jana Kazimierza*, vol. I, p.350.

The Swedes, in a brazen show of their bravado, on 7 November, sent a strong sally that supposedly killed up to 200 Imperial infantrymen, while, on 8 November, they attacked the positions of the Polish regiments of Lubomirski (under Giza) and Grudziński, killing a few and taking two prisoner. Despite these energetic actions, the situation of the Swedish garrison was slowly turning for the worse. Heavy losses during the fight and illnesses reducing their fighting strength, many bastions, towers and gates were damaged by constant artillery fire. The townsfolk were not very eager to support the defence, seeing how the prolonged fight was destroying the town. Of course, the situation of the besieging army was not great, either. The Imperials in particular were suffering due to hunger, illnesses and worsening weather conditions. De Souches, writing to Montecuccoli, was to even comment that, due to losses, he was 'afraid that he is going to lose his violin in the middle of the dance'.[46] The Poles were taking losses as well, but, overall, it seems that their situation was a bit better, especially as the Polish supply system was doing its best to provide food to the troops. Moreover, in early November, three regiments of national cavalry and one squadron of dragoons were sent away to block Malbork, lowering the number of 'mouths to feed' and easing a bit of the logistic burden.

After the arrival of infantry reinforcements, the allied Council of War decided to commit to the general assault. The commanders believed that they had a sufficient force to do so and that the Swedes were weakened enough to give them a chance for success in such an attack. Despite de Souches' objections, Lubomirski ordered to start the preparations. The soldiers were to prepare fascines, bags with sand (to fill the moat), 500 assault ladders and mobile gangways that men could use to cross the moat. The engineers focused on grenades, firebombs and other fire projectiles that could be thrown at the walls by cannons, mortars and 'earth mortars'. The initial attack, which was aimed to capture Bazarowa Island, had to be postponed, as a deserter from amongst the besieging ranks shared with the Swedes the plans for the attack. On 13 November, the Polish infantry committed to a surprise attack on the left side of the Old Town bastion, identified as a weak point of the defence. While Lubomirski's regiment (led by Giza), with heavy losses, made a diversionary attack, a part of Paweł Celari's regiment, under Captain Wojciech Osowski, managed to sneak into the temporarily unmanned bastion and dig in. The Swedes immediately counterattacked, supported by their artillery from the city walls. They managed to push out the Poles through the moat, but the stubborn Osowski returned with his men and yet again captured the bastion. Another Swedish counterattack, this time led by Hamilton's Scots, caused heavy Polish losses: Osowski was captured, and the remnants of his unit were forced to retreat. Celari sent out fresh companies from his regiments, which managed recapture the bastion. The weary Swedes and Scots decided to return to the walls. The Poles tried to push through after them but were stopped by heavy Swedish fire. Despite that, Celari's men managed to keep their position in the captured bastion.

---

46   Nowak, *Oblężenie Torunia w roku 1658*, p.88.

SIEGE OPERATIONS

A new Swedish counterattack was launched late at night on 14 November, when a in heavy fight, with frequent hand-to-hand combat and using hand grenades, the Poles were forced out from the bastion and onto the other side of the moat. The Swedes did not man the recaptured position, though, and returned to the walls. While the Polish foreign infantry paid a heavy price and did not manage to keep their presence within the Swedish positions, they did focus the attention of the defenders on this part of the line, while, in fact, the main assault was to be launched on a much wider part of the defence lines on 16 November. The allies were to attack in seven points, attempting to capture as many bastions as possible:

Place of attack	Assault force	Notes
Frontal attack on Old Town bastion, known as 'Smaller Chevalier'	Lubomirski's infantry regiment under Giza	
Left part of Old Town bastion	Celari's infantry regiment	Same bastion that regiment fought for on 13 November
Another bastion next to two previous	Alten-Bockum with Royal Guard Dragon regiment	
Section bastion[47]	General Grodzicki with his infantry regiment and parts of Cernezzi's and Grudziński's regiment	
St. Catherine's bastion	De Souches with Imperial infantry and dragoons	
New bastion (next to Vistula river)	Jan Sapieha's dragoon regiment, Bogusław Leszczyński's infantry regiment	
Bazarowa Island	Jan Zamoyski's infantry regiment under de Buy, Royal Guard reiters under Bieliński, Lubomirski's dragoons under Pniewski, three banners of Polish cavalry (cossack style?), part of Lubomirski's reiter regiments, part of Imperial cuirassier regiment Ratschin, attached 20 files of infantry (possibly Imperial)	Infantry was to cross the rivers on boats and as passengers on cavalry and dragoons' horses

The rest of the infantry regiments were kept in reserve, mostly next to the Old Town bastion. The assault started near midnight from 16 to 17 November, with heavy fire from mortars and cannons. Eyewitnesses were impressed and shocked alike with the display of these deadly fireworks, seeing heavy stones, fire balls and heavy grenades being shot towards the walls. The assault columns all struck almost simultaneously. Interestingly, next to the assigned

---

47 Name in German (*Abschnitts-Bollwerck*) comes from the fact that transverse rampart was here connect with double line of old city walls.

troops, a large number of armed camp servants took part in the fight, always eager to fight when facing a chance for looting. Lubomirski was personally in charge of the attacks on the Old Town bastion, seeing it as a crucial place of the assault. The regiments attacking here took heavy losses from musket fire and hand grenades, especially while the forward companies were cutting through the palisades protecting any approach to the bastions. The initial attack stalled and was forced to retreat, 'as Swedish fire was so intense, that it looks that bullets fall [on the Poles] like hail',[48] so Lubomirski supported it with soldiers from the reserve units: the regiment of Wilhem Butler, Aleksander Lubomirski and Ernest Magnus Grotthauz. At the same time, General Major Celari, leading his men through the left side bastion, was wounded, 'as [he was an] obese man and was pushed by Swedish pikes' and fell down into the moat.[49] He was saved by the timely intervention of an officer from his unit, Major Jakub Celari, but the attack failed, and the Poles were repulsed. General Grodzicki and the regiments under his command were initially more successful, reaching the top of the Swedish earthworks, but the murderous salvoes from muskets and the explosions of hand grenades decimated the forward companies and pushed the attack back to the moat. Alten-Bockum's dragoons had more luck, as their designated bastion was not manned at all. De Souches and his Imperial soldiers attacked later than the Polish forces and paid a steep price for their delay. While they managed to approach St. Catharine's bastion, the Swedish defence was very heavy, and de Souches lost many in killed and wounded. At around 0400 hours, he sent a messenger to Lubomirski, asking for reinforcements. By then, the Field Hetman already used the majority of his reserve force, throwing the Polish foreign infantry in assaults against the Old Town bastion. The last intact unit was the Foot Guard regiment under Wolff, and Lubomirski was not keen on sending them to support his allies. The Imperial assault was then met by a furious Swedish counterattack, which forced de Souches to sound the retreat. The defenders of the New bastion also managed to repulse the attack, stopping the Polish dragoons and infantry. The struggle for the Swedish redoubts on Bazarowa Island was very intense, with the attackers approaching the island on boats and while keeping to swimming horses. Initially, the Poles

A Polish horseman (likely from cossack cavalry) and an Imperial or Polish foreign infantry musketeer during the siege of Toruń in 1658. Isidoro Affaitati, 1659 (Biblioteka Uniwersytecka, Toruń).

---

48 Kochowski, *Historya panowania Jana Kazimierza*, vol. I, p.352.
49 Kochowski, *Historya panowania Jana Kazimierza*, vol. I, p.352.

managed to capture one redoubt and surround the second, with a part of the Swedish force retreating via the bridge towards the town. They were reinforced by reiters sent to secure the bridge, though, and quickly counterattacked de Buy's forces. Apparently, the Imperial cuirassiers were unwilling to support the Polish troops in the struggle, 'to send 100 dismounted men, as horses were useless there due to number of trenches', and spent the whole fight just orderly standing on the beach.[50] In vicious melee, during which allegedly the combatants were even tearing out the pikes from their opponents hands and breaking them, the Swedes started to gain the upper hand.[51] After the long fight, at around 0600 hours (after all other assaults were ended), de Buy decided to take his wounded and dead and retreat from the island. It seems that not all of the latter were evacuated, as the victorious Swedes found on the battlefield around 60 killed Poles and Imperials.

As mentioned before, Lubomirski was throwing almost all of his reserves at the Old Town bastion, hoping to break through this position and gain the entry to the city. Five regiments of foreign infantry were slowly moving towards the city walls, capturing one Swedish position after another. They were under the constant heavy fire of Swedish musketeers and cannons, with hand grenades taking a heavy toll on attackers as well. A few times, infantry from both sides clashed in bloody hand-to-hand combat. Swedish Lieutenant Colonel Bock, in charge of the defence of this part of the wall, was twice shot and one struck with a Polish pike, so he had to be carried to the city proper. The stubborn Poles managed to capture two lines of trenches, destroy part of the palisades and dig in, trying to keep the beachhead in the defence lines. Seeing it as a crucial point of the assault, von Bülow himself arrived near the Old Town bastion to take care of the defence. He ordered the evacuation of the cannons and soldiers from the bastion, leaving a small rearguard that was supposed to leave their position when ordered to and to lead the Polish attack into an artillery ambush, where the Poles could be hit with grapeshots from the city walls. At the same time, Lubomirski sent to the attack his last reserve, the Royal Foot Guard under Wolff. The officers of the Guard were to carry on with capturing the rest of the bastion or, if faced with too strong of a defence, to destroy the remaining palisades and evacuate their own dead and wounded. Apparently, the Swedish rearguard, in the chaos of the battle, did not hear the orders to retreat. This allowed the Polish Guard to push them out from the bastion and carry into the Old City Gate. The Swedish grapeshots, at least partially, hit their own retreating soldiers, but they did manage to force the Poles away from the gate. The Old Town bastion was finally in Polish hands, after at least nine assaults that took close to five-and-half hours and cost Lubomirski's infantry many in killed and wounded. The Poles did capture there three cannons and one mortar, but all of them were spiked by the retreating defenders. A very nice surprise for the victorious infantry was the large supply of food and beer that was found in the captured bastion.

---

50 *Portfolio królowej Maryi Ludwiki*, vol. II, pp.199–200.
51 Nowak, *Oblężenie Torunia w roku 1658*, p.112.

From all the main points of the assault, the allies managed to capture the vital Old Town bastion and one of the unmanned, less important bastions next to it. While it was seen as a bit of success, which should have fairly quickly led to the surrender of the town (more about this later), the price of the assault was heavy. Sources vary in the estimates of killed Poles and Imperials, with figures as low as 60 and as high as 1,000 men. It seems that the closest to the truth is the estimate of 400 killed in the infantry alone (including 200 during the assaults on the Old Town bastion) and at least 600 wounded. Kochowski also added that in 'many places that night lots of camp followers were killed'.[52] Amongst the dead were five Imperial and 12 Polish officers, including Captain Klebek from Hetman Lubomirski's infantry regiment, Captain Pozowski from Aleksander Lubomirski's infantry regiment and Captain Berg from Zamoyski's regiment. General Celari was injured, and Lieutenant Colonel del Pace from Grodzicki's infantry regiment was heavily wounded. The Swedes claimed to have lost only 16 killed and 25 wounded, which seems to be, typical for the period, a lowering of their own losses. Tadeusz Nowak, basing it on various, mostly German-language sources, estimates Swedish losses as up to 200 killed and 300 wounded. The bloody toll on the officers was especially high, with a quarter of those present at the garrison killed or wounded.[53]

After a short truce, allowing both sides to collect their dead and wounded, the Poles tried to negotiate, hoping that the assault lowered Swedish morale and made them more willing to discuss a surrender. Von Bülow showed that this clearly was not the case, declining further talks, refusing to call Jan II Kazimierz by the Swedish royal title (as Polish Vasa kings claimed it since Sigismund III) and sending new forays against the Imperial positions. Seeing that the Swedes were unwilling to negotiate, the Poles started preparing for a new assault. Three batteries (in total 11 cannons) were set up near the Old Time bastion, which at the same time was reinforced by further earthworks. A further reinforcement of the infantry arrived at the Polish camp as well: the remaining companies of Butler's and Grotthauz's regiments and the full regiment of the foreign infantry of Michał Kazimierz Radziwiłł. The Polish position in the bastion captured by Alten-Bockun's dragoons was strengthened, while another bastion in the first line, near Chełmińska Gate, abandoned by the Swedes, was manned by further units of the Polish foreign infantry. However, it seems that, by that time, conflict within the allied camp had escalated a lot. De Souches, dejected by the high losses of his troops so far, was against further assaults. Lubomirski was of the opinion that another assault was the correct course of action and should be carried out. The Queen was arguing with de Souches, showing French–Austrian animosity. The King, in a rather unusual twist, although maybe mostly impacted by the scale of losses amongst the Polish troops, was supporting de Souches against Lubomirski. As such, no further attack was agreed upon, and the activities against Toruń focused on artillery fire and, annoying for the defenders but rather lacking in success, barrages from Getkant's 'earth mortars'.

---

52 Kochowski, *Historya panowania Jana Kazimierza*, vol. I, p.353.
53 Nowak, *Oblężenie Torunia w roku 1658*, pp.112–14.

Hoping that maybe contact with Generalissimo Adolph Johann, in charge of the Swedish army in Prussia, would convince the defenders to lay down their arms, the allies allowed von Bülow on 2 December to send his envoys to Malbork. While awaiting response, both sides continued with artillery fire exchange, while the besiegers, from time to time, had to deal with the Swedish sallies as well. Considering that both their powder and food supplies were getting low, the defenders were getting less and less active in such endeavours. There was also growing pressure from Toruń's City Council, as the burghers were hoping for the surrender of the city and possible amnesty from the Polish King. It is highly probable that, by that point, the Imperials were in fact looking to lift the siege over the winter and just leave the blockade force while the majority of the allied army would be spread over the winter quarters. The Poles were against it, though, hoping to force the surrender of the city as soon as possible and only after that deploy the army to winter quarters. The Imperials were seen as a very burdensome ally by then since, in a similar way to 1629, when they were present in Prussia against the Swedes, they demanded a high price for their help, providing way too high a number of their troops allegedly present that needed to be paid for, while in fact their ranks were decimated by death, illnesses and desertion.

It seems that the long siege was really testing the patience of Queen Ludwika Maria herself, as, at the beginning of December, she asked her secretary to arrange the purchase in France of 'three or four of the best books about fortifications, that would include also ways of art of siege craft; maybe also few [more] books about artillery'.[54] Luckily, she did not have to employ her newly obtained skills as a military engineer. Starting from 14 December, both sides agreed for a truce, and long negotiations regarding the surrender of the city began. The Swedes knew by now that they could not count on help from Douglas' army fighting in Courland, knowing also that Adolph Johann did not have enough soldiers in Prussia to organise a relief operation. Interestingly, Imperial officers did not take part in the negotiations, so the final act of surrender was agreed upon between the Poles, Swedes and city burghers. The document, signed by both sides on 23 December, in 20 very detailed articles, specified the conditions of the surrender. Toruń and its inhabitants were to receive a full pardon and confirmation of all its previous privileges. All prisoners would be exchanged unless they had already decided to join the army of their captors. The Swedish garrison would be allowed to leave with their weapons, all flags and drums, and, under armed escort, it would march to Malbork. The Swedes were to take with them all their field cannons, two mortars and four 6-pdr cannons. The Poles would also provide horses and carts to transport the Swedish wounded and sick to Malbork. Those that could not be transported would stay in Toruń, where they would receive quarters, food and medical help. No soldiers from the garrison (except for the already mentioned prisoners) were allowed to switch to the Polish, Imperial or Brandenburg service, with all deserters to be handed back to the Swedes. The Poles would respect the graves of all the Swedish soldiers

---

54 *Portfolio królowej Maryi Ludwiki*, vol. II, p.205.

buried in Toruń. Von Bülow would give over to Polish commissioners all the remaining cannons and ammunition; he would also guarantee that the Swedes would not leave in the town any mines or any other 'trickery'.[55] While it seems that these were very generous terms, we need to remember that it was already mid-December, so the besiegers could expect heavy losses from the cold, hunger and illness if their troops would have to remain along the city. The Polish command may also have been hoping that such fair treatment would affect the soldiers in the garrisons in Elbląg and Malbork, making them more eager to surrender once the allied force approach those cities. They were false hopes, though, as despite blockades and sieges in 1659, both fortresses remained in Swedish hands for the rest of the war.

Finally, on 30 December 1659, the decimated Swedish garrison left Toruń. Only approximately 500 men left the city,[56] with a further 500 sick and wounded left as per the conditions of surrender. Pufendorf mentioned only 190 infantry and 110 cavalry leaving Toruń, but it is more than likely that he meant only those that were still in shape to fight, so the other 200 would be the wounded and sick transported on carts.[57] The rest of the garrison died during the siege or succumbed to wounds and illnesses. Pufendorf, as the main reasons for the surrender of Toruń, mentioned the lack of a chance for the relief of and the heavy losses amongst the garrison, which on one side prevented a proper defence across all city walls, while on the other negatively affected the morale of the Swedish soldiers and civilians.[58]

Two Polish foreign infantry regiments under General Celari were to be stationed in Toruń as a new garrison. General Grodzicki was nominated as Polish military governor of Royal Prussia. The rest of the units marched to designated winter quarters. After six months of siege, Toruń was finally in Polish hands. The besiegers paid a heavy price for the success, though. The Imperial corps that, in September, had approximately 5,000 men by the end of the siege was reduced to 1,200 cavalry (including dragoons) and 400 infantry. Losses amongst the infantry were especially serious, as it lost three-quarters of its number. On one side, the Imperials were affected by the nearly constant Swedish sallies that focused their attention on de Souches' men. On the other, the corps suffered due to illnesses, hunger and a high rate of desertion. Polish losses are more difficult to count, considering the lack of proper musters of the units, loss of many documents from the war and tendency of the officers to present the paper strength of their regiments and companies for accounting purposes. The difference between the strength of units before and after the siege would indicate that approximately 2,600 men were lost from amongst infantry and dragoons, with losses amongst cavalry – indirectly involved in the fights – in probably the low hundreds. This would give the minimal Polish losses as approximately 3,000 killed in fights or dead due to illnesses, wounds or hunger. The siege was, at least for the conditions of the war in Poland, very long despite the concentration of

---

55   Nowak, *Oblężenie Torunia w roku 1658*, pp.192–95.
56   *Diary of General Patrick Gordon*, vol. I, p.276.
57   Pufendorf, *Siedem ksiąg o czynach Karola Gustawa króla Szwecji*, p.506.
58   Pufendorf, *Siedem ksiąg o czynach Karola Gustawa króla Szwecji*, p.503.

a rather strong besiege force. The allies lacked the proper artillery, though, and often suffered due to the lack of powder and cannonballs. There was practically no attempts to use mines to destroy the Swedish bastion, which again could have been caused by the lack of proper equipment, although de Noyers mentioned that the besieging army did not have any engineers able to deal with mines anyway.[59] The massive assault that took place 16 to 17 November caused pretty high losses amongst the attackers, although it led to capturing some of the Swedish positions and, what is probably more important, also led to heavy losses amongst the garrison.

---

59   *Portfolio królowej Maryi Ludwiki*, vol. II, p.167.

9

Example of a 'Low-Level' Campaign: Actions in Livonia and Courland 1657–1660

During the Deluge, Livonia and Courland were secondary theatres of war; campaigns waged there were on a lower scale and involved much smaller forces than in the other areas. As there are quite a lot of primary sources available for this conflict, I think it may be interesting to present in this chapter an overall description of this campaign, with its 'small war' encounters and number of siege operations.[1] In October 1657, a 'division of left wing' of the Lithuanian army, led by Field Hetman Gosiewski, started a new offensive against the Swedish forces in Livonia. Gosiewski's forces had 'on paper' 10,592 horses and portions, so they should have been approximately 9,500 men. In reality, the army was much smaller since, due to previous losses and war attrition, the units were well below their strength. The initial phase of the operations went well, as the Lithuanians were able to capture almost 20 castles (including Treiden and Wolmar) and set up a blockade of the crucial port of Riga. At the beginning of December 1657, part of division, led by Camp Master Samuel Komorowski, started the siege of Parnau. The Lithuanians lacked artillery and infantry, so, after eight weeks of unsuccessful efforts, they had to lift the siege. In early winter 1658, the Lithuanian cavalry had a few small encounters with the Swedes, although the scale and subsequent losses of the involved forces vary depending on the source. Pufendorf wrote about a sally of Swedish troops under General Simon Grundel-Helmfelt, who was to defeat a detachment of Gosiewski's force near farm Ulenborg on the night from 6 to 7 January 1658. The Swedes allegedly burnt the Lithuanian camp and captured more than 40 prisoners,

---

1   Unless noted, the description is based on: Bobiatyński, *Michał Kazimierz Pac*, pp.31–62; Leszek Podhorodecki, 'Kampania polsko-szwedzka 1659 r. w Prusach i Kurlandii', *Studia i Materiały do Historii Wojskowości*, IV (1958), pp.233–44; Andrzej A. Majewski, 'Działania wojenne w Księstwie Kurlandii i Semigalii w latach 1658-1660', in Mirosław Nagielski (ed.), *Z dziejów stosunków Rzeczypospolitej Obojga Narodów ze Szwecją w XVII wieku* (Warszawa: Wydawnictwo DiG, 2007), pp.225–45; Majewski, *Marszałek wielki litewski Aleksander Hilary Połubiński (1626-1679)*, pp.159–78.

EXAMPLE OF A 'LOW-LEVEL' CAMPAIGN: ACTIONS IN LIVONIA AND COURLAND 1657–1660

three cannons and 12 flags, losing only 13 killed and 17 wounded.[2] In the same month, 'rising star' of the Lithuanian army *Rotmistrz* Michał Pac led four banners of cossack-style cavalry in a skirmish against General Major Fabian Aderkas' cavalry outside Parnau.[3] Interestingly, two of the Lithuanian banners attacked on foot, and the whole group was even able to pursue the Swedes close to the city's gate. Here, a few companions were shot dead by the garrison, while the horses of the Lithuanians were panicked by straw set up in fire by the Swedes. A few days later, the Swedes led an attack from Parnau into the Lithuanian camp but were forced back into the town. In a direct hand-to-hand fight, Pac was able to severely wound Swedish Colonel Iskiel, cutting off his army, but, in return, he was wounded in the leg. In February 1658, Gosiewski ordered the majority of his troops to winter quarters in Courland and Samogitia, leaving only a small garrison of troops scattered in Livonia. In summer the same year, the Swedes started to prepare an offensive to take back control over Livonia. In July 1658, their forces in the regions were as follows:[4]

- 3,232 infantry in garrison forces
- 2,534 infantry in field army (five regiments)
- 3,021 cavalry in field army (16 regiments and squadrons).

Despite their units being well under strength, with some regiments of cavalry being the equivalent of one or two companies, they took the initiative and gradually recaptured all Lithuanian gains. Through July and August 1658, the weak Lithuanian outposts were being defeated one by one, with some places – like castle Helmet – being destroyed after their surrender, as the Swedes did not have enough soldiers to garrison them all. By autumn the same year, the last three Lithuanian fortresses in Livonia – Wolmar, Ermes and Ronneburg – were lost. In September, Field Marshal Robert Douglas, with 3,000 soldiers, entered Samogitia, taking the offensive into Lithuanian soil. Gosiewski sent one national cavalry regiment (*pułk*) under Michał Kazimierz Pac to capture some prisoners and establish more information about the enemy, their strength and their plans. Pac had under his command six banners of cossack-style cavalry and one banner of dragoons, so the force was well suited for the reconnaissance mission. The Lithuanians clashed with the strong (1,000 horses) vanguard of the Swedish forces over the bridge over the river Musza (Mūša). According to Poczobut Odlanicki, Pac's force managed to easily break the Swedish reiters despite getting under heavy fire.[5] During the fight, they captured 11 prisoners and brought news that Douglas set up camp in Doblena in Courland. Unfortunately, at the same time, the Muscovites started their offensive against the Lithuanians, forcing the

---

[2] Pufendorf, *Siedem ksiąg o czynach Karola Gustawa króla Szwecji*, p.476.
[3] In 1663, Pac became Lithuanian Field Hetman. At the beginning of 1667, he was promoted to Grand Hetman and held this office until his death in 1682.
[4] Mankell, *Uppgifter rörande svenska krigsmagtens styrka, sammansättning och fördelning sedan slutet af femtonhundratalet*, pp.340–41.
[5] Poczobut Odlanicki, *Pamiętnik Jana Władysława Poczobuta Odlanickiego*, p.23.

Lithuanians to split their forces since Grand Hetman Sapieha's division was not able to fight the new invasion on its own. Gosiewski divided his division: the majority of his force under Samuel Komorowski was sent to fight the Swedes in Courland, while Gosiewski himself, with some cavalry, marched to Vilnius, as he was under the impression that some sort of truce could be negotiated with the Muscovites. The Hetman was surprised on 21 October at Werki by a much stronger Muscovite army: his troops took heavy losses, and Gosiewski, along with many of his officers, was captured. More details about the scale of losses are provided in Appendix VII. Since the right wing division under Grand Hetman Sapieha did not support Gosiewski's troops, it led to a worsening of the conflict between both parts of the Lithuanian army. After some turmoil due to Gosiewski's capture, Samuel Komorowski was nominated as *regimentarz* to lead the left wing division during the Field Hetman's absence.

Douglas captured the main Courland city of Mitawa (Mitau) in October 1658, taking Prince Jacob Kettler and his family captive. Komorowski was not able to recapture any of the places taken by the Swedes. His forces were composed mostly from cavalry (the majority of it were cossack cavalry banners) and some dragoons, so he focused on harassing the Swedish forces instead. The Lithuanians set up their camp at Janiszki, from which they started to send out groups of cavalry to harass the Swedes in Courland. Poczobut Odlanicki wrote that the cavalry clashes were very frequent and very intense.[6] At the beginning of November, Pac, with his regiment, 'destroyed few hundred Swedes near Mitau'. Poczobut Odlanicki, probably with a typical-for-any-diary dose of exaggeration, wrote that more than 300 killed Swedes were later counted on the battlefield while a further 50, mostly officers, were captured. The Lithuanians were to lose only two killed companions from cossack-style cavalry and two killed dragoons, which seems far too low an estimate for the rather intense and bloody fight.[7] Courland volunteer forces, likely a mix of armed local nobility and their peasant subjects, was also fighting against the Swedes, attacking smaller outposts and patrols. For example, on early January 1659, they killed 24 Swedish soldiers in Sackenhusen.[8]

Winter, as was often the case, brought some respite and rest for both sides. Units from both sides were stationed in winter quarters, while the

A Lithuanian cossack cavalryman or Tatar with captured Cossacks. He is unarmoured and equipped with a sabre and bows. From the drawing of Abraham von Westervelt. 1651 (Muzeum Wojska Polskiego, Warszawa, photo from author's archive).

---

6 Poczobut Odlanicki, *Pamiętnik Jana Władysława Poczobuta Odlanickiego*, p.23.
7 Poczobut Odlanicki, *Pamiętnik Jana Władysława Poczobuta Odlanickiego*, pp.24–25.
8 Pufendorf, *Siedem ksiąg o czynach Karola Gustawa króla Szwecji*, p.584.

EXAMPLE OF A 'LOW-LEVEL' CAMPAIGN: ACTIONS IN LIVONIA AND COURLAND 1657–1660

Lithuanians sent home their district troops and levy of nobility supporting the regular army. There were, of course, still some small-scale cavalry fights, like the one near Janiszki when, in early January 1659, a Lithuanian force managed to defeat Douglas's troops. According to the Lithuanian relation, their four banners (one hussars, one *pancerni* and two cossack cavalry banners) broke through 400 Swedes, killing most of them and taking more than 20 prisoner. As often with such relations, the losses of the victorious side were suspiciously low: just one companion and one retainer killed.⁹

Lithuanian cavalry from the period of 1649-1651 as drawn by Abraham von Westervelt. The unit on right is clearly hussar, the two others are cossack cavalry or light horse. From the drawing of Abraham von Westervelt. 1651 (Muzeum Wojska Polskiego, Warszawa, photo from author's archive).

In the early spring of 1659, the Swedes prepared yet another offensive. In March, Aderkas managed to recapture three smaller castles, while Gustav Armfeld scattered Lithuanian detachments, capturing three flags.¹⁰ In April and May, Douglas gathered under his command a new field army, after assembling some reinforcements from Ingria and Estonia. He had 11 regiments of cavalry (61 companies) with a total of 1,722 men and five regiments of infantry (28 companies) with a total of 1,213 men, supported by a small artillery train with six field cannons and probably some siege pieces as well. As in 1658, his units were severely depleted, with some cavalry regiments being the size of the reinforced company.¹¹ Nonetheless, this force included many veteran officers and soldiers, and it was facing also severely undermanned Lithuanian forces. The Swedish plan was for Douglas to move to Courland and, from there, join General Wirtz's corps, which was marching from Prussia. In early May 1659, the Lithuanians signed a temporary truce with the Muscovites so that Komorowski could use his whole division to fight against the Swedes again. On 18 May, at Zydylia, Douglas defeated a part of the

---

9 *Die 19 January 1659 z Listu Chorążego Kazimierza Chłusowicza do Jego Mości Pana Porucznika Chrapowickiego*, Saint Petersburg Institute of History, collection 32, box 660/2, p.132.
10 Pufendorf, *Siedem ksiąg o czynach Karola Gustawa króla Szwecji*, p.584.
11 Daniel Staberg, *Livonian Field Army, April and May 1659* (unpublished article in the author's archive), pp.1–2.

Lithuanian troops, causing them heavy losses. Komorowski was able to stop Douglas' offensive, though, and prevent two Swedish forces from joining. In June, the Lithuanians received reinforcements from their Brandenburg allies, with a small 'division' under Colonel Georg von Schönaich arriving in the theatre of the war. He initially had two regiments/squadrons (four companies each) of reiters and two companies of dragoons, approximately 640 reiters and 160 dragoons. In August, he was reinforced by another squadron of reiters (three companies) and one company of dragoons, in total approximately 400 men.[12] On 23 June, Lithuanian Colonel Teofil Schwarzhoff defeated a group of 1,000 Swedish cavalry at Sałaty. The Swedish commander, General Aderkas, was captured. When Douglas started to retreat towards Courland, he was harassed by 2,500 Lithuanian cavalry led by Pac. On 16 August 1659, the Lithuanians started a siege of the castle in Goldynga, and, on 31 August, Komorowski's troops were joined by the majority of Sapieha's division under the command of Aleksander Hilary Połubiński. He was supposed to lead two banners of hussars, 17 banners of cossack cavalry, two banners of Tartar light horse, 10 units of dragoons[13] and two banners of haiduks, although we do not have confirmation if all of these planned units did in fact take part in this operation.[14]

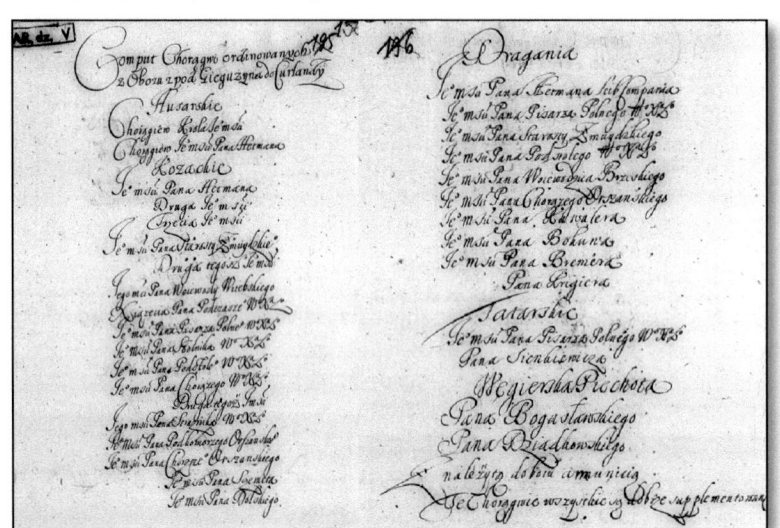

A list of the Lithuanian units from the division of Grand Hetman Sapieha that were to be sent in late summer 1659 under the command of Połubiński to Courland to fight against Swedes. They are listed in the following order: hussars (two banners), cossack cavalry (17 banners), dragoons (10 units), Tatar light horse (two banners), Hungarian infantry (two banners), all with 'enough ammunition and well supplemented (manned)' (AGAD, Warsaw).

The siege of Goldingen became somewhat personal to Komorowski, as, on 16 August, his brother, *Rotmistrz* Eliasz Komorowski, was killed 'from ambush' by a Swedish musketeer.[15] The circumstances of his death are a bit unclear, as the Lithuanians and Swedes had a temporary truce at the time and were supposed to cease fire for the negotiations. Lacking infantry, artillery and powder, the Lithuanian operation was more alike to a blockade than a real siege. On 3 September, Douglas attempted to come with help to the besieged town but was forced to retreat by the Lithuanians. His forces were then pursued by two groups of Lithuanian cavalry (each group 20-banners strong, probably mostly cossack cavalry and light horse). Pac led soldiers from Komorowski's division, and Colonel Samuel Kmicic led soldiers from Sapieha's division. Douglas was able to set up camp near Bowsk, and the Lithuanian cavalry

---

12 Sławomir Augusiewicz, *Przebudowa wojska pruskiego w latach 1655-1660. U źródeł nowożytnej armii* (Oświęcim: Wydawnictwo Napoleon V, 2014), pp.274–75.
13 Some of them were regiments, others squadrons or free companies.
14 AGAD, AR V, no. 11208/I, pp.156–57.
15 Poczobut Odlanicki, *Pamiętnik Jana Władysława Poczobuta Odlanickiego*, p.27.

EXAMPLE OF A 'LOW-LEVEL' CAMPAIGN: ACTIONS IN LIVONIA AND COURLAND 1657–1660

stayed in the area to harass him. On 24 September, the Lithuanians were surprised by a counterattack of the Swedish cavalry, with one group of 1,000 men led by Douglas and another group of 800 men striking both Lithuanian detachments at the same time. Kmicic's troops fled the battlefield, leaving Pac's troops to fight alone against Douglas' group. Pac managed to surprised Douglas when the Swedish soldiers were resting in some village. In the ensuing fight, up to 500 Swedes were killed or captured; the Lithuanians also managed to capture 10 standards. Douglas retreated with the rest of his troops to Bowsk.

In the meantime, on 19 September, the Lithuanians achieved great success, forcing the decimated garrison of Goldingen to finally surrender. According to Poczobut Odlanicki, 400 reiters and more than 700 infantrymen from the garrison were enlisted into the Lithuanian force. On 25 of September, two Courland nobles, named Rumb and Klisser, who served as officers in the Swedish army were beheaded as 'traitors'.[16] The same day, another Swedish outpost, Ventspils, was captured by Lithuanians supported by some loyal Courland volunteers. It seems that the majority of its garrison were ex-Danish soldiers, who, after some initial clashes, 'throw down their weapons and refused to fight', forcing the commandant of Ventspils, Lieutenant Colonel Bickerton, to surrender. Officers were set free to return to Riga, while all rank-and-files joined the Lithuanian army.[17] The main Lithuanian army moved then to besiege Szkrund (the operation started on 30 September), but reinforcements were sent to Pac, who was staying with his cavalry near Bowsk. *Rotmistrz* Krzysztof Szumski led 80 horses of hussars, one *pancerni* and one cossack cavalry banner from Komorowski's division, while *Rotmistrz* Marcjan Ogiński led a group of troops from Sapieha's division. On 10 October, Pac met those troops at Poswol, and he led them to Arenburg, where Douglas had his camp. The Lithuanian vanguard under Lieutenant Grabiński of Jerzy Karol Hlebowicz's cossack cavalry banner managed to capture six prisoners, who provided some information about the Swedish strength and deployment. Another reconnaissance force, composed from a few light cavalry banners, was harassing the Swedes on 14 October, capturing another eight prisoners. On 21 October, Pac's group attacked the main Swedish forces. First, they were able to destroy the Swedish vanguard (killing 40 and taking 30 prisoner) and then, near the river Musza, encountered the main Douglas' force. The Lithuanian cavalry was able to push the Swedes back towards camp; Douglas himself was saved by the counterattack of his reiters. Another Lithuanian attack was stopped by the infantry and artillery defending the Swedish camp. The next day, Douglas started to retreat, pursued by the Lithuanian cavalry. While hard pressed and losing more men from those attacks, the Swedes did not go down without a fight, causing some losses amongst the attacking Lithuanians. After a few days of skirmishing, once Douglas' troops crossed the river Musza, Pac's forces broke the contact and returned to their camp. King Jan Kazimierz hoped that, with the Swedish field army no longer a treat and with the majority of fortresses already recaptured, the Lithuanians

---

16   Poczobut Odlanicki, *Pamiętnik Jana Władysława Poczobuta Odlanickiego*, p.29.
17   Pufendorf, *Siedem ksiąg o czynach Karola Gustawa króla Szwecji*, p.585.

would be able to easily force the rest of them to surrender, especially when using the artillery captured in Goldingen.[18]

From late September, a stronger Brandenburg corps under Prince Bogusław Radziwiłł was also operating in this theatre of the war. Radziwiłł had under his command approximately 2,000 men in 14 to 15 companies of reiters, one dragoon company and nine companies of infantry, with some artillery support. Initially, this force captured Lipawa (Libau) on 3 October and then moved to besiege Grobin, where he was joined by Georg von Schönaich and his troops, who left the Lithuanian army camp at Goldingen.[19] They captured Grobin on 19 October, which led to a conflict with Lithuanians who were trying to set up their own garrison. Radziwiłł objected to that, leaving his own troops there instead. The next day, Komorowski and Połubiński took part in a feast in Radziwiłł's camp. It was a farewell meeting, as the main Brandenburg force, under Prince Bogusław Radziwiłł, was leaving for Prussia, with just von Schönaich's detachment stationed in Grobin as garrison. On 21 October, while returning from the Brandenburg camp, Samuel Komorowski died suddenly. There were strange rumours about the cause of his death, as gossip (even in the form of the drawings published later) spread that he had fallen asleep on the cart while drunk and was strangled by his own scarf, which was stuck in the wheel of the cart. It seems, though, that he in fact died due to apoplexy. Of course, the sudden death of their *regimentarz* completely paralysed the left wing division, as different factions were trying to take over the command. Soldiers of the foreign *autorament* voted for Maciej Gosiewski, the brother of the captured Field Hetman, to be their *regimentarz*, as they were hoping to retain the status of an independent division and not be moved under the control of Sapieha. The Grand Hetman's commander in the area, Aleksander Hilary Połubiński, did not use the opportunity to take over Komorowski's former troops. In fact, on 25 October, the units of both divisions split: Połubiński took Sapieha's soldiers towards Mitau, while Maciej Gosiewski with the 'left division' marched towards Bowski, where Pac was already operating with a detachment of cavalry. Połubiński's reconnaissance group, led by Lieutenant Grabiński, defeated a group of Swedish cavalry, forcing Douglas to retreat towards Mitau where the Swedes set up a new camp three miles from the town.[20] Meanwhile, on 27 October, Pac started a blockade of Bowsk, and, on 2 November, his cavalry was joined by the rest of the division, led by Maciej Gosiewski. In the next few days, there were many heated discussions between the officers of the 'left division', with many colonels vying for the right to replace Komorowski. Pac fiercely clashed with reiter Colonel Teofil Schwarzhoff, which almost led to a fight when Pac was trying to shoot from his pistol and Schwarzhoff was grabbing his pallasch. Despite such conflicts, on 5 November, during the general gathering of the 'left division', Michał Kazimierz Pac was chosen as the new *regimentarz*. Despite his youth

---

18 AGAD, AR III, no. 7, p.57; Poczobut Odlanicki, *Pamiętnik Jana Władysława Poczobuta Odlanickiego*, pp.31–32.
19 Augusiewicz, *Przebudowa wojska pruskiego w latach 1655-1660*, pp.277–78.
20 AGAD, AR V, 12080, pp.16–17.

EXAMPLE OF A 'LOW-LEVEL' CAMPAIGN: ACTIONS IN LIVONIA AND COURLAND 1657–1660

(he was born in 1624) and not having much military experience, he had strong support at the Royal Court. His uncle, Lithuanian Grand Chancellor Kazimierz Zygmunt Pac, was supporting the promotion of his cousin, while King Jan II Kazimierz was looking to increase the role of the officers loyal to him in the Lithuanian army. On 29 October, Michał Kazimierz Pac was nominated to the vacant (after Komorowski's death) office of Lithuanian Camp Master, and, on 11 November, the *Senat* Council confirmed his role as *regimentarz*.

While the new commander of the 'left division' was definitely a good cavalry officer, he lacked experience in utilising infantry and artillery. He lost many months on besieging Bowsk; moreover, he sent most of his infantry and some cannons to help Połubiński, who was besieging Mitawa.[21] The Swedes were also making frequent forays from both Mitawa and Bowsk, often causing losses amongst the besiegers. On 28 December, two cavalry lieutenants from Połubiński's command, Grabiński and Michałkiewicz, were captured. On 30 December, a sally from Bowsk surprised Pac's soldiers, killing six officers and some infantrymen.[22] The Lithuanian commander continued his pointless attacks against Bowsk, a few times throwing his soldiers at the fortress walls, where they took heavy losses. One of the dragoon companies, probably formed from former Swedish soldiers, deserted to the defenders. Lacking food and suffering from illnesses, the siege operation took a heavy toll on the Lithuanians. One assault on the castle, which took place on 28 February 1660, was a very costly mistake, with many soldiers, two captains and three lieutenants killed. At the beginning of March 1660, the last Lithuanian units left their positions near Bowsk, realising the futility of their operation. Połubiński, suffering from the same problems as Pac, was more successful, though. Despite the loss of approximately 200 killed during the few months of the siege, he was finally able to force the garrison of Mitau to surrender on 9 January 1660. Just over 500 surviving Swedish soldiers, with seven flags, two cannons and one mortar, were allowed to leave the fortress and were escorted to Riga.[23] Pufendorf commented rather harshly that General Major Valentin Meier surrender Mitau castle 'for not reason, as he had there enough food and 350 healthy infantrymen'. It seems that the Swedish officer was even imprisoned for his decision in Riga, after arriving there with the surviving soldiers.[24] Połubiński left 800 men as the new garrison of Mitawa and despatched his remaining infantry and dragoons to support Pac at Bowsk, but, as we have already seen, even those reinforcements did not help the Camp Master's troops. With the end of the war against Sweden, most of the Lithuanian troops from Courland and Livonia were now to be relocated to fight against the Muscovites, taking part in the Battles of Połonka and Basia.

---

21 AGAD, AR V, 12080, p.29.
22 Poczobut Odlanicki, *Pamiętnik Jana Władysława Poczobuta Odlanickiego*, p.33.
23 AGAD, AR V, 12080, pp.29, 34; Poczobut Odlanicki, *Pamiętnik Jana Władysława Poczobuta Odlanickiego*, p.34.
24 Pufendorf, *Siedem ksiąg o czynach Karola Gustawa króla Szwecji*, p.585.

Conclusion

Silver medal celebrating the Treaty of Oliwa in 1660 (Muzeum Narodowe, Kraków).

The war with Sweden, waged between 1655 and 1660, was one of the most traumatic and long-reaching experiences of the Polish–Lithuanian Commonwealth in the seventeenth century. Combined with the conflict against Muscovy, it led to a massive loss of life and destruction throughout the whole country, with its impact being felt for many years after the war. It was also a painful lesson for both the Polish and Lithuania military, with a string of poor performances and many defeats in the opening stages of the conflict. The period of recovery started quickly, though, and, already in 1656, we start to see the first successes achieved not only during partisans' attacks or cavalry raids but also during open battles against the Swedish invaders. Despite Transylvanian, Cossack and Brandenburg involvement on the Swedish side, the Commonwealth's armies, from 1657 supported by Imperial troops as well, gradually started to gain the upper hand. The later stage of the war saw the creation of the wider anti-Swedish coalition and led to a Polish auxiliary division being despatched to Denmark. This period also brought about changes in the organisation of both the Polish and Lithuanian armies, with a large increase of the presence of foreign *autorament*, especially infantry and dragoons, connected with many siege operations and plans to renew operations against the Muscovites. The hard-won war against the Swedes did not stop the Commonwealth's military operations, as they continued from 1660 to 1664, this time against the Muscovites, while between 1665 and 1666, the country and its military were involved in the civil war known as Lubomirski's rebellion (*rokosz Lubomirskiego*). Only from 1667, after the Treaty of Andrusowo was signed with Muscovy, could the Commonwealth enjoy a brief period of piece, which ended a few years later with the outbreak of the new war, this time against the Ottomans.

The 1655–1660 war clearly showed the many weak sides of the Polish and Lithuanian warfare. Constant issues with the lack of pay led soldiers to

CONCLUSION

loot their own local populations and to raise confederations (mutinies) of disgruntled troops. Internal politics, full of bickering between pro- and anti-royal factions, often negatively affected military operations or cooperations between different divisions and armies. The fact that practically the whole Polish regular army decided, in late 1655, to switch to the Swedish side clearly shows issues with morale, internal problems within the country and the position of King Jan II Kazimierz amongst the Polish and Lithuanian nobles. On the other hand, starting in 1656, the Commonwealth's military started to recover, with many reorganisations of its structure and command chain, during which talented officers were promoted to important offices within the army. The wars against the Swedes and the Muscovites also led to an increase of the number of professional soldiers, who served within the ranks for many years and gradually raised within the units and army's structures. It provided a great fundament for the later successes of Jan Sobieski as a hetman and a king, with a large part of his officers' corps starting their careers during the Deluge.

Colour Plates Commentary

A1. King Jan II Kazimierz

While there are some paintings depicting Jan II Kazimierz in Polish attire, we decided to present him with Western-style clothing and armour in the way he would have fought at Zborów in 1649, Beresteczko in 1651 and Warsaw in 1656. In the latter battle, he had to look like the many Swedish, Brandenburg or foreign officers in the Polish service, with blackened armour of very good quality and long leather cavalry boots. According to de Noyers, during the retreat of the Polish and Lithuanian armies on the third day of the battle (30 July 1656), the King was mistaken by some Brandenburg officer (ex-Polish soldier) for 'some German officer' and was shouted at, 'come over my friend, come over to us, you will be welcomed here and you will find here better [service] than amongst those cowardly Poles'. The enraged King, recognising the officer from his court, was to answer, 'Traitor! One day I will have you hang!'. After the battle, the Brandenburg officer allegedly made the comment that he did not recognised the King; otherwise, he would have courtly bowed to him.

Jan II Kazimierz showed on many occasions his personal bravery on the battlefield, at both Zborów and Beresteczko calming down waving troops and restoring order. At Warsaw, he tried to organise the support of the other cavalry for the hussars' charge, ordering banners 'as sergeant, quartermaster and ordinary soldier', but, despite his requests and even tears, the other soldiers were not willing to take part in the charge. On the final day of the battle, with his sword in hand, the King was leading the retreat of the infantry regiments. We presented him with the so-called 'regiment', a baton used as a symbol of rank of an important officer not only in Western-European armies but also in foreign *autorament* in the Commonwealth's armies.

A2. Queen Ludwika Maria

Queen Ludwika Maria (as Marie Louise Gonzaga was known in Poland) had a keen interest not only in the Commonwealth's politics but also in the military matters, supporting King Jan II Kazimierz on many occasions and

COLOUR PLATES COMMENTARY

raising the morale of the soldiers during siege operations. We decided to present her in the most famous episode of her 'military career', from the second day of the Battle of Warsaw (29 July 1656). When observing the fight from the safety of the Polish field fortifications, she noticed that the fire from a two-cannon battery set up on the left bank of the Vistula river did not hit the Swedish and Brandenburg forces. She ordered for the horses from her own carriage to be used to move the cannons to Kępa Potocka, on the bank of the river, from which they started a much more successful fire. Her haircut, dress and jewellery are based on the period paintings. Additional parts of the Queen's attire presented here are based on a source describing the event, as she is covered with a Tatar *burka*, an overcoat normally made from camel fur or (like here) from wool. She is sitting on the infantry drum, holding a scope with which she was checking the progress of the fight. It is possible that she looked very similar in 1658, while, on many occasions, she was inspecting the siege lines at Toruń.

B1. Aleksander Hilary Połubiński

As one of the most important Lithuanian commanders during the war, Połubiński was also the lieutenant in charge of the elite Royal hussar banner in the Lithuanian army. He led the famous charge of hussars during the second day of the Battle of Warsaw on 29 July 1656. That is why we decided to present him in the attire of a high-ranking hussar, based on the portrait of another Lithuanian commander, Michał Kazimierz Pac. He has good quality armour, worn over a white *kontusz*, with a red, fur-lined *delia* coat worn over them. His footwear are longer boots made from yellow saffian (Morocco leather), common amongst the Polish military. When in a fight, he would have probably used a *szyszak* helmet of the similar type that can be seen with the hussar companion on plate B2. In his hand, he has a *buzdygan* mace, which was not only a symbol of a cavalry officer's rank but could also, if needed, be used as a weapon. At the side he has sabre, a clear symbol of the Commonwealth's nobility.

B2. Winged Hussar Companion

His main clothing is the Hungarian-style dolman, over which he is wearing a breastplate. Another piece of armour is the *szyszak* helmet. The series of the post-1648 conflicts put much financial strain on the soldiers, so, even amongst the hussars, many companions were unable to afford more elaborate armour or even some elements of it (which is why the companion is missing arm-guards). Tight purple trousers are covered up to the knees with long boots made from yellow saffian. Over the dolman, he has a leopard pelt (often just called *lampart* in Polish, no matter which cat it came from), which has red lining matching his clothing. If he would have been equipped with a wing, it would have been attached to his horse's saddle, not to the soldier's back – just as we can see in Dahlbergh's drawings of the horses captured during second day of the Battle of Warsaw in 1656. He is armed with a sabre while, in the right hand, he has an estoc (*koncerz*). With its long, straight blade, it was carried in a special scabbard under the saddle, usually on the left side of the horse. It was used while mounted once the lance was crushed or lost or in a situation when a hussar lacked a lance, as was often the case during campaigns. Alternative to the estoc, a soldier could carry a pallasch; it was matter of individual choice, though. As with other cavalry, a hussar would normally also have pistols in holsters. The helmet and armour are based on the surviving trophies from Skokloster Castle in Sweden.

C1. *Pancerni* Companion

Here is a very well-equipped companion from a *pancerni* banner, although, at the same time, he could be serving in cossack cavalry or even levy of nobility. He has long chainmail (*kolczuga*) worn over a red *żupan*, while his head is protected by a *misiurka* helmet; there are also *karwasze* arm-guards. The Eastern-style *kałkan* shield was not required as a part of the equipment mentioned in recruitment letters, although it seems to have been common enough amongst Polish cavalry. The soldier should be equipped with 'three firearms'. In fact, we can see a spanner-like tool on his belt used for wheellock pistols kept at the horse's saddle in holsters. Instead of a long firearm, though, he has a bow, often used by companions as a symbol of status and an efficient weapon on its own. For hand-to-hand combat, he has not only a sabre but also a *czekan* warhammer.

C2. Cossack Cavalryman from Czarniecki's Division, 1660

This soldier, serving in one of the cossack cavalry banners from Stefan Czarniecki's division, is good example of how soldiers had to adjust to different conditions during a campaign. He took part in the campaign in Denmark, so his clothing is mix of Eastern and Western elements. He has a short blue *żupan*, according to Pasek (who was also serving in this division), made from drill fabric (*drelich*). It is shorter than those usually worn in Poland, as it comes together with long German riding boots, typical for reiters. While he does not have chainmail like *pancerni*, he is at least protecting his head with a *misiurka* helmet; there are also *karwasze* arm-guards, although of a different type than those used by the *pancerni* companion seen on C1. He is armed with a sabre and *bandolet* carbine (which could be used from saddle), with a pistol or two held in holster with his horse.

COLOUR PLATES COMMENTARY

D1. Light Horseman/Volunteer

While we named this soldier as a 'light horseman/volunteer', the presented figure – based on a few drawings of Polish horsemen from the period – could be used as a representation of many more types: levy of nobility, mounted partisans and retainers (or even poorer companions) from cossack cavalry banners of the regular armies. His clothing consists of the common combination: he wears a red *kontusz* outer garment worn over a blue *żupan* (the bottom of it is visible, as it is slightly longer than the *kontusz*). He has brown long boots, as he was not able to afford the more expensive saffian ones. On his head, we can see a fur-brimmed cap; many types of these caps were worn by soldiers and civilians alike. He is lacking any sort of armour, while his weapons are a sabre and wheellock pistol. Of course, depending on availability and his own wealth, such a cavalryman could have been equipped with other weapons as well: a bow, *bandolet* carbine and additional hand-to-hand weapons like a pallasch or *nadziak*.

D2. Reiter

In the 1650s, the armour used by Western-style cavalry was often out of favour, so reiters tended to rely on buff-coats – either with long sleeves or sleeveless. This reiter is equipped with the former version, giving him a bit of extra protection during a fight. With a sword at the belt and pistols in holsters (with the horse), his other important weapon is the carbine, often mentioned in Holsten's description of German mercenary reiters in the Swedish and Polish service. The sword could be exchanged for a sabre, especially when no other weapon was available, as Gordon had to rely on the old Polish sabre he found after losing his equipment during a fight against the Poles. Long riding boots and a wide-brim hat are other Western-style elements, although during long campaigns, especially against the Muscovites in Ukraine, more local clothing (e.g., shorter boots, *żupan* garments and fur caps) could be used.

E1. Dragoon

Despite dragoons having been a part of the foreign *autorament*, they were at least partially recruited from amongst local – Polish and Lithuanian – populations and so often combined Western and Eastern influence into their clothing. This dragoon is based on Patrick's Gordon depiction of the private company of Konstanty Lubomirski. The unit, being composed of Polish soldiers, was led by a Dutch captain and had 'blue cloaks after the Dutch manner and fashion'. He has infantry boots with garters and buckles. The dragoon obtained a more local fur-brimmed cap instead of a Western-style hat. He is armed with a matchlock musket, as he was not trained (or expected) to shoot when mounted. As a sidearm, this dragoon is equipped with a locally obtained Polish sabre. Other units that we know of would have had Western-style swords, described in sources as *szpady*. Dragoons were not required to use pistols, although some soldiers managed to get one or a pair as a useful additional weapon when fighting mounted. His clothing is based on the painting, 'The Dance of Death', from Bernardine Monastery in Cracow, dated circa 1670.

E2. Foreign or Lan Infantry

Here is a musketeer serving in a foreign infantry regiment or lan infantry raised by Polish provinces. The main part of his clothing is based on the regulations for lan infantry from Halicz Land. He has a blue *palendrak* (balandran), with lining made from white *kir* and with six white buttons. His red coat is in a Western-style cut, as this colour can be found in some voivodeship regulations. The headgear is a Montero cap, which seems to be one possible explanation for the 'hooded German cap' used by lan infantry from Sandomierz Voivodeship. He is armed with a matchlock musket and sabre, while, in his hand, he is holding an axe used as additional weapon and engineering tool.

F1. Polish Haiduk

Here is a haiduk with a *żupan* in typical 'infantry colour' – blue with yellow lining. Over it, he is wearing a *delia* coat, with the same combination of colours. Red trousers and good-quality yellow leather shoes could indicate a soldier from a hetman's banner or some well-funded private unit. The headgear is a Hungarian *magierka* cap, very popular in Poland since Bathory's reign; as it was a common theme, it had some feathers attached to it. While his side weapons are typical for that type of infantry – a sabre and axe – his firearm is not. He is armed with a *cieszynka* rifle, a hunter gun named after the town of Cieszyn in Silesia. Patrick Gordon had a chance to see them being used during one attack against the Swedes: 'Their ryfled gunnes, being heavy and takeing a very little bulletnot much bigger as a good pease, and not much powder, shoot very just without making a loud report'. As such, it was not a weapon used by regular army haiduks and would be more likely found to be used by privately raised haiduks or some local units.

F2. Highland Peasant Partisan

Polish Highlanders (*górale*) were very quickly raised to fight against the Swedish invaders, 'defending land and their religion'. They armed themselves with whatever weapon was available, from simple firearms to scythes and other tools, until they could use some captured Swedish weaponry and put it to good use. The Highlander presented here is armed with a heavy *rusznica*

COLOUR PLATES COMMENTARY

caliver and a local *ciupaga*, a shepherd's axe that was used as a walking stick, tool and weapon. As a non-regular, he would have been fighting in his typical clothing. His long *koszula* shirt and *hołośnie* trousers are made from cheap, grey cloth. Over them, he is wearing a *kożuch* made from sheepskin. On his feet, we can see *kierpce* shoes made from leather. The blue part of the fur-brimmed cap adds some colour to the overall attire.

Flag Plates Commentary

Unless noted otherwise, all are seventeenth-century Olof Hoffman's drawings from the original flags, kept in Armémuseum in Stockholm.

G1. Banner of cossack or light cavalry. Dimensions of the flag: 108x59cm, with a flagpole of 210cm. (Armémuseum, Stockholm)

G2. Flag of the winged hussars or *pancerni* unit, as indicated by the motif and size of it. Dimensions of the flag: 320x159cm, with a flagpole of 245cm. (Armémuseum, Stockholm)

H1–2. Flag with a so-called '*Aaron*', the coat of arms of the Catholic Archdiocese of Cracow. It could indicate one of the private units of Bishop Piotr Gembicki: dragoons or haiduks. The Latin motto, '*Tandem bona causa triumphat*', means 'A good cause triumphs in the end', while '*Vincedre aut mori*' means 'Either dead or victorious'. Dimensions of the flag: 120x107cm, with a flagpole of 220cm. (Armémuseum, Stockholm)

I1–2. Cavalry or dragoon flag, with the date of 1654, indicating a newly raised unit or newly issued standard for the already existing unit. Dimensions of the flag: 164x164cm, with a flagpole of 85cm. (Armémuseum, Stockholm)

J1–2. Photo of the surviving Tatar light cavalry flag, most likely from the Polish army, captured by the Swedes in 1655 or 1656. Above the two crossed sabres, we can see *Shahada* (Islamic creed) 'There is no God but Allah. Mohammed is the prophet of Allah'. Dimensions of the flag: 244x146cm, with a flagpole of 185cm. (Armémuseum, Stockholm)

K1. Infantry flag with the Cross of Burgundy, a very popular motif on the standards of Polish infantry throughout the whole seventeenth century. Dimensions of the flag: 205x185cm, with a flagpole of 290cm. (Armémuseum, Stockholm)

K2. Another flag with a highly decorated motif, possibly of wing hussars or *pancerni*. Dimensions of the flag: 334x173cm, with a flagpole of 255cm. (Armémuseum, Stockholm)

L1. Flag associated with reiters or dragoons of the Royal Guard. Dimensions of the flag: 106x138cm, with a flagpole of 254cm. (Armémuseum, Stockholm)

L2. Another flag associated with the Royal Guard (reiters or dragoons). Dimensions of the flag: 104x128cm, with a flagpole of 317cm. (Armémuseum, Stockholm)

FLAG PLATES COMMENTARY

M1–2. Third flag associated with Jan II Kazimierz's Royal Guard, either reiters or dragoons. It is much smaller than the other, though, with dimensions of 56x63cm and no flagpole. (Armémuseum, Stockholm)

N1. Flag of cavalry or dragoons, captured at Warsaw in 1656. Dimensions of the flag: 230x175cm, with a flagpole of 230cm. (Armémuseum, Stockholm)

N2. Infantry flag captured during the Battle of Warsaw in 1656. Dimensions of the flag: 168x231cm. (Armémuseum, Stockholm)

O1. Cavalry or dragoon flag, captured during the Battle of Warsaw in 1656. Dimensions of the flag: 251x187cm, with a flagpole of 230cm. (Armémuseum, Stockholm)

O2. Infantry flag, possibly captured in 1657 at Brześć Litewski. Dimensions of the flag: 293x245cm, with a flagpole of 258cm. (Armémuseum, Stockholm)

P1–2/R1–2. Company flags of the Royal Foot Guard regiment of Colonel Fromhold Ludinghausen von Wolff. The regiment took part in the defence of Cracow and afterwards, despite the truce, was captured by the Swedes near Będzin in November 1655. The flags vary slightly in size, with an average of 175x180cm and a flagpole of 295cm. (Armémuseum, Stockholm)

S1. One of the company flags from Gdańsk (Danzig) White regiment of the town militia in 1646. It is almost certain that the design of the flags was the same during the Deluge, as they were based on different areas of the town. Each flag had, next to the drawing, a list of the officers of the company (captain, lieutenant and ensign). From Adam Jakub Martini's *Kurtze Beschreibung vnd Entwurff alles dessen...*, published in 1646 in Gdańsk. (Biblioteka Narodowa, Warszawa)

S2. One of the company flags from Gdańsk Red regiment of the town militia in 1646. From Adam Jakub *Martini's Kurtze Beschreibung vnd Entwurff alles dessen...*, published in 1646 in Gdańsk. (Biblioteka Narodowa, Warszawa)

Appendix I

Stefan Czarniecki's Division in Denmark (1658–1659) and in the Campaign against the Muscovites (1660)

Denmark 1658–1659

In September 1658, Stefan Czarniecki took his division to Denmark to support the allied military effort against the Swedes there. Most of his troops were those that served under his command in the last few campaigns of the war, amongst them a Royal regiment of national cavalry and his own dragoon regiment. Thanks to the presence of two diarists – Pasek and Łoś – and surviving documents, Jan Wimmer was able to reconstruct the larger part of this division:[1]

Royal regiment under Stefan Czarniecki:

- Three banners of hussars: a Royal banner under Gabriel Wojniłłowicz (174 horses), Stefan Czarniecki under Hieronim Pągowski (170) and Wł. Myszkowski (121).
- 15 banners of *pancerni* and cossack cavalry: a Royal banner (189), Franciszek Myszkowski under Piotr Borzęcki (122), Stefan Czarniecki under Piotr Mężyński (149), Wacław Leszczyński under Władysław Skoraszewski (131), Kazimierz Piaseczyński under Kazimierz Bazalski (105), Jan Myśliszewski (75), Aleksander Cetner (150), Jan Dembiński (103), Konstanty Wiśniowiecki (137), Samuel Leszczyński (116), Adam Działyński under Aleksander Polanowski (125), Andrzej Firlej (100), Jakub Rokitnicki under Wolborski (121), Kazimierz Widlica Domaszewski (91) and Mikołaj Daniłowicz (100)

---

1 Wimmer, *Wojsko polskie w drugiej połowie XVII wieku*, pp.118–19.

STEFAN CZARNIECKI'S DIVISION IN DENMARK (1658–1659)

- Wallachian banner of Kazimierz Piaseczynski under Tomasz Ratowski (86)
- Tatar banner of Michał Antonowicz (88)
- *Semeni* banner of Franiciszek Kobylecki (107)

Regiment under Krzysztof Żegocki:

- Cossack cavalry banner of Krzysztof Żegocki (100)
- Dragoon company of Krzysztof Żegocki (100)
- Wallachian banner of Wacław Teleżyński (90)
- Tatar banner of Stefan Moszkowski (93)

Regiment under Piotr Opaliński:

- Seven cossack cavalry banners, formed from levy of nobility and district troops from Wielkopolska, from 1 July 1658 included into the *komput* as regular units: Krzysztof Grzymułtowski (150), Piotr Opaliński (155), Jan Opaliński (99), Jarosz Pogorzelski (100), Adam Czarnkowski under Mikołaj Skrzetuski (100), Jan Gniński (87) and Klemens Branicki under Kułak (127)[2]
- Five cossack cavalry banners, composed of district troops from Wielkopolska, so not being a part of the *komput*. Their strength is unknown, although most likely on average they had 100 horses each.

Dragoon regiment of Stefan Czarniecki under Lieutenant Colonel Jan Tedtwin: 1,000 portions.

In total, the division had a paper strength of 5,067 horses and portions, so, after a reduction due to 'dead pays', it should have had approximately 4,500 men. Most likely, it was even weaker, though, as Pasek mentioned a high rate of desertion amongst the troops from Wielkopolska. We also have to add at least two or three times more men of armed servants that accompanied the division, as in certain circumstances (e.g., during assaults on fortresses) they were used to supplement the regular troops.

While, in autumn 1659, Czarniecki took the majority of his troops back to Poland, he left a combined regiment under Colonel Kazimierz Piaseczyński in Denmark. It was up to 1,000 men (plus accompanying servants) in nine banners, and amongst the units left with him we can find Piaseczyński's cossack cavalry banner, Myśliszewski's cossack cavalry, Teleżyński's Wallachians and two unidentified (probably cossack cavalry) banners under Lieutenant Stanisław Korczewski and Jan Koziński.[3] It is also possible that Piaseczyński's Wallachians and Żegocki's dragoons were present as well.[4] They took part in the allied victory at Nyborg on 14 November 1659, although Piaseczyński died leading one of the charges.

---

2   It is possible that this last banner was, in fact, part of Żegocki's regiment.
3   Łoś, *Pamiętnik towarzysza chorągwi pancernej*, p.89.
4   Wimmer, *Wojsko polskie w drugiej połowie XVII wieku*, p.123.

Campaign of 1660

After they returned to Poland and rested in the winter quarters, it was decided that the division would be sent to today's Belarus to support the Lithuanian army against the Muscovites. While the core of the division, including most of the Royal regiment, was kept under the command of Czarniecki, there were some changes. Piotr Opaliński's regiment was detached from it; also, some banners either changed the name of their *rotmistrz* or were disbanded. Additionally, some new troops were added, including those of the Royal Guard. The new organization looked as follows:[5]

- Two banners of hussars: a Royal banner under Gabriel Wojniłłowicz (201 horses) and Stefan Czarniecki under Piotr Kossakowski (at the Battle of Połonka) and later under Władysław Skoraszewski (the battle at the Basia) (184 horses)
- 28 banners of *pancerni*, cossack cavalry and Tatar and Wallachian light horses, in total 2,809 horses. Amongst them was a Royal *pancerni* banner (184 horses), Stefan Czarniecki's banner (135 horses), Michał Kozubek's Wallachian banner (60 horses)[6] and Michał Antonowicz's Tatar banner (84 horses)
- Reiter squadron under Colonel Jan Ernest Korff (253 horses), in three companies: Korff's, *Rotmistrz* Władysław Szmeling's and *Rotmistrz* Krzysztof Fryderyk Glaubicz
- Two companies of dragoons from Jan Ernest Korff's regiment (128 horses), under Major Sebastian Jan Lichtenhan and Captain Johann Erffort Furster
- Dragoon regiment of Stefan Czarniecki under Lieutenant Colonel Jan Tedtwin: 1,000 portions
- *Semeni* banner of Franciszek Kobylecki: 100 horses
- Two dragoon companies of Krzysztof Żegocki: each 87 portions

During the campaign, one cossack cavalry banner – of Adam Działyński under Aleksander Polanowski – left the division and marched to Hetman Potocki's forces in Ukraine. Three new units joined Czarniecki's division during campaign, though. It was the cossack cavalry banner of Stanisław Czarniecki under Lieutenant Konstanty Górski (120 horses), reiter company of Stanisław Czarniecki (81 horses) and cossack cavalry banner of Karol Łużecki under Lieutenant Jan Cieciszewski (98 horses).

---

5 Wimmer, *Wojsko polskie w drugiej połowie XVII wieku*, p.127; Marcin Gawęda, *Połonka-Basia 1660* (Warszawa: Dom Wydawniczy Bellona, 2005), pp.320–24.
6 The former banner of Kazimierz Piaseczyński, who died in Denmark.

Appendix II

Polish Auxiliary Corps Sent to Support the Lithuanians in Late Autumn 1654

Below is a list of the Crown (Polish) troops that were sent in the late autumn of 1654 to support the Lithuanian army against the Muscovites. The composition of this auxiliary force was fairly unusual, being a mix of foreign troops (as the Lithuanian ones took heavy losses during the campaign of 1654) and Tatar light cavalry, which were to provide the Lithuanian army with strong reconnaissance units. The Polish foreign troops took heavy losses during the campaign, and, despite being ordered to return to Poland (to face the Swedish invasion), most were disbanded in summer 1655 or partially switched to the Brandenburg army in Ducal Prussia. Some stayed in the Lithuanian army; others returned to take part in the defence of Poland against the Swedish invasion. Below, the horses and portions mentioned next to the units are the paper strength at the beginning of the fourth quarter of 1654. When possible, the further fate of all units after their campaign alongside the Lithuanians is mentioned:[1]

Foreign infantry and dragoons:

- Prince Bogusław Radziwiłł foot regiment, under Wilhelme Patterson (later under Jan Berk) – 1,044 portions: After the campaign, the unit remained as part of the Lithuanian army, serving as a garrison force in Słuck. Later, part of the regiment, as a unit in the service of Prince Bogusław Radziwiłł, took heavy losses when defending Tykocin against Sapieha's forces.
- Royal Guard Foot regiment, under Fromhold von Ludingstausen Wolff – 1,200 portions: The unit took heavy losses during the campaign and was recalled to Poland in summer 1655, recruiting to fill in the ranks while en

---

1   Bobiatyński, *Od Smoleńska do Wilna. Wojna Rzeczypospolitej z Moskwą 1654-1655*, *passim*; Bobiatyński, 'Działania posiłkowego korpusu koronnego na terenie Wielkiego Księstwa Litewskiego w latach 1654-1656', pp.61–81; Nagielski, 'Losy jednostek autoramentu cudzoziemskiego w drugiej połowie 1655 roku (lipiec-grudzień)', pp.131–39.

route. Part of the defence of Cracow, in autumn 1655, was captured by the Swedes.
- Royal Guard dragoon regiment, under Fryderyk Mohl (since July 1655 under Jan Henryk von Alten Bockum) – 600 portions: Part of the unit took part in the defence of Malbork, while one company was protecting King Jan II Kazimierz when he left Poland.
- Ludwik Weyher dragoon regiment – 541 portions: After returning to Poland in summer 1655, it took part in the defence of Malbork.

Reiter regiments:

- Royal Guard regiment under the command of Henryk Wallenrodt, led by Marcin Wallenrodt – 350 horses: On 11 July 1655, a royal order was issued to Marcin Wallenrodt, requesting him to return to Poland while the regiment was to be reinforced by a squadron of 200 reiters composed of the disbanded units of Denhoff and Seweryn Kurdwanowski.[2] The regiment was to arrive in Poland 'in three Sundays' to take part in the campaign against the Swedes.[3] The unit was disbanded in summer 1655 during the march to Prussia, though, while Henryk Wallenrodt, probably with some part of the regiment, joined the Brandenburg army.[4]
- Salomon Sacken – 250 horses: It was disbanded in summer 1655 during the return to Poland.
- Squadron of Dietrich von Lessgewang[5] (since July 1655 under Botho Heinrich von Eylenburg) – 324 horses: A royal order to return to Poland 'in three Sundays' was issued to its colonel on 10 July 1655.[6] During the march home, the squadron was disbanded, this one in early autumn 1655. Von Lessgewang, Major Georg Friedrich von Kanitz and Lieutenant Georg Venediger all joined the Brandenburg army in Prussia, which could indicate that some of their reiters did so, too.[7]
- Zygmunt Denhoff – 250 horses: It was disbanded in summer 1655 and merged with a Royal Guard regiment.
- Jakub Weyher – 357 horses: The unit was decimated in fights against the Muscovites, as, in the third quarter of 1655, it dropped to 95 horses. On 10 July 1655, it was issued a royal order to return to Poland 'in three Sundays'.[8] Unlike many other reiter units, it did return and was fighting in the defence of Prussia against the Swedes. It disbanded in early 1657.
- Banner (company) of Bogusław Leszczyński – 100 horses: It was probably disbanded in the summer or autumn of 1655. It is also possible that Seweryn Kurdwanowski was in charge of this unit, which could indicate that it was merged with a Royal Guard regiment.

---

2 Possibly a *rotmistrz* from another regiment or squadron, as there is no indication that he led an independent unit.
3 AGAD, Metryka Koronna (MK), no. 195, pp.189–92.
4 Augusiewicz, *Przebudowa wojska pruskiego w latach 1655-1660*, pp.130–32.
5 The officer was known in Poland as Teodor Lesquant or Leskwant.
6 AGAD, MK, no. 195, pp.192–94.
7 Augusiewicz, *Przebudowa wojska pruskiego w latach 1655-1660*, p.130–31.
8 AGAD, MK, no. 195, pp.192–94.

POLISH AUXILIARY CORPS SENT TO SUPPORT THE LITHUANIANS IN LATE AUTUMN 1654

Tatar light cavalry (name of *rotmistrz*):

- Mustafa Sudycz – 120 horses: In summer 1655, it returned to Poland and, from October 1655, was in the Swedish service. It switched back to the Polish service in spring 1656 but was punished for its long service to Karl X Gustav by losing pay for the last quarter of 1655 and first half of 1656. It was in the Polish army for the rest of the war.
- Halembek Morawski, from July 1655 under Bechtiar Morawski – 120 horses: It had further service as Sudycz's banner.
- Adam Falkowski – 120 horses: It had further service as Sudycz's banner.
- Jan Sielecki – 120 horses: It had further service as Sudycz's banner.
- Adam Taraszewski – 120 horses: It had further service as Sudycz's banner.
- Court banner of cossacks and Tatars under Murza Bohdanowicz – 150 horses: The unit did not return to Poland but was incorporated into the Lithuanian army.
- Probably also banners of Bohdan Murza and Mikołaj Pohojski – 100 horses each: It had further service as Sudycz's banner.

Appendix III

Polish and Imperial Army Besieging Toruń (Thorn), Summer–Winter 1658

The siege of Toruń by the Polish and Imperial armies is described in chapter eight. The allied troops arrived there in a few phases, with de Souches' Imperials and Polish Sapieha's cavalry being present near the city from July 1658. In this appendix, I want to present all the units that took part in the siege, from both the Polish and Imperial armies. The list is based on the works of Tadeusz Nowak and Jan Wimmer, with some additional information from other sources quoted in the text.[1]

Polish Troops

A. Infantry – 13 units – 10,458 portions = approximately 9,400 soldiers. Unless noted, all units were foreign infantry:

- Regiment of Jerzy Lubomirski, Marshal and Crown Field Hetman – 1,676 portions
- Regiment of Jan Zamoyski – 783 portions
- Regiment of General Major Wilhelm Butler – 1,107 portions
- Regiment of General Major Pawel Celari – 720 portions
- Regiment of General of Crown Artillery Krzysztof Grodzicki – 931 portions
- Regiment of General Major Ernst Magnus Grotthauz – 908 portions
- Regiment of Andrzej Cernezzi – 327 portions
- Regiment of Bogusław Leszczyński – 496 portions
- Regiment of Aleksander Lubomirski – 1,200 portions
- Regiment of Andrzej Karol Grudziński – 1,200 portions

---

1 Nowak, *Oblężenie Torunia w roku 1658*, passim; Wimmer, *Wojsko polskie w drugiej połowie XVII wieku*, pp.116–18. Wimmer corrected some errors in regard to Nowak's identification of the units and their strength.

POLISH AND IMPERIAL ARMY BESIEGING TORUŃ (THORN), SUMMER–WINTER 1658

- Regiment of Michał Radziwiłł, Lithuanian Cup-Bearer – 710 portions
- Regiment of Royal Foot Guard under General Major Fromhold Ludingshausen Wolff – 400 portions
- Banner of Polish infantry of Jerzy Lubomirski, Marshal and Crown Field Hetman – 100 portions

B. Dragoons – 6 units – 2,529 portions = approximately 2,270 soldiers:

- Regiment of Royal Guard under Jan Henryk von Alten-Bockum – 858 portions
- Regiment of Jan Sapieha, Crown Field Writer – 553 portions
- Regiment of Józef Łączyński – 494 portions
- Squadron of Aleksander Koniecpolski, Crown Standard-Bearer – 400 portions
- Company of Jerzy Lubomirski, Marshal and Crown Field Hetman under Captain A. Pniewski – 100 portions
- Company of Andrzej Morstin – 124 portions

C. Reiters – 2 units – 1,108 portions = approximately 1,000 soldiers:

- Regiment of Jerzy Lubomirski, Marshal and Crown Field Hetman under Colonel de Oedt – 891 horses
- Banner of Royal Guard (part of the dragoon regiment) – 217 horses

D. National cavalry – six regiments, with a total of 59 banners – 6,670 horses = approximately 6,000 soldiers:

- Jerzy Lubomirski, Marshal and Crown Field Hetman: one banner of hussars, 16 banners of *pancerni* and cossack cavalry and one banner of Tatars
- Aleksander Koniecpolski, Crown Standard: 11 banners of cossack cavalry and one Wallachian banner
- Jan Zamoyski, Voivode of Sandomierz: one banner of hussars and three banners of cossack cavalry
- Jan Sobieski: seven banners of cossack cavalry and one banner of Tatars
- Jan Sapieha, Crown Field Clerk: seven banners of cossack cavalry, three banners of Tatars and one Wallachian banner
- Dymitr Wiśniowiecki: five banners of cossack cavalry and one Wallachian banner

Total army approximately 18,700 soldiers

E. Artillery – between 18 and 27 cannons, mostly small calibre

F. Imperial corps led by General de Souches – about 3,500 soldiers in July 1658, up to 5,000 soldiers:[2]

---

[2] For additional information about the Imperial troops, see: Alphons von Wrede, *Geschichte der K. Und K. Wehrmacht* (Wien: W. Seidel und Sohn, 1898), vol. II, *passim*; (Wien: W. Seidel und

- Infantry regiment de Souches (*Regimentst-Inhaber*[3] Ludwig Raduit de Souches, under Lieutenant Colonel Cividelli) – approximately 650 men
- Dragoon regiment Spankau (Spancko) (*Regimentst-Inhaber* Paris von Spankau) – 679 men in April 1658
- Dragoon regiment Flettinger (Fletting/Fleffinger) (*Regimentst-Inhaber* Johann Flettinger, Lieutenant Colonel Philip von Longueval) – 887 men in April 1658
- Cuirassier regiment Heister (*Regimentst-Inhaber* Gottfried von Heister, under Lieutenant Colonel Otto Wilhelm von Berlepsch) – 513 men in April 1658 (without the two companies that were a part of the garrison of Cracow)
- Cuirassier regiment Ratschin (*Regimentst-Inhaber* Joachim von Ratschin) – 493 men in April 1658 (without the four companies still in Bohemia). Three companies from Bohemia rejoined the regiment at Toruń in September 1658.
- Cuirassier regiment Knigge (*Regimentst-Inhaber* Jobst Hilmar von Knigge) – 597 men in April 1658
- Six field cannons and two mortars
- Reinforcements in August: infantry regiment Nicola (*Regimentst-Inhaber* Christoph Nicola, under Lieutenant Colonel Pazmann) – approximately 600 men
- Reinforcements in September: five companies from infantry regiment de Mers (*Regimentst-Inhaber* Franz von de Mers und la Corona) – approximately 400 men

---

Sohn, 1901), vol. III, *passim*; and (Wien: W. Seidel und Sohn, 1901), vol. III, part 2, *passim*.

3   'Colonel-Owner' of the regiment. It was often just a nominal command (in the same way as in the Polish army), and, during a campaign, the regiment was under the command of its lieutenant colonel.

Appendix IV

Lithuanian Forces Loyal to Grand Hetman Janusz Radziwiłł – Autumn 1655

In this appendix, readers can find a list of the Lithuanian troops that, after the Kiejdany Treaty from October 1655, stayed loyal to Janusz Radziwiłł, who pledged support to the Swedish Crown. While most Lithuanian units, especially national cavalry, left his army and joined the anti-Swedish side, some soldiers stayed on Radziwiłł's side. They were mostly foreign *autorament* troops or those directly connected to the Hetman. The list includes all identified units, and it is based on the article by Andrzej Rachuba from 2007, with some added additional comments and (in square brackets) the paper strength of the units, based on the surviving muster lists from 1654 and 1655.[1] Of course, we need to remember that, after the hard-fought battles against the Muscovites, during those two years, the units would have been much reduced despite some additional recruitment.

It is worth adding that, despite the presence of many officers and their signatures on the document of the treaty, there is no guarantee that their full units were present in Kiejdany and supported their decision. Gradually, more and more of those units left Kiejdany and either scattered, rejoined the loyal Lithuanian army rebuilding under the command of Sapieha or even switched to the Swedish army. At the end of this appendix, there are a few names of the other officers signing treaty, of whose units were not identified:

- Husaria banner of Hrehory Mirski, Grand Lithuanian Guardian. Lieutenant Hieronim Mirski was Hrehory's son. [83 horses]
- Husaria banner of Jerzy Karol Hlebowicz, Starosta of Zmudz. Lieutenant of this banner, Jan Bychowiec, fled to the anti-Radziwiłł troops. [120 horses]
- Cossack cavalry banner of Samuel Komorowski, Grand Camp Master [200 horses]

---

1   Rachuba, 'Oficerowie armii litewskiej z armii szwedzkiej i oficerowie armii szwedzkiej z armii litewskiej w latach 1655-1600', pp.155–56.

- Cossack cavalry banner of Bogusław Sluszka, Court Vice Treasurer. Lieutenant Łukasz Białobrzeski [150 horses]
- *Rotmistrz* Samuel Wysocki from his cossack cavalry banner [100 horses]. The unit was not present, as it deserted.
- Cossack cavalry banner of *Rotmistrz* Hrehory Kazimierz Podbereski [150 horses]. The unit may not have been present, as it was later, under *Rotmistrz* Zygmunt Adam Słuszka, serving in the 200 horses in Hetman Sapieha's army.
- Reiter regiment of Janusz Radziwiłł [6 companies, 660 horses]
- Reiter company of Ernest Jan Korff [120 horses]
- Reiter regiment of Lithuanian Grand Hetman Wincenty Gosiewski – Lieutenant Colonel Krzysztof von Grotthuss [possibly 480 horses]
- Dragoon regiment of Ernest Jan Korff under Major Richard von Puttkamer [750 horses]
- Dragoon regiment of Erdman von Gantzkow, Standard-Bearer of Dorpat under Major Johann von Eckeln-Huelsen [400 horses]
- Dragoon regiment of Maciej Gosiewski probably scattered after 9 September 1655 when Hetman Gosiewski (Maciej was his brother) was arrested in Kiejdany. It is possible that only part of regiment became a part of Radziwiłł's forces. [full regiment had a paper strength of 1,000 horses]
- Dragoon squadron of Samuel Komorowski [204 horses]
- Possibly the dragoon company of Jerzy Karol Hlebowicz under Captain Johann von Neustadten [100 horses]
- Foreign infantry regiment of Janusz Radziwiłł, under Lieutenant Colonel Jan von Ottenhausen [1,050 portions]. The regiment was destroyed during the Battle of Szepielewicze, and it was slowly rebuilt. After Kiejdany, it switched to the Swedish army, where its nominal commander was Prince Adolf Johan.
- Foreign infantry regiment Wilhelm Ernest Korff, Starosta of Orlen, including Lieutenant Colonel Krzysztof von Korff and Major Lorens vcon Vietinghoff-Scheel [694 portions]
- Foreign infantry company of Colonel Samuel Abramowicz [176 portions]
- Polish–Hungarian infantry banner of Hetman Janusz Radziwiłł under Samuel Bohdan Juszkiewicz [200 portions]
- Polish–Hungarian infantry banner of Hetman Janusz Radziwiłł under Jan Dmochowski [100 portions]
- Polish–Hungarian infantry banner of Marcin Błędowski [100 portions]

Further troops were under the command of Prince Bogusław Radziwiłł in Podlasie, including the units under the name of Hetman Radziwiłł:

- Husaria banner of Grand Hetman Janusz Radziwiłł (without officers though) [169 horses]
- Cossack cavalry banner of Grand Hetman Janusz Radziwiłł (without officers though) [150 horses]
- *Pancerni*/cossack cavalry banner of Prince Bogusław Radziwiłł under Lieutenant Wolan [120 horses]
- Reiter company of Prince Bogusław Radziwiłł under Major Otto Butler [158 horses]

LITHUANIAN FORCES LOYAL TO GRAND HETMAN JANUSZ RADZIWIŁŁ – AUTUMN 1655

- Dragoon regiment of Prince Bogusław Radziwiłł under Lieutenant Colonel Eberhard von Puttkamer [700 portions]
- Dragoon life company of Grand Hetman Janusz Radziwiłł under Captain Jan Borkowski and Captain Dawidson [possibly 100 horses]

Officers of the unidentified units who also signed the treaty:

- Colonel Ernest von Nolde: In previous campaigns, he was serving in foreign infantry.
- Colonel Otto von Vietinghoff
- Lieutenant Colonel Reinhold Tyzenhauz: In previous campaigns, he was serving in a reiter unit.
- Major Detloff (Teofil) Schwarzhoff: In previous campaigns, he was serving in a reiter unit.
- Captain Jan Roguski
- Lieutenant Aleksander Mierzeński
- Lieutenant Świerzyński

Appendix V

Two Lithuanian Army Lists from 1661

In this appendix, I would like to present lists with the units of the Lithuanian army from 1661. While they are not perfectly accurate, missing some units or adding some volunteer ones, they can give a good idea of the composition and strength of both Lithuanian divisions after the end of the fights against the Swedes.

The first *komput* is the one published in the diary of Jan Poczobut Odlanicki.[1] It is divided into two divisions and dated from September 1661:

Right wing division, under the command of Lithuanian Grand Hetman Sapieha

Formation	*Rotmistrz* or colonel	Strength	Additional notes
Hussars	King Jan II Kazimierz	200	
	Grand Hetman Sapieha	200	
***Pancerni* (just one banner) and cossack cavalry (rest of units)**	Grand Hetman Sapieha	200	*Pancerni* banner under Lieutenant Ogiński
	Grand Hetman Sapieha	150	Cossack cavalry banner under Lieutenant Kosiło
	Grand Hetman Sapieha	150	Cossack cavalry banner under Lieutenant Anferowicz
	Michał Kazimierz Radziwiłł	120	
	Jerzy Karol Hlebowicz	120	'Black' banner under Lieutenant Gabiński
	Jerzy Karol Hlebowicz	120	'White' banner under Lieutenant Wiażewicz
	Zygmunt Adam Słuszka	120	'Red' banner

---

1   Poczobut Odlanicki, *Pamiętnik Jana Władysława Poczobuta Odlanickiego*, pp.180–85.

TWO LITHUANIAN ARMY LISTS FROM 1661

Pancerni (just one banner) and cossack cavalry (rest of units)	Zygmunt Adam Słuszka	120	'Blue' banner under Lieutenant Michalski
	Krzysztof Wołodkowicz/ Wołotkiewicz	120	
	Władysław Wołłowicz	120	
	Aleksander Hilary Połubiński	120	
	Mikołaj Judycki	120	
	Jan Sosnowski	120	
	Marcjan Aleksander Ogiński	120	
	Krzysztof Sapieha	120	
	Władysław Jerzy Chalecki	120	
	Stanisław Jan Lipnicki	120	
	Mikołaj Szemet	120	
	Samuel Kmicic	120	
	Aleksander Judycki	120	
	Michał Leon Obuchowicz	120	
	Jan Karol Dolski	120	
	Kazimierz Bobrownicki	120	
Tatar light horse	Konstanty Jarmołowicz	120	
	Ułan	120	
	Połubiński	120	Under Murza
Hungarian infantry	Grand Hetman Sapieha	120	Under Bolesław Działkowski/ Dziatkowski
	Grand Hetman Sapieha	120	Under Krzysztof Posudziewski/ Posudziejowski, former private unit of Hetman
	Grand Hetman Sapieha	100	Under Stanisław Skarbek
	Grand Hetman Sapieha	100	Under Andryasz Jankowski
Dragoons	Grand Hetman Sapieha	200	Free company
	Grand Hetman Sapieha	400	Squadron under von Kalkstein, divided into four banners
	Jerzy Karol Hlebowicz	400	Squadron of four banners
	Aleksander Hilary Połubiński	400	Squadron of four banners
	Michał Kazimierz Radziwiłł	200	Free company of two banners
Foreign infantry	Grand Hetman Sapieha	800	Regiment under Colonel Egidiusz de Bremer de Britmar, divided into eight companies

Left wing division, under Lithuanian Field Hetman Wincenty Korwin Gosiewski

Formation	*Rotmistrz* or colonel	Strength	Additional notes
Hussars	Field Hetman Gosiewski	200	Under Lieutenant Kazimierz Chwalibóg Żeromski
	Field Hetman Gosiewski	200	Under Lieutenant Adam Maciej Sakowicz
	Krzysztof Pac	120	
	Kazimierz Dowmont Siesicki	120	
Pancerni (where noted) and cossack cavalry (rest of units)	Field Hetman Gosiewski	200	*Pancerni* banner under Lieutenant Jan Ichnatowicz Łubiański
	Field Hetman Gosiewski	250	Cossack cavalry under Lieutenant Piotr Rudomino Dusiacki
	Field Hetman Gosiewski	150	Cossack cavalry under Lieutenant Andrzej Chrapowicki
	Krzysztof Pac	120	
	Michal Kazimierz Pac	120	
	Krzysztof Odachowski	120	
	Konstanty Władysław Pac	120	
	Albrycht Kostanty Ciechanowiecki	120	
	Hrehory Kazimierz Podbereski	120	
	Kroszyński	120	
	Wiktoryn Konstanty Mleczko	120	
	Polski	120	
Reiters	Szkultyn	600	Regiment under Lieutenant-Colonel Roguski; six companies
	Field Hetman Gosiewski	200	Squadron under Teperman, divided into two companies: under Krzysztof Meyer and Andrzej Olszer/Elszer
	Teofil Schwarzhoff (Szwarzoch)	400	Regiment divided into four companies; two under Schwarzhoff and two under Plater brothers (Gotard Jan and Jan Andrzej)

TWO LITHUANIAN ARMY LISTS FROM 1661

Tatar light horse	Lit	120	
	Paweł Kazimierz Iwaszkiewicz	120	
	Florian Szlager	120	
	Dawid Rejżewski/ Rojrzewski	120	
	Field Hetman Gosiewski	120	Under Dawid Baranowski
Dragoons	Field Hetman Gosiewski	200	Free company
	Lach Podbereski	120	
	Michal Kazimierz Pac	300	Squadron divided into three banners
	Pac/Jeśman[2]	800	Regiment divided into eight companies
	General-Major Maciej Gosiewski[3]	600	Regiment divided into six companies
	Konopacki[4]	600	Regiment divided into six companies
Hungarian infantry	Twarowski	100	
	Konstanty Mordas Bykowski	100	It was unit of Field Hetman Gosiewski
Foreign infantry	Field Hetman Gosiewski	1200	Regiment under Mateusz Remer/ Rejmer, divided into 12 companies
	Fryderyk Eberhard Bockum (Alten-Bockum)	600	Regiment divided into six companies
	Jakub Jaspers	600	Regiment divided into six companies

The second *komput* was included in the writing of Lithuanian noble and diplomat Stefan Franciszek Medeksza.[5] It is also from 1661, although it does not mention the month. Some of the units are incorrectly switched between wings; others are missing, but Medeksza added some of volunteer units into the regular army:

---

2 Document incorrectly list this unit as foreign infantry.
3 Document incorrectly list this unit as foreign infantry.
4 Document incorrectly list this unit as foreign infantry.
5 Stefan Franciszek Medeksza, *Księga pamiętnicza wydarzeń zaszłych na Litwie 1654-1668* (Kraków: Akademia Umiejętności, 1875), pp.250–56.

Right wing division, under the command of Lithuanian Grand Hetman Sapieha

Formation	*Rotmistrz* or colonel	Strength	Additional notes
Hussars	King Jan II Kazimierz	200	Under Lieutenant Aleksander Hilary Połubiński
	Grand Hetman Sapieha	200	Under Lieutenant Władysław Jerzy Chalecki
Pancerni (just one banner) and cossack cavalry (rest of units)	Grand Hetman Sapieha	200	*Pancerni* banner under Lieutenant Jan Jacelk Ogiński
	Grand Hetman Sapieha	150	Cossack cavalry banner under Lieutenant Jerzy Władysław Kosiło
	Michał Kazimierz Radziwiłł	200	Under Lieutenant Stanisław Szczygielski
	Jerzy Karol Hlebowicz	150	'Black' banner under Lieutenant Jan Władysław Grabiński
	Jerzy Karol Hlebowicz	120	'White' banner under Lieutenant Jerzy Piotr Wiażewicz
	Krzysztof Wołodkowicz/ Wołotkiewicz	120	Under Lieutenant Michał Stanisław Wołodkowicz
	Krzysztof Potocki	120	Under Lieutenant Dąbrowa
	Aleksander Hilary Polubiński	200	Under Lieutenant Kotowski
	Zygmunt Adam Słuszka	200	'Blue' banner under lieutenant Jerzy Władysław Michałkiewicz
	Zygmunt Adam Słuszka	150	'Red' banner under Lieutenant Kosarzewski
	Krzysztof Sapieha	200	
	Marcjan Aleksander Ogiński	150	Under Lieutenant Ogiński
	Władysław Jerzy Chalecki	150	Under Lieutenant Nowicki
	Mikołaj Judycki	150	Under Lieutenant Andrzej Wołodkowicz
	Samuel Kmicic	200	Under Lieutenant Krzysztof Steckiewicz
	Stanisław Jan Lipnicki	150	Under Lieutenant Władysław Wołk
	Michał Leon Obuchowicz	120	Under Lieutenant Mikołaj Komorowski
	Krzysztof Stetkiewicz/ Steckiewicz	200	
	Kamiński	120	Under Lieutenant Kamiński
	Kazimierz Bobrownicki	150	Under Lieutenant Górski
	Aleksander Judycki	120	

Pancerni (just one banner) and cossack cavalry (rest of units)	Jan Karol Dolski	120	
	Mikołaj Szemet	120	
	Mikołaj Chlewiński	120	
	Działowicz	100	
	Samuel Oskierko	200	
	Dionizy Muraszko	150	
	Staniszewski	120	
Tatar and Wallachian (just one banner) light horse	Konstanty Jarmołowicz	150	
	Dymitr Czerkas	120	Wallachian banner, in service since May 1661
	Aleksander Hilary Polubiński	120	Under *rotmistrz* Murza
	Abramowicz	120	
	Murza the Older	100	
	Roman Sienkiewicz	100	
	Mustafa Baranowski	100	
	Hasanowicz	120	Possibly Assan Assanowicz
	Hułan Głuchy (the Deaf)	150	
	Hasan/Assan	120	
	Samuel Murza Juszyński	150	
	Ułan	120	
Foreign autorament[6]	Mikołaj Judycki	680	Dragoon regiment
	Bohun	700	Seven banners
	Aleksander Hilary Polubiński	420	
	Stanisław Massalski	500	400 of the original unit + 100 newly recruited by Hor
	Marcjan Aleksander Ogiński	400	
	Jerzy Karol Hlebowicz	360	
	Samuel Kmicic	140	Dragoons
	Stanisław Jan Lipnicki	200	Two banners
	Ilchin (Chilchen)	240	
	Adam Kraszport	120	Hetman's dragoons
	Piotr Kasztel (Castelli)	120	Hetman's dragoons
	Klat (Wilhelm von Klodt)	120	
	Demonow	500	Squadron of four banners

---

6   Infantry and dragoons (division didn't have reiters) are listed as one group, only two of them are named as 'dragoons' in original list.

Foreign autorament	Mateusz Reymer	600	Squadron of six banners[7]
	Szuman	200	Two banners
	Samuel Oskierko	200	Two banners
Hugarian infantry	Dziarkowski	120	Possibly Hetman Sapieha's unit under Bolesław Działkowski/Dziatkowski
	Andrzej/Andryasz Jankowski	120	Possibly former private unit of Hetman Sapieha
	Wichorowski	200	Volunteers
	Łobaczewski	120	Volunteers
	Iwan	120	

Left wing division, under Lithuanian Field Hetman Wincenty Korwin Gosiewski

Formation	*Rotmistrz* or colonel	Strength	Additional notes
Hussars	Field Hetman Gosiewski	200	Under Lieutenant Kazimierz Chwalibóg Żeromski
	Field Hetman Gosiewski	200	Under Lieutenant Adam Maciej Sakowicz
	Krzysztof Pac	120	
	Kazimierz Dowmont Siesicki	120	
Reiters	Field Hetman Gosiewski	120	Under *rotmistrz* Deperman (Teperman)
	Bogucki	552	Dragoon regiment under Lieutenant-Colonel Roguski; six companies
	Teofil Schwarzhoff (Szwarzoch)	100	There were in fact two companies under his command
	Plater	100	One of two units under Plater brothers (Gotard Jan and Jan Andrzej)
Pancerni (just one banner) and cossack cavalry (rest of units)	Field Hetman Gosiewski	200	*Pancerni* banner under Lieutenant Jan Ichnatowicz Łubiański
	Field Hetman Gosiewski	200	Cossack cavalry banner under Lieutenant Piotr Rudomino Dusiacki
	Field Hetman Gosiewski	200	Cossack cavalry banner under Lieutenant Andrzej Chrapowicki
	Krzysztof Pac	120	Under Lieutenant Kozubski

---

7   Hetman Gosiewski's regiment, incorrectly counted amongst Hetman Sapieha's division here.

TWO LITHUANIAN ARMY LISTS FROM 1661

Pancerni (just one banner) and cossack cavalry (rest of units)	Michał Kazimierz Pac	150	Under Lieutenant Okolski
	Konstanty Władysław Pac	120	Under Lieutenant Szpendowski
	Hrehory Kazimierz Podbereski	120	Under Lieutenant Inatowicz
	Samuel Andrzej Abramowicz	120	Under Lieutenant Stanisław Abramowicz
	Krzysztof Odachowski	120	Under Lieutenant Odachowski
	Albrycht Kostanty Ciechanowiecki	120	
	Kroszyński	120	Under Lieutenant Białłozor
	Komorowski Younger	120	Under Lieutenant Polski
	Wiktoryn Konstanty Mleczko	120	Under Lieutenant Salomonowicz
	Bonifacy Teofil Pac	120	Under Lieutenant Zabłocki. It was former reiter banner of Stefan Niewiarowski under Lieutenant Colonel Dawid Jordan, converted into cossack cavalry in May 1661
Tatar light horse	Krzysztof Vorbek-Lettov	150	
	Dawid Rejżewski/Rojrzewski	150	
	Former banner of Paweł Kazimierz Iwaszkiewicz	150	
	David or Mustafa Baranowski	120	Unit of Field Hetman Gosiewski
	Kulbicki	120	
Dragoons (regiments and squadrons) of Field Hetman Gosiewski	Lieutenant Colonel Konopacki	500	Regiment
	General Major Maciej Gosiewski	600	Regiment
	Jeśman	600	Former regiment of chancellor Pac
	Jeśman	200	Additional squadron, attached to the regiment above
	Sakowicz	400	Squadron

Dragoons (free companies)	Field Hetman Gosiewski	200	Life company
	Michal Kazimierz Pac	120	
	Lech Podbereski	150	
	Chwalibóg Żeromski	150	
	Albrycht Konstanty Ciechanowiecki	100	Former company of Niewiarowski
	Krzysztof Eperiesz	120	
	Wilhelm Tyzenhauz	100	
	Siesicki	200	
	Wiktoryn Konstanty Mleczko	100	
	Teofil Szwarcoch	200	
	Chalecki	100	
	Konstanty Władysław Pac	100	
	Żardyn	100	
	Unit of Discalced Carmelites	100	Probably paid by Discalced Carmelites of Vilnius
Foreign infantry	Field Hetman Gosiewski	600	Regiment under Lieutenant Colonel Mateusz Reymer
	Field Hetman Gosiewski	600	Regiment under Lieutenant Colonel Jakub Jaspers
	Jerzy Barsotti (Barsoty)	400	Squadron
Hungarian infantry	Hieronim Michał Iwanowski	200	

Appendix VI

Letter of Passage for Patrick Gordon (July 1661)

In late June 1661, Patrick Gordon decided to leave the Polish service. He had hopes to take part in the recruitment for the Imperial army, with plans to become captain of the horse regiment raised with other British officers. While Hetman Lubomirski was not too pleased to lose such an excellent commander, nonetheless he agreed. Gordon asked to receive a 'writt of passe'; in return, Lubomirski answered that the Scot should write it himself. The diarist did so, commenting that he wrote 'in plaine termes, without any hyperbollical or superfluous praise or expressions'. The Hetman read it over and passed it to his secretary, Bartłomiej Pestrzecki, telling him to write a new one, as Gordon 'deserveth a better recommendation'. On 7 July 1661, the new pass was delivered to Gordon, and he included its Latin text in his diary.

As it is a very interesting example of a source from the period, not only as a letter of passage but also a written recommendation of the discharged officer, I thought it would be good to include its full version in this appendix. I will present the English translation taken from Dmitry Fedosov's edition from 2010.[1] Such letters or passports were often provided to foreigners leaving the Polish or Lithuanian service to help them with their safe passage through the country. When Hieronim Chrystian Holsten left the Polish army in 1663, he asked Field Hetman Lubomirski to issue him with a document 'like I am still in his service and only received few months' leave to go to Prussia'. It seems that the German soldier was well liked, as he not only received a passport from Lubomirski but also another one from Grand Hetman Potocki.[2] Unfortunately, the documents issued to Holsten did not survive to today, making the one provided to Gordon an even more valuable primary source:

> Jerzy Sebastian Lubomirski, Count of Wiśnicz and Jarosław, Prince of the Holy Roman Empire,[3] Great Marshal of the Kingdom of Poland and Field Hetman of

---

1 *Diary of General Patrick Gordon*, vol. II, pp.122–25.
2 Holsten, *Przygody wojenne 1655-1666*, p.84.
3 The title was awarded to his father, Stanisław Lubomirski (1583–1649), by Emperor Ferdinand III in 1647.

the Army, Wojewoda of Lesser Poland,[4] Starosta of Kraków, Chmielnik, Nieżyn, Kazimierz, Olsztyn and Perejasław.

To all and sundry persons of whatever estate, grade, merit, dignity, office and pre-eminence, who shall see, read or hear this letter, we present our kindest respects. Whoever shall shine forth by their excellent feats, especially those whose generous courage reveals itself in military fame – all such must be decorated for their merits with honour and glory by commanders under whose leadership they fight, as full justice does require. Therefore, we have decided that the worthy Patrick Gordon, by birth a Scotsman, scion of a noble family in his homeland, who during eighteen months acted as regimental quartermaster in our Regiment of Dragoons, and for twelve months as captain-lieutenant in the Company of our Bodyguards,[5] who is [now] asking to be discharged by us, and desires to leave for other lands in other to seek his fortune there, should not by any means be deprived of testimony of his distinguished services.

Thus, before all and sundry to whose notice these presents will come, we do attest that in all wars, battles and campaigns during his service against many enemies of this Kingdom, namely, Swedes, Muscovites and Cossacks, he has taken part and fought bravely, and performed his duty of a good soldier as well as officer so diligently, that he has both gained praise and honour for himself, and proved most equal to the name of the Scottish nation, famed everywhere for military prowess.

Therefore, we not only grant for the foresaid Patrick Gordon, according to military law and custom, the free and honourable discharge and ample testimonial of his merits, but also bid all and sundry respect him, insofar as it befits every one according to their dignity and rank, as one who proved the best, brave and faithful warrior for His Sacred and Most Serene Royal Majesty our Most Gracious Prince, for the Republic, and for ourselves; so that, whether he decides to transfer to Scotland, his native country, or to the other lands, he would be especially regarded as one discharged properly, freely and honourable; in all places given a safe passage, return and lodging; treated with all respect, benevolence and kindness, and considered worthy of any promotion in military ranks and advancement in offices and grades. In confirmation whereof we have cause give him the present letters of free discharge and commendation, with the signature in our own hand and our ordinary seal. Given in Warsaw on July 2nd in the year of our Lord 1661.

Jerzy Lubomirski   P[lace of] S[seal]
Bartłomiej Pestrzecki
Secretary to His Excellency

---

4   Małopolska.
5   A life company of dragoons.

Appendix VII

Register of the Prisoners Taken at the Battle of Werki on the Day 21 October 1658

The Battle of Werki in 1658 was a huge blow to the Lithuanian army, affecting Hetman Gosiewski's division and having a major impact on the further activities of the Lithuanian forces for next few years. Depending on the source, between 50[1] and 100[2] men were killed, and another 100 were taken prisoners. While it does not seem like a large loss, considering that many of the captured were important officers, we can better understand why the defeat was much more serious than just by looking into the numbers of killed and captured. Thanks to Poczobut Odlanicki and Vorbek-Lettow, we can reconstruct quite a detailed list of those captured, especially based on the latter's diary. I added additional comments to better identified units mentioned in the original texts. The title of the appendix is taken from Vorbek-Lettow's writing; I also followed his diary when compiling the list, with some further annotations:[3]

Killed:

- Lieutenant Bogusław Rudomino from Hetman Gosiewski's cossack cavalry banner
- Schwarzhoff brothers Fromhold and Wilhelm, who were serving as *rotmistrz* of the two of Gosiewski's reiter companies
- Captain Lieutenant Benedykt, unidentified reiter company

---

[1] Vorbek-Lettow, *Skarbnica pamięci,* p.282.
[2] Poczobut Odlanicki, *Pamiętnik Jana Władysława Poczobuta Odlanickiego,* p.23.
[3] Vorbek-Lettow, *Skarbnica pamięci,* pp.282–83; Poczobut Odlanicki, *Pamiętnik Jana Władysława Poczobuta Odlanickiego,* pp.23–24.

Captured:

- Lithuanian Field Hetman Wincenty Korwin Gosiewski
- Colonel Stefan Niewiarowski[4]
- Lieutenant Jan Aleksander Ichnatowicz-Łubiański from Hetman Gosiewski's *pancerni* banner
- Lieutenant Sołohub from the hussar banner of Kazimierz Dowmont Siesicki: This unit was created in 1656 as cossack cavalry, but I was not able to find confirmation that it was converted into hussars until 1661.
- Lieutenant Aleksander Mierzeński/Mierzyński from Prince Bogusław Radziwiłł's *pancerni* banner
- Colonel Mikołaj Szkultyn/von Schultze von Islitz from Gosiewski's reiter regiment
- Giovanni Battista Frediani, Italian, 'captain of artillery'
- Companions from Gosiewski's hussar banner of Lieutenant Żeromski: Złoty, Ostrowski, Rybiński, Kosakowski, Skinder, Doroszkowski and Gnoiński
- Companion Poniatowski from second Gosiewski's second hussar banner of Lieutenant Adam Maciej Sakowicz
- Companions from the other banners: Suchodolski, Terebesz the Younger, Węcławski, Protaszewicz, Milnicki, Szlagier (standar-bearer from Hetman Gosiewski's cossack cavalry banner), Burba, Abramowicz, Walicki, Werbiński, Staszkiewicz, Łochowski, Wowejko, Lachnicki, Władysław Jawgieł, Zaleski, Gaudens and Lipnicki the Younger[5]
- Retainers from different banners:[6] (none of them were a noble, as they lack the word '*pan*' before their names) Pokucki, Pożarski, Pojurski, Bielski, Romanowski, Marcinkiewicz, Rzeczow, Piotrowski, Zaleski, Harbut, Miałkowski, Kaszycki, Chomski, Tuszewski, Kurazewicz, Gozicki and Michałowski
- Two surgeons
- From the banner of Krzysztof Vorbek-Lettow:[7] a retainer killed, one horse killed, another horse shot three times. All of Krzysztof's wagons with their horses were captured; one of the drivers was killed as well.

---

4 He was in charge of five companies of reiters, although not all of them may have been present during the battle.
5 Son of Stanisław Jan Lipnicki, who was the *rotmistrz* of a cossack cavalry banner and colonel of one of the regiments of national cavalry.
6 The list did not include any reiters, whose number had to have been amongst both the killed and captured, as a few companies were present at Werki.
7 Maciej's son. He had a Tatar light banner, but the list mentioned 'his hussar banner'. He previously was serving as a companion in Gosiewski's hussar banner, so it possible that he kept the retinue under his name in this unit.

Appendix VIII

Letters of Marshal Lubomirski and General Würtz

In early February 1657, after hearing news of the Transylvanian army approaching Poland, Jerzy Sebastian Lubomirski decided to lift the unsuccessful siege, or rather blockade, of Cracow to march against the new enemy. In a very courteous letter, he announced to the Swedish commander of Cracow, General Paul Würtz (Wirtz), that he needed to abandon his positions and their current rivalry. Of course, Würtz answered in a very similar manner, leading to a rather bizarre exchange of apologies, promises and threats. As both of these letters are included in the memoir of the French ambassador to Karl X Gustav, Hugues de Terlon, I would like to present their translation in this appendix as an example of a very interesting war correspondence between two generals.[1]

Letter from Grand Marshal Lubomirski to General Würtz:

My Lord,
The fact that we oppose each other and have duties based on our offices drawn us so seriously into military operations, that it seems we cannot equally share the glory. Circumstances of the war means right now, that while by leaving [the area of] Cracow I improve your situation but also do not abandon some gains for myself. Surviving such serious siege in foreign country, so far away from king, your Lordship's ruler, [and] facing so many dangers it clear example of Your virtues. I am certain that those that in future will judge the current events, wo not condemn me for my current decision, despite the fact that it is happening just before spring, in my own country, where there is plenty of different food.

I was forced to do it [lift the siege], despite signs of the weaking of the besieged town and its [growing] lack of resistance, as more matters more important than capturing the city called my attention. It is vital to protect the most important [things]. Moving against the new enemy, whose plans are different than marching to relief the city, are now became the main task.

---

1   Terlon, *Pamiętniki ambasadora Ludwika XIV przy królu Szwecji Karolu X Gustawie, 1656-1660*, pp.48–49.

It is said that any act of hostility is allowed during the fervour of the fight, yet it is prudent to show some restrain during the war, as it is often main way leading to achieving the peace. I do hope that neighbouring areas [around Cracow] wo not suffer too much due to Your treatment, especially those places from which You can gain many private and public benefits, thanks to salt that is mined there.[2] Because of that I am sending you Mr Morsztyn, who knows those salt mines very well and he will be able to discuss them with You according to my wishes. I can assure you that I will always give evidence of Your foresight and bravery, even more so as I am certain that, once I will retake our own lands taken by You against all laws and justice, I expect You to show me respect [then].

I feel I have enough strength and bravery, to achieve the success. Once that happen, full of generous competitiveness, I shall be able to discuss with You all the kindness that you have shown me, in exchange for those that I have offered to You. There is enough order in virtue, so it can be shown between enemies.

I remain Your most humble and obedient servant
Jerzy Lubomirski

Answer from General Würtz to Grand Marshal Lubomirski:

My Lord,
From the letter of Your Grace, delivered to me by Mr Morsztyn, that new enemy is forcing You to redirect all your forces and to abandon the siege of the city. It will allow Your Grace great opportunity to show your virtues, although I doubt that you can achieve success. It would be much more useful and cautious to focus on [peaceful] solutions than risking that You can fail in your hopes.

I have no doubt about Your bravely, I must also admit that often Fate is on Your side. I doubt though, that You can resist such great [incoming] storm. Not thanks to my achievements but thanks to Your kindness I managed to obtain respect mentioned in Your letter. Because of that I feel even more strongly obliged to faithfully proclaim Your glory, [which You] obtained not through strength and violence but through the right behaviours.

While the local people, due to their words, actions and insults are not worthy [of mercy] but [are safe] thanks to indulgence of King [Karl X Gustav], my lord, for whom protecting the people is more important than destroying the country. His desire for glory makes him more willing to show some ease to [captured] provinces than to ruin them. Out treatments towards them [locals] will be adequate to their behaviour towards us, especially for those from town of Wieliczka and salt mine. Mr Morsztyn will inform you, what we agreed upon in this matter.

I join Your Grace in praising the glorious circumstances which free Him from the futile venture, which was the siege of this city [of Cracow].

I assure Your Grace about my friendliness and bid [You] good rest.

I remain Your most humble and obedient servant.
P. Wirtz
[Dated] Cracow, 10 February 1657

---

2   A salt mine in Wieliczka near Cracow.

Appendix IX

Administrative Division of the Polish–Lithuanian Commonwealth

Poland was divided into two large provinces (Wielkopolska and Małopolska), with Royal Prussia often counted as part of the former. Within each province, there was a number of voivodeships (*województwa*), along with some duchies or lands of special status. Each voivodeship was divided into a number of counties (*powiaty*); some also included lands (*ziemie*) that were also divided into further counties. Voivodeships were, in the majority of cases, named after their capitol. The Grand Duchy of Lithuanian was divided into one duchy and nine voivodeships. Below, in italics, is the Polish version of the name, after it the capitol of the voivodeship or land.

Greater Poland Province (Wielkopolska)

- Brześć Kujawski Voivodeship (*województwo brzesko-kujawskie*, capitol Brześć Kujawski)
- Inowrocław Voivodeship (*województwo inowrocławskie*, Inowrocław)
- Kalisz Voivodeship (*województwo kaliskie*, Kalisz)
- Łęczyca Voivodeship (*województwo łęczyckie*, Łęczyca)
- Mazowsze Voivodeship (*województwo mazowieckie*, Warszawa)
- Poznań Voivodeship (*województwo poznańskie*, Poznań)
- Płock Voivodeship (*województwo płockie*, Płock)
- Podlasie Voivodeship (*województwo podlaskie*, Drohiczyn)
- Rawa Voivodeship (*województwo rawskie*, Rawa)
- Sieradz Voivodeship (*województwo sieradzkie*, Sieradz)

Lesser Poland Province (Małopolska)

- Bełz Voivodeship (*województwo bełzkie*, Bełz)
- Bracław Voivodeship (*województwo bracławskie*, Bracław)
- Czernichów Voivodeship (*województwo czernichowskie*, Czernichów)
- Kijów Voivodeship (*województwo kijowskie*, Kijów)
- Kraków Voivodeship (*województwo krakowskie*, Kraków)
- Lublin Voivodeship (*województwo lubelskie*, Lublin)
- Podolia (Podole) Voivodeship (*województwo podolskie*, Kamieniec Podolski)
- Ruhenia (Ruś) Voivodeship (*województwo ruskie*, Lwów)
- Sandomierz Voivodeship (*województwo sandomierskie*, Sandomierz)
- Wołyń Voivodeship (*województwo wołyńskie*, Łuck)
- Duchy of Siewierz (*księstwo siewierskie*, Siewierz), demesne in Silesia, controlled by the Bishop of Cracow

Royal Prussia (Prusy Królewskie)

- Chełmno Voivodeship (województwo chełmińskie, Chełmno)
- Malbork Voivodeship (*województwo malborskie*, Malbork)
- Pomeranian Voivodeship (*województwo pomorskie*, Gdańsk)
- Duchy of Warmia (*Księstwo Warmińskie*, episcopal principality of Warmia, Lidzbark Warmiński)

Grand Duchy of Lithuania

- Duchy of Samogita (*księstwo żmudzkie*, Worna) was divided into 28 counties known as *trakty*.
- Brześć Litewski Voivodeship (*województwo brzesko-litewskie*, Brześć Litewski)
- Mścisław Voivodeship (*województwo mścisławskie*, Mścisław)
- Mińsk Voivodeship (*województwo mińskie*, Mińsk)
- Nowogródek Voivodeship (*województwo nowogrodzkie*, Nowogrodek)
- Połock Voivodeship (*województwo połockie*, Połock)
- Smoleńsk Voivodeship (*województwo smoleńskie*, Smoleńsk)
- Troki Voivodeship (*województwo trockie*, Trakai)
- Wilno Voivodeship (*województwo wileńskie*, Vilnius)
- Witebsk Voivodeship (*województwo witebskie*, Witebsk)

Polish Livonia (Inflanty Polskie)

While practically in whole under Swedish occupation throughout a large part of the first half of the seventeenth century, it was divided into three voivodeships, and nobles still received official titles from those:

- Wenden Voivodeship (*województwo wendeńskie*, Wenden)
- Dorpat Voivodeship (*województwo dorpackie*, Dorpat)
- Parnawa Voivodeship (*województwo parnawskie*, Parnawa)

After the Treaty of Oliwa, the Swedes ceased their rights to the southern part of Livonia, although, until 1667, it was under Muscovite occupation. After the Treaty of Andruszów, this territory returned to Poland. Therefore, all three voivodeships were replaced with one known as Livonian Voivodeship (*województwo inflanckie*, Dyneburg), also known (from 1677) as the Duchy of Livonia (with the King of Poland being the Duke of Livonia).

Vassal States

- Duchy of Courland and Semigallia (*Księstwo Kurlandii i Semigalii*)
- Autonomous district of Pilten (*powiat piltyński*), near Courland
- Ducal Prussia (Prusy Książęce, Królewiec), from 1657, was no longer a vassal of the Polish Crown.
- Lauenburg and Bütow Land (*ziemia lęborsko-bytowska*, Bytów and Lębork), from 1637, was an independent land within Pomerania Voivodeship and, from 1657, was a part of Brandenburg and only counted as a Polish vassal 'on paper'.

Bibliography

Archival Sources

Archiwum Główne Akt Dawnych (AGAD) [The Central Archives of Historical Records in Warsaw]
Archiwum Publiczne Potockich (APP), no. 7.3
Archiwum Skarbu Koronnego (ASK) II, IV, 82, 85
Archiwum Warszawskie Radziwiłłów (AR) 2.1, II, III, VII, X, XI
Archiwum Zamoyskich (AZ) 334, 463, 3112
Metryka Koronna (MK), no. 195
Zbiór Anny z Potockich Ksawerowej Branickiej, no. 5

Archiwum Narodowe w Krakowie [National Archive in Cracow]
Zbiór dokumentów papierowych, no. 658
Zbiór Zygmunta Glogera, no. 619

Archiwum Narodowe w Poznaniu (APPoz.) [National Archive in Poznań]
Gr. Pozn., 693

Biblioteka Jagiellońska (BJ) [Jagiellonian Library]
no. 8842/IV

Biblioteka Kórnicka PAN [Kórnik Library]
no. 350
no. 352
no. 356
Extraktschreiben von unrterschiedlichen Orten aus Großpolen (PAN Kórn. 1119)

Biblioteka Książąt Czartoryskich (BCzart.) [Czartoryski Library]
no. 352
no. 2749

Biblioteka Narodowa [National Library]
Kopiariusz korespondencji Bogusława Radziwiłła oraz innych materiałów historycznych i publicystyczno-literackich z lat 1657–1672

Riksarkivet, Stockholm
Z Bochynia taki raty chcieli na tydzień do Łowicza, Riskarkivet Stockholm, Extranea IX Polen, 143

Saint Petersburg Institute of History
32, box 660/2

Skokloster Samlingen (SkS)
337

Printed Primary Sources

Akta grodzkie i ziemskie z czasów Rzeczypospolitej Polskiej (Lwów: Księgarnia Seyfartha i Czajkowskiego, 1884), vol. X

Akta grodzkie i ziemskie z czasów Rzeczypospolitej Polskiej (Lwów: Księgarnia Seyfartha i Czajkowskiego, 1911), vol. XXI

Akta grodzkie i ziemskie z czasów Rzeczypospolitej Polskiej (Lwów: Księgarnia Seyfartha i Czajkowskiego, 1931), vol. XXIV

Akty izdavaemye Vilenskoju Arheograficeskou Kommissieu (*AVAK*) (Vilna: Tipografia A. G. Syrkina, 1909), vol. XXXIV

Ascheberg, Rutger von, *Dziennik oficera jazdy szwedzkiej 1621-1681* (Kraków: Wydawnictwo Eternum, 2014)

Bobiatyński, Konrad; Gawron, Przemysław; Kossarzecki, Krzysztof; Kroll, Piotr; Majewski, Andrzej A.; Milewski, Dariusz; and Nagielski, Mirosław (eds), *Korespondencja wojskowa hetmana Janusza Radziwiłła w latach 1646-1655*, vol. II. *Listy.* (Warszawa: Wydawnictwo Neriton, 2020)

Chrapowicki, Jan Antoni, *Diariusz. Część pierwsza: lata 1656-1664* (Warszawa: Instytut Wydawniczy Pax, 1978)

Diary of General Patrick Gordon of Auchleuchries 1635-1699 (Aberdeen: University of Aberdeen, 2009), vol. I

Diary of General Patrick Gordon of Auchleuchries 1635-1699 (Aberdeen: University of Aberdeen, 2009), vol. II

Druszkiewicz, Stanisław Zygmunt, *Pamiętniki 1648-1697* (Siedlce: Wydawnictwo Akademii Podlaskiej, 2001)

Dwa pamiętniki z XVII wieku Jana Cedrowskiego i Jana Floriana Drobysza Tuszyńskiego (Wrocław-Kraków: Zakład Imienia Ossolińskich-Wydawnictwo, 1954)

'Dyaryusz Michał Obuchowicza, Strażnika Wielkiego Księstwa Litewskiego, pisany przez czas więzienia w Moskwie', in *Pamiętniki historyczne do wyjaśnienia spraw publicznych w Polsce XVII wieku posługujące, w dziennikach domowych Obuchowiczów i Cedrowskiego pozostałe* (Wilno: Nakładem A. Assa Księgarza, 1859), pp.65–104

Erik Dahlberghs dagbok (1625-1699) (Upsala & Stockholm: Almqvist & Wiksells Boktryckeri AB, 1912)

Grabowski, Ambroży (ed.), *Ojczyste spominki w pismach do dziejów dawnej Polski* (Kraków: Nakładem Józefa Cypcera, 1845), vol. I

Gramont, Antoine de, *Iz istorīi moskovskago pokhoda Īana Kazimira, 1663-1664 g.g.* (Yuriev: Tipografiâ K. Mattisena, 1929)

Holsten, Hieronim Chrystian, *Przygody wojenne 1655-1666* (Warszawa: Instytut Wydawniczy Pax, 1980)

Ingres albo wjazd królowej [Ludwiki Marii] do Gdańsk 11 lutego 1646 (Kraków: Walerian Piątkowski, 1646)

Ingres triumfalny do Warszawy Ludwiki Marii Gonzagi, królowej polskiej w r. 1646 (Warszawa: Piotr Elert, 1646)

Jakuba Michałowskiego, wojskiego lubelskiego a później kasztelana bieckiego Księga Pamiętnicza (Kraków: Drukarnia C.K. Uniwersytetu, 1864)

Jemiołowski, Mikołaj, *Pamiętnik dzieje Polski zawierający (1648-1679)* (Warszawa: Wydawnictwo DiG, 2000)

Jerlicz, Joachim, *Latopisiec albo kroniczka* (Warszawa: Kazimierz Władysław Wóycicki, 1853), vol. I

Jerlicz, Joachim, *Latopisiec albo kroniczka* (Warszawa: Kazimierz Władysław Wóycicki, 1853), vol. II

Kochowski, Wespazjan, *Historya panowania Jana Kazimierza* (Poznań: N Kamieński, 1859), vol. I

Kochowski, Wespazjan, *Historya panowania Jana Kazimierza* (Poznań: N Kamieński, 1859), vol. II

Kochowski, Wespazjan, *Lata Potopu 1655-1657* (Warszawa: Wydawnictwo Ministerstwa Obrony Narodowej, 1967)

Laskowski, Otton. (ed.), 'Relacjā obrotów wojennych pod Tykocinem roku 1656', *Przegląd Historyczno-Wojskowy*, X:2 (1938), pp.255–57

Lasota, Eryk, and Beauplan, Wilhelm, *Opis Ukrainy* (Warszawa: Państwowy Instytut Wydawniczy, 1972)

Leszczyński, Samuel, *Potrzeba z Szeremetem, hetmanem moskiewskim i z Kozakami w Roku Pańskim 1660 od Polaków wygrana*, edited by Piotr Borek (Kraków: Collegium Columbinum, 2008)

Łoś, Jakub, *Pamiętnik towarzysza chorągwi pancernej* (Warszawa: Wydawnictwo DiG, 2000)

Medeksza, Stefan Franciszek, *Księga pamiętnicza wydarzeń zaszłych na Litwie 1654-1668* (Kraków: Akademia Umiejętności, 1875)

Nagielski, Mirosław (ed.), *Relacje wojenne z pierwszych lat walk polsko-kozackich powstania Bohdana Chmielnickiego okresu "Ogniem i Mieczem" (1648-1651)* (Warszawa: Wydawnictwo VIKING, 1999)

Nagielski, Mirosław; Bobiatyński, Konrad; Gawron, Przemysław; Kossarzecki, Krzysztof; Kroll, Piotr; Majewski, Andrzej A.; and Milewski, Dariusz (eds), *Korespondencja wojskowa hetmana Janusza Radziwiłła w latach 1646-1655*, vol. I. *Diariusz kancelaryjny 1649-1653* (Warszawa: Wydawnictwo Neriton, 2019)

'Najdawniejsza taryfa okupu szwedzkiego z Warszawy w roku 1655', *Starożytności Warszawy* (Warszawa: Aleksander Wejnert, 1856), series 2, vol. IV

Nowak, Tadeusz, 'Nieznane materiały do wojny szwedzkiej 1656 z b. Archiwum Radziwiłłów w Warszawie', *Przegląd Historyczny*, 47:4 (1956), pp.713–20

Oświęcim, Stanisław, *Dyaryusz 1643-1651* (Kraków: Nakładem Akademii Umiejętności, 1907)

Pamiętniki Samuela i Bogusława Kazimierza Maskiewiczów (Wrocław: Zakład Narodowy im. Ossolińskich-Wydawnictwo, 1961)

Pasek, Jan Chryzostom, *Pamiętniki* (Warszawa: Państwowy Instytut Wydawniczy, 1963)

Pisma polityczne z czasów panowania Jana Kazimierza Wazy, 1648-1668. Publicystyka, eksorbitancje, projekty, memoriały. Volume I. 1648-1660 (Wrocław-Warszawa-Kraków-Gdańsk-Łódź: Wydawnictwo Polskiej Akademii Nauk, 1989)

Poczobut Odlanicki, Jan Władysław, *Pamiętnik Jana Władysława Poczobuta Odlanickiego (1640-1684)* (Warszawa: Drukarnia Michała Ziemkiewicza, 1877)

Portfolio królowej Maryi Ludwiki (Poznań: Drukarnia i księgarnia Nowa, 1844), vol. I

Portfolio królowej Maryi Ludwiki (Poznań: Drukarnia i księgarnia Nowa, 1844), vol. II

Przeździecki, Aleksander (ed.), 'Zdobycie Warszawy przez Szwedów w 1656 r. opisane w listach królowej polskiej Marii Ludwiki', in *Biblioteka Warszawska* (Warszawa: Drukarnia Stanisława Strąbskiego, 1851), vol. III

Pufendorf, Samuel, *Siedem ksiąg o czynach Karola Gustawa króla Szwecji*, translated and edited by Wojciech Krawczuk (Warszawa: Wydawnictwo DiG, 2013)

Rachuba, Andrzej (ed.), *Metryka Litewska. Księga wpisów nr 131* (Warszawa: Wydawnictwo DiG, Instytut Historii PAN, 2001

Rachunki podskarbstwa litewskiego 1648-1652, wydane z współczesnego rękopisy znajdującego się w bibliotece Eustachego Hr. Tyszkiewicza (Wilno: Nakładem i Drukiem Józefa Zawadzkiego, 1855)

Radziwiłł, Albrycht Stanisław, *Pamiętnik o dziejach w Polsce. Tom 3. 1647-1656* (Warszawa: Państwowy Instytut Wydawniczy, 1980)

Radziwiłł, Bogusław, *Żywot xięcia Bogusława Radziwiłła, przez niego samego napisany* (Poznań: Drukarnia na Garbarach, 1841)

Relacye nuncyuszów apostolskich i innych osób w Polsce od roku 1548 do 1690 (Berlin-Poznań: Księgarnia B. Behra, 1864), vol. II

Rudawski, Wawrzyniec Jan, *Historja Polska od śmierci Władysława IV aż do pokoju oliwskiego* (Petersburg-Mohylew: Nakładem Bolesława Maurycego Wolffa, 1855), vol. II

Rządy sejmikowe w epoce królów elekcyjnych 1572-1795. T.2. Lauda i instrukcye 1572-1674 (Warszawa: Druk Józefa Bergera, 1888)

Skorobohaty, Aleksander D., *Dziennik* (Warszawa: Wydawnictwo DiG, 2000)

Stanisława Oświęcima Dyarusz 1643-1651 (Kraków: Akademia Umiejętności, 1907)

Tarnowski, Jan, *Consillium rationis bellicae* (Tarnów: Publisher unknown, 1558)

Terlon, Hugues de, *Pamiętniki ambasadora Ludwika XIV przy królu Szwecji Karolu X Gustawie, 1656-1660* (Wrocław: Towarzystwo Przyjaciół Ossolineum, 1999)

Urkunden und Actenstücke zur Geschichte des Kurfürsten Friedrich Wilhelm von Brandenburg (Berlin: Preußische Kommission bei der Preußischen Akademie der Wissenschaften, 1884), vol. VIII

Voget, Peter, *Wahrhafftiger und gründlicher Bericht von Belager- und Eroberung der Haupt-Schantze in der Dantziger Nährung zwischen der Theilung des Weissel-Strohmes von den Schweden Anno M DC LVI. auffgeführet und befestiget von den Dantzigern aber Anno M DC LIX* (Danzig: Dawid Fryderyk Rhete, 1661)

Volumina Legum (Petersburg: Nakładem i drukiem Jozafata Chryzki, 1859), vol. IV

Vorbek-Lettow, Maciej, *Skarbnica pamięci. Pamiętnik lekarza króla Władysława IV* (Wrocław-Warszawa-Kraków: Zakład Narodowy im. Ossolińskich-Wydawnictwo, 1968)

Wierzbowski, Stanisław, *Konnotata wypadków w domu i w kraju zaszłych od 1634 do 1689 r.* (Lipsk: Księgarnia Zagraniczna, 1858)

Wydźga, Jan Stefan, *Historia Abo Opisanie wielu Poważnieyszych Rzeczy ktore się działy podczas Woyny Szwedzkiey w Krolestwie Polskim od Roku Pańskiego 1655. w Miesiącu Lipcu, aż do Roku 1660, Miesiącu Maiu trwaiącey, w sobie zamykaiące, y do wiadomości potomnym Wiekom Podane* (place of publish unknown, date between 1661 and 1665)

'Zabytek historyczny o Pińsku', in *Athenauem* (Wilno: Nakład i druk T. Glucksberga, 1841), vol. VI

Zbiór dyplomatów rządowych i aktów prywatnych, posługujących do rozjaśnienia dziejów Litwy i złączonych z nią krajów (od 1387 do 1710 r.) (Vilnius: J. Zawadzki, 1858), vol. I

Printed Secondary Sources

Augusiewicz, Sławomir, *Prostki 1656* (Warszawa: Dom Wydawniczy Bellona, 2001)

Augusiewicz, Sławomir, *Przebudowa wojska pruskiego w latach 1655-1660. U źródeł nowożytnej armii* (Oświęcim: Wydawnictwo Napoleon V, 2014)

Biernacki, Witold, *Łojów 1649* (Zabrze-Tarnowskie Góry: Wydawnictwo Inforteditions, 2014)

Bobiatyński, Konrad, 'Działania posiłkowego korpusu koronnego na terenie Wielkiego Księstwa Litewskiego w latach 1654-1656', *Studia i Materiały do Historii Wojskowości*, XLI (2004), pp.61–81

BIBLIOGRAPHY

Bobiatyński, Konrad, 'Husaria litewska w dobie walk z Kozakami oraz wojskami moskiewskimi w latach 1648-1667', in *W boju i na paradzie. Husaria Rzeczypospolitej w XVI-XVII w.* (Warszawa: Arx Regia, Wydawnictwo Zamku Królewskiego w Warszawie – Muzeum, 2020), pp.109–28

Bobiatyński, Konrad, *Michał Kazimierz Pac. Wojewoda wileński, hetman wielki litewski* (Warszawa: Wydawnictwo Neriton, 2008)

Bobiatyński, Konrad, *Od Smoleńska do Wilna. Wojna Rzeczypospolitej z Moskwą 1654-1655* (Zabrze: Inforteditions, 2004)

Borcz, Andrzej, *Przemyśl 1656-1657* (Warszawa: Dom Wydawniczy Bellona, 2006)

Ciesielski, Tomasz, *Od Batohu do Żwańca. Wojna na Ukrainie, Podolu i o Mołdawię 1652-1653* (Zabrze: Wydawnictwo Inforteditions, 2007)

Fredholm von Essen, Michael, *Charles X's War. Volume I – Armies of the Swedish Deluge, 1655-1660* (Warwick: Helion & Company, 2021)

Fredholm von Essen, Michael, *Charles X's War. Volume II – The Wars in the East. 1655-1657* (Warwick: Helion & Company, 2022)

Frost, Robert, *After the Deluge. Poland-Lithuania and the Second Northern War 1655-1660* (Cambridge: Cambridge University Press, 1993)

Frost, Robert, *The Northern Wars. War, State and Society in Northeastern Europe, 1558-1721* (London: Routledge, 2000)

Gawęda, Marcin, *Od Beresteczka do Cudnowa. Działalność wojskowa Jerzego Sebastiana Lubomirskiego w latach 1651-1660* (Zabrze-Tarnowskie Góry: Wydawnictwo Inforteditions, 2013)

Gawęda, Marcin, *Połonka-Basia 1660* (Warszawa: Dom Wydawniczy Bellona, 2005)

Górski, Konstanty, *Historya artyleryi polskiej* (Warszawa: Księgarnia E Wende i S-ka, 1902)

Kersten, Adam, *Stefan Czarniecki 1599-1665* (Lublin: Wydawnictwo Uniwersytetu Marii Curie-Skłodowskiej, 2006)

Kossarzecki, Krzysztof, 'Działania wojenne nad Dźwiną w latach 1662-1667', in Karol Łopatecki (ed.), *Organizacja armii w nowożytnej Europie. Struktura-urzędy-prawo-finanse* (Zabrze: Wydawnictwo Inforteditions, 2011)

Kotlhjarchuk, Andrej, *In the Shadows of Poland and Russia. The Grand Duchy of Lithuania and Sweden in the European Crisis of the mid-17th Century* (Huddinge: Södertörns högskola, 2006)

Kotłubaj, Edward (ed.), *Życie Janusza Radziwiłła* (Oświęcim: Wydawnictwo Napoleon V, 2016)

Kroll, Piotr, 'Wykorzystanie husarii koronnej na ukraińskim obszarze działań wojennych w latach 1648-1667', in *W boju i na paradzie. Husaria Rzeczypospolitej w XVI-XVII w.* (Warszawa: Arx Regia, Wydawnictwo Zamku Królewskiego w Warszawie – Muzeum, 2020), pp.129–50

Kubala, Ludwik, *Wojna brandenburska w roku 1656 i 1657* (Lwów: H. Altenberg, G. Seyfarth, E. Wende i Sp, 1914)

Kubala, Ludwik, *Wojna moskiewska r. 1654-1655* (Warszawa: Nakład Gebethnera i Wolffa, 1910)

Kubala, Ludwik, *Wojna szwecka w roku 1655 i 1656* (Lwów: H. Altenberg, G. Seyfarth, E. Wende i Sp, 1913)

Łopatecki, Karol, and Walczak, Wojciech, *Mapy i plany Rzeczypospolitej XVII w. znajdujące się w archiwach w Sztokholmie* (Warszawa: Ministerstwo Kultury i Dziedzictwa Narodowego, 2011), vol. I

Majewski, Andrzej A., 'Działania wojenne w Księstwie Kurlandii i Semigalii w latach 1658-1660', in Mirosław Nagielski (ed.), *Z dziejów stosunków Rzeczypospolitej Obojga Narodów ze Szwecją w XVII wieku* (Warszawa: Wydawnictwo DiG, 2007), pp.225–46

Majewski, Andrzej A., *Marszałek wielki litewski Aleksander Hilary Połubiński (1626-1679). Działalność polityczno-wojskowa* (Warszawa: Instytut Historyczny Uniwersytetu Warszawskiego, 2014)

Majewski, Andrzej A., 'Military accounts of the Grand Lithuanian Hetman Paweł Jan Sapieha of the years 1655-1662', *Res Historia*, 49 (2020), pp.568–87

Mankell, Julius, *Uppgifter rörande svenska krigsmagtens styrka, sammansättning och fördelning sedan slutet af femtonhundratalet* (Stockholm: Tryckt hos C.M. Thimgren, 1865)

Nagielski, Mirosław, *Bitwa pod Warszawą 1656* (Warszawa: Dom Wydawniczy Bellona, 2007)

Nagielski, Mirosław, 'Chorągwie husarskie Aleksandra Hilarego Połubińskiego i króla Jana Kazimierza w latach 1648-1666', *Acta Baltico-Slavica*, 15 (1983), pp.77–137

Nagielski, Mirosław, 'Gwardia przyboczna Władysława IV (1632-1648)', *Studia i Materiały do Historii Wojskowości*, XXVII (1984), pp.113–45

Nagielski, Mirosław, *Liczebność i organizacja gwardii przybocznej i komputowej za ostatniego Wazy (1648-1668)* (Warszawa: Wydawnictwo Uniwersytetu Warszawskiego, 1989)

Nagielski, Mirosław, 'Losy jednostek autoramentu cudzoziemskiego w drugiej połowie 1655 roku (lipiec-grudzień)', in Bogusław Dybaś (ed.), *Wojny północne w XVI-XVIII wieku* (Toruń: Towarzystwo Naukowe w Toruniu, 2007)

Nowak, Tadeusz, 'Kampania wielkopolska Czarnieckiego i Lubomirskiego w roku 1656', *Rocznik Gdański*, XI (1938), pp.67–162

Nowak, Tadeusz, 'Kasper Kasprzycki, nieznany bohater z czasów "Potopu"', *Przegląd Historyczny*, 50:2 (1959), pp.225–47

Nowak, Tadeusz, *Oblężenie Torunia w roku 1658* (Toruń: Nakładem Wydawnictwa Naukowego w Toruniu, 1936)

Nowak, Tadeusz, 'Polska artyleria koronna przed wojną 1655-1660 i podczas jej trwania', in Jan Wimmer (ed.), *Wojna polsko-szwedzka 1655-1660* (Warszawa: Wydawnictwo Ministerstwa Obrony Narodowej, 1973), pp.100–26

Orłowski, Damian, 'Potop szwedzkie na ziemi wieluńskiej', *Rocznik Wieluński*, 7 (2007), pp.25–45

Paradowski, Michał, *Despite Destruction, Misery and Privations…: The Polish Army in Prussia during the War against Sweden 1626-1629* (Warwick: Helion & Company, 2020)

Paradowski, Michał, *We Came, We Saw, God Conquered: The Polish-Lithuanian Commonwealth's Military Effort in the Relief of Vienna, 1683* (Warwick: Helion & Company, 2021)

Płosiński, Jacek, *Potop szwedzki na Podlasiu* (Zabrze: Wydawnictwo Inforteditions, 2006)

Podhorodecki, Leszek, 'Kampania polsko-szwedzka 1659 r. w Prusach i Kurlandii', *Studia i Materiały do Historii Wojskowości*, IV (1958), pp.203–46

Polska w okresie Drugiej Wojny Północnej 1655-1660. Volume I. Rozprawy (Warszawa: Państwowe Wydawnictwo Naukowe, 1957)

Polska w okresie Drugiej Wojny Północnej 1655-1660. Volume II. Rozprawy (Warszawa: Państwowe Wydawnictwo Naukowe, 1957)

Polska w okresie Drugiej Wojny Północnej 1655-1660. Volume III. Bibliografia (Warszawa: Państwowe Wydawnictwo Naukowe, 1957)

Rabka, Rafał, 'Kampania Ochmatowska 1654-1655. Część I', *Studia i Materiały do Historii Wojskowości*, XLIII (Białystok: Ośrodek Nadań Historii Wojskowej Muzeum Wojska w Białymstoku, 2007), pp.177–206

Rachuba, Andrzej, 'Oficerowie armii litewskiej z armii szwedzkiej i oficerowie armii szwedzkiej z armii litewskiej w latach 1655-1660', in Bogusław Dybaś (ed.), *Wojny północne w XVI-XVIII wieku* (Toruń: Towarzystwo Naukowe w Toruniu, 2007), pp.151–63

Rachuba, Andrzej, 'Oficerowie cudzoziemskiego autoramentu w armii Wielkiego Księstwa Litewskiego w latach 1648-1667', in Zbigniew Karpus and Waldemar Rezmer (eds), *Od armii komputowej do narodowej (XVI-XX w.)* (Toruń: Wydawnictwo UMK, 1998), pp.57–71

Rachuba, Andrzej, 'Uwagi do problemu kampanii Wincentego Gosiewskiego w Prusach Książęcych jesienią 1656 roku', *Kwartalnik Historyczny*, CIX:3 (2002), pp.171–81

Rachuba, Andrzej, 'Wysiłek mobilizacyjny Wielkiego Księstwa Litewskiego w latach 1654-1667', *Studia i Materiały do Historii Wojskowości*, XLIII (2007), pp.43–60

Skworoda, Paweł, *Warka-Gniezno 1656* (Warszawa: Dom Wydawniczy Bellona, 2003)

Staberg, Daniel, *Livonian Field Army, April and May 1659* (unpublished article in the author's archive)

Staręgowski, Bartosz, *Formacje zbrojne samorządu szlacheckiego województw poznańskiego i kaliskiego w okresie panowania Jana Kazimierza (1648-1668)* (Warszawa: Wydawnictwo DiG, 2022)

Staręgowski, Bartosz, 'Organizacja, struktury i udział w walkach regimentu piechoty Bogusława i Jana Leszczyńskich w latach 1658-1662', *Przegląd Historyczno-Wojskowy*, 2 (2020), pp.10–41

Szczotka, Stanisław, *Chłopi obrońcami niepodległej Polski w okresie potopu* (Kraków: Spółdzielnia Wydanicza "Wieś", 1946)

Wagner, Marek, *Słownik biograficzny oficerów polskich drugiej połowy XVII wieku* (Oświęcim: Wydawnictwo Napoleon V, 2013), vol. I

Wagner, Marek, *Słownik biograficzny oficerów polskich drugiej połowy XVII wieku* (Oświęcim: Wydawnictwo Napoleon V, 2014), vol. II

Wimmer, Jan, 'Materiały do zagadnienia liczebności i organizacji armii koronnej w latach 1655-1660', *Studia i Materiały do Historii Wojskowości*, IV (1958)

Wimmer, Jan, *Polska-Szwecja. Konflikty zbrojne w XVI-XVII wieku* (Oświęcim: Wydawnictwo Napoleon V, 2013)

Wimmer, Jan, *Wojsko polskie w drugiej połowie XVII wieku* (Warszawa: Wydawnictwo Ministerstwa Obrony Narodowej, 1965)

Wrede, Alphons von, *Geschichte der K. Und K. Wehrmacht* (Wien: W. Seidel und Sohn, 1898), vol. II

Wrede, Alphons von, *Geschichte der K. Und K. Wehrmacht* (Wien: W. Seidel und Sohn, 1901), vol. III

Wrede, Alphons von, *Geschichte der K. Und K. Wehrmacht* (Wien: W. Seidel und Sohn, 1901), vol. III, part 2